W9-CNK-678

The Complete Small Business Guide

WITHDRAWN FROM LIBRARY

WITHDRAWN FROM LIBRARY

WITHDRAWN FROM LIBRARY

MONTGOMERY COLLEGE
ROCKVILLE CAMPUS LIBRARY
ROCKVILLE, MARYLAND

THE COMPLETE SMALL BUSINESS GUIDE

A SOURCEBOOK FOR NEW AND SMALL BUSINESSES

COLIN **BARROW**

EIGHTH EDITION

CAPSTONE

415255
NOV 0 3 2007

Published in 2006 by Capstone Publishing Ltd (A Wiley Company) The Atrium, Southern Gate Chichester, West Sussex, PO19 8SQ, England Phone (+44) 1243 779777

Copyright © 2006 Colin Barrow

Email (for orders and customer service enquires): cs-books@wiley.co.uk
Visit our Home Page on www.wiley.co.uk or www.wiley.com

All Rights Reserved. No part of this publication may be reproduced, stored in a retrieval system or transmitted in any form or by any means, electronic, mechanical, photocopying, recording, scanning or otherwise, except under the terms of the Copyright Licensing Agency Ltd, 90 Tottenham Court Road, London, W1P 0LP, UK, without the permission in writing of the Publisher. Requests to the Publisher should be addressed to the Permissions Department John Wiley & Sons, Ltd, The Atrium, Southern Gate, Chichester, West Sussex, PO19 8SQ, England, or e-mailed to permreq@wiley.co.uk, or faxed to (44) 1243 770620.

Designations used by companies to distinguish their products are often claimed as trademarks. All brand names and product names used in this book are trade names, service marks, trademarks or registered trademarks of their respective owners. The Publisher is not associated with any product or vendor mentioned in this book.

This publication is designed to provide accurate and authoritative information in regard to the subject matter covered. It is sold on the understanding that the Publisher is not engaged in rendering professional services. If professional advice or other expert assistance is required, the services of a competent professional should be sought.

Colin Barrow has asserted his right under the Copyright, Designs and Patents Act 1988, to be identified as the author of this work.

Other Wiley Editorial Offices
John Wiley & Sons, Inc. 111 River Street, Hoboken, NJ 07030, USA
Jossey-Bass, 989 Market Street, San Francisco, CA 94103–1741, USA
Wiley-VCH Verlag GmbH, Pappellaee 3, D-69469 Weinheim, Germany
John Wiley & Sons Australia, Ltd, 33 Park Road, Milton, Queensland, 4064, Australia
John Wiley & Sons (Asia) Pte Ltd, 2 Clementi Loop #02–01, Jin Xing Distripark, Singapore 129809
John Wiley & Sons Canada Ltd, 22 Worcester Road, Etobicoke, Ontario, Canada, M9W 1L1
Wiley also publishes its books in a variety of electronic formats. Some content that appears in print may not be available in electronic books.

British Library Cataloguing in Publication Data
A catalogue record for this book is available from the British Library

ISBN13   978-1-84112-686-9
ISBN10   1-84112-686-1

Typeset in 10/13 pt Minion by Sparks – www.sparks.co.uk
Printed and bound in Great Britain by TJ International Ltd, Padstow, Cornwall
This book is printed on acid-free paper responsibly manufactured from sustainable forestry in which at least two trees are planted for each one used for paper production.
10 9 8 7 6 5 4 3 2 1

CONTENTS

PREFACE TO THE 8TH EDITION

Since the first edition of this book came out nearly a quarter of a century ago the climate for those aspiring to start or to grow their own business has changed profoundly. Once the prerogative of the brave or foolhardy, entrepreneurship is now on the cusp of becoming a near compulsory part of school education, in the United Kingdom at any rate. In 1982 barely 1.8 million people in the UK ran their own business compared with over 4 million in 2005.

The explosion of entrepreneurship has not been confined to the UK. Across Europe over 25 million people are either self-employed or engaged in a business venture of their own making. The breath of entrepreneurship has even reached former bastions of centrally planned economies such as China and the Russian Federation. Indeed there is evidence at least in the top political echelons in these two countries that perhaps they have more successful entrepreneurs than they can currently stomach.

The most profound change, however, is not so much in numbers of business start-ups but in the wealth of research and help and advisory services that have sprung up to help and sustain new business founders. There is strong evidence beginning to emerge that suggests that those entrepreneurs who take the time and trouble to prepare and to plan their strategies carefully have a significantly greater chance of success than those who do not.

This book is aimed at those who are seriously interested in starting their own business, or in expanding an existing one. Those starting up in business for the first time or undertaking their first stages of expansion very often do not know where that help is, or just how much it can do for them. This book is a guide to these organizations and their services, and the important directories, books and periodicals that will provide up-to-date information on each main topic. Enough information is generally included to allow a choice of service and organization, or of publications to find and read.

I am delighted that Capstone are bringing out this, the eighth edition, and hope that it saves some of you at any rate a few sleepless nights and makes the path to success a little less lonely and arduous.

Section 1

WHY SMALL FIRMS MATTER... AND WHY THERE IS SO MUCH HELP ON OFFER

Why small firms matter

One important thing to strike anyone thinking seriously about starting up their first business is just how many organizations there are around that appear to be able to offer a helping hand, or to have timely and valuable advice to offer. This book lists nearly a thousand such people and organizations. Many of those organizations are either directly or indirectly linked to, or inspired by, some government initiative. Apart from the obvious desire to be seen in a favourable light by voters – and there are over forty million owner-managers with votes in the US and Europe alone, a number that could be doubled if spouses are included – there are practical reasons too.

The most compelling reason why small firms matter so much was brought to light first by an American academic, David Birch, over three decades ago. Whilst conducting research at MIT (The Massachusetts Institute of Technology) Birch demonstrated that it was these fledgling enterprises, employing fewer than twenty workers, that were responsible for over two-thirds of the increase in employment in the United States. This revealing statistic was seized upon, especially as it was largely confirmed to be valid for much of the developed world, as the signal for governments, and others, to step up their efforts to stimulate and encourage enterprise.

Small firms had been a neglected part of most countries' economies for most of the post-Second World War years. In the United Kingdom, various studies including the influential Bolton Committee Report, commissioned by the government to investigate the state of the small business sector, had identified that the sector was starved of equity capital and experienced management, but until Birch's paper no one accepted quite how important new and small firms were to a country's economic well-being.

Alongside this recognition of the significance of new business, Birch's research also revealed their fragility. He estimated that roughly 8 million enterprises operating in America closed every year, meaning ' every five to six years, we have to replace half of the entire US economy'. These findings on small-firm failure rates have been shown in study after study, throughout the world. Birch's research and many subsequent studies show that depending on macroeconomic conditions, only about half of all small firms will survive more than five years.

In the years since Birch's research was first published there has been a dramatic increase in new business creation. In the UK alone the small business population has more than doubled from 1.9 million to nearly 4 million. However, the failure rates remained worryingly high. There is a general agreement that the main reasons for small business failure are the lack of management expertise and under-capitalization, aside, that is, from the effects of macroeconomic mismanagement.

Arising from these twin findings that new firms are both vital and fragile have come a plethora of government initiatives both to foster and protect small firms during their formative years. The private sector has not been slow to recognize that if so many entrepreneurs need help, and governments are keen to put money into initiatives, then there must be profitable opportunities for them. The

American Small Business Agency with its army of advisers and support services, the UK's Business Links, and the website www.boutiques-de-gestion.com/ for French-speakers are examples of government small business initiatives designed to ensure new ventures have an easier passage into the business world.

The banks' small business advisers, Business Angel Networks and the 4,000 or so business incubators around the world are examples of the private sector seeing ways of doing well by doing good.

There is also compelling evidence to suggest that the more entrepreneurial a country is, the more wealthy it becomes, as Fig. 1.1, constructed from research data from the respected Kauffman Centre for Entrepreneurial Leadership shows. One further reason governments may find small firms worthy of support is their apparent employment resilience during economic downturns. Fig. 1.2, constructed from data produced by the European Observatory for SME Research, an EC financed research project, seems to suggest that small firms shed employees much more slowly than large ones when the going gets tough. That may well be because when you only employ two or three people, firing what amounts to a half or a third of your workforce is difficult to do and still remain in business. The fact that one or two of those employees may be members of the owner's family may also have a bearing on this reluctance to let people go when work levels dip.

Why people start up in business

It's clear why governments are so keen to foster entrepreneurship. New businesses create jobs for individuals and increased prosperity for nations, which are both primary goals for any government. If those new firms don't throw people out of work

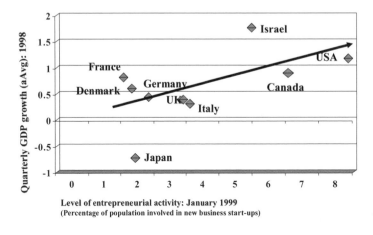

Fig. 1.1 Level of entrepreneurial activity and growth in GDP (source: Kauffman Center for Entrepreneurial Leadership, Autumn 1999).

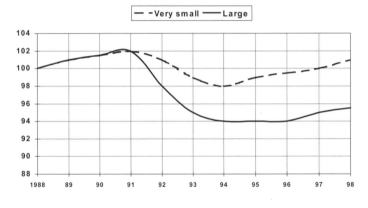

Fig. 1.2 Employment by size and class, Europe 1988–98. Base = 100 in 1988. Small firms are less vulnerable to employment fluctuations over the business cycle (source: European Observatory for SME Research, October 1997).

when recessions start to bite, supporting them becomes doubly attractive.

But people don't start businesses or grow existing ones simply to please politicians or to give their neighbours employment.

There may be many reasons for considering self-employment. Most people are attracted by the idea of escaping the daily grind of working for someone else and being in charge of their own destiny. Other reasons frequently given for taking this step are:

- being able to make your own decisions
- continuation of the business through the next generation
- creating employment for the family
- being able to capitalize on specialist skills
- earning your own money when you want
- having flexible working hours for existing or family commitments
- taking a calculated risk on your own abilities
- reducing existing stress and worry
- having satisfaction in your own work and achievements
- being your own boss
- working without having to rely on others.

The central themes connecting all these reasons for self-employment seem to revolve around personal satisfaction, which can be seen as making work as much fun as any other aspect of life and wealth creation, and which is essential if an enterprise is going to last any length of time.

Personal satisfaction (fun)

No one particularly enjoys being told what to do and where and when to do it. Working for someone else's organization brings all those disadvantages; and in addition, most jobs have little real security. Even in countries where the culture of a job for life runs deep, such as Japan, in practical terms career spans are much shorter. Somewhere between six and nine years is the average time an employee stays with one firm. But if you work for yourself you can, in theory at least, construct your own work pattern and give yourself a job for life, albeit a changing one. The only person to blame if your job is boring, repetitive or takes up time that should perhaps be spent with family and friends is yourself.

Another source of personal satisfaction comes from the ability to ' do things my way'. Employees are constantly puzzled and often irritated by the decisions their bosses impose on them and on the organizations. All too often, managers in big firms say that they would never spend their own money in the manner in which they are encouraged or instructed by the ' powers that be'. They also feel constrained by 'company policy', which seems to set out arbitrary standards for dealing with customers and employees alike. Big firms often fall into the trap of thinking that just because they are big and have been around a long time, what they are doing must be right.

IBM fell into that trap. After growing to dominate the computer world in much the same way as Microsoft has, and facing similar accusing voices, the company stumbled and nearly fell. The outside view of the company was encapsulated in the phrase used at that time to describe their staff: 'Button-down shirt, button-down mind'. IBM badly fumbled desktop computing, handing over the two most critical PC architectural control points – the system's software and the microprocessor – to Microsoft and Intel. Since any clone maker could acquire the operating system software from Microsoft and the microprocessor from Intel, making PCs became a brutal commodity business. In 1990 IBM was in serious trouble and newcomer Microsoft was in the ascendancy. By 2000 IBM had recovered itself and was a world-class business once again. Itself, a rare example of a stunning recovery. Britain's Marconi and Marks & Spencer will do well if they can manage a similar turnaround. But stories abound about executives in these three firms (and many others besides) who knew that their firm's arrogance and 'if it ain't broke so why fix it' mentality was bound to lead them into trouble.

Running your own firm allows you to do things in a way that you think the market and your employees believe to be right for the time. Until, of course, you become big and successful yourself!

Wealth creation (making money)

Americans and Asians are unambivalent about their desire to be successful in business and hence make money. However, there is still a certain nervousness about admitting to wanting to make money in most European cultures, although that is changing fast.

For example, two decades ago 70% of the richest 500 people in the UK inherited their money, with many coming from the traditional 'landed gentry' such as the Duke of Westminster and the Queen. A minority of the very wealthy were what might be called ' self-made' first generation entrepreneurs. Today the ratio is reversed. The vast majority of the current, seriously rich are people who started up their own business. Bill Gates (Microsoft), Larry Ellison (Oracle), Richard Branson (Virgin), Jim Clarke (Netscape), Barry Haigh (Innovex), and Anita Roddick (Body Shop) are just some examples of dollar billionaires who started up in the past few decades.

Apart from doing the lottery, starting your own business is the only possible way to achieve full financial independence. That is not to say it is without risks. In truth, most people who work for themselves do not become mega rich. But many do and many more become far wealthier than they would probably have become by working for someone else.

Business starters have something else going for them today when it comes to creating wealth. Most countries have recognized the value of entre-preneurship, and vie with each other to make their business climate more ' friendly' towards them, or in many cases to actually woo entrepreneurs themselves to emigrate to their more favourable regime. In the UK, for example, the last Labour government under Callaghan presided over a punitive income and capital gains tax system that made it all but impossible to create personal wealth. Whilst various Conservative governments whittled these taxes down, by the turn of the century entrepreneurs still faced a 40% capital gains tax when they sold their business, unless they took drastic (and not necessarily reliable) measures such as selling up all their UK assets (including their home) and moving overseas.

From April 2002 the capital gains tax on the sale of most businesses that are at least two years old was reduced to just 10%. This very low level of capital gains tax was designed to encourage more people to start up businesses, to sell them once they have reached either the level of wealth that they aspire to, or their level of managerial and business competence, and then to either start up again or to finance other entrepreneurial ventures by becoming business angels.

There are disadvantages too

Running your own business is not just about per-sonal satisfaction and creating wealth. It means taking more risks than working for someone else. If the business fails, you could stand to lose far more than your job. If, like most owner-managers, you opt for sole trader status, you could end up personally liable for any business debts incurred. This could mean having to sell up your home and other assets, to meet your obligations. In these cir-cumstances not only will all your hard work have been to no avail, you could end up worse off than when you started. Also, winding up a business is far from fun or personally satisfying.

How many and what sort of people start businesses and what type of business do they go into?

At one level, statistics on small firms are very pre-cise. Government collect and analyse the basic data on how many businesses start (and close) in each geographic area and what type of activity they undertake. Periodic studies give further insights into how new and small firms are financed or how much of their business comes from overseas mar-kets. After that the 'facts' become a little more hazy and we have to rely on ad hoc studies by banks, academics and others, perhaps with a particular axe to grind.

These are the basic facts known about who starts firms and what they do.

How many people start up?

The first fact about the UK small business sector is how big it is. There were an estimated 4 million businesses in the UK at the start of 2005. The vast majority of these (99%) had less than 50 employees and they provided 46% of the UK non-government employment and 38% of sales turnover. Large businesses are in the minority; there are only around 6,000 firms that have 250+ employees. This compares with 1.9 million three decades ago.

What sorts of people start up businesses?

The propensity to start a business is not evenly distributed across the population as a whole. Certain demographic factors such as geographic areas, age groups and so forth seem to influence the number of start-ups at any one time.

Age

Research by Barclays Bank shows that people over 50 now account for 15% of all start-ups in the UK – a growth of 50% in the last ten years. Barclays' study also shows that people aged 50+ are much more likely to research and prepare business plans when starting in business.

It's not just older people who are likely to start up or their own. According to those running Shell's Livewire project, which aims to help the under-25s get a business off the ground, over one in three young people say that they would like to start their own businesses, and around 50,000 young people decide to set up in business each year. The desire to be their own boss, and the opportunity to create a better future are two of the main reasons given by those who start up.

Geography

Some countries, and some regions within countries, seem to be more attractive to start up a business in, if the relative numbers of people starting up are anything to go by. For example, the Global Entrepreneurship Monitor (GEM), a joint research initiative led by London Business School and Babson College, has produced a measure which it uses to compare national rates of entrepreneurial activity called the Total Entrepreneurial Activity (TEA) Index. It is calculated by summing two measures:

1 The nascent entrepreneurship prevalence rate, i.e. the proportion of working age adults actively involved in the creation of a firm which they would own in whole or in part.

2 The new firm owner-management prevalence rate, i.e. the proportion of working age adults owning and managing new firms (less than 3 years old).

The latest TEA index is shown in Fig. 1.3, produced using GEM's data.

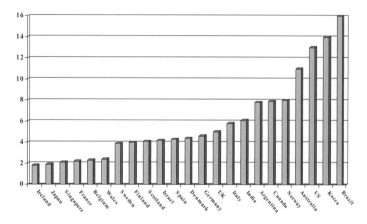

Fig. 1.3 Total entrepreneurial activity prevalence rates by country (TEA index).

This shows Ireland and Japan to be near the bottom of the league table with the US, Korea and Brazil at the top.

Even within countries entrepreneurial skills (or propensities) do not appear evenly spread. Fig. 1.4 comes from UK government published data.

These figures suggest that more than three times as many people in London start a business as do those in the North East. At the very least you are more likely to feel lonely as an entrepreneur in that area, or in Wales and Scotland, than you would in say London or the South East. If the chart set out to show where farmers are likely to be located, London would probably feature at the low end of the spectrum and Wales and Scotland at the high end.

Sex

There is little information available on women's entrepreneurship or women-owned businesses in the UK. The Women's Unit, a government sponsored initiative, has produced some facts about women business starters in both the UK and elsewhere in Europe. Although women make up half the population in Europe, they currently own less than a third of small businesses. Women currently start up an estimated 35% of small businesses in the UK. This reflects the steady growths in female self-employment over the last 20 years. In Ger-

many the proportion is nearer 26% and in Sweden just 25% of women run their own business.

- Self-employment tends to be a midlife choice for women, with the majority starting up businesses after the age of 35.
- Half the self-employed women have at least one or more dependent children, and a fifth have at least one child under five.
- Women are more likely than men to choose self-employment because of family commitments (a fifth compared with 2%).
- The types of businesses women run reflect their pattern of occupation in employment. Public administration, education and health account for 22% of women in self-employment; distribution, hotels and restaurants another 21%.
- There are large regional variations in the proportion of self-employed who are women, from over a third in inner London, to less than a fifth in Northern Ireland, Greater Manchester and West Yorkshire.
- In financing a new business, women tend to prefer using personal credit cards or re-mortgaging their home, while men prefer bank loan finance and government and local authority grants.

Education

There is a popular myth that under-educated 'self made men' dominate the field of entrepreneurship. Anecdotal evidence seems to throw up enough examples of school or university drop-outs to support the theory that education is unnecessary, perhaps even a hindrance, to getting a business started. After all, if Bill Gates and Richard Branson can give higher education a miss, it can't be that vital.

However, the facts such as they are, show a rather different picture. Research in the US shows the higher educated the population, the more likely entrepreneurship takes place. Educated individuals are more likely to identify gaps in the market or understand new technologies.

In Germany, a study on the education level of entrepreneurs showed that whilst 21% of owner-

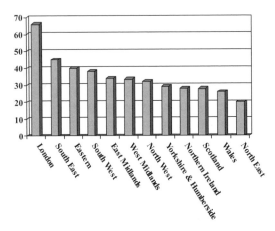

Fig. 1.4 Business registration rates per 10,000 population (Source: *Regional Trends 2001*).

managers had received higher education, nearly one in three who employed five people or more had higher education. A revealing statistic if ever there was one. The GEM study referred to above showed that whilst only 30% of Scots entrepreneurs are women, those who have completed higher education are four times more likely to start a business than those who have not. The most entrepreneurial men are those with vocational education from a further education college.

- clothes shop
- café
- landscape gardener
- recording studio
- graphic designer
- hairdresser
- car mechanic
- website designer
- aromatherapist
- hand-made toys.

What types of business are most popular?

The Government's Small Business Service produced the following statistics on sectors (Fig. 1.5). In terms of the sheer number of enterprises it would appear the UK is more a nation of estate agents rather than of small shopkeepers.

The Government figures are for the small business population as a whole. Barclays Bank's SME research team produce statistics on the sectors that people favour most at the current time. Retailers account for 21% of all start-ups in 2000 and catering accounted for 6%. Property and financial services between them only accounted for 4% of new business start-ups.

According to Shell's Livewire project, the top ten business start-up ideas that young people investigate, though not necessarily start-up, are:

What are the key ingredients of success?

People very often start a business because they have been sacked, made redundant, passed over for promotion, or reached an age where opportunities seemed to have dried up. Whilst any of these events may be the trigger for wanting to start up a business, in themselves they are no guarantee of success.

In fact, there is no sure-fire way to guarantee success in business. However, it's fair to say that two factors significantly influence the likely outcome of any venture. To launch a new business or to grow your own venture successfully calls for a particular type of person. The business idea must also be right for the market and the timing must be spot on. The business world is full of products and

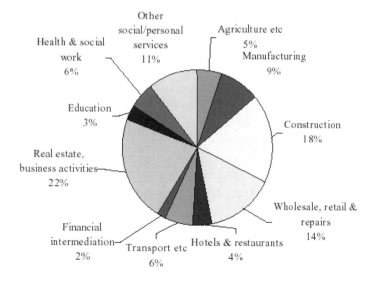

Fig. 1.5 Smaller firms (under 50 employees) by sector.

services that were ahead of their time. Many of the new ventures that were launched in the Internet frenzy were well ahead of the market, as too few consumers were connected and methods of online payment were considered too insecure. Hard work and luck also have a part to play.

You

The business founder is frequently seen as someone who is always bursting with new ideas, is highly enthusiastic, hyperactive and insatiably curious. But the more you try to create a picture of the typical small business founder, the more elusive he or she becomes. Many efforts have been made to 'divine' the characteristics of people who are best suited to become small business founders with limited success. In fact, the only reliable indicator is that someone with a parent or sibling who runs a business is highly likely to start a business himself or herself. Unfortunately this rule applies equally to doctors, accountants and teachers as it does to entrepreneurs.

The following fairly broad characteristics are generally accepted as being desirable, if not mandatory.

- **Total commitment:** Small business founders have complete faith in their business idea. That's the only way that they can convince all the doubters that they are bound to meet on the way. But blind faith is not enough. That commitment has to be backed up with a sound business strategy.
- **Able to work hard:** Hard work should not be confused with long hours. There will be times an owner-manger has to put in 18-hour days, but that should not be the norm. But even if you do work long hours and enjoy them – that's fine. 'Enthusiasts' can be very productive. Workaholics, on the other hand, have a negative kind of black, addictive, driven quality where output (results) become less important than inputs. This type of hard work is counterproductive.

- **Acceptance of uncertainty:** Managers in big business, on the other hand, tend to seek to minimize risk by delaying decisions until every possible fact is known. This response to uncertainty is one that challenges the need to operate in the unknown. There is a feeling that to work without all the facts is not prudent or desirable. Entrepreneurs, on the other hand, have known that by the time the fog of uncertainty has been completely lifted, too many people will be able to spot the opportunity clearly. In point of fact, an entrepreneur would usually only be interested in a decision that involved accepting a degree of uncertainty and would welcome, and on occasion even relish, that position. An essential characteristic of someone starting a business is a willingness to make decisions and to take risks. This does not mean gambling on hunches. It means carefully calculating the odds and deciding which risks to take and when to take them.
- **Good health:** Apart from being able to put in long days, the successful small business owner needs to be on the spot to manage the firm every day. Owners are the essential lubricant that keeps the wheels of the small business turning. They have to turn their hands to anything that needs to be done to make the venture work, and they have to plug any gaps caused either by other people's sickness or because they just can't afford to employ anyone else for that particular job. They themselves cannot afford the luxury of sick leave. Even a week or so's holiday would be viewed as something of a luxury in the early years of a business life.
- **Self-discipline:** One of the most common pitfalls for the novice business man or woman is failing to recognize the difference between cash and profit. Cash can make people 'feel' wealthy, and if it results in a relaxed attitude to corporate status symbols such as cars and luxury office fittings, then failure is just around the corner. The owner-manager needs strong personal discipline to keep him or herself and the business on the schedule the plan calls for. This

is the drumbeat that sets the timing for everything in the firm. Get that wrong and wrong signals are sent to every part of the business both inside and out.

- **Originator/innovator characteristics:** Most people recognize innovation as the most distinctive trait of business founders. They tend to tackle the unknown; they do things in new and difficult ways; they weave old ideas into new patterns. But they go beyond innovation itself and carry their concept to market rather than remain in an ivory tower.
- **Good all-rounder:** Small business founders are rarely geniuses. There are nearly always people in their business who have more competence, in one field, than they themselves could ever aspire to. But they have a wide range of ability and a willingness to turn their hands to anything that has to be done to make the venture succeed. They can usually make the product, market it and count the money, but above all they have the self-confidence that lets them move comfortably through uncharted waters.
- **Planner/organizer characteristics:** Business founders need to be results-oriented. Successful people set themselves goals and get pleasure out of trying to achieve them as quickly as possible and then move on to the next goal. This restlessness is very characteristic.

Self-evaluation for prospective small business owners

The following self-evaluation questions probe only those areas that are important to successfully starting up a business, and can be controlled or affected by the individual. A good score is not a guarantee of success and a poor score does not necessarily bode failure. But if you do the evaluation and get one or two people who know you well to rate you too, it should throw up some things to consider carefully before taking the plunge.

If the statement is rarely true, score 1; if usually true, score 2; and if nearly always true, score 3.

1 I know my personal and business objectives.
2 I get tasks accomplished quickly.
3 I can change direction quickly if market conditions alter.
4 I enjoy being responsible for getting things done.
5 I like working alone and making my own decisions.
6 Risky situations don't alarm me.
7 I can face uncertainty easily.
8 I can sell my business ideas and myself.
9 I haven't had a day off sick for years.
10 I can set my own goals and targets and then get on with achieving them.
11 My family are right behind me in this venture – and they know it will mean long hours and hard work.
12 I welcome criticism – there is always something useful to learn from others.
13 I can pick the right people to work for me.
14 I am energetic and enthusiastic.
15 I don't waste time.

A score of 30 plus is good; 20–30 is fair; below 20 is poor. A high score won't guarantee success but a low one should cause a major re-think.

The idea

Every business begins with an idea. It may be an entirely new product or service or it could just be a new twist to something that is already on the market. Alternatively you could offer an established product or service in an area where it is either unavailable or where you think current demand is not being met fully. Being better, cheaper or faster, and if possible having all three of those attributes can deal you a winning hand.

Great ideas can be very simple and often come from personal experience. Anita Roddick, co-founder of the Body Shop, used to travel widely and noticed that in developing countries people used natural beauty preparations such as cocoa butter to protect the skin. Back in England when she tried to buy natural oils and creams she found they could only be bought in huge quantities. She asked around and soon found that many other people were interested in buying natural, cruelty-free products, provided of course that the price was competitive and they could be bought in small quantities. Roddick set out to find some suppliers and was soon in business.

Sam Walton set up his first Wal-Mart shop in a hamlet near Bentonville, Arkansas in 1962, because retailers such as Kmart and Sears dominated the large towns. Lacking customers, staff and suppliers, Walton had to do things differently. He offered incentives such as profit sharing for the staff and partnerships for suppliers. Customers got friendly service and ' everyday low prices'. These ideas hardly seem world-beaters today, but four decades ago they were nothing short of revolutionary.

Today Wal-Mart is the world's top global retailer and its $220 bn annual sales exceed the sum of the sales of its four biggest competitors. Sears and Kmart, who dominated the market when Walton started in business, are not in the same league.

The key to finding out if your business idea will work lies in researching the market to see if enough people want what you plan to sell, and see what other similar and competing products or services are already about. It is often helpful to start off with a shortlist of two or three possible ideas, which you can refine, and research before deciding which one to run with.

The idea you run with should ideally be one which suits your aspirations and skills, and for which there is evidence of a market that is ripe for development.

What goes wrong?

There is a considerable misinformation in circulation about the number of failing businesses. The most persistent and wrong statistic is that 70% (some even quote 90%) of all new businesses fail. The failure rate is high, but not that high, and in any case the term ' failure' itself, if the word is used to mean a business closing down, has a number of subtly different nuances.

Whilst there are millions of small businesses starting up, many of these survive only a rela-

tively short time. Corporate life generally is on the decline. Less than a third of America's leading companies operating 30 years ago still exist today. But over half of all independently owned ventures will have ceased trading within five years of starting up. One comprehensive study (Kirchoff) of all 814,000 firms started up in the US, in a particular year, followed their destinies for eight years (see Fig. 1.6). That research indicated that only 18% were failures, in that the founders had no real say in the final event. A higher proportion (28%) opted for a voluntary closure, usually when they discovered that the business they had started was losing money, or that in some other way the venture was unsatisfactory. Of the remaining 54% about half sold out, or in some other way changed their ownership, perhaps moving from a partnership to trading through a limited company. Some of these ownership changes were no doubt symptoms of success brought about by business growth, but some would indubitably have been rescue operations in which a stronger competitor saved a drowning firm. Only 28% of all the start-ups in Kirchoff's study survived as independent entities, which after all is the primary goal of most people starting a business.

The European Observatory study (Fig. 1.7) carried out a few years later than Kirchoff, and using a smaller sample, came to a similar conclu-

Fig. 1.6 Eight year destinies of all 814,000 US firms founded in 1978 (Source: *Entrepreneurship and Dynamic Capitalism*, Kirchhoff, 1994).

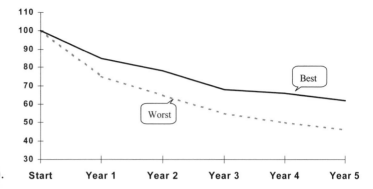

Fig. 1.7 Survival rate of new enterprises in Europe: the best and the worst experiences (Source: European Observatory for SME Research, October 1997).

sion on survival rates. However, this study added one important extra fact. The failure rate in the early years is much higher than in later years, and by year 5 of a firm's life the failure curve is flattening off.

The office of the Official Receiver lists the following causes for business failures:

- insufficient turnover
- poor management and supervision
- lack of proper accounting
- competition
- not enough capital
- bad debts
- excessive remuneration to the owners.

These are for the most part symptoms rather than causes. The causes of failure come under the following general headings.

Nothing new to say

Many people starting up in business have no clear idea as to why people should buy from them rather than their existing supplier of competitive products and services. Indeed, many would-be entrepreneurs have little or no idea what governs their potential customers' purchase decisions. Trying to sell sausages to consumers who are largely preoccupied with buying sizzle can be an unproductive exercise. If there is nothing unique about your product or service, or the way you plan to do business, you must surely question why anyone would want to buy from you. It may only be that

your opening hours are different, and customers feel that matters; or that you keep your promises while operating in sectors such as building or the motor trade, which are renowned for low integrity. But you must have an edge that matters in the market.

Lack of expertise

Starting a business from scratch calls for remarkable versatility. The owner-manager types the invoices with one finger in the evenings, does the books at the weekend, sells on Monday, makes the goods from Tuesday and delivers when he or she can. People whose only experience has been in a large firm may find it difficult to become a jack-of-all-trades. But whilst being able to turn your hand to many tasks, you still need some experience of the industry you plan to start up in. Going into an entirely new area forces the business starter into a near impossibly steep learning curve. Not only do they have to learn how to start a business and all the new tasks that involves, but also they have to learn about a new market with customers, suppliers and workers about whom they know practically nothing.

All learning has to be bought at some price. For those lacking expertise of the sector they are going into, this learning is often gained by making mistakes, which in turn consumes scarce cash resources. That fact goes some way to explaining why small firm failure rate is so much steeper at the outset.

At no time does this lack of expertise show up faster and with more disastrous consequences than during a recession. It is during such periods that lots of people are propelled into entrepreneurship through redundancy, or forsake their own industries believing that the best opportunities lie elsewhere. However, it is clear that the further you move away from the what you know and understand in terms of products or services and customers or markets, the less your chances of success are. The lowest risk route to market is to build on either your product/service expertise, or on your knowledge of the market, and ideally on both.

Cash flow crisis

Too few new and small businesses prepare cash flow forecasts at the outset and maintain a permanent one-year projection when they begin to trade. Received wisdom is that all forecasts are wrong, which can lead the unwise to believe they are a waste of time. Paradoxically it's exactly because events are so unpredictable that cash flow projections are essential. Expenses occur that were not anticipated; customers take longer than expected to find and they take longer still to pay up. These and a dozen other unforeseen and to some extent unforeseeable factors make it vital to make a realistic estimate of the likely timing of cash movements in and out of the business, whilst building in a margin of safety.

One other factor to remember is that cash that flows into a business isn't subject to any automatic deductions as, for example, is a pay cheque from an employer. Too often, entrepreneurs yield to the temptation to use this cash to maintain their living standard, and when the bills come in – from suppliers, for National Insurance, for Value Added Tax – they can't pay them. It's no surprise that the Inland Revenue and the Customs and Excise put more businesses into liquidation than anyone else.

No management accounts

Cash management is only one aspect of the financial information an owner needs to control in the business. Profit and loss accounts, balance sheets and key performance ratios such as gross margin, debtor days and stock turn all have a part to play in a prudent and well-run business. It is not merely useful to understand the basics of accounting; for company directors it is a legal requirement. It is an offence for the directors of a limited company to continue trading once they know – or should have known – their business is in trouble.

Poor financial control is a major reason why many firms fail. Owner managers often leave financial questions to their accountants to sort out at the year-end. They often have the erroneous belief that keeping the books is an activity somehow divorced from the ' real' task of getting customers or making products. By the time the first set of figures are produced, perhaps up to eighteen months after trading commenced, most small businesses are already too far down the road to financial failure to be saved. The final accounts become all too final and a good business proposition has been ruined by financial illiteracy, something that with a modicum of outside help and advice could easily have been prevented.

Falling out

Hidden in all the reasons why some small firms fold is the failure in relationship between business partners. If the business is going to have any chance of success, it is essential that the partners can work together harmoniously and trust each other. Business partners need to be temperamentally suited, have complementary skills and be prepared to compromise with each other without falling out.

There are no hard and fast rules about selecting a business partner, but most successful partnerships seem to occur where people have known each other for some time, ideally as business associates rather than just as friends.

Getting it right

Without exception, all the fundamental reasons and causes of business failure could be anticipated and be addressed in advance by taking some relatively simple measures that cost little. At best, taking such measures would allow the business to succeed and prosper, perhaps even beyond the founders' early hopes and dreams. At worst, they could ensure that if the business does have to close down it can do so in an orderly way, with as little pain and cost to every one involved as is possible.

Write a business plan

Perhaps the most important step in launching any new venture or expanding an existing one is to prepare a business plan. Such a plan must include your goals for the enterprise, both short and long term; a description of the products or services you will offer and the market opportunities you have anticipated for them; and finally, an explanation of the resources and means you will employ to achieve your goals in the face of likely competition.

Preparing a comprehensive business plan along these lines takes time and effort, but very little cost. In our experience at Cranfield on our new enterprise programmes, anything between 200 and 400 man hours are needed, depending on the nature of your business and how much data you have already gathered. Not surprisingly, fewer than one in five new businesses prepare a business plan at the outset. Less than 50% of firms employing up to 20 people have a current business plan. However, it has to be remembered that most new ventures fail. Preparing a business plan is essential if you are both to crystallize and focus your ideas, and test your resolve about entering or expanding your business. Once completed, your business plan will serve as a blueprint to follow which, like any map, improves the user's chances of reaching the destination.

Despite the obvious benefits, thousands of would-be entrepreneurs still attempt to start without a business plan. The most common among these are businesses that either appear to need little or no capital at the outset, or whose founders have funds of their own; in both cases it is believed unnecessary to expose the project to harsh financial appraisal.

The former hypothesis is usually based on the easily exploded myth that customers will all pay cash on the nail, and suppliers will wait for months to be paid. In the meantime, the proprietor has the use of these funds to finance the business. Such model customers and suppliers are thinner on the ground than optimistic entrepreneurs think. In any event, two important market rules still apply: either the product or service on offer fails to sell like hot cakes and mountains of unpaid stocks build up, all of which eventually have to be financed; or it does sell like hot cakes and more financially robust entrepreneurs are attracted into the market. Without the staying power that adequate financing provides, these new competitors will rapidly kill him off.

Those would-be entrepreneurs with funds of their own, or worse still, have borrowed from 'innocent' friends and relatives, tend to think that the time spent in preparing a business plan could be more usefully (and enjoyably) spent looking for premises, buying a new car, or installing a computer. In short, anything that inhibits them from immediate action is viewed as time wasting.

As most people's perception of their business venture is flawed in some important respect, it follows that jumping in at the deep end is risky – and unnecessarily so. Flaws can often be discovered cheaply and in advance when preparing a business plan; they are always discovered in the marketplace, invariably at a much higher and usually fatal cost.

There was a myth at the start of the Internet boom that the pace of development in the sector was too fast for business planning. The first generation of dotcom businesses and their backers seemed happy to pump money into what they called a 'business' or 'revenue' model. These 'models' were little more than brief statements of intent supported by little more than wishful thinking. A few months into the new millennium, a sense of realism came to the Internet sector. Now, only ventures with a well-prepared business plan have any chance of getting off the ground or being supported in later stage financing rounds.

Section 11 gives detailed guidance on preparing viable business plans and where to get help in writing it.

Learning from others: a business plan example

This example business plan shows both how to structure a business plan and the types of information needed to give credence to your arguments. Much of the rest of this book is intended to show you exactly where you can find such evidence and data as will support (or refute) your plans.

Safari Europe Business Plan

Executive summary

For the past five years Karen Kehoe has been a founder director of a very successful outdoor clothing shop in Bristol, Adventure Works. Last year that business made £120,000 profit on sales of £850,000 and employed seven people.

Adventure Works recently took on an agency from European Adventure Holidays, one of the largest and most respected tour operators in the market. With virtually no marketing effort, some 200 adventure holidays have been sold by Karen in the past six months, netting £40,000 in commissions. Sales of insurance policies and other services have added to this total, and could potentially add much more. From desk and field market research carried out on 300 clients, Karen is certain that there is considerable potential in the adventure travel business. In particular one important segment of that market, the professional, 25- to 35-year-olds who want to adventure travel in Europe, is not having its needs properly met.

Karen Kehoe plans to sell her shares in the clothing shop and invest the proceeds in a new business, Safari Europe. The business will operate from a self-contained facility within the existing shop,

with its own entrance and shop window onto the main street.

The company believes that by concentrating on one market segment, the 25- to 35-year-old professionals, and one geographic destination, Europe, it will be able to deliver a significantly superior service to anything currently on the market.

Published research shows that tourism is a fast-growing business sector and Europe is the favoured location for most travellers. Adventure holidays, though a relatively new and small market, looks set for explosive growth.

Karen has selected a small team, some of whom have worked with her in the clothing shop for several years. She has worked as the manager of a branch of a high street travel agent, and other members of the staff have extensive travel, selling, and computer skills, all of which will be invaluable to the new venture.

Safari Europe expects that by concentrating full time on selling adventure holidays, clients will increase from the present level of 200 in six months, achieved with only a part time effort, to at least 660 in the first year, 1400 in the second, and 2100 in the third. To help achieve this growth Karen has identified three other tour operators she wishes to represent and has begun negotiations with them. Selling between two and three holidays a day will allow the business to reach cash flow break-even in year 1, while making a modest profit. This compares with the 1.3 holidays currently being sold each day.

By year 2 post-tax profits should be £180,000, and in year 3 nearly £300,000.

To achieve these results the company needs to invest in website and database software and systems, and in refurbishing the shop premises. Our market research demonstrates that sales of travel services via the Internet accounts for approaching £3 billion a year's worth of business. It is the fastest growing business-to-consumer activity on the Internet.

In all, about £75,000 will be needed to fund the business during its formative months. A further £10,000 needs to be available to deal with unforeseen events, although a sensitivity analysis has been carried out which shows this is unlikely to be required.

Karen will be investing £25,000 of her own money in the business, and seeking £60,000 from outside. The purpose of this business plan is to attract other shareholders to invest in a highly profitable venture. Return on shareholders capital by year 3 will be close to 100 per cent. This opportunity may appeal to Karen's partners in the clothes shop or to a business angel.

Alternatively, she is considering loan finance made up of a £25,000 short-term loan and an overdraft facility of £35,000.

The business and its management

History and position to date

Increasingly, shop customers have asked for advice on adventurous places to go on holiday. Last year Adventure Works took on an agency from European Adventure Holidays, one of the largest and most respected tour operators in this market and began to promote and sell their products. In the six months that we have been selling travel agency products, some 200 holidays, at an average cost of £2000, have been sold. Adventure Works' commission on the sales has been £40,000 (10 per cent commission). In addition, 35 insurance policies have been sold at an average price of £100, yielding £1050 (30 per cent commission).

Mission

Safari Europe has as its mission, to be the leading provider of hassle-free European adventure holidays to the 25- to 35-year-old young professionals market, initially operating within a 25-mile catchment area, but quickly starting to sell its services worldwide, via the Internet. Sales of travel services is the fastest growing category of business-to-consumer activity on the Internet. In 2006 the value of this market will be an estimated £2.7 billion

The emphasis will be on providing a complete specialist service, based on having a detailed knowledge of the holiday destination and adventure activities being offered. Our market research shows that the major criticism our type of client has of existing travel agencies, is that they 'know nothing about their products, they just open the catalogue and read', to quote one of the many disappointed adventure holidaymakers.

Also, by using our experience in the Adventure Works clothing shop, we will be able to both advise and direct our clients to sources of the type of travel equipment they will need to get the very best out of their holiday experience.

Objectives

Our financial objectives are to be operating at, or close to, cash flow break-even by the end of the first year. We aim to be profitable from year 1 onwards; then we will aim to earn at least £180,000 post-tax profit in the second year, and nearly £300,000 in the third. Our profit margin on sales by year 3 will be a respectable 7 per cent.

We also intend that the business should be fun. The present staff are passionate about adventure holidays, and we intend to maintain their enthusiasm by constant product and skill training. We will only recruit new people who share our vision.

Legal structure

The business will be set up as a limited company in the next few weeks. This structure will clearly separate the travel business from the shop and make it possible to attract the risk capital that will be required when the business starts to grow. For example, an Air Travel Operator's Licence (ATOL) will eventually be required, which in turn calls for a business to have a minimum paid-up share capital of £25,000.

At a later stage the business may wish to sell and issue airline tickets and to create its own charter holidays. This will require membership of the International Air Traffic Association (IATA) and an Association of British Travel Agents (ABTA) bonding. However, in the period covered by this business plan we intend to operate only as the appointed agents for a number of tour operators. As such, we can shelter under their licences and bonds.

Professional advisers

We have taken legal advice on the formation of our company from Browne, Browne, and Browne, a local firm of business solicitors. We have also talked directly with the various regulatory authorities. We will be taking professional advice on database systems and on website construction and Internet trading systems, from Solomon Burt Associates, the London-based software and systems design house.

Products and Services

Tour agency products

We currently are appointed agents for European Adventure Holidays (EAH), a leading supplier in the market. At present EAH offer some 40 different adventure holiday packages throughout Europe, covering such areas as: horse trekking in Iceland; above-the-clouds trekking on islands and remote mountain regions in such areas as Corsica and Norway; van-supported, inn-to-inn bicycling; mountain biking and hiking adventure tours throughout France, Germany, Italy, and Austria; ballooning across the Alps.

We intend to seek to be appointed agents by three other major adventure holiday tour firms, with whom we are currently in negotiation.

Services

We will offer a comprehensive range of complementary services to support the adventurous holidaymaker that will ensure they have a safe, enjoyable, and memorable experience. These services will include: insurance, both personal and effects; pre- and post-holiday briefing packs; a directory of advice and information services covering each country and adventure activity.

Proprietary position

Whilst at present we are offering only other companies' adventure holidays we have protected our position in a number of ways.

Firstly, we have a two-year agency agreement with European Adventure Holidays that gives us access to all their holiday products, both existing and new. This contract is dependent on our achieving sales of at least 250 holiday packages a year. We intend to negotiate similar agreements with future suppliers, although sales targets with them will be lower to reflect their relative market position.

Secondly, we intend to maintain a high service element to our business, extending our range of value-added services. In this way we will seek to build up a high level of repeat business. Customer loyalty is vital to our profitable growth.

Guarantees and customer protection

Our clients will be protected financially against either our or our tour operators' failure, by virtue of the ABTA bonding held by our principals. We will only use holiday providers who can provide 24-hour emergency support services for clients whilst on holiday.

Markets and Competitors

Markets, projections, and market segments

The world travel market is forecast to expand at a 4.1 per cent average annual growth rate until 2010. This is faster than economic growth generally, which is expected to be around 2.4 per cent per annum.

The European market, whilst not the fastest growing, will be the most important destination, accounting for over 50 per cent of all international arrivals (see Table 1.5, Appendix).

France, Italy, and Spain are the most important destinations within Europe (Table 1.6, Appendix). This is why we have selected as our initial partners, tour operators with appropriate products in these countries.

Figures for the size and projected growth of adventure holidays are sketchy, but one recent study (World Adventure Travel Data Corp.) gave the figures shown in Table 1.1.

Our own market study confirms that Europe is likely to be the largest destination market for adventure holidays. Our study shows only 30 per cent

Table 1.1   Adventure Travel Holidays – World forecast (million arrivals): 1990–2010

Destination	1990	1997	2003	2010
Europe	0.25	0.60	1.60	2.35
N. America	0.45	0.60	1.40	2.20
Rest of World	0.10	0.25	0.95	1.10
Total	**0.85**	**1.45**	**3.95**	**5.65**

Age	1990 (%)	2010 (%)
16–24	61	38
25–35	20	31
36–45	15	26
46+	4	6
	100	**100**

of adventure travellers to be under 24, whilst the World Adventure Travel Data study claims 61 per cent. We feel the difference is caused by our survey sample being confined to relatively affluent people who had spent at least £200 in adventure clothing.

One further emerging market-segment for adventure holidays is corporate clients. Our market research suggests that up to 20 per cent of adventure holidays are sold at this top-price end of the market.

Competition and competitive advantage

There are no adventure holiday specialist travel agents in the Bristol area. However, there are many in capital and secondary cities such as London, Paris, Lyon, Madrid, Barcelona, and Frankfurt. There are also a number of direct marketing and Internet providers. These are the types of competitors we expect to face.

- General travel agents, who have added adventure holidays to their range. These agents often have little or no knowledge of adventure destinations or activities. They sell literally from the page, offering limited advice, information, and support. According to our market study 40 per cent of adventure holidays are booked through these general travel agents, but only 33 per cent of clients would use them again. Adventure tour operators advertise their holidays in the press attracting about 25 per cent of all adventure holiday clients. However, clients have to shop around several tour operators to find what they want, and they cannot get unbiased advice, or much help with information. Only 45 per cent would go back to a tour operator for their next holiday.

- Independent travellers make up 15 per cent of those going on adventure holidays, and 65 per cent of those would travel that way again. We need to persuade this group that our superior product knowledge and service is worth their consideration.

- Internet providers sell only 5 per cent of adventure travel holidays. However, 70 per cent would buy their next holiday via the Internet. There is plenty of scope to offer a superior website. We believe that by having daily face-to-face contact with clients we will be better able to manage a fresh, vital, and relevant website aimed at the specific needs of our market segment.

- Specialist adventure travel agencies only sell about 15 per cent of holidays at present, but we feel that this is due partly to lack of client awareness and partly to the comparative rarity of such outlets. Some 65 per cent of those using specialist adventure holiday travel agents would use them again, which is many more than would use either a tour operator direct or a general travel agent. However, these agents were criticized for having such a wide range of activities and destinations that their sales agents knew little about them. Our research shows that whilst 41 per cent of clients take adventure holidays in Europe only 23 per cent of the 5000 adventure tours on offer are for European destinations.

We feel that by concentrating on European destinations, which is the largest market for both holidays in general and adventure holidays in particular, we *will be able to have superior product knowledge. We will only need to know perhaps 100 destinations and activities well, rather than have only a passing knowledge of the 5000 adventure holidays on offer.*

Our market research has also shown that many adventure travel agents are catering for the backpacker market, consisting mostly of very cost-conscious under 24-year-olds. This can lead to very different types of clients ending up at the same destination, with some consequent dissatisfaction. It is also evident that the backpacker market requires a much lower level of service and information, than do the more affluent professional 25- to 35-year-olds.

Customer needs and benefits

We believe that by concentrating on the European market, offering a limited but extensive range of types of holiday, and aiming our service specifically at affluent professionals, we can meet the needs of our clients in a way not being achieved by any of our competitors.

Our market study has shown that this group has specific needs that are not currently being met, as 65 per cent of those taking adventure holidays would not buy from the same source again. In particular they want their travel agent to have comprehensive knowledge of the destination (87 per cent); to have an efficient administration system in which they can have confidence (84 per cent); to go on holiday with similar professional people (81 per cent); and to be offered useful advice and ancillary services such as insurance (79 per cent).

Competitive Business Strategy

Pricing policy

The normal commission paid to travel agents for this type of holiday is in the 10 to 15 per cent range. Whilst European Adventure Holidays, the first agency we have been appointed to, pay us at the lower end of the scale, they are a prestigious firm to represent. Having them in our portfolio will enable us to negotiate much higher commissions from our

new principals. Accordingly we are planning on an average travel agency commission of 11 per cent rising to 13 per cent by the end of year 3. Commission on insurance and other services will be 30 per cent, throughout.

Promotional plans

Our market research shows that editorial has the greatest impact on people's choice of an adventure holiday, closely followed by having the right 'shop window' and having a recommendation from a friend, relation, or colleague. General press advertising seems to be fairly ineffective in this sector, and even specialist press advertising only draws in 14 per cent of clients. (See Appendix, Summary of Findings from our Market Research.)

Accordingly, our promotional plan is as follows:

Public Relations (PR). We will put considerable effort into preparing and disseminating a regular flow of press releases. These will be based on stories about our destinations, activities, corporate clients, and our staff. We will use a freelance PR adviser to help us write copy and target editors.

Shop Front. We plan to have an exciting, informative, and actively managed display window. There will be a video display showing holidays in progress. Different destinations can be selected from outside the window via a control panel, otherwise the scenes will rotate on a random basis.

Website. We will have a well-managed website. This is fast becoming a major promotional channel and we believe it will increase in importance over time. Also it is the easiest way for us to have a global presence at the outset. (See Appendix, Internet Growth and the Sale of Travel Services.)

Advertising. We will undertake a small amount of specialist-press advertising in order to enhance our PR activity. There is considerable research to support the argument that the more often a potential client hears about you, the more likely they are to approach you when they have a need for your type of service.

Database. Our database will retain full details of all our clients, the holidays they have taken, and their post-holiday appraisal data. We will use this data to provide incentives to our delighted clients prompting them to recommend our services to friends, relatives, colleagues, and employers.

Direct Mail. We will write to all past shop clients announcing the establishment of the travel business, and offering them a special introductory adventure holiday package.

Wider factors affecting strategy

The general economic climate in this city is good. A large influx of new businesses relocating from London and its surrounds has added to the area's prosperity. There is now a large and growing young professional population.

Tourism in general looks set to grow (see Appendix), Europe looks like continuing to be the major destination, and the Internet will be an important channel into this market.

Tourism is becoming a heavily regulated business sector. Whilst we have avoided most of the regulatory problems by becoming an appointed agent for a large established tour operator, in the future we will need our own ABTA bonding and ATOL registration.

Operations

Sales

Excellent selling skills are vital in our type of business, so everyone will be fully trained in selling. Every month we will audit each other by observing half a day's selling activity and giving feedback on strengths and weaknesses in skills.

Record keeping

We will keep records of every sales contact. Data such as source of enquiry; client's needs; previous holidays; and job, income, and status, will be recorded. By having superior information on clients and prospects we intend to offer a truly personal service.

Premises

It is vital that the travel business has both a shop front facing onto the main street, and a visible separate entrance. It is intended that clothing shop clients will be able to move between the premises without going outside. We will be renting $70m^2$ ($750ft^2$) of space at a cost of £18,000 per annum, fully serviced. In addition, we will need to spend £15,000 on internal refurbishments. We plan to do some of this work ourselves. Also a further £2500 will be needed for office equipment such as desks and chairs.

Capacity

Our offices can accommodate five sales desks. Each sales desk has a capacity to handle four clients per hour, which means over the year we could handle up to 40,000 enquiries. With our average conversion rate of 1 in 5 we could service 9600 clients from our present facilities. This is well above the numbers we are anticipating in the business plan.

Opening hours

The telephone will be staffed 24 hours a day by live operators. During the period 9.00 a.m. to 6.00 p.m. this will mostly be done by our staff. However, overload calls during the day and out-of-hours calls will go to our live telemarketing bureau. People consider holiday decisions at home in the evenings after discussion with friends and partners. We want to be available as their first point of contact with an informed friendly service.

We believe that as our clients will mostly be busy working professional people, out-of-hours access to our services is also a key way in which we can differentiate ourselves.

Equipment

We will be renting an integrated telephone and database system from the outset. This will allow any of up to ten sales staff to answer calls and have full on-screen data on clients and products. As *service is one of our key differentiators, it is essential that all of us have full access to all relevant data speedily and efficiently.*

Staffing

From the outset, all staff will have job descriptions, a career and training history file, and a record of appraisals.

New staff will take the travel agency psychometric aptitude test, and then spend time with each member of the Adventure Works Travel team.

All staff will undergo full product training, and will spend at least four weeks a year on site at key travel destinations.

Quality control

We will be developing outline scripts to help sales staff manage enquiries. This will ensure that all incoming phone calls are dealt with in the same way and to a similar high standard.

We will encourage people enquiring about holidays to give us feedback on:
- *Our ability to handle their enquiry.*
- *The way we manage between booking the holiday and taking the holiday.*

- *The client's reactions to the holiday, in terms of whether it meets their expectations.*

Forecasts and Financial Data

Sales forecast

Our enquiry-to-sales conversion rate on the adventure travel holidays sold to date, whilst operating within the outdoor clothing shop, has been 33 per cent. For the purposes of our sales forecast, we are assuming that only 20 per cent of enquiries will actually result in an adventure holiday being booked. This is a very conservative estimate.

We expect there to be a steady build-up of clients coming from the clothing shop to talk to us about holidays (see table below). However, the number of new enquiries generated by our promotional activity will also build up during the year, gradually overtaking enquiries from the clothes shop. This is a trend we expect to continue.

Based on the projection below, we are forecasting to sell 660 adventure travel holidays next year at an average price of £2125.

Once insurance and other service sales are added in we expect to generate an income of £160,948 over the 12 months (Table 1.2).

In year 2 we are forecasting £373,843 in commission, and in year 3 we plan to reach £590,926.

Table 1.2   Sales forecast projection

	Q1	Q2	Q3	Q4	Year total
Enquiries Generated Through Promotion	200	425	425	750	1,800
Adventure Shop Enquiries	300	300	450	450	1,500
Total Enquiries	**500**	**725**	**875**	**1,200**	**3,300**
Holidays Sold	100	145	175	240	660
Average Holiday's Cost	2,000	2,000	2,250	2,250	2,125
Commission Received	20,000	29,000	43,312	59,136	151,448
Commission on Insurance & Other Services Received	1,000	2,000	3,000	3,500	9,500
Total Commission & Fees Earned	**21,000**	**31,000**	**46,312**	**62,636**	**160,948**

Cash flow projections and sensitivity analysis

The cash flow projections for year 1 show that after the owner has put in £25,000 the business will need additional short-term financing of about £50,000. For the last two months of the year we are forecasting a positive cumulative cash flow, and a year-end cash surplus of £11,937.

We have also done a sensitivity analysis to assess the impact on cash flow, if our sales of holidays were 10 per cent less than projected. We do not believe this to be a likely event. But even if it were to occur, our short-term financing needs would still not exceed £50,000 in any month. However, this scenario would leave the company with a small (£1450) negative cash position at the year end.

In our cash flow projection we have assumed the whole £50,000 additional financing has come from a bank loan. We have allowed for interest on the full amount for the whole period. In practice, we would hope to finance part of this at least by an overdraft amount equal to the money actually required. In this way we believe we have made a prudent, conservative provision.

Profit and loss account

We expect to make a small after-tax profit in the first year of £21,898. This is before the owner's drawings. Any owner's drawings will be contingent on performance being better than that expected in the plan (Table 1.3).

Balance sheet

The balance sheet at the end of year 1 shows a healthy surplus of current assets over current liabilities. We have shown a conservative funding position, which does not include any of the additional capital that we hope to secure.

Performance ratios

We plan to move our gross profit up from 11 per cent in year 1, to 13 per cent in year 3. These figures look quite low, but it should be remembered that our income is really the sales commission we earn, not the full price of an adventure holiday.

Our profit before tax is a more accurate measure of performance. This we expect to move from 2 per cent at the outset, up to 8 per cent by year 3.

Commission generated and profit per employee will be amongst the highest in the industry. At Brooker's Travel, for example, profit per employee never exceeded £19,500 (Table 1.4).

Break-even

To break even we will need to sell between 2 and 3 holidays a day. This compares with our present sales of 1.3 holidays a day, based on our part-time effort out of the clothing shop. So we feel confident that break-even can be attained within a reasonable period.

Table 1.3 Projected profits in years 1 to 3

	Year 1	Year 2	Year 3
Turnover	1,416,071	3,115,356	4,545,588
Less cost of sales	1,255,123	2,741,513	3,954,662
Gross profit	**160,948**	**373,843**	**590,926**
Less expenses	133,575	145,750	207,000
Profit before tax	**27,373**	**228,093**	**383,926**
Provision for tax	5,474	45,619	87,276
Profit after tax	**21,898**	**182,474**	**296,650**

	Year 1	Year 2	Year 3
Gross profit (%)	11	12	13
Profit before tax %	2	7	8
Commission generated per employee	£45,985	£83,076	£98,487
Profit per employee	£7,535	£41,471	£63,987

Table 1.4   Profit before tax

Financing Requirements

Funds required and timing

The two major investments we plan to make are:

Website and Database Development (this will cost us £25,000). The database system is one of our key differentiators. It will allow us to offer superior service and ensure a high level of repeat business and referrals. The website is vital if we are to reach this wide and disparate global market. The group of potential clients we have chosen as our target market (affluent, professional 25- to 35-year-olds) are prime users of the Internet. Even those people in our locality will expect to be able to research our offers on the Internet before coming to the shop

Shop Premises Development (this will cost us £17,500). We have to look professional and to have an efficient work environment. If our staff do not have the right tools we can hardly expect them to deliver superior performance. If clients see amateur premises, they will not be inspired to spend thousands of pounds and entrust their adventure holiday plans to us.

Both these investments need to be made at the outset to ensure the business creates the right impression from the start. We only get one chance to make a first impression.

We have decided to lease our telephone and computer systems as this is a rapidly changing area and we need to have access to the very latest technology. Financing packages from equipment suppliers are currently very attractive.

Funding options

The owner plans to invest £25,000 of her own money (the proceeds of the sale of her share of the

clothing shop business). The cash flow projections show that the business will require a further £50,000 of working capital during the early months of the first year's trading. We think we should provide for £60,000 to allow for unforeseen eventualities. We are considering two options for raising this.

Option 1: The sale of equity, perhaps to the original shop partners, of between £25,000 and £100,000. This would provide some capital to allow for growth. Any shortfall could be funded by overdraft or a bank loan.

Option 2: Approach our bank with a view to raising a medium-term loan of £25,000 and an overdraft facility of £35,000. Karen Kehoe could, with family help, provide any lender with security for part, if not all, of this facility.

Business Controls

Financial

We will be using a computer-based financial management system. This will allow us to analyse the profitability of sales of different holidays through each tour operator. In this way we can review our sales and marketing activities on a regular basis. It will also allow us to reward staff on the basis of profit achieved rather than just on sales.

Sales and marketing

We will also be using a contact-management system that will allow us to monitor the effectiveness of different promotional strategies and of different marketing messages.

The cornerstone of our strategic advantage lies in having superior data on prospects and clients.

Appendix: Market Research

Table 1.5   International arrivals by world regions: updated forecast for the years 2000 and 2010 (millions)

	1975	1995*	1996*	2000	2010	Average annual growth rate 1990–2010
Europe	153.8	338.2	347.4	397	525	3.1
East Asia/Pacific	8.7	84.5	90.1	122	229	7.6
Americas	50.0	110.1	115.5	138	195	3.7
Africa	4.7	18.7	19.4	25	37	4.6
Middle East	3.6	11.3	15.1	14	21	4.9
South Asia	1.6	4.5	4.5	6	11	6.7
World total	**222.3**	**567.4**	**592.1**	**702**	**1,018**	**4.1**

Source: Global Stats Corp. 2005

Table 1.6   Indicators of tourism demand in 2006

	International tourist arrivals (thousands)	Nights spent by foreign tourists (millions)	International tourism receipts (millions ECU)
Austria	17,173	63.8	11,168
Belgium	5,560	12.8	4,776
Denmark	1,614	10.8	2,814
Finland	835	3.3	1,320
France	60,110	54.3	20,742
Germany	14,847	35.5	12,408
Greece	10,130	39.6	3,138
Ireland	4,231	14.0	2,059
Italy	31,052	113.0	20,993
Luxembourg	767	2.3	4,776
Netherlands	6,574	19.7	4,946
Portugal	9,706	22.2	3,330
Spain	44,886	107.8	19,431
Sweden	683	7.9	2,652
United Kingdom	22,700	164.9	14,366
EU	230,868	672.0	124,143
Iceland	190	0.8	127
Liechtenstein	59	0.1	n/a
Norway	2,880	7.1	1,826
EEA	233,997	680.0	126,096
Switzerland	11,500	34.0	7,236
Europe	245,497	714.0	133,332

Source: Global Stats Corp. 2005

Summary of findings from our market research

Part 1: from a sample of 300

300 clients of Adventure Works were surveyed, who had made purchases in excess of £200 in the past six months.

The key responses are shown in Fig. 1.8. From this we can see that only 20 per cent of our sample had never taken or considered taking an adventure holiday. Whilst they had not yet taken such a holiday, 30 per cent had at least actively considered doing so. And 10 per cent are regular users, taking at least one adventure holiday each year.

Part 2: from those 186 respondents who have taken at least one adventure travel holiday (Fig. 1.9)

Gender:	Male 65%	Female 35%
Status:	Married 21%	Single 79%

The 25- to 35-year-olds appears to be the largest group, accounting for 40 per cent of adventure holidaymakers.

Over 40 per cent of adventure holidaymakers are in the £20,000 plus income bracket. Nearly 20 per cent earn in excess of £25,000 (Fig. 1.10).

Most of those taking adventure holidays spend in excess of £2000 per head per holiday. Those spending over £3000 per head tend to be 25- to 35-year-old professionals. Those spending under £2000 are in the lower income and lower age groups (Fig. 1.11).

Our research shows that Europe is the most popular destination for adventure holidaymakers (Fig. 1.12). However, only 1200 of the 5000 adventure tours on the market are for European destinations. Africa, which only attracts 7 per cent of the market, has 16 per cent of the tours aimed at it (Table 1.7).

Table 1.7 The 5,000 major tours offered by region (Adventure research, August 2005)

Europe	1,200
North America	1,000
India	600
Africa	810
Far East	675
Other	715

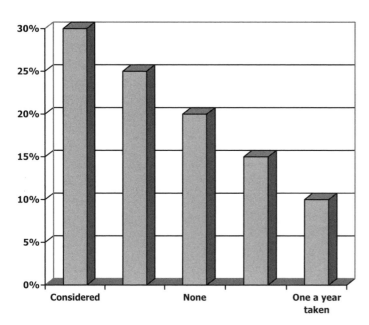

Fig. 1.8 Percentage of sample taking and not taking adventure holidays

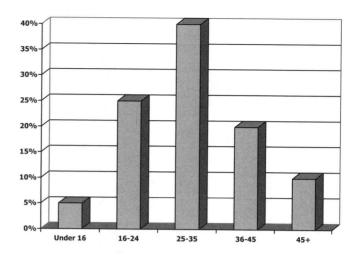

Fig. 1.9 Percentage by age

It follows that the European market has scope for expansion, and that if we concentrate on that market we only have to have detailed knowledge of upmarket European tours, rather than all 5000. In that way we can have the advantage of superior knowledge in our chosen market.

Fig. 1.13 shows one of the most powerful results of our research. Whilst general travel agents may be the most likely to be used by those taking an adventure holiday, they are the least likely place for those clients to return to.

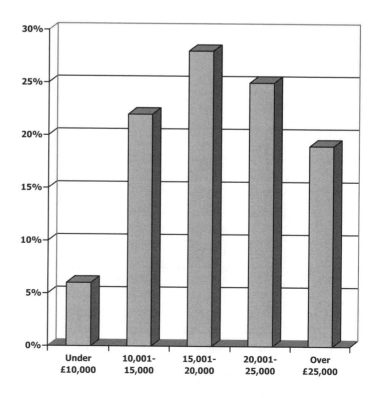

Fig. 1.10 Percentage by income group

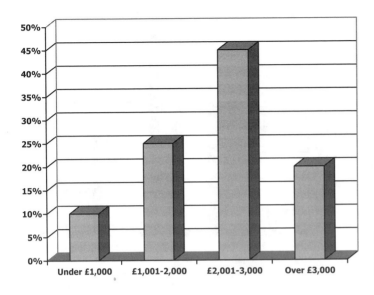

Fig. 1.11   Percentage average spend on adventure holidays per head per holiday

Whilst specialist adventure travel agents, such as the business we are setting up, only account for 15 per cent of the market, 65 per cent of clients would use them again. We aim by superior service to better this ratio.

Fig. 1.14 demonstrate the power of editorial comment. The next most effective way to reach potential clients is via the travel agent's shop window. Both the general press and the adventure/travel press do not appear to have much effect on buyers in this market.

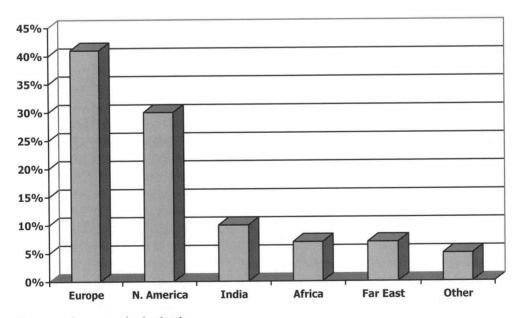

Fig. 1.12   Percentage by destination

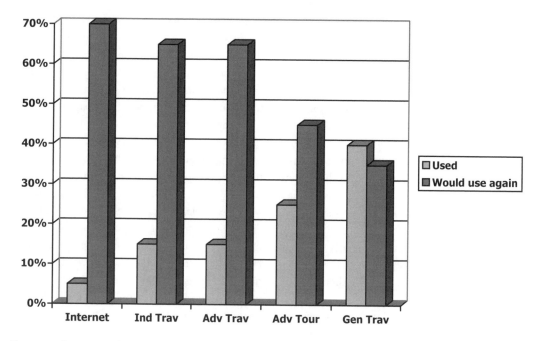

Fig. 1.13   Percentage by source of purchase of last adventure holiday – and whether they would use again

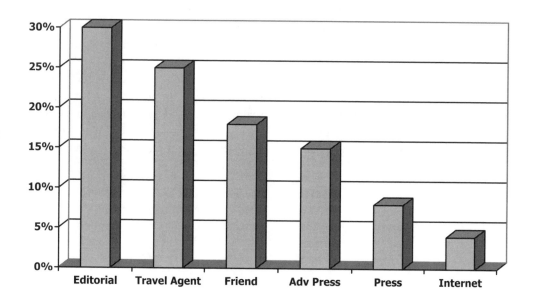

Fig. 1.14   Percentage of where you heard about your last adventure holiday

Be well informed

All this implies that in order to keep out of the failure statistics it is vital for the owner or manager of a new or small business to be better informed.

There are now thousands of organizations and even more publications that can provide the much-needed information for small business. Many of these organizations have only recently come into being, and many are still in a state of flux. There has been a parallel growth in other organizations, some shaping their policies to recognize the needs of small ventures, and others being wholly new activities. So 'entrepreneurs' have plenty of help to turn to, and evidence is beginning to emerge that those who take this advice improve their chances of survival significantly.

One reason advanced for not taking advice is that doing so would involve taking the risk that someone else would steal the business idea and get to market first. There are at least two good reasons for dismissing this argument. The first is that there is no shortage of so-called great business ideas. What is in short supply are people with the ability, resourcefulness and tenacity to bring those ideas to market place. The second reason is based around the argument that attaining ' first mover advantage', or ' the element of surprise', to use the military strategist's language, is worth paying almost any price. This principle is one of the most enduring in business theory and practice. Entrepreneurs and established giants are always in a race to be first. Research from the 1980s that purported to show that market pioneers have enduring advantages in distribution, product-line breadth, product quality and, especially, market share underscores this principle.

Beguiling though the theory of first mover advantage is, it is probably wrong. A thorough review of the research studies that supported this theory was published four years ago in the *Sloan Management Review*, and the findings were found to be flawed. (The authors of this paper also drew on many other studies that lent support to their views.) Amongst the many errors in the earlier research, the authors of the Sloan paper revealed that the questions used to gather much of the data were at best ambiguous, and perhaps dangerously so. For example, the term, 'one of the pioneers in first developing such products or services,' was used as a proxy for 'first to market'. In fact, the only compelling evidence from all the research was that nearly half of all firms pursuing a first to market strategy were fated to fail, whilst those following fairly close behind were three times as likely to succeed.

Finding help and advice

Those starting up in business for the first time or undertaking their first stages of expansion very often do not know where that help is, or just how much it can do for them. The rest of this book is a guide to these organizations and their services, and the important directories, books and periodicals that will provide up-to-date information on each main topic. Enough information is generally included to allow a choice of service and organization, or of publications to find and read. The decision to include or exclude an entry is based on two criteria. Does the organization (or directory) provide either a service or information of specific help to a new or small business? Would the entry simply extend the reader's choice without necessarily extending the possible reward?

Section 2

SOURCES OF GENERAL HELP AND ADVICE FOR SMALL FIRMS

Each working day over 10,000 people use the services of a small business advisory organization. Most are simple telephone enquiries but others involve face-to-face counselling sessions – perhaps to help raise money or to cope with an in-depth tax problem. There are now several hundred organizations specifically concerned with providing help, advice and resources (including finance) for small businesses and those starting them. For the most part, these services are provided free or at a very low cost, at least at the outset. In order to give a better understanding of their nature and purpose it will help to look at them in seven groups:

1 National Government help for small firms, which covers the help on offer by the main government agencies concerned with small-business matters in England, Scotland, Wales, Northern Ireland and the Irish Republic.
2 Business Links delivering locally certain government initiatives, and some developed locally by the Link and other partners.
3 Local Enterprise Agencies (LEAs) are companies limited by guarantee, typically set up as partnerships between big companies and organizations in the private sector and local authorities, with support from central Government to promote economic regeneration by the setting up of small firms.
4 Sector specific services. As well as schemes of general help, assistance and advice, some organizations provide services to small and new start-ups in particular sectors.

5 Help with, and in, particular locations. Details of organizations set up to help find business premises, or to advise on any special support on offer in an area that could influence your choice of where to locate.
6 Small business associations. Self-help groups and sub-groups of general business associations.
7 Small business websites. There are now many websites offering help and advice to new and small businesses. Some are simply offshoots of small business magazines, but others offer a wider range of services.

1 National Government help for small businesses

The various governments in the British Isles and the government of Eire have a number of initiatives and advisory services to help small firms. As well as the services listed below that cover the general range of offerings, other such initiatives are covered in more detail in the relevant sections of this book.

Department of Trade and Industry

The main Government bodies concerned with business in the UK are the Department of Trade and Industry (www.dti.gov.uk/) in England; Scottish Enterprise (www.scottish-enterprise.com/) in Scotland; the Welsh Development Agency (www.

wda.co.uk/) in Wales and The Local Enterprise Development Unit (LEDU) in Northern Ireland (www.ledu-ni.gov.uk/).Whilst they each operate independently, in practice they offer broadly similar forms of help and assistance for small and new business start-ups.

Government small-business support services

These are the major small-business support services on offer in the United Kingdom. You can get more information on these services either by phoning the relevant service provider in your country or by visiting their website.

Some of these services are described in more detail in other sections of this book (consult the index for details).

General support

- A number of free booklets that give advice on matters such as starting a business, employing staff, and finance have been prepared and copies can be ordered online from websites.
- Those who are presently unemployed but wanting to move into self-employment can find out from their local Jobcentre about suitable work-based training. Young people can get further help with starting a business under the New Deal. Parts of the UK have been designated as 'Employment Zones' and in these the Department for Education and Employment will be providing extra help to get such businesses off the ground.
- The Government-created Phoenix Fund encourages entrepreneurship in disadvantaged communities and amongst disadvantaged groups. It includes provision to put in more resources so that local organizations can in turn give more help to new and growing businesses.
- The Small Business Service (SBS) Small Firms Loan Guarantee Scheme guarantees loans from banks and other financial institutions for small businesses with viable business propos-

als, which have tried and failed to obtain a conventional loan because of a lack of security.
- The SBS Smart scheme provides grants to individuals and small/medium sized businesses to review, research, or develop technologies leading to commercial products.
- The Trade Partners UK Export Awards for Smaller Businesses (www.tradepartners.gov.uk/export) provides practical encouragement to help you to exploit niche markets.
- Small/medium sized firms can also benefit from a range of regionally based schemes aimed at new and small businesses and which are supported by European Structural Funds (which promote competitiveness throughout Europe).
- Enterprise Grants are on offer via the DTI which are a form of financial assistance for small and medium sized enterprises investing in projects in the Assisted Areas and Enterprise Grant Areas of the English Regions.

Help to improve business performance

- The 'A Great Place to Work' (www.dti.gov.uk/greatplacetowork/) website contains ideas and advice to help you build a successful workplace.
- The SBS National Business Improvement Services are designed to help firms compare their business performance against others and show how to adopt the latest good/best practice to sharpen up a firm's operations.
- There are also a range of best practice guides and tools to help identify management best practices, techniques, and technologies and which provide practical guidance on specific best practice issues.
- From Quality to Excellence(www.dti.gov.uk/quality/) is a DTI website to help organizations improve their reputation for providing quality products and services. The website covers the whats and hows of the quality-to-excellence journey, as well as the tools needed along the way.

Help to expand a business

- The DTI has a wide range of services geared to helping businesses to export including market research, sales leads, and trade missions overseas. For further information visit the Trade Partners UK website listed above.
- The Regional Selective Assistance scheme aims to attract investment and create/safeguard jobs in the Assisted Areas, through grants for larger projects with fixed capital costs > £500,000.
- Corporate Venturing can be a powerful mechanism for growth. It generally involves investments by larger companies in new or expanding small business, with parties sharing risks and resources equally for mutual benefit. The DTI helps put entrepreneurs and big firms in contact with each other to foster corporate venturing.
- 'Business Angels' are private individuals wanting to invest in growth businesses. DTI supports the National Business Angels Network that brings together companies and potential investors.
- UK online for business can help a new or small business to use the Internet and other technologies to reach new customers.
- The Department for Education and Employment (DfEE) operates The New Deal, which provides financial support towards salary and training costs for companies employing young and long-term unemployed people.

Help with innovation and technology

- Business Links (and equivalent offices outside England) have Innovation Technology Counsellors available to give you local advice and also to help you to tap into European Research and Development initiatives.
- The SBS Smart scheme provides grants to individuals and small/medium sized businesses to review, research, or develop technologies leading to commercial products.
- There are a range of programmes run to help industry to profit from knowledge and technology from the higher education and other institutions.
- There are a number of initiatives to help exploit particular new technologies: for biotechnology – Biowise, and Manufacturing for Biotechnology; for computer and communications technologies – UKISHELP; for lasers – the Association of Industrial Laser Users; and for improving controls in manufacturing – the Advanced Control Technology Transfer Programme.
- The International Technology Service – keeps companies aware of new technological developments and management best practice from across the world.
- LINK is a mechanism for supporting collaborative research partnerships between UK industry and the research base. It provides financial support to individual programmes of pre-competitive science and technology research.
- The Foresight programme aims to develop visions of the future and bring together the knowledge and expertise of business, science and government to increase national wealth and quality of life.
- NMS (the National Measurement System) is the UK's national infrastructure of laboratories, which delivers world-class measurement science and technology, providing traceable and increasingly accurate standards of measurement for use in trade, industry, academia and government.
- The European initiative known as Eureka encourages international collaborations between companies and other organizations.
- Businesses can tap into a range of regionally based schemes that are designed to help them benefit from innovative ideas and technological advances and which are supported by European Structural Funds. They are normally administered by Government Offices in the English regions and delivered through your local Business Link (and equivalent offices outside England), Training and Enterprise Councils, etc. Further information is available from these organizations or the National

Assembly for Wales, the Scottish Executive and the Northern Ireland Office.

- www.innovation.gov.uk – this site, run by the DTI's Future and Innovation Unit, aims to help organizations understand innovation, why it is important and how the best organizations manage it.
- An R&D tax credit for small firms was introduced in 2000 to help small and medium-sized companies undertake R&D either for the first time or encourage them to undertake even more R&D. Further information is available on the Inland Revenue's website. At the same time new Guidelines were introduced on the definition of R&D for tax purposes. The Guidelines, published by the Secretary of State, will benefit both large and small companies by providing added certainty for their tax affairs.
- The Patent Office helps small firms to protect their business ideas, inventions and logos by offering advice about patents, designs, trademarks and copyright and provides a range of free literature.

Help with environmental matters

- A guide to the Packaging (Essential Requirements) Regulations
- Envirowise, formerly the Environmental Technology Best Practice Programme (ETBPP), provides information to help you increase competitiveness by the use of cost-effective cleaner technology and waste minimization techniques.
- If you are looking to reduce your firm's energy consumption, then the Energy Efficiency Best Practice programme can show you how.
- If you are intending to dispose of white goods or computer equipment you might like to see the guides the DTI have about how these can be re-used.
- Comments are invited from business people on the various consultation papers, such as those setting out the requirements of the proposed EC Directives on Waste from Electrical and Electronic Equipment (WEEE) and Restrictions on the Hazardous Substances in Electrical and Electronic Equipment (RoHS).

Help for particular industries

The DTI also provides schemes of help, assistance and advice that are particular to certain industries. If your business operates or will operate in one of these areas it may well be worth exploring further:

- Aerospace and Defence
- Agriculture, horticulture and food
- Automotive
- Biotechnology and the Biotechnology: Looking Forward Report
- Boat and Shipbuilding
- Coal – Coal Operating Aid Scheme
- Construction
- Design
- Electronics
- Engineering
- Forging 2020 and Castings 2000+
- Minerals
- Oil, Gas and Petrochemicals
- Plastics
- Metalforming 2000
- Space Technology
- Steel
- Surface Engineering 2000 and the National Surface Engineering Centre
- Textile and Clothing
- Tourism, arts and sports
- Waste Management.

Help with regulations

- DTI regulates company matters such as competition, fair trading, aspects of employment law and trade union affairs.
- NMS (the National Measurement System) improves trade. NMS increases and underpins the regulatory framework for commercial activity, while removing unnecessary burdens on business. It supports the foundation of accredited certification, calibration and inspection that reduces the need for UK suppliers to be assessed by each of its customers. Mutual recognition, at European and international level, further reduces the need for multiple assessment of suppliers and consequently helps to reduce trade barriers.

- Guidance on regulations issued by other Departments can be found on the Direct Access Government website.
- The Regulatory Impact Unit (RIU), based in the Cabinet Office works with other government departments, agencies and regulators to help ensure that regulators are fair and effective.
- The ITSA's website has guidance for business about trading standards.

Help with European matters
European Information – How to find it.

- Our Standards and Technical Regulations Directorate provides advice through a series of Product Standards booklets on a number of European directives and the UK regulations that implement these.
- DTI also maintains a UK Contact List of the people you can speak to across Government about Single Market Legislation.
- HM Treasury's website maintains detailed information about the implications for business of the Access business of the Euro.

England

Department of Trade and Industry
Small Firms Business Support
Ashdown House
1 Victoria Street
London SW1H 0ET
Tel: 020 7215 5000
www.dti.gov.uk

Wales

Welsh Development Agency
Plas Glyndwr
Kingsway
Cardiff CF10 3AH
Tel: 01443 845500
Fax: 01443 845589
www.wda.co.uk

Northern Ireland

Formerly known by the uninspiring name, LEDU (Local Enterprise Development Unit), Invest Northern Ireland, formed in April 2002 by the Northern Ireland Government is the main economic development organization and single entry point for all entrepreneurial activity in the region.

Invest Northern Ireland
Upper Galwally
Belfast
BT8 6TB
Tel: 028 9023 9090
Fax: 028 9049 0490
http://www.investni.com/

Scottish Enterprise

Delivers a service for small businesses in Scotland that includes the range of services on offer in England through Business Link.

Scottish Enterprise
5 Atlantic Quay
150 Broomielaw
Glasgow
G2 8LU
Tel: 0141 248 2700
Fax: 0141 221 3217
Email: network.helpline@scotent.co.uk
(www.scottish-enterprise.com/)
There are direct links from this website to the entire network of Scottish Enterprise's local offices.

The Irish Republic

County Enterprise Boards
The County Enterprise Boards are an initiative launched by the Department of Enterprise, Trade and Employment. Their primary aim is to promote enterprise and job creation at local level and to assume responsibility for business areas not already covered by the state industrial develop-

ment agencies, e.g. small firms, start up projects, service projects.

There are 35 County Enterprise Boards covering all county and city areas in the state. The Boards have 14 members drawn from elected members of the local authority, the social partners, state agencies, and community/other representatives. The Boards have considerable autonomy and deal with companies with up to 10 employees. Funding for the Boards comes from the Government and the European Union through the Operational Programme for Local Rural Development.

The Boards provide support in the form of grants, loans, and advice Each project is assessed individually and already many small businesses have been helped to get started successfully.

Financial Supports: Grants are available to eligible small businesses that can demonstrate significant innovation to cover part of the cost of conducting feasibility studies, employing additional staff (including the owner/manager himself or herself in the case of a start-up enterprise), or acquiring capital assets. These grants are strictly at the discretion of the Board and may be made on a refundable or non-refundable basis.

Mentoring Service: Occasionally, developing businesses encounter a specific problem or want to undertake a specific project that requires skills beyond the normal range of the owner/manager. Our local panel of 'mentors', supplemented as necessary by the Enterprise Ireland Panel, are all experienced business executives and consultants who are skilled in working with the owner/manager to specify the problem, identify solutions and implement them. This service is available free, subject to approval of the assignment by our Board.

Pre-enterprise Training: A variety of courses for people who are working towards setting up their own business are run regularly in several centres around the county. These are provided in conjunction with community-based enterprise support organizations and are free of charge.

Open Learning: Setting up a business is a very time-consuming activity and it is not always possible to conform to the set schedule of a traditional training programme. For this reason, some boards have invested in a wide range of interactive computer-based training programmes.

Small Business Networking MEDIAN: Owner/managers are unanimous in saying that they often feel isolated in running their business. For this reason, the Board supports a network for small business owners, which is dedicated to helping them develop their business.

Financial Health Check: Using the latest in dedicated financial analysis software, Boards can provide you with an in-depth analysis of your business's financial performance based on one or more sets of financial accounts. The written report you receive is an essential aid to monitoring the financial health of your business and understanding exactly what your accounts are telling you.

Tradenet: Boards partners in Tradenet, the Internet business network for small businesses in the Dublin–Belfast Economic Corridor. This online network of businesses is like a vast business-to-business buy-and-sell and is capable of delivering business opportunities direct to your desktop every day. At their offices, we demonstrate this new technology as well as providing a backup service to users and those who do not yet have an online connection.

Empower: Empower is a nationwide e-business initiative provided by the City and County Enterprise Boards which will assist small businesses as follows: e-business training, mentoring, web access, technical assistance and networking. The 3 million campaign that aims to supply e-commerce support to over 6,000 small businesses by means of direct incentives.

Financial Assistance Programme

The Board operates a Financial Assistance Programme that consists of grant aid and equity in the form of preference shares.

Manufacturing and service businesses, including tourism projects, are eligible for grant aid in respect of three categories. Feasibility Studies, Capital Equipment and Creation of Employment.

The Enterprise Board has 3 grants available.

- Feasibility Study Grant (up to 50% of the cost, maximum €4000);
- Capital Grant (up to €50,000); and
- Employment Grant (up to €5000 per new employee).

The Employment Grant may also apply to a person starting up his/her own business. The Enterprise Board is precluded from grant aiding projects involving capital expenditure in excess of £100,000 and/or employing more than 10 persons.

(Dialling from outside of Eire, use the International code 00 353 and drop the first 0 in the number.)

A comprehensive directory of all 35 County Enterprise Boards can be found at http://www.startingabusinessinireland.com/dirceb.htm

Enterprise Ireland

Established on 23 July 1998, Enterprise Ireland combines the resources of the former Irish Trade Board, Forbairt and the in-company training activities of FÁS.

Enterprise Ireland is the government organization charged with assisting the development of Irish enterprise. Their mission is:

'… to work in partnership with client companies to develop a sustainable competitive advantage, leading to a significant increase in profitable sales, exports and employment.'

Clients are mainly Irish manufacturing and internationally traded services companies employing ten or more people, and overseas food and natural resources companies operating in Ireland. Enterprise Ireland also administers national and EU supports for building technological innovation capability and co-operation between industry and higher educational institutions.

Five categories of support are available (for more information, see its brochure on financial support):

1. Exploring new opportunities: preliminary funding to exploit new ideas for businesses with 10 to 250 staff or high potential start-ups (HPSUs).
2. HPSUs based on technological innovation or rapidly developing niche market.
3. Existing company expansion, where more than 10 people are already employed.
4. Building international competitiveness: a new Competitiveness Fund for SMEs offers assistance to businesses with 10 to 250 staff, that have not received more than €200,000 in support over the past three years.
5. Research and development: Support under the Research Technology and Innovation (RTI) Competitiveness Scheme for significant R&D projects.

Enterprise Ireland's services include:

- Access to business angels and venture capital funds
- Assistance with intellectual property and technology transfer
- Benchmarking
- Design support
- Incubation and workspaces
- Linkages with EU technology support programmes
- Market information and supports
- Mentoring
- Support for e-commerce/e-business.

Enterprise Ireland also supports a range of other initiatives targeted at developing enterprise, including an annual Student Enterprise Awards competition.

Dublin (Central)
Enterprise Ireland,
Glasnevin,
Dublin 9, Ireland.
Tel: +353–1-808 2000
Fax: +353–1-808 2020

Starting a Business in Ireland (http://www.start-ingabusinessinireland.com) is a really helpful website that describes and provides web links directly to over 700 organizations, in both the North and South of Ireland, which offer assistance and support to start-ups. The site is masterminded by Brian O' Kayne, author of *Starting a Business in Ireland*, published by Oak Tree Press, 4th edition 2005.

2   Business Link (and its equivalent in Scotland, Wales and Northern Ireland)

The contact point for much of the small business support services in each country not delivered directly by a government department is through a Business Link, or its equivalent outside of England. These are supported by the government through its Small Business Service, which is the latest in a long line of 'branding' that has been applied to government and quasi-government small business initiatives.

In England, advice on general business matters and access to information on any Government small business assistance can be obtained from one of 40 or so Business Links that cover the country (website: www.businesslink.gov.uk; tel: 0845 600 9 006; minicom: 0845 606 2666).

For most of Scotland, small business services are provided by the network of Scottish Business Shops (website: www.sbgateway.com; tel: 0845 609 6611).

The Highlands are covered by Highlands and Islands Enterprise-Scotland (website: www.hie.co.uk; tel: 01463 715400).

Invest Northern Ireland, formed in April 2002 by the Northern Ireland Government is the main economic development organization and single entry point for all entrepreneurial activity in the region (website: http://www.investni.com/; tel: 028 9023 9090

In Wales, small business services are offered by the Welsh Development Agency (website: www.wda.co.uk; tel: 01443 845500)

All these sites provide links to your nearest small firms advisory service.

Business Link aim to improve an entrepreneur's chances of success by encouraging them to do research and planning and ask for help when it's needed. For in-depth advice related to your personal circumstances, your local Business Link operator offers a comprehensive business start-up service. Experienced advisers will work with you to develop your plans and help you access the full range of business support service providers who can assist you.

In particular they provide pre-start-up help and advice to enable would-be business starters to:

- assess themselves against the attributes and skills needed to launch and run a business;
- discover the range of issues that they'll need to consider in developing a business proposition;
- decide on the right sort of finance to start and grow their business;
- become aware of – and find – the regulations that apply when starting a business;
- decide what type of business is most appropriate; and
- understand the steps required for informing public authorities that they are launching a business.

Finance and money

Depending on your circumstances and geographic area, there may be special initiatives or grants that are available and suitable for your business needs. Business Links can advise on such grants as well as helping prepare your case for bank or equity finance.

They can also offer advice and help on the basics of accounting and bookkeeping and on practical issues on managing working capital effectively, such as making sure you get paid on time.

People

For most small businesses, people are one of the most important resources. The lack of suitably skilled staff is seen as a major obstacle to small-business expansion. Business Links can help you put plans in place to develop your staff, enhance their skills and improve their effectiveness to your business. Their 'Investors In People' programme helps both the business founder and their employees to perform better by ensuring adequate training, and ensures all the appropriate personal function requirements such as job descriptions, contracts of employment and personal development plans are in place.

Sales and marketing

To be successful, a business needs a constant flow of new customers and the means to ensure they become loyal and profitable in the longer term. This means understanding customers – knowing what they want, need and will pay for.

Entrepreneurs need to keep abreast of changes in the market and understand how these will affect their customers. They also need to be aware of what competitors are doing and find unique ways to sell their own products and services.

Business Links can provide practical help with ideas on:

- finding, winning and keeping profitable customers;
- developing your business by launching new products, entering new markets and starting to export;
- planning and using a wide variety of marketing communications, advertising, PR, direct mail, and the Internet;
- making use of information about competitors; and
- learning about new markets.

E-commerce and IT

E-commerce is not just about technology. It is about making technology work to achieve the best outcomes for your business. Business Links advise on both the business issues involved in making e-commerce happen, as well as the technical issues such as security basics, site design and development.

They also advise on choosing and using computers and IT systems and have access to a network of advisers, often based at the Business Link premises.

Management and operations

Once your business is established you need to keep it running well and look for ways to improve performance. Most businesses face decisions about property and premises. Entering inappropriate leasing agreements is an area where many small businesses have come unstuck. Business Links provide a topic guide on *Property & Premises* that includes guidance sourced from some of the UK's most authoritative experts. They also offer information on Supply Chain Management, and all the logistical problems associated with getting products from where you make or assemble them to where the customer wants them.

Business improvement

Business Links offer information on two areas where small businesses can learn from, and beat, their large organization counterparts: Process Improvement and Quality Improvement. They also offer information and access to a Benchmarking service, which lets small firms compare themselves with the best of their peers and so learn where and how to improve performance.

If you want to go beyond merely improving what you are doing to create something distinctive and innovative, the Business Link also offers information on innovation.

The Link can provide a Personal Business Adviser (PBA); usually an experienced business person, and often professionally qualified or even a former business owner themselves, to help with business improvement and innovation, as well as with a range of other business issues.

Regulations and tax

Regulation and taxes are an unwelcome but essential part of an entrepreneur's business life. Whether you are taking on your first employee, have ideas and intellectual property you want to protect, or want to know about tax and VAT, Business Links offer some practical guidance.

All the regulatory information on their site has been provided by or checked by the relevant government department to provide authoritative material, and is linked directly via the Business Link website.

- To read the individual pieces of legislation guidance published by other government departments, visit Direct Access Government (DAG).
- Information about local trading standards and regulations is available from your local authority. Available websites are listed on the UK Online website. The network of Local Business Partnerships around the country provides a framework to enable business and Local Authorities to work together and streamline the regulation process.
- Visit the Inland Revenue website to view their *Starting Up in Business* guide to cutting through the red tape.

Special initiatives

At any one time, there is a range of government initiatives that may be able to help your small business. Some, like Smart, are intended to help fund the development of advanced technology. Others are focused on helping specific groups, such as Women in Business and Ethnic Minorities. This topic area maintains signposts and overview documents of government initiatives that are relevant to small business. Here are some current topic areas.

The Small Business Research Initiative, which aims to increase the success of smaller firms in obtaining contracts from Government bodies to conduct research and development.

Grants under the Finance & Money topic area lists and describes all the currently available grants for new and small businesses, together with contact details.

For example, in Scotland, through the Proof of Concept Fund, leading-edge Scottish technologies are supported in getting innovation from the lab into the global marketplace. The £30m Fund – launched in 1999 and currently supporting 44 ground-breaking projects – is available to budding entrepreneurs working in Scottish Universities, Research Institutes and NHS Trusts. The fund concentrates on early-stage ideas that have typically reached patent level, and could lead to the creation of new businesses, or licensing innovative technologies. Successful bidders must demonstrate that their ideas have originality and true commercial potential.

Feedback

If you can't find answers to your questions on the website, you can email your question which will be answered promptly. You will be asked for a contact phone number in case the person working on your enquiry needs more information.

Knowledge repository and online toolbase

Business Link maintains hundreds of short, sharp articles on every aspect of starting, growing and selling a business and has dozens of online tools for such activities as writing business plans, benchmarking and carrying out market research

To find your nearest Business Link office, just enter your postcode in the space provided on their website (www.businesslink.gov.uk) or call their help line (0845 600 9 006). Alternatively, contact the most convenient Business Link yourself.

Business Links

Business Link Bedfordshire and Luton
The Chamber
The Business Competitiveness Centre
Kimpton Road

Luton
LU2 0SX
Tel: 0845 390 1345
Fax: 01582 522450
Email: info@chamber-business.com
Website: www.chamber-business.com

Business Link for Berkshire and Wiltshire
Emlyn Square
Swindon
SN1 5BP
Tel: 0845 600 4141
Fax: 01793 485186
Email: info@blbw.co.uk
Website: http://www.blbw.co.uk/

**Business Link for Berkshire and Wiltshire
– Salisbury**
22 Bedwin Street
Salisbury
SP1 3UT
Tel: 01722 424184
Fax: 01722 415447
Website: http://www.blbw.co.uk/

**Business Link for Berkshire and Wiltshire
– Trowbridge**
Bryer-Ash Business Park
Bradford Road
Trowbridge
BA14 8HE
Tel: 0845 600 4141
Fax: 01225 774018
Website: http://www.blbw.co.uk/

**Business Link for Berkshire and Wiltshire
– Chippenham**
Temple Court
8 The Causeway
Chippenham
SN15 3BT
Tel: 01249 705004
Fax: 01249 448270
Website: www.businesslinkberksandwilts.co.uk

**Business Link for Berkshire and Wiltshire
– Reading**
Thames Tower
37–41 Station Road
Reading
Berkshire
RG1 1LX
Tel: 0845 600 4141
Fax: 0118 951 6410
Email: info@blbw.co.uk
Website: www.blbw.co.uk

**Business Link for Berkshire and Wiltshire
– Newbury**
2b Northbrook Court
Park Street
Newbury
RG14 1EA
Tel: 01635 567140
Fax: 01635 567141
Website: www.blbw.co.uk

Birmingham CCI
Chamber House
75 Harborne Road
Edgbaston
Birmingham
B15 3DH
Tel: 0121 607 0809
Fax: 0121 455 8670
Email: info@birminghamchamber.org.uk
Website: www.bci.org.uk

Business Link for the Black Country
Dudley Court South
Waterfront East
Brierley Hill
DY5 1XN
Tel: 0845 113 1234
Fax: 01384 360560
Email: info@bccbl.com
Website: www.bccbl.com

Business Link Cheshire and Warrington
International Business Centre
Delta Crescent
Westbrook
Warrington
WA5 7WQ
Tel: 0845 345 4025
Fax: 01925 715 005
Email: info@blinkcw.co.uk
Website: www.blinkcw.co.uk

Business Link County Durham
IMEX Business Centre
Abbey Road
Durham
DH1 5JZ
Tel: 0191 374 4000
Fax: 0191 374 4010
Email: gateway@blcd.co.uk
Website: www.blcd.co.uk

Business Link Cumbria
Capital Building
Hilltop Heights
London Road
Carlisle
CA1 2NS
Tel: 0845 600 9006
Fax: 01228 613258
Email: info@businesslinkcumbria.co.uk
Website: www.businesslinkcumbria.co.uk

Business Link Derbyshire
Commerce Centre
Canal Wharf
Chesterfield
S41 7NA
Tel: 0845 601 1038
Fax: 01246 233228
Email: info@businesslinkderbyshire.co.uk
Website: www.businesslinkderbyshire.co.uk

Business Link Wessex
Wates House
Wallington Hall
Fareham

PO16 7BJ
Tel: 0845 458 8558
Fax: 01329 223 223
Email: info@businesslinkwessex.co.uk
Website: www.businesslinkwessex.co.uk

Business Link for East Lancashire
Business Services (East Lancashire) Limited
Red Rose Court
Clayton Business Park
Clayton-le-Moors
Accrington
BB5 5JR
Tel: 0800 696696
Fax: 01254 604604
Email: bleastlancs@bleastlancs.co.uk
Website: www.bleastlancs.co.uk

Business Link Gloucestershire
Chargrove House
Main Road
Shurdington
Cheltenham
GL51 4GA
Tel: 01242 863863
Fax: 01242 864101
Email: info@glos.businesslink.co.uk
Website: www.glos.businesslink.co.uk

Business Link for Greater Merseyside
St Nicholas House
4th Floor
Old Churchyard
Liverpool
Merseyside
L2 8TX
Tel: 0845 330 0151
Fax: 0845 330 0150
Email: information@bl4gm.co.uk
Website: www.bl4gm.co.uk

Business Link Hertfordshire
45 Grosvenor Road
St Albans
AL1 3AW
Tel: 01727 813813

Fax: 01727 813404
Email: info@mybusinesslink.co.uk
Website: www.mybusinesslink.co.uk

Business Link Kent Limited
26 Kings Hill Avenue
West Malling
ME19 4AE
Tel: 0845 722 6655
Fax: 01732 841109
Email: info@businesslinkkent.com
Website: www.businesslinkkent.com

Business Link Leicestershire
Charnwood Court
5b New Walk
Leicester
LE1 6TE
Tel: 0845 070 0086
Fax: 0116 258 7333
Mini: 0116 258 7340
Email: enquiries@blleics.co.uk
Website: www.blleics.co.uk

Business Link Lincolnshire & Rutland
Welton House
Limekiln Way
Lincoln
LN2 4WH
Tel: 0845 757 4000
Fax: 01522 574005
Email: enquiry@matrixbusinesslink.co.uk
Website: http://www.bllr.co.uk/

Business Link for Manchester
Chamber Business Enterprises
Churchgate House
56 Oxford Street
Manchester
M60 7HJ
Tel: 0845 608 3388
Fax: 0161 236 4160
Email: info@chamber-link.co.uk
Website: www.chamber-link.co.uk

Milton Keynes Oxfordshire and Buckingham-shire SBS
Business Link Solutions
Eastern Bypass
Thame
Oxfordshire
OX9 3FF
Tel: 0845 606 4466
Fax: 0870 161 5860
Email: info@businesslinksolutions.co.uk
Website: www.businesslinksolutions.co.uk

Business Link Norfolk
PO Box 36
Swaffham
PE37 7WZ
Tel: 0845 721 8218
Fax: 01760 726 727
Email: success@businesslinknorfolk.co.uk
Website:www.businesslinknorfolk.co.uk

Business Link North and Western Lancashire
Leyland House
Lancashire Enterprise Business Park
Centurion Way
Farington
Leyland
PR26 6TY
Tel: 01772 450500
Fax: 01772 450501
Email: info@bllancs.co.uk
Website: www.businesslinklancashire.co.uk

Business Link North Manchester
Wigan Investment Centre
Waterside Drive
Wigan
WN3 5BA
Tel: 01942 705750
Fax: 01942 705296
Email: info@blnm.co.uk
Website: www.businesslinknorthmanchester.org.uk

Northamptonshire Chamber
Opus House

Anglia Way
Moulton Park
Northampton
NN3 6JA
Tel: 08457 566 566
Fax: 01604 670 362
Email: info@businesslinknorthants.org
Website: www.businesslinknorthants.org

Business Link for Northumberland
Wansbeck Business Centre
Wansbeck Business Park
Rotary Parkway
Ashington
NE63 8QZ
Tel: 01670 813322
Fax: 01670 813355
Email: info@n-bs.co.uk
Website: www.n-bs.co.uk

Shropshire Business Link
Trevithick House
Stafford Park 4
Telford
TF3 3BA
Tel: 0845 754 3210
Fax: 01952 208208
Email: enquiries@blwm.com
Website: www.businesslink.gov.uk/blwm

Business Link Somerset
Creech Castle
Taunton
Somerset
TA1 2DX
Tel: 0845 721 1112
Fax: 01823 274 862
Email: enquiry@blsl.co.uk
Website: www.businesslinksomerset.co.uk

Business Link Staffordshire
Commerce House
Festival Park
Stoke-on-Trent
ST1 5BE
Tel: 07002 202122

Fax: 01782 274394
Email: info@staffs.businesslink.co.uk
Website: http://www.businesslinkstaffordshire.
co.uk/

Business Link for South Yorkshire
Reresby House
Bowbridge Close
Templeborough
Rotherham
S60 1BY
Tel: 0800 073 7474
Fax: 01709 386330
Email: enquiries@blsy.com
Website: www.blsy.com

Sussex Enterprise
Greenacre Court
Station Road
Burgess Hill
RH15 9DS
Tel: 0845 678 8867
Fax: 01444 259255
Email: info@sussexenterprise.co.uk
Website: www.sussexenterprise.co.uk

Business Link Tees Valley Ltd
Tees Valley Business Centre
2 Queens Square
Middlesbrough
TS2 1AA
Tel: 01642 806666
Fax: 01642 341425
Email: info@tees.businesslink.co.uk
Website: www.teesbusinesslink.co.uk

Business Link Tyne and Wear
Business & Innovation Centre
Sunderland Enterprise Park East
Wearfield
Sunderland
SR5 2TA
Tel: 0191 516 6767
Fax: 0191 516 6777
Email: info@businesslinktw.co.uk
Website: www.businesslinktw.co.uk

Business Link West Yorkshire
Unit 4
Meadow Court
Millshaw Business Park
Leeds
LS11 8LZ
Tel: 0845 833 6000
Fax: 0113 383 7700
Email: info@blwy.co.uk
Website: www.blwy.co.uk

3   Local Enterprise Agencies (LEAs)

There are some 250 Enterprise Agencies in the UK who deliver business support services under contract to Business Link and are sometimes located in the same premises. The agencies' key purpose is to promote economic regeneration by the setting up of small firms. Local Enterprise Agencies (LEAs) are companies limited by guarantee, typically set up as partnerships between big companies and organizations in the private sector and local authorities, with support from central Government depending on their individual circumstances.

LEAs are independent and are controlled by no single group of sponsors. The private sector generally retains the largest sponsorship stake, and almost invariably the LEA will be chaired by a local business person. LEAs have great, in-depth experience of the local small and medium (SME) enterprise economy, with the ability to draw on a local network of specialist skills, such as accountants, lawyers and banks.

Typically LEAs directly or indirectly provide advice and information, counselling and training on a comprehensive range of business issues, as well as very often providing shared workspace with access to some business services. They are involved with all types of SME, including pre-starts, start-up, sole traders, partnerships, cooperatives, and limited companies.

Business counselling

As a direct consequence of private sector sponsorship, LEAs are able to offer start-up companies and small business firms free business counselling, a service that remains unique. Business counselling and follow-up is at the heart of all Enterprise business training.

LEAs provide a wide variety of training. All provide training in business planning and other pre-start essentials. In addition, most LEAs offer training for established businesses in topics such as marketing, exporting, management development, financial management, managing people, etc.

Consultancy

All LEAs provide start-up advice. Many can also assist more established businesses with strategy, business planning and raising finance; total quality and ISO9000; marketing and exporting; and so on. LEAs are partners in Business Links and, if they are unable to help directly, can signpost you to appropriate assistance locally.

Managed workspace

Nearly half the Enterprise Agencies operate managed workspace for small firms, offering tenants a sheltered working environment in which the landlord is also the business adviser. Length of tenure can vary, but all offer easy in, easy out terms. This gives agencies a first hand insight into the critical early years in the life of the start-up small firm.

Central contact points for the LEA's umbrella organizations are:

Business in the Community
137 Shepherdess Walk
London N1 7RQ
Tel: 0870 600 2482
Email: information@bitc.org.uk

www.bitc.org.uk
www.business-impact.org.uk

Who include recruiting sponsoring organizations for LEA management amongst their activities.

National Federation of Enterprise Agencies (NFEA)
Trinity Gardens
9–11 Bromham Road
Bedford MK40 2UG
Tel: 01234 345055
Fax: 01234 354055
www.nfea.com

NFEA maintains a current directory of all its members on its website.

Their members constitute a network of independent, but not for profit, Local Enterprise Agencies committed to responding to the needs of small and growing businesses by providing an appropriate range of quality services. These particularly, but not exclusively, target pre-start, start-up and micro businesses, and assist in building their ability to survive, to sustain themselves and to grow.

The NFEA also offer an online version of the range of services provided by the local agencies themselves at http://www.smallbusinessadvice. org.uk/

Enterprise Agency Directory

Listed by country or region and then alphabetically by town or district, as appropriate.

England

Northern region
Northumbria Centre for Enterprise
South East Northumberland Enterprise Trust
Lintonville Parkway
Ashington
Northumberland
NE63 9JZ

Contact: Allan Bell
Tel: 01670 508402
Fax: 01670 528407
Email: allanbell@senet-ict.co.uk
Website: www.senet-ict.co.uk

Business Link County Durham (Wear Valley Development Agency)
Wear Valley Business Centre
27 Longfield Road
South Church Enterprise Park
Bishop Auckland
DL14 6XB
Contact: Ms Geraldine Pinder
Tel: 01388 776688
Fax: 01388 777116
Email: Geraldine.Pinder@blcd.co.uk
Website: www.wvda.co.uk

Chester-Le-Street and City of Durham Enterprise Agency Ltd
Chester-le-Street Office
CDC Enterprise Agency
1 High Chare
Chester-le-Street
Co. Durham
DH3 3PX
Contact: Mr R Batty
Tel: 0191 389 2648
Fax: 0191 387 1684
Email: enquiries@cdcbp.org.uk
Website: www.cdcbp.org.uk

Derwentside Industrial Development Agency
Steel House
Ponds Court Business Park
Genesis Way
Consett
Co. Durham
DH8 5XP
Contact: Eddie Hutchinson
Tel: 01207 580 011
Fax: 01207 591 477
Email: dida@dida.co.uk
Website: www.dida.co.uk

Teesdale Enterprise Agency
Enterprise House
Harmire Enterprise Park
Barnard Castle
Co Durham
DL12 8XT
Contact: Jack Woodhouse
Tel: 01833 696 600
Fax: 01833 631 909
Email: enquiries@teesdaleenterprise.co.uk
Website: www.teesdaleenterprise.co.uk

Darlington Business Venture
6th Floor
Northgate House
St Augustine's Way
Darlington DL1 1XA
Contact: Brian Coady
Tel: 01325 289610
Fax: 01325 467926
Email: enquiries@dbv-northeast.co.uk
Website:www.dbv-northeast.co.uk

Chester-Le-Street and City of Durham Enterprise Agency Ltd
Durham Office
CDC Enterprise Agency
The Lodge
Laburnum Avenue
Durham City
DH1 4HA
Contact: Mr R Batty
Tel: 0191 384 5407
Fax: 0191 386 8673
Email: enquiries@cdcbp.org.uk
Website: www.cdcbp.org.uk

East Durham Development Agency
4th Floor Lee House
Peterlee
County Durham
SR8 1BB
Contact: Ken Greenfield, Chief Executive
Tel: 0191 586 3366
Fax: 0191 518 0332

Email: ken.greenfield@blcd.co.uk
Website: www.edda.co.uk

Project North East
Design Works
William Street
Gateshead
NE10 0JP
Contact: Alison Robson
Tel: 0191 495 0066
Fax: 0191 495 3207
Email: robson@projectne.co.uk
Website: www.pne.org

Project North East
7–15 Pink Lane
Newcastle upon Tyne
NE1 5DW
Contact: Chief Executive
Tel: 0191 261 6009
Fax: 0191 245 3785
Email: info@projectne.co.uk
Website: www.pne-bss.org

Project North East
1 Pink Lane
Newcastle Upon Tyne
NE1 5DW
Contact: Christine Dryden
Tel: 0191 2616009
Fax: 0191 2330206
Email: christine.dryden@pne.org
Website: www.pne.org.uk

Tyne & Wear Enterprise Trust Ltd
Portman House
Portland Road
Newcastle Upon Tyne
NE2 1AQ
Contact: Liz Blair
Tel: 0191 244 4000
Fax: 0191 244 4001
Email: l.blair@entrust.co.uk
Website: www.nfea.com

Sedgefield Borough Business Services (SBBS)
Bede House
St Cuthbert's Way
Aycliffe Industrial Park
Newton Aycliffe
Co Durham
DL5 6DX
Contact: Janet Johnson, Chief Executive
Tel: 01325 307270
Fax: 01325 307226
Email: enquiries@sbbs.org.uk
Website: www.sbbs.org.uk

Tyneside Economic Development Company Ltd
Tedco Business Centre
Viking Industrial Park
Jarrow
Tyne & Wear
NE32 3DT
Contact: Mrs J. Dodds
Tel: 0191 428 3300
Fax: 0191 428 3388
Email: bussupport@tedco.org
Website: www.tedco.org

Yorkshire & Humberside region
West Yorkshire Enterprise Agency Ltd
Annexe 1
Batley Business & Technology Centre
Technology Drive
Grange Road
Batley
West Yorkshire
WF17 6ER
Contact: Sandra Wood
Tel: 01924 516700
Fax: 01924 424 863
Email: enquiries@wyea.co.uk
Website: www.wyea.co.uk

Doncaster Business Advice Centre Ltd (DONBAC)
Business Link Doncaster
White Rose Way
Doncaster

DN4 5ND
Contact: Bryce Staniland
Tel: 01302 761 000
Fax: 01302 739 999
Email: bstaniland@btinternet.com
Website: www.donbac.co.uk

Grimsby and Cleethorpes Area Enterprise Agency
10–14 Hainton Avenue
Grimsby
North East Lincolnshire
DN32 9BB
Contact: Paul Scott, Acting Chief Executive
Tel: 01472 312 121
Fax: 01472 312 131
Email: pharness@experienceenterprise.co.uk
Website: www.experienceenterprise.org

West Yorkshire Enterprise Agency Ltd
Croft Myl
West Parade
Halifax
West Yorkshire
HX1 2EQ
Contact: Andrea Smith
Tel: 01422 343 898
Fax: 01422 343 899
Email: enquiries@wyea.co.uk
Website: www.wyea.co.uk

SIRIUS (Saltend Community Development Company Ltd)
8 St Augustine's Gate
Hedon
East Yorkshire
HU12 8EX
Contact: Alan Gordon-Freeman
Tel: 01482 890146
Fax: 01482 899253
Email: info@sirius-hull.co.uk
Website: www.sirius-hull.co.uk

Hull Area Business Advice Centre Ltd
The Enterprise Centre
4 Bowlalley Lane

Hull
HU1 1XR
Contact: Colin Hanslip
Tel: 01482 607100
Fax: 01482 607102
Email: colin.hanslip@habac.co.uk
Website: www.habacltd.co.uk

Rotherham Enterprise Agency
12 The Crofts
Snail Hill
Rotherham
S60 2DJ
Contact: John Lewis
Tel: 01709 386 239
Fax: 01709 389237
Email: j.lewis@rotherhamchamber.org.uk
Website: www.rotherhamchamber.org.uk

Scarborough Enterprise Agency
Scarborough Business Centre
Auborough Street
Scarborough
North Yorkshire
YO11 1HT
Contact: Chris Jinks
Tel: 01723 354454
Fax: 01723 363633
Email: admin@scarboroughenterprise.org
Website: www.scarboroughenterprise.org

South Humber Business Advice Centre Ltd
Berkeley House
Doncaster Road
Scunthorpe
DN15 7DQ
Contact: Derek Marshall
Tel: 01724 270 444
Fax: 01724 276 684
Email: marshalld@SoHBAC.co.uk
Website: www.SoHBAC.co.uk

Sheffield Enterprise Agency
Albion House
Savile Street
Sheffield

S4 7UD
Contact: Sandra Edwards
Tel: 0114 281 4621
Fax: 0114 281 4624
Email: enquiries@senta.co.uk
Website: www.senta.co.uk

West Yorkshire Enterprise Agency Ltd
New Commerce House
192 Westgate
Wakefield
West Yorkshire
WF2 9SR
Contact: Paul Tansey
Tel: 01924 299 299
Fax: 01924 201 288
Email: enquiries@wyea.co.uk
Website: www.wyea.co.uk

York Business Development Ltd
The Fishergate Centre
4 Fishergate
York
YO10 4FB
Contact:
Tel: 01904 731562
Fax: 01904 731568
Email: info@ybac.co.uk
Website: www.yorkbac.co.uk

North Western region
Hyndburn Enterprise Trust
Globe Centre
St James Square
Accrington
Lancashire
BB5 0RE
Contact: Aileen Evans
Tel: 01254 600 625
Fax: 01254 600 627
Email: info@hyndburnenterprisetrust.co.uk
Website: www.hyndburnenterprisetrust.co.uk

Furness Enterprise Ltd
Trinity Enterprise Centre
Furness Businesss Park

Iron Works Road
Barrow in Furness
Cumbria
LA14 2PN
Contact: Harry Knowles
Tel: 01229 820611
Fax: 01229 820438
Email: hknowles@furnessenterprise.co.uk
Website: www.furnessenterprise.co.uk

Blackburn and District Enterprise Trust Ltd
Number One@The Beehive
Lions Drive
Shadsworth Business Park
Blackburn
BB1 2QS
Contact: John Ball
Tel: 01254 844144
Fax: 01254 844120
Email: info@enterprisetrust.co.uk
Website: www.enterprisetrust.co.uk

Business Link Fylde Coast Ltd
 Blackpool Challenge Partnership
Blackpool Technology Management Centre
Faraday Way
Bispham
Blackpool
FY2 0JW
Tel: 01253 470 200
Fax: 01253 470 201
Email: enquiries@bcp-ltd.co.uk
Website: www.bcp-ltd.co.uk

Bolton Business Ventures Ltd
46 Lower Bridgeman Street
Bolton
BL2 1DG
Contact: Paul Davidson
Tel: 01204 391 400
Fax: 01204 380 076
Email: info@bbvonline.net
Website: www.bbvonline.net

Bolton Incubator Centre Ltd
Endeavour House
98 Water Meeting Roads
The Valley
Bolton
BL1 8SW
Contact: Paul Davidson
Tel: 01204 546600

Cumbria Chamber of Commerce & Industry Limited
Enterprise Centre
James Street
Carlisle
Cumbria
CA2 5DA
Contact: Viv Dodd
Tel: 01228 534120
Fax: 01228 515602
Email: info@cumbriachamberofcommerce.co.uk

Chorley Local Enterprise Agency
34 Market Street
Chorley
Lancashire
PR7 2SE
Contact: Mrs Mavis Pearson
Tel: 01257 266166
Fax: 01257 241766

Ribble Valley Enterprise Agencies
Suite 3
The Printworks
Hay Road
Ribble Valley Enterprise Park
Barrow
Clitheroe
Lancs
BB7 9WA
Contact: Aileen Evans
Tel: 01254 828820
Fax: 01254 822858
Email: info@ribblevalleyenterpriseagency.co.uk
Website: www.ribblevalleyenterpriseagency.co.uk

Cumbria Rural Enterprise Agency Ltd
Lake District Business Park
Mintbridge Road
Kendal
Cumbria
LA9 6NH
Contact: Bob Clark
Tel: 01539 726624
Fax: 01539 730928
Email: bob@crea.co.uk
Website: www.crea.co.uk

South Ribble Business Venture
Centurion House
Centurion Way
Farington
Leyland
PR25 3GR
Contact: Tony Harrison
Tel: 01772 422242
Fax: 01772 623446
Email: pheyworth@bvg.org.uk
Website: www.bvg.org.uk

Cariocca Enterprises Manchester Ltd
Unit 55
Cariocca Business Park
2 Hellidon Close
Ardwick
Manchester
M12 4AH
Contact: Patrick Umeh
Tel: 0161 273 6605
Fax: 0161 273 6613
Email: umeh@cariocca.co.uk
Website: www.cariocca.co.uk

Manchester Business Consortium
1st Floor
Fourways House
57 Hilton Street
Manchester
M1 2EJ
Contact: Paul Shambrook
Tel: 0161 2361168
Fax: 0161 2361178

Email: enquiries@manchester-business.co.uk
Website: www.manchester-business.co.uk

Moss Side & Hulme Agency for Economic Development
Alexandra House
Ground Floor
2 Southcobe Walk
Moss Side
Manchester
M15 5NX
Contact: Sam Hill
Tel: 0161 226 0033
Fax: 0161 226 9437
Email: aed@aed.org.uk

Trafford Business Venture
Nelson House,
Park Road,
Timperley,
Cheshire.
WA14 5AB
Tel: 0161 976 4243
Fax: 0161 976 4245
Email: enquiries@tbv.co.uk
Website: www.tbv.org.uk

Pendle Enterprise Trust Ltd
Pendle Business Centre
Trafalgar Court
Commercial Road
Nelson
Lancs
BB9 9BT
Contact: Shirley White
Tel: 01282 698001
Fax: 01282 611634
Email: shirley@trust4business.co.uk
Website: www.trust4business.co.uk

Cumbria Rural E A Ltd
Rural Enterprise Centre
Redhills
Penrith
Cumbria
CA11 0DT

Contact: Bob Clark
Tel: 01768 891555
Fax: 01768 892666
Email: linda@crea.co.uk
Website: www.crea.co.uk

Preston Business Venture Ltd

108 Deepdale Road
Preston
Lancashire
PR1 5AR
Contacts: Philip Morris CEO, Carol Douglas
Tel: 01772 825 723
Fax: 01772 888 676
Email: enquiries@prestonbusinessventure.co.uk
Website: www.prestonbusinessventure.co.uk

Rochdale Borough Chamber

Dane Street
Rochdale
OL12 6XB
Contact: Don Brearley
Tel: 01706 344 031
Fax: 01706 641 811
Email: d.brealey@rochdalechamber.co.uk

Salford Hundred Venture

Business Link House
33–35 Winders Way (off Frederick Road)
Salford
Manchester
M6 6BU
Contact: Mike Finnie
Tel: 0161 742 4424
Fax: 0161 742 4401
Email: info@shv.org.uk
Website: www.shv.org.uk

Business Link West Lancashire

1 Westgate
Pennylands
Skelmersdale
Lancashire
WN8 8LP
Tel: 01695 51999
Email: info@westlancs.businesslink.co.uk

Warrington Business Venture

International Business Centre
Delta Crescent
Westbrook
Warrington
Cheshire
WA5 7WQ
Contact: Margaret Dandy
Tel: 01925 715175
Fax: 01925 715177
Email: everyone@wbv.org.uk
Website: www.warringtonbusinessventure.co.uk

West Cumbria Development Agency

Westlake Science & Technology Park
Moore Row
Whitehaven
Cumbria
CA24 3JZ
Contact: Godfrey Holden
Tel: 01946 696 201
Fax: 01946 696 202
Email: enquiry@wcda.co.uk
Website: www.wcda.co.uk

South Western region
Bath Enterprise Ltd

Abbey Chambers
Abbey Church Yard
Bath
BA1 1LY
Contact: Ian Storey
Tel: 01225 338 383
Fax: 01225 443 220
Email: enquiries@bath.blw.westec.co.uk

North Devon Enterprise Agency

5 The Quay
Bideford
Devon
EX39 2XX
Contact: Angi Lowe – Administrator
Dane Stanley – Director
Tel: 01237 426 416
Fax: 01237 426443
Email: info@ndea.org.uk

Website: www.ndea.org.uk

Brave Enterprise Agency
The Coach House
2 Upper York Street
Bristol
BS2 8QN
Contact: John Fitzgerald
Tel: 0117 944 5330
Fax: 0117 944 5661
Email: info@brave.org.uk
Website: www.brave.org.uk

East Devon Enterprise Agency Ltd
East Devon Business Centre
Heathpark
Honiton
Devon
EX14 1SF
Contact: Sue Bond
Tel: 01404 413500
Fax: 01404 46865
Email: info@heartofdevon.com
Website: www.heartofdevon.com

Enterprise South Devon
Teignbridge Business Centre
Cavalier Road
Heathfield
Newton Abbot
Devon
TQ12 6TZ
Contact: Tracey Higgins (operations manager)
Tel: 08456 447 558
Fax: 01626 837001
Email: info@enterprisesouthdevon.co.uk
Website: www.enterprisesouthdevon.co.uk

West Devon Business Information Point Ltd
Bridge House
Rooms 2, 3 & 4
25 Fore Street
Okehampton
Devon
EX20 1DL
Contact: Stewart Horne

Tel: 01837 659059
Fax: 01837 659314
Email: team@bipwestdevon.biz
Website: www.bipwestdevon.biz

West Cornwall Enterprise Trust Ltd
Carrick Business Centre
Beacon House
Commercial Road
Penryn
TR10 8AR
Contact: Mike Adams, chairman
Tel: 01326 378 737
Fax: 01326 378 643
Email: mike.adams@wcet.co.uk

West Cornwall Enterprise Trust Ltd
(Head Office)
Penwith Business Centre
Longrock Industrial Estate
Penzance
Cornwall
TR20 8HL
Contact: Jayne Spencer
Tel: 01736 352007
Fax: 01736 352002
Email: Jayne.spencer@wcet.co.uk
Website: www.enterprisewestcornwall.co.uk

Enterprise Plymouth Ltd
City Business Park
Stoke
Plymouth
Devon
PL3 4BB
Contact: Sheila Parkes
Fax: 01752 609240
Email: enquiries@epl.org.uk
Website: www.businessadvicecentre.co.uk

Mid Cornwall Enterprise Trust Ltd
Westhaul Park
Par Moor Road
St Austell
Cornwall
PL25 3RF

Contact: Alan Moore
Tel: 01726 813 079
Fax: 01726 814 251
Email: enterprise@mcet.demon.co.uk
Website: www.mcet.org.uk

Great Western Enterprise
Third Floor
The Forum
Marlborough Road
Swindon
Wiltshire
SN3 1QN
Contact: Lynne Bamford
Tel: 01793 645150
Fax: 01793 645151
Email: lynne.bamford@greatwesternenterprise.
co.uk
Website: www.greatwesternenterprise.co.uk

Mid Devon Enterprise Agency
The Factory
Leat Street
Tiverton
Devon
EX16 5LL
Contact: Sue Bond
Tel: 01884 255 629
Fax: 01884 243 031
Email: info@heartofdevon.com
Website: www.heartofdevon.com

North Somerset Enterprise Agency T/A Business Link West (North Somerset)
The Link Centre
Oldmixon Crescent
Weston-Super-Mare
North Somerset
BS24 9AY
Contact: Angela Hicks
Tel: 01934 418 118
Fax: 01934 629 541
Email: enquiries@weston.blw.westec.co.uk
Website: www.blweston.severn.co.uk

London Agencies
CENTA Business Services
Centa House
61 Birkenhead Street
London
WC1H 8BB
Contact: Jane Howden
Tel: 020 7278 5757
Fax: 020 7278 3466
Email: jhowden@centa.co.uk
Website: www.centa.co.uk

New LEntA Limited
One London Limited
28 Park Street
London
SE1 9EQ
Contact: Trevor Phillips
Tel: 020 7403 0300
Fax: 020 7403 1742
Email: Trevor.phillips@one-london.com
Website: www.citypartners.co.uk

One London Business Advice Service
Wandsworth Challenge Partnership
Unit 17–19 Arndale Walk
Southside Shopping Centre
London
SW18 4BX
Contact: Vivienne Scantlebury
Tel: 020 8870 1451
Fax: 020 8874 4195
Email: vivienne.scantlebury@one-london.com
Website: www.one-london.com

Brent Business Venture
38–40 High Street
Harlesden
London
NW10 4LS
Contact: Clair Ferguson
Tel: 0870 7570303
Fax: 0870 9617347
Email: judith@bbv.co.uk
Website: www.bbv.co.uk

Haringey Business Development Agency
2nd Floor
312 High Road
Haringey
London
N15 4BN
Contact: Dr Effiong Kaplan
Tel: 0208 376 6262
Fax: 0208 880 9344
Email: info@hbda.org.uk
Website: www.hbda.org.uk

East London Small Business Centre
Universal House
88–94 Wentworth Street
London
E1 7SA
Contact: Tim Heath
Tel: 0207 377 8821
Fax: 0207 375 1415
Website: www.goeast.org
Website: www.elsbc.com

HBV Enterprise
34–38 Dalston Lane
London
E8 3AZ
Contact: Sally Agass, chief executive
Tel: 020 7254 9595
Fax: 020 7254 8686
Email: mail@hbv.org.uk
Website: www.hbv.org.uk

Greenwich Enterprise Board
26 Burney Street
Greenwich
London
SE10 8EX
Contact: Graham Hart (business services manager)
Tel: 0208 305 2222
Fax: 0208 858 7010
Email: Graham Hart@geb.co.uk
Website: www.geb.co.uk

Business Focus
Donegal House
73 Tweedy Road
Bromley
Kent
BR1 1RG
Contact: Mike Ellis
Tel: 0845 4664700
Fax: 0845 4664701
Email: info@business-focus.co.uk
Website: www.business-focus.co.uk

Croydon Business Venture Ltd
Acorn House
74–94 Cherry Orchard Road
Croydon
CR9 6DA
Contact: Norman Pierce
Tel: 0208 681 8339
Fax: 0208 680 1996
Email: info@cbvltd.co.uk
Website: www.cbvltd.co.uk

Portobello Business Centre
2 Acklam Road
London
W10 5QZ
Contact: Abim Olabenjo
Tel: 0207 460 5050
Fax: 0207 968 3660
Email: abim@pbc.co.uk
Website: www.pbc.co.uk

West London Enterprise Agency Ltd
2nd Floor, Regal House
London Road
Twickenham
Middlesex
TW1 3QS
Contact: Charles Herrod
Tel: 0208 891 3742
Fax: 0208 8924874
Email: wlea57@hotmail.com

Enfield Enterprise Agency
Enfield Business Centre
201 Hertford Road
Enfield
Middlesex
EN3 5JH
Contact: Linda Moult
Tel: 020 8443 5457
Fax: 020 8443 5312
Email: info@enfieldenterpriseagency.co.uk
Website: www.enfieldenterpriseagency.co.uk

Harrow in Business
Enterprise House
297 Pinner Road
Harrow
Middlesex
HA1 4HS
Contact: Allen Pluck
Tel: 0208 4276188
Fax: 0208 861 5709
Email: info@hib.org.uk
Website: www.hib.org.uk

West Midlands region
Business Enterprise Support Limited
Fyrest House
Wetmore Road
Burton upon Trent
DE14 1SN
Contact: Peter St.John-Harris
Tel: 01283 537151
Fax: 01283 537130
Email: info@enterprisesupport.org
Website: www.enterprisesupport.org

Black in Business Birmingham (3b)
Unit 7
3b Business Village
Alexandra Road
Handsworth
Birmingham
B21 OPD
Contact: Goriola Sonola
Tel: 0121 523 1820
Fax: 0121 554 8823

Email: goriola@3b.org.uk
Website: www.3b.org.uk

Birmingham Enterprise Ltd.
Waterlinks Enterprise Centre
69 Aston Road
North Aston
Birmingham
B6 4EA
Contact: Wendy Maughan
Tel: 0121 359 2221
Fax: 0121 359 2230
Email: wendy@birmingham-enterprise.co.uk
Website: www.tng.uk.com

Birmingham Enterprise Ltd
Southside Business Centre
249 Ladypool Road
Sparkbrook Road
Birmingham
B12 8LF
Contact: Wendy Maughan
Tel: 0121 446 4444
Fax: 01299 693 6399
Email: wendy@birmingham-enterprise.co.uk
Website: www.tng.uk.com

Cannock Chase Enterprise Agency
The Hollies Business Centre
Hollies Road
Cannock
Staffordshire
Contact: Paul Saunby
Tel: 0800 4588797
Fax: 01283 537130
Email: paul@busentsupport.demon.co.uk

Coventry & Warwickshire Chamber of Commerce
Oak Tree Court
Binley Business Park
Harry Weston Road
Coventry
CV3 2UN
Contact: Paul Warwick

Tel: 024 7665 4321
Fax: 024 76450242
Email: paulw@cw-chamber.co.uk
Website: www.cw-businesslink.co.uk

Enterprise Link Dudley
Dudley Court
South Waterfront East
Brierley Hill
West Midlands
DY5 1XN
Contact: David Lindsay
Tel: 0845 22 234
Fax: 01384 868 400
Email: davidlindsay@babl.com
Website: www.enterpriselinkdudley.co.uk

Lichfield Enterprise Agency
District Council House
Frog Lane
Lichfield
Staffordshire
WS13 6YZ
Contact: Paul Saunby
Tel: 0800 4588797
Fax: 01283 537130
Email: paul@busentsupport.demon.co.uk

Solihull Business Enterprise Ltd
142 Lode Lane
Solihull
B91 2HP
Contact: Tony Lowe
Tel: 0121 704 1456
Fax: 0121 711 1051
Email: sbe@solihull.businesslink.co.uk

Stafford Enterprise Ltd
1st Floor Civic Offices
Riverside
Stafford
ST16 3AQ
Contact: Tony Brookes
Tel: 01785 257 057
Fax: 01785 220 612

Email: manager@staffentp.demon.co.uk
Website: www.staffordenterprise.org

North Staffs & District Business Initiative
Commerce House
Festival Park
Etruria
Stoke-on-Trent
ST1 5BE
Contact: Jill Levens
Tel: 01782 202 222
Fax: 01782 202 448
Email: jill.l@business.org.uk
Website: www.business.org.uk

Tamworth Enterprise Agency Ltd
Philip Dix Centre
Corporation Street
Tamworth
Staffordshire
B79 7DN
Contact: Paul Saunby
Tel: 0800 4588797
Fax: 01283 537130
Email: paul@busentsupport.demon.co.uk

Walsall Enterprise Agency Ltd
1st Floor Challenge Building
Hatherton Road
Walsall
West Midlands
WS1 1YG
Contact: Joy Henry
Tel: 01922 654 711
Fax: 01922 654 717
Email: aboajaj@walsall.gov.uk

Wolverhampton Enterprise Ltd
Lichfield Chambers
Exchange Street
Wolverhampton
WV1 1TS
Contact: Fred Pickerill
Tel: 01902 312 095
Fax: 01902 714 476

South Eastern region

Basingstoke & Andover Enterprise Centre
Business Centre
Beech Hurst
Weyhill Road
Andover
SP10 3AJ
Contact: David Lewis
Tel: 01264 332092
Fax: 01256 476040
Email: advice@bandec.org.uk
Website: www.bandec.org.uk

Enterprise First
11 Wellington Street
Aldershot
Hants
GU11 1DX
Contact: Peter Scares
Tel: 01252 319 272
Fax: 01252 319 384
Email: info@enterprisefirst.co.uk
Website: www.enterprisefirst.co.uk

Berkshire and Buckinghamshire Enterprise Agency
Wing House
Britannia Street
Aylesbury
Bucks
HP20 1QS
Contact: Grace Branker
Tel: 0118 958 5715
Fax: 0118 956 6884
Email: bbea@iname.com
Website: www.bbea.demon.co.uk

Oxfordshire Business Enterprises Ltd
The Colin Sanders Innovation Centre
Mewburn Road
Banbury
Oxfordshire
OX16 9PA
Contact: Chris Carr
Tel: 0870 2403686
Fax: 01295 817601

Email: info@oxonbe.co.uk
Website: www.oxonbe.co.uk

Technology Enterprise Kent
St James House
Castle Street
Canterbury
Kent
CT1 2QD
Contact: Linda Bailey
Tel: 01227 470 234/780 044
Fax: 01227 472665
Email: enquiries@technologyenterprise.co.uk
Website: www.technologyenterprise.co.uk

West Sussex Area Enterprise Centre Limited
The Enterprise Centre
2nd Floor
Greenacre Court
Station Road
Burgess Hill
RH15 9DS
Contact: John De Groot
Tel: 0845 2301054
Fax: 0845 2301064
Email: info@enterprise-centre.co.uk
Website: www.enterprise-centre.co.uk

Eastbourne & District Enterprise Agency Ltd
Minster House
York Road
Eastbourne
East Sussex
BN21 4PR
Contact: Customer service manager
Tel: 01323 413 500
Fax: 01323 412 470
Videolink: 01323 411522
Email: info@edeal.org.uk
Website: www.edeal.org.uk

Shepway Business Centre
Shearway Business Park
Shearway Road
Folkestone
Kent

CT19 4RH
Contact: John Earl
Tel: 01303 270022
Fax: 01303 270476
Email: john.earl@shepwaybc.co.uk
Website: www.shepwaybc.co.uk

Enterprise Agency of North Kent
Unit 4
The Courtyard
7a Manor Road
Gravesend
Kent
DA12 1AA
Contact: Diana J Porges
Tel: 01474 327 118
Fax: 01474 335 884
Email: info@businessnorthkent.co.uk
Website: www.businessnorthkent.co.uk

Ten Sixty Six Enterprise
Summerfields Business Centre
Bohemia Road
Hastings
East Sussex
TN34 1UT
Contact: Graham Marley
Tel: 01424 205500
Fax: 01424 205501
Email: info@1066enterprise.co.uk
Website: www.1066enterprise.co.uk

**South East Hampshire Enterprise Agencies
(SEHEA)**
Regional Business Centre
Harts Farm Way
Havant
Hampshire
PO9 1HR
Contact: Tim Austin
Tel: 023 9244 9449
Fax: 023 9244 9555
Email: tima@sehea.co.uk
Website: www.sehea.co.uk

Isle of Wight Enterprise Agency
Mill Court
Furrlongs
Newport
Isle of Wight
PO30 2AA
Contact: John Reddecliff
Tel: 01983 535 353
Fax: 01983 554555
Email: john@iwea.co.uk
Website: www.iwea.co.uk

Maidstone Enterprise Agency
2 Westree Road
Maidstone
Kent
ME16 8HB
Contact: Douglas Lawson
Tel: 01622 675 547
Fax: 01622 682 513
Email: info@thechamber.inmaidstone.com
Website: www.inmaidstone.com

Thames Business Advice Centre
Osney Mead
Oxford
OX2 0DR
Contact: Roger Cowdrey
Tel: 01865 249 279
Fax: 01865 792 269
Email: tbac@mail.oxlink.co.uk
Website: www.oxlink.co.uk/business/tbac

South West Hampshire Enterprise Agencies Ltd
Solent Business Centre
Millbrook Road West
Southampton
SO15 0HW
Contact: Neil Hendricks
Tel: 02380 788 088
Fax: 02380 704 046
Email: neil.hendricks@hampshire.businesslink.
co.uk

Enterprise Agency of West Kent
West Kent Business Centre

3–4 River Walk
Tonbridge, Kent
TN9 1DT
Contact: Diana Porges
Tel: 01732 360133
Fax: 01732 354131
Email: info@businesswestkent.co.uk
Website: www.businesswestkent.co.uk

Surrey Business Advice
19a High Street
Woking
Surrey
GU21 6BW
Contact: Michael Instone
Tel: 01483 728 434
Fax: 01483 751147
Email: sbe@sbe.org.uk
Website: www.surreybusinessadvice.org.uk

The Enterprise Centre – Worthing
Portland House
Richmond Road
Worthing
West Sussex
BN11 1HR
Contact: Kathy Lewis
Tel: 01903 228 622
Fax: 01903 228 628
Email: kathylewis@enterprise-centre.co.uk
Website: www.enterprise-centre.co.uk

East Midlands region
Derby and Derbyshire Business Venture
Innovation House
Riverside Park
Raynesway
Derby
DE21 7BF
Contact: John O'Reilly
Tel: 0845 6011038
Fax: 01332 548088
Email: John.O'Reilly@derbyshire.org
Website: www.derbyshire.org

Erewash Partnership
The Old Police Station
Wharncliffe Road
Ilkeston
Derbyshire
DE7 5GF
Contact: Derek Hogg
Tel: 0115 944 3944
Fax: 0115 944 3955
Email: derek@erewash-partnership.com
Website: ww.erewash-partnership.com

Kettering Business Venture Trust
The Business Exchange
Rockingham Road
Kettering
Northamptonshire
NN16 8JX
Contact: Lyn McGinn – Managing Director
Tel: 01536 513 840
Fax: 01536 523 209
Email: lyn@kbvt.co.uk
Website: www.kbvt.co.uk

**Mansfield Sutton & Kirby Enterprise Agency
(Manskep)**
The Old Town Hall
Market Place
Mansfield
Nottingham
NG18 1HX
Contact: John Whiteley
Tel: 01623 621773
Fax: 01623 648 579
Email: jwhiteley@manskep.com
Website: www.manskep.co.uk

Newark Business Venture
The Bearings
Bowbridge Road
Newark
Nottinghamshire
NG24 4BZ
Contact: Stuart Parr (manager)
Tel: 01636 708326

Fax: 01636 613023
Email: sparr@nnbv.co.uk
Website: www.newarkbusinessventure.co.uk

Newark Enterprise Agency
The Firs
67 London Road
Newark
Nottinghamshire
NG24 1RZ
Contact: John Whiteley
Tel: 01636 640 666
Fax: 01636 605 558
Email: jwhiteley@manskep.com
Website: www.manskep.co.uk

Nottingham Business Venture
Enterprise House
Shipstones Business Centre
Northgate
New Basford
Nottingham
NG7 7FN
Contact: Richard Dearden (chief executive)
Tel: 0115 9705550
Fax: 0115 9706471
Email: enquiries@nbv.co.uk
Website: www.nbv.co.uk

East Anglian region
Braintree District Enterprise Agency Ltd
Corner House
Market Place
Braintree
Essex
CM7 3HQ
Contact: Carol Marshall
Tel: 01376 328 221
Fax: 01376 550 126
Email: carol.marshall@essex.businesslink.co.uk

Cambridge Enterprise Agency
71a Lensfield Road
Cambridge
CB2 1EN
Contact: Lisa Collins

Tel: 01223 323 553
Fax: 01223 576 553
Email: cea@cambsenterprise.co.uk
Website: www.cambsenterprise.co.uk

Mid-Essex Enterprise Agency
8 Brockley Road
Chelmsford
Essex
CM2 2HQ
Contact: Geoff Powdrill
Tel: 01245 496712
Fax: 01245 347 455
Email: GeoffPowdrill@midessexenterprise
agency.co.uk

Braintree District Enterprise Agency Ltd incorporating Uttlesford Enterprise
Council Offices
46 High Street
Great Dunmow
Essex
CM6 1AN
Contact: Jim Rowley, DMS FIBA MIMgt
Tel: 01799 510490

Mid-Anglian Enterprise Agency (MENTA)
The Vision Centre
5 Eastern Way
Bury St Edmunds
IP32 7AB
Interview facilities available at Haverhill.
Please contact Bury St Edmunds
Office to arrange appointment.
Contact: Albert Cook (director)
Tel: 01284 760 206
Fax: 01284 767 157
Email: albert.cook@menta.org.uk
Website: www.menta.org.uk

NWES – Great Yarmouth
Queens Road
Great Yarmouth
Norfolk
NR30 3HT
Contact: Admin

Tel: 01493 850 204
Fax: 01493 330 754
Email: gy@nwes.org.uk
Website: www.nwes.org.uk

WENTA Business Services
1–11 Bridge Street
Hemel Hempstead
Hertfordshire
HP1 1EG
Contact: Abi Jenkin
Tel: 0870 870 0891
Fax: 0870 870 0892
Email: admin@wenta.co.uk
Website: www.wenta.co.uk

Huntingdonshire Enterprise Agency Ltd
Centenary House
St Mary's Street
Huntingdon
Cambs
PE29 3PE
Contact: Teresa Leone
Tel: 01480 450 028
Fax: 01480 455 710
Email: hea@cambsenterprise.co.uk
Website: www.huntssenterprise.co.uk

Ipswich Enterprise Agency
Felaw Maltings
44 Felaw Street
Ipswich
Suffolk
IP2 8SJ
Business Counselling available at Leiston TEL:
01728 833122
Contact:
Tel: 01473 407 001
Fax: 01473 407 301
Email: info@suffolkenterprise.co.uk
Website: www.suffolkenterprise.co.uk

North East Suffolk Business Centre
Pinbush Road
Lowestoft
Suffolk

NR33 7NQ
Contact: Eva Warner
Tel: 01502 501620
Fax: 01502 511834
Email: eva.warner@nwes.org.uk
Website: www.nwes.org.uk

Lowestoft Enterprise Trust Ltd
North East Suffolk Business Centre
Pinbush Road
South Lowestoft Industrial Estate
Lowestoft
Suffolk
NR33 7NQ
Contact: Brian Barker
Tel: 01502 501 620
Fax: 01502 511834
Website: www.enterprise-services.co.uk

Forest Enterprise Agency Trust
Epping Forest Business Centre
Langston Road
Loughton
Essex
IG10 3UE
Contact: Michael Mulvaney
Tel: 01992 564 800
Fax: 01992 564 801
Email: michael.mulvaney@essex.businesslink.co.uk

InterBusiness Group
Head Office:
The Business Centre
Kimpton Road
Luton
Beds
LU2 0LB
Satellite Office in Ampthill. Please contact
Head Office in Luton for appointments.
Tel: 01582 522448
Fax: 01582 533450
Email: blb@beds.businesslink.co.uk
Website: www.beds-luton-business.co.uk

Fens Business Enterprise Trust Ltd
Fenland Business Centre

Longhill Road
March
Cambridgeshire
PE15 0BJ
Contact: Neil Dick
Tel: 01354 660 900
Fax: 01354 660021
Email: info@enterprisefenland.com
Website: www.enterprisefenland.com

Business Link Milton Keynes & North Bucks
Tempus
249 Midsummer Boulevard
Milton Keynes
Bucks
MK9 1EU
Contact: Alan J Wade
Tel: 01908 259000
Fax: 01908 230130
Email: enquiry@mk-chamber.co.uk
Website: www.businessadvicemk.demon.co.uk

Norwich Enterprise Centre
6 Upper Goat Street
Norwich
NR2 1EW
Contact: Kelly Stamp
Tel: 01603 677510
Fax: 01603 677518
Email: kelly.stamp@neatbusiness.co.uk
Website: www.neatbusiness.co.uk

Peterborough Enterprise Programme
no address available
Contact: Katie Hart
Tel: 01733 232010
Fax: 01223 576553
Email: pep@cambsenterprise.co.uk
Website: www.peterenterprise.co.uk

Stevenage Business Initiative
Business & Techology Centre
Bessemer Drive
Stevenage
Herts
SG1 2DX

Business Counselling available at Hertford.
Please contact Stevenage Office.
Contact: Doug King
Tel: 01438 315 733
01438 310101
Fax: 01438 310 001
Email: info@sbi-herts.co.uk
Website: www.sbi-herts.co.uk

St Albans Enterprise Agency STANTA
Unit 8, St Albans Enterprise Centre
Long Spring
Porters Wood
St Albans
Herts
AL3 6EN
Contact: Mel Hilbrown
Tel: 01727 837760
Fax: 01727 851 200
Email: advice@stanta.co.uk
Website: www.stanta.co.uk

Braintree District Enterprise Agency Ltd incorporating Uttlesford Enterprise
Council Offices
London Road
Saffron Walden
Essex
CB11 4ER
Contact: Jim Rowley, DMS FIBA MIMgt
Tel: 01799 510428

Southend Enterprise Agency Ltd
Enterprise House
853/855 London Road
Westcliff on Sea
Essex
SS0 9SZ
Contact: Mr Anthony Vincent (chairman)
Tel: 01702 471 118
Fax: 01702 470 598
Email: info@southend-enterprise.com
Website: www.southend-enterprise.com

Watford Enterprise Agency WENTA
The WENTA Business Centre

Colne Way
Watford
Herts
WD24 7ND
Contact: Chris Pichon
Tel: 0870 870 0891
Fax: 0870 870 0892
Email: admin@wenta.co.uk
Website: www.wenta.co.uk

Southend Enterprise Agency Ltd
Enterprise House
853/855 London Road
Westcliff on Sea
Essex
SS0 9SZ
Contact: Mr Anthony Vincent
Tel: 01702 471 118
Fax: 01702 470 598
Email: info@southend-enterprise.com

Scotland

Highlands & Islands Enterprise Network
Tel: 01463 234171
Website: www.hie.co.uk

Highlands & Islands Enterprise
Inverness Retail and Business Park
Inverness IV2 7GF
Scotland
Contact: Gavin Cameron &
Jacqui Campbell
Tel: 01463 234171
Fax: 01463 244469
Email: hie.general@hient.co.uk

Argyll & Islands Enterprise
Enterprise Centre
Kilmory Industrial Estate
Argyll
PA31 8SH
Contact: Mr Paul Anfield (business information
manager)
Fax: 01546 603 964
Email: aie@hient.co.uk

Website: www.hie.co.uk/aie

Caithness & Sutherland Enterprise
Tollemache House
High Street
Thurso
Caithness. KW14 8AZ
Contact: Lynne Johnston
Tel: 01847 896115
Fax: 01847 893383
Email: case@hient.co.uk

Inverness & Nairn Enterprise
The Green House
Beechwood Business Park North
Inverness IV2 3BL
Contact: Ms. Yvonne Crook/Ms. Fiona Robb
Tel: 01463 713504
Fax: 01463 712002
Email: ine.general@hient.co.uk

Lochaber Limited
St Mary's House
Gordon Square
Fort William. PA33 6DY
Contact: Tina Davenport
Tel: 01397 704326

Moray Badenoch & Strathspey Enterprise Ltd
The Horizon Scotland complex
The Enterprise Park
Forres
Moray IV36 2AB
Tel: 01309 696000
Fax: 01309 696001
mbse@hient.co.uk

Orkney Enterprise
14 Queen Street
Kirkwall. KW15 1JE
Contact: Ruth Kilpatrick
Tel: 01856 874638
Fax: 01856 872915
Email: oe@hient.co.uk

Ross & Cromarty Enterprise
69–71 High Street
Invergordon
Ross-shire. IV18 0AA
Contact: Suzanne Stewart
Tel: 01349 853666
Fax: 01349 853833
Email: race@hient.co.uk

Shetland Enterprise
Toll Clock Shopping Centre
26 North Road
Lerwick
Shetland.
ZE1 0DE
Contact: Valerie Treneman
Tel: 01595 693177
Fax: 01595 693208
Email: hie.general@hient.co.uk

Skye & Lochalsh Enterprise
Kings House
The Green
Portree
Isle of Skye.
IV51 9BS
Contact: Gordon Bushnell
Tel: 01478 612841
Fax: 01478 612164
Email: sale@hient.co.uk

Western Isles Enterprise
9 James Street
Stornoway
Isle of Lewis. HS1 2QN
Contact: Fiona Mckenzie
Tel: 01851 703703
Fax: 01851 704130
Email: wie@hient.co.uk

Scotland (other than Highlands and Islands)

Scottish Enterprise Head Office
5 Atlantic Quay
150 Broomielaw
Glasgow

G2 8LU
Contact: Administration
Tel: 0141 248 2700
Fax: 0141 221 3217
Email: network.helpline@scotent.co.uk

Scottish Enterprise Ayrshire
17–19 Hill Street
Kilmarnock
KA3 1HA
Tel: 01563 526623
Fax: 01563 543636
Email: ayrshire@scotent.co.uk

Scottish Enterprise Borders
Bridge Street
Galashiels
TD1 1SW
Tel: 01896 758991
Fax: 01896 758625
Email: seb-enquiry@scotent.co.uk

Scottish Enterprise Dumfries & Galloway
Solway House
Dumfries Enterprise Park
Tinwald Downs Road
Dumfries
DG1 3SJ
Tel: 01387 245000
Fax: 01387 246224
Email: sedg.enquiries@scotent.co.uk

Scottish Enterprise Dunbartonshire
2nd Floor, Spectrum House
Clydebank Business Park
Clydebank
Glasgow
G81 2DR
Tel: 0141 951 2121
Fax: 0141 951 1907
Email: dunbartonshire@scotent.co.uk

Scottish Enterprise Edinburgh and Lothians
Apex House
99 Haymarket Terrace
Edinburgh

EH12 5HD
Tel: 0131 313 4000
Fax: 0131 313 4231
Direct Fax for Liz: 0131 313 6005
Email: lothian@scotent.co.uk

Scottish Enterprise Fife
Kingdom House
Saltire Centre
Glenrothes
Fife
KY6 2AQ
Tel: 01592 623000
Fax: 01592 623149
Email: fife@scotent.co.uk

Scottish Enterprise Forth Valley
Laurel House
Laurelhill Business Park
Stirling
FK7 9JQ
Tel: 01786 451919
Fax: 01786 478123
Email: forthvalley@scotent.co.uk

Scottish Enterprise Glasgow
Atrium Court
50 Waterloo Street
Glasgow
G2 6HQ
Tel: 0141 204 1111
Fax: 0141 248 1600
Email: glasgow@scotent.co.uk

Scottish Enterprise Grampian
27 Albyn Place
Aberdeen
AB10 1DB
Tel: 01224 252000
Fax: 01224 213417
Direct Fax for Louise Cooper: 01224 252127
Email: segrampianenquiries@scotent.co.uk

Scottish Enterprise Lanarkshire
New Lanarkshire House
Dove Wynd

Strathclyde Business Park
Bellshill
ML4 3AD
Tel: 01698 745454
Fax: 01698 842211
Email: selenquiry@scotent.co.uk

Scottish Enterprise Renfrewshire
27 Causeyside Street
Paisley
PA1 1UL
Tel: 0141 848 0101
Fax: 0141 848 6930
Email: renfrewshire@scotent.co.uk

Scottish Enterprise Tayside
45 North Lindsay Street
Dundee
DD1 1HT
Tel: 01382 223100
Fax: 01382 201319
Email: set.reception@scotent.co.uk

Northern Ireland

North Down Development Organisation Ltd
Enterprise House
Balloo Avenue
Balloo IndustrialEstate
Bangor
BT19 7QT
Contact: Lynne Vance
Tel: 028 9127 1525
Fax: 028 9127 0080
Email: mail@nddo.co.uk
Website: www.nddo.u-net.com

Acorn the Business Centre
2 Riada Avenue
Garryduff Road
Ballymoney
BT53 7LH
Tel: 028 2766 6133
Fax: 028 2766 5019
Email: enquiries@acornbusiness.co.uk
Website: http://www.acornbusiness.co.uk

Ballymena Business Development Centre Ltd
Galgorm Industrial Estate
62 Fenaghy Road
Ballymena
BT42 1FL
Tel: 028 2565 8616
Fax: 028 2563 0830
Email: info@ballymenabusinesscentre.co.uk
Website: http://www.bbdc.co.uk

East Belfast Enterprise Park Ltd
308 Albertbridge Road
Belfast
BT5 4GX
Contact: Steve Pollard
Tel: 028 9045 5450
Fax: 028 9073 2600
Email: info@eastbelfast.org
Website: http://www.eastbelfast.org

Fermanagh Enterprise Ltd
Enniskillen Business Centre
Lackaghboy Industrial Estate
Tempo Road
Enniskillen
BT74 4RL
Tel: 028 6632 7348
Fax: 028 6632 7878
Email: info@fermanaghenterprise.com
Website: http://www.fermanaghenterprise.com

Glenwood Enterprises Ltd
Springbank Industrial Estate
Poleglass
Belfast
BT17 OQL
Contact: Eamon Foster
Tel: 028 9061 0311
Fax: 028 9060 0929
Email: Glenwood Enterprises Ltd
Website: www.glenwoodbc.com

North City Business Centre
2 Duncairn Gardens
Belfast
BT15 2GG

Contact: Michael McCorry
Tel: 028 9074 7470
Fax: 028 8224 9451
Email: info@oecl.co.uk
Website: http://www.oecl.co.uk

Ortus
Twin Spires Centre
155 Northumberland Street
Belfast
BT13 2JF
Contact: James McCreary
Tel: 028 9031 1002
Fax: 028 9031 1005
Email: Ortus
Website: www.ortus.org

Ormeau Enterprises Ltd
Ormeau Business Park
8 Cromac Avenue
Belfast
BT7 1EL
Contact: Patricia McNeill
Tel: 028 9033 9906
Fax: 028 9033 9937
Email: Ormeau Enterprises Ltd
Website: www.ormeaubusinesspark.com

Townsend Enterprise Park
28 Townsend Street
Belfast
BT13 2ES
Contact: George Briggs
Tel: 028 9089 4500
Fax: 028 9089 4502
Email: admin@townsend.co.uk
Website: www.townsend.co.uk

Workspace (Draperstown) Ltd
7 Tobermore Road
Draperstown
BT45 7AG
Tel: 028 7962 8113
Fax: 028 7962 8975
Email: info@workspace.org.uk
Website: http://www.workspace.org.uk

Work West Enterprise Agency
301 Glen Road
Belfast
BT11 8BU
Contact: Claire Ferris
Tel: 028 9061 0826
Fax: 028 9062 2001

Castlereagh Enterprises Ltd
Enterprise Drive
Carrowreagh Road
Dundonald
BT16 0QT
Contact: Jack McComiskey
Tel: 028 9055 7557
Fax: 028 9055 7558
Website: www.castlereagh.com

Lisburn Enterprise Organisation Ltd
Enterprise Crescent
Ballinderry Road
Lisburn
BT28 2BP
Contact: Aisling Owens
Tel: 028 92661160
Fax: 028 9260 3084
Website: www.lisburn-enterprise.co.uk

Mallusk Enterprise Park Ltd
Mallusk Enterprise Park
Mallusk Drive
Newtownabbey
BT36 4GN
Contact: Melanie Humphrey
Tel: 028 9083 8860
Fax: 028 9084 1525
Email: info@mallusk.org
Website: www.mallusk.org

Ards Business Centre Ltd
Jubilee Road
Newtownards
Co Down
BT23 4YH

Contact: Margaret Patterson
Tel: 028 9181 9787
Fax: 028 9182 0625
Email: postbox@ardsbusiness.com
Website: www.ardsbusiness.com

Wales

In Wales the services provided by Enterprise Agencies is provided by Business Connect Wales. Connect Wales: 08457 96 97 98, Website www.businessconnect.org.uk

See also under Business Link for other details of services provided by Business Connect.

4　Sector-specific services

As well as schemes of help, assistance and advice that are particular to certain industries provided by the DTI (see above) these organizations provide services to small and new start-ups in their sectors.

UK Steel Enterprise Ltd

UK Steel Enterprise Ltd, formerly British Steel (Industry) Ltd, was originally established in 1975 by the then British Steel Corporation and is a subsidiary of Corus Group plc, the company formed from the merger of British Steel and Koninklijke Hoogovens in 1999.

Their objective is to help in the economic regeneration and development of those areas of the UK that have been affected by changes in the steel industry. They do this directly by helping small businesses – new and existing – to grow and create job opportunities. They also support other organizations with similar aims. Businesses engaged in most manufacturing and industrial activities are eligible for support, as are those engaged in providing a service to industry. They do not have to have any connection with Corus or the steel industry other than being based in a steel area.

More than 3,700 businesses have been directly assisted with finance or workspace (some with both). These businesses are estimated to have created more than 60,000 new jobs.

They have two main programmes for small businesses, finance and premises and operate in 21 present and former steel areas.

- **Finance**: They have provided £50 million to over 2,400 businesses, of which: £40 million has been provided as loan or share capital, invested in more than 1,700 businesses. £10 million has been provided in other ways. They have continued to invest around £2m of risk capital (shares and loans) in about 50 businesses each year. Further information about the size and type of businesses they have financed is shown right.
- **Premises**: They have developed 570 self-contained workspace units, totalling 480,000 sq ft, at a cost of £18m. Whilst a few are conversions of larger, existing buildings, most are part of purpose-built business centres. These units were developed with the needs of small businesses, particularly new enterprises, in mind. Most sites provide light industrial units and offices, in a mix of sizes, and a range of business support services. Some of the workspace complexes have since been transferred to other owners. At any one time, they have around 250 units available, totalling 225,000 sq ft, at various locations. They are available on flexible terms. They have two Innovation Centres, in Teesside and Sheffield, and have redeveloped and expanded their largest site, Cardiff Bay Business Centre. Over 1,400 businesses have been supported through their premises since the first, Clyde Workshops, was opened in 1979.

For general enquiries please contact their head office:

The Innovation Centre
217 Portobello
Sheffield
S1 4DP
Tel: 0114 273 1612
Fax: 0114 270 1390
Email: ho@uksteelenterprise.co.uk

Yorkshire, Humberside and the Midlands
The Innovation Centre
217 Portobello
Sheffield
S1 4DP
Tel. 0114 270 0933
Fax. 0114 224 2222
Email: yorks@uksteelenterprise.co.uk

Scotland
Grovewood Business Centre
Strathclyde Business Park
Bellshill,
Lanarkshire
ML4 3NQ
Tel. 01698 845045
Fax. 01698 845123
Email: scot@uksteelenterprise.co.uk

North of England
The Innovation Centre
Vienna Court
Kirkleatham Business Park
Redcar
TS10 5SH
Tel. 01642 777888
Fax. 01642 777999
Email: north@uksteelenterprise.co.uk

Tourist Boards

The Tourist Boards in England, Scotland and Wales have a role to play in helping new tourism businesses, such as restaurants, hotels, guest houses, pubs, holiday parks, souvenir and local interest shops and cafés to get started, or to help the 127,000 existing tourism businesses to expand. Their services come under three main headings.

Funding for tourism projects

The Tourist Boards provide information on how new and existing tourism projects have accessed the funds they needed. Their funding page is regularly updated with news and articles specifically related to tourism. Recent articles cover sources of funds for resort regeneration; rural tourism; sustainable tourism; and accessibility.

They also provide information on what funds are currently available to you and your projects. They have up-to-the-minute news about current funding opportunities for the whole range of not-for-profit and public sector organizations. Included are: European grants; the Lottery; urban and rural regeneration funding; sponsorship; charitable trusts and corporate grants

Insights: The Tourism Intelligence Marketing Service

Insights is one of the most comprehensive reference publications on tourism. It is a one-step source of the latest marketing information, market analysis and statistics. The English Tourism Council's bi-monthly subscription provides the latest market information for the tourism market, in an easy-to-use A4 binder format or CD-ROM.

The Pink Booklet

This publication explains nearly sixty pieces of legislation affecting anyone running a tourism accommodation business. The guide is practical, easy to use and contains a wealth of up-to-date information. Thousands of accommodation businesses have already benefited from using previous editions of *The Pink Booklet*.

For general enquiries contact the relevant country Tourist Board.

English Tourist Authority
Thames Tower
Black's Road
London W6 9EL
Tel: (+44) (0)20 8846 9000
Fax: (+44) (0)20 8563 0302
Website: www.britishtouristauthority.org/
For enquiries on working with the BTA on a specific tourism business project, telephone: 020 8563 3186, fax: 020 8563 3352 or Email: tradehelpdesk@bta.org.uk

Scottish Tourist Board
23 Ravelston Terrace
Edinburgh EH4 3TP
Tel: 0131 332 2433
Fax: 0131 343 1513
Website: www.holiday.scotland.net

Wales Tourist Board
Brunel House
2 Fitzalan Road
Cardiff
CF24 0UY
Tel: 029 2049 9909
Fax: 029 2048 5031
Website: www.visitwales.com

Northern Ireland Tourist Board
St Anne's Court
59 North Street
Belfast BT1 1NB
Tel: +44 (0) 28 9023 1221
Minicom (011232) 233228
Fax: (011232) 240960
Website: www.discovernorthernireland.com

Rural businesses

In response to foot and mouth disease, and the problems that has created for rural businesses, the Government has set up a Helpline (0845 600 9 006) which operates at local rate between 08:00 to 20:00hrs Mon-Sat. They also issue leaflets with general advice, and contact details for further help to contact points such as banks and post offices. Their website (www.countryside.gov.uk) also provides details of telephone lines and web links to government contacts providing information and help for rural businesses announced by the Government's Rural Task Force. Such help includes reduced rates bills and extensions to payment of tax. The special Tax Helpline is 0845 300

0157 – local rate – open 08:00 to 24:00hrs seven days a week.

Phone: 0845 600 9 006 (local rate between 08:00 to 20:00hrs Mon-Sat)

5   Help with property and where to locate your business

Apart from estate agents and other more conventional sources of help and advice on where to locate a business, the following organizations are set up to help in this area, or to advise on any special support on offer in an area that could influence your choice of where to locate.

English Partnerships

English Partnerships is the national force for property regeneration and development. They work in partnership to create new jobs and investment through sustainable economic regeneration and development in the English regions.

English Partnerships focuses on national and cross-regional coordination, where this adds value to the Government's regeneration agenda and the work of the Regional Development Agencies (see below); and their primary goal is to ' help to provide quality places for people to live and work, to the highest standards of design, sustainability and environmental benefit'.

Englishsites.com is an interactive database of strategic development sites in England, managed by English Partnerships, which is the service most likely to be of help to entrepreneurs.

Englishsites.com provides a fast, accurate and up-to-date information service on the best sites currently available to companies considering expanding, investing or relocating in the English regions. The database was re-launched in January 2001 after an exhaustive updating process to ensure that all information was current and accurate.

The database currently holds approximately 200 sites, and uses a powerful search facility that allows a user to search for a site using a number of criteria, including size, location, distance to motorway and airports, and the level of grants available.

Outside of England you should contact one of the country help agencies listed above to find what help is on offer with premises and location.

English Partnership contact points:
Corporate Headquarters
110 Buckingham Palace Road
London
SW1W 9SA
Tel: + 0044 (0)20 7881 1600
Fax: + 0044 (0)20 7730 9162
Email: mail@englishpartnerships.co.uk
Website: www.englishpartnerships.co.uk

St George's House
Kingsway
Team Valley
Gateshead
Tyne and Wear
NE11 0NA
Tel: + 0044 (0)191 487 6565
Fax: + 0044 (0)191 487 5690

Central Business Exchange II
414–428 Midsummer Boulevard
Central Milton Keynes
MK9 2EA
Tel: + 0044 (0)1908 692692
Fax: + 0044 (0)1908 691333

Arpley House
110 Birchwood Boulevard
Birchwood
Warrington
WA3 7QH
Tel: + 0044 (0)1925 651144
Fax: + 0044 (0)1925 411493

Jordan House
Hall Court
Hall Park Way
Telford

TF3 4NN
Tel: + 0044 (0)1952 293131
Fax: + 0044 (0)1952 293132

Enterprise Zones

There are number of Enterprise Zones (EZs) operating in the UK, though the scheme in its present form is due to be wound up in October 2006.

Companies locating in EZs are exempt from the requirement to pay business rates during the life of the zone. For a building of 20,000 square feet this could result in a saving of up to £25,000 per annum during the life of the zone.

The incentives generally take the form of rent-free periods, cash incentives to sign a lease or a contribution towards the cost of fitting out a building. Our experience is that companies could expect rent-free periods of one month per year of lease, although more attractive incentives may be available on properties within EZs.

Alternatively if a company chooses to construct a building in an Enterprise Zone directly rather than leasing from a developer, significant tax allowances associated with the construction cost may be available (i.e. 100% tax relief against the construction cost is available in the year of construction).

Benefits summary
The following benefits are available, for the period of designation of the Zone, to
both new and existing industrial and commercial enterprises in an EZ:

- 100% allowances for corporation and income tax purposes for capital expenditure on industrial and commercial buildings.
- Exemption from the National Non-Domestic Rate on industrial and commercial property.
- A greatly simplified planning regime; developments that conform with the published scheme for each Zone do not require individual planning permission.
- Those statutory controls remaining in force (e.g. planning) are administered more speedily.

- Applications from firms in EZs for certain customs facilities are processed as a matter of priority and certain criteria relaxed.
- Government requests for statistical information are reduced.

Operating Enterprise Zones
Lanarkshire EZ
John McManus
Lanarkshire Development Agency
New Lanarkshire House
Dove Wynd
Strathclyde Business Park
Bellshill
Lanarkshire ML4 3AD
Tel: 441698 745454
Fax: 441698 842211

East Midlands EZ Nos 1, 2 &3: Holmewood
Mel Pretious
Development and Leisure Dept.
North East Derbyshire DC
Council House
Saltergate
Chesterfield
Derbyshire S40 1LF
Tel: 441246 212685
Fax: 441246 212620

East Midlands EZ No 4: Manton Wood
Bob Dean
Local Plans Unit
Bassetlaw DC
Queens Buildings
Potter Street
Worksop
Nottinghamshire S80 2AH
Tel: 441909 533190
Fax: 441909 482622

East Midlands EZ Nos 5 & 6: Crown Farm
Steven Baker
Property Services
Mansfield DC
Civic Centre
Chesterfield Road South

Mansfield
Nottinghamshire NG17 7BH
Tel: 441623 656656 ext 3231
Fax: 441623 420197

East Midlands EZ No 7: Sherwood Business Park
Peter Johnson
Assistant Director Planning & Estates
Ashfield DC
Urban Road
Kirkby-in-Ashfield
Nottinghamshire NG19 8DA
Tel: 441623 457352
Fax: 441623 457590

Dearne Valley EZ Nos 1–6:
Peter Bright
Marketing Manager, Marketing Team
Dearne Valley Partnership
Manvers House
PO Box 109
Wath-upon-Dearne
Rotherham S63 7YZ
Tel: 441709 760207
Fax: 441709 879199

East Durham EZ Nos 1–6:
Ken Greenfield
Chief Executive, East Durham Development
Agency
4th Floor
Lee House
Peterlee
County Durham SR8 1DB
Tel: 44191 586 3366
Fax: 44191 518 0332

Tyne Riverside EZ Nos 8–11:
Ms Madelaine Rourke
Investment Officer, INTO
105 Howard Street
North Shields
Tyne & Wear NE30 1NA
Tel: 44191 200 6060
Fax: 44191 200 6110

Other Government initiatives to help with location

Assisted areas

The government has designated certain areas as Assisted Areas, and there could be grants available which might encourage you to locate in an inner city or one of the poorer regions. Such grants may make your business idea more viable and are worth investigating. An area that has been designated as having Assisted Area status offers the following help:

- Regional selective assistance (RSA), which provides grants of up to 15 per cent of the fixed costs of a project investing over £500,000. Higher grants are awarded for quality projects involving high skilled sustainable jobs. Eligible costs include property and plant and machinery relating to the expansion, modernizing or establishment of a new company.
- Enterprise grants (EG), which are aimed at small- and medium-sized businesses with projects investing up to £500,000. Enterprise grants are available in the English regions in the Assisted Areas and additional areas of special need. Grants are up to a maximum of 15 per cent of project costs (£75,000). Scheme criteria are similar to RSA, but there are some regional variations. Scotland operates a small business (RSA-based) scheme, and Wales also offers RSA to small and large businesses. Details of RSA and EG are available from your local Business Link, or outside of England contact one of the country agencies listed above.
- Other types of help provided at the local level, such as training for small business managers in, say marketing, start-up grants, rate relief during the start-up period. Local areas (represented by the local authority or chamber of commerce) are expected to present a strategic plan for regenerating the area, and showing that partnership funding (for example from local businesses or direct from local authority budgets) is committed to the plan. The local area then directs how the funds will be used

– that is, what projects will be eligible, what form assistance will take. The aim is to focus help more directly at local needs.

Regional Development Agencies (RDAs)

Regional Development Agencies (RDAs) were formally launched in eight English regions on 1 April 1999. The ninth, in London, was established on 3 July 2000 following the establishment of the Greater London Authority (GLA). They aim to coordinate regional economic development and regeneration, enable the English regions to improve their relative competitiveness and reduce the imbalances that exists within and between regions. (For access to similar services outside of England, contact the country agencies listed above.)

RDAs have the following statutory purposes:

- to further economic development and regeneration;
- to promote business efficiency, investment and competitiveness;
- to promote employment;
- to enhance development and application of skill relevant to employment; and
- to contribute to sustainable development.

Agencies' specific functions are:

- formulating a regional strategy in relation to their purposes;
- regional regeneration;
- taking forward the Government's competitiveness agenda in the regions;
- taking the lead on regional inward investment;
- developing a regional Skills Action Plan to ensure that skills training matches the needs of the labour market; and
- a leading role on European funding.

Local authorities have a significant stake in the work of the RDA. Four of the thirteen RDA board members are drawn from local government – with the choice reflecting a balance between type and size of authority, as well as geographical and political spread.

RDAs are accountable to ministers and Parliament, but there will also be arrangements in place to ensure that the RDAs are responsive to regional views, and that they give an account of themselves to those with an interest in their work, including Chambers of Commerce

RDA contact details:

OneNorthEast
One NorthEast
Stella House
GoldCrest Way
Newburn Riverside
Newcastle upon Tyne
NE15 8NY
Tel: 0191 229 6200
Fax: 0191 229 6201
General website: http://www.onenortheast.co.uk
Regional Economic Strategy: http://www.onestrategynortheast.co.uk

North West Development Agency
Renaissance House
Centre Park
Warrington
Cheshire
WA1 1XB
Tel: 01925 400 100
Fax: 01925 400 400
Website: http://www.nwda.co.uk

Yorkshire Forward
Victoria House
2 Victoria Place
Leeds
LS11 5AE
Tel: 0113 3949600 (8.30–17.30)
Fax: 0113 243 1088
Website: http://www.yorkshire-forward.com

Advantage West Midlands
3 Priestley Wharf, Holt Street,
Aston Science Park
Birmingham

B7 4BN
Tel: 0121 380 3500
Fax: 0121 380 3501
Email: neilskitt@advantagewm.co.uk
Website: http://www.advantage-westmidlands.
co.uk

East Midlands development agency
Apex Court
City Link
Nottingham
NG2 4LA
Tel: 0115 988 8300
Fax: 0115 8533666
Email: info@emd.org.uk
Website: http://www.emda.org.uk

East of England Development Agency
The Business Centre
Station Road
Histon
Cambridge
CB4 9LQ
Tel: 01223 713 900
Fax: 01223 713 940
Email: knowledge@eeda.org.uk
Website: http://www.eeda.org.uk

South West of England Regional Development Agency
Sterling House
Dix's Field
Exeter
EX1 1QA
Tel: 01392 214 747
Fax: 01392 214 848
Website: http://www.southwestrda.org.uk

SEEDA Headquarters
Cross Lanes
Guildford
GU1 1YA
Tel: +44 (0)1483 484200
Fax: 01483 484 247
Website: http://www.seeda.co.uk

LDA Headquarters
4th Floor
Romney House
Marsham Street
London,SW1P 3PY
Tel: 0207 984 ext no.
Fax. 0207 983 4801
Email: seeda@seeda.co.uk
Website: http://www.lda.gov.uk

LDA
Devon House
58–60 St Katharine's Way
London
E1W 1JX
Tel: 020 7954 4500
Textphone: 020 7954 0010
Email: info@lda.gov.uk
Website: www.lda.gov.uk

Specialised local help schemes
Even outside Assisted Areas, some special help is available to certain types of business in rural areas. Village post offices and village shops qualify automatically for 50 per cent relief against business rates – at the discretion of the local authority, this can be increased to 100 per cent relief. Certain other village businesses can also get help with rates at the discretion of the local authority. In this context, a village means a community with a population of 3,000 or less in a designated rural area. There is a list of Development Areas and Intermediate Areas (both known as Assisted Areas) available from the DTI. Contact your local Business Link or its equivalent outside of England (see country agencies above) for more information on what help is available. This includes information on what EU grants may be available.

You may see firms advertising as specialists in telling you about grants; however, they could simply end up charging you for information you can get free from your local Business Link or RDA.

6 Small business associations

The following are some the key private initiatives and self-help groups for small businesses in the UK.

British Association of Women Entrepreneurs

The British Association of Women Entrepreneurs (BAWE) is a non-profit professional organization for UK-based women business owners affiliated to the world association of women business owners, Les Femmes Chefs d'Entreprises Mondiales (FCEM).

The President of BAWE and Council members promote British entrepreneurship world-wide, and includes representation at the Council of Europe (Strasbourg); the United Nations (New York); the OECD (Paris); ILO (Vienna) and the EU (Brussels) whenever 'Women in the Economy' is on the agenda. BAWE is a member of The Confederation of British Industry, works closely with the Department of Trade and Industry, the Institute of Directors, the Chambers of Commerce and other organizations to promote the interests of women business owners. Recent trading partners have been found in Eastern Europe, USA, South Africa, Malaysia, Germany, Belgium, Jordan, Egypt, Canada and Australia.

BAWE, founded in 1954, encourages the personal development of member entrepreneurs and provides opportunities for them to expand their business through:

- informal and formal networking;
- the BAWE website for marketing and advertising;
- national and international trade missions and conferences;
- mentoring, training and accessing capital; and
- information exchange through the use of the Internet.

Full membership in BAWE is open to all women who own or control a company whatever its size.

Their own capital and livelihood must be at risk, either as individuals or in partnerships or as majority stakeholders in companies. Members of BAWE are encouraged to take an active interest in supporting their fellow members and the aims of BAWE and FCEM.

Associate membership is open, by invitation, to women who might not fulfil the above criteria, but who have an interest in women business owners and support the aims and objectives of BAWE, or are in the early stages of creating their own business and would benefit from involvement in this professional organization.

There is a £125.00 joining fee, which includes one year's membership of BAWE.

BAWE
Suite E,
123–125 Gloucester Place,
London W1H 3PJ
Tel: +44 (0)20 7935 0085
Fax: +44 (0)20 7486 6016
Website: http://www.bawe-uk.org/

The British Chambers of Commerce

Though not aimed exclusively at small businesses, The British Chambers of Commerce do offer an extensive range of services for business-starters. Their national network of accredited chambers is managed and developed by their business membership and monitored at the national level, to ensure they deliver appropriate products and services to prescribed standards. They are funded by membership subscriptions.

Currently over 135,000 businesses belong to a Chamber in the accredited network, from growth-oriented start-ups to local and regional subsidiaries of multinational companies, in all commercial and industrial sectors, and from all over the UK.

Benefits of membership
British Chambers of Commerce have access to a range of benefits, all geared to help businesses big or small to succeed and grow. With over 2500 staff, covering more than 100 locations, their net-

work provides a ready-made management support team for any business, anywhere in the UK.

Business training, information resources, networking and savings on essential overheads, all of which are tailored to individual business needs, are all on offer from local Chamber. Increasingly, many of their services are also available online.

Some specific membership benefits include the following.

- A total vehicle management service, providing fleet solutions for businesses of all sizes, and added benefits including free AA cover and accident management.
- Unlimited access to free 24-hour, professional advice on commercial and employment law, health and safety and tax related issues.
- Guaranteed discounts on gas and electricity from one of the UK's leading energy suppliers.
- A stakeholder pension solution.
- A complete, comprehensive package in insurance cover which is relevant to the minefield of legal problems a business faces today.
- A professional and confidential counselling service for employees, to help support and improve company performance.
- A range of healthcare packages to suit every business size at discounted rates.

The British Chambers of Commerce are also part of the global network of Chambers of Commerce, and for existing or potential exporters there is simply no better route to the global marketplace.

Their regular surveys, consultations and reports provide grassroots business opinion, and have strong influence on government ministers and officials, MPs, and other decision makers and opinion formers.

For more information about the work of the British Chambers of Commerce, contact your local accredited Chamber, take a look through their website, or write to the address below.

The British Chambers of Commerce
Manning House
65 Petty France,
St James Park,
London SW1H 9EU
Tel. 020 7654 5800
Fax. 020 7654 5819
Email: info@britishchambers.org.uk
Website: http://www.chamberonline.co.uk/

The BCC Directory of Approved and Accredited members is available, price £40.00. Or you can locate your nearest accredited chamber on their website http://www.britishchambers.org.uk/

Business Clubs UK

Business Clubs UK is the federation of business clubs, groups and associations throughout Great Britain and Ireland. They provide a direct link between business and government. It is dedicated to assisting existing clubs to thrive and establishing new business clubs where non exist.

Joining a Business Club is a way to become part of the UK's biggest inter-trading community, with access to the wealth of expertise and information held by almost 500 Business Clubs, groups and associations and thousands of their members.

Products and services for members include legal insurance and bookkeeping systems, as well as free membership of the BCUK \ Virgin Online Business Club business portal.

You can access each of these clubs through the Business Clubs UK website.

Members list
- Andover Women in Business Club
- Bexley Business Club
- Bournemouth Business Breakfast Club
- Business Breakfast Club Southampton
- Business Club Peterborough
- Business Enterprise Network Ltd Sunderland
- Business Forum Cardiff
- Business Network Warrington
- CENTRIM Network for Learning and Innovation
- Caithness Business Club
- Carlisle Business Forum
- Centre for Business Excellence Newcastle

- Chorley & South Ribble Business Club
- City Business Club
- Coordinate Metrology Association
- Coventry Regional Environmental Management Panel
- Darlington & District Business Club
- Durham Business Club
- East Durham Business Club
- Federation of Small Business (FSB)
- Forum of Private Business
- Gloucestershire Business Breakfast Club
- Gwent Business Forum
- Hackney Chamber of Commerce
- Hetton and Houghton Business Club Ltd
- Home Business Alliance (HBA)
- LACS
- Mid Wales Manufacturing Group
- Moseley Traders Association
- ewport Business Club
- ngb2b
- North Devon Business Club
- North London Enterprise Club Limited
- Optimum Business Solutions
- Park Lane College
- Pembrokeshire Business Club
- Pembrokeshire in Business
- Preston Business Club
- Riverside North Business Group
- Romney Marsh & Rye Business Club
- Shrewsbury Business Club
- Scottish Business Alliance
- South East Cheshire Investors In People Club
- Staffordshire Business & Environment Network
- TEC South East Wales Corporate Club
- Techinvest
- The-bag-lady.co.uk
- The Business Club
- The Business Connection
- Watford & West Herts Chamber of Commerce
- WENTA Small Business Club
- West Berkshire Business Club
- West Lancashire Business Club
- West London Business Network
- West Wales Chamber of Commerce
- Women in Business
- Women in Management
- Women into the Network

Further information can be found on: www.bcuk.co.uk, www.onlinebusinessclub.net
Contact Tony Appleton, Managing Director of Business Clubs UK, Tel. 01302 771763.
Contact: Terry Rees (BCUK in Wales) Tel: 01437 760960, Email: Terry@bcuk.co.uk

Country Land and Business Association (CLA)

The CLA was formed in 1907 as the Central Land Association. In 1918 it became The Central Landowners' Association, and in 1949 became The Country Landowners' Association. Now known as the Country Land and Business Association, the CLA has a membership of about 50,000.

The Country Land and Business Association in England and Wales has as its primary objective, to safeguard the interests of private landowners and rural businesses. They have two main functions – to exert political pressure through authoritative briefing and lobbying of policy-makers, and to provide the best advice and services for their members.

They use their political skills, policy expertise, legal and taxation knowledge and public relations techniques to put across the case for businesses in the rural economy and private landownership. They are constantly lobbying ministers and Government departments, Opposition representatives, statutory bodies, regional agencies, local authorities and voluntary organizations.

Their specialists in land use, legal and taxation affairs give unbiased and confidential advice on many subjects, and work to ease the burden of regulation and taxation on all rural businesses. The issues covered include agriculture, forestry, public access, conservation, mineral extraction, land values, capital grants, employment, water resources, water quality, oil exploration and wayleaves.

They help members to exploit the full potential of their business assets, whether related to food and timber production, energy generation, recreation and tourism, or more novel enterprises. They actively promote new uses for old buildings to help regenerate the rural economy, stimulate jobs and help to keep the countryside alive.

There are 16 regional offices, supported by dedicated professional advisers, which provide local information, help and support to members, and also promote the case for the rural economy with regional and local authorities, public agencies and voluntary bodies.

Business membership costs £108. CLA business members become part of a network of contacts, including key customers and suppliers, and can participate alongside the CLA in many shows and events around the country.
Headquarters:

Country Land and Business Association
16 Belgrave Square
London
SW1X 8PQ
Telephone: +44 (0)20 7235 0511
Fax: +44 (0)20 7235 4696
Email: mail@cla.org.uk

Regional offices:

CLA Wales Office and CLA Powys – Brecon/ Radnor
Hoddell Farm
Kinnerton
Presteigne
Powys
LD8 2PD
Tel: 01547 560484
Fax: 01547 560493
Email: info.wales@cla.org.uk
Email: val.taylor@cla.org.uk
Website: http://www.cla.org.uk

CLA North Wales – Anglesey/Caernarfon, Clwyd and Meirionnydd
Dinam
Llangaffo
Anglesey

LL60 6LR
Tel: 01248 440 479
Fax: 01248 440 418
Email: JudithM@clanwales.demon.co.uk

CLA South and West Wales – Dyfed, Glamorgan & Monmouthshire
Llewellyn Humphreys & Co
Napier House
Spilman Street
Carmarthen
Dyfed
SA31 1JY
Tel: 01267 237812/3
Fax: 01267 221519
Email: jonathana@claswwales.demon.co.uk

CLA Eastern – Norfolk & Suffolk
Aspen Grove Farm,
Assington Green
Stansfield,
Sudbury,
Suffolk
CO10 8LY
Tel: 01284 789201
Fax: 01284 789559
Email: info.eastern@cla.org.uk

CLA Bedfordshire, Cambridgeshire, Essex & Hertfordshire/Middlesex
Brick House Farm
Berden
Bishops Stortford
Hertfordshire
CM23 1AZ
Tel: 01279 777391
Fax: 01279 777532
Email: richarde@claeastcos.demon.co.uk

CLA South East – Kent, Surrey and Sussex
Roughfield Farm Office
London Road
Hurst Green
East Sussex
TN19 7QY
Tel: 01580 879667

Fax: 01580 879668
Email: johnb@claseast.demon.co.uk

CLA Berkshire, Buckinghamshire, Hampshire and Oxfordshire

Brookfields House
Westridge
Highclere
Newbury
Berkshire
RG20 9RX
Tel: 01635 255412
Fax: 01635 255413
Email: andrewd@clathames.demon.co.uk

CLA Isle of Wight

Thorley Lodge
Thorley
Yarmouth
Isle of Wight
PO41 0SX
Tel: 01983 760202
Fax: 01983 760203
Email: info.southeast@cla.org.uk

CLA South West – Somerset, Dorset, Wiltshire and Gloucestershire

Country Land & Business Association
South Wing
Tauntfield
South Road
Taunton
Somerset
TA1 3ND
Tel: 01823 323393
Fax: 01823 323818
Email: alistairs@clawessex.demon.co.uk

CLA South West – Devon & Cornwall

Halthaies
Bradninch
Exeter
Devon
EX5 4LQ
Tel: 01392 202070
Fax: 01392 882490

Email: info.southwest@cla.org.uk

CLA West Midlands – Warwickshire, Shropshire, Staffordshire, Herefordshire and Worcestershire

Knightley
Woodseaves
Staffordshire
ST20 OJW
Tel: 01785 284722
Fax: 01785 284733
Email: info.westmidlands@cla.org.uk

CLA North West – Cumbria, Lancashire and Cheshire

Dalton Hall Stable Yard
Burton
Carnforth
Lancashire
LA6 1NJ
Tel: 01524 782209
Fax: 01524 782248
Email: info.north@cla.org.uk

CLA East Midlands – Derbyshire, Lincolnshire, Northamptonshire, Leicestershire/Rutland and Nottinghamshire

The Hayloft
Sutton Lodge
Sutton Bassett
Market Harborough
Leics LE16 8HL
Tel: 01858 468949
Fax:01858 432250
Email: info.eastmidlands@cla.org.uk

CLA Yorkshire

Old Toll Booth
Market Place
Easingwold
YORK
YO61 3AB
Tel: 01347 823803
Fax: 01347 823846
Email: info.yorkshire@cla.org.uk

Experience Counts Ltd

Experience Counts promotes the breadth of experience and knowledge of individuals who, at a relatively early age, have achieved business success in their careers at senior management level, and have decided to retire from full-time work. Now financially independent, they are actively interested in continuing to use their expertise, particularly with entrepreneurs and other SMEs.

They target a wide range of individuals with this background, including those with international experience such as former UK expatriates and other nationals now resident in the UK or abroad. They maintain a portfolio of members whose credentials have been reviewed and verified by them, and will introduce these individuals to any business, or other public or private organization, only if they can demonstrate that they have the qualities and experience required.

Experience Counts Ltd
8 Cavendish Crescent
Bath BA1 2UG
United Kingdom
Tel: +44 (0)1225 471567
Fax: +44 (0)1225 471678
Email: info@experience-counts.com
Website: www.experience-counts.com

The Federation of Small Businesses (FSB)

The Federation is a national organization with 165,000 members, protecting small firms' interests and fighting for their rights. The Federation maintains Press and Parliamentary Offices at Westminster, in Glasgow, Cardiff and Belfast; an Administration Office at Blackpool, and Regional Offices elsewhere in the U.K. The professional staffs are complemented by 31 regional committees and over 200 branch committees, manned by small businessmen and women who donate some of their spare time to the Federation.

For people thinking of starting their own business they offer legal, environmental, fire and premises tips, as well as many other issues which the small business person may have to address as they grow. Plus information on other agencies that might be of use or assistance when starting up.

Membership costs range from £100 per annum, including a one-off registration fee of £30 for a person working on their own, up to £650 for a firm employing more than 101 people. (Prices exclude VAT.)

The Federation has the resources to take major test cases of importance to small business through the expensive legal process leading to the House of Lords and the European Courts if necessary. They have been particularly effective in dealing with taxation and employment matters.

Amongst the benefits on offer (provided by a partner organization, Abbey Legal Protection Ltd (ALP) is an underwriting service specializing in legal and professional fees insurance. In addition, ALP's in-house solicitors, barristers and tax experts provide legal and taxation advice lines, including litigation and representation services.

The range of services available to FSB members from ALP is set out below.

Advice
• Legal & tax advice lines

Insurance
• Legal & accountancy costs re tax
• Legal & accountancy costs re VAT
• Employment disputes
• Health & safety
• Criminal prosecutions statutory licences
• Data protection
• Property protection
• PAYE disputes
• Jury service information
• Employment law
• Precedent documents
• Specimen letters
• Legal news

Federation contact points are as follows:

Head office
Federation of Small Businesses
Sir Frank Whittle Way
Blackpool Business Park
Blackpool
Lancashire
FY4 2FE
Tel: 01253 336000
Fax: 01253 348046
Website: www.fsb.org.uk

FSB UK Lobbying Office
This deals with all UK press and Parliamentary affairs/enquiries. Their address is:

Federation of Small Businesses
2 Catherine Place
Westminster
London SW1E 6HF
Tel: 020 7592 8100
Fax: 020 7233 7899

FSB Scottish Lobbying Office
This deals with all Scottish press and Parliamentary affairs/enquiries. Their address is:

Federation of Small Businesses
6 Rutland Court Lane
Edinburgh
EH3 8ES
Tel: 0131 228 3772
Fax: 0131 228 3804

FSB Welsh Lobbying Office
This deals with all Welsh press and Parliamentary affairs/enquiries. Their address is:

Federation of Small Businesses
6 Heathwood Road
Birchgrove
Cardiff CF4 4JP
Tel: 029 2052 1230
Fax: 029 2052 1231

FSB Northern Ireland Lobbying Office
This deals with all Northern Ireland press and Parliamentary affairs/enquiries. Their address is:

Federation of Small Businesses
3 Farrier Court
Glengormley
Newtownabbey
Co Antrim BT36 7XB
Tel: 028 9084 4079
Fax: 028 9034 2441

Birmingham and West Midlands region
Federation of Small Businesses
Tintern House
Abbey Road
Malvern
Worcestershire WR14 3HG
Tel: 01684 566787
Fax: 01684 566907
Email: wmpu.policy@fsb.org.uk

Federation of Small Businesses
347a Garstang Rd
Fulwood
Preston
Lancashire PR2 9UP
Tel: 01772 712033
Fax: 01772 788033
Email: lancscumbreg@fsbdial.co.uk

Federation of Small Businesses
65 High Street
Lincoln LN5 8AD
Tel: 01522 523380
Fax: 01522 511423
Email: region102@fsbdial.co.uk

Federation of Small Businesses
Tower House
Fishergate
York
North Yorkshire YO10 4UA
Tel: 0I904 629777
Fax: 01904 629666
Email: admin.northyorks@fsb.org.uk

North East region
Federation of Small Businesses
205 Ouseburn Buildings
Albion Row
East Quayside
Newcastle upon Tyne NE6 1LL
Tel: 0191 276 6770
Fax: 0191 276 6770
Email: northeasthq@fsbdial.co.uk

East Sussex
Federation of Small Businesses
3 High St
Polegate
East Sussex BN26 5HA
Tel: 01323 482018
Fax: 01323 483352
Email: eastsussex@fsb.org.uk

Forum of Private Business Ltd

The mission of the FPB is, through a growing membership, to influence laws and policies that affect private businesses and support members to grow profitably. The Forum researches and distributes a referendum a number of times each year and keeps both members and government aware of how small firms feel about key topical issues. Membership fees are based on a sliding scale dependent on the number of referendums you take part in.

Membership of the Forum brings the following benefits.

- A direct influence on laws and policies affecting your business, e.g. employment law, uniform business rates, taxation, red tape, bank services, late payment.
- Information on tap when you need it with unlimited FREE access to the Member Information Service, on any issue affecting your business.
- User-friendly management tools to help your business stay within the law – as you complete, you comply. They include: *FPB Employment Manual* (produced with TUC), *FPB Health &*

Safety Audit (produced with TUC), *FPB Bank Finance Review* (produced with Institute of Chartered Accountants), *FPB Credit Control Audit.*
- Free access to VUSME (the Virtual University for Small and Medium Sized Enterprises).
- Grant search.

The Forum of Private Business Ltd
Ruskin Chambers
Drury Lane
Knutsford
Cheshire, WA16 6HA
Tel: +44 (0)1565 634467
Fax: +44 (0)1565 650059
Email: fpbltd@fpb.co.uk
Website: www.fpb.co.uk

The Forum of Private Business in Scotland
Unit 4 Alpha Centre
Stirling University Innovation Park
Stirling FK9 4NF
Tel/fax: +44 (0)1786 472450
Email: g@fdowds.freeserve.co.uk
Website: www.fpb.co.uk

Institute of Directors

The IoD has decades of experience in helping directors improve themselves, and their businesses. As well as providing training and coaching (including up to 30% discounts for IoD members on training courses) they offer a programme of national and local events that are ideal for networking.

The IoD hosts some of the most prestigious events in the UK business calendar. From the Annual Convention at the Royal Albert Hall, to the more informal Sporting Lunches, there will be an event to meet your needs.

Membership

To become a member you must be over 21, and be a 'director', of an 'entity' which is a solvent, going concern of 'substance' as broadly defined below, and have been:

- A director for a minimum of 3 years, having been in business for a minimum of 7 years, or
- A director for a minimum of 1 year, having been in business for a minimum of 5 years and have attended the IoD course 'The Role of a Company Director'.

For the purposes of IoD membership, the following definitions apply:

A 'director' must be a member of the body that is responsible for and accountable for the strategic business direction and corporate governance of the 'entity', and makes the decisions that determine its prosperity and integrity.

Membership fees

Election fees are payable once only, on application, together with the first year's membership fee.

- Applicants resident in the European Union (including UK) £195
- Applicants resident outside the European Union £147
- Applicants under 30 years old £95

Group discounts are available for applicants from the same company applying at the same time.

Annual fee

Payable annually together with first year Election fee (see above). Members and Associates resident in the European Union (including UK):

- 1 year £204
- 2 years £408
- 3 years £612
- 4 years £816
- 5 years £1,020
- Life £4,080

Members and Associates resident outside the European Union:

- 1 year £154
- 3 years £462
- 5 years £770
- Life £3,080

To find out more about any aspect of membership, please Email: join-iod@iod.com or telephone 020 7766 8888.

Director Training Courses: maximizing your potential

All courses are designed by directors for directors and are facilitated by subject experts who are business leaders themselves. Some courses are offered for either the SME or the complex organization, reflecting the differing needs.

In addition to individual courses, two programmes are run for directors. The Essential Director's Programme covers the core issues faced by all directors. The Company Direction Programme builds on this to cover functional areas for which directors may not have had previous responsibility.

- Company Direction Programme
- Essential Director's Programme
- Directors' Skills
- Business Presentations and Public Speaking
- Chairing Successful Meetings
- Generating Ideas & Accelerating Solutions
- Improving Employee Motivation
- Keys To Personal Effectiveness
- Negotiating Skills and Techniques
- Transformational Leadership
- Effective Board
- Board Decision Making
- Handling Boardroom Politics
- Role of Company Directors & the Board in Complex Organizations
- Role of Company Directors & the Board in SMEs
- Role of Company Director in SME Birmingham
- Role of Company Director in SME Edinburgh
- The Role of Company Chairman
- The Role of Company Secretary

- The Role of Finance Director
- The Role of Managing Director Edinburgh
- The Role of Managing Director in Complex
- The Role of Managing Director in SME
- The Role of Non-Executive Director
- Finance
- A Director's Introduction to the City
- Buying and Selling Companies
- Finance for Non-Financial Director Birmingham
- Finance for Non-Financial Director Edinburgh
- Finance for Non-Financial Directors
- Strategy & Leadership
- Building Corporate Reputation
- Developing Strategic Thinking
- Developing Strategic Thinking Edinburgh
- Effective Marketing Strategies Complex Organizations
- Effective Marketing Strategies Edinburgh
- Effective Marketing Strategies in SMEs
- Effective Marketing Strategy Birmingham
- Getting The Best From Your Team
- Improving Business Performance
- Improving Business Performance Edinburgh
- Leading Major Change
- Leading and Directing Change
- Organizing For Tomorrow
- Organizing for Tomorrow Edinburgh
- People Mean Business
- People Mean Business Edinburgh
- Strategic Business Direction Birmingham
- Strategic Business Direction Edinburgh
- Strategic Business Direction in Complex Organizations
- Strategic Business Direction in SMEs.

Your local IoD

IoD London

116 Pall Mall

London SW1Y 5ED

Tel: 020 7839 1233

116 Pall Mall is located in the heart of London's West End. Its nearest underground stations are Piccadilly Circus, Green Park and Charing Cross. All are only a short walk away. There is also a railway station at Charing Cross and there are NCP car parks nearby.

IoD Edinburgh

The Royal Scots Club

30 Abercromby Place

Edinburgh BH3 6QE

Tel: 0131 557 5488

The Club is about 10 minutes' walk from Prince's Street and Waverley mainline station. Ample parking is available in the city.

IoD Nottingham

Trent Bridge Cricket Ground

Nottingham NG2 6AQ

Tel: 0115 982 3011

Email: iodnotts@iod.com

The ground is a few minutes' drive from the city centre and the mainline train station. Ample parking is available at the ground and is free to members (except on match days).

IoD Manchester

Lancashire County Cricket Club

Manchester M16 0PX

Tel: 0161 282 4152

Manchester city centre and its mainline train links are within easy reach from Lancashire County Cricket Club at Old Trafford, which is just yards from the Metrolink station. There is ample parking at the ground.

IoD Belfast

Ulster Reform Club

4 Royal Avenue

Belfast BT1 1DA

Tel: 028 9023 2880

Fax: 028 9023 2881

IoD Bristol

Castlemead Building

Bristol BS1 3AG

To book a private meeting room, call 0117 917 5800, Fax: 0117 917 5808

To contact the IoD South West Regional Office at IoD Bristol, call 0117 917 5801

This address is just a short taxi ride or a 10–15 minute walk from Templemead mainline station.

IoD Birmingham
1 Victoria Square
Birmingham B1 1BD
Tel: 0845 070 9992

The Small Business Bureau

Since its formation in 1976 the Small Business Bureau has:

- Established a close working relationship with government Ministers and Westminster, and European Members of Parliament.
- Organized annually the largest conference of its kind for small businesses within Europe.
- Established an effective nationwide policy-making role through its Policy Unit.
- Established an influential, informative newspaper *Small Business News*, which has a nationwide circulation.
- In 1986 formed 'Women into Business'.
- In 1990 inaugurated the Annual National 'Women into Business' Awards ceremony in Westminster.
- Established links within Europe to contribute to policymaking in the European Parliament and Commission.
- Pressed continually – and successfully – for the easing of legislative, financial and bureaucratic burdens on small business.
- Published regular information bulletins and discussion documents.
- Cooperated effectively with allied groups within the UK and overseas.
- Generated increasing national awareness of the needs and the contribution of small businesses to the economy and employment.
- Campaigned successfully for the Loan Guarantee Scheme, the Enterprise Investment Scheme and Venture Capital Trusts. In addition the SBB took the lead in the elimination of the impact of inheritance tax on unquoted companies.

- In 1997 initiated the African Caribbean Westminster Initiative.
- In 1998 inaugurated a National 'Women into Business' conference.

Membership usually costs £115, but they have been known to have special offers – for example, from time to time they have had a special price of £58.75 per annum including VAT for people joining online.

Subscriber benefits include:

- a copy of the quarterly newspaper 'Small Business News'
- a discount to all conferences and SBB functions
- access to National and European information on a wide range of issues concerning small businesses
- the opportunity to publicize their own particular initiatives and publish articles in *Small Business News*
- direct access to a business network
- the opportunity of increasing their business profile through the Bureau's many contacts
- complimentary copies of documents produces by the Small Business Bureau Policy Unit.

The Small Business Bureau Limited
Curzon House
Church Road
Windlesham
Surrey GU20 6BH
Tel: 01276 452010/452020
Fax: 01276 451602
Website: www.smallbusinessbureau.org.uk/

The Stoy Centre for Family Business

Stoy Centre for Family Business
8 Baker Street, London W1M 1DA
Tel: 0207 486 5888
Fax: 0207 487 3686).
Email grow-how@bdo.co.uk.
The Centre for Family Business is an organization dedicated to protecting and enhancing the

interests of its members. The Centre has evolved out of the interest and expertise of Stoy Hayward. Because family businesses can face more complex issues than other companies, the Centre's activities are directed to these special needs, including:

* succession planning
* personal and corporate taxation
* training for the next generation
* retirement planning and finance
* developing a family constitution
* communication.

Other services to members include:

* Invitations to VIP lunches with leading politicians or opinion-formers
* A quarterly newsletter targeted at family businesses giving you information on all the latest developments
* Access to BDO's GrowHow service to help firms develop new ideas to grow their firms.

The Telework Association

The Telework Association, also known as the TCA, is Europe's largest organization dedicated to the promotion of teleworking. Over 2,000 people and organizations have joined since they started in 1993. The TCA believes that teleworking can benefit people by increasing the quality of life and improving access to work.

How can they help you?

* **Individual teleworkers:** the TCA provides advice on how to approach teleworking, information on technology, examples of how other people progress – and uniquely – information about work opportunities. In the bi-monthly magazine *Teleworker*, and in a weekly electronic bulletin the TCA sends out updates and information about full-time and temporary telework opportunities.
* **Corporate teleworking schemes:** the TCA believes that in order for teleworking to become mainstream, businesses have to realize

the advantages and pursue workable schemes for good business reasons. The TCA advises businesses, as well as disseminating information through its publications.

* **Telecottage managers:** a source of reliable information on local resource centres/telecottages, the TCA has pioneered this approach and provides up-to-date information on the subject.

Benefits

The TCA is a company limited by guarantee. This structure is a not-for-profit company and limits the liability of members. Membership is open to individuals and companies. Individual members have full voting rights. A board of nine elected by the membership ensure that a strategy and the operation of the TCA reflect the needs of the teleworking community.

Handbook

The *Teleworking Handbook* is the most comprehensive guide on teleworking yet produced. The 352-page book has been developed with assistance from Lloyds Bank, BT, Hewlett-Packard, insurers Tolson Messenger and the EU. Sales of the handbook already total 10,000.

Magazine

Teleworker is the TCA's full colour 28-page magazine which is published on a bi-monthly basis. Sections cover headlines, telecottages, organizations, home work, and technology. A reference section includes a listing of telecottages in the UK and Ireland, work opportunities and discounted offers on products and services.

Membership costs between £35 and £150 dependent on status (self-employed or company).

The Telework Association
WREN
Kenilworth
Warwickshire CV8 2BR
Tel: 024 7669 6986
Fax: 024 7669 6538
Email:teleworker@tca.org.uk

Trade associations

Trade associations can be a valuable source of information and advice for anyone starting a business in a sector that is comparatively new to them, or where there are major changes taking place and where timely information is of the essence. Trade associations keep on top of the latest legislation that is likely to effect their sector and monitor trends and events of general importance.

Since 1996 Trade Associations in the UK have been encouraged to follow these Best Practice guidelines.

- Represents the whole of a commercial or industrial sector and seeks to cover all products, services and processes.
- Members represent a substantial proportion of sector (both in terms of output and numbers).
- Governing council includes representatives from the largest companies in the sector and a good cross-section of other members. Meets sufficiently regularly to direct action/strategy.
- Broadly-based membership with both large and small businesses and the key players.
- Enjoys active participation of a representative cross-section of its members. Is responsive to their views.
- Is properly resourced. Successful both in generating income from members' subscriptions and from sales of services to members, and to others.
- Is professional in its approach. Attracts and retains high calibre staff. Pulls in services of high level people from member companies for representation and policy development purposes when necessary.
- Has a business plan (annual/3 year) that sets out its mission, a clear strategy and priority areas. Developed in consultation with members. Monitors progress rigorously against it.
- Makes full use of information technology to minimize costs and improve quality of its services to members.

- Promotes cooperation within the sector, and between the sector, its customers and suppliers, to enhance international competitiveness.
- Forms appropriate links with other representative bodies, to ensure that services are supplied to its members with the minimum of duplication, and in the most effective manner.
- Adopts best management practices in quality assurance, financial management and control, and training and development of staff.
- Prepared to work with non-members and cooperates with other associations in allied sectors on matters of joint concern.

Benefits of membership of a trade association include:

- **Professional development:** Regular programmes, generally on a monthly basis, feature knowledgeable speakers addressing timely and critical topics of international trade. Additionally, special programmes provide in-depth educational knowledge and training in important aspects of international trade, such as Basics of Export; How to Do Business in a Foreign Country.
- **Networking opportunities:** Regular and special programmes afford opportunities for members to meet one another, exchange experiences, and make important contacts. Trade association membership represents men and women with a wide and deep knowledge of trade who usually enjoy exchanging ideas and experiences.
- Membership directories, listing members alphabetically and by area of expertise/interest, provide further opportunities for networking. Annual trade expos afford opportunities for member companies to showcase their products and/or services, and for attendees to broaden their knowledge of available goods and services.
- **Communication:** Newsletters keep the membership informed of association activities, introduce new international resources, and provide timely information on a wide range of

topics of local, regional, national, and international interest.

- **Member premiums:** Members of a trade association are eligible for the member benefits offered by their association, as well as opportunities provided by member associations for their members to obtain reduced rates on a wide variety of international trade services and publications.
- **Industry voice:** As part of a group of knowledgeable international trade professionals, members can exert influence on regulations affecting their industry.

There are two main ways in which you can find out more about which is the most appropriate trade association for you to consider joining.

From your desk via http://www.brainstorm.co.uk/TANC/Directory/Welcome.html where you can search the Directory of Trade Associations alphabetically, or list all the trade associations and browse through to see who suits your purposes best. Alternatively you can visit another site, http://www.martex.co.uk/trade-associations/index.htm, run by the UK Trade Associations Forum, which provides an online directory. Everyone listed from the Aberdeen Fish Curers & Merchants Association to the Yacht Brokers, Designers & Surveyors' Association.

The second route is to visit your local reference library and look at a hard copy of one of these directories of Trade Associations.

Women Into Business

Women Into Business aims:

- To give successful businesswomen a higher national profile and greater visibility so as to publicize and acknowledge their achievements and contributions to the economy.
- To set up a counselling service run by businesswomen for businesswomen whereby senior successful entrepreneurs who are aware and sympathetic to the unique problems facing businesswomen will counsel and assist smaller

businesswomen as well as potential entrepreneurs.
- To ensure that Government Policies encourage women to set up in business. Also that they recognize the significant contribution that they make to the Small Business sector.

Women Into Business
The Small Business Bureau Limited
Curzon House
Church Road
Windlesham
Surrey GU20 6BH
Tel: 01276 452010/452020
Fax: 01276 451602
Website: www.smallbusinessbureau.org.uk/

7   Small business websites

There are now literally dozens of websites offering help and advice to new and small businesses. Some are simply offshoots of small business magazines, but others offer a wider range of services. This is a cross-section of such sites, but a trawl using a search engine will reveal many more, though the extra ' volume' may not add much to the sum of the help available.

www.bankrate.com/brm/biz_home.asp
American site linked to the online magazine, Bankrate.com
Full of useful advice and tips for business starters. The advice is helpful
in any country and the range is wide if somewhat eccentric. How A Janitorial Business Can Clean Up, vies with Cleaning Up After A Computer Crash for your attention.

www.better-business.co.uk:
Whether you are a self-employed professional, managing a small business or planning to start one, this site contains useful facts, tips, contacts and moneymaking ideas. It provides the latest news for small businesses, a list of contacts and Internet links and free factsheets. The Bargain

Centre offers discounts on software and the Business Library reviews the latest business books.

www.bizhot.co.uk/

Business Hotline Publications was set up in 1991 to produce high quality, unbiased information for small and medium-sized businesses. Two of their main publications, *Directors' Briefing* and *Start-up Briefing*, can be accessed free of charge, once you have registered on their site. They also offer a number of other publications, including *ExpertInsert*, *BizBites*, and *Start-up Guide*.

They aim to cover the full range of business issues, from employment contracts, tax and designing your website to renting an office, running a board meeting and financing your business.

Help with each of the following topics is available on this website:

1   Writing a business plan
2   Forming a business
3   Researching your market
4   Marketing
5   Pricing
6   Effective PR
7   Direct mail
8   Advertising
9   Writing an advertisement
10   Selling to new customers
11   Customer care
12   Purchasing
13   Negotiation
14   Choosing and using an accountant
15   Financing your business
16   Grants
17   Simple book-keeping
18   Budgeting
19   Credit control
20   Tax and NI
21   VAT
22   Searching for premises
23   Property licences
24   Setting up an office
25   Introduction to computers
26   Insurance
27   Recruiting and interviewing
28   Business law and using a solicitor
29   Employment law
30   Buying a franchise.

www.businesseurope.com/

Business Europe aim to provide information to aid better-informed decision-making and direct action. The site is provided in English, French and German and much of the information is completely free. All you have to do is register. Their team of journalists focuses purely on events relevant to SMEs and daily report the news that matters. They aim to add value through their own research, insight and business experience. They compile an extensive range of guides for the management of new or unfamiliar events, legal and tax issues, finance and operational elements. Business Europe can help you identify and establish the best hiring process for your business, advise on advertising, employment terms, contract staff and job sharing. Their discussion forums look at how to improve employee conditions and efficiency with teleworking, flexi-time and the imminent benefits of third-generation telecommunications

Business Europe has strategic partnerships with blue chip organizations, Small Business Service franchises, trade bodies, chambers of commerce, SME organizations and business institutions to provide expertise, special services and discounts to people using the service.

The guides cover the following topics and also provide links to more detailed advice and assistance.

- Accounting
- File a complaint against an accountant
- Find an accountant
- Evaluate accountancy software packages
- Calculate National Insurance Contributions
- Examine audit exemptions for SMEs
- Capital finance
- Obtain a soft loan
- Assess your grant eligibility
- Understand grants
- Buy a business with personal equity or seller-finance

- Find grants to finance your business
- Banking
- Set up a business bank account
- Understand BACS
- Keep your bank charges under control
- Assess your euro banking needs
- Anticipate your bank charges
- Business planning
- Source products from overseas
- Be aware of business etiquette
- Find an existing business to buy
- Prepare your business for sale
- Cash flow
- Receive payments for exports
- Grow your business with barter
- File for bankruptcy
- Deal with insolvency
- Manage your petty cash
- Euro
- Assess your euro banking needs
- Receive payments in euros
- Arrange euro payment services
- Understand the implications of the European Monetary Union
- Set up a euro account
- Insurance
- Make an insurance claim
- Evaluate personal accident and sickness insurance
- Choose an insurance policy
- Become aware of employer's liability
- Evaluate life insurance
- Tax
- Understand the Climate Change Levy
- Understand corporation tax
- Understand IR35
- Register for VAT
- Make a VAT return.

www.businesszone.co.uk/

Sponsored by BT, BusinessZONE is a virtual community for SME and SOHO professionals. It draws together a compendium of information and tools to help business people conduct their business online and save them time and money.

They have a range of Expert Business Guides and up to the minute business news.

www.clearlybusiness.com/about.htm

Voted 'Best Business Portal' in the Internet Business Awards 2001, Clearlybusiness is a leading small business website in the UK. Launched in June 2000, Clearlybusiness has already helped over 105,000 businesses start up and grow offering a wealth of practical information, tools and services to help you build a better business.

Backed by Barclays and Freeserve, Clearlybusiness is a joint venture, but at the same time remains a separate business entity.

If you have a burning question about running your business their experts are online to help, or you can cast your vote on the big issues facing business every week.

www.ecommercetimes.com/small_business/index.shtml

An American site concentrating on e-business issues. It has Small Business Advisor site that addresses the issues that concern small business owners, clearly and in plain language.

www.ehow.com/home/home.jsp

An American version of Business Europe. The site covers the universe and operates by inviting you to ask the question, How to... ...

In the small business section there are three main areas: starting up, operating a business and taking a business online. The questions answered range from the precise How to Start a Kennels, to general questions such as how to take board minutes.

www.enterprisenetwork.co.uk

The *Sunday Times* Enterprise Network is a membership organization delivering tailored knowledge to entrepreneurs seeking to grow their businesses. This is achieved through a website, the business section in the *Sunday Times*, live events, *Enterprise Focus* magazine, The Help Desk and other media.

- Many publications and research reports are available free to members in hard copy.
- An online forum enables members to network directly with each other.
- A quarterly magazine focuses in-depth on specific business issues.
- A linked listing of members' websites can be browsed to find out about and do business with members.
- A members' networking list provides contact details of members who have opted in.
- An email with practical tips and business tools is sent to members monthly.
- A help desk is at hand to answer your enquiries.
- Special offers worth around £500 a year are available to every member.
- Workshops, seminars and other live events address core small business issues.

Whilst some of these benefits are available to all users of this website, many are available only to members.

For complete access to Enterprise Network's full range of information and services both on and off the website, a fee of £50 + VAT per annum is required

www.everywoman.co.uk/

Everywoman business channels have been put together to provide women with the tools and resources they need for growing or starting a business, looking for work solutions, seeking career advice or developing new business ideas. Key areas such as legal, finance, planning and technology have all been designed to keep members up-to-date when searching for facts, advice and opinions.

- **Bulletin boards:** For networking and additional resources the bulletin Boards are an beasy way to network with other members of the everywoman community. The latest industry events posted on the networking board – feel free to add your own. If your business could benefit from skills you don't possess you could barter your services with other skilled women on the Barter Board.
- **Infobank:** Their Infobank has a range of associations and organizations able to offer advice and support.
- **Ask the experts:** They have a team of experts available to answer your questions. They cover an array of subjects in many areas of business, including: employment law, copyright and intellectual property right issues, public relations, tax, career and life coaching.
- **Sponsors:** All sponsors are experts in their field, with extensive knowledge and a wealth of business experience. They are also keen supporters of women in business and include IBM, Natwest and Netaccount.
- **Library search:** You can check out their library, which contains articles on many topics including accounting, tax, health & safety, VAT, business planning, advertising and marketing. Their search engine has been designed to help you find what you are looking for and the following is an example of the areas you can get current information on:
  - Financial information – for best value loans or credit cards
  - Legal services – to find a law consultant, solicitor or book-keeper in your area
  - Tax advice – for great value, tax advice
  - Business news – for the latest news stories
  - Date for your diary – details on forthcoming trade exhibitions
  - Networking events.

Membership is free.

europe.businessweek.com/smallbiz/

The section of *BusinessWeek* online devoted to small firms. Access to hundreds of articles, tips and resources of interest to those in or about to start-up. A useful resource area for finding out about finance and links to a further 100 business information sources.

www.is4profit.com

Launched in May 2000 as an independent, one-stop, business information and advisory service for the SME sector, the site's design encompasses expert guidance on business planning, legal and personnel management issues, group purchasing facilities, cash flow protection and first steps in e-commerce. Other facilities include a B2B member directory to help source suppliers and customers.

www.smallbusinessadvice.org.uk

Offers a free and independent source of information and advice for:

- entrepreneurs
- owner-managers
- self-employed

who are starting or running a business with fewer than 10 staff and based in England.

It is run by the National Federation of Enterprise Agencies (NFEA), which is a network of independent, but not for profit, Local Enterprise Agencies committed to responding to the needs of small and growing businesses by providing an appropriate range of quality services; particularly, but not exclusively, targeting pre-start, start-up and micro businesses and assisting in building their ability to survive, to sustain themselves and to grow.

www.office.com/

Office.com aims to be the first stop on the web for small businesses looking for resources to help them be more productive and competitive in today's environment. This site is a gateway for finding practical information on how to run or start a business, best-of-breed business products and services, and links to resources on how to transform their companies into thriving e-businesses. Site users can search for relevant news that affects their industry and companies and can access more than 500 databases from the world's leading electronic information services such as Dun & Bradstreet, Lexis-Nexis and more.

www.sba.gov/starting/

The US Small Business Administration main web-site, and although much of the information is US-orientated, an awful lot of it will prove useful anywhere. The sections entitled Start-up Kit, Do your Research, Business Plans and Shareware, are worth a look-over by anyone serious about starting up.

The Business Plan section has the template for a complete business plan and the Shareware section has several hundred quite respectable software programmes covering everything from basic accounting to marketing databases.

www.success4business.com

success4business.com is a free online resource from Lloyds TSB that helps you build and manage a successful business. By registering, you get access to personalized information about the things that matter to your business, up-to-the-minute news and solutions to the key issues that affect businesses like yours. Lloyds TSB business banking customers also get the opportunity to promote their business in the directory, access to exclusive content and the opportunity to join the success4business.com community.

www.virginbiz.net/

Virginbiz.net was launched in October 1999 to cater for the vast number of UK small businesses keen to grow using the web. Over the last year they have developed a range of information and services to help companies make the most of the opportunities offered by e-commerce, from providing the nuts and bolts of building a website, to aiding with online marketing strategies.

Virginbiz.net has brought together online tools and services, essential to anyone serious about making an impact on the Internet. This is all backed up with in-depth information offering guidance and support to users throughout their business lifecycle. Access is free and open to everyone, 24 hours a day.

Virginbiz.net employs 25 people, based at their London headquarters in Piccadilly. They are partnered with Freecom.net, who deal with all Virginbiz.net's Customer Support and Technical Support.

www.womanowned.com/

Started by a woman entrepreneur in 1997, the site has lots of information for would-be business starters. You can start by taking an online quiz to see if you have what it takes, and go on to use a checklist and see if your business idea looks like a winner or a lemon.

www.startups.co.uk

A site with case studies, start-up guides, directories, templates and discussion forums for would-be and recent business starters.

www.which.net

Which? online is an independent service that provides access to product reports and consumer information from a wide range of *Which?* publications, as well as being an Internet access provider. The website has a forum where consumer experts will answer your queries, and exclusive features containing information on matters such using the Small Claims Court. By becoming a member, you will also qualify for buying products at competitive prices.

Section 3

BUSINESS OPPORTUNITIES

Whilst every business begins with an idea, it does not necessarily have to be your own idea. It has to be a viable idea, which means there have to be customers out in the market who want to buy from you, and there have to be enough of them to make you the kind of living you want. It may be an idea you have nursed and investigated for years, or it may be someone else's great idea that is just too big for them to exploit on their own. A franchised business is one example of a business idea that has room for more than one would-be business starter to get involved with. Franchises can be run at many levels, ranging from simply taking up a local franchise, through to running a small chain of two to five such franchises covering neighbouring areas. It can even be extended to taking a master franchise to run a country network, or you could consider using franchising as a way to grow and extend your own great business concept.

There are four main ways to identify a business opportunity.

- Start up yourself with your own idea or invention, or use someone else's idea.
- Buy a business either in whole or in part in one of a number of ways.
- Join a co-operative.
- Take up a franchise opportunity.

This section reviews these ways of identifying business opportunities. You will still need to go through the market research processes described in Section 5 to see if there is a market and, if so, how best to reach it. Going through the process of generating business opportunities will hopefully result in several ideas that you think are worth exploring. The final part of this section, 'Is the business right for you?', will help you choose which opportunity to develop as a business proposal.

Starting up by yourself

You may want to develop your own unique ideas for a product or service and, if so, setting up your own business from 'the drawing board' may be the only option. Many people start businesses because they want to do things 'the right way', after working for an employer who appeared to make a mess of things. This usually means they want to do things 'their own way'. It is much easier to do things 'your own way' in a new business, rather than, say, buying someone else's business that already has its routines and working practices established.

Often people who start up their own businesses do not have enough money to buy into an existing operation, so the 'Do It Yourself' approach is the only alternative.

Advantages of starting up your own business include the following.

- It may be possible to start the business in your spare time. This will allow you to gain more confidence in the future success of your proposed venture before either giving up your job or pumping your life savings into the venture.
- If you have limited money to invest in your new venture, you may not need to spend it all at the start of the project. This also means that

if things do start to go wrong, it will be easier to restrict the losses.

- Starting a business is not just about money. Setting up and running a successful business has the potential to give you a feeling of personal achievement which may not be there to quite the same extent if you buy someone else's business, for example.

Disadvantages of setting up your own business include these.

- Your business will take time to grow. It may not be able to support your current personal financial obligations for many months or years.
- There is a lot of one-off administration involved in setting up a new business such registering for VAT and PAYE, getting business stationery, setting up phone, fax and Internet connections at your trading premises, and registering your business name, in addition to actually trading. These tasks can be very time-consuming and frustrating in the short term, and very costly in the long run if you get them wrong. Unfortunately, these tasks are often not easily delegated and can be expensive if you get other people to do them. If you buy a business or take up a franchise, these basic administrative tasks should have already been dealt with (these areas are covered in Section 7).
- Statistically, the risk of failure is higher for 'start-up' businesses than for businesses with a trading record of over five years (see Section 1 for the data on this).
- As a result of this perceived riskiness, it is generally more difficult to borrow money to fund a start-up than to borrow to invest in an established profitable business.

A gap in the market

The classic way to identify a great opportunity is to see something that people would want to buy if only they knew about it. The case studies below show how other businesses founders have identified such gaps and successfully launched their own businesses.

Case studies: spotting a gap in the market

Easy Tele-language is a company which specializes in teaching modern European languages over the phone. It is run by 29-year-old Karine Hetherington, who got the idea for it while she was teaching English in Paris. 'I noticed that a lot of the language schools gave lessons over the telephone. It seemed like such a simple but effective idea. Clients could learn on a one-to-one basis, at a time convenient to them, and also without having to travel to lessons. People are also a lot less self-conscious when there's a telephone between themselves and the teacher.'

When she came back to Britain, she was amazed to find the same technique wasn't used here. Three years later, her business was booming. The company employs more than 20 language teachers and is looking to increase that number. 'The demand has been phenomenal, far greater than I ever anticipated,' she says. 'It's been extremely hard work and pretty nerve-racking at times, but definitely worth it.'

David Sinclair, 24, runs a fast food bagel company. David's idea was sparked during an overseas trip: 'When I was backpacking my way round America on Greyhound buses,' he says, 'at one station in Vermont I saw a huge queue at what turned out to be a bagel stand. I'd hardly ever heard of bagels, even though they were sold all over the States.' When he returned home he discovered that bagels were only sold as fast food in a handful of outlets: 'They were very much a Jewish secret.' He piloted the idea by taking a small stall on Liverpool Station for three months and took advice from the Graduate Enterprise Programme run by the Cranfield School of Management. Within two years he had opened eight bagel shops.

A new approach to an old idea

Sometimes with little more than a slight adjustment an old idea can be given a whole new lease of life. For example, the game Monopoly, with its emphasis on the universal appeal of London street names, has been launched in France with Parisian 'rues' and in Cornwall using towns rather than streets.

Case study: taking a new approach

Roger Freebody, managing director of Trees Unlimited, took the traditional approach to artificial Christmas trees and turned it on its head. His central idea was to escape from old-fashioned manufacturing-led tradition and to innovate and try new marketing approaches, such as offering a choice of colours. While Porth Textiles, Britain's then largest manufacturer of decorations, garlands and plastic trees, was collapsing with debts of £8 million, Freebody and his colleagues launched Trees Unlimited on the back of a whole new range of coloured trees from brown to pink. Their success is proof that Christmas trees do not have to be green.

Using the Internet

Many of the first generation of Internet start-ups had nothing unique about their offer other than that it was 'on the Net'. Any new entrant to a market with nothing particularly distinctive to make it better – in the customer's eyes at least – will end up competing on price. New and small businesses are less able to win price wars than bigger and better established competitors.

But using the Internet to take an old idea and turn it into a new and more cost-efficient business can be a winner, as the case study below illustrates.

Case study: winning on the Internet

Harold had worked in a car salvage business for five years when he decided he would like to be his own boss. The salvage business consisted largely of broken-down motor cars, rusty puddles of water and lots of used notes changing hands. A less likely business to start on the Internet it was hard to think of. His employer had two sites situated strategically at motorway junctions to cover as much of the country as possible. Once recovered from an accident, the insurance company assesses the vehicle – those that are beyond repair are sold for scrap after the spare parts have been salvaged. The rest were sold at auction by his employer or one of his competitors. Historically, all vehicles were held and sold at the company's premises, which effectively acts as a car showroom. Prospective purchasers would visit, view and buy vehicles in the traditional way, much like a second-hand car dealership. This meant that traders who were located in prime positions had access to both the best buys and the best customers. Some customers from out of the area would visit occasionally, but not often because it was too time-consuming to take a day out browsing on the off chance of finding a good deal.

But for Harold, having a prime site was too expensive a proposition. He had read about e-business and felt that it offered the possibilities of opening up the market, so more buyers could be enticed into an auction. Also if the auctions could be conducted online, Harold could use a less expensive site to store the vehicles, as access was less important to buyers, who could have their purchases delivered to them.

Harold bought an off-the-shelf software package which enabled him to come up with a no-mess, no-fuss website. He had all the features of an online auction up and working within six weeks. He ran a promotional campaign, including advertising in local and trade publications to spread the word. He emailed his network of business contacts to start spreading the news by word of mouth. Harold started small, with just a dozen cars for sale, but quickly built up his stock. He was able to do this because all his vehicles are sold and paid for in a matter of days. His previous employer took up to three months to get his money back after buying in stock.

Over 100 serious buyers attend Harold's online auctions, compared with a physical auction, which would be lucky to attract 50. Having a wider and larger audience ensures better prices, too.

Solving unsolved problems

Sometimes customers are just not having their needs met by existing suppliers. Big firms very often don't have the time to pay attention to all of their customers properly, as it is just not economic. If there are enough people with needs and expectations that are not being met, as in the case study below, that could constitute an opportunity for a new small firm to start up.

Case study: unsolved problems

For Tim Waterstone, the basic concept of his bookshop chain, Waterstone's, came from wandering around Manhattan bookshops on his frequent solo trips to the United States. They were brilliant places: lively and consumer-led with huge stocks, accessible staff and long opening hours. He felt book buyers in Britain were frustrated at not being able to browse outside normal working hours, as bookshops in Britain stuck pretty much to regular shop opening times. Also, they were staffed by shop assistants who knew plenty about merchandising but little or nothing about books. This meant that unless a customer knew exactly what book they were looking for, they were unlikely to get much help to find it.

Although Waterstone felt he was on to a winning idea at the time, as he had a job he did nothing about it. Sometimes, even when you have

recognized a new way to get into an old business, there is not sufficient impetus to get going. But once Waterstone was made redundant, a trip to the dole office acted as a catalyst. It was the most horrific experience of his life. Not waiting for his turn, he rushed out and sat in his car. Instead of trying to get a new job, he formulated the Waterstone's concept. High street banks turned him down. He then went to a finance house and struck lucky. He pledged his house and committed £6000 savings and £10,000 borrowed from his father-in-law, raising the rest through the Government Loan Guarantee Scheme. Three months later, the first Waterstone's opened. Based on a simple store plan that an art student sketched out for £25, Waterstone filled the shop with the type of books that appeal to book lovers, not best-seller buyers. Late hours, Sunday trading (where possible) and bonus schemes for his highly literate staff led to dazzling sales. Within eight years, Waterstone's had some 40 shops employing 500 people with a turnover of £35+ million. He sold the business out to WHSmith for nearly £60 million and was invited to stay on and run it – less than a decade after his dole queue experience.

Inventions

Inventions are all too often almost the opposite of either identifying a gap in the market or solving an unsolved problem. Inventors usually start by looking through the other end of the telescope. They find an interesting problem and solve it. There may or may not be a great need for whatever it is they have invented. The Post-it Note is a good example of inventors going out on a limb to satisfy themselves rather than to meet a particular need or even solve a burning problem. Scientists at 3M, the giant American company, so the story goes, came across an adhesive that failed most of their tests. It had poor adhesion qualities as it could be separated from anything it was stuck to. There was no obvious market but they persevered and pushed the product onto their marketing department, saying the new product had unique properties in that it would stick 'permanently, but temporarily.' The rest, as they say, is history.

Sadly, most inventions are not so successful.

Bookham Technology is a stunning example of an entrepreneur recognizing a business opportunity for an e-business, then doggedly setting out to create and acquire the technology that would allow him to realise his dream. The personal billion pounds he made when the firm floated on NASDAQ and the London Stock Exchanges in May 2000 was perhaps a well-deserved reward.

Case study: inventing an opportunity

Bookham Technologies, founded by Andrew Rickman, could well have been an example of a high technology start-up in search of a market. With an honours degree in Mechanical Engineering from Imperial College, London and a PhD from the University of Surrey, Rickman certainly had the makings of a boffin. But an MBA from Cranfield leavened his fervour for technology as an end in itself.

'Back in 1988 I came across the forerunners of the Internet and it struck me at the time that optical fibre was going to become a very important part of the Internet because it was the best way of transmitting lots and lots of information,' he says.

Rickman is part academic, part new-economy entrepreneur and part traditional businessman. He spurns the dressed-down uniform of the e-world for a sober suit, white shirt and tie, and is at his most animated explaining at a blackboard how data travels down optical cables.

Communication via optical fibres, rather than copper wires, uses light instead of electrical signals to carry and process information and is ideally suited to the heavy data traffic of the Internet age. Fibreoptic cables have been used for at least 10 years but the optical components at each end of the cables were expensive, involving the hand assembly of tiny lasers, filters and lenses.

This was the problem that Rickman set out to solve. He says: 'Our vision at the beginning of the business was to find a way of integrating all of the functions needed in optical components on to a chip in the same way that the electronics industry has done.'

This simplification would allow automated volume manufacture, bringing down cost and allowing the growth in use of the Internet. 'The only thing that is likely to prevent the continued exponential growth in the use of the Internet is that cost reduction in use does not come down fast enough,' he says.

The business started in a room above the garage of his home, with his wife as company secretary. But the idea did not stem from academic research; instead, Rickman designed the business model to meet a market need rather than to exploit an existing technology. He says: 'I had briefly worked in the venture capital community and at the outset of Bookham formulated a model for the ideal technology company. We saw the market opportunity and then went looking for the technology. That is the right way to do it.'

Once the initial scientific breakthroughs had been made, the company raised private equity finance, totalling $110 million over several rounds, and had backing from 3I, Cisco, Intel and others.

'It was a very long road to travel with substantial challenges but now we are producing tens of thousands of components, scaling up in a way that has not been seen in the UK,' he says.

Bookham, like CISCO, is a supplier of 'picks and shovels' to the Internet market. By 2001, they employed 400 people and had listed on the London Stock Exchange and the NASDAQ.

Before deciding to go ahead with a business idea based on an invention, you should seek as much help and advice as possible. See Sections 4 and 7 for the relevant sources of help and advice.

Using other people's ideas

You may not have a business idea of your own, but nevertheless feel strongly that you would like to work for yourself. There is nothing unusual about this approach. Sometimes an event such as redundancy (as with Tim Waterstone), early retirement or a financial windfall may prompt you into searching for a business idea. Business ideas themselves very often come from the knowledge and experience gained in previous jobs, but then take time to come into focus. Often you will need a good flow of ideas before one arrives that appeals to you and that appears viable. You can trawl for ideas and opportunities by reading magazines such as Business Opportunity Digest, which, as the name suggests, presents the bones of a number of ideas each month. Or you can read papers and periodicals which advertise other people's opportunities. Almost all papers and many general magazines too, have sections on opportunities and ideas for small business.

When answering advertisements for other people's business ideas, do take precautions to ensure you are not simply about to become a victim of someone else's fraudulent venture. The Advertising Standards Authority (ASA) warns that not all 'Get rich quick' offers are genuine. These advertisements can lure even quite sophisticated people into bogus schemes. The ASA believes that 'fooling all of the people all of the time' is entirely possible when the product or service is interesting or persuasive enough. Recent complaints include a mailshot saying: 'No more telephone bills for you – ever.' For £7.50, GP Services of Huntingdon offered to disclose details of a technique which had been 'tried, tested and proven', which required no equipment or capital and which was 'currently being used throughout the UK'. The method was just to contact British Telecom's customer services department and ask to be disconnected. Upholding complaints against the firm, the authority ruled that it 'exploited consumers' credulity'.

Case study: fraudulent opportunities

In March 2001, three champagne fraudsters who were exposed by Financial Mail *were convicted of cheating investors out of £4 million. Julian Blee, Craig Dean and Lee Rosser operated the House of Delacroix, which offered Champagne Lantz as an investment in 1996 and 1997.*

Their slogan claimed, 'The biggest party for a thousand years is about to run out of fizz,' and they predicted huge profits for customers who resold their bubbly in pre-millennium auctions at Sotheby's or Christie's. But in January 1997, Financial Mail *warned that Lantz was unknown in wine circles and Delacroix's Paris address was just a message-taking service. In any event, champagne producers already had four years' stock in hand, more than enough to supply the world's millennium demand.*

In 1997, Delacroix ceased trading and investors were told they must pay to import their champagne to Britain, or sell it back to the French producer at a big loss. The Serious Fraud Office discovered that no auctions had been arranged and that, in any event, neither Sotheby's nor Christie's would touch the unknown Lantz.

The 'Paris-based' House of Delacroix was found to have operated from Wimbledon, southwest London and Amsterdam. The champagne, for which investors paid £30 a bottle before tax, compared unfavourably with cheaper supermarket bubbly.

Blee surrendered to police in February 1999; Dean was later extradited from Portugal, where he was running a company marketing cognac as an investment; and Rosser was extradited from Spain last year. Southwark Crown Court in London heard that they used false names, made false claims about their expertise and returns on investments, and drew 'unusually large amounts of cash' from Delacroix's bank account. Rosser and Blee had been jailed previously for a £6 million whisky fraud.

Sources of help and advice with finding business ideas

Websites

The following is a small cross section of the hundreds of websites that offer information on business ideas small and big, many of which can be started from home with minimum working capital.

Business Opportunity Profiles (BOPs)

At website: http://www.cobwebinfo.com/
They provide practical, fact sheet style guides to starting up 390 types of business.

Each BOP follows a standard format providing concise, clear and relevant information covering:

* market
* customers
* competition
* promotion
* start-up costs
* training and qualifications
* legal
* further reading
* useful addresses.

Recent titles include:

* baby clothes and equipment shop
* care agency
* dental services
* designer clothing shop
* estate agent – residential property
* knitting services
* maternity clothing shop
* nightclub
* off-licence
* personal shopper
* property maintenance service
* residential letting agent
* software developer
* sub post office
* typing and word processing
* women's clothing shop
* virtual office assistant.

Business Opportunity Profiles are available from £425 plus VAT for a single user, twelve-month subscription

Entrepreneur.com

At their business opportunities site, http://www.entrepreneur.com/bizoppzone/0,4997,,00.html they give details of over 400 ideas for starting your own business in some 60 different categories ranging from advertising to water businesses.

Each opportunity has information on start-up costs and suggestions for further research. They also have a series of checklists to help you evaluate a business opportunity to see if it's right for you. The checklists are:

* business analysis checklist
* business start-up cash needs
* competitor analysis worksheet
* personal goals worksheet.

http://www.homebizwomen.com

They publish new *Women's Business Success Stories* every month. Their ideas are designed for people who are considering their first home business, or who do not have a lot of business experience, and who do not have a lot of money to invest in starting a business.

http://www.homeworkinguk.com/

… has a site http://www.homeworkinguk.com/ bizopps.htm listing dozens of current business ideas in the UK.

http://www.powerhomebiz.com/

Free site with archives of dozens of articles on such topics as: how to turn a hobby into a money-making business, the top ten ways to make money at home and so forth.

Power Homebiz Guides

… is an online magazine offering a wide range of information and tools for home businesses. Their guides are designed to provide ideas, facts and resources to stimulate the entrepreneurial mind.

http://www.workathomeplace.com/home_business.htm

Hundreds of ideas for starting a home business. Heavily US biased, but the ideas are generic and adaptable.

Publications

Whatever business idea you are thinking about, the chances are good that someone will have started something similar before. Judging by the volume of books published, there is also a good chance they will have written about their experiences. If you already have an idea of the sort of sector in which you would like to work up a business idea, then finding such a book should be fairly easy, using an Internet booksellers search engine.

This is a cross section of the sort of books that have been published in the past few years, to give a flavour of what is on the market.

- *101 Internet Businesses You Can Start from Home: How to Choose and Build Your Own Successful E-Business,* Susan Sweeney, Maximum Press, July 2001, £14.69.
- *Ultimate Start-Up Directory*; a comprehensive collection of 1350 start-up ideas in more than 30 industries, including home-based, part-time and Internet opportunities, James Stephenson Entrepreneur Press; December 1, 2002, $16.90.
- *Growing Profits: How to Start and Operate a Backyard Nursery,* Michael Harlan, Moneta Publications, April 2000, $17.95.
- *How to Make Big Money Starting a Business: Five Businesses That Can Generate Over $250,000 with Little or No Investment,* Donny Lowy, Xlibris Corporation, December 2000, $20.99.
- *How to Start a Home-Based Antiques Business,* Jacquelyn Peake, Globe Pequot Press, October 2000, $17.95.
- *How to Start a Home-Based Gift Basket Business,* Shirley George Frazier, Globe Pequot Press, October 2000, $17.95.

- *How to Start a Home-Based Writing Business,* Lucy Parker, Globe Pequot Press, August 2000, $18.95.
- *How to Start a Magazine,* James B. Kobak, M. Evans and Company Inc, January 2002, $33.95
- *101 Small Business Ideas for Under $5000,* Corey Sandler, Janice Keefe, John Wiley & Sons, April 2005, $13.57.
- *Home-Based Business For Dummies* Paul Edwards, Sarah Edwards, Peter Economy, John Wiley & Sons, February 2005, $19.99.
- *Kitchen Table Publisher: The Master Manual: How to Start, Manage & Profit from Your Own Homebased Publishing Company,* Thomas A. Williams, Venture Press (FL), March 2000, $59.95.
- *Retail in Detail: How to Start and Manage a Small Retail Business,* Ronald L. Bond, Oasis Press, May 2001, $16.95.
- *Starting Over: How to Change Careers or Start Your Own Business,* Stephen M. Pollan, Warner Books, March 1997, $15.99.
- *The Couple's Business Guide: How to Start and Grow a Small Business Together,* Amy Lyon, Perigee Books/Berkley Pub Corp., June 1997, $16.00.
- *Turn Your Passion Into Profits: How to Start a Business of Your Dreams,* Janet Victoria Allon, Hearst Books, August 2001, price $25.
- *Upstart Start-Ups! How 25 Young Entrepreneurs Overcame Youth, Inexperience, and Lack of Money to Create Thriving Businesses,* Ron Lieber, Broadway Books, September 1998, $15.00.

Buying a business

This way into business is particularly well suited to people who have extensive experience of general business management but lack detailed technical or product knowledge.

When you buy an established business, you will not only pay for the basic assets of the business, but also the accumulated time and effort that the previous owners spent growing the business to its present state. This extra asset can be thought of as 'goodwill' of the business. The better the business, the more the 'goodwill' will cost you.

Advantages of buying a business include these factors.

- You will buy some of the experience and expertise you do not have. It is much easier and almost invariably less costly to learn from the mistakes that other people have made in the past, rather than making all these mistakes again yourself.
- You will gain both access to your potential customers. and the credibility of a trading history from the outset, which can save months if not years of hard work in building relationships.
- If the business you buy is already profitable, you could pay yourself a living wage from the outset.
- An established business is usually less risky than a start-up and so it may be easier to get bank finance.

Disadvantages of buying a business include these.

- When you buy an established business there is always the risk you will buy the existing unsolved problems and mistakes of the person who is selling it.
- Identifying the right potential acquisition and negotiating purchase can take a very long time, and there is no guarantee that you will succeed at your first attempt.
- The professional fees associated with buying a business can be a very significant, though necessary, cost. If you buy a very small business, you should expect that the total professional fees associated with the transaction will be a major percentage of the total cost of your investment – perhaps as much as 15 or 20%. Experienced solicitors and accountants are vital to this process. They are your safeguard to ensure that you know exactly what you are buying.

The different ways to buy a business

There are a number of different ways to achieve the benefits associated with buying a business.

- Buy the whole business. If the business you want is owned by a company, you can buy all the shares in that company to acquire the business. This is advantageous if you want to maintain the trading name of the company or do not want to bring the change of ownership to the attention of customers or suppliers. If the business is a partnership or sole trader, you can buy out the existing owners. This will mean you will get all of the business, both the bad bits and the good bits. If there are some particularly onerous obligations you are taking over from the previous owners, this should be reflected in the price you pay.
- Buy bits of the business. A business is made up of various assets and liabilities. Some of these will be valuable to you and some may be of no use at all. For example, you may wish to buy the customer list and stocks of an existing business but may not wish to take on the property it trades from or its existing liabilities. This can be a good way of avoiding being landed with problems inherited from the old business.
- Buy a part of a business. If the business you want to get into is going to be more than you can afford, it may make sense to buy a part of that business. If it's a company then you will end up with a proportion of the shares and become a shareholder. You may or may not also become a director of that business. If the business is run by a sole trader or a group of partners, you will become a partner in that enterprise too. You need to be aware of the reputation of your prospective business partners. Ask around and get references if appropriate. Going into business with them means you will take on their reputation by association. Always formalize the relationship with your business partners by a comprehensive and professionally drafted legal agreement. (See Section 7 for the legal aspects of this area.)

- Management Buy Outs (MBOs). This term is applied to the sale of a business to the existing management team. Large companies are continuously reviewing their overall operating strategy. They often seek to dispose of, or close down, businesses they have acquired in the past that are not sufficiently profitable or that do not fit in with their future plans. If you work in such a business, this may be the way to get into your own enterprise, though you will have to share that ownership with others. Big firms often favour buy-out teams, as selling out to the management makes better headlines than closing a business down or making people redundant. Financial backers like them too, as both the management team and the business idea are to some extent proven, or at least the problems are more visible (and hence solvable, in theory at least).
- Management Buy Ins (MBIs). This term is applied to the purchase of a stake in a business by an external manager or management team. As with MBOs, MBIs tend to be transactions backed by external investors such as venture capital (VC) firms. (See Section 7.) The opportunity for an MBI exists where current management is poor, or lacks expertise and, consequently, the business is under-performing. In this way the business gets the injection of expertise it requires and the new managers share in the future profits they expect to generate. This could be an alternative to buying a part of the business from an existing owner. In essence the existing owner sells out to a VC, who in turn lets you acquire a share in return for some money and your expertise.
- BIMBOs. This strange sounding title stands for buy-in management buy out. This occurs when some of a company's existing management team join with a new incoming manager(s), backed by a VC to buy the business.

Negotiating the deal

Buying a business is a specialist task. If your usual advisers are general practitioners, who don't have relevant experience, ask them to refer you to a specialist for this particular transaction. (See Sections 6 and 7 for contact points.)

You need to set some ground rules before you start negotiating to buy a business.

- Decide how much you are willing to spend before you start negotiations. Don't forget to include the professional advisers' fees in this equation.
- Always negotiate 'subject to contract'. This means that no negotiations are binding until the final contract is agreed.
- Be prepared to walk away from the deal if it doesn't 'feel' right, however far down the line you have got.

Once the general terms of the sale are agreed, including the price, request the opportunity to review the business's affairs, in detail, to check that you are buying what you think you are buying. This checking process is called 'due diligence'. Generally, there will be legal aspects (e.g. confirming ownership of assets in the business and the validity of contracts), and financial aspects (e.g. reviewing asset values and checking for unrecorded liabilities) pertinent to the review. These will be carried out by your solicitor and accountant.

However, if the business you're buying is in an industry that is particularly risky or specialized, it will be worth getting the assistance of an industry expert. Don't try to do the review by yourself, or with inexperienced advisers. Accountants and solicitors have checklists and procedures to make sure they cover all the major risk areas, so important issues don't get missed. Taxation related issues can also arise at this stage. These can prove extremely costly in the future, if not dealt with correctly in the sale agreement.

Sources of help and advice with buying a business

BusinessesForSale.com
40 Bowling Green Lane

Clerkenwell
London EC1R ONE
United Kingdom
Telephone: +44 (0)20 7864 9700
Fax: +44 (0)20 7713 8661
Email: info@businessesforsale.com
http://www.businessesforsale.com/

They provide a comprehensive range of services to facilitate the buying and selling of a business in the most effective manner possible.

They offer professional intermediaries and business owners/buyers a cost-effective channel to advertise their details to a wide audience. There are over 16,000 firms on the site at any one time.

Businesses on the site range from a Mobile Food Trailer at £4500 to a Fast Food Master Franchise at £2 million.

Christie & Co
50 Victoria Street
London SW1H 0NW
Tel: +44 (0) 20 7227 0700
Fax: +44 (0) 20 7227 0701
Email: enquiries@christie.com
Website: http://www.christie.com/
Regional offices:

Christie & Co
Edgbaston House
3 Duchess Place
Hagley Road
Birmingham B16 8NH
Tel: +44 (0) 121 456 1222
Fax: +44 (0) 121 455 0114
Email: birmingham@christie.com

Christie & Co
5 Logie Mill
Beaverbank Office Park
Logie Green Road
Edinburgh EH7 4HG
Tel: +44 (0) 131 557 6666
Fax: +44 (0) 131 557 6000
Email: edinburgh@christie.com

Christie & Co
Kings Wharf
The Quay
Exeter EX2 4AN
Tel: +44 (0) 1392 285600
Fax: +44 (0) 1392 285601
Email: exeter@christie.com

Christie & Co
Beacon House
Queens Road
Clifton
Bristol BS8 IQU
Tel: +44 (0) 117 933 1500
Fax: +44 (0) 117 933 1501
Email: bristol@christie.com

Christie & Co is one of the leading business agents in the UK, operating both nationally and internationally, specializing in the hotel, licensed, leisure, care and retail markets.

Claimed as Europe's largest database of businesses for sale, Christies was set up in 1935 by George Christie, who with his partners founded a practice in London's West End, the location for the company's present headquarters

As well as a searchable website, their publications concerning business for sale include:

- *Business First.* A full-colour monthly publication listing newly available businesses and price reductions.
- *Hotel Opportunities.* A full-colour brochure listing hundreds of hotels and guest houses for sale throughout the United Kingdom and worldwide. (Three times per year.)
- *Healthcare Opportunities.* A full-colour brochure listing hundreds of healthcare businesses for sale throughout the United Kingdom. (Three times per year.)
- *Retail Opportunities.* A full-colour brochure listing hundreds of retail businesses for sale throughout the United Kingdom. (Three times per year.)
- *Public House, Restaurant and Wine Bar Opportunities.* A full-colour brochure listing hundreds

of licensed businesses for sale throughout the United Kingdom and worldwide. (Three times per year.)

Daltons Weekly
Daltons Weekly C.I. Tower,
St George's Square,
New Malden, Surrey
KT3 4JA
Tel: 020 8329 0100
Fax: 020 8329 0101
Website: www.daltons.co.uk/

Daltons Business justly claims to be the UK's leading businesses for sale website. If your goal is to be your own boss, then they can help find a business that suits your needs and your purse. Within this site, you can access the details of thousands of shops, businesses and franchises on the market both throughout the UK and overseas. If you're also an existing business owner, with a business to sell in the UK, you can have it valued by leading business transfer agents using their free valuation service.

To find your business or franchise, you can search by business type, location or price.

Grant Thornton
Melton Street
Euston Square
London
NW1 2EP
Tel: 020 7383 5100
Fax: 020 7383 4715
Website: www.companiesforsale.uk.com/

Companiesforsale.uk.com is a service owned and operated by Grant Thornton, a firm of chartered accountants. They specialize in owner-managed businesses transactions between £2m and £75m.

They have a dedicated team of specialists based in 7 regions throughout the country, and with 43 offices in the UK, plus representation in over 100 countries worldwide, access to a national and international network of advisers is available to the owner-manager.

You can register at no cost and receive these benefits.

- Updates by e-mail of the opportunities they receive that match your criteria.
- You can specify a number of different industry sectors, geographical regions or turnover levels for companies that are of interest to you. If you wish to receive all new opportunities you can select 'all' to each of these categories.
- By registering you will also receive news of deals completed.

Lakey & Co
11 Broad Street, Pershore,
Worcestershire WR10 1BB
Tel: 01386 554200
Email: info@lakeygroup.co.uk
Website: www.lakeygroup.co.uk/

The Lakey & Co group was established in 1983 and is one of the leading agencies specialising in the sale of businesses. They have a network of local regional offices, and sell businesses nationally.

Nationwide Businesses Ltd
11a High Street
Purley
Surrey
CR8 2AF
Tel: 020 8763 1777
Fax: 020 8763 0727
Email: Info@NationwideBusinesses.com
Website: www.nationwidebusinesses.co.uk/

Nationwide Businesses Ltd has details on over 1500 businesses for sale in the UK. From their site you can do all this:

- Request full business details and decide on which businesses you want to see.
- Arrange appointments. They will contact the owners on your behalf to arrange meetings and viewings.
- Verify the income. They will get you accounts, VAT returns, copies of takings figures.

- Agree a price. All offers are subject to contract.

BCMS Tradeplan Ltd

Plantagenet House, Kingsclere Park, Kingsclere,
Newbury, Berkshire, RG20 4SW
Tel: +44 (0)1635 299616
Fax:: +44 (0)1635 299502
Email: melanie.byard@tradeplan.com
Website: www.tradeplan-ma.co.uk/
and at:

Northern UK Office

Dr Mike Sweeting
BCMS Tradeplan Ltd
Belasis Business Centre
Belasis Hall Technology Park, Coxwold Way
Billingham, Cleveland, TS23 4EA
Tel: +44 (0)1642 345685
Fax: +44 (0)1642 345691
Email: mike.sweeting@tradeplan.com

US Office:

Mr Howard Lalgee
BCMS M&A LLC
5008 Green Bay Road, Suite 3
Kenosha, WI 53144–1790
USA
Tel: +1 262 657 9222
Fax: +1 262 657 9223
Email: BCMS-USA@pitnet.net

BCMS operate throughout the world in the field
of finding and qualifying:

- buyers for shareholders that are looking to sell
  their business
- suitable acquisition targets for organizations
  that are looking to buy companies
- investment partners
- joint venture/trade partners.

Established in 1989 BCMS now undertakes more
than 600 projects every year on behalf of a wide
variety of small and large clients alike. They claim
their database has 82 million companies, which
enables them to search worldwide for suitable
opportunities

UKBusinessBase.com

This service is only offered via their website.
Website: http://www.ukbusinessbase.com/
Developed in conjunction with Harvey Silver
Hodgkinson, a long-established business transfer
agent, they offer an online searchable database of
businesses for sale. In addition they offer links to
other professional advisers in your area who can
help with raising finance or with the legal aspects
of the transaction.

One interesting feature on their website is a
listing of the most popular businesses and regions.
In June 2005, these were the listings for sector and
area, with the number of opportunities listed in
brackets.

Business sector

Hot Food Take-Away (196)
Newsagent (142)
Public House (110)
Hair Salon (109)
Restaurant (101)
Business Opportunities (97)
Hotel (94)
General Store (84)
Café (74)
Sandwich Bar (71)

Geographic area

Greater Manchester (211)
Lancashire (194)
Nationwide (183)
Cheshire (142)
Greater London (106)
Leicestershire (100)
West Midlands (79)
Surrey (66)
Nottinghamshire (65)
Dorset (64)

Books and publications

*   *Buying and Selling a Business Made E-Z,* Arnold S. Goldstein, Made E-Z Products, May 2001, $14.95.
*   *Buying and Selling of Private Companies and Businesses,* Simon Beswick LLB, Butterworths, September 2001, $97.49.
*   *Buying and Selling a Business: A Step-by-Step Guide,* Robert F. Klueger, John Wiley & Sons, August 2004, $11.87.
*   *Buying and Selling Your Business: Including Forms, Formulas, and Industry Secrets,* William W. Bumstead, John Wiley & Sons, February 1998, $110.00.
*   *How to Buy and Sell a Business: How You Can Win in the Business Quadrant,* (Rich Dad's Advisors Series), Garrett Sutton, Robert T. Kiyosaki, Warner Books, April 2003, $16.95.
*   *The Essentials of Buying & Selling a Business,* Verne A. Bunn, Research & Education Association, February 2000, $6.95.

Joining a cooperative

If making money is much lower on your list of priorities for starting up in business than being involved in the decisions of an ethical enterprise, then joining a cooperative or starting your own is an idea worth exploring.

Although the most commonly known cooperatives are the high street shops and supermarkets, there is another less visible but none the less important variety – the workers' cooperative. In 1844, 28 workers in northern England formed the first successful workers cooperative. They were weavers, shoemakers, cabinetmakers, tailors, printers, hatters, and engineers. They called themselves the Rochdale Equitable Pioneers Society, taking their name from the town they lived in, Rochdale, 12 miles north of Manchester.

There are over 1500 workers' cooperatives in the UK with over 40,000 people working in them. In the United States, there are 47,000 cooperatives generating over $100 billion in sales output.

There are cooperatives that sell bicycles, furniture, camping equipment, appliances, carpeting, clothing, handicrafts, and books. There are cooperative wholesalers, like those in the hardware, grocery, and natural foods businesses. There are cooperatives that disseminate news and cooperatives for artists.

There are cooperative electric and telephone utilities. There are cooperatively managed banks, credit unions, and community development corporations. There are thousands of farm cooperatives, along with cooperatives that provide financing to farm cooperatives.

There are subscriber-owned cable TV systems and parent-run day-care centres. There are cooperatively organized employee-owned companies, cooperative purchasing groups for fast-food franchises, and, of course, various kinds of cooperative housing.

There are co-ops that provide health care, such as health maintenance organizations and community health clinics. There are cooperative insurance companies. There are cooperative food stores, food-buying clubs, and discount warehouses.

Definition

A cooperative is an autonomous association of persons united voluntarily to meet their common economic, social and cultural needs and aspirations through a jointly owned and democratically controlled enterprise.

Values

Cooperatives are based on the values of self-help, self-responsibility, democracy, equality, equity and solidarity. In the tradition of their founders, cooperative members believe in the ethical values of honesty, openness, social responsibility and caring for others.

Principles

The cooperative principles are guidelines by which cooperatives put their values into practice.

- **1st Principle: Voluntary and Open Membership.** Cooperatives are voluntary organizations, open to all persons able to use their services and willing to accept the responsibilities of membership, without gender, social, racial, political or religious discrimination.
- **2nd Principle: Democratic Member Control.** Cooperatives are democratic organizations controlled by their members, who actively participate in setting their policies and making decisions. Men and women serving as elected representatives are accountable to the membership. In primary cooperatives, members have equal voting rights (one member, one vote), and cooperatives at other levels are also organized in a democratic manner.
- **3rd Principle: Member Economic Participation.** Members contribute equitably to, and democratically control, the capital of their cooperative. At least part of that capital is usually the common property of the cooperative. Members usually receive a limited compensation, if any, on capital subscribed as a condition of membership. Members allocate surpluses for any or all of the following purposes: developing their cooperative, possibly by setting up reserves, part of which at least would be indivisible; benefiting members in proportion to their transactions with the cooperative; and supporting other activities approved by the membership.
- **4th Principle: Autonomy and Independence.** Cooperatives are autonomous, self-help organizations controlled by their members. If they enter into agreements with other organizations, including governments, or raise capital from external sources, they do so on terms that ensure democratic control by their members and maintain their cooperative autonomy.
- **5th Principle: Education, Training and Information.** Cooperatives provide education and training for their members, elected representatives, managers and employees so they can contribute effectively to the development of their cooperatives. They inform the general public – particularly young people and option leaders – about the nature and benefits of co-operation.
- **6th Principle: Cooperation Among Cooperatives.** Cooperatives serve their members most effectively and strengthen the cooperative movement by working together through local, national, regional, and international structures.
- **7th Principle: Concern for Community.** Cooperatives work for the sustainable development of their communities through policies approved by their members.

The main attraction of workers' cooperatives is the greater level of involvement in decision-making and the ethical standards implied in their principles.

The Industrial Common Ownership Movement (ICOM)

The Industrial Common Ownership Movement (ICOM) is the UK federation for workers' cooperatives, and can provide information to the public and to its members on aspects of setting up and running cooperatives. It can also undertake promotional activities on their behalf.

ICOM is the Industrial Common Ownership Movement Limited, a non-profit membership organization promoting and representing democratic employee owned businesses throughout the UK.

Since 1971 it has pioneered the cause of democratic employee ownership, especially in the form of worker cooperatives. It is also involved in developing other innovative forms of cooperation, including an increasing number of cooperative consortiums made up of small businesses or self-employed individuals.

ICOM has drawn up sets of model rules for secondary or marketing cooperatives – used often by people or groups (including cooperatives) that want to provide an agency service for themselves; for nursery cooperatives; for community cooperatives – which can include members of the community on the management committee; and many more. Details can be obtained from ICOM's Legal Office.

For further details, contact:

ICOM
Holyoake House
Hanover Street
Manchester M60 0AS
Tel: 0161 246 2959
Email: icom@icom.org.uk
Website: www.icof.co.uk/icom/

Publication
New Sector Magazine
Society Place
West Calder
EH55 8EA
Tel: 01506 871370
Fax: 01506 873079
Email: office@newsector.co.uk
Website: www.newsector.co.uk/

New Sector is the magazine of workers' cooperatives and community-owned businesses in the UK, and tries to establish worldwide links with others involved in local economic development work.

It is published by a joint venture company on behalf of ICOM, Community Business Scotland Network (CBS Network) the Wales Cooperative Centre and Social Economy Agency Northern Ireland.

See also Enterprise Agencies on page **43**.

Franchising

Franchising is a marketing technique used to improve and expand the distribution of a product or service. The franchisor supplies the product or teaches the service to the franchisee, who in turn sells it to the public. In return for this, the franchisee pays a fee and a continuing royalty, based usually on turnover. They may also be required to buy materials or ingredients from the franchisor, giving them an additional income stream. The advantage to the franchisee is a relatively safe and quick way of getting their own business, but with the support and advice of an experienced organization close at hand.

Franchisors can expand their distribution with the minimum strain on their own capital and have the services of a highly motivated team of owner-managers. Franchising is not a path to great riches, nor is it for the truly independent spirit, as policy and profits will still come from 'on high'.

Franchising in the UK and Europe is a relatively young industry. Body Shop is scarcely 30 years old, and the whole franchise concept spread only slowly in the decades after the first really major British franchise, Wimpy, got going in the mid 1950s. Since then, however, development has been very rapid; more rapid, perhaps, than most people realize. Now, there are few sectors of the economy, be it babysitting, fast food or knitwear that don't have a franchise operation working in them. If you glance at the franchise directory that follows, it may reveal some firms that you were not aware of as franchises at all.

Here are some results from the latest (2005) annual franchise survey produced by the National Westminster Bank and the British Franchise Association.

- There are 718 franchise systems in operation in the UK.
- There are an estimated 327,000 people employed in franchising.
- The average initial cost of starting a franchise is £42,200 (including franchise fee, working capital, equipment and fittings, stock and materials).
- 88% of franchisees claim to be profitable.
- The average turnover for franchised businesses is £291,000.

- On average, franchisees pay an estimated 7.7% of their sales in recurring fees to their franchisors.
- The two biggest sectors are Business & Commercial Services and Property Services.
- 80% of all franchisees are married.
- 79% of franchisees are male.
- The average age for a franchisee is 45.
- Two-thirds (65%) of franchisees were in salaried employment immediately before taking out their current franchise.

Franchising can be a good first step into self-employment for those with business experience but no actual experience of running a business – often the case with those who are looking for something to do following a corporate career. However, while franchising eliminates some of the more costly, and at times disastrous, bumps in the learning curve of working for yourself, it is not an easy way to riches either. Whilst nearly ninety per cent of franchisees report they are trading profitably, the number of those claiming high levels of profitability remains low at under 10 per cent. Wild claims are made about how much safer a franchise is when compared with a conventional start-up. Whilst it is true that the long-established big franchise chains are relatively safe (though a few big names have got into trouble), the smaller and newer ones are as vulnerable as any other venture in their early formative years.

Types of business franchise

Franchises can be clustered under these three main headings.

- **Job franchises:** These require a financial investment in the £7000–20,000 range, and could be described as 'buying a job' – however, with back-up in the way of training, customer leads, advertising etc. from the franchisor. Suitable for someone with little capital, but having a specific area of expertise or willing to be trained in it, e.g. cleaning or vehicle repair and maintenance services.

- **Business franchises:** These require a higher level of investment, typically in the range of £20,000–120,000 in stock, equipment and premises. There are large numbers of business franchises available in such areas as retailing, food services and business services such as High Street printing shops.
- **Investment franchises:** Here you are talking about initial investments of over £120,000. Hotels and some of the larger and more established fast food outlets come into the top range of this category at around £750,000.

Definitions of a franchise

A formal definition of a franchise is set out by the British Franchise Association (BFA), the industries main trade body, as follows:

A contractual licence granted by one person (the franchisor) to another (the franchisee) which:

a) permits or requires the franchisee to carry on during the period of a franchise a particular business under or using a specified name belonging to or associated with the franchisor; and

b) entitles the franchisor to exercise continuing control during the period of the franchise over the manner in which the franchisee carries on the business which is the subject of the franchise; and

c) obliges the franchisor to provide the franchisee with assistance in carrying on the business which is the subject of the franchise (in relation to the organization of the franchisee's business, the training of staff, merchandising, management or otherwise); and

d) requires the franchisee periodically during the period of the franchise to pay to the franchisor sums of money in consideration for the franchise or for goods or services provided by the franchisor to the franchisee; and

e) is not a transaction between a holding company and its subsidiary (as defined in Section 154 of the Companies Act 1948) or between subsidiaries of the same holding company or between an individual and a company controlled by him.

The last clause establishes the important distinction between a franchise and an agency; though this official definition is certainly useful, it does not mention a number of aspects that are important from the point of view of the person taking up a franchise. It does not indicate that an initial fee is usually payable by the franchisee, nor does it stress that the subject of the franchise should be a tried and tested commercial operation (though running a pilot scheme is a condition of membership of the BFA). It does not mention that the business, once set up, is the property of the franchisee, nor does it warn him of the degree of control he may be subject to under clause b). Further, it gives no indication of the extent of the back-up services that the franchisee might reasonably expect to get for his money. In other words, the BFA definition is not a sufficient standard against which to check the franchise contract.

The British Franchise Association expects its members to follow its code of practice, set out below.

1. BFA Code of Practice shall be based on that established by the Advertising Standards Association and shall be modified from time to time in accordance with alterations notified by the ASA. The BFA will subscribe fully to the ASA Code unless, on some specific issue, it is resolved by a full meeting of the Council of the BFA that the ASA is acting against the best interests of the public and of franchising business in general on that specific issue; in this case the BFA will be required formally to notify the ASA, setting out the grounds for disagreement.

2. No member shall sell, offer for sale, or distribute any product or render any service, or promote the sale or distribution thereof, under any representation or condition (including the use of the name of a 'celebrity'), which has the tendency, capacity, or effect of misleading or deceiving purchasers or prospective purchasers.

3. No member shall imitate the trademark, trade name, corporate identity, slogan, or other mark or identification of another franchisor in any manner or form that would have the tendency or capacity to mislead or deceive.

4. Full and accurate written disclosure of all information material to the franchise relationship shall be given to prospective franchisees within a reasonable time prior to the execution of any binding document.

5. The franchise agreement shall set forth clearly the respective obligations and responsibilities of the parties and all other terms of the relationship, and be free from ambiguity.

6. The franchise agreement, and all matters basic and material to the arrangement and relationship thereby created, shall be in writing and executed copies thereof given to the franchisee.

7. A franchisor shall select and accept only those franchisees who, upon reasonable investigation, possess the basic skills, education, personal qualities and adequate capital to succeed. There shall be no discrimination based on race, colour, religion, national origin or sex.

8. A franchisor shall exercise reasonable surveillance over the activities of his franchisees to the end that the contractual obligations of both parties are observed and the public interest safeguarded.

9. Fairness shall characterize all dealings between a franchisor and its franchisees. A franchisor shall give notice to its franchisee of any contractual breach and grant reasonable time to remedy default.

10. A franchisor shall make every effort to resolve complaints, grievances and disputes with its franchisees with good faith and good will through fair and reasonable direct communication and negotiation.

Take advice

Whilst membership of the BFA and adhering to a code of practice is a hopeful indicator, it is not sufficient guarantee to either the probity or the viability of the franchise opportunity. You should be looking for a shortlist of as many as six opportunities, acquiring as much advice as you can get from franchisors, from franchisees, from your bank and from other professional advisers. Before deciding on a particular franchise it is essential that you consult your legal and financial advisers.

You must also ask the franchisor some very searching questions to prove his competence. You will need to know if he has operated a pilot unit in the UK – an essential first step before selling franchises to third parties. Otherwise, how can he really know all the problems, and so put you on the right track? You will need to know what training and support is included in the franchise package, the name given to the start-up kit provided by franchisors to see you successfully launched. This package should extend to support staff over the launch period and give you access to back-up advice.

You will need to know how substantial the franchise company is. Ask to see their balance sheet (take it to your accountant if you cannot understand it). Ask for the track record of the directors (including their other directorships).

Organizations

Franchise Association
British Franchise Association
Thames View
Newtown Road
Henley-on-Thames
Oxon RG9 1HG
Tel: (44) (0)1491 578050

Fax: (44) (0)1491 573517
Email: mailroom@british-franchise.org.uk
Website: http://www.british-franchise.org/

The British Franchise Association is the single regulatory body for franchising in the UK. The BFA is a non-profit making body responsible for developing and promoting fair and ethical franchising through its member franchisor companies.

They conduct research on the sector, support training programmes on franchise awareness, and liaise with clearing banks to help with start-up finance.

Banks

Many of the clearing banks have departments specializing in franchising; see these in Section 6.

HSBC Franchise Unit
24th Floor
8 Canada Square
London E14 5HQ
Contact: Cathryn Hayes
Tel: 020 7992 1062
Fax: 020 7991 4604
Email: franchiseunit@hsbc.com
Website: www.ukbusiness.hsbc.com

Lloyds TSB plc
Business Banking
Canon's House PO Box 112
Canon's Way
Bristol BS99 7LB
Contact: Mr Alick Jones
Tel: 0117 943 3089
Email: franchising@lloydstsb.co.uk
Website: www.lloydstsbbusiness.co.uk/

The Royal Bank of Scotland plc
Franchise Department
PO Box 20000
The Younger Building
Drummond House
3 Redheughs Avenue
Edinburgh EH12 9RB

Contact: Mr Alan Smart – National Franchise Manager
Tel: 0800 521 607
Fax: 0131 523 5059
Email: alan.smart@rbs.co.uk
Website: www.rbs.co.uk/franchise

Chartered accountants
Beresfords
Castle House
Castle Hill Avenue
Folkestone
Kent CT0 2TQ
Contact: PhillipHindle
Tel: 01303 850992
Fax: 01303 850979
Email: beresefors@folkestone1.demon.co.uk

Rees Pollock
35 New Bridge Street
London
EC4V 6BW
Contact: Mr W. A. Pollock
Telephone: 020 7778 7200
Fax: 020 7329 6408
Email: info@reespollock.co.uk
Web site: www. reespollock.co.uk

Watson Dunne & Co
Oakfield House
378 Brandon Street
Motherwell
ML1 1XA
Contact: Mr Terry Dunne
Tel: 01698 250251
Fax: 01698 250261
Email: WatsonDunn@aol.com

FranAccounts
ALB House
4 Brighton Road
Horsham
West Sussex RH13 5BA
Contact: Mr Jon Hiller
Tel: 01403 255788
Fax: 01403 255704

Email: info@franaccounts.co.uk

Morris & Co
Ashton House
Chadwick Street
Moreton
Wirral CH46 7TE
Contact:Mr Phil Harrison
Tel: 0151 678 7979
Fax: 0151 606 0909
Email: franchise@moco.co.uk
Website: www.moco.co.uk

Franchise consultants
BDO Stoy Hayward
Management Consultants
8 Baker Street
London W1M 1DA
Contact: Mr Max McHardy
Tel: 020 7486 5888
Email: max.mchardy@bdo.co.uk
Website: www.bdo.co.uk

CFM Consulting
Bywood
37Arbrook lane
Claygate
Esher
Surrey KT10 9EG
Tel: 01372 470010
Fax: 01372 470027
Website: www.cfmconsulting.demon.co.uk

Franchise Development Services
(FDS London & South East)
1 Huguenot Court
Princelet Street
London E1 5LP
Contact: Mr Nick Williams
Tel: 0870 350 337
Email: nickw@fdsltd.com
Website: www.franchise-group.com

Franchise Options
56 Carters Close
Sherington

Newport Pagnell
Buckingham MK16 9NW
Contact: Mr Paul Tough
Tel: 01908 616300
Fax: 01908 616300
Email: paultough@franchiseoptions.co.uk

Horwath Franchising (London & South-East)
London & Oxford
Contact: Mr Brian Duckett
Tel: 0870 458 6682
Email: brian@horwathfranchising.co.uk
Website: www.horwathfranchising.co.uk

TDA- Enterprising Futures
4 Thameside Centre
Kew Bridge Road
Brentford
Middlesex TW8 9HF
Contact: Mr P. Tough
Tel: 0208 568 3040
Fax: 0208 569 9800
Email: vmdunn@tdaconsulting.co.uk

Solicitors
Addleshaw Goddard
100 Barbirolli Square
Manchester M2 3AB
Contact: Mr G. Lindrup
Tel: 0161 9346255
Fax: 0161 9346060
Email: garth.lindrup@addleshawgoddard.com

Brodies
15 Atholl Crescent
Edinburgh EH3 8HA
Contact: Mr J. C. A. Voge
Tel: 0131 228 3877
Email: julian.voge@brodies.co.uk

Chambers & Co
Jonathan Scott Hall
Thorpe Road
Norwich NR1 1UH
Contact: Mr J. Chambers
Tel: 01603 616155

Email: chambers@paston.co.uk

Eversheds
Senator House
85 Queen Victoria Street
London EC4V 4JL
Contact: Mr M. Mendelsohn
Tel: 0207 919 4862
Email: chriswormald@eversheds.com

Levy & Macrae
266 St Vincent Street
Glasgow G2 5RL
Contact: Mr A. Caplan
Tel: 0141 307 2311
Email: tonycaplin@lamac.co.uk

Mundays
Cedar House
78 Portsmouth Road
Cobham
Surrey KT11 1AN
Contact: Mrs Nicola Broadhurst
Tel: 01932 590500
Fax: 01932 590220
Email: nicola.broadhurst@mundays.co.uk

Osborne Clarke
Apex Plaza
Forbury Road
Reading
Berkshire RG1 1AX
Contact: Mr Mark Antingham
Tel: 01189 252042
Fax: 01189252043
Email: Mark Antingham@osborneclarke.com
Website: www.osborne-clarke.co.uk

Owen White
Senate House
62–70 Bath Road
Slough
Berks SL1 3SR
Contact Mr Anton Bates
Tel: 01753 536846
Email: anton.bates@owenwhite.com

Parker Nullen
45 Castle Street
Salisbury
Wilts SP1 3SS
Contact: Mr M. Lello
Tel: 01722 412000
Fax: 01722 411822
Email: mark.lello@parkerbullen.com

Taylor Wessing
Carmelite
50 Victoria Embankment
Blackfriars
London EC4Y ODX
Contact: Mr C. Lloyd
Tel: 0207 3007000
Email: c.lloyd@taylorwessing.com

Wragg & Co
55 Colmore Row
Birmingham B3 2AS
Contact: Mr Michael Luckman
Tel: 0121 233 1000
Email: michael_luckman@wragge.com

Publications

Magazines
Business Franchise Magazine
2nd Floor
83–84 George Street
Richmond
Surrey TW9 1HE
Contact: Sally Giles
Tel: 0208 332 9995
Fax: 0208 332 9307
Email: editor@circlepublishing.net

Franchise World
Highlands House
165 The Broadway
Wimbledon
London SW19 1NE
Contact: Mr Robert Riding
Tel: 020 8605 2555
Fax: 020 8605 2556

Email:info@franchiseworld.co.uk

The Franchise Magazine
Franchise House
56 Surrey Street
Norwich NR3 1FD
Contact: Simon Carpenter-Foster
Tel: 01603 6203001
Email: enquiries@fdsltd.com

Books

- *Bond's Top 100 Franchises: An In-Depth Analysis of Today's Top Franchise Opportunities,* Robert Bond, Source Book Publishers, 2004, $33.95.
- *Complete Idiot's Guide to Franchising*, J. Amos, Alpha Books, August 1, 2005, £10.
- *Guide to Franchising*, Martin Mendelsohn, Thomson Learning, 2004, £27.99.
- *The Franchise Annual Directory*, Ted Dixon, Donna House, Lisa Carpenter, Info Franchise News, 2001, $43.95.
- *Franchises & Business Opportunities: How to Find, Buy and Operate a Successful Business*, Andrew A. Caffey, Entrepreneur Press, 2002, $12.95.
- *Franchising for Dummies*, Dave Thomas, Michael Seid, Hungry Minds Inc., 2000, $19.99.
- *Franchising for Free*, D. Foster, John Wiley and Sons, 1988, $19.95.
- *How to Buy a Franchise*, James A. Meaney, Sphinx Publishing, July 2004, £10.00.
- *Taking up a Franchise*, C. Barrow, G. Golzen, H. Kogan, Kogan Page, London, 2001, £12.95.
- *The 220 Best Franchises to Buy: The Sourcebook for Evaluating the Best Franchise Opportunities*, Lynie Arden, Broadway Books, 2000, $19.95.
- *Ultimate Book of Franchising*, Rieva Lesonsky *et al.*, Entrepreneur Press, March 1 2004, £10.49.

Franchise opportunity directory

The following is a comprehensive but by no means exhaustive directory of current franchise organizations. The directory is divided in two; the first section being opportunities requiring less than

£25,000 initial investment, and the second section for those over £25,000.

After the directory there is a list of websites that maintain lists of franchise opportunities.

Under £25,000 start-up capital required

Agency Express
The Old Church
St Matthews Road
Norwich
NR1 1SP
Contact: Tony Marsh
Tel: 01603–620 044
Fax: 01603–613 136
Email: enquiries@agencyexpress.co.uk
Website: www.agencyexpress.co.uk

- Business description: Specialist estate agents board contractors
- Industry sector: Estate services
- BFA membership: Full member
- Franchise type: Management
- Minimum personal investment: N/A
- Minimum total investment: £11,950

AIMS Partnership plc
3 Park Road
Regent's Park
London
NW1 6AS
Contact: Louise Berwin
Tel: 020 7616 6629
Email: central@aims.co.uk
Website: www.aims.co.uk

- Business description: Accountants for business
- No. of franchise outlets: 36
- Year business started: 1992
- Start-up capital (minimum): To cover office equipment
- Initial fee: Minimum of £750 to maximum of £5650
- Management fee: On a sliding scale, 12.5% down to 6.25%

Amtrack Express Parcels Ltd
Northgate Way
Northgate
Aldridge
West Midlands
WS9 8ST
Contact: David Scott
Tel: 01922 747 031
Email: marketing@amtrak.co.uk
Website: www.amtrak.co.uk

- Business description: Overnight and international parcel company
- No. of franchise outlets: 340
- Year business started: 1987
- Start-up capital (minimum): £19,000 (to include working capital)
- Initial fee: £12,500 (usually)
- Management fee: Nil

Apollo Blinds Ltd
Unit 10B, Park View Industrial Estate
Hartlepool
TS25 1PE
Tel: 01429 851500
Fax: 01429 851501
Email: franchising@apolloblinds.co.uk
Website: www.lds.co.uk/franchise/apollo

- Business description: Window furnishings retailer
- No. of franchise outlets: 58
- Year business started: 1970
- Start-up capital (minimum): £15,000
- Initial fee: £9999
- Management fee: Nil

ASC Partnership plc
3 Park Road
Regent's Park
London
NW1 6AS
Contact: Louise Berwin
Tel: 020 7616 6628
Email: central@asc.co.uk
Website: www.asc.co.uk

- Business description: Finance for business
- No. of franchise outlets: 30
- Year business started: 1969
- Start-up capital (minimum): £10,000 to cover office equipment
- Initial fee: £7500 minimum to £47,500 maximum
- Management fee: On a sliding scale, 15% down to 7.5%

Best Training
Best House
66 Ock Street
Abingdon
OX16 5BZ
Contact: Neil Eades
Tel: 01235 559000
Fax: 01235 554206
Email: training@best.co.uk

- Business description: Computer training programmes
- No. of franchise outlets: 15
- Year business started: 1991
- Start-up capital: Total investment around £26,000 + VAT
- No fees, just buy materials from Best Training

Blazes Fireplace & Heating Centres Ltd
23 Standish Street
Burnley
Lancashire
BB11 1AP
Tel: 01282 831176
Fax: 01282 424411
Email: info@blazes.co.uk
Website: www.blazes.co.uk

- Business description: Fireplace retailers
- No. of franchise outlets: 31
- Year business started: 1989
- Start-up capital (minimum): £15,000 cash
- Initial fee: £8000
- Investment 20K up to 50K
- Management fee: 8% net sales

Card Connection
Park House
South Street
Farnham
Surrey
GU9 7QQ
Contact: Robina Every
Tel: 01252 892 323
Fax: 01252 892 339
Email: ho@card-connection.co.uk
Website: www.card-connection.co.uk

- Business description: Greeting card publishers distributing through a network of franchisees
- Industry sector: Greeting card distribution
- BFA membership: Full member
- Franchise type: Single operator manual
- Minimum personal investment: £15,000
- Minimum total investment: £35,000

Chem-Dry
Harris Research Inc./Chem-Dry
1530 North 1000 West
Logan, UT 84321, USA
Phone: 1–800-ChemDry (1–800–243–6379)
International Call: 1–435–755–0099
Email: charlie@chemdry.com
Website: www.chem-dry.com

- Business description: A worldwide franchise company with patented systems and solutions, serving the domestic, commercial and insurance carpet and upholstery cleaning sectors.
- No. of franchise outlets: 523 (nationwide)
- Year business started: 1987
- Start-up capital (minimum): £17,950 + VAT
- Initial fee: £8000
- Management fee: £154.57 per month

Chemex
Spring Road
Smethwick
West Midlands
B66 1PT
Contact: Richard Sarjent
Tel: 0121 525 4040

Fax: 0121 525 4922
Email: info@chemicalexpress.co.uk
Website: www.chemexinter.com

- Business description: Mobile supply of hygiene and cleaning products to industry
- Year business started: 1985
- Start-up capital (minimum): £16,900
- Initial fee: £7000
- Management fee: 7.5%

CICO Chimney Linings Ltd
Westleton
Saxmundham
Suffolk
IP17 3EF
Contact: RJ Hadfield
Tel: 01728 648608
Email: cico@chimney-problems.co.uk
Website: www.chimney-problems.co.uk

- Business description: Lining of domestic and non-domestic chimneys
- No. of franchise outlets: 20
- Year business started: 1982
- Start-up capital (minimum): £21,000
- Initial fee: £8000
- Management fee: 7.5%

Countrywide Grounds Maintenance
Teejay Court
Alderley Road
Wilmslow
SK9 1NT
Contact: Simon Stott
Tel: 01625 529000
Email: franchise@countrywidegrounds.co.uk
Website: www.countrywidegrounds.co.uk

- Business description: National grounds maintenance contractors
- No. of franchise outlets: 51
- Year business started: 1986
- Start-up capital (minimum): £20,000
- Initial fee: £27,750
- Management fee: 10%

Decorating Den
Railway House
WTE Station Road
Membury
Longbridge
Ilminster
Somerset
TA19 9DW
Tel: 01406 55700
Fax: 01460 53003

- Business description: Mobile interior design and supply
- No. of franchise outlets: Nil
- Year business started: 1970 (USA); 1989 (UK)
- Start-up capital (minimum): Nil
- Initial fee: Nil
- Investment up to 10K
- Management fee: 11.7%

Dor-2-Dor
Clare Lodge
41 Holly Bush Lane
Harpenden
AL5 4AY
Contact: Jeff Frankling
Tel: 01582 462744
Email: dor2dor@val-u-pakxom
Website: www.dor-2-dor.com

- Business description: Door-to-door leaflet distribution
- No. of franchise outlets: 35
- Year business started: 1994
- Start-up capital (minimum): £1500
- Initial fee: £1500
- Management fee: 10% (£35 monthly minimum)

Drinkmaster Ltd
Plymouth Road
Liskeard
Cornwall
PL14 3PG
Contact: Margaret Bunton
Tel: 01579 342082

Fax: 01579 325003
Email: ahobson@drinkmaster.co.uk
Website: www.drinkmaster.co.uk

- Business description: Drinks and vending systems
- No. of franchise outlets: 45
- Year business started: Company established 1962 (franchise established 1995)
- Start-up capital (minimum): £10,500
- Initial fee: £7000
- Management fee: TBA

Fix-a-Chip Ltd
The Car Smart Centre
Vermont
Washington
NE37 2AX
Contact: Bryan Stapley
Tel: 0191 417 0577
Fax: 0191 415 7214
Website: www.lds.co.uk/franchise/fixachip

- Business description: Mobile minor vehicle repairs
- No. of franchise outlets: 36
- Year business started: 1995
- Start-up capital (minimum): £6000
- Initial fee: £15,000
- Management fee: 10%

The Garage Door Company (Scotland) Ltd
Unit 7
Russell Road Industrial Estate
Russell Road
Edinburgh
EH11 2NN
Contact: Allan Macreath
Tel: 0131 337 3332
Email: sales@garage-door.co.uk
Website: www.garage-door.co.uk

- Business description: Installation, supply and repair of doors, gates, operators
- No. of franchise outlets: 9
- Year business started: 1977

- Start-up capital (minimum): £19,500
- Initial fee: £500
- Management fee: 6% of sales

Globalink
Globalink House
Honeybridge Lane
Dial Post
Horsham
West Sussex
RH13 8NX
Contact: Phil Gaffer
Tel: 0870 770 1616
Fax: 0870 770 1617
Email: info@globalinkgroup.com
Website: www.globalinkgroup.com

- Business description: Telecommunications
- Industry sector: IT & Communication
- BFA membership: Provisional list
- Franchise type: Management
- Minimum personal investment: N/A
- Minimum total investment: £ 20,000

In-toto Kitchens
Shaw Cross Court
Shaw Cross Business Park
Dewsbury
WF12 7RF
Contact: David Watts
Tel: 01924 487900
Email: info@intoto.co.uk
Website: www.intoto.co.uk

- Business description: Fitted kitchen retailer
- No. of franchise outlets: 30
- Year business started: 1979
- Start-up capital (minimum): £15,000
- Initial fee: £5000
- Management fee: Nil

Kendlebell Ltd
32 London Road
Guildford
Surrey
GU1 2AB

Tel: 0870 161 4144
Fax: 0870 161 4099
Website: www.kendlebell.com

- Business description: Telephone answering service for small businesses
- No. of franchise outlets: 8
- Year business started: 1997
- Start-up capital (minimum): £10,000
- Initial fee: £10,000
- Management fee: 10%

Keytracker Franchising Ltd
Keyper House
19 Whitehall Road
Halesowen
B63 3JR
Contact: Steve Reed
Tel: 0121 585 0123
Email: franchising@keytracker.com
Website: www.keytracker.com

- Business description: Key, lock or valuable item tracking system business
- No. of franchise outlets: 6
- Year business started: 1997
- Start-up capital (minimum): £12,000
- Initial fee: £9750
- Management fee: Nil

Martin & Co
23 Hinton Road
Bournemouth
Dorset
BH1 2EF
Tel: 01202 201221
Fax: 01202 201325
Website: www.martinco.com

- Business description: Residential lettings and management
- No. of franchise outlets: 21
- Year business started: 1986
- Start-up capital (minimum): Variable
- Initial fee: £6900 + VAT
- Management fee: 9% of gross income

MollyMaid
Bishop House South
The Bishop Centre
Bath Road
Taplow
Maidenhead
SL6 0NY
Contact: Pam Bader
Tel: 0800 500 950
Fax: 01628 663 700
Email: ukho@mollymaid.co.uk
Website: www.mollymaid.co.uk

- Business description: Domestic cleaning services
- Industry sector: Cleaning services
- BFA membership: Full member
- Franchise type: Management
- Minimum personal investment: £7,800
- Minimum total investment: £17,800

O'Briens Irish Sandwich Bar
11–14 Bond Court
Leeds
West Yorkshire
LS1 2JZ
Tel: 0113 2470444
Fax: 0113 2470555
Website: www.obriensonline.com

- Business description: Upmarket sandwich bars
- No. of franchise outlets: 35
- Year business started: 1988
- Start-up capital (minimum): £40,000–£100,000
- Initial fee: £9000 + VAT
- Management fee: 6% of net turnover

Oscar Petfoods
Bannister Hall Mill
Higher Walton
Preston
PR5 4DB
Contacts: Martin Dancy; Janet Walmsley
Tel: 01772 647909

Fax: 01772 647939
Email: discover@oscars.co.uk
Website: www.oscars.co.uk

- Business description: Pet food delivery and pet care service
- No of franchise outlets: 140
- Year business started: 1990
- Start-up capital (minimum): £4000–8000
- Initial fee: £6,000–15,000
- Management fee: £75 per month

Paint Technik Ltd
PO Box 5066
Leighton Buzzard
LU7 7YS
Contact: Stephen Wood
Tel: 01525 373777
Fax: 01525 373877
Email: painttechnikk@dial.pipex.com
Website: http://dscpace.dial.pipex.com/town/place/rceio

- Business description: Mobile automotive refinishing, smart repairs
- No. of franchise outlets: 90
- Year business started: 1990
- Start-up capital (minimum): £20,000
- Initial fee: £14,995
- Management fee: £1000 p.a.

PlumbLocal
Melville House
High St
Dunmow
Essex
CM6 1AF
Contact: Steve Baker
Tel: 0800 781 4922
Fax: 0845 090 8823
Email: franchises@plumblocal.co.uk
Website: www.plumblocal.co.uk/franchises/index.html

- Business description: Domestic and commercial plumbing service

- Industry sector: Property emergency
- BFA membership: Associate
- Franchise type: Single operator manual
- Minimum personal investment: £10,000
- Minimum total investment: £21,500

Practical Car & Van Rental
21–23 Little Broom Street
Camp Hill
Birmingham
B12 0EU
Contact: B. Agnew
Tel: 0121 772 8599
Fax: 0121 766 6229
Website: www.practical.co.uk

- Business description: Car and van rental
- No. of franchise outlets: 190
- Year business started: 1984
- Start-up capital (minimum): £6000
- Initial fee: From £5000
- Management fee: TBA

Rainbow International
Spectrum House
Lower Oakham Way
Oakham Business Park
Mansfield
NG18 5BY
Contact: Ian Hadley
Tel: 01623 675100
Fax: 01623 422466
Email: info@rainbow.licomnet.com
Website: www.rainbowintl.co.uk

- Business description: Carpet and upholstery cleaning, part of Dwyer Group, Texas
- No. of franchise outlets: 70
- Year business started: UK 1988
- Start-up capital (minimum): £10,000
- Initial fee: £21,000
- Management fee: 9% of gross turnover

Ribbon Revival Ltd
Caslon Court
Pitronnerie Road

St Peter Port
Guernsey
GY1 2RW
Contact: Mick Underdown
Tel: 01481 729552
Email: ribbonrev@post.guernsey.net
Website: www.ribbonrevival.net

- Business description: Desktop printers – sales, servicing, consumables
- No. of franchise outlets: 45
- Year business started: 1993 (UK)
- Start-up capital (minimum): £20,000
- Initial fee: Varies with territory
- Management fee: 9%

Ripples Ltd

PO Box 136, Kingswood
Bristol
Avon
BS30 6YE
Contact: Roger Kymo
Tel: 0117 932 4613
Fax: 0117 932 4475
Email: enquiries@ripples.ltd.uk
Website: www.ripples.ltd.uk

- Business description: Top range retail bathrooms
- No. of franchise outlets: 10
- Year business started: 1988 (UK)
- Start-up capital (minimum): £15,000
- Initial fee: £15,000
- Management fee: 5%

Riverford Organic Vegetables

Wash Barn
Buckfastleigh
Devon
TQ11 0LD
Contact: Martin Swarbrick
Tel: 01803 762720
Fax: 01803 762718
Email: franchise@riverford.co.uk
Website: www.riverford.co.uk

- Business description: Fresh organic produce direct to your door
- Industry sector: Organic Food/Drink Distribution
- BFA membership: Full member
- Franchise type: Single operator manual
- Minimum personal investment: £12,500
- Minimum total investment: £22,000

Rosemary Conley Diet & Fitness Clubs

Quorn House
Meeting Street
Quorn
Loughborough
LE12 8EX
Contact: Heather Shaw
Tel: 01509 620222
Email: rcdf@the-rosemary-conley-group.co.uk
Website: www.the-rosemary-conley-group.co.uk

- Business description: Health and beauty clubs
- No. of franchise outlets: 175
- Year business started: 1993 (UK)
- Start-up capital (minimum): £15,000
- Initial fee: £12,800
- Management fee: £11 per class, per week

Stainbusters

15 Windmill Avenue
Woolpit Business Park
Bury St Edmunds
IP30 9UP
Contact: Lorrie Finlay
Tel: 0800 783 4721
Email: franchise@stainbusters.co.uk
Website: www.stainbusters.com

- Business description: Carpet and furnishing dry cleaning
- No. of franchise outlets: 37
- Year business started: 1994
- Start-up capital (minimum): £5500
- Initial fee: £9950
- Management fee: 10% (+ 2.5% advertising levy)

TaxAssist Direct Ltd
112–114 Thorpe Road
112/114 Thorpe Road
Norwich
Norfolk
NR1 1RT
UK
Tel: 01603 447402
Fax: 01603 619992
Website: www.taxassistdirect.info

- Business description: Accountancy and financial assistance to small businesses
- No. of franchise outlets: 54
- Year business started: 1995
- Start-up capital (minimum): £15,000
- Initial fee: £11,750
- Management fee: 9%

Techclean Services
VDU House
Old Kiln Lane
Churt
Farnham
GU10 2JH
Contact: D. Cooper
Tel: 01428 713713; 0800 281940
Fax: 01428 713798
Email: techclean@easynet.co.uk
Website: www.techclean.com.uk

- Business description: Cleaning of hi-tech equipment
- No. of franchise outlets: 52 UK, 20 overseas
- Year business started: 1987
- Start-up capital (minimum): £10,000
- Initial fee: £13,500
- Management fee: 15% of turnover

Tongue Tied Ltd
Savan House
49 Goldstone Villas
Hove
BN3 3RT
Contact: John Shouler
Tel: 01273 723988

Email: sales@tongue-tied.co.uk
Website: www.tongue-tied.co.uk

- Business description: Translation and interpreting services
- No. of franchise outlets: 5
- Year business started: 1989; 1997 (UK)
- Start-up capital (minimum): £5000
- Initial fee: £6995
- Management fee: Nil

Ventrolla Ltd
11 Hornbeam Square South
South Harrogate
HG2 8NB
Contact: Lesley Spence
Tel: 01423 859323
Fax: 01423 859321
Email: info@ventrolla.co.uk
Website: www.ventrolla.co.uk

- Business description: Sash window renovation specialists
- No. of franchise outlets: 17
- Year business started: 1985
- Start-up capital (minimum): £15,000
- Initial fee: £15,500
- Management fee: 10% of sales

Over £25,000 start-up capital required
247
Granby Chambers
1 Halford St
Leicester
LE1 1JA
Contact: Les Armitage
Tel: 0845 225 5025
Fax: 07043 301684
Website: www.247staff.net/franchise

- Industry sector: Employment/Training
- BFA membership: Provisional list
- Franchise type: Single operator exec
- Minimum personal investment: £12,000
- Minimum Total Investment: £40,000

Action Bikes plc
3–5 St John's Road
Isleworth
TW7 6NA
Contact: Ian Johnstone
Tel: 020 8560 9494
Fax: 020 8758 9368
Website: www.action-bikes.com

- Business description: Franchise cycle shops
- No. of franchise outlets: 50
- Year business started: 1991, from a core family business established in the 1930s
- Start-up capital (minimum): £59,500
- Initial fee: £9500
- Management fee: 6% + 1.5% advertising/marketing

Alphagraphics
Thornburgh Road
Eastfield
Scarborough
YO11 3UY
Contact: Andrew Dalton
Tel: 01723 502222
Fax: 01723 502368
Email: a.dalton@alphagraphics.co.uk
Website: www.alphagraphics.co.uk

- Business description: Design, copy, print bureau
- No. of franchise outlets: 14
- Year business started: 1988
- Start-up capital (minimum): £50,000
- Initial fee: £24,000
- Management fee: Royalties on sales, sliding scale 10%, 7%, 5%

Aquaid Franchising Ltd
51 Newnham Road
Cambridge
CB3 9EY
Contact: Paul Searle
Tel: 01223 508109
Website: www.aquaid.co.uk

- Business description: Providing water coolers and water to businesses
- No. of franchise outlets: 7
- Year business started: 1999
- Start-up capital (minimum): £50,000
- Initial fee: £8000
- Management fee: 10%

AutoShine Express
Whitburn Rd
Birniehill
Bathgate
West Lothian
EH48 2HR
Contact: Andrew Stephenson
Tel: 01506 650 959
Fax: 01506 634 968
Email: info@autoshine-express.co.uk
Website: www.autoshine-express.co.uk

- Business description: Vehicle wash and car care centre
- Industry sector: Auto cleaning
- BFA membership: Provisional list
- Franchise type: Management
- Minimum personal investment: £30,000
- Minimum total investment: £60,000

Business Post Ltd
Nepshald Lane South
Gildersome
Leeds
Yorkshire
LS27 7JQ
Contact: Michelle Recardo
Tel: 01133 074834
Fax: 01133 074831
Email: michelle.recardo@business-post.com
Website: www.businesspost.biz

- Business description: UK and worldwide delivery of mail and parcels. Business Post is one of the largest independent UK parcel and express mail delivery companies
- No. of franchise outlets: 41
- Year business started: 1971

- Start-up capital (minimum): £100,000–250,000
- Initial fee: £15,000 + VAT and business base fee
- Management fee: £100,000–250,000

Card Connection Ltd
Park House
South Street
Farnham
GU9 7QQ
Contact: Tony Winchester
Tel: 01252 892323
Fax: 01252 892338
Email: ho@card-connections.co.uk
Website: www.card-connections.co.uk

- Business description: Distribution of greeting cards
- No. of franchise outlets: 80
- Year business started: 1992
- Start-up capital (minimum): £25,000
- Initial fee: £15,000
- Management fee: Nil

Cash Generator Ltd
63/74 Oakhill Trading Estate
Worsley Road North,
Walkden
Manchester
M28 3PT
Contact: Brian Lewis
Tel: 01204 574444
Fax: 01204 577711
Email: info@cash.generator.thruthe.net
Website: www.cashgenerator.net

- Business description: Buying goods from the public for instant cash, selling pre-used items and discounted new products with no-quibble guarantees, instant cash raising and cheque cashing services
- No. of franchise outlets: 22
- Year business started: 1994
- Start-up capital (minimum): £85,000
- Initial fee: £7950

- Management fee: 5.5% of turnover

County Homesearch International plc
The Sight Centre
Newham Quay
Truro
TR1 2DP
Contact: Jonathan A. Haward
Tel: 01872 223349
Email: headoffice@county-homesearch.co.uk
Website: www.county-homesearch.co.uk

- Business description: Providers of a bespoke home finding service
- No. of franchise outlets: 25
- Year business started: 1991
- Start-up capital (minimum): £25,000
- Initial fee: £15,000
- Management fee: 7.5%

Driver Hire Group Services Ltd
Progress House
Castlefields Lane
Bingley
BD16 2AB
Contact: Alan Cawthorne
Tel: 01274 551166
Email: info@ driver-hire.co.uk
Website: www.driver-hire.co.uk

- Business description: Specialist employment agency (drivers)
- No. of franchise outlets: 78
- Year business started: 1983
- Start-up capital (minimum): £25,000 + working capital
- Initial fee: £15,000
- Management fee: 5% management, 2% administration, 1% advertising

Direct Workwear
9 Beacon Ave
Quorn
Leicestershire
LE12 8EW

Contact: Paul Venn
Tel: 0845 351 9969
Website: www.directworkwear.co.uk

- Business description: Personal protective clothing and equipment
- Industry sector: Workwear
- BFA membership: Provisional list
- Franchise type: Single operator manual
- Minimum personal investment: £14,000
- Minimum total investment: £32,000

DP Furniture Express
Colima Avenue
Sunderland Enterprise Park
Sunderland
Tyne & Wear
SR5 3XF
Contact: Allan Mitchell
Tel: 0191 516 2600
Fax: 0191 516 9528
Website: www.dp-fx.com

- Business description: Specialist pine furniture retail outlets
- Industry sector: Furniture shops
- BFA membership: Full member
- Franchise type: Retail
- Minimum personal investment: £70,000
- Minimum total investment: £125,000

Durham Pine Ltd
Colima Avenue
Hylton Riverside
Sunderland
SR5 3XF
Contact: Rita Ferenson
Tel: 0191 516 9300
Email: les@durhampine.com
Website: www.durhampine.com

- Business description: Pine furniture retailer
- No. of franchise outlets: 37
- Year business started: 1986
- Start-up capital (minimum): £45,000
- Initial fee: £10,000

- Management fee: 5% of monthly takings

Energie Fitness Clubs
Blusky House
13 Britten Grove
Old Farm Park
Milton Keynes
MK7 8PP
Contact: Jonathan Holden
Tel: 01908 646984
Fax: 01908 270498
Website: www.energiefitnessclubs.com

- Business description: Fitness clubs
- Industry sector: Fitness & Weight
- BFA membership: Provisional list
- Franchise type: Retail
- Minimum personal investment: £35,000
- Minimum total investment: £100,000

Fast Food Systems Ltd (T/A Southern Fried Chicken)
Unit 1 Headley Park
9 Headley Road
East Woodley
Reading
RG5 4SQ
Contact: A.J. Withers
Tel: 01189 441100
Email: sales@fast-food-system.co.uk
Website: www.southern-fried-chicken.com

- Business description: Fried chicken sales retailer
- No. of franchise outlets: 650
- Year business started: 1980
- Start-up capital (minimum): £65,000
- Initial fee: Nil
- Management fee: Nil

The Food Weighouse Ltd
4 Walkerville Industrial Park
Catterick
DL9 4SA
Contact: Richard Russell
Tel: 01748 834646

Email: info@thefoodweighouse.co.uk
Website: www.thefoodweighouse.co.uk

- Business description: Loose food retailing
- No. of franchise outlets: 31, plus 23 company shops
- Year business started: 1988
- Start-up capital (minimum): £35,000
- Initial fee: £3000
- Management fee: Nil

Greencare Ltd
Greencare House
Sharpness
GL13 9UD
Contacts: Malcolm Macleod; Rebecca Lee
Tel: 01453 511366
Email: sales@greencare.co.uk
Website: www.greencare.co.uk

- Business description: Recycling service provider to businesses
- No. of franchise outlets: 25
- Year business started: 1993
- Start-up capital (minimum): £25,000
- Initial fee: £10,000
- Management fee: Nil

Hudson's Coffee Houses
Kyros Business Services Ltd
Wassell Grove Business Centre
Wassell Grove Lane
Stourbridge
DY9 9JH
Contact: Rita Ferguson
Tel: 08701 044233
Fax: 08701 044234
Website: www.hudsonsfood.com

- Business description: Gourmet Coffee House & Food Shop
- Industry Sector: Restaurants
- BFA membership: Provisional list
- Franchise type: Retail
- Minimum personal investment: £30,000

- Minimum total investment: £85,000

Initial City Link Ltd
Wellington House
61/73 Staines Road West
Sunbury-on-Thames
TW16 5LR
Tel: 01932 822622
Fax: 01932 785560
Website: www.city-link.co.uk

- Business description: Parcel delivery
- No. of franchise outlets: 70
- Year business started: 1969
- Start-up capital (minimum): £25,000
- Initial fee: Variable
- Management fee: 10%

Kall Kwik Printing (UK) Ltd
Kall Kwik House
106 Pembroke Road
Ruislip
HA4 8NW
Contact: Janet Twining
Tel: 01895 872000
Email: franchise.sales@kallkwik.co.uk
Website: www.kallkwik.co.uk

- Business description: Print, copy and design
- No. of franchise outlets: 187
- Year business started: 1978
- Start-up capital (minimum): £135,000
- Initial fee: £4500
- Management fee: 10%

McDonald's Restaurants Ltd
Franchising Department
3 Cross Lane
Salford
Manchester
M5 4BN
Tel: 0161 253 4116
Fax: 0161 253 4184
Website: www.mcdonalds.co.uk

- Business description: Quick service restaurant
- No. of franchise outlets: 245
- Year business started: 1974
- Start-up capital (minimum): £35,000
- Initial fee: £30,000
- Management fee: Nil

Metro-Rod plc
Vale House
100 Vale Road
Windsor
Berkshire
SL4 5JL
Contact: Charles Sindall
Tel: 01753 829 400
Email: wendy.ayres@thameswater.co.uk
Website: www.metrorod.co.uk

- Business description: Drain care and repair
- No. of franchise outlets: 40
- Year business started: 1983
- Start-up capital (minimum): £45,000
- Initial fee: £15,000
- Management fee: 25%

Mr Cod Ltd
6–7 High Street
Woking
GU21 1BG
Contact: J.A. Brewer
Tel: 01438 755407

- Business description: Fast food takeaway/restaurant selling fish and chips and American fried chicken
- No. of franchise outlets: 8
- Year business started: 1980
- Start-up capital (minimum): £35,000–75,000
- Initial fee: Variable

Nevada Bob Ltd
The Rotunda
Broadgate Circle
London
EC2M 2BN
Contact: Phil Smith

Tel: 020 7628 4999
Email: mitch@nevadabob.co.uk
Website: www.nevadabobsgolf.co.uk

- Business description: Golf retail
- No. of franchise outlets: 39
- Year business started: 1990
- Start-up capital (minimum): £160,000
- Initial fee: £47,500
- Management fee: 3% royalty

PAPERfix
Unit 1
Elmfield Business Park
Lotherton Way
Garforth
Leeds
LS25 2JY
Contact: Ted Girtchen
Tel: 0845 6017376
Fax: 0845 6018536
Website: www.paperfix.co.uk

- Business description: Servicing and sales of binders, laminators and paper handling equipment
- Industry sector: Business svcs/equip
- BFA membership: Provisional list
- Franchise type: Single operator manual
- Minimum personal investment: £13,000
- Minimum total investment: £25,570

PDC Copyprint
1 Church Lane
East Grinstead
RH19 3AZ
Contact: Stephen Ricketts
Tel: 01342 315321
Email: pdc@pdc-intl.demon.co.uk
Website: www.pdccopyprint.co.uk

- Business description: High Street business printers (print, design, copying)
- No. of franchise outlets: 35
- Year business started: 1982

- Start-up capital (minimum): £37,000 (total £111,000)
- Initial fee: £6500
- Management fee: 10% reducing to 5%

Pitman Training Group plc
Pitman House
Audby Lane
Wetherby
LS22 7FD
Contact: James O'Brien
Tel: 01937 548562
Fax: 01937 584575
Email: franchising-opportunities@pitman-train-ing.com
Website: www.pitman-training.co.uk

- Business description: Computer training and education training centres
- No. of franchise outlets: 80
- Year business started: 1992
- Start-up capital (minimum): £50,000
- Initial fee: £25
- Management fee: Nil

Pitman Training Group
Sandown Lane
Sandbeck Way
Wetherby
West Yorkshire
LS22 7DN
Contact: Mike Cressey
Tel: 01937–548 562
Fax: 01937–586 761
Website: www.pitman-training.com

- Business description: IT training centres
- Industry sector: Employment/Training
- BFA membership: Full member
- Franchise type: Management
- Minimum personal investment: £20,000
- Minimum total investment: £50,000

Prontaprint Ltd
106 Pembroke Road,

Ruislip
Middlesex
HA4 8NW
Contact: Julian Minwalla
Tel: 01895 872000
Fax: 01895 872110
Email: franchiseseales@prontaprint.com
Website: www.prontaprint.com

- Business description: Franchise, print, copy, design and communication services
- No. of franchise outlets: 245
- Year business started: 1972
- Start-up capital (minimum): £35,000
- Initial fee: £12,500 + VAT
- Management fee: 10% of turnover

Pizza Hut
Enterprising Futures Ltd
500 Chiswick High Rd
London
W4 9RG
Contact: Franchise team
Tel: 0870 241 0697
Website: www.pizzahut.co.uk

- Business description: Pizza delivery, take-away outlets
- Industry sector: Fast food
- BFA membership: Provisional list
- Franchise type: Retail
- Minimum personal investment: £50,000
- Minimum total investment: £135,000

Recognition Express Ltd
Wheatfield Way
Hinckley Fields
Hinckley
Leicestershire
LE10 1YG
Contact: Ian Taylor
Tel: 01455 445555
Fax: 01455 445576
Email: post@recognition.co.uk
Website: www.recognition-express.com/franchise

- Business description: Business-to-business services
- No. of franchise outlets: 26
- Year business started: UK 1979
- Start-up capital (minimum): £50,000
- Initial fee: £10,000
- Management fee: 10%

Safeclean
152 Milton Park
Abingdon
OX14 4SD
Contact: M. Graham
Tel: 01235 833009
Email: safeclean@valspar.com
Website: www.safeclean.co.uk

- Business description: Furnishing care specialists
- No. of franchise outlets: 70
- Year business started: 1971
- Start-up capital (minimum): £25,000
- Initial fee: £15,950 + VAT
- Management fee: 10% of gross turnover

Scenic Blue
The Plant Centre
Brogdale Road
Faversham
Kent
ME13 8XZ
Contact:Tony Mundella
Tel: 01795 533 266
Fax: 01795 591 059
Website: www.scenicblue.co.uk

- Industry sector: Garden/Landscaping
- BFA membership: Associate
- Franchise type: Management
- Minimum personal investment: £12,000
- Minimum total investment: £40,000

Select Appointments Plc
Regent Court, Laporte Way

Luton
Bedfordshire
LU4 85B
Contact: Lorraine Ratcliffe
Tel: 01582 811600
Fax: 01582 811611
Website: www.select.co.uk/franchise

- Business description: Recruitment services
- No. of franchise outlets: 11
- Year business started: 1980 (franchised 1994)
- Start-up capital £25,000 (total investment £90,000)
- Initial fee: £12,500
- Management fee: 7% of gross turnover

Sevenoaks Video & Vision
111 London Road
Sevenoaks
TN13 1BH
Contact: Malcolm Blockley
Tel: 01494 431290
Fax: 01494 431460
Email: peterborough@sevenoakssoundandvision.com
Website: www.sevenoakshifi-peterborough.co.uk

- Business description: Specialist retailers of hi-fi, video, home cinema
- No. of franchise outlets: 22
- Year business started: 1972
- Start-up capital (minimum): £75,000
- Initial fee: £10,000
- Management fee: 5% of turnover

Sign a Rama
7 Herald Business Park
Golden Acres Lane
Coventry
CV3 2SY
Contact: Martyn Ward
Tel: 02476 659 933
Fax: 02476 659 944
Website: www.sign-a-rama.com

- Business description: Full service sign centres
- Industry sector: Signs
- BFA membership: Associate
- Franchise type: Retail
- Minimum personal investment: £30,000
- Minimum total investment: £80,000

Signs Express Ltd
The Old Church
St Matthews Road
Norwich
NR1 1SP
Contact: Jan Corbett
Tel: 01603 625925
Email: fran@signsexpress.co.uk
Website: signsexpress.co.uk

- Business description: Sign services
- No. of franchise outlets: 65
- Year business started: 1989
- Start-up capital: £72,000
- Initial fee: £16,500
- Management fee: 7.5% of gross turnover

Snappy Snaps
10–12 Glenthorne Mews
Hammersmith
London
W6 0LJ
Contact: Hugh Jones
Tel: 020 8742 7474
Email: info@snappysnaps.co.uk
Website: www.snappysnaps.co.uk

- Business description: Photo processing
- No. of franchise outlets: 67
- Year business started: 1983
- Start-up capital (minimum): £30,000
- Initial fee: £12,500
- Management fee: 6%

Thrifty Car Rental
The Old Court House
Hughendon Road
High Wycombe
HP13 5DT

Contact: Graham Bullock
Tel: 01494 474767
Fax: 01494 474732
Email: flightfm@thrifty.co.uk
Website: www.thrifty.co.uk

- Business description: Car and van rental
- No. of franchise outlets: 68
- Year business started: 1990
- Start-up capital (minimum): £80,000
- Initial fee: £17,500 + VAT
- Management fee: 5%

Travail Employment Group Ltd
24 Southgate Street
Gloucester
GL1 2DP
Contact: Steve Mills
Tel: 01452 420700
Website: www.travail.co.uk

- Business description: Temporary and permanent recruitment services
- No. of franchise outlets: 40
- Year business started: 1977
- Start-up capital (minimum): £65,000
- Initial fee: £10,000
- Management fee: 7.25% of sales

Tumble Tots (UK) Ltd
Blue Bird Park
Bromsgrove Road
Hunnington
Halesowen
B62 0TT
Contact: David Hunt
Tel: 0121 585 7003
Fax: 0121 585 6891
Email: tumbletots.uk@btinternet.com.
Website: www.tumbletots.com

- Business description: Active physical play for pre-school children
- No. of franchise outlets: 80
- Year business started: 1979

- Start-up capital (minimum): Circa £25,500 to include working capital and vehicle
- Initial fee: £5800 (licence fee for two years)
- Management fee: Licence is then renewed annually and an annual fee is payable

Urban Planters
202 Pasture Lane
Bradford
BD7 2SE
Contact: Nick Gresty
Tel: 01274 579331
Email: anything@urbanplanters.co.uk
Website: www.urbanplanters.co.uk

- Business description: Rental and maintenance of indoor plants
- No. of franchise outlets: 8
- Year business started: 1965
- Start-up capital (minimum): £50,000 (includes £20,000 working capital)
- Initial fee: £12,000
- Management fee: 7.5% of sales invoiced

VIP Bin Cleaning Ltd
The Coach House
Commercial Road
Dereham
Norfolk
NR19 1AE
Contact: Mark Harvey
Tel: 01362 851185
Email: vipbin@globalnet.co.uk
Website: www.lds.co.uk/franchise/vip

- Business description: Wheelie-bin cleaning
- No. of franchise outlets: 40
- Year business started: 1995
- Start-up capital (minimum): £10,500
- Initial fee: £7500
- Management fee: £75 per week
- Proportion of start-up capital that can be arranged: Approx. 70%

Wiltshire Farm Foods
Apetito Ltd
Canal Rd
Trowbridge
BA14 8RJ
Contact: Ben Haynes
Tel: 01225 756 015
Fax: 01225 756 069
Email: ben.haynes@apetito.co.uk
Website: www.wiltshirefarmfoods.com

- Business description: Private home meals delivery
- Industry sector: Home delivery
- BFA membership: Full member
- Franchise type: Single operator manual
- Minimum personal investment: £50,000
- Minimum total investment: £50,000

Websites with UK franchise opportunities listed

- www.businessfranchise.com
- www.business-opportunities.net
- www.franchisebusiness.co.uk
- www.franchisecompany.co.uk
- www.franchisedirect.co.uk
- www.franchise-group.com
- www.franchisesolutions.com
- www.startups.co.uk
- www.whichfranchise.com

Is the business right for you?

One way to see if your business concept is likely work for you is to try to position your proposition in terms of risk (see Fig. 3.1).

As you can see, there are trade-offs. Doing something that has been around for years and everyone knows about may be easy, but may be too competitive to make much money. Better, or new and different, products aimed at existing and proven markets are usually good bets. However, if you are a high risk-taker, then aiming unproven

Product *Market*	Similar product/service	Better product/service	New and different product/service
Existing well established market	*No/No* *Price war*	*Yes/Yes* *Low risk*	*Yes* *Mod risk*
New but identified market	*Yes/Yes* *Low risk*	*Yes* *Moderate*	*?* *High risk/reward*
Unknown market yet to be created	*Yes* *Moderate risk*	*? High risk/reward*	*No/No* *Very high cost*

Fig. 3.1 New business start-ups, risk and the product/market position.

products into markets that don't yet exist might be the area to concentrate your search for opportunities. If these pay off they usually pay off well. But more often than not they fail. Most Internet-based ventures launched in the bubble era from 1998 to 2000 were of this nature.

Once you have decided on your attitude to risk, the following exercise might help your decision process.

Take a sheet of paper and draw up two columns. In the left-hand column, list all your hobbies, interests and skills. In the right-hand column, translate them into possible business ideas. Table 3.1 gives an example.

Table 3.1 Sample list: business ideas related to hobbies, interests and skills.

Interest/skills	Business ideas
Motor cars	Motor car dealer/repair garage/home tuning service
Restaurants	Restaurant/home catering service/bakery shop providing produce for freezer outlets
Gardening	Supplier of produce to flower or vegetable shop/running a nursery/running a garden centre/landscape design
Typing	Typing authors' manuscripts from home/typing back-up service for busy local companies/running a secretarial agency

Having done this exercise, you need to balance the possibilities against the criteria; which are most important to you? These might be: small amount of capital required; good anticipated profit; secure income; work satisfaction; no need to learn new skills; variety of work; the possibility of working hours that suit your lifestyle; opportunity to meet new people; minimal paperwork; opportunity to travel.

Select your criteria

You may have other criteria not on this list. Decide the most important criteria and place them in order of importance. Allocate each chosen criterion a weighting factor of between 1 and 5. Now list the possible business opportunities you have identified from the first exercise and measure them against the graded criteria.

A simple example: Jane Clark, an ex-secretary with school-age children needed work because her husband had been made redundant and was busy looking for another job. She wasn't in a position to raise much capital, and she wanted her hours to coincide with those of her children. She wanted to run her own show and she wanted to enjoy what she did. The criteria she selected are shown in Table 3.2.

Since minimal capital was a very important criterion for Jane she gave it a weighting factor of 5, whereas the opportunity to meet interesting people, being far less important to her, was only weighted 1.

Criteria	Weighting factor (out of 5)
Minimal capital required	5
Possibility of work hours that suit lifestyle	5
No need to learn new skills	4
Minimal paperwork	3
Work satisfaction	2
Opportunity to meet interesting people	1

Table 3.2   Sample weighting table.

Jane then gave each of her three business ideas a rating, in points (out of 5), against these criteria. A secretarial agency needed capital to start, so was given 1 point. Back-up typing needed hardly any money and was allocated 5 points. Her worked-out chart is shown in Table 3.3.

The weighting factor and the rating point multiplied together give a score for each business idea. The highest score indicates the business that best meets Jane's criteria. In this case, typing authors' manuscripts scored over back-up typing since Jane could do it exactly when it suited her.

Help and advice

Help with fundamental life decisions is not easy to come by. The basic economic decisions are not impossible. Judgement and arithmetic usually clear the field of the very worst ideas. Here is one organization that may be able to help you with evaluating business opportunities before you take the plunge.

Invest-Tech Limited
27 Ardmeen Park
Blackrock
Co. Dublin
Ireland
Tel: 00 353 1 283 4083
Fax: 00 353 1 278 2391
Email: info@planware.org
Website: www.planware.org

Invest-Tech have a free series of what they refer to as 'White Papers' that explain the issues surrounding starting up a business. One of those papers is 'Getting New Business Ideas'. The direct link is: www.planware.org/ideas.htm.

Needless to say, they have a range of more sophisticated software that they hope, once your appetite has been suitable whetted, you may be persuaded to buy

The package they have to help evaluate business ideas is entitled Quick Insight and costs $239 including delivery.

Table 3.3   Sample chart showing application of weightings to ideas.

Criteria	Weighting factor	Points score		
		Secretarial agency	Back-up typing	Authors' manuscripts
Minimal capital	5x	1 = 5	5 = 25	4 = 20
Flexible hours	5x	1 = 5	3 = 15	5 = 25
No new skills	4x	2 = 8	5 = 20	5 = 20
Work satisfaction	3x	4 = 12	1 = 3	3 = 9
Minimal paperwork	2x	0 = 0	4 = 8	5 = 10
Meeting people	1x	4 = 4	3 = 3	4 = 4
Total score		34	74	88

They claim that by taking just two hours with Quick Insight to find out if your bright business idea will really succeed in the market place, you will get a clear perspective of its potential before you invest more time and effort. The software also offers suggestions for improvement.

Quick Insight is interactive, and allows you to examine the underlying reasoning used to reach each of its conclusions. You can review how your input influenced the conclusion and, if desired, change your answer to see how the conclusion changes. When you are satisfied with the analysis you can create a printed report of about 50 pages. The report will include:

- a success potential rating of your product or service concept

- a written summary describing steps that might improve the success potential
- observations of inconsistencies and areas requiring attention.

A book that will be useful is:

- *Evaluating Business Opportunities: A No-Hype Approach for Choosing the Right Business for You* by Paul Edward Hadinger, Batesville THINC Corp., $20.00, 1997.

It has 22 chapters, all useful, but Chapter 2, which covers topics such as honest self-assessment, taking measure of yourself and the impact of personal health, should help you decide your priorities.

Section 4

EXPLOITING HIGH AND NOT SO HIGH TECHNOLOGY

Technology presents considerable opportunities to inventors and users alike. It also presents a number of problems. Inventors have difficulty in communicating their ideas to commercial organizations. These ideas are often a long way from being a recognizable product at the time when most help (financial or otherwise) is needed. A growing number of institutions, organizations and services now aim to provide just this understanding and assistance. On the other hand, there are many small businesses that could make considerable use of new technology, if only they knew how. The Internet, computers and mobile communications systems are just the most obvious developments, allowing tasks to be done quickly or more effectively, frequently leaving the entrepreneur free to perform more other tasks. The following material should give you an appreciation of the sort of help that is on hand to help innovators and inventors bring their wares to market.

Accelerators, incubators, innovation centres and science parks

Tempting though it might be to believe that business accelerators are an Internet phenomenon, incubators, science parks, innovation centres, technology parks and a whole variety of other names have been coined over the years to describe the task that accelerators perform, or rather, try to perform. The first serious attempt at incubation is credited to a near-derelict building near New York in 1959 and the name came into common usage more by way of a joke than as a serious description of the task in hand. One of the incubator's first tenants was involved in incubating real chickens. Several waves of accelerators followed this inauspicious start and by the 1980s several hundred such facilities were scattered around the US, Canada and Europe and Australia. Later incubator progressions took in the developing economies and the Internet variation, which came into being in the mid-1990s, swept across the US, Europe, India, China, Malaysia, Singapore, The Philippines and elsewhere, bringing the total to some 4000 facilities worldwide.

One particularly revealing statistic shows the split between 'private for profit' incubators and those more established incubators sponsored by the states and universities. In the US, of the 950 incubators, some 300 fall into the 'for profit' category. The rest of the world lays claim to 2500 incubators, but only the same number, 300, are in the 'for profit' category (see Fig. 4.1).

Varieties of accelerators and incubators now co-exist in the market, with radically different aims and objectives. Some, such as those founded by entrepreneurs and venture capital firms, the 'for profit' variety, only want to get rich by helping entrepreneurs to get rich. That goal at least has the merit of transparency. Some have revenue models that can make the incubator rich without necessarily benefiting anyone else that much. Governments and local governments are more concerned with job creation than wealth, and universities, another major player, want jobs for the students and funding for faculty research, rather than riches themselves. Big corporate firms run private incubators to encourage firms who might buy their

Incubator growth

Incubators by region/country

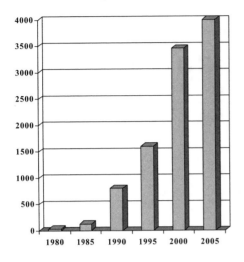
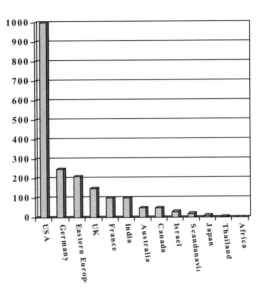

Fig. 4.1 The growth of the world incubator industry (source: author's estimates from various published sources).

products or services or create career opportunities for their more entrepreneurial and potentially less fickle employees.

These incubators are havens for entrepreneurs with innovative or technology-based business ideas that need more help than most to be brought to fruition. Such ventures usually have more potential than other business starters, but they are also more risky. No one knows how many entrepreneurs graduate from these incubators each year. But it's a reasonable supposition that each of the estimated 4000 incubators has two or three graduates each year. So 10,000 or so 'eggs' are hatched in a safe environment each year. That's not a big number in terms of business start-ups. Across Europe and the US, somewhere between 3 and 4 million new businesses get going in most years. But for the entrepreneurs, some of them at any rate, who get into an incubator, their chances of success are better than if they went it alone. There is not much conclusive evidence to show that the incubator sponsors have done so well.

How to get into an accelerator

There is almost invariably an application proc-

ess to getting into any business incubator. All that varies is the process itself. Some incubators positively invite and encourage the informal approach, some are highly structured, some have their own models and techniques that they believe can sort the wheat from the chaff. All the application processes take time and if it didn't you would have cause for concern. After all, if they take in anyone without any serious consideration as to what they can do to help their businesses, that particular incubation process is unlikely to be of much value. Most application processes require some sort of a business plan. It may be little more than an executive summary to be done online with your application. Or it may be a more comprehensive written document setting out your latest thinking on what is so special about you and your big idea. Then come the interview and, after that, the decision.

Most accelerators have details of their application process on their websites, as well as case examples of successful clients. Some have business plan application templates to help in the process. You can expect it to take anything from a couple of weeks to a couple of months to get through the process (see Fig. 4.2).

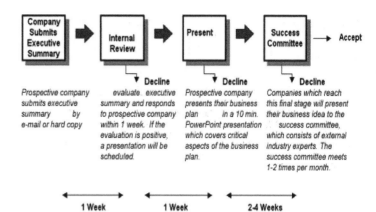

Fig. 4.2 Incubator acceptance time frame.

How much will incubation cost?

If you are just paying rent and paying for services as you use them as, say, in the Cranfield or St John's Innovation Centres, then the cost of being in an incubator is transparent. Such 'not-for-profit' incubators are usually aimed at non-business-educated people who have good ideas to create traditional small businesses, usually with little technology involved. These incubators are frequently government-funded, often located in underdeveloped cities and provide mentoring, business development and office space. The typical equity stake required ranges from none to nominal (some require CEOs to give back to the community).

But if giving an incubator an equity stake in your business is involved, as it surely will be in any 'for profit' incubator, then the cost can run the scale from a few per cent of the business to being an outrageously expensive 30–50%. It's not always clear that the more you pay, the more value you get. It depends on your business needs and the scale of the opportunity you want to exploit.

The directory below lists UK accelerators across the country. For the most part these are open to more or less any type of venture with either a technology, innovation or knowledge industry bias. In some cases, for example where 'bio' appears in the description, there may be a focus on a particular industry.

Directory of UK business accelerators, incubators and science parks

Aberdeen Science and Technology Park
27 Albyn Place
Aberdeen
AB10 1DB
Tel: 01224 252000
Fax: 01224 213417
Email: info@Scotent.co.uk
Website: www.astp.co.uk

Animal Health Technology Transfer Complex
University of Glasgow Veterinary School
Garscube Estate
Bearsden Road
Glasgow
G61 1QH
Tel: 0141 330 2690
Fax: 0141 942 7215
Email: info@vet.gla.ac.uk
Website: www.gla.ac.uk

AntFactory
Prospect House
80–100 New Oxford Street
London
WC1A 1HB
Tel: 020 7947 5000
Fax: 020 7947 5001
Email: uk@antfactory.com
Website: www.antfactory.com

Aston Science Park
Love Lane
Birmingham
B7 4BJ
Contact: Derek Harris (Chief Executive)
Tel: 0121 250 3502
Fax: 0121 250 3567
Email: info@astonsciencepark.co.uk
Website: www.astonsciencepark.co.uk

Babraham Bioincubator
Babraham Hall
Babraham
Cambridge
CB2 4AT
Tel: 01223 496205
Fax: 01223 496020
Email: info@babraham.co.uk
Website: www.bi.bbsrc.ac.uk

Bainlab
40 The Strand
London
WC2N 5HZ
Tel: 020 7848 9477
Fax: 020 7969 9498
Website: www.bainlab.com

Bangor Innovation & Technology Centre
c/o Snowdonia BIC
Llys y Fedwen
Parc Menai
Bangor
LL57 4BF
Tel: 01248 671101
Fax: 01248 671101
Email: info@Gwynedd.gov.uk

Barnsley Business and Innovation Centre Ltd
Innovation Way
Barnsley
S75 1JL
Tel: 01226 249590
Fax: 01226 249625
Email: info@bbic.co.uk
Website: www.bbic.co.uk

Basildon & Local District Enterprise Agency
Samson House
Arterial Road
Basildon
SS15 6DR
Tel: 01268 410400
Fax: 01268 543515
Email: basenterprise@lineone.net

BioAdventures
5 South Avenue
Clydebank Business Park
Clydebank
G81 2LG
Tel: 0141 951 3450
Fax: 0141 951 3451
Website: www.bioadventures.com

Bioincubator York Ltd
Innovation Centre
York Science Park
University of York
YO10 5DG
Tel: 01904 433 5251
Fax: 01904 433 5101
Email: inb@york.ac.uk
Website: www.york.ac.uk

Bioscience Centre
International Centre for Life
1st Floor
East Wing
Times Square
Scotswood Road
Newcastle upon Tyne
NE1 4EP
Tel: 0191 230 5440
Fax: 0191 230 5441
Email: general@centre-for-life.co.uk
Website: www.centre-for-life.co.uk

Bioscience Innovation Centre (Sittingbourne)
Sittingbourne Research Centre
Woodstock House
Winch Road
Sittingbourne

ME9 8AG
Tel: 01795 411500
Fax: 01795 411511
Email: info@bio-innovations.co.uk
Website: www.src-uk.com

Birmingham Research Park
Vincent Drive
Edgbaston
Birmingham
B15 2SQ
Tel: 0121 471 4988
Fax: 0121 472 5739
Email: BRPL@bham.ac.uk
Website: www.bham.ac.uk

Blythe Valley Innovation Centre
Property Services
University of Warwick Science Park
Barclays Venture Centre
Sir William Lyons Road
Coventry
CV4 7EZ
Tel: 024 76323003
Fax: 024 76323231
Email: info@uwsp.co.uk
Website: www.uwsp.co.uk

Bournemouth University Business Incubation Centre
Studland House
12 Christchurch Road
Bournemouth
BH1 3NA
Tel: 01202 595417
Fax: 01202 595314
Email: phogarth@bournemouth.ac.uk
Website: www.bournemouth.ac.uk

Brainspark PLC
The Lightwell
12–16 Laystall Street
London
EC1R 4PA
Tel: 020 7843 6600
Fax: 020 7843 6601

Email: info@brainspark.co.uk
Website: www.brainspark.co.uk

Brunel University Enterprise Centre
Uxbridge
UB8 3PH
Tel: 01895 239234
Fax: 01895 203099
Email: info@brunel.ac.uk
Website: www.brunel.ac.uk

BT Brightstar
Adastral Park
Martlesham Heath
Ipswich
IP5 3RE
Tel: 01473 647434
Fax: 01473 648707
Email: info@btbrightstar.com
Website: www.btbrightstar.com

Campus Ventures
University of Manchester
Oxford Road
Manchester
M13 9PL
Tel: 0161 273 5110
Fax: 0161 273 5111
Email: info@campus-ventures.co.uk
Website: www.campus-ventures.co.uk

Cardiff Business Technology Centre
Senghennydd Road
Cathays
Cardiff
CF24 4AY
Contact: Eileen Turner (Centre Administrator)
Tel: 029 20647000
Fax: 029 20647009
Email: enquiries@cbtc.co.uk
Website: www.cbtc.co.uk

Carrington Business Park Ltd
Carrington
Manchester
M31 4DD

Tel: 0161 776 4000
Fax: 0161 775 8995
Email: info@cbpk.com
Website: www.cbpk.com

Centre for Advanced Industry
NEMI
Royal Quays
North Shields
NE29 6DE
Tel: 0191 293 7000
Fax: 0191 293 7001
Email: jrw@nemi-cai.co.uk
Website: www.nemi-cai.co.uk

Challenge Enterprise Centre
Sharps Close
Portsmouth
PO3 5RJ
Tel: 02392 651701
Fax: 02392 651801

Cherwell Innovation Centre
77 Heyford Park
Upper Heyford
Bicester
OX6 3HD
Tel: 01869 238000
Fax: 01869 238001
Email: info@oxin.co.uk
Website: http://www.oxin.co.uk

Chilworth Business Incubator
Chilworth Science Park
Southampton
SO16 7JF
Contact: Don Fox
Tel: 02380 767420
Fax: 02380 766190
Email: cclcml@aol.com; d.fox@csp-ltd.com
Website: www.chilworthsciencepark.com

Chrysalis Project
Institute for Enterprise (UNIEI)
Business School
University of Nottingham

Jubilee Campus
Wollaton Road
NG8 1BB
Tel: 0115 846 6609
Fax: 0115 846 6650
Email: info@nottingham.ac.uk
Website: www.nottingham.ac.uk

CIRCE Ltd
Wheldon Road
Castleford
WF10 2JT
Tel: 01977 712712
Fax: 01977 712713
Email: info@circe.co.uk
Website: www.circe.co.uk

CMGI
Sygnus Court
Market Street
Maidenhead
SL6 8AD
Tel: 01628 588504
Fax: 01628 588519
Email: info@cmgi.co.uk
Website: www.cmgi.com

Coach House Small Business Centre
2 Upper York Street
Bristol
BS2 8QN
Tel: 0117 944 5530
Fax: 0117 944 56661
Email: admin@brave.org.uk
Website: www.brave.org.uk

Cobweb Incubator Ltd
8 The Coles Shop
Merton Abbey Mills
London
SW19 2RD
Tel: 020 543 9390
Fax: 020 543 8748
Email: info@pmpe.co.uk

Cornwall Science Park
South West Investment Group
Trevint House
Strangways Villas
Truro
TR1 2PA
Tel: 01872 223883
Fax: 01872 242470
Email: swigservicesltd@btinternet.com

Coventry University Technology Park
The Technology Centre
Puma Way
Coventry
CV1 2TT
Contact: Sharon Simkiss
Tel: 024 76838140; 024 76838145
Fax: 024 76221396
Email: info@coventry.ac.uk

Cranfield Innovation Centre
University Way
Cranfield Technology Park
Cranfield
MK43 0BT
Tel: 01234 756000
Fax: 01234 752514
Website: www.cranfield.org

DDL Internet Incubator
Dawnay Day Lander Ltd
9–11 Grosvenor Gardens
London
SW1W 0BD
Tel: 020 7979 7575
Fax: 020 7979 7585
Email: info@d21.com
Website: www.d21.com

Derwentside Business Development Complex
Consett Business Park
Villa Real
Consett
DH8 6BP
Tel: 01207 218239
Fax: 01207 218300

Email: info@derwentside.org.uk
Website: www.derwentside.org.uk

Doncaster Business Innovation Centre
Barnsley & Doncaster TEC
Innovation Way
Barnsley
S75 1JL
Tel: 01226 248088
Fax: 01226 291625
Email: info@bdtec.co.uk
Website: www.bdtec.co.uk

Dundee Incubator Co Ltd
Technopole House
PO Box 6932
Dundee
DD2 5YE
Tel: 01382 360226
Fax: 01382 360226
Email: info@dundeeincubator.co.uk
Website: www.dundeeincubator.co.uk

Edinburgh Technology Transfer Centre
Kings Buildings
Mayfield Road
Edinburgh
EH9 3JL
Tel: 0131 472 4700
Fax: 0131 662 4678
Email: info@ed.ac.uk

Farnborough Innovation Centre
DEM-Room 101
X92 Building
DERA
Farnborough
GU14 0RX
Tel: 01252 550000
Fax: 01252 550001

Flintstone Technologies plc
8–10 Malew Street
Castletown
Isle of Man
IM9 1AB

Tel: 01624 825472
Fax: 01624 825660
Email: info@flintstone.com
Website: www.flintstone.com

Foundation for Entrepreneurial Management
London Business School
Sussex Place
Regents Park
London
NW1 4SA
Tel: 020 7262 5050
Fax: 020 7724 7875
Email: info@lbs.ac.uk
Website: www.lbs.ac.uk

Framlingham Technology Centre
Station Road
Framlingham
Woodbridge
Suffolk
IP3 9EE
Tel: 01728 727003
Fax: 01728 724318
Email: info@minima.co.uk
Website: www.framtec.com

Generics Group AG
Harston Mill
Harston
Cambridge
CB2 5NH
Tel: 01223 875200
Fax: 01223 875201
Website: www.generics.co.uk

Gloucestershire Innovation Centre Ltd
Southgate House
Southgate Street
Gloucester
GL1 1UD
Tel: 01452 553000
Fax: 01452 563016
Email: Info32@innovation-centre.org.uk
Website: www.innovation-centre.org.uk

GorillaPark
42–46 Princelet Street
London
E1 5LP
Tel: 020 7920 2500
Fax: 020 7920 2501
Email: info@gorillapark.com
Website: www.gorillapark.com

Greenwich Business Innovation Centre
16 Warren Lane
Woolwich
London
SE18 6BW
Tel/Fax: 020 8854 2511

Harefield Mediparc
Trafalgar House Property Ltd
10 Bedford Street
London
WC2E 9HE
Tel: 020 7648 5600
Fax: 020 7648 5606

Harris Knowledge Park
Adelphi Building
University of Central Lancashire
Preston
PR1 2HE
Tel: 0800 195 0055
Fax: 01772 892994
Email: info@uclan.ac.uk
Website: www.ulcan.ac.uk/hkp

Hillington Park Innovation Centre
1 Ainslie Road
Hillington Park
Glasgow
G52 1RU
Tel: 0141 585 6300
Fax: 0141 585 6301
Email: info@innovationcentre.org
Website: www.innovationcentre.org

Himalaya UK
1 Kemp House

152–160 City Road
London
EC1V 2NP
Tel: 020 7608 8530
Fax: 020 7608 8539
Website: www.himalaya.fr

Hothouse
Peter Jost Enterprise Centre
Byrom Street
Liverpool
L3 3AF
Tel: 0151 231 2136
Fax: 0151 231 2486
Email: info@livjm.ac.uk
Website: www.thehothouse.org.uk

Huddersfield Business Generator
Suite S14
2nd floor
The Kirklees Media Centre
7 Northumberland Street
Huddersfield
HD4 7BQ
Tel: 01484 346780
Fax: 01484 346781
Email: info@architechs.com
Website: www.hud.ac.uk/busgen

IdeaLab-Europe
58–59 Haymarket
5th Floor
London
SW1Y 4QX
Tel: 020 7968 4700
Fax: 020 7930 4310
Website: www.idealab.com

Ideas Hub
40 Portman Square
London
W1H 6LT
Tel: 020 7487 1300
Fax: 020 7487 1301
Email: info@ideashub.com
Website: www.ideashub.com

Imargo Ltd
Aston Science Park
Love Lane
Birmingham
B7 4BJ
Tel: 0121 333 3848
Fax: 0121 333 3858
Email: admin@imargo.co.uk

Imperial College Company Maker Ltd
Imperial College
47 Prince's Gate
Exhibition Road
London
SW7 2QA
Tel: 020 7594 6597
Fax: 020 7594 6561
Email: info@ic.ac.uk
Website: www.icinnovations.co.uk

Incubation Partnership
The Campus Ventures Centre
The University of Manchester
Oxford Road
Manchester
M13 9PL
Tel: 0161 276 8355
Fax: 0161 273 5111
Email: info@incubationapartnership.co.uk
Website: www.incubationpartnership.co.uk

Innova Science Park
Urban Regeneration Unit
London Borough of Enfield
PO Box 61
Civic Centre
Silver Street
Enfield
EN1 3XY
Tel: 020 8967 8427
Fax: 020 8982 7331
Website: www.thesciencepark.com

Innovation Centre (Sheffield)
217 Portobello Road
Sheffield

S1 4DP
Tel: 0114 273 1612
Fax: 0114 270 1390
Email: innovcentre@uksteelenterprise.co.uk
Website: www.uksteelenterprise.co.uk

Internet Capital Group (Europe)
Cassini House
57 St James's Street
London
SW1A 1LD
Tel: 020 7959 1100
Fax: 020 7959 1199
Website: www.internetcapital.com

Inverness Business Technology Centre
Inverness and Nairn Enterprise
The Green House
Beechwood Business Park North
Inverness
IV2 3BL
Tel: 01463 713504
Fax: 01463 712002
Email: thegreenhouse@hient.co.uk
Website: www.business-incubator.co.uk

Larne Enterprise Development Company Ltd
LEDCOM Industrial Estate
Bank Road
Larne
Co Antrim
BT40 3AW
Tel: 028 28 270742
Fax: 028 28 275653
Email: info@ledcom.org
Website: www.ledcom.org

Leeds Innovation Centre
103 Clarendon Road
Leeds
LS2 9DF
Tel: 0113 384 5845
Fax: 0113 384 5846
Email: info@leeds-innovation-centre.fsbusiness.
co.uk
Website: www.leedsinnovationcentre.co.uk

Lee Valley Technopark
Ashley Road
Tottenham
London
N17 9LN
Tel: 020 8880 3636
Fax: 020 8880 3442
Email: technopark@lvc.leevalley.co.uk
Website: www.lvc.leevalley.co.uk

Lisburn Enterprise Organisation Ltd
Enterprise Crescent
Ballinderry Road
Lisburn
Co Antrim
BT28 2BP
Tel: 028 92 661160
Fax: 028 92 603084
Email: center@lisburn-enterprise.co.uk
Website: www.lisburn-enterprise.co.uk

London BIC Ltd
Business Innovation Centre
Innova Park
Mollison Avenue
Enfield
EN3 7XU
Tel: 020 8350 1350
Fax: 020 8350 1351
Email: info@londonbic.com
Website: www.londonbic.com

London Bioscience Innovation Centre
Royal College Street
London
NW1 0TU
Tel: 020 7388 4674
Email: info@oxin.co.uk
Website: www.oxin.co.uk

The London Science Park at Dartford
Civic Centre
Home Gardens
Dartford
Kent
DA1 1DR

Contact: Susie Mayell
Tel: 01322 343073
Fax: 01322 343951
Email susie.mayell@dartford.gov.uk

Loughborough Innovation Centre
Loughborough University
LE11 3TU
Contact: Tim Bacon
Tel: 01509 228890
Fax: 01509 228892
Email tim.bacon@charnwoodbc.gov.uk
Website: www.loughborough-innovation.com

Malvern Hills Science Park
Geraldine Road
Malvern
Worcester
WR14 3SZ
Contact: Nigel Shaw (Manager)
Tel: 01684 585200
Fax: 01684 585201
Email: enquiries@mhsp.c.uk
Website: www.mhsp.co.uk

Manchester Innovation Centre Ltd
Manchester Incubator Building
Grafton Street
Manchester
M13 9XX
Tel: 0161 606 7200
Fax: 0161 606 7300
Email: mail@manbio.com
Website: www.maninv.com

MENTEC
Deiniol Road
Bangor
Gwynedd
Wales
LL57 2UP
Tel: 01248 672600
Fax: 01248 672601
Email: info@gwynedd.gov.uk
Website: www.gwynedd.gov.uk

Merlin Ventures
12 St James's Square
London
SW1Y 4RB
Tel: 020 7849 6003
Fax: 020 7976 1444
Email: mailbox@merlin-ventures.co.uk
Website: www.merlin-ventures.co.uk

Merseyside Innovation Centre Ltd
131 Mount Pleasant
Liverpool
L3 5TF
Tel: 0151 708 0123
Fax: 0151 707 0230
Email: info@micltd.co.uk
Website: www.micltd.co.uk

Metro New Media
35 Kingsland Road
London
E8 2AA
Tel: 020 7729 9992
Fax: 020 7739 7742
Email: info@mnm.co.uk
Website: www.metronewmedia.co.uk

Metrocube
Sir John Lyon House
5 High Timber Street
London
EC4N 3NX
Tel: 020 7420 7717
Fax: 020 7420 7701
Email: info@metrocube.com
Website: www.metrocube.com

Mountjoy Research Centre
University of Durham Science Park
Stockton Road
Durham
DH1 3UP
Tel: 0191 374 2580
Fax: 0191 374 2591
Email: info@durham.ac.uk
Website: www.dur.ac.uk

MRC Technology
1–3 Burtonhole Lane
Mill Hill
London
NW7 1AD
Tel: 020 8906 3811
Fax: 020 8906 1395
Email: info@nmir.ac.uk
Website: www.cc.mrc.ac.uk

NEMI Centre for Advanced Industry
Coble Dene
Royal Quays
North Shields
NE29 6DE
Tel: 0191 293 7000
Fax: 0191 293 7001
Email: info@nemi-cai.co.uk
Website: www.nemi-cai.co.uk

New Greenham Park Enterprise Cenetre
8 Venture West
New Greenham Park
Newbury
RG19 6HW
Tel: 01635 817442
Email: info@greenham-common-trust.co.uk
Website: www.newburyhub.co.uk

New Media Spark
3rd Floor
33 Glasshouse Street
London
W1R 5RG
Tel: 020 7851 7777
Fax: 020 7851 7770
Email: enquiries@newmediaspark.com
Website: www.newmediaspark.com

North East of England Business Innovation Centre
Wearfield
Sunderland Enterprise Park
Sunderland
SR5 2TA
Tel: 0191 516 6023

Fax: 0191 516 6143
Email: info@northeast-bic.co.uk
Website: www.Sunderlandtec.uk.com

North Lanarkshire Business Incubation Centre
The Atrium Business Centre
North Caldeen Road
Coatbridge
ML5 4EF
Tel: 01236 702020
Fax: 01236 702021
Email: 101715.1376@compuserve.com

Northern Technologies Innovation Centre
Brunswick Street
Nelson
BB9 0PQ
Tel: 01282 724200
Fax: 01282 724201
Email: info@northerntech.co.uk
Website: www.innovation-centre.co.uk

Nottingham Trent Business Park
City Link
The Island Business Quarter
Nottingham
NG2 4LA
Tel: 0115 948 6046
Fax: 0115 948 6185
Email: n.b.park@ntu.ac.uk
Website: www.ntu.ac.uk

Ormeau Business Park
8 Cromac Avenue
Belfast
BT7 2JA
Tel: 028 90 339906
Fax: 028 90 339937
Email: info@ormeaubusinesspark.com
Website: www.ormeaubusinesspark.com

Oxford Science Park
Robert Robinson Avenue
Oxford
OX4 4GA
Contact: Shannon Blaszko (Manager)

Tel: 01865 784000
Fax: 01865 784004
Email: shannon.blaszko@oxfordsp.com
Website: www.oxfordsp.com

Peabody Trust (Westferry)
90–162 Milligan Street
London
E14 8AS
Tel: 020 7377 8821
Fax: 020 7375 1415
Email: info@goeast.org
Website: www.goeast.org

Pentlands Science Park
Penicuik
EH26 0PZ
Tel: 0131 445 6116
Fax: 0131 445 6256
Email: george.walker@pentlands.co.uk

Pera Innovation Park
Nottingham Road
Melton Mowbray
LE12 0PB
Tel: 01664 501501
Fax: 01664 501261
Email: info@pera.com
Website: www.pera.com

Peterborough Workspace Ltd
28–29 Maxwell Road
Woodston
Peterborough
PE2 7JE
Tel: 01733 390707
Fax: 01733 390622
Email: admin@peterborough-workspace.co.uk
Website: www.peterborough.workspace.co.uk

Plus Technology Ltd
Joseph Wright House
34 Iron Gate
Derby
DE1 3GA
Tel: 01332 368568

Fax: 01332 368768
Email: info@plus-tech.com

PricewaterhouseCoopers Venture Partners
32 Farringdon Street
London
EC4A 4EA
Tel: 020 7213 1944
Fax: 020 7212 1768
Email: uk.venturepartners@uk.pwcglobal.com
Website: www.pwcglobal.com

Progeny Bioventures
Surrey Technology Centre
Guildford
Tel: 07712 191810
Fax: 01483 295836
Email: progeny@angletechnology.co.
Website: www.angletechnology.com

Project North East
Hawthorn House
Forth Banks
Newcastle upon Tyne
NE1 3SG
Tel: 0191 245 2209
Fax: 0191 261 1910
Email: info@projectne.co.uk
Website: www.silicon-alley.co.uk

Qubis Ltd
10 Malone Road
Belfast
BT9 5BN
Tel: 028 90 682321
Fax: 028 90 663015
Email: info@qubis.co.uk
Website: www.qubis.co.uk

Scottish Microelectronics Centre
The Kings Buildings
West Mains Road
Edinburgh
EH9 3JF
Tel: 0131 650 7474
Fax: 0131 650 7475

Email: info@ee.ad.ac.uk
Website: www.scotmicrocentre.co.uk

Sheffield Science and Technology Park
The Cooper Buildings
Arundel Street
Sheffield
S1 2NS
Tel: 0114 221 1800
Fax: 0114 221 1801
Email: info@sci-tech.org.uk
Website: www.sci-tech.org.uk

Shetland Business Innovation Centre
North Cremista Industrial Estate
Lerwick
Shetland
ZE1 0PX
Tel: 01595 742100
Fax: 01595 742122
Email: info@sbic.shetland.co.uk
Website: www.shetlandbusiness.com

Sir Frank Whittle Business Centre
Great Central Way
Butlers Leap
Rugby
CV21 3XH
Tel: 01788 551500
Fax: 01788 550621
Email: info@warwickshire.gov.uk
Website: www.warwickshire.gov.uk

Snowdonia Business Innovation Centre
Parc Menai
Bangor
LL59 4BF
Tel: 01248 671101
Fax: 01248 671102
Email: info@bic-eryri.wales.com
Website: www.bic-eryri.wales.com

Software Business Network
CSSA
20 Red Lion Street
London

WC1R 4QN
Tel: 020 7395 6739
Website: www.sbn.org.uk

South Bank Technopark
90 London Road
London
SE1 6LN
Tel: 020 7928 2900
Fax: 020 7928 3908
Website: www.sbu.ac.uk/Litc/sbt

South Ribble Enterprise Park
Capitol Way
Walton-Le-Dale
Preston
PR5 4AQ
Tel: 01772 422242
Fax: 01772 623446
Email: info@srbv.demon.co.uk
Website: www.srbv.co.uk

South Wiltshire Incubator and Biotechnology
8 Centre One
Old Sarum Park
Salisbury
SP4 6BU
Tel: 01722 415026; 01722 415027
Fax: 01722 415028
Email: nse@dial.pipex.com

Springvale Innovation Centre
Synergy Centres Ltd
Millennium House
1 Millennium Way
Springvale Business Park
Belfast
BT12 7AL
Tel: 028 90 288836
Fax: 028 90 288850
Email: info@synergycentres.org

St Albans Enterprise Centre
Low Spring
St Albans
AL3 6EN

Tel: 01727 837760
Fax: 01727 851200
Email: advice@stanta.co.uk
Website: www.stanta.co.uk

St Cross Innovation Centre
St Cross Business Park
Monks Brook
Newport
PO30 5WB
Tel: 01983 550300
Fax: 01983 550550
Email: info@iwpartnership.com
Website: www.iwpartnership.com

St John's Innovation Centre Ltd
Cowley Road
Cambridge
CB4 0WS
Tel: 01223 420252
Fax: 01223 420844
Email: info@stjohns.co.uk
Website: www.stjohns.co.uk

Staffordshire & Black Country Business Innovation Centre
Staffordshire Technology Park
Staffordshire County Council
County Property Service
Green Hall
Lichfield Road
Stafford
ST17 4LA
Contact: Paul Adams
Tel: 01785 277706
Fax: 01785 277712
Email: paul.adams@staffordshire.gov.uk
Website: www.thebic.co.uk

StarTech Partners Ltd
4 Woodside Place
Glasgow
G3 7QF
Tel: 0141 353 5230
Fax: 0141 332 2928
Email: info@startech.co.uk

Website: www.startech.co.uk

Stirling University Innovation Park Ltd
Scion House
Stirling University Innovation Park
Stirling
FK9 4NF
Contact: Sandie McGee (Manager)
Tel: 01786 448333
Fax: 01786 458033
Email: sandie.mcgee@suip.co.uk
Website: www.innovation.stir.ac.uk

Strathclyde University Incubator Ltd
141 St James Road
Glasgow
G4 0LT
Tel: 0141 552 7287
Fax: 0141 552 3886
Email: info@suilimited.com
Website: www.suilimited.com

Surrey Technology Centre
The Surrey Research Park Office
30 Frederick Sanger Road
Surrey Research Park
Guildford
GU2 7EF
Tel: 01483 579693
Fax: 01483 568946
Email: info@surrey.ac.uk
Website: www.surrey-research-park.com

Sussex Innovation Centre
Science Park Square
Falmer
Brighton
BN1 9SB
Tel: 01273 704400
Fax: 01273 704499
Email: info@sussexinnovation.co.uk
Website: www.sinc.co.uk

Tamar Science Park Ltd
ITTC Building
1 Davy Road

Derriford
PL6 8BX
Tel: 01752 772200
Fax: 01752 772227
Email: ittc@sciencepark.org.uk
Website: www.sciencepark.org.uk

Tapton Park Innovation Centre
Brimington Road
Tapton
Chesterfield
S41 0TZ
Tel: 01246 231234
Fax: 01246 230055
Email: admin@tapton.co.uk
Website: www.tapton.co.uk

TechnoCentre
Coventry University Technology Park
Puma Way
Coventry
CV1 2TT
Tel: 024 7623 6262
Fax: 024 7623 6024
Email: info@coventry.ac.uk
Website: www.coventry.ac.uk

Technology and Software Incubator Centre
University of Ulster
Magee College
Northland Road
Derry
BT48 7JL
Tel: 028 71 375651
Fax: 028 71 375652
Email: info@ulst.ac.uk
Website: www.ulst.ac.uk

Technology House Business Incubation Unit
Lissadel Street
Salford
M6 6AP
Tel: 0161 278 2552
Fax: 0161 278 2421
Email: info@salford.ac.uk
Website: www.technology-house.com

TEDCO Business Centre
Viking Industrial Park
Jarrow
NE32 3DT
Tel: 0191 428 3300
Fax: 0191 428 3388
Email: info@TEDCO.btinternet.com

Thames Gateway Technology Centre
University of East London
Docklands Campus
4 University Way
London
E16 3RD
Tel: 020 8223 3388
Fax: 020 8223 3327
Email: info@uel.ac.uk
Website: www.tgtc.co.uk

Torrent Valley Enterprise Centre
Tullyleek
Donaghmore
Dungannon
Co. Tyrone
Tel: 028 87 761729
Fax: 028 87 767060

Catalyst for Success Limited
The Turnpike
Marketing Catalyst Ltd
London Road
Wymondham
NR18 9SS
Tel: 01953 605000
Fax: 01953 605800
Email: info@marketing-catalyst.co.uk
Website: www.marketing-catalyst.co.uk

UK Steel Enterprise Ltd (formerly British Steel Industry Ltd)
The Innovation Centre
217 Portobello Road
Sheffield
S1 4DP
Tel: 0114 224 2424
Fax: 0114 224 2222

Email: innovation.centre@bsi.onyzxnet.co.uk
Website: www.innovation-centre.co.uk

Univentures International Ltd
Woodhouse Business Centre
Wakefield Road
Normanton
WF6 1BB
Tel: 01924 891125
Fax: 01924 892207
Email: info@univentures.co.uk
Website: www.univentures.co.uk

University of Exeter
Northcote House
The Queen's Drive
Exeter
EX4 4QJ
Tel: 01392 263181
Fax: 01392 263187
Email: business@ex.ac.uk
Website: www.ex.ac.uk

University of Exeter Innovation Centre
Rennes Drive
Exeter
EX4 4RN
Tel: 01392 262394
Fax: 01392 263686
Email: innovation@exeter.ac.uk
Website: www.exeter.ac.uk

University of Leeds
Leeds
LS2 9JT
Tel: 0113 233 4121
Fax: 0113 233 3988
Email: info@leeds.ac.uk
Website: www.leeds.ac.uk

University of Reading Science & Technology Centre
The University of Reading
Earley Gate
Reading
Berkshire

RG6 6BZ
Contact: Alison Ansell (Director)
Tel: 0118 931 8978
Fax: 0118 931 8979
Email: a.ansell@reading.ac.uk
Web www.reading.ac.uk/stc

University of Salford Incubator Unit
Technology House
Lissadel Street
Salford
M6 6AP
Tel: 0161 278 2553
Fax: 0161 278 2701
Email: info@salford.ac.uk
Website: www.technology-house.com

University of Teesside Business Development & Growth Programme
Borough Road
Middlesbrough
TS1 3BA
Tel: 01642 384400
Fax: 01642 384411
Email: info@tees.ac.uk
Website: www.tees.ac.uk

University of Wales College of Medicine Spinout Programme
c/o Research & Consultancy Division
Cardiff University
55 Park Place
Cardiff
CF10 3AT
Tel: 029 3087 6957
Fax: 029 3087 4189
Email: thewlisdp@cardiff.ac.uk
Website: www.spinoutwales.co.uk

University of Wales Swansea Innovation Centre
University of Wales Swansea
Singleton Park
Swansea
SA2 8PP
Tel: 01792 295562
Fax: 01792 295613

Email: innovation@swansea.ac.uk
Website: www.swansea.ac.uk

University of Warwick Science Park
Barclays Venture Centre
Sir William Lyons Road
Coventry
CV4 7EZ
Tel: 024 7632 3000
Fax: 024 76323001
Email: info@uwsp.co.uk
Website: www.uwsp.co.uk

University of Westminster Innovation Studios
Harrow Campus
Watford Road
Harrow
HA1 3TP
Tel: 020 8357 7303
Fax: 020 8357 7326
Email: info@nmk.co.uk
Website: www.nmk.co.uk

UUTECH Incubators at the University of Ulster
University of Ulster at Jordanstown
Shore Road
Newtownabbey
BT37 0QB
Tel: 01232 368019
Fax: 01232 366802
Email: info@ulst.ac.uk
Website: www.ulst.ac.uk/research/uutech/tech-tran.html

Valleys Innovation Centre
Economic Development Unit
Rhondda Cynon Taff CBC
Valleys Innovation Centre
Navigation Park
Abercynon
CF45 4SN
Tel: 01443 665000
Fax: 01443 665001
Email: invest@rhondda-cynon-taff.gov.uk
Website: www.invest.rhondda-cynon-taff.gov.uk

Victory Business Centre
Victory House
Somers Road North
Portsmouth
PO1 1PJ
Tel: 02392 826225
Fax: 02392 864023

Wellpark Enterprise Centre
120 Sydney Street
Glasgow
G31 1JF
Tel: 0141 550 4994
Fax: 0141 550 4443
Email: info@wellpark.co.uk
Website: www.wellpark.co.uk

Westlakes Ventures Ltd
Westlakes Science & Technology Park
Ingwell Hall
Moor Row
Cumbria
CA24 3JZ
Contact: Diana Wilson-Long
Tel: 01946 595200
Fax: 01946 595202
Email: dwl@westlakesproperties.co.uk
Website: www.westlakessciencepark.co.uk

WHEB Partnership
213 The Foundry
156 Blackfriars Road
London
SE1 8EN
Tel: 020 7721 7285
Fax: 020 7721 7286
Email: wheb.partnership@virgin.net
Website: www.whebpartnership.co.uk

Workspace
The Business Centre
Draperstown
Magherafelt
BT45 7AG
Tel: 028 79 628113
Fax: 028 79 628975

Email: info@workspace.org.uk
Website: www.workspace.org.uk

Workstation

15 Paternoster Row
Sheffield
S1 5FZ
Tel: 0114 279 6511
Fax: 0114 279 6522
Email: admin@workstation.org.uk
Website: www.showroom.org.uk

Associations

These are the umbrella organizations for most of the world's 4000 business accelerators. The National Business Incubation Association (NBIA) is probably the oldest incubator association. It was formed in 1985 by industry leaders, growing from about 40 members in its first year to about 1130 members in 2001. The Association is primarily composed of incubator developers and managers, but technology commercialization specialists, educators and business assistance professionals are also well represented. Its mission is to provide training and act as a clearing house for information on incubator management and development issues and on tools for assisting start-up and fledgling firms. The UK Science Park Association, also, is a well-established organization with a strong network and valuable information and help for innovative entrepreneurs.

These associations usually maintain directories of their members on their websites, so if you want to locate outside the UK, this could be a good starting point.

Association of Lithuanian Innovation Networks

c/o Kaunas Innovation Centre
K Donelaicio Street 73
LT-3006 Kaunas
Lithuania
Tel: 00 37 07 300 691
Fax: 00 37 07 300 692
Email: P.Milius@cr.ktu.lt

Website: www.ediaclit.vtk.ktu.lt

Baltic Association of Science/Technology Parks & Innovation Centres (BASTIC)

Ehitajatee 5
EE-0026 Tallinn
Estonia
Tel: 00 372 620 20 13
Fax: 00 372 738 30 41
Email: raivot@edu.ttu.ee
Website: www.edu.ttu.ee

Bedrijfs Technologisch Centrum Twente BV (btc)

Postbus 545
NL-7500 AM Enschede
Netherlands
Tel: 00 31 53 48 36 35 5
Fax: 00 31 53 43 37 41 5
Email: info@btc-twente.nl
Website: www.btc-twente.nl

Britech (British-Israel Technology Foundation)

Wyvols Court
Swallowfield
Reading
RG7 1WY
Tel: 0118 988 0275
Fax: 0118 988 0375
Email: enquiries@britech.org
Website: www.britech.org

European Business & Innovation Centre Network

Avenue de Tervuren 168
B-1150 Brussels
Belgium
Tel: 00 32 2 77 28 90 0
Fax: 00 32 2 77 29 57 4
Email: info@ebn.be
Website: www.ebn.be

ELAN Association des Dirigeants de Pépinières d'Entreprises

C/o Atecval
Prolgue Voie No.1

BP 27/01 Labege Innopole
F-31312 Labege Cedex
France
Tel: 00 33 561 39 10 31
Fax: 00 33 561 39 86 89

France Technopoles
C/o Atlanpole Château de la Chantrerie
Château de la Chantrerie BP 90702
F-44307 Nantes Cedex 3
France
Tel: 00 33 240 25 227 03
Fax: 00 33 240 25 10 88
Email: balducchi@atlanpole.fr
Website: www.atlanpole.fr

Hungarian Association for Innovation
Október huszonharmadika u.16
H-1117 Budapest
Hungary
Tel: 00 33 1 18 69 61 5
Fax: 00 36 1 18 52 18 1

IASP International Association of Science Parks
c/o Parque Tecnológico de Andalucía
Sede Social
Maria Curie 35
E-29590 Campanillas
Málaga
Spain
Tel: 00 34 95 26 19 19 7
Fax: 00 34 965 26 19 19 8
Email: iasp@isapworld.org
Website: www.iaspworld.org

Latvian Association of Technological Parks Innovation Centers and Business Incubators
Aizkrauklesstr. 21
LV-1006 Riga
Latvia
Tel: 00 371 2 25 58 66 3
Fax: 00 371 2 75 41 21 8

NBIA National Business Incubation Association
20 East Circle Drive
Suite 190
Athens, Ohio 45701-3571
Tel: 00 1 740 59 34 33 1
Fax: 00 1 740 59 31 99 6
Email: dadkins@nbia.org
Website: www.nbia.org

PBICA Polish Business & Innovation Centres Association
Rubiez 46
PL-61612 Poznan
Poland
Tel: 00 48 61 86 59 65 1
Fax: 00 48 61 86 59 56 8
Email: soipp@soipp.org.pl
Website: www.soipp.org.pl

Russian National Business Incubators Association Academy of Management & the Market
Zazepa Street 41
RUS-113054
Moscow
Russia
Tel: 00 7095 56 48 18 3
Fax: 00 7095 95 57 93 7
Email: kagan@morozov.ru
Website: www.morozov.ru

Society of Science & Technology Parks of the Czech Republic
Novotneho lavka 5
CZ-11668
Praha 1
Czech Republic
Tel: 00 420 2 21 08 22 74
Fax: 00 420 2 21 08 22 76

Spice-Group (ICECE)
c/o Zentrum am Zoo Geschaftsbauten AG
Hardenbergplatz 2
D-10623 Berlin
Germany
Tel: 030 26 47 07 0

Fax: 030 26 47 07 33
Email: zaz@zoobogen.de
Website: www.zoobogen.de

Stiftung Technopark Zurich
(Club de Schweizer Technologieparks)
Technoparkstrasse 1
CH-8005 Zurich
Switzerland
Tel: 00 41 1 445 10 10
Fax: 00 41 1 445 10 01

**TII European Association for the Transfer
of Technology, Innovation & Industrial
Informations**
3 rue des Capucins
L-1313
Luxembourg
Tel: 00 352 46 30 35
Fax: 00 352 46 21 85
Email: tti@sitel.lu
Website: www.sitel.lu

**Ukrainian Business Incubators & Innovation
Centers Association**
Petscherski Spusk 3
UA-01023 Kiev
Ukraine
Tel: 00 38 044 23 56 21 0
Fax: 00 38 044 23 56 21 0
Email: ligor@prime.net.ua
Website: www.prime.net.ua

UK Business Incubation
Aston Science Park
Love Lane
Birmingham
B7 4BJ
Tel: 0121 250 3538
Fax: 0121 250 3542
Email: malcolm.buckler@ukbi.co.uk
Website: www.ukbi.co.uk

**United Kingdom Science Park Association
(UKSPA)**
Aston Science Park

Love Lane
Aston Triangle
Birmingham
B7 4BJ
Tel: 0121 693 4850
Fax: 0121 333 5852
Email: infor@ukspa.org.uk
Website: www.ukspa.org.uk

**United Nations Industrial Development
Organization Headquarters**
PO Box 300
A-1400
Vienna
Austria
Tel: 00 43 1 26026
Fax: 00 43 1 2692669
Email: unido@unido.org
Website: www.unido.org

**VTO Vereinigung der Technologiezentren
Osterreichs**
Wehrgrabengasse 1–5
A-4400 Steyr
Austria
Tel: 00 43 7252 88 41 05
Fax: 00 43 7252 88 41 11
Email: vtoe@inna.at
Website: www.inna.at

Publications

*Incubators: A Realist's Guide to the World's New
Business Accelerators* by Colin Barrow, John Wiley
& Sons, 2001, £12.99. A guide to finding the right
accelerator for your type of venture, as well as
pointers on getting in and getting out again, once
your business is up and running.

Other organizations who can help and advise with exploiting high and not-so-high technology

Association of Independent Computer Specialists (AICS)

Bismore
Eastcombe
Stroud
GL6 7DG
Tel: 0701 070 1118
Email: admin@aics.org.uk
Website: www.aics.org.uk

AICS is a trade association whose members are committed to 'setting and maintaining the highest technical and ethical standards in the independent provision of computer-related services'. By 'independent' they mean 'free to trade within the law without being obliged to acknowledge the authority, control or influence of any third party.'

They believe that character and technical competence are more important than paper qualifications. Applicants for full membership must therefore satisfy the Council that they have a minimum of five years' relevant experience and are of 'good repute' as attested by two referees. Every member is required to abide by the Association's 10-point Code of Practice and failure to do so may lead to expulsion.

The Big Idea

The Nobel Exhibition Trust
The Harbourside
Irvine
KA12 8XX
Tel: 08708 404030
Fax: 08708 403130
Email: info@bigidea.org.uk
Website: www.bigidea.org.uk

Claimed as the World's first inventor centre, The Big Idea opened in 2000 as a permanent Millennium attraction funded by the National Lottery, European Development Fund and the private sector. It is a hands-on exhibition devoted to the process of inventing.

The Big Idea is a living laboratory for people who wish 'to think, to dream, to discover, to innovate and to invent.' The Big Idea's goal is to stimulate people to ask the questions – 'why?' and 'why not?'

British Council

Information Services Management
Bridgewater House
58 Whitworth Street
Manchester
M1 6BB
Website: www.britishcouncil.org/science/science/pubs/ukitt.htm

The British Council publishes a directory, *Essential Sources of Information on Innovation and Technology Transfer*, which is available on this website, or in hard copy from the above address. This directory lists in 91 pages essential sources of information on innovation and technology transfer under the following headings:

- general resources
- innovation
- technology transfer
- intellectual property
- finance for innovation
- entrepreneurship
- science parks, incubators and spin-outs.

The Chartered Institute of Patent Agents

Staple Inn Buildings
High Holborn
London
WC1V 7PZ
Tel: 020 7405 9450
Fax: 020 7430 0471
Email: mail@cipa.org.uk
Website: www.cipa.org.uk

The Chartered Institute of Patent Agents (CIPA) is the professional and examining body for patent agents (also known as patent attorneys) in the United Kingdom. The Institute was founded in 1882 and was incorporated by Royal Charter in 1891. It represents virtually all the 1400 registered patent attorneys in the United Kingdom, whether they practise in industry or in private practice. Total membership is over 2700 and includes trainee patent attorneys and other professionals with an interest in intellectual property matters.

Despite the historic name of the Institute, patent attorneys have always been qualified to advise on trade marks, designs and copyright as well as patents (collectively known as intellectual property).

The Institute sees its role as falling under the following headings, of which the last two will be of particular interest to small businesses:

- advising the UK government and other international bodies on policy and practice matters;
- maintaining a code of conduct for its members to observe;
- providing training for its members, both pre- and post-qualification;
- organizing patent clinics for members of the public;
- providing informative publications for the general public.

Computing Services and Software Association (CSSA)

20 Red Lion Street
London
WC1R 4QN
Tel: 020 7395 6700
Fax: 020 7404 4119
Email: cssa@cssa.co.uk
Website: www.cssa.co.uk

CSSA runs a free service, 'FITS' (Finding an IT supplier), aimed at finding IT software and services suppliers that suits particular requirements. Association members are expected to uphold standards in the industry. FITS will give you immediate access to these companies, plus the knowledge that they are both reputable and experienced. You can use FITS by searching the CSSA database directly online.

CSSA's Business Growth Consulting Services have developed a range of systematic approaches that are intended to make a positive, tangible difference to the sales effectiveness of your organization.

The Design Council

34 Bow Street
London
WC2E 7DL
Tel: 020 7420 5200
Fax: 020 7420 5300
Website: www.design-council.org.uk

The Design Council is a registered UK charity founded by the Department of Trade and Industry. It exists to 'inspire the best use of design by the United Kingdom, in the world context, to improve prosperity and well-being.'

Amongst other aids the Design Council have developed is a website design tool to help SMEs manage the process of designing a web presence. It aims to help entrepreneurs:

- find and choose the right supplier, based on their business needs – this includes finding designers and design companies to work with, and assess the calibre of those people or organizations and their suitability for working with them on a particular project
- understand and manage the web design process
- develop a design brief
- use a series of tools that help in the process of website design
- prepare a business for the changes a website brings.

The site has six sections, which can be downloaded as a Word document.

In the resources section you can download a range of templates to help you with particular stages. There is also a diagram which shows the different stages you may go through, and gives you an overview of the process.

They have helpfully used the terms which are used by suppliers. You will notice that on the first time such a word appears, a question mark will appear next to it. If you click on this, a definition will appear to give you more detail.

eBusiness Clubs

Tel: 020 7565 2000
Email:info@ebusinessclubs.co.uk
Website: www.ebusinessclubs.co.uk

Launched on 15 January 2002, this is a new initiative to help small firms exploit the multi-billion pound e-commerce market, with the following announcement:

> World-leading companies in the technology and banking sectors have today (15 January) partnered with the British Chambers of Commerce and the DTI led programme, UK online for business, to set up a support network of eBusiness Clubs to help more SMEs do business online.

> The cross sector partnership is a collaboration between UK online for business, BT, Cisco Systems Ltd, Hewlett-Packard, Intel, Lloyds TSB and Chambers of Commerce.

> The UK-wide initiative will see the initial creation of 16 eBusiness Clubs to support and encourage firms to use technology to succeed in business. Companies that join the clubs will receive information, guidance and practical business solutions to help firms integrate e-commerce solutions into everyday business processes.

For further details on finding an e-business Club near to you, look on the directory at this website: www. Ebusinessclubs.co.uk

European Business Innovation Network (EBIC)

168 Avenue de Tervuren
Box 25
B-1150 Brussels
Tel: 00 32 2 772 89 00

Fax: 00 32 2 772 95 74
Email: ebn@ebn.be
Website: www.ebn.be

EBN is the leading network for Business & Innovation Centres (BICs) and similar organizations in Europe. There are now more than 150 European Commission-recognized BICs in regions throughout Europe, from the Algarve in Portugal to the east of Finland, from the west coast of Ireland to Košiče in the east of the Slovak Republic. You can find contact details for any of the 150 BICs on their website.

These Business & Innovation Centres are a regional focal point for innovators and entrepreneurs, co-operating with other organizations to ensure an A–Z range of assistance to new and existing SMEs: from detection and assessment of innovative business ideas, through business planning guidance, launch advice and business accommodation, to post-start-up support.

European Patent Office

Website: www.european-patent-office.org
The European Patent Office runs a service similar to that provided by the Patent Office (see information on the UK Patent Office on page 171. They have several free databases available online. Of particular interest to entrepreneurs are:

- esp@cenet – free patent searching
- European Patent Attorneys database
- European Patent Convention database.

Fachinformationszentrum (FIZ)

http://patents.fiz-karlsruhe.de

Fachinformationszentrum (FIZ) Karlsruhe is a non-profit organization set up to provide information and information services for academic and industrial research & development, as well as for business and administration. In co-operation with its partners in the USA and Japan, FIZ Karlsruhe is operating the host STN (Scientific and Technical Information) International, offering public access to databases with scientific, technical, and supplementary business information. In its function as European STN Service Center, FIZ Karlsruhe offers access to more than 200 electronic databases in almost all fields of science and technology, including patents.

They offer access to all major international and national patent databases, including the following.

- APIPAT (API EnCompass Patent database) covers worldwide patents relating to the petroleum refining, petrochemical, natural gas and energy industries, including those on alternate energy sources and environmental effects of energy.
- Caplus covers worldwide literature from all areas of chemistry, biochemistry, chemical engineering and related sciences from 1967 to the present.
- CAOLD (pre-1967 Chemical Abstracts database) contains records for Chemical Abstracts (CA) references from 1907–1966.
- DRUGPAT (IMSworld Drug Patents International database) provides evaluated international patent family analysis for more than 1500 pharmaceutical compounds, either on the market or under active development.
- Derwent World Patents Index provides information on patent publications from the 40 most important patent-issuing authorities in the world.
- DGENE (Derwent Geneseq) contains information on nucleic acid and protein sequences extracted from the original (basic) patent documents published by 40 patent offices worldwide.
- EUROPATFULL (European Patents Fulltext database) covers the full text of European patent applications and granted European patents published by the European Patent Office (EPO) since January 1996.
- IFIPAT (IFI Patent database) contains the front page and bibliographic data, abstracts and complete claims from US utility patents, reissue patents and defensive publications, and Statutory Invention Registrations (S.I.R.).

- IFICDB (IFI Comprehensive DataBase) provides, in addition, a more in-depth indexing of chemical-related patents by fragmentation codes and role indicators.
- IFICLS (IFI Current Legal Status Database) provides information on the current legal status of US patents.
- INPADOC (the International Patent Documentation File) contains bibliographic and family data for patent documents and utility models of 67 patent-issuing organizations, including the European Patent Office (EPO) and the World Intellectual Property Organization (WIPO). Legal status data from 28 patent-issuing organizations are included.
- JAPIO provides the most comprehensive English-language access to Japanese unexamined patent applications (Kokai Tokkyo Koho), covering all mechanical, electrical, chemical and physical technologies. English-language titles and abstracts.
- PTDPA (German Patent Database) contains citations on scientific and technological patents, patent applications and utility models published by 'Deutsches Patent- und Markenamt' (German Patent and Trademark Office) in the *Patentblatt*, including applications filed at the European Patent Office and the World Intellectual Property Organization (WIPO) designated for Germany. Covers period since 1981.
- PATDD contains the bibliographic data of patent publications of the former German Democratic Republic (GDR) published, up to 2 October 1990, in *Bekanntmachungen* by the former Patent Office of the GDR.
- PATOSDE (Patent-Online-System Deutschland database) contains a variety of German Patent and Trademark Office publications: patent applications and examined patent applications since 1968, granted patents (*Patentschriften*) since 1980, and utility models (*Gebrauchsmuster*) since 1983.
- PATIPC contains the text and graphics (chemical structure images) of the International Patent

Classification (IPC) as published by the World Intellectual Property Organization (WIPO) and the German Patent and Trademark Office (DPMA).

- PATOSEP (PATent Online System EuroPa) contains extracts from patent applications and granted patents published by the European Patent Office since 1978, with titles in English, German and French.
- PATOSWO (PATent Online System WOrld) contains bibliographic information and English abstracts of international patent applications (PCT applications) published by the World Intellectual Property Organization (WIPO) in the *PCT-Gazette* since 1978.
- PCTFULL (Patent Cooperation Treaty Full Text) which covers the full text of PCT (Patent Cooperation Treaty) published applications issued under the auspices of the World Intellectual Property Organization (WIPO) since 1983.
- USPATFULL contains the complete text of US patents and current classifications for all patents issued by the US Patent and Trademark Office (USPTO) from 1975 to the present.

For online access an account is required, which can be set up online within minutes. If you do not want to do the online searching yourself, you can use their search service.

Foresight

Foresight Directorate
Department of Trade and Industry
1 Victoria Street
London
SW1H 0ET
Fax: 020 7215 6715
Website: www.foresight.gov.uk

Foresight is a Department of Trade and Industry initiative launched in 1994 following a major review of government science, engineering and technology policy, which aims to:

- develop visions of the future – looking at possible future needs, opportunities and threats and deciding what action is needed
- help companies to reshape their business strategies and build sustained competitive advantage
- build bridges between business, science and government, bringing together the knowledge and expertise of many people across all areas and activities in order to increase national wealth and quality of life.

Innovation Relay Centre (IRC) Gateway

Website: http://irc.cordis.lu
If you are:

- an owner of an innovative technology and you are unsure of how to market your innovation
- looking for new technologies to exploit
- searching for an innovative solution to a technology need

then contacting an Innovation Relay Centre will almost certainly be to your advantage.

In 1995, the European Commission established the IRC network and by April 2000, it consisted of 68 Innovation Relay Centres (IRCs) throughout Europe, including the EU, Bulgaria, Czech Republic, Cyprus, Estonia, Hungary, Iceland, Israel, Latvia, Lithuania, Norway, Poland, Romania, Slovak Republic, Slovenia and Switzerland. These centres have been created in order to help the transfer of innovative technologies to and from European companies, mainly between SMEs. The IRCs are innovation support service providers, mainly hosted by public organizations such as university technology centres, chambers of commerce, regional development agencies or national innovation agencies. Most IRCs are set up as consortia. Each centre is staffed by personnel who have extensive knowledge of technology.

All IRCs are linked by an efficient Internet-based Business Bulletin System, so that technology offers or requests can rapidly be conveyed across Europe. A scheme involving mandatory information templates ensures that all necessary details are given in order to facilitate a sensible appraisal of the technology. The system also ensures that only relevant organizations are approached when searching for partners and/or technologies.

An IRC will support entrepreneurs with the marketing of a technology and/or know-how of innovative products that involve some technical collaboration between the transferring companies and/or research institutes. They do not assist with the selling of products.

Whilst IRCs do not have funds themselves, they will signpost companies seeking assistance to the relevant national contact points.

IRCs regularly organize transnational missions and brokerage events. They pre-arrange meetings, provide a venue, make the travel and accommodation arrangements and generally ease the process of technology transfer. These transnational activities generally target a particular industrial sector.

IRC England
UK Innovation Relay Directory
Beta Technology Limited
Barclay Court
Doncaster Carr
DN4 5HZ
Tel: 0130 232 2633
Fax: 0130 238 8800
Email: info@betatechnology.co.uk
Website: www.betatechnology.co.uk

ChamberLink
Churchgate House
56 Oxford Street
Manchester
M60 7HJ
Contact: Chris Greenhalgh
Tel: +44 161 238 4555
Fax: +44 161 237 4186
Email: chris.greenhalgh@c-b-e.co.uk

Coventry University Enterprises Ltd
The Technocentre
Puma Way
Coventry
CV1 2TT

Tel: 024 7623 6236
Fax: 024 7623 6024
Email: mirc@coventry.ac.uk
Website: www.mirc.org.uk

Defence Diversification Agency
Defence Diversification Agency
A1 Building
Room 1013
DERA
Ively Road
Farnborough
GU14 0LX
Tel: 01252 39 5755
Fax: 01252 39 3318
Email: djphillips@dera.gov.uk
Website: www.seirc.org.uk

IRC North-Nord Manche
RTC North Ltd
1 Hylton Park,
Wessington Way
Sunderland
SR5 3HD
Contact: Mikel Echevarria
Tel: +44 191 516 4400
Fax: +44 191 516 4401
Email: mikel.echevarria@rtcnorth.co.uk
Website: www.rtcnorth.co.uk

Kent Technology Transfer Centre Ltd
Research and Development Building
University of Kent
Canterbury
CT2 7PD
Tel: +44 1227 824308
Fax: +44 1227 763424
Email: john.miller@technologyenterprise.co.uk

NIMTECH
Suite 14
The Globe
St James' Square
Accrington
BB5 0RE
Fax: 01254 231715

Email: langley.d@enterprise.plc.uk
Website: www.nimtech.co.uk

RTC North Ltd
1 Hylton Park
Wessington Way
Sunderland
SR5 3HD
Tel: 0191 516 4400
Fax: 0191 516 4401
Email: relay@rtcnorth.co.uk
Website: www.rtcnorth.co.uk

IRC East of England
St John's Innovation Centre Ltd
Cowley Road
Cambridge
CB4 0WS
Tel: 01223 421117
Fax: 01223 420844
Email: relaycentre@stjohns.co.uk
Website: www.stjohns.co.uk/eeirc

IRC South West England
South West Innovation Relay Centre
4th Floor
100 Temple Street
Bristol
BS1 6EA
Tel: 0117 933 0277; 0117 933 0275
Fax: 0117 933 0240
Email: swirc@southwestrda.org.uk
Website: www.southwest-irc.org.uk

Thames Valley Technology Ltd
Magdalen Centre
The Oxford Science Park
Oxford
OX4 4GA
Tel: 01865 784888
Fax: 01865 784333
Email: alec.moore.lseirc@tvt.co.uk
Website: www.tvt.co.uk/seirc/

IRC Midlands
Coventry University Enterprises Ltd
The Technocentre
Puma Way
Coventry
CV1 2TT
Contact: John Latham
Tel: +44 24 7623 6236
Fax: +44 24 7623 6024
Email: mirc@coventry.ac.uk
Website: www.mids.demon.co.uk

IRC North of England
The Regional Technology Centre for the North East and Cumbria Ltd
1 Hylton Park
Wessington Way
Sunderland
SR5 3HD
Contact: Sarah Hart
Tel: 0191 516 4400
Fax: 0191 516 4401
Email: sarah.hart@rtcnorth.co.uk
Website: www.rtcnorth.co.uk

IRC Northern Ireland
Invest NI
17 Antrim Road
Lisburn
BT28 3AL
Contact: Marshall Addidle
Tel: +44 (0) 2890698824
Fax: +44 (0) 2890490490
Email: irc@investni.com
Website: www.investni.com/irc

IRC Scotland
Targeting Innovation
Third Floor
Atrium Court
Glasgow
G2 6HQ
Contact: Caroline Gray-Stephens
Tel: +44 141 572 1609
Fax: +44 141 572 1608
Email: caroline@targetinginnovation.com

Website: www.ircscotland.net

Targeting Technology Ltd
6.08 Kelvin Campus
Maryhill Road
West of Scotland Science Park
Glasgow
G20 0SP
Tel: 0141 946 0500
Fax: 0141 945 1591
Email: dgreenlees@targetingtechnology.co.uk
Website: www.ircscotland.net

Business Information Source Ltd
Innovation Support Team
The Green House
Beechwood Business Park North
Inverness
IV2 3BL
Tel: 01463 667269
Fax: 01463 712002
Email: norma.macdonald@hient.co.uk
Website: www.bis.uk.com

Stirling University Innovation Park Ltd
SUIP Limited
Unit 4
Scion House
Stirling University Innovation Park
Stirling
FK9 4NF
Tel: 01786 458052
Fax: 01786 458033
Email: kirsty.hall@suip.co.uk
Website: www.suip.co.uk

IRC Wales
Welsh Development Agency
Plas Glyndwr
Kingsway
Cardiff
CF10 3AH
Contact: Sandra Lopes
Tel: +44 29 2082 8739
Fax: +44 29 2036 8229
Email: sandra.lopes@wda.co.uk

Web: www.walesrelay.co.uk

The Institute of International Licensing
Suite 73
Kent House
87 Regent Street
London
W1R 7HF
Tel: 020 7287 0200
Fax: 020 7287 0400
Email: iilp.web@virgin.net
Website: freespace.virgin.net/iilp.web/index.htm

The Institute of International Licensing has the following aims and services:

- to establish professional standards for those engaged in licensing practice
- to provide a forum for the exchange of ideas and information relating to international licensing
- to assist companies and individuals to obtain the services of qualified licensing practitioners on a fee-paying basis.

The Institute of Inventors
19–23 Fosse Way
Ealing
London
W13 0BZ
Tel: 020 8998 3540
Fax: 020 8998 4372
Email: mikinvent@aol.com
Website: www.newgadgets.freeserve.co.uk

The Institute of Inventors is a voluntary, non-profit Inventors' Club, founded in 1964 and run by unpaid volunteer professional engineer-inventors. Their purpose is to help all private inventors – with evaluation of new ideas, gadgets and inventions, prototype drawings and development, patent specification, drawings and applications, and licensing of intellectual property to maximize inventors' chances of earning money on inventions with merit. They have 1200 members and annual membership costs £120.

The Institute of Patentees and Inventors
Suite 505A
Triumph House
189 Regent Street
London
W1B 4JY
Tel: 020 7434 1818
Fax: 020 7434 1727
Email: enquiries@invent.org.uk
Website: www.invent.org.uk

The Institute of Patentees and Inventors claims that each year approximately 20,000 patents are applied for by UK residents. About 20% of these applications are by individuals, rather than companies or academic institutions. With the success rate of getting patented ideas to the market being only 2%, the inventor needs all the assistance available. The Institute of Patentees and Inventors is a non-profit-making association of over 1000 members who pay an annual subscription (£75). It offers its members advice and guidance on all aspects of inventing from idea conception to innovation and development.

The Institute has among its membership not only inventors but patent agents, marketeers and others who can provide expert advice to its membership on the complex issues relating to invention and innovation. These issues cover not only intellectual property rights but also topics as diverse as originality searching, manufacturing practices, pricing practices, presentation techniques, funding and other subjects relating to the exploitation of an invention.

A journal, *Future and the Inventor*, is produced and issued to members at least once per annum. The journal contains information pertinent to inventors and details the forthcoming activities of the Institute.

The International Inventions Fair, held each year as part of the Tomorrow's World Live Exhibition, is supported by the Institute.

The Institute holds members' meetings at which invited speakers talk on various subjects relating to the invention and innovation process.

Visits to places of interest for members are also arranged when appropriate.

The Institute's Faculty of Education has developed, in conjunction with the Open College Network, a number courses on the invention process which are run for inventors and those interested in the invention and innovation process. The courses lead their participants through the complex procedures and stages of developing an idea into a marketable and potentially successful development. The Faculty is also developing further educational courses for inventors.

www.intellectual-property.gov.uk
This site is the government-backed home of UK intellectual property on the Internet. They hope to bring you all the answers to your questions and all the resources you need to find your way through the IP (intellectual property) jungle of copyright, designs, patents and trade marks.

They have on their site answers to most of the most persistent questions in this area, covering for example:

- What is intellectual property or IP?
- How do I get protection for my idea/material?
- How will my idea/material benefit from IP?
- How do I enforce my rights?
- Do I always need permission to use IP?
- How do I get permission to use someone's material?
- Why is intellectual property important to medicine?
- Can I patent computer software?

International Exhibition of Inventions, New Techniques and Products
Rue du 31 Decembre
CH-1207 Geneva
Switzerland
Tel: 00 41 22 736 59 49
Fax: 00 41 22 786 00 96
Email: promex@worldcom.ch
Website: www.inventions-geneva.ch

Now in it its thirty-first year, this claims to be the world's premier exhibition for and about inventors. It is held under the patronage of the Swiss Federal Government. The last exhibition claimed 686 exhibitors from 44 countries from all five continents. Licences were negotiated worldwide for over $30 million of new inventions and innovative ideas.

International Federation of Inventors Societies (IFIA)
PO Box 299
1211 Geneva 12
Switzerland
Fax: 00 41 22 789 3076
Email: invention-ifia@bluewin.ch
Website: www.invention-ifia.ch

IFIA is a non-profit, non-governmental organization created by seven European inventor associations in 1968. Today, its membership is drawn from more than 100 countries. Their website contains links to their 100 member organizations and to 345 other organizations of probable use to inventors, organized under the following headings:

- inventor associations
- innovation centres
- foundations
- patent administrations
- universities
- invention exhibitions
- patent attorneys
- companies
- other organizations
- individual members.

They also include on their website details of reference books, guides, surveys, studies, conferences, seminars, workshops, expert group meetings, lectures, competitions and awards for inventions, illustrative exhibits related to inventors and inventions and information on consultative services.

International Technology Service
Website: www.dti.gov.uk/mbp/its/its.html

(Links to these services via website)

Aiming to help UK firms become and remain competitive at home and overseas, the International Technology Service is a government initiative that keeps them aware of new technological developments and management practices from across the world. The four elements are:

- information, in particular:
  - *Online Technology Information* – bringing together technical developments and policy information from overseas.
  - *Global Watch* – a monthly magazine of important technology developments from around the world. It leads readers to Global Watch Online.
  - British embassy science and technology web sites – British embassies in Bonn (Germany), Paris (France), Tokyo (Japan), Washington (USA) and Seoul (Korea) provide information on current scientific and technological developments and policies within their specific countries.
- Missions – for first-hand experience of overseas management technologies and practices.
- International technology promoters – for help with accessing specific technologies or information from overseas.
- Secondments – for financial and practical help to second key UK managers or specialists to a world-class overseas company for between three months and a year.

Inventors Bible
MOI Solutions
24 Stephen Lane
Sheffield
S35 8QZ
Email: solutions@moi.demon.co.uk
Website: www.inventorsbible.co.uk

MOI Solutions provides a service to inventors which is part email support (at £17.50 per quarter), part book (*The Inventors Bible*, priced £95), and part CD-ROM (containing a comprehensive set of over 60 files to enable you to undertake your inventing activities smoothly, including: an accounting package; standard letters; confidentiality agreements; successful funding applications; business plans; project proposals; and questionnaires).

The *Inventors Bible* contains over 300 pages split into 11 chapters, including:

- creativity
- business development
- personal development
- market research
- patenting and intellectual property
- financial assistance
- design and prototypes
- marketing and exploitation
- directory.

Underpinning all of this is the comprehensive yet simple-to-use planning system that enables all activities to be undertaken in the right order and for the right purpose – a prerequisite for success.

Inventors Digest
Website: www.inventorsdigest.com

This site is designed for anyone who has ever said, 'I've got a great idea … Now what do I do?' It also claims to be the spot for anyone who's searching for the next great product! The first issue of *Inventors Digest* rolled off the presses in June 1985. Now the site has a comprehensive range of services aimed at the inventing entrepreneur. One of the many useful features of the site is the directory of inventors exhibitions and trade shows. In January 2002 the list of forthcoming events for the next quarter included the following:

- North Dakota Inventors Congress. Workshops and Expo (www.ndinventors.com)
- Rocky Mountain Inventors Congress Denver, Colorado – Workshops and Invention Expo (www.RMInventor.org)
- Midwest Inventors Conference & Resource Expo, Flint, Michigan (tel: +1 810 232 7101)

- Pulse of Innovation Trade Show, Long Island, NY – Invention Trade Show (email: lcarter@lift. org).

Microsoft bCentral
Website: www.bcentral.co.uk

Microsoft bCentral is the online destination for Microsoft's smaller business customers. They hope this site will be the place that you come for 'business-critical information, advice and services', to use Microsoft's own jargon. Their aim is to support entrepreneurs and their businesses and to show them how technology can help to make a business more productive and more successful. And of course to sell their own products!

They try to do this in a number of ways:

- helping you to get more out of your existing technology investments with information on support, contact information, 'tips and tricks' and 'how-to's'
- highlighting new technologies and why they're important to you
- bringing things to you by providing a stepping stone to both Microsoft websites and the Internet in general
- selecting the web-based services that will help you get more done, more easily and cheaply.

Their services seem pretty comprehensive if their subject index is any guide:

- marketing
- eBusiness
- marketing basics
- online marketing
- planning
- trading abroad
- websites
- finance
- banking
- business health
- cash management
- planning
- starting up

- tax
- technology
- windows
- office
- server/other products
- buyers guide
- Internet and networks
- administration
- consumer rights
- get organized
- legal
- people management
- starting up
- services
- buying software
- business books
- office supplies
- get online
- online tax returns.

The National Computing Centre Limited
Oxford House
Oxford Road
Manchester
M1 7ED
Tel: 0161 228 6333
Fax: 0161 242 2499
Email: info@ncc.co.uk
Website: www.ncc.co.uk

Looking for a virtual IT research department, saving time and money otherwise spent on procuring information from many sources? The National Computing Centre could be the answer. It is an independent membership and research organization whose mission is to help organizations manage technologies, processes and people to deliver effective IT solutions. This objective is achieved by creating and sharing relevant knowledge. NCC members benefit by being kept informed of current IT issues via published guidelines, surveys, research and also special interest groups. The membership spans universities, government bodies, SMEs and blue chip corporations.

Their services include:

- **NCC Salary Finder:** accesses up-to-date and reliable salary data based on the NCC *Salaries and Staff Issues in IT* survey to give calculations according to job type, location, size of department and industry sector
- **IT Services Directory:** provides a one-stop reference to meet all IT requirements for suppliers and manufacturers of IT products and related services. NCC members have full access to all the information and non-members can use a limited version
- **IT Encyclopedia (members only):** this quarterly updated encyclopedia contains more than 15,000 IT definitions, illustrations, photos, charts and diagrams. It covers the field from micro to mainframe.

The membership packages include monthly publications, access to knowledge networks, information on benchmarking, and advice by email and telephone as well as reductions on places for their IT conferences, discounts on web hosting packages and access to software tools. (Membership packages are tailored to fit each organization's needs, so to find out how much it costs you have to send them your details.)

National Inventors Hall of Fame
221 South Broadway Street
Akron, OH 44308-1505
Tel: 00 1 330 762 4463
Fax: 00 1 330 762 6313
Website: www.invent.org

The National Inventors Hall of Fame was established in 1973 by the US Patent and Trademark Office and the National Council of Intellectual Property Law Associations.

It is a not-for-profit organization that aims to recognize inventors and invention everywhere, to promote creativity and to advance the spirit of innovation.

On the website you can search the short stories of the inventors in the Hall of Fame for inspiration: everyone from Acheson (carborundum) to Zworykin (cathode ray tube) is listed.

PatentCafe.com, Inc.
441 Colusa Avenue
Suite D
Yuba City, CA 95991
Tel: 00 1 530 671 0200
Fax: 00 1 530 671 0201
Website: www.patentcafe.com

Launched in 1996, PatentCafe has established itself as a navigational directory for creators and professionals needing informational resources related to patents, trade marks and copyrights.

Among other things they are a developer and distributor of products, services and information management tools used in the creation, protection, enforcement and commercialization of patents, trade marks and other intellectual property. They also have an extensive collection of news, advice, software, books, legal, insurance and financial products, intellectual asset management tools, patent analytics management tools and educational support materials, on or off the web.

Their products, information and services reach every segment of the intellectual property community, including patent attorneys, inventors, researchers, entrepreneurs, government agencies, engineers and scientists, law students, corporate intellectual property and M&A managers.

Patent Information Network
The British Library
96 Euston Road
London
NW1 2DB
Tel: 020 7412 7919 (British patents); 020 7412 7902 (foreign patents)
Email: patents-information@bl.uk
Website: www.bl.uk/services/information/patents/patentsnetork.html

The Patent Information Network is a group of 13 public and academic libraries which aims to supply regional access to the technological and commercial information available in patent documentation. You can access the library nearest you from their website.

Research associations

Research associations are the centres of knowledge in their respective field. Every field of science and technology has such a centre, so the business idea you are pursuing will almost certainly fall within their remit. These organizations have extensive information systems and can usually guide enquirers to the appropriate sources of data or help.

Some of their services are free and available on the Internet. However, from being government inspired and funded when set up, these organizations are for the most part private enterprise initiatives concerned with supporting a membership and making money themselves.

The list below is indicative rather than exhaustive and gives an idea of the range of associations. A search of the web will uncover the association that covers your chosen area.

BHR Group
The Fluid Engineering Centre
Cranfield
MK43 0AJ
Tel: 01234 750422
Fax: 01234 750074
Email: fluid@bhrgroup.com
Website: www.bhrgroup.co.uk

BIBRA Toxicology International
Woodmansterne Road
Carshalton
SM5 4DS
Tel: 020 8652 1040
Fax: 020 8661 7029
Email: help@tnobibra.co.uk
Website: www.bibra.co.uk

Covers the following industries:

• food and drink
• pharmaceutical

- consumer health
- chemical
- agrochemical.

Biotechnology and Biological Sciences Research Council (BBSRC)
Polaris House
North Star Avenue
Swindon
SN2 1UH
Tel: 01793 413200
Fax: 01793 413201
Website: www.bbsrc.ac.uk

Brewing Research International
Lyttel Hall
Nutfield
Redhill
RH1 4HY
Tel: 01737 822272
Fax: 01737 822747
Email: bri@brewingresearch.co.uk
Website: www.brewingresearch.co.uk

Brick Development Association Ltd
Woodside House
Winkfield
Windsor
SL4 2DX
Tel: 01344 885651
Fax 01344 890129
Email: brick@brick.org.uk
Website: www.brick.org.uk

BLC Leather Technology Centre Ltd
Leather Trade House
Kings Park Road
Moulton Park
Northampton
NN3 6JD
Tel: 01604 679999
Fax: 01604 679998
Email: info@blcleathertech.com
Website: www.blcleathertech.com

Building Research Establishment(BRE)
Bucknalls Lane
Garston
Watford
WD25 9XX
Tel: 01923 664000
Email: enquiries@bre.co.uk
Website: www.bre.co.uk

CERAM Research Ltd
Queens Road
Penkhull
Stoke-on-Trent
ST4 7LQ
Tel: 01782 764444
Fax 01782 412331
Email: enquiries@ceram.co.uk
Website: www.ceram.co.uk
For ceramics and materials expertise.

Construction Industry Research and Information Association (CIRIA)
6 Storey's Gate
London
SW1P 3AU
Tel: 020 7222 8891
Fax: 020 7222 1708
Email: enquiries@ciria.org.uk
Website: www.ciria.org.uk

Engineering and Physical Sciences Research Council
Polaris House
North Star Avenue
Swindon
SN2 1ET
Tel: 01793 444100
Website: www.epsrc.ac.uk

Fabric Care Research Association (FCRA)
Forest House Laboratories
Knaresborough Road
Harrogate
HG2 7LZ
Tel: 01423 885977
Fax: 01423 880045

Email: FCRA@compuserve.com
Website: www.fcra.org.uk

Furniture Industry Research Association International (FIRA)
Maxwell Road
Stevenage
SG1 2EW
Tel: 01438 777700
Fax: 01438 777800
Website: www.fira.co.uk

Food Research Association
Randalls Road
Leatherhead
KT22 7RY
Tel: 01372 376761
Fax: 01372 386228
Email: help@lfra.co.uk
Website: www.lfra.co.uk

Forest Products Research Centre
Buckinghamshire Chilterns University College
Queen Alexandra Road
High Wycombe
HP11 2JZ
Tel: 01494 605104
Fax: 01494 605051
Email: fprc@bcuc.ac.uk
Website: www.bcuc.ac.uk/technology/FPRC/

The Horticulture Research International Association
Horticulture Research International
Wellesbourne
Warwick
CV35 9EF
Tel: 01789 470382
Fax: 01789 470552
Email: HRI.Association@hri.ac.uk
Website: www.hri.ac.uk

Institute of Materials
1 Carlton House Terrace
London
SW1Y 5DB

Tel: 020 7451 7300
Fax: 020 7839 1702
Email: Admin@materials.org.uk
Website: www.instmat.co.uk

Medical Research Council
20 Park Crescent
London
W1N 4AL
Tel: 020 7636 5422
Fax: 020 7436 6179
Website: www.mrc.ac.uk

The Paint Research Association
8 Waldegrave Road
Teddington
TW11 8LD
Tel: 020 8614 4800
Fax: 020 8943 4705
Website: www.pra.org.uk

Production Industry Research Association (PERA)
Pera Innovation Park
Melton Mowbray
LE13 0PB
Tel: 01664 501501
Fax: 01664 501554
Email: marketing@pera.com
Website: www.pera.com

Paper Industry Research Association International (PIRA)
Randalls Road
Leatherhead
KT22 7RU
Tel: 01372 802050
Fax: 01372 802239
Email: infocentre@pira.co.uk
Website: www.piranet.com

TRADA (Timber Research and Development Association) Technology Ltd
Stocking Lane
Hughenden Valley
High Wycombe

HP14 4ND
Tel: 01494 569600
Fax: 01494 565487
Website: www.trada.co.uk

TRADA Technology Ltd
The Business Centre
Templeborough Enterprise Park
Bowbridge Close
Rotherham
S60 1BY
Tel: 01709 720215
Fax: 01709 720178

TRADA Technology Ltd
Office 30
Stirling Business Centre
Wellgreen Place
Stirling
FK8 2DZ
Tel: 01786 462122
Fax: 01786 474412

Small Business Research Initiative
Small Business Service
Kingsgate House
66–74 Victoria Street
London
SW1E 6SW
Email: mike.burrows@sbs.gsi.gov.uk
Website: www.sbs.gov.uk/sbri/sbri.asp

The Small Business Research Initiative (SBRI) is designed to increase the success of smaller firms in obtaining contracts from government bodies to conduct research and development. The initiative was inspired by the US Small Business Innovation Research Programme.

The R&D procurement programmes of government departments and the Research Councils (worth up to £1 billion in total) are being opened up to smaller firms. The government departments involved will aim to buy at least 2.5% of their R&D requirements from smaller businesses.

The Research Councils will move to meet the same targets over time. The target is for £50 mil-lion of government research to be bought from smaller firms.

The SBRI aims:

*   to strengthen those existing small firms whose businesses are based upon providing R&D – by increasing the size of the market
*   to encourage other smaller businesses to increase their R&D capabilities and capacity – to exploit the new market opportunities and
*   to create opportunities for starting new technology-based or knowledge-based businesses.

Businesses must meet certain criteria to participate in the SBRI:

*   they should have fewer than 250 employees
*   their annual turnover must not be greater than €40 million (about £26 million) or alternatively their balance sheet total should not higher than €27 million (about £17 million)
*   they must be independent (that is, less than 25% of the business is owned by enterprises that do not conform to the other criteria – this rule need not apply to investments that are held by public investment corporations, venture capital companies or other institutional investors provided that they do not exercise control over the business).

Charities, university spin-offs, individuals and groups are eligible to participate if they fulfil the above criteria.

The research opportunities offered under the SBRI will also be publicized on the individual sites of the participating government departments and the Research Councils.

SMART awards
Website: www.sbs.gov.uk/SMART/

Small Firms Merit Award for Research and Technology (SMART) awards are Department of Trade and Industry (DTI) grants for individuals and small businesses in England to develop innovative new products and processes. Businesses need to contact their local Business Link to apply for an award. Businesses compete for the grants, which are given for various types of project.

- **Technology Reviews:** Grants of up to £2500 for individuals and small and medium-sized firms (those with fewer than 250 employees) towards the costs of expert reviews against best practice.
- **Technology Studies:** Grants of up to £5000 for individuals and small and medium-sized firms (fewer than 250 employees) to help identify technological opportunities leading to innovative products and processes.
- **Micro Projects:** Grants of up to £10,000 to help individuals and micro-firms (fewer than 10 employees) with developing low-cost prototypes of products and processes involving technical advances and/or novelty.
- **Feasibility Studies:** Grants of up to £45,000 for individuals and small firms (fewer than 50 employees) undertaking feasibility studies into innovative technologies.
- **Development Projects:** Grants of up to £150,000 for small and medium-sized firms (fewer than 250 employees) undertaking development projects.
- **Exceptional Development Projects:** Also for small and medium-sized firms (fewer than 250 employees), a small number of exceptional high cost development projects may attract grants of up to £450,000.

There are similar schemes in Scotland run by the Scottish Office Education and Industry Department; in Wales by The National Assembly for Wales Industry and Training Department, and in Northern Ireland by the Department of Economic Development's Industrial Research and Technology Unit. The website has direct links to these providers.

Technology Means Business
Website: www.technologymeansbusiness.org.uk

Entrepreneurs looking for answers to these IT questions should find answers from this government-sponsored accreditation service.

- Who should I turn to?
- How will ICT apply to my business?
- How should I develop my ICT strategy?
- What do I need to do?

Any SME within the UK looking for credible information and communications technology (ICT) advice can contact any adviser with the TMB accreditation, who can help you to adopt, integrate and use ICT to your business' advantage.

Technology Means Business aims to be the industry standard accreditation for those providing integrated business and information and communications technology (ICT) advice to SMEs.

Key benefits the service offers to SMEs are:

- access to high quality ICT advice focused on business needs
- up-to-date advice on the latest technology and links to other sources of useful business information
- reduction in the time and risk associated with choosing an adviser or supplier
- reassurance of the adviser's or supplier's credibility and ability to:
  - understand the role of ICT in business
  - understand issues facing SMEs
  - keep the use of jargon to a minimum
  - help integrate ICT into business strategy
  - help identify how the full integration and utilization of ICT can develop business
  - assist in managing the process of change.

UK Patent Office
Website: www.patent.gov.uk

The Patent Office is responsible for intellectual property (copyright, designs, patents and trade marks) in the UK. On their website they have full details on all matters connected with intellectual property. All details concerning UK copyright, designs, patents and trade marks, including costs and application procedures, are given on their website There are also links to the relevant patent-granting bodies in 75 other countries from Algeria to Uzbekistan.

Their free leaflets, guidance notes, manuals (with text on the website) and services include:

- What is a Patent: the definition of a patent
- Benefits of Patent Protection: why you should protect your patent
- How to apply for a Patent: what you need to do to apply for a patent both in the UK and abroad, and assistance available to inventors and innovators
- Patents in Detail: further information about applying for a patent and what options are available to you after grant
- Forms and Fees: all forms relating to patents and their fees
- Patent Law and Legal Decisions: the patents rules and results of legal disputes
- Patent Notices & PDJ: Patents and Designs Journal, search delivery targets and patent practice notices
- Reference Material: Manual of Patent Practice and Patent Classification schemes; Hearing Officers' Manual; Litigation Section Manual and Deciding Patent Disputes in the Patent Office
- Record Searches: search for patent records
- Glossary of Terms: definitions of the technical terms used in the field.

This information is mirrored for trade marks, copyright and designs.

United Inventors Association

PO Box 23447
Rochester
NY 14692
Tel: 00 1 585 359 9310
Fax: 00 1 585 359 1132
Email: UIAUSA@aol.com
Website: www.uiausa.com

Formed in 1990 solely for educational purposes.

The mission of the UIA is to provide leadership, support and services to inventor support groups and independent inventors. Membership is extended to these as well as to others who provide reputable service and support to the inventor community. Their Bookstore link lists useful books, publications and journals.

United States Patent and Trademark Office

General Information Services Division
US Patent and Trademark Office
Crystal Plaza 3
Room 2C02
Washington, DC 20231
Website: www.uspto.gov

Provides for the US market a service similar to UK Patent Office (see page 171). Booklets, information and hundreds of useful web links are all listed and described on the site.

World Intellectual Property Organization (WIPO)

Small and Medium-Sized Enterprises Division
World Intellectual Property Organization
34 chemin des Colombettes
1211 Geneva 20
Switzerland
Fax: 00 41 22 338 8760
Email: sme@wipo.int
Website: www.wipo.int

If you are wondering what 'intellectual property' means, or what relevance it could possibly have to the creation or success of an SME, then this website could be the right place to look for answers. WIPO examines intellectual property (IP) from the perspective of SMEs and analyses the possibilities offered by the IP system for improving their performance and competitiveness.

The Intellectual Property for Business section of their website provides a succinct and reader-friendly overview of the main reasons why attention should be focused on the IP system, along with practical tips on how to make the best use of it. Explanations in business-oriented language, often in the form of questions and answers, examine how the IP system helps SMEs to face some of their everyday business challenges, as well as the basic steps required to protect, manage, license and enforce IP rights.

The Intellectual Property in Electronic Commerce section offers an introduction to IP issues related to e-commerce.

Under Activities, they provide a panoramic view of the type of assistance WIPO offers for promoting the use of the IP system by SMEs, including information on past and forthcoming events as well as on useful information and reference material.

The Links section contains more detailed information on specific issues or related matters and links to other sources of information on IP.

Their target audience worldwide includes not just the end-users of the IP system – namely, entrepreneurs – but also the providers of IP services, as well as partners and support institutions at the international, regional, national and local levels. Through this website, they hope to reach out also to the public, private and civil society organizations that are working to improve the prosperity and sustainability of the SME sector worldwide

E-commerce

E-commerce covers a range of activities that can be carried out online to make your business more efficient. These solutions extend across the supply chain, from ordering your raw materials right through to after-sales service. It can incorporate market intelligence gathering, customer relationship management and a whole range of back office procedures.

By using integrated e-commerce solutions a small business can level the playing field with big business and have a similar level of efficiency but at an affordable cost. The mainstream areas that can be incorporated into an integrated e-commerce solution include:

- having a virtual storefront, electronic mall or business-to-business commerce system
- being able to process sales transactions, identify buying patterns and preferences, customize promotions, savings and incentives, track orders, maintain customer sales information and keep a record of sales contact activity
- integrate front-end sales processes with your back-end system such as stock and debtors, using your existing technology and software. This saves duplication of entries and systems, as one entry runs across all the necessary transactions
- account authorizing, processing and credit card transactions systems
- flexible and cost-effective solutions for global payment processing, fraud prevention, tax calculation, export compliance, territory management, delivery address verification and fulfilment management.

Other areas of your business that can be conducted online using the same software and processes as the rest of your online activities include:

- recruitment and selection of staff using online agencies
- employment records
- customer satisfaction surveys using integrated questionnaire analysis software
- online accounting and financial report generation to provide better business controls
- market research information on customers, competitors, market segments and overseas markets
- brochure, catalogue, leaflet and price list generation
- purchasing of supplies and materials.

In the UK there has never been a better time to invest in IT. Since the 2000 Budget, a measure meant to help small firms equip themselves with new technology has been in force. All IT spending attracts accelerated write down for tax purposes, in the year in which that equipment is bought. Normally such expenditure has to be spread over several years when claiming the tax relief. The measure applies to any company, partnership or sole trader which satisfies two of the following criteria:

- turnover of under £2.8 million
- a balance sheet total of not more than £1.4 million
- not more than 50 employees.

The concession covers computers, connecting peripheral kit, cabling, WAP phones and most other IT equipment.

Trading online

There are nearly 40 million people in the UK with Internet connections, up from under 8 million in October 1999, and over £100 billion of sales are made over the Internet. Worldwide, the figures are more elusive and more impressive. Some 600 million are on the Internet and the sales via that channel are now in the thousands of billions.

You need two things, apart from some fairly minimal computer hardware costing no more than £1000, to get into E-business. A shop front, and means of accepting payment online.

Shop front

There are two main methods of getting an online shop front:

- **A server-based subscription service:** A server-based store lets you create and manage a web store using just a web browser using only an inexpensive local computer. The subscription can include hosting too. You'll pay a set-up fee and a monthly subscription fee, which makes it an easy payment system for small businesses, rather than a major investment up front. The host is responsible for backing up and securing your store. However, because the store is managed via a web browser, your Internet connection gives you access to your store, so you are only as efficient as your connection. If you have a slow connection you'll find building and running a sizeable store can be a headache. These stores can all look rather similar, as they're designed for wide appeal.

  Server-based services include:
  - ShopCreator at www.shopcreator.com. A subscription-based service costing anything from £450 to £3500, depending on whether you want a simple system for up to 50 products, or want something to handle currencies, credit, customer tracking and 1000 products
  - Ecomm Store 2.0 at www.trellian.com/ecommstore costs from $39.95 and is based around a flexible database which can handle up to 12 user-defined fields. Order processing is handled on a secure site for $15 a month
  - Digital StoreFronts at www.digitalstore-fronts is a fairly similar product, costing $49 per month plus a further $19.95 for providing an online shopping cart.

- **PC-based store:** An out-of-the-box store builder runs on your own local computer – so you'll need a powerful computer capable of managing your site and supporting the application. You'll also need to find an Internet Service Provider (ISP) to host the site (these are listed in most web magazines) and you will be responsible for maintaining it and uploading any changes to the ISP. There are a variety of packages built to fit a budget of a few hundred pounds, although you'll need to add on hosting charges, plus the time and cost of updating and uploading the site. You will also need to consider what type of customer payments the software supports. As some people will not pay online by credit card, you'll have to ensure that you can accept cash on delivery (COD) or cheque with order as well. Examples of off-the-shelf software include:
  - Actinic Catalogue 5 at www.actinic.co.uk. Priced at £350, this software creates an e-commerce site that's ready to go. It covers all

main payment methods and has gateways to many merchant accounts (see below)

- ecBuilder Pro 6 at www.multiactive.com is priced at $399. As well as being a wizard-based store designer, ecBuilder automatically submits your website to the top 10 search engines as part of the deal.
- Dataflex Business Systems Ltd at www.egenie.co.uk have designed an easy to use but powerful shop front. They claim that within minutes a complete Internet novice can create an impressive website with full e-commerce facilities. Priced at £275.

Paying online

Although you can start to trade online by accepting payment on delivery by cheque, eventually you will have to accept credit cards. There are three ways to open up this method of payment.

Merchant accounts

If you want to be able to take credit card transactions on your website, the best route is to get a 'merchant account'. This is arranged with a 'card acquirer' – a virtual bank which processes card payments for you, then levies charges on your merchant account and transfers the balance into your bank account. Start-ups often find merchant status difficult to obtain – but a good personal banking record may suffice.

Merchant account providers include:

- www.worldpay.com
- www.netbanx.com
- www.creditcardprocessor.com
- www.secpay.com
- www.securetrading.com
- www.gap-online.co.uk/ecommerce.htm
- www.smarterfinance.com/uk
- www.datacash.com
- www.chargil.com

Payment Service Providers (PSPs)

Payment service providers (PSPs) act as go-betweens for customers and online traders, providing online authorization and processing of payments. When a customer confirms an order on your site, their payment details go directly to the PSP's secure server. The provider arranges authorization, deducts a fee, and puts the balance in your account. A PSP is a safe way of selling online, and most High Street banks prefer you to use them even if you do have a merchant account, because it's safer to authorize a small number of PSPs than to rely on each trader to be secure.

You pay higher fees than you would with merchant status, and wait for payment, but it is by far the easiest way to get paid online.

PSPs include:

- www.ccnow.com
- www.iFulfill.com
- www.netbanx.com
- www.ibill.com
- www.kagi.com
- www.clickbank-com

Electronic cash

Electronic cash allows customers to save credits online, either by cash, cheque, credit card or smart card. These can then be spent on your site. Customers have to have an electronic cash account before they can start spending, which is bound to narrow your market.

Electronic cash services include:

- www.paypal.com
- www.nochex.com
- www.digicash.com (Ecash)

Many of the organizations listed earlier in this section can help you with the e-commerce aspects of your strategy, in particular the accelerators and eBusiness Clubs.

Section 5

FINDING OUT ABOUT YOUR MARKET

Sizing up the market

You need to ensure that there are enough customers out there, with sufficient money to spend, to create a viable market place for your products or services. You must also see who else will be competing against you for their business. In other words, you need to research your market. This is something that potential financial backers – be they banks or other institutions – will insist on. And in this they are doing you a favour. Many businesses started with private money (such as redundancy payments) fail because the market was not thoroughly researched at the outset. Whatever your business idea, you must undertake some well-thought-out market research before you invest any money or approach anyone else to invest in your venture. You do not always have to pay professional companies to do your research, although sometimes it may make good sense to do so. You can often gather information effectively (and cheaply) yourself. This 'DIY' market research will have three purposes.

- To build credibility for the business idea, the entrepreneur must prove, first to his or her satisfaction and later to outside financiers, that he or she thoroughly understands the marketplace for the new product or service. This will be vital if resources are to be attracted to build the new venture.
- To develop a realistic market entry strategy for the new business, based on a clear understanding of genuine customer needs and ensuring that product quality, price, promotional methods and distribution chain are mutually supportive and clearly focused on target customers.
- To ensure you have sufficient information on customers, competitors and markets so that your market entry strategy or expansion strategy is at least on the target, if not on the bull's eye itself. If you miss the target altogether, which you could well do without research, you may not have the necessary cash resources for a second shot.

The military motto 'Time spent in reconnaissance is rarely time wasted' holds true for business as well. You will need to research in particular:

- **your customers:** who will buy your goods and services? What particular customer needs will your business meet? How many of them are there, are their numbers growing or contracting, how much do they spend and how often do they buy?
- **your competitors:** which established businesses are already meeting the needs of your potential customers? What are their strengths and weaknesses? Are they currently failing their customers in some way that you can improve on?
- **your product or service:** could or should it be tailored to meet the needs of particular groups of customer? For example, if you are starting up a delivery business, professional clients may require a 'same day service', whilst members of the public at large would be happy to get goods in a day or two, provided it was less costly

- **the price you should charge:** all too often small firms confine their research on pricing to seeing what the competition charges and either matching it or beating it. That may be a way to get business, but it is not the best route to profitable business. You need to know what price would be perceived as being too cheap, what would represent good 'value for money' and what would be seen as a rip-off, so you can pitch in at the right price for your offering
- **which promotional material will reach your customers:** what newspapers and journals do they read and which of these is most likely to influence their buying decision?
- **your location:** from where could you reach your customers most easily and at minimum cost?
- **how will you sell most effectively:** can you use telesales, the Internet or a catalogue, or will customers only buy face-to-face either from a salesperson or from a retail outlet?

Research, above all else, is not just essential in starting a business but, once launched, should become an integral part in the ongoing life of the business. Customers and competitors change; products and services don't last forever. Once started, however, ongoing market research becomes easier, as you will have existing customers (and staff) to question. It is important that you regularly monitor their views on your business (as the sign in the barber shop stated: 'We need your head to run our business') and develop simple techniques for this purpose (e.g. questionnaires for customers beside the till, suggestion boxes with rewards for employees).

Hasten slowly

Procter & Gamble test-marketed the home dry-cleaning product 'Dryel' on 150,000 households for more than three years before introducing the product in 1999. Contrast this with how Drugstore.com tested the water. Before its launch in February 1999, the online company spent less than a week surveying only about 100 people. Around that time, market research for many online companies was reduced to slapping up a website and hoping for the best.

Drugstore's financial performance makes sorry reading. Its latest quarterly accounts, known in the US as a 'Form 10-Q', which give details of its financial performance to 30 September 2001, show a loss of $34,506,000 on sales of $34,978,000. Over the nine months to that date they had lost over $100 million on the same amount of sales. Shareholders had lost $0.39 for every $1 they had put in and the share price was a fraction of its price at launch.

Now that this practice has stopped, it seems likely that new Internet firms will have to act a bit more slowly and follow some of the old rules of marketing, while maybe at the same time speeding up these traditional practices. With so many Internet firms, being first to market has translated into little more than being first out of it.

The seven steps to good market research

Researching the market need not be a complex process, nor need it be very expensive. The amount of effort and expenditure needs to be related in some way to the costs and risks associated with the business. If all that is involved with your business is simply getting a handful of customers for products and services that cost little to put together, then you may spend less effort on market research than you would for, say, launching a completely new product or service into an unproven market that required a large sum of money to be spent up front. However much or little market research you plan to carry out, the process needs to conducted systematically. There are seven stages you need to go through to make sure you have properly sized up your business sector.

They are briefly described below and covered more fully under the headings 'Desk research' and 'Field research' later in this section.

Step 1: Formulate the problem

Before embarking on your market research you should first set clear and precise objectives, rather than just setting out to find interesting general information about the market. The starting point for a business idea may be to sell clothes, but that is too large and diverse a market to get a handle on. So that market needs to be divided up into, say, clothes for men, women and children, and then further divided into clothes for working, leisure, sport and social occasions. This process is known as segmenting the market. A further segment could cover special occasions such as weddings. Even once you have narrowed your idea down to, say, smart clothes for women, the definition of what is smart will differ for each age group. Most businesses end up selling to several different market segments, but when it comes to detailed market research you need to examine each of your main segments separately.

So, for example, if you are planning to open a shop selling to young, fashion-conscious women, amongst others, your research objective could be: to find out how many women aged 18–28, in the income range £25,000+ p.a., live or work within two miles of your chosen shop position. That would give you some idea if the market could support a venture such as this.

Step 2: Determine the information needs

Knowing the size of the market in the example given above may require several different pieces of information. For example, we will need to know the resident population, which may be fairly easy to find out. But we would also like to know something about people who come into our catchment area to work, for leisure purposes, on holiday or for any other major purpose. There may, for example, be a hospital, library, railway station or school nearby that also pulls potential customers to a particular area.

Step 3: Where can you get the information

This will involve either desk research in libraries or on the Internet or field research, which you can do yourself or get help in doing. These areas are covered later in this section.

Step 4: Decide the budget

Market research will not be free, even if you do it yourself. At the very least there will be your time. There may well be the cost of journals, phone calls, letters and field visits to plan for. At the top of the scale could be the costs of employing a professional market research firm.

Starting at this end of the scale, a business-to-business survey comprising 200 interviews with executives responsible for office equipment purchasing decisions cost one company £12,000. Twenty in-depth interviews with consumers who are regular users of certain banking services cost £8000. Using the Internet for web surveys is another possibility, but that can impose too much of your agenda onto the recipient and turn them away from you.

Doing the research in-house may save costs but may limit the objectivity of the research. If time is your most scarce commodity, it may make more sense to get an outside agency to do the work. Using a reference librarian or university student to do some of the spadework need not be prohibitively expensive (see the examples for Birmingham Library Information Direct on page 214). Another argument for getting professional research is that it may carry more clout with investors.

Whatever the cost of research, you need to assess its value to you when you are setting your budget. So if getting it wrong will cost £100,000, then £5000 spent on market research may be a good investment.

Step 5: Select the research technique

If you can't find the data you require from desk research you will need to go out and find the data yourself. The options for such research are described later in this section under the heading 'Field Research'.

Step 6: Construct the research sample population

It is rarely possible or even desirable to include every possible customer or competitor in your research. So you have to decide how big a sample you need to give you a reliable indication as to how the whole population will behave.

Stage 7: Process and analyse the data

The raw market research data needs to be analysed and turned into information to guide your decisions on price, promotion, location and the shape, design and scope of product or service itself.

Desk research

Once you have your research objective and know the questions you want answers to, the next step is to see if someone else has the answers already. Market research conjures up images of people with clipboards accosting you in the street – and you might well have to do that. But much of the information you need will already be published, so some of your market research activity, at least, can be done in a comfortable chair either at home on the Internet, or in a good library. For instance, the official Census of Population will supply you with demographic data on size, age and sex of the local populace, and there is a wealth of government and other published statistics to enable you to work out the size and shape of the market nationwide and the expenditure per head of population. This type of research is called desk research and it is well worth doing first.

Let's look first at the types of information that is out there.

Market data and sources

Much of the information listed below is costly. Some data costs hundreds of pounds and some is only available to subscribers who have paid thousands of pounds to have it on tap. Fortunately, the cost to you need not be too much. Indeed, in many cases it may cost you nothing at all. Your library (or an Internet link to a library) may have the relevant directory, publication or research study on its shelves. If you are a member of a chamber of commerce, a trade association, small business association or are taking or have taken a small business course (see Section 8), the chances are you will have access to much of the data, and perhaps more, for free.

But even if it does cost something in time and money, getting the data will almost invariably help you make better decisions. If you think knowledge is expensive you should try ignorance!

Market research data

The number of directories and data-gathering services is enormous. A small selection of the most important of these is set out below, divided into UK and overseas sections.

Most of these organizations are international in nature and operate wherever business is to be done profitably. Whatever your sector or interest, the chances are there is a directory or information service.

Most of these services are fee-paying and sometimes expensive. However, access to much of the data can be gained on a pay-as-you-use basis. Often the data is available through an intermediary such as a library (See 'Libraries and library information sources' on page 214), in which case the data may well be free to visitors and available through their specialist services either at a modest cost or perhaps even free if you are a library member. Some libraries may make some of the data available online.

UK market data
Bank of England
Threadneedle Street
London
EC2R 8AH
Tel: 020 7601 4444
Fax: 020 7601 5460
Email: enquiries@bankofengland.co.uk
Website: www.bankofengland.co.uk

The Bank of England publishes information on all aspects of its work in many formats; much of it available on their website. The search facility enables one to find either the complete document (presented in one of two ways – either as a web page or as a PDF file) or a summary of the contents and/or details of how to obtain the publication from the Bank.

Hard copies of all publications (including those not available on this site) can be obtained by contacting the Public Enquiries Group.

Aside from a vast array of data on how the economy is working, the following small business reports are regularly produced, and make interesting and informative reading:

- Quarterly Report on Small Business Statistics (start-ups and failures, all by sector and geographic area)
- The Financing of Technology-based Small Firms reports
- Finance for Small Firms
- Smaller Exporters – A Special Report
- The Financing of Ethnic Minority Firms in the UK
- Finance for Small Businesses in Deprived Communities.

BENNS Media Directory

Benns
Miller Freeman UK Ltd
Riverbank House
Angel Lane
Tonbridge
TN9 1SE
Tel: 01732 362666
Fax: 01732 367301
Website: www.millerfreeman.co.uk

Directory covering the media industry across all of its sectors within the UK. Guide to newspapers, periodicals, broadcasting, reference publications and electronic media. Europe and World editions also available. Priced at £152 per volume. Not yet on the Internet.

BRAD (British Rate and Data)

BRAD Group
EMAP Media
33–39 Bowling Green Lane
London
EC1R 0DA
Tel: 020 7505 8000
Website: www.brad.co.uk

BRAD is a monthly classified directory of media in the UK and the Republic of Ireland that carry advertising. Media are broken down into: national and regional newspapers, consumer press, business press, new and electronic media (mostly Internet sites), television, video, cinema, radio, and posters and outdoor. This information is also available via subscription through BRADnet and BRADbase. The BRAD group also publish Genesis, Alf and mailing list service, Target Direct.

British Companies
Website: www.britishcompanies.co.uk

An annotated listing of links to British companies and organizations that deal in consumer products, organized into several dozen categories.

British Services
Website: www.britishservices.co.uk

An annotated listing of British companies and organizations that provide services, organized by category.

Companies House
Tel: 0870 333 3636 (call centre and telesales)
Website: www.companieshouse.co.uk

and at

Companies House Cardiff
Crown Way
Cardiff
CF14 3UZ
Tel: 029 20 388588
Monday to Friday, 0900–1700

Companies House Edinburgh

37 Castle Terrace

Edinburgh

EH1 2EB

Monday to Friday, 0900–1700

Companies House London

21 Bloomsbury Street

London

WC1B 3XD

Fax: 029 20 380900

Monday to Friday, 0900–1700

Prospect House Leeds Ltd

Prospect House

32 Sovereign St

Leeds

LS1 4BJ

Monday to Friday, 0900–1600

Expansys Ltd

Rutherford House

40 Pencroft Way

Manchester

M15 6GG

Monday to Friday, 0900–1600

Visiting any of the offices you are able to get the following information instantly from in-house computer screens:

- company number
- company type
- date of incorporation
- a list of all documents filed in the last five years
- details of serving directors and secretaries and of those who have resigned since 1991
- a list of disqualified directors
- images of accounts online to view or print (Cardiff and London)
- document packages
- a choice of three company reports
- mortgage information (Cardiff and London)
- insolvency details.

You can order print-outs of the information shown on the screen and you can use the online ordering system to order a full search on microfiche, available within two hours at Cardiff, London and Edinburgh, or the following day at the other offices.

You can order records of Scottish companies from the English and Welsh offices and records of English and Welsh companies from the Scottish offices. These inter-registry searches will be ready by 0900 the following day if you order by 1500.

Alternatively, you can use their Internet service, Companies House Direct (website: www.companieshouse.co.uk).

Online services include:

- **WebCHeck:** make your own selection of easily downloadable company reports, returns and accounts at the online shop
- **CD-ROM Directory:** pin down key information with accurate searches on over 1.7 million live and recently dissolved companies.
- **CH Monitor:** a surveillance service for pre-ordering specified documents submitted by the companies you wish to monitor.

Prices range from 10p per page of information copied on site, to £6.50 for a microfiche of a company's accounts. A special delivery of data can cost £25.

The dedicated call centre is able to deal with most general queries on matters relating to Companies House. Callers requiring more specific help can be routed to the relevant sections. Staff at the call centre can also take orders for company searches, which are then dispatched by post or fax. The minimum credit card payment is £5.

ICC Business Information

Victoria House

64 Paul Street

London

EC2A 4NG

Tel: +44 (0)20 7426 8555

Fax: +44 (0)20 7426 8514

Email: clientservices@icc.co.uk

Website: http://www.icc.co.uk

Founded in 1969, ICC is one of the leading providers of British and Irish business information, possessing unrivalled knowledge of all 5.2 million UK and Irish companies.

Profile reports are available for all four million limited companies (both live and dissolved) registered at Companies House since 1968, whether they have been analysed by ICC or not. The report provides the following information on the company:

- the registered address
- date of incorporation
- account filing details
- type of company
- principal activity statement
- principal SIC code (Standard Industry Classification code – classifying a particular business activity)
- ownership information
- company secretary
- abbreviated accounts for three years
- filing history.

Overview reports are available for over 750,000 analysed companies (by ICC). The report is divided into the following six sections:

- **statutory information:** registered name and address, previous name(s), issued capital, type of accounts filed, company type, date of incorporation and all relevant filing dates
- **directory information:** confirms the trading address (where available), telephone and fax numbers, region, bankers, auditors, SIC codes (Standard Industry Classification code – classifying a particular business activity) and the principal activities statement
- **risk information:** details County Court judgments, risk score for the last four years and the latest recommended credit and contract limit
- **account information:** shows an abbreviated profit and loss account and balance sheet for the company
- **company and industry comparison:** compares ratios and percentages of company performance against companies in the same industry type
- **directors information:** lists the Company Secretary and all notified directors.

Financial reports are available for all 750,000 analysed companies (by ICC). There are 13 sections available, detailing five years' worth of accounts, including:

- **statutory information:** details of registered name and address, date of incorporation, type of accounts filed, accounts and annual return filing dates, and issued capital
- **directory information:** where available, confirms the trading address, telephone and fax numbers, principal activities with the main SIC codes (Standard Industry Classification code – classifying a particular business activity) and details of the auditors and the bank
- **risk information:** details the latest 10 County Court judgments, the risk score for the last four years, a recommended credit and contract limit and the holding structure of the company
- **ownership:** breaks out group structure and all live subsidiaries ranked by turnover
- **profit and loss account:** details all items for the last five years, indicating where relevant notes exist
- **balance sheet:** displays the last five years' worth of balance sheet items, indicating where notes are cross-referenced
- **cash flow:** displays cash flow figures for up to five years, showing cash flow from operating activities and cash flow from finance
- **accounts notes:** holds information on items extracted from the latest set of notes, such as exports, audit fees, intermediate assets, bank overdraft, and finance due to directors and group
- **ratios:** lists the main liquidity, performance, employee and gearing ratios
- **growth rates:** provides percentage growth measurements for 1/2/3/4-year periods

- **filing history:** displays every change of name, all mortgage documents and one of each other filing type.

The **company directors report** is available on all companies. It covers all 4.2 million directors, showing a company's directors as reported in the last stated set of accounts. The report provides the following information:

- home address
- date of birth
- occupation
- appointment date
- number of current directorships
- number of past directorships.

The **individual directors report** provides details of current and previous directorships of specified individuals, including:

- address
- occupation
- date of birth
- date of appointment
- number of present directorships
- number of resignations since June 1996.
- original documents.

In addition to analysed reports, Company Plus provides users with access to the original documents as filed by companies at Companies House in PDF format.

You have to open a Company Plus account to access the comprehensive range of UK Company Data provided by ICC information. There is, however, no charge for opening an account with Company Plus, searching the Company Plus database or viewing the top-line information on any company. You only pay if you access a report, and you will always be asked to confirm that you wish to purchase a report before you access it.

Directory of UK Associations
A.S.K. Hollis
Hollis Directories Ltd

Harlequin House
7 High Street
Teddington
TW11 8EL
Tel: 020 8977 7711
Fax: 020 8977 1133
Website: www.hollis-pr.com/publications/ask.htm

Over 5000 associations, pressure groups, unions, institutes, societies and more are profiled in this publication, representing every interest area from abrasives through to zoos, from industrial, professional and business sectors to government, charities and the consumer. Price £150.

Directory of Directories
Albedo Systems Ltd
268 Amhurst Road
London N16 7UP
Tel: 020 7923 2267
Email: information@albedo.co.uk
Website: www.albedo.co.uk

AlephSearch is maintained by Albedo Systems, and contains links to selected web-based directories, both unspecialized and specialized, from Accommodation to Zoology. The directories cover the world, but fairly thinly!

Dun & Bradstreeet
European and UK Headquarters
Holmers Farm Way
High Wycombe
HP12 4UL
Tel: 01494 422000
Fax: 01494 422260
Email: customerhelp@dnb.com
Website: www.dnb.com

D&B, as they are generally known, have been one of the world's leading providers of business information for 160 years.

D&B's information and technology solutions help businesses reduce credit risk, find profitable customers and manage vendors efficiently. They claim to have the largest company database available, with information on 66 million businesses and branches worldwide.

Businesses also use D&B's information and technology to authenticate and verify potential trading partners online, increasing their trust and confidence in e-commerce transactions. Over 90% of the Business Week Global 1000 rely on D&B as the source for information they need to make their business a success.

Their services include:

- D&B Authentication & Verification Services
- D&B Business Information Report: detailed business information and financial risk assessment on companies outside Europe
- D&B CAMEO Consumer Classifications: consumer classification and analysis systems to identify and target new consumer customers
- D&B Client Certificates
- D&B Collection Services
- D&B Compact Report: identification and business information for low-level credit decisions
- D&B Company Document Service: copies of Companies House original documents
- D&B Comprehensive Report: a complete picture of a company's financial position
- D&B Country Report: comprehensive information for evaluating risks and opportunities across the globe, providing a unique insight into the relative performance of different countries.
- D&B Country RiskLine: individual country reports from International Risk & Payment Review – analysis of political, commercial and economic risk covering over 130 countries worldwide
- D&B Data Exchange: access to quality consumer datasets to build and enhance your database and direct marketing campaigns
- D&B Demograf Software: convert raw consumer data into market intelligence and knowledge
- D&B Key British Enterprises for the Internet: details on the corporate background, deci-

sion-makers, capital, markets and branches of the UK's leading enterprises
- D&B MarketPlace® UK: identify prospects and acquire profitable new customers with D&B's list and labels
- D&B Monitoring Service: alerts to both positive and negative changes in a customer's, supplier's or competitor's business performance.

Experian
Talbot House
Talbot Street
Nottingham
NG1 5HF
Tel: 0115 941 0888
Fax: 0115 934 4905
Website: www.uk.experian.com

Experian helps organizations find the best prospects and make fast, informed decisions to improve and personalize their relationships with their customers. It does this by combining intelligent decision-making software and systems with some of the world's most comprehensive databases of information on consumers, businesses, motor vehicles and property. Experian is a subsidiary of GUS plc. It also has offices in London and Edinburgh.

The Holway Report
2 St Georges Yard
Farnham
GU7 7LW
Tel: 01252 740900
Fax: 01252 740919
Email: mail@ovumholway.com
Website: www.holway.co.uk/publications/holwayreport/index.htm

Published every year for the past 14 years, the Holway Report is acknowledged as the bible of the UK SITS (Software and IT Services) industry. The Holway Report is perhaps the most respected – and most used – research document on the UK SITS market. Customers include almost every one of the leading UK SITS companies, as well as many from overseas, and most of the investment community. Its research is quoted extensively and has been used in the prospectuses of nearly every UK IPO in recent years.

Since 2001, the Holway Report has become a continuous service, with the whole report available online. Using a simple, web-based interface, you can now find your way quickly to the analysis you need.

The company profiles, financial data and ranking tables are updated regularly, so that you can get an instant, up-to-date picture of over 400 companies.

In addition, the Industry Report (Volume 1) is also available on paper, for those who need a reference guide on their bookshelf.

Their ranking tables are available for download, allowing you to sort, manipulate and present them in the way that suits you best. Also in the report are:

- **acquisitions:** a review and detailed listing of all the main acquisitions undertaken in the last year, including prices paid and recent trading record
- **companies quoted on the Stock Exchange:** a review of the performance, and valuation trends, of the companies in the sector quoted on the UK main and AIM markets as well as NASDAQ
- **company profiles:** including their own comment, not just bland facts and figures, and covering over 400 of the leading companies operating in the UK market
- **company financial datasheets:** one page summaries of the 1000 leading companies operating in the UK, showing detailed profit and loss and balance sheet items for the last five years
- **company ranking tables:** over 30 different rankings of the top 1000 companies.

However, the hard copy costs £2500, so you will probably have to find a library or research provider who can supply you the bits you need.

ICC Information Limited
Field House
72 Oldfield Road
Hampton
TW12 2HQ
Tel: 020 8481 8847
Fax: 020 8941 6014
Email: ipdatasupport@icc.co.uk
Website: www.icc.co.uk

Founded in 1969, ICC has grown to become one of the leading business information providers of British and Irish company information.

For accurate, up-to-date analysed reports, document searches or copies of original company documents, ICC is the definitive source of information on UK and Irish companies.

ICC produces and maintains a database of all 1.6 million live, and 3.8 million dissolved, limited liability companies in the UK.

To ensure up-to-date information, ICC have at least one share in approximately 95% of British quoted companies, as well as sourcing reports from Companies Registration Office in the UK.

Insight Research
46 Sandwich House
Sandwich Street
London
WC1H 9PR
Tel: 020 7383 4546
Fax: 020 7383 0579
Email: info@insightresearch.co.uk
Website: www.insightresearch.co.uk

Insight specialise in grocery reports. They cover such subjects as consumer loyalty, home shopping and the changing role of the grocery buyer.

All reports are priced at £495 and summaries are available on the website.

Jordan's Ltd
21 St Thomas Street
Bristol
BS1 6JS
Tel: 0117 923 0600

Email: customersupport@jordans.co.uk
Website: www.jordans.co.uk

Jordan's is a leading provider of UK business information and services. Jordan's services include company formations and company secretarial services, software solutions, trade mark and domain name registration, company searches and conveyancing services

Their specific services include:

- JordanWatch online business information
- UK company search
- UBIS – unincorporated business information
- international company search
- monitoring services
- Jordan's Company Database
- bespoke data services
- FAME (financial analysis software – UK companies)
- new company information services
- shareholder information
- business surveys
- AMADEUS (financial analysis software).

Kelly's
Website: www.kellys.co.uk

Kelly's directories are published by Reed Publications. They cover a wide range of business activities in the UK. Kellysearch.com is the latest version of the long-established Industrial Directory. The website contains all of the product and service listings that users of their hard copy directories are used to, plus many more.

Because the website is a live source of information they can keep you up to date with the latest in company details, news and special features. The website is completely free to use and allows you to search their extensive database of over 140,000 UK companies and over 100,000 product and service headings.

Key Note Ltd
Field House
72 Oldfield Road

Hampton
TW12 2HQ
Tel: 020 8481 8750
Fax: 020 8783 0049
Email: info@keynote.co.uk
Website: www.keynote.co.uk

Key Note has built a reputation as an expert provider of market information, producing highly respected off-the-shelf publications which cover a comprehensive range of market sectors, from commercial and industrial to service and consumer titles.

Their report gallery has a listing of literally hundreds of reports, covering everything from activity holidays to women's magazines.

The executive summary – a generous 1000 words – plus a full index is available free for every report, which should make it clear whether the report is worth buying or a trip to a major reference library, which may well have a copy to view, is necessary.

Reports are priced from around £300 upwards, with most in the £500 to £700 range.

Kompass United Kingdom
Reed Business Information
Windsor Court
East Grinstead House
East Grinstead
RH19 1XA
Tel: 0800 0185 882
Email: jmason@reedinfo.co.uk
Website: www.kompass.com

Kompass claims to have details of 1.6 million UK companies, 23 million key product and service references, 3.2 million executive names, 744,000 trade and brand names and 50,000 Kompass classification codes in their UK directory.

They also create directory information in over 70 countries.

Their website has a free access area which a user may access without registration, giving access to the following:

- limited search criteria – products/services, company/trade names, and geographical (worldwide, regions or countries)
- limited company lists
- limited number of full company profiles (partial profiles contain only the contact details).

mad.co.uk
Centaur Communications
50 Poland Street
London
W1F 7AX
Tel: 020 7970 4937
Email: danielle@mad.co.uk
Website: www.mad.co.uk

mad.co.uk is the online community for the marketing, media, new media, advertising and design industries. As well as producing up-to-the-minute news, mad.co.uk incorporates the content from 15 of Centaur's leading industry publications including *Marketing Week*, *Design Week*, *New Media Age* and *Creative Review*.

By using mad.co.uk you can access in-depth and up-to-the-minute news, features, analysis and reports from a wide variety of industry titles giving you greater, specific knowledge of your industry and a competitive advantage over your peers.

Alongside up-to-the-minute industry news there are also extensive publication archives going back to 1985 that allow you to research topics by performing simple searches using keywords and offering results in date and relevance order.

Information is also pulled together from each of the publications and placed on 38 content-specific channels, covering nine main areas including New Media, Advertising and Below the Line Marketing. This offers you the chance to tailor the content you see to your particular areas of interest.

Users are provided with an online bookstore (www.mad.co.uk/books), with a list and reviews of recommended industry titles.

You have to spend a couple of minutes filling in their registration form, but after that you will have access to the mad.co.uk home page stories and have the opportunity to take a 30-day free trial

giving you full subscriber access to the site. Subscription costs £223.25 p.a.

Marketing & Creative Handbook
Suite 5
74 Oak Road
Horfield
Bristol
BS7 8RZ
Tel: 0117 944 6144
Fax: 0117 944 6377
Email: mchpages@mch.co.uk
Website: www.mch.co.uk

Printed on A4 glossy paper, these publications contain full colour advertisements and editorial-style entries with precise descriptions of each company's specialization, enabling you to see at a glance the wealth of advertising, marketing and creative services that are available within your own local area. Each region of UK has its own directory, costing £25. The basic text is available for free on the website.

Media Pocket Book
NTC Publications Ltd
Farm Road
Henley-on-Thames
RG9 1EJ
Tel: 01491 411000
Fax: 01491 571188

A statistical profile of British commercial media. Contains data on audiences, ad rates and ad spend for all media plus key data on economics, demographics, digital TV and radio, ambient media and the Internet. Price £26.00.

Media UK Internet Directory
Media UK
2 King's Court
Skelmanthorpe
Huddersfield
HD8 9DY
Tel: 0701 0701 218
Fax: 0701 0701 219

Website: http://directory.mediauk.com

Complete listing of all online media in the UK. Includes radio, television, magazines and newspapers with industry resources. A useful touch for publicity-conscious entrepreneurs is a tutorial on writing a press release.

Mintel International Group Ltd
18–19 Long Lane
London
EC1A 9PL
Tel: 020 7606 4533
Email: info@mintel.com
Website: www.mintel.com

A privately owned independent company, established and respected for over 27 years, Mintel publish over 400 reports every year examining every conceivable consumer market.

There are detailed reports on hundreds of specific market sectors. For example:

* baby food and drink
* barbeque foods
* beachware
* bras and pants
* bicycles
* bridal wear
* british lifestyles.

That's just a handful of the entries under B. The other end of the alphabet looks like this:

* yoghurt market (the) – US report
* yoghurts
* yoghurts (Irish series)
* youth and leisure
* youth and sport
* youth holidays.

Reports cost several hundred pounds, but you can view the introduction and main headings. Most are available free in business libraries.

They also offer a number of reports on the US and European markets.

National Statistics
Website: www.statistics.gov.uk

The National Statistics website contains a vast range of official UK statistics and information about statistics, which can be accessed and downloaded free. There are 13 separate themes. Each one deals with a distinct and easily recognizable area of national life.

The range of data is mind-boggling. For example, within the Economy section it is possible to drill down to Household Final Consumption Expenditure which includes personal expenditure on goods, both durable and non-durable, on second-hand goods, and on services. This shows trends in usage of almost everything you can think of.

Net Profit Publications
8 The Leathermarket
Weston Street
London
SE1 3ER
Tel: 020 7403 1140
Fax: 020 7403 4160
Email: info@netprofit.co.uk
Website: www.net-profit.co.uk

Net Profit, founded in 1996, is a research-based consultancy and publisher that helps organizations raise return on their investment in key business processes.

Their aims are to:

* maximise return on your website investment
* help you understand how others tackle the problems you face
* allow you to measure yourself against other organizations
* gather the evidence that helps you make a business case.

The strengths they claim are:

* a unique database of originally-researched case studies and website analysis

- a continuous scanning operation for best and worst practice worldwide
- the most reliable and comparable database of new economy statistics
- six years' experience and a blue chip client base
- an ability to communicate in plain business English.

Their areas of expertise are:

- website effectiveness
- electronic channels
- supply chains
- knowledge management
- business statistics (net figures).

A recent report was *Winning Strategies on the Internet*, published in association with *Management Today* and priced at £450.

Research Index Ltd

94 West Parade
Lincoln
LN1 1JZ
Tel: 01522 524212
Fax: 01522 514257
Email: info@researchindex.co.uk
Website: www.researchindex.co.uk

Research Index, part of the Creditfax Group, is a database that indexes the headlines of news, views and comments on industries and companies worldwide, as reported in the UK national press and a range of quality business magazines. Every significant daily and Sunday newspaper, business magazine and periodical is indexed. The website is a free way to find out what the press has to say about competitors or suppliers

Sources of Unofficial UK Statistics

Gower Publishing Ltd
Gower House
Croft Road
Aldershot
GU11 3HR

Tel: 01252 331551
Fax: 01252 355505
Email: orders@bookpoint.co.uk
Website: www.gowerpub.com

Sources of Unofficial UK Statistics gives details of almost 900 publications and services (including electronic publications) produced by trade associations, professional bodies, banks, consultants, employers' federations, forecasting organizations and others, together with statistics appearing in trade journals and periodicals. Titles and services are listed alphabetically by publisher and each entry contains information, where available, on subject, content and source of statistics, together with frequency, availability and cost, and address, telephone and fax details for further information. This edition also includes details of Internet sites and information on whether statistics are available on those sites. The book concludes with a title index and a subject index to the entries. It's 368 pages long and costs £65.00.

The Stationery Office

Website: www.thestationeryoffice.com
and at

The Stationery Office

16 Arthur Street
Belfast
BT1 4GD
Tel: 028 90 238451
Fax: 028 90 235401
Email: belfast.bookshop@tso.co.uk

The Stationery Office

68–69 Bull Street
Birmingham
B4 6AD
Tel: 0121 236 9696
Fax: 0121 236 9699
Email: birmingham.bookshop@tso.co.uk

The Stationery Office

33 Wine Street
Bristol

BS1 2BQ
Tel: 0117 926 4306
Fax: 0117 929 4515
Email: bristol.bookshop@tso.co.uk

The Stationery Office Oriel Bookshop
18–19 High Street
Cardiff
CF10 1PT
Tel: 02920 39 5548
Fax: 02920 38 4347
Email: cardiff.bookshop@tso.co.uk

The Stationery Office
71 Lothian Road
Edinburgh
EH3 9AZ
Tel: 0870 606 5566 or 0131 228 4181
Fax: 0870 606 5588 or 0131 622 7017
Email: edinburgh.bookshop@tso.co.uk

The Stationery Office
123 Kingsway
London
WC2B 6PQ
Tel: 020 7242 6393 or 020 7242 6410
Fax: 020 7242 6394
Email: london.bookshop@tso.co.uk

The Stationery Office
9–21 Princess Street
Albert Square
Manchester
M60 8AS
Tel: 0161 834 7201
Fax: 0161 833 0634
Email: manchester.bookshop@tso.co.uk

The Stationery Office (tSO) has over 200 years' experience in publishing official and regulatory information for the UK's government, Parliament and other government and world organizations such as the IMF (International Monetary Fund). Britain's largest publisher by volume, tSO has an unrivalled expertise across a wide range of services, including maintaining 27 websites.

tSO was created in September 1996, when most of the assets and commercial activities of Her Majesty's Stationery Office (HMSO) were sold to The Stationery Office Group Ltd (TSOL).

One of their websites, clicktso.com is a business and professional online bookstore offering a comprehensive range of management titles from leading business publishers as well as quick and simple access to over 1 million UK publications, including tSO's complete catalogue of official government publications.

You can order online 24 hours a day, seven days a week and pay for all orders by using your credit card or via an account. There is the additional benefit of being able to manage your account and track your orders online.

Verdict Research Limited
Newlands House
40 Berners Street
London
W1T 3DU
Tel: 020 7255 6400
Fax: 020 7637 5951
Email: retail@verdict.co.uk
Website: www.verdict.co.uk

Verdict Research Limited one of the UK's leading authority on retailing – supplying retailers, consumer goods and related manufacturers and suppliers with in-depth retail analysis. A typical report is priced at £990. The company's website provides a searchable index of all the reports by retailer or product sector.

Who Owns Whom
Dun & Bradstreeet
European and UK Headquarters
Holmers Farm Way
High Wycombe
HP12 4UL
Tel: 01494 422000
Fax: 01494 422260
Email: customerhelp@dnb.com
Website: www.dnb.com

This is a worldwide company directory file that links a company to its corporate family, showing the size of the corporate structure, family hierarchy, and key information on the parent company, headquarters, branches, and subsidiaries worldwide. Corporate family structure information is provided in one easy-to-read online record. They use their parent company, Dun & Bradstreet, for their data as well as using interviews conducted by the Dun & Bradstreet staff of business analysts located around the world, government sources, large volume mailings and third party sources.

As well as for the UK, *Who Owns Whom* directories are produced for the USA and some European and Asian countries.

(Contact details as for Dun & Bradstreet and linked from their website)

Willings Press Guide
Hollis Directories Ltd
Harlequin House
7 High Street
Teddington
TW11 8EL
Tel: 020 8943 3138
Fax: 020 8943 5141
Website: www.willingspressguide.com

Willings Press Guide is a comprehensive guide to newspapers, magazines, business and specialist publications in both the UK and worldwide. It also includes TV and radio.

UK edition costs £180, as does the international version. They offer a free trial on their website.

The Youth Research Group (YoRG)
4 Pinetrees
Portsmouth Road
Esher
KT10 9LF
Tel: 01372 468554
Fax: 01372 469788
Website: www.yorg.com

YoRG's surveys are completed in school classes by 6–16 year olds playing on multimedia worksta-

tions as they respond intuitively to their software. They don't bore them with books of multiple choice answers that are worse than homework. Their research programme involves them completely by using technology they love and understand. The survey sample consists of three waves of 7000 respondents, conducted once each school term. Of this sample, 2000 respondents complete all three waves, to allow for brand and attitude tracking annually. The remainder of the sample are new respondents in each wave. This authoritative sample is applied to investigate Information Modules which are also complemented by new 'Hot Topics' throughout the year. Results are obtained within three weeks of commissioning.

There are free profiles of various age groups and sexes on the website.

International market data

Many of the providers listed in the UK section above also provide data on the international market. For example, Benn's have Europe and World editions; Dun & Bradstreet have extensive coverage of the US, Europe and Asia; Jordan's have an International Company Search service; Kelly's, Keynote and Kompass all have international coverage, as does Mintel and Willing's Press Guide. Who Owns Whom have guides covering Australia and the Far East, mainland Europe and a North American edition.

These data providers have not been listed again here, but clearly if one of them provides data you need for the UK there is a fair chance they will do so for other markets. Over and above those providers, the following data providers operate primarily overseas. Only providers who offer some sort of online service are listed, so only the web address only has been given. Those that produce their information in hard copy and book form will, in all probability, be available in or through major reference or university libraries (see 'Libraries' on page **214**)

No attempt has been made to cover the whole of the international scene. However, a reasonable cross-section is provided, to give an idea of the sort of data that is being routinely produced and is available with a modest amount of desk research.

Where the source name is not the same as the title on the top line it is given at the bottom of each entry.

AME Info
Website: www.ameinfo.com

A business directory providing access to 200,000 companies from 14 Middle East countries. Also includes company news and news from selected industries, exhibitions and events, travel guide, country facts and much more.

Provided by: AME – Arabian Modern Equipment Establishment (email: klaus@ameinfo.com).

AskAlix
Website: www.askalix.com

A European business directory (using Dun & Bradstreet's data) that searches for businesses by the keywords. Currently lists businesses in the United Kingdom, Ireland, Germany, France, the Netherlands, Luxembourg, and Sweden. Search by name, product or service and by location.

Provided by: Miami International Limited (email: info@askalix.com).

Big Book
Website: www.bigbook.com

Listings for businesses in the United States. You can search by business name, location and/or category. Listings include address, phone number and a street map showing the business's location.

Provided by: BigBook (email: bigbook@northnet.com.au).

Business Directory of Thailand
Website: www.thaiindex.com

'Electronic yellow pages, which lists name of businesses and companies by categories. Information

on over 20,000 companies classified in over 1000 categories.'

Provided by: Only The Best Info (Thailand) Co., Ltd. (email: info@thaiindex.com).

Cap Gemini Ernst & Young
Website: www.capgemini.co.uk

This is an IT services and management consultancy with offices throughout Europe. They publish strategic reports on IT and Internet issues, extracts of which can be found on their website.

ChemConnect
Website: www.chemconnect.com

Directory of chemical suppliers, including an online trading exchange for buyers and sellers to connect. Links to chemistry journals and websites of interest to chemists.

Provided by: ChemConnect, Inc. (email: info@chemconnect.com).

Computer Technology Research Corporation
Website: www.ctrcorp.com

An internationally recognized and respected research and publishing company. Their reports cover major technologies, trends, products, companies and markets concerning the computer industry. Some report data is free, the rest is catalogued and priced on the website.

Corporate Information
Website: www.corporateinformation.com

Business information site covering the main world economies. The site can be searched in four ways.

1 **Research a company:** type in the name of a company and you'll get a list of sites that cover the company. Over 350,000 profiles are indexed by search engine.

2 **Research a country's industry:** select one of 30 industries and 65 countries and get a list of companies in that particular industry, a list of

relevant links and a short write-up about the industry.

3 **Research by country:** there is a link library with thousands of links. Select from one of over 100 countries and you'll be able to research companies, industries and economic information.

4 **Research reports:** you can read research reports about over 15,000 companies. Each research report analyses sales, dividends, earnings, profit ratios, research and development, inventory, etc.

Dodona

Website: www.dodona.co.uk

Dodona compiles reports on the European and international cinema and film markets and each report contains country, analysis, company information and forecasts. Summary analysis and statistics are given in press releases on the website and there is an email alerting facility for details of new reports.

dNet

Website: www.d-net.com

Database of business directories. Directories are not online, but this helps locate a type of directory, indicates whether it comes in print, CD-ROM or otherwise, and gives contact information for how to purchase it. Also a database of mailing lists and labels.

Provided by: dNet Online Services, Inc.

dot com directory

Website: www.dotcomdirectory.com

'The dot com directory™ is one of the most comprehensive resources available to locate business information about companies on the web. Whether you are a directory user or a business that needs a better way to reach the online market, we believe you'll find what you're looking for in the dot com directory™!' Get links to companies' websites, company overviews, subsidiaries/divi-

sions and financial information. Use the site's search engine or browse by category.

Provided by: Network Solutions, Inc.

e complaints

Website: www.ecomplaints.com

A free website service where consumers can instantly register their experiences and obtain information on how to complain effectively. They can also research the complaint history of companies providing the goods and services they want to buy.

You could use this site to track a competitor's performance, but only if they are in the US. However, even in the UK you could get some idea of the sort of problems that crop up in your industry and so be better prepared to meet your customer's expectations.

Euromonitor

Website: www.euromonitor.com

Euromonitor International is a leading global information provider with 28 years of research expertise. They provide instant access to in-depth strategic analysis and up-to-date market statistics for dozens of global industries

You can download data direct, have reports despatched by email or order a hard copy version.

Reports cover sectors ranging from alcohol to tourism and are not free, but you can see what's available and get an idea of its content before you buy, or try to track a report down in a library or elsewhere on the Internet.

Europages – European Business Directory

Website: www.europages.com

'Europages provides 500,000 company addresses from over 30 European countries, hundreds of company brochures, access to key business information and links to yellow pages throughout Europe.' This site has information that is searchable, company catalogues, phone numbers, product information, email capability, and economic information. The site can be viewed in English, German, Spanish, French, Italian and Dutch.

Provided by: Khalfat Ourida-Elke (email: ok@europages.com).

European Commerce Directory (EuroDir)
Website: www.eurodir.com

'European Commerce Directory (EuroDir) is a business database of more than 100,000 companies, especially in Central and Eastern Europe. It contains addresses, telephone and fax numbers, web site URLs and more about your potential business partners, distributors, resellers, suppliers, corporate clients, etc.' The database is searchable by name, product, country and industry.

Provided by: Hexium Corporation (email: hexium@hexium.com).

Food for Thought
Website: www.fft.com

Swiss-based independent research company specializing in European food and food service data. Over 114 food and drink products and markets in 22 counties are covered, including East Europe. Just launched a service to cover North America, Canada and Mexico.

Forrester Research
Website: www.forrester.com

A US company which, following its purchase of UK-based Fletcher Research, has a strong presence in Europe. Their great strength lies in the Internet and e-commerce in general. Hundreds of IPOs have relied on their data to support the sales forecasts in their business plans. Much of their published data can be accessed on their website on a 90-day free trial basis.

FT.com
Website: www.ft.com

Has global, UK and US sites, as well as full coverage of Asia, the Middle East, South America and

Africa. The site is free, all you have to do is register. Once registered, you also get:

- daily industry-specific news bulletins sent to you by email
- a portfolio that tracks share prices, market news and broker recommendations.

Their new Business.com directory enables you to access 25,000 business categories and subcategories, as well as hundreds of thousands of business-oriented websites. In addition, it incorporates over 10,000 company profiles and 58 Business.com industry profiles. The main site contains 10 million news articles sourced from 2000 leading publications worldwide. Updated every 10 minutes.

The *Financial Times* itself publishes approximately 240 surveys annually, which appear with copies of the newspaper most days of the week. Topics include financial markets, global industries, business management and developed and emerging countries. FT.com publishes these surveys as soon as they are available, as well as providing an index of previous surveys.

Provided by: Pearson PLC.

Hoover's Online
Website: www.hoovers.com

An important source of company information – news, special industry features, business book bestsellers, a powerful free database of 8500 companies, and perhaps the best company profiles available anywhere.

Provided by: The Reference Press, Inc. (email: lglass@hoovers.com).

Lexis-Nexis
Website: www.lexis-nexis.com

Lexis-Nexis have literally dozens of databases covering every sector you can think of. But most useful for entrepreneurs researching competitors is Company Analyzer.

Company Analyzer creates a comprehensive company reports drawn from 36 separate sources – with up to 250 documents per source. So when you get tired of scouring different databases to find out all there is to know about a competitor, customer or supplier you could consider using Company Analyzer to access legal, business, financial and public records sources with a single search.

Company Analyzer also provides access to accurate information about parent and subsidiary companies and their directors to highlight potential conflicts of interest.

Provided by Reed Elsevier.

MagPortal.com: Magazine Articles on Business
Website: www.MagPortal.com/c/bus/

A searchable, browsable directory of magazine articles related to business topics that are available online. Topics covered include: Briefs; Consultants; Diversity; Financing & Incubators; Future Trends; Industries; International Business; Job Search & Career; Marketing; Office Products & Services; Recruiting & Personnel; Regional; Small Business; Strategy & Management; Technology Management; Work Life & Environment. Updated every few days.

Provided by: Hot Neuron LLC (email: support@magportal.com).

Moreover
Website: www.moreover.com

'Moreover uses dynamic indexing technology to deliver up-to-the-minute news, business intelligence, and other information across the web.'

Provided by: Moreover.com (email: edmanager@moreover.com).

News Directory.com
Website: www.newsd.com

NewsDirectory is a guide to all online English-language media. This free directory of newspapers, magazines, television stations, colleges, visitor bureaux, governmental agencies and more can

help you get to where you want to go, or find sites you didn't know about. It is a simple and fast site that can be used to access all the news and information that you can handle.

You will find that NewsDirectory is logically organized so that links can provide you with easy access to thousands of periodicals worldwide. You can link to:

- over 3600 newspapers
- over 4800 magazines
- hundreds of television stations plus
- colleges, visitor bureaux, governmental agencies and travel links.

More than 14,500 links in all.

PJB Publications Ltd
Website: www.pjbpubs.co.uk

An independent UK publisher of newsletters, business reports and directories covering global pharmaceutical, diagnostic, animal health and agrochemicals markets. The reports are segmented into four core groups:

- **scrip reports:** up to 30 reports a year on pharmaceutical markets
- **theta reports:** reports on medical devices, diagnostics, biotechnology
- **clinica reports:** up to 15 a year on medical devices and diagnostics
- **agrow reports:** agrochemical reports.

Report prices start at £395 and there are details of reports on the website, forthcoming reports and online ordering.

The Small Business Exchange
Website: www.sbeinc.com

A US site that provides vital, timely information for small businesses, including bid opportunities, legislative and financial information, marketing and pricing information, and customer profiles. You can access thousands of public sector bids and

430,000+ companies with complete profiles. Click on one of the links to view the services they offer for the specific needs of your industry.

The Small Business Exchange collects information for bids and proposals for the construction, commodities, business services and professional services industries throughout the US. They also have a comprehensive database containing information on over 350,000 companies, including small, minority-owned and woman-owned businesses and disadvantaged business enterprises.

Standard & Poor's
Website: www.standardandpoors.com

Standard & Poor's was established in 1860, to provide independent insight, analysis and information to the financial community to help them determine value in the market place. They are a pre-eminent global provider of independent financial analysis and information on companies, their shareholders and their directors.
Provided by: McGraw Hill.

Statistics
Countries have their own government sites for national statistics data. Below are listed some of the main sites, which in turn have links to other sources of general statistical data.

http://stats.bls.gov
US site of the Bureau of Labor Statistics, this contains lots of statistical material on the American economy and labour force.

www.insee.fr/va/keyfigur/index.htm
French National Statistics Organisation.

www.statistik-bund.de/e_home.htm
German National Statistics Organisation.

http://petra.istat.it
Italian National Statistics Organisation.

http://europa.eu.int/en/comm/eurostat/serven/part6/6theme.htm
Site of Eurostat, the EEC statistical organization.

gopher://gopher.undp.org:70/11/ungophers/popin/wdtrends
United Nations World Population Figures.

Sweets
Website: www.sweets.com

This is the database (parts are provided free online) that helps the construction community by providing access to real-time industry news, projects, building products and industry-leading workflow applications. It aims to provide the design and construction community with comprehensive, timely and accurate sales, marketing, information and knowledge.
Provided by: McGraw-Hill.

Telebase
Website: www.telebase.com

Telebase designs, manages and markets online information services that help people find the information they need from some 500 databases from the world's leading electronic information services, including: Dun & Bradstreet, LexisNexis, Experian, Thomson & Thomson, Standard & Poor's and the like. Available directly and under private label from more than 25 distributors via the Internet, these products provide quick and simple, single-point access to a wealth of detailed business and research information. You can search a wide variety of general interest, specialized or technical publications, along with over 100 international and US national and regional news sources, and gather detailed company information from premier business sources.
Provided by: Office.com Inc.

Thomas's Register
Website: www.thomasregister.com

ThomasRegister.com is one of the world's leading

resources for information on industrial products and services. They provide details on more than 170,000 American and Canadian manufacturers, with extensive company and product information. The site also provides secure online ordering and links to thousands of manufacturers and online catalogues. You can search by product, company or brand name. You need to register for free membership to use the site, and hard copies of the various registers are about £129 + VAT.

Provided by: Thomas Publishing Company.

Totally Business.com
Website: www.totallybusiness.com

This site provides market information in several areas:

* business news and research
* industry news and research
* technology news and research.

TradStat
Website: www.tradstatweb.com

TradStat gives you statistics detailing 90% of world trade at the touch of a button. You can use TradStat to:

* assess market share and track competition
* monitor trends in trade flows
* identify potential trading partners
* monitor price fluctuations
* track the movement of products around the globe.

TradStat compiles official government trade statistics from reporting countries and presents them electronically so you can find the exact data you require.

Not free, but could save an awful lot of time and may be available via some libraries.

Provided by: The Dialog Corporation.

Travel and Tourism Research (TTR)
Website: www.t-ti.com

Travel and Tourism Research has details of its reports on the site plus free tourism trends statistics with basic data taken from some reports.

Provided by: Corporate Intelligence group.

How to carry out desk research

There are three main ways to get 'desk research'. Via the Internet, visiting a library to read their physical or online directories, or by commissioning someone else, perhaps a market research agency or business studies students carrying out a supervised project.

Using the Internet

The Internet can be a powerful source of desk research. It has some particular strengths and weaknesses that you need to keep in mind when using it.

* Weaknesses of the Internet:
  * strong US bias
  * patchy coverage
  * often there is lack of authority.
* Strengths of the Internet:
  * access is cheap and information can be free
  * good for background information
  * information can be obtained quickly
  * wide geographic scope
  * more organizations now have their own web pages.

It would be a brave or foolhardy entrepreneur who started up in business or set out to launch new products or services without at least spending a day or two 'surfing' the Internet.

There are two main ways to gather market research information on the Internet. The first is by using directories, search engines or telephone directories. This can be seen as a passive action, simply gathering in data that is already out there. Some of the libraries listed later also provide routes to market research data on the Internet. These have the advantage over pure search engines of having had their content vetted by an information specialist. The second and more active way to use the Internet for market research is to use bulletin or message boards, newsgroups and chat rooms to elicit the data you require.

Search engines and directories

Using automated software, search engines send out 'spiders', or 'crawlers', that make copies of the pages they find on the web. The search engine automatically stores copies of these pages and indexes some or all of the words on the page. Then, when a surfer types in a search, the engine looks up the words in its index and calls up the appropriate web addresses. The engine doesn't actually go out on the web each time a search is requested. There are a variety of different types of search engines, and each uses a different way of determining how different pages are ranked. Even if a company doesn't register with any search engines or directories, web crawlers will still visit sites and find pages to list.

You need to know something of how search engines work to make the best use of them both for market research and to market your business more effectively.

How search engines work

Online searching services are often grouped under the single heading of 'search engines'. There are, however, two distinct services, 'directories' and 'search engines', both of which contain the key to unlock the wealth of information contained in billions of web pages throughout the Internet. Directories and search engines differ mainly in the way each compiles its database of information.

Directories

Directories depend on people for compiling their information. You and millions of other people from around the world submit their website URLs (your website address, for example, www.mybusiness.com) with a brief description of the content (see Fig. 5.1).

Volunteer editors view the website, see if it's appropriate for their directory, and then place it in a category. Each category is further subdivided into more specific categories. For example, clicking on the category 'business' will lead you to a further score of subheadings (see Fig. 5.2).

Each of these subheadings could have tens or even thousands of subheadings and so on until the end area is precisely defined. So starting with 'business', the trail could then lead to 'associations', then to 'small business' and finally, say, to the National Federation of Independent Businesses, one of the 50 or so small business associations listed. That organization will have a one-line description which lets the searcher know what they have found and therefore whether or not it is likely to meet their needs (see Fig. 5.3).

Search engines

Unlike directories, in the case of search engines

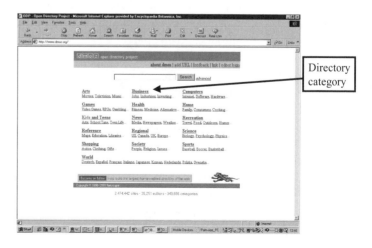

Fig. 5.1   A web directory.

- Associations@ *(14)*
- Business Software@ *(1,195)*
- Business Travel@ *(209)*
- Classifieds@ *(504)*
- Cooperatives *(51)*
- Directories@ *(447)*
- E-Commerce *(1,951)*
- Economics@ *(1,772)*
- Employment *(1,741)*
- History@ *(73)*

- Industries *(106,079)*
- International Business and Trade *(674)*
- Investing *(5,125)*
- Major Companies *(6,325)*
- News and Publications@ *(545)*
- Opportunities *(8,271)*
- Resources *(1,139)*
- Small Business *(973)*
- Training and Schools *(723)*
- Venture Capital *(1,218)*

Fig. 5.2   Searching a web directory.

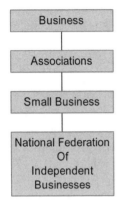

The largest advocacy organization representing small and independent businesses in the United States.

Fig. 5.3   Directory 'trail'.

You searched for " Small Business Association"

- 79% Syndicate Web design Ltd.
- 76% Psychoanalysis an the public sphere. Free associations.
- 76% National Housing Act.
- 75% IDFORUM 05/98: Re Chris Rust, Professional Associations
- 75% small sailing boats, sail boat plans, dinghies and trailers
- 71% EMBA Youth Organisation
- 70% Professional Organisations
- 69% Ashdale Business Web link

Fig. 5.4   Search engine results.

no human interaction takes place with the websites submitted. Instead, search engines have three major elements to them that attempt, with varying degrees of success, to arrive at the end result the 'surfer' is trying to get to. For example, putting in a search for 'Small Business Association' in one major search engine came up with the results shown in Fig. 5.4. That list is very different from the one produced by the directory example above.

Search engines often fall short of the ideal in terms of the results they produce. Many aren't able to correct simple spelling mistakes. And they don't recognize synonyms like 'laptop' and 'notebook', treating them as totally different things, so leading to completely different results. However, understanding how they work will help you ensure your entries into the system increase the chances of people finding your site. And in any event, search engines are getting better all the time.

The elements that make up the search engine and try to replicate the human intervention in directories are:

- **The spider (also called the crawler):** The spider visits a web page, reads it and then follows links to other pages within the site. The spider is looking for HTML (Hypertext Markup Language) 'tags' or markers. Some such tags are obvious and visible. Others, such as Meta and Comment tags, are invisible to those who view the web page. These and other tags can be woven into a web page to make it more likely that a particular page will be detected by the spider. The spider then returns to the site on a regular basis, such as every month or two, to look for changes.

- **The index (also called a catalogue):** Everything the spider finds goes into the second part of the search engine, the index. The index can best be thought of as a colossal digital book holding a copy of every web page found by the spider. This 'book' is updated every time a web page changes. Until a web page is entered into the index it is not available to those searching with a search engine. Hence the longer the interval between each time a site is 'spidered' as this process is known, the less likely it is that information searched for will be relevant or current.

- **The software:** Search engine software is the third element of a search engine. This is the program that sifts through the millions of pages recorded in the index to find matches to a search. It will also rank those matches according to certain criteria to suggest which pages are most relevant. In the example shown in Figure 5.4, a percentage score is given to each result suggesting which is most likely to be the site with the required information.

Hybrid search engines

Hybrid search engines list sites in two ways. They have directories, in which human editors have organized sites into categories. They also have a search engine component, in which a spider crawls the web to build an index of web pages. This is an attempt to gain the accuracy of description that can come from some intelligent human intervention, but using a machine, the spider, do the intensive, expensive donkey work.

Metasearch engines

A metasearch engine is a service that will automatically submit parallel queries on several different search engines simultaneously and then return a single list of results. Some metasearch engines rely entirely on their software to carry out the search. Some allow for some human intervention by the searcher themselves. For example, you can limit the search engines to be included in the search or add a further layer of speciality to the search. Metasearch engines only return the top tier of matches from any specific search engine. That in turn makes it vitally important that your site is one of those found.

Speciality search engines

New models of search engine are continuously being developed. For example, many sites provide their own internal search engines. As well as allowing visitors to find things quickly on the site, these can keep visitors on a site even while they are looking outside the site for information. Your main messages and business name are in front of them throughout the search process.

Community 'portals' are websites devoted to specific themes or markets. These too have their own special search capabilities tailored to work best in the portal's environment.

Other models of search engine link the results they give to how much the registering company is prepared to pay for their listing. Under this model the pages in the index are not ranked by page content, but by the highest cost-per-click bid. This can be a powerful way to drive people to your site, but you have to be sure the people you are attracting really want what you have to offer. If you are running a recruitment consultancy, for example, this could be one way of making sure your site appears before that of your competitors in any web search.

Determining ranking

When you enter a word or phrase into a search engine the engine, as we have seen, ranks its findings using some logical criteria. Key word density is one important way that search engines decide which web page is most relevant to a particular keyword search. The keyword density is calculated by dividing the total number of words on the page by the number of keywords on the page.

The search engine then uses a specific algorithm that takes the keyword density of the various types of visible and invisible tags contained in the web page into account. Some search engines put more relevance on pages that have many other web pages linked to them, whilst others claim to read all the text and base their ranking mostly on that criterion.

Business search engines

The most useful sites for entrepreneurs include the following.

www.allsearchengines.com

Started in 1998, this site lists and describes, together with links, *all search engines!!*

http://altavista.com

Good for broad searching but you can be overwhelmed by too many hits. There is a strong US bias but you can restrict your search to 'domain: uk'. AltaVista is a true search engine. It searches for words on the page and seems to give no preference to page titles. They match *some* of your search words, not necessarily *all*, and the results are not always very relevant. There are some useful features, though. For example, you can see how many other sites link to yours by searching for 'link:http://yourURL'.

www.business.com

With more and more information about companies (and their products and services) being published online every day, the Internet is getting harder and harder for business professionals to navigate. The mission at Business.com is to help you find exactly what you're looking for. To do this, they've built a business-focused search engine and directory.

Developed by a team of industry experts and library scientists, the Business.com directory contains more than 400,000 listings within 25,000 industry, product and service subcategories. So, whether you're seeking general industry background or specifics about a particular product line, Business.com will deliver the most useful and relevant results every time. Try it for yourself and compare their search results with those of a general search engine. It's pretty impressive.

www.bizlink.org

Bizlink is a selective list of top quality Internet sites, electronic resources and print business materials. This is an electronic pathway to the latest business data, from company and industry information to international trade research on: companies; industries; starting a business; international business; business forms; marketing & demographics; taxes; patents & trade marks.

http://dmoz.org

Similar to Yahoo!, but with some human intervention. DMOZ Open Directory uses volunteer editors to build and maintain each category in their directory. Once your site has been accepted into the Open Directory, your site will be listed on partner sites that use the Open Directory data, such as AOL Search, AltaVista, HotBot, Google, Lycos, Netscape Search, etc.

www.easysearcher.com

Easy Searcher 2 is a compilation of the best 400 search engines available on the Internet. These engines include the WWW engines that Internet users are familiar with as well as highly specialized search engines that will only search for information on specific topics. The search engines are displayed by means of drop-down menus, which are listed under their appropriate category.

www.excite.com

Allowing local searches in UK, France, Germany or European sites, this search engine gives percentage values to the relevance ranking, which can also be useful.

www.google.com

Over 2 billion web pages searched in seconds. A great all-round site that rarely fails to put you on the right track.

www.virtualpet.com/industry/rdindex2.htm

The Industry Research Desk portal links to several hundred mostly American industry portals and communities for specific industries. Provides tools for researching specific companies, industries, and manufacturing processes.

www.lycos.com

Using structured subject listings or searching by keyword, this site also allows search for image or sounds. Lycos is less a search engine than a means of selling you Lycos services. If you ignore what looks like a directory and use the search box only, you will gain access to the World Wide Web. Some site descriptions are not very descriptive.

www.mamma.com

Mamma.com – The Mother of All Search Engines – is one of the top meta search engines on the Internet today, with a vast network, presently servicing over 7.9 million unique users per month. It is a

'Smart Meta Search Engine'. When the user enters a query, proprietary technology simultaneously queries a series of search engines and properly formats the words and syntax for each source being probed. Mamma then creates a virtual database, organizes the results into a uniform format and presents them by relevance and source. In this manner, Mamma.com provides the end-user with a highly relevant and comprehensive set of search results.

www.metacrawler.com
MetaCrawler queries many of the Web's top search engines simultaneously, retrieving the best search results across the Internet and organizing them in a uniform format, ranking them by relevance.

www.metaplus.com
Metaplus is a listing or launch pad of sites by subject area.

www.northernlight.com
Since January 2002 Northern Light, with an online business library of over 70 million pages of full-text, authoritative content from more than 7100 sources, has been offered to paying enterprise customers using Northern Light's patented classification technology, and will continue offering custom web searching for enterprise customers.

www.smallbusinessportal.co.uk
The Small Business Research portal provides links to Internet sites that will be helpful to fellow small business researchers, policy-makers and support agencies. The site hopes to become the definitive portal for small business research. There is a useful section on research tools and a link to Amazon's small business books.

The portal receives commission on books bought through Amazon. Any profits will be donated to the Prince's Youth Trust to help young people start businesses.

www.smallbizsearch.com
This site is organized as a searchable directory, just like Yahoo!, but because it only accepts sites relevant to small businesses, does not experience the relevancy problems that major search engine suffer. It runs through Entrepreneur.com's website.

http://smallbiz.searchking.com
A searchable directory for small business owners, entrepreneurs, proprietors and freelancers. Find everything you need to run your business – in the US! But useful for ideas wherever you are.

www.yahoo.com
Yahoo! is the original, and still the most popular, way to access the World Wide Web. Although, at root, it is a directory, Yahoo! has linked with Google's search engine to take over when it cannot find what you are looking for internally. This creates a list of Categories that match your search-words, then a list of web *sites*, followed by web *pages* from Google. It works well when searching for companies.

This site is structured into subject areas but also allows keyword searching across categories, as always there is a strong US bias unless you use the UK version (www.yahoo.co.uk).

www.ukindex.co.uk
This list of UK sites is a quick way to check if UK information is available. It is in effect a comprehensive index of UK Internet sites.

Telephone directories
There are business telephone directories available on the Internet and a smaller selection of residential directories also. These are the online equivalent to the yellow pages or the national telephone books. Some have English versions of the search screen but many are only in the original language and the level of searching and ease of use varies considerably. You can use these directories to identify the names and location of competitors.

www.eyp.co.uk
UK business telephone directory (yellow pages) searchable by location, subject category or com-

pany name, results are listed alphabetically 10 to a page with a random start letter.

www.globalyp.com/world.htm
List of links to telephone directories, mostly business (yellow pages), available on the Internet. Coverage is worldwide and some most surprising countries are available. Search capabilities are variable, as is English language availability.

www.worldpages.com
List of links to telephone directories, mostly business (yellow pages), available on the Internet. Mostly USA.

www.zip2.com
The Zip2 Business Directory searchable directory lists over 16 million US businesses and allows searching by city, via a map, searching near an address (i.e. for finding businesses close to where you live) and also provides door to door directions between two addresses in the same metropolitan area.

Bulletin or message boards
Bulletin boards, or message boards as they are often known, are used for discussions, announcements and general communications between wide groups of people who often have some interest or purpose in common. They are the electronic equivalent of the notice boards you see in schools, supermarkets or any place that people pass fairly frequently. They have the great advantage over their physical counterparts of being able to reach a large audience around the world very quickly.

You can either trawl the Internet and place messages on other businesses' message boards, or you could set up an area on your own website (see Fig. 5.5).

You could draw attention to your website by posting messages letting people know in a discreet way about your products and services. Obviously, to be effective you have to find the right bulletin board for your type of business. In much the same way, asking if anyone knows where you can get a second-hand pram is more likely to yield results if the notice in a supermarket than, say, in the a place frequented mostly by pensioners.

But most importantly, you can use message boards as an ideal place to generate discussions of interest to your potential customers and so find out answers to your market research questions. For example, if you were planning to go into business as a financial adviser you could include discussion groups on your website related to the various services you were considering offering. If everyone seems interested in your tax clinic and the response for inheritance trusts is poor, then that knowledge may help you decide what services to start out with (see Fig. 5.6).

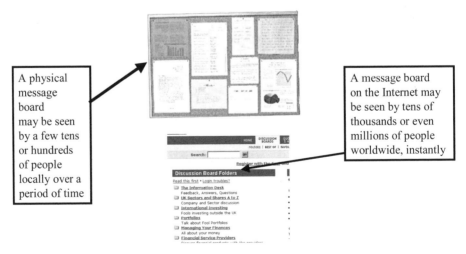

Fig. 5.5   Message boards.

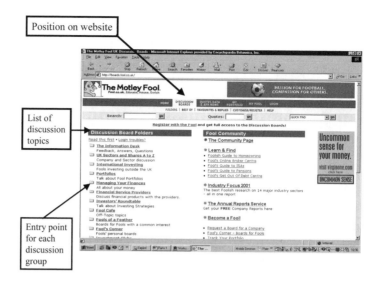

Fig. 5.6 Message and discussion boards.

Even if you don't have your own website yet, you can still use message boards in much the same way by going to someone else's website and joining in discussions there. As long as you choose a relevant site that has visitors that could buy your products and services, then there is much valuable data to be got. If we use our hypothetical person setting up in financial services, then using the Motley Fool site to generate a discussion about aspects of the venture could yield valuable data.

Newsgroups

Like message boards, newsgroups are a way to communicate with selected groups of people over the Internet. They have been around a lot longer than the Internet, having first appeared at Duke University around 1979. Like email, newsgroups are usually text-based, but they require a special piece of software called a 'newsreader'. Similarly, just as in email, images and other types of files can be attached to messages and your newsreader can display multimedia content as well (see Fig. 5.7).

The advantages of a newsgroup over email is that messages appear in a threaded list clustering topics, questions and answers together in a logical hierarchical framework. This can be a powerful way to generate a lot of highly relevant information quickly (see Fig. 5.8).

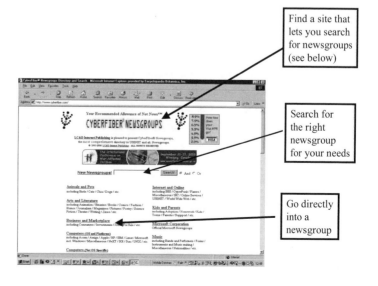

Fig. 5.7 Finding a newsgroup.

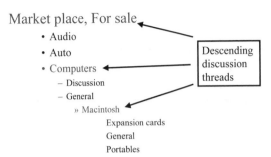

Fig. 5.8   Newsgroup discussion thread.

For example, let's suppose you want to find out about a computer system from other users before you launch out in competition. You could find an appropriate newsgroup that covers the topic 'Business and Market Place'. Then follow the threads, For sale, Computers and Macintosh. Here you can pick a newsgroup to find out specifically about Macintosh portables, for example. Continuing down the threads would take you into PCs and so on.

Newsgroup information is updated fairly frequently so you have to read information quickly, as unlike email it will be deleted automatically after a specified time.

Cyberfiber (www.cyberfiber.com) is one site that lists thousands of newsgroups with direct links to their sites.

Chat rooms

As the name suggests, these are websites where messages can be exchanged by many people who are online at the same time. The messages are generally brief and use shorthand and acronyms that can be almost unintelligible to a newcomer. Chat rooms are often used by businesses to get groups of customers to discuss issues of concern to both parties. It can be used as a valuable market research tool in much the same way as a focus group. Its great advantages over the telephone or a real focus group are that you automatically have a written record of the discussion and it is very inexpensive to set up. Real-time software tools have been developed for business users, for example, allowing 'whiteboards' to be shown on users' screens, much as a flip chart might be used in a meeting room. Chat rooms can

be used for customer support or passing on topical and timely information.

COINs (Communities of Interest)

Some websites have developed to provide an extensive range of content that helps a certain community (customers, suppliers and other interested parties) find extra value in visiting and using their website. This could be industry news, business tools such as sample software, or just a place to exchange views and information with people with similar interests.

Joining communities that include people from your market – customers, competitors and suppliers – can be a powerful way to get first-hand and really current market data.

You can find communities by looking on the websites of big firms, and help organizations in your sector. There is usually a title in the banner on the website inviting you into a community. www.clearlybusiness.com is a good example.

Cybercafés

Even if you don't have easy access to the Internet, you are never too far from a cybercafé. These are places you can conduct all your online research and perhaps even meet up with potential partners, backers or customers.

www.netcafes.com maintain a worldwide directory of current Internet cafés – but you have to be online to read it! They list 4208 Internet cafés in 140 countries.

A1 Internet Cafe
19 Leinster Terrace
London
W2 3ET
Tel: 020 7402 1177
Fax: 020 7262 92 39
Email: a1ic@aol.com
Website: www.a1ic.co.uk

access4all
39 Thurloe Street
Opposite South Kensington Underground
London

SW1
Tel: 020 7581 8272
Fax: 020 7581 8294
Email: a4a@visto.com

@the cafe
6–8 Chapel Pl
Headingley
Leeds
Tel: 0113 294 4270
Email: info@thecafe.co.uk
Website: www.thecafe.co.uk

Battersea.net
40 St Johns Hill
Battersea
London
SW11 1RZ
Tel: 020 7738 0015
Email: post@battersea.net
Website: www.battersea.net

Biblio@Tech
631 Fulham Rd
London
Tel: 020 7460 4343
Fax: 020 7736 6066
Email: thecybercentre@postmaster.co.uk
Website: www.thecybercentre.co.uk

brain caf
10 Tariff Street
Back Piccadily
Tel: 0161 907 3123
Email: brain@xtml.u-net.com

Bushbang cyber cafe
49 The Broadway
Stratford
London
E15 4BQ
Tel: 020 8227 1008
Fax: 020 8227 1001
Email: info@bushbang.com
Website: www.bushbang.com

Bytes
475 Falls Road
Belfast
Tel: 01232 242050
Email: bytes@worknet.thegap.com

C@fe Net
40 Sheen Lane
East Sheen
London
SW14 8LW
Tel: 020 8255 4022
Email: CafEmail@cafenet.uk.com
Website: www.cafenet.uk.com

Cafe Internet
28 North John Street
Liverpool
L2 9QN
Tel: 0151 255 1112
Email: len@gowing.u-net.com
Website: info@cafeliv.u-net.com

Cafe Internet
2nd Floor
Waterstones
153–157 Sauchiehall Street
Glasgow
G2 3EW
Tel: 0141 353 2484
Email: glasgow@cafeinternet.co.uk
Website: www.cafeinternet.co.uk/glasgow/

Cafe Internet
22–24 Buckingham Palace Road
Victoria
London
SW1A 0QP
Tel: 020 7233 5786
Fax: 020 7233 5786
Email: cafe@cafeinternet.co.uk
Website: www.cafeinternet.co.uk

Chelsea.com Computer and Internet Centre
391 King's Road
Chelsea
London
SW10 0LR
Tel: 020 7351 5511
Fax: 020 7351 1144
Email: info@chelsea-net.com
Website: www.chelsea-net.com

Cibo @ the Net
448 Chiswick High Road
London
W4 5TT
Tel: 020 8994 4510
Fax: 020 8994 4510
Email: cibonet@hotmail.com

Comms Port
471 Great Western Road
Glasgow
G12 8HL
Email: gwradmin@commsport.com

CommsPort Limited
35 Shandwick Place
Edinburgh
EH2 4RG
Tel: 0131 228 6322
Fax: 0131 228 6322
Website: www.commsport.com

Connections
5 Colinton Rd
Edinburgh
EH10 5DP
Tel: 0131 446 9494
Website: www.heimdall-scot.co.uk

cyber buffs
696 High Rd
Leytonstone
London
E11 3AA
Tel: 020 8539 9696
Email: Cyberbuffsltd@hotmail.com

Website: www.cyberbuffs.co.uk

Cyber cafe
229 Great Portland Street
London
W1N 5HD
Tel: 020 7631 8359
Email: info@cybercafe.org.uk
Website: www.cybercafe.org.uk

Cyber Gallery
420 Essex Road
London
N1 3PJ
Tel: 020 7354 5005
Fax: 020 7354 0025
Email: cybergallery@itcraft.com
Website: www.thecybergallery.co.uk

Cyber Park
1 Hogarth Place
London
SW5 0QT
Tel: 020 7259 2680
Fax: 020 7259 2688
Email: info@cyberpark.demon.co.uk
Website: www.cyberpark.demon.co.uk

CYBERGATE
3 Leigh Street
London
WC1H 9EW
Tel: 020 7387 3810
Fax: 020 7387 3810
Email: cybergate@c-gate.com
Website: www.c-gate.com

Cyberia Manchester
12 Oxford Street
Manchester
Tel: 0161 236 6300
Email: barbie@cyberiacafe.net
Website: www.manchester.cyberiacafe.net

Cyberia Ealing
73 New Broadway
Ealing
London
W3
Tel: 020 8840 3131
Fax: 020 8840 4123
Email: ealing@cyberiacafe.net
Website: www.ealing.cyberiacafe.net

Cyberia Edinburgh
88 Hanover Street
Edinburgh
Tel: 0131 220 4403
Email: manager@cybersurf.co.uk
Website: www.cybersurf.co.uk

Cyberia London
39 Whitfield Street
London
W1P 5RE
Tel: 020 7681 4200
Fax: 020 7209 0984
Email: cyberia@cyberiacafe.net
Website: www.cyberiacafe.net/cafes/london.html

Cyberspace@doddington.co.uk
263–265 Battersea Park Road
London
SW11
Tel: 020 7498 1952
Fax: 020 7498 6392
Email: Cyberspace@doddington.co.uk

Cybervalley
The Valley Leisure Centre
Newtownabbey
Antrim
BT36 7LJ
Tel: 01232 866088
Website: www.cybervalley.co.uk

databoxcafe.com
91 High Street
Teddington

TW11 8HG
Tel: 020 8943 2277
Fax: 020 8940 9640
Email: info@databoxcafe.com
Website: www.databoxcafe.com

databoxcafe.com
4 Red Lion Street
Richmond upon Thames
TW9 1RW
Tel: 020 8208 940 9540
Fax: 020 8208 940 9640
Email: info@databoxcafe.com
Website: www.databoxcafe.com

Declare computer studios
58 Kenway Road
Earls Court
London
SW5 0RA
Tel: 020 7835 0203
Fax: 020 7835 0204
Email: earlscourt@declare.com
Website. www.declare.com

Declare computer studios
Top Floor Camden Lock Market
206 Chalk Farm Road
London
NW1 9AF
Tel: 020 7482 0102
Fax: 020 7482 0104
Email: camden@declare.com
Website: www.declare.com

Dot Com Internet Cafe and Bar
3–5 Thorpe Close
London
W10 5XL
Tel: 020 8964 5484
Fax: 020 8964 8776
Email: dotcom@dotcom.uk.com
Website: www.dotcom.uk.com

easyEverything
Tel: 020 7907 7808
Fax: 020 7482 2857
Email: james.h@easyEverything.com
Website: www.easyEverything.com

Five stores at Victoria, Kensington High Street, Oxford Street, Tottenham Court Road and Trafalgar Square, with 2300 computers in all.

Ecafe
40 Golders Green Road
London
NW11
Tel: 020 8922 7113
Email: leo@netcomuk.co.uk
Website: www.ecafelondon.com

EFE Kensington
41b Kensington High Street
London
W8 5ED
Tel: 020 7937 2077
Fax: 020 7376 2368
Email: acmw@efe.co.uk
Website: www.efe.co.uk/internetcafe.htm

The Egg Café
The Acorn
16–18 Newington
Liverpool 1
L1 4ED
Tel: 0151 707 2755
Email: cafe@surfnet.u-net.com
Website: www.personal.u-net.com/~surfnet/cafe.htm

electricFrog
42–44 Cockburn Street
Edinburgh
Tel: 44 (0) 131 226 1505
Email: admin@electicfrog.co.uk
Website: www.electricfrog.co.uk

Ezeeworld
898 Garratt Lane

Tooting
London
SW17 0NB
Tel: 020 8767 7499
Fax: 020 8767 2379
Email: admin@ezeeworld.co.uk
Website: www.ezeeworld.co.uk

Falls Road Bytes Centre
475 Falls Road
Belfast
Tel: 01232 242050
Email: bytes@worknet.thegap.com

FirstNET Online
1A Brougham Place
Edinburgh
EH3 9HW
Tel: 0131 229 7557
Email: greg@fol.net.uk
Website: www.askfol.com

Fulham.eBar
42–48 New Kings Road
London
SW6 4LS
Tel: 020 7384 9746
Fax: 020 7384 9747
Email: info@ebar.co.uk
Website: www.ebar.co.uk

Global Cafe
15 Golden Square
London
W1R 3AG
Tel: 020 7287 2242
Fax: 020 7734 8968
Email: dbcox@hotmail.com
Website: http://gold.globalcafe.co.uk

Input Output Centres
Marylebone Library
nr Baker Street
London
NW1
Tel: 020 7486 3161

Fax: 020 7486 4151
Email: iocentre@iocentre.co.uk
Website: www.iocentre.co.uk

Intercafe
25 Great Portland Street
London
W1
Tel: 020 7631 0063
Fax: 020 7631 0063
Email: managers@intercafe.co.uk
Website: www.intercafe.co.uk

International Telecom Centre
52 High Street
Royal Mile
Edinburgh
EH1 1TB
Tel: 0131 558 7114
Fax: 0131 558 7114
Email: itcedinburgh@hotmail.com
Website: www.btinternet.com/~itc1

Internet Cafe
122 Great Street
Belfast
Tel: 028 90 286945
Email: hootieman_2000@yahoo.co.uk

The Internet Centre
The Plaza
120 Oxford Street
London
W1N 9DP
Tel: 020 7580 5558
Fax: 020 7436 0747
Email: info@askinternet.com

Internet Exchange
47–49 Queensway
London
W2 4QH
Tel: 020 7792 5790
Fax: 020 7792 5790
Email: admin@internet-exchange.co.uk
Website: www.internet-exchange.co.uk

Internet Exchange
125–127 Baker Street
London
W1M 1FG
Tel: 020 7224 5402
Fa. 020 7224 5402
Email: admin@internet-exchange.co.uk
Website: www.internet-exchange.co.uk

Internet Exchange
117 Putney High Street
London
SW15 1SS
Tel: 020 8785 1485
Fax: 020 8785 1485
Email: admin@internet-exchange.co.uk
Website: www.internet-exchange.co.uk

INTERNET INTERNET
48–49 Crawford Street
London
WIH 1HA
Tel: 020 7724 3060
Email: admin@internet-internet.net
Website: www.internet-internet.net

Internet Lounge
24A Earl's Court Gardens
Earl's Court
London
SW5 0SZ
Tel: 020 7370 1734
Fax: 020 7244 0916
Email: info@internetlounge.co.uk

Kaleida
448 Wilmslow Rd
Manchester
Tel: 0161 291152
Email: office@kscope.u-net.com

Link Cafe
569 Sauchiehall Street (near Charing Cross inter-section)
Glasgow
Tel: 0141 564 1052

Fax: 0141 564 1054
Email: info@linkcafe.co.uk
Website: www.linkcafe.co.uk

Megabyte Cyber Cafe
14 Hyde Park Corner
Leeds
Tel: 0113 275 4715
Fax: 0113 275 2931
Email: info@megabytecybercafe.co.uk
Website: www.megabytecybercafe.co.uk

Mile End, NetLearn
1 Roman House
9–10 College Terrace
Mile End
London
E3 5AN
Tel: 020 8981 1333
Fax: 020 8981 7333
Email: Mark@nll.co.uk
Website: www.netlearnsolutions.com

NETHOUSE INTERNET CAFE
138 Marylebone Road
Near Baker Street
London
NW1
Tel: 020 7224 7008
Fax: 020 7224 7008
Email: info@nethousecafe.co.uk
Website: www.nethousecafe.co.uk

NUTOPIA – Cyberlounge Launchpad
42 Shelton Street
Covent Garden
London
WC2H 9HZ
Tel: 020 7837 8887
Fax: 020 7837 8887
Email: info@nutopia.net
Website: www.nutopia.net

Offshore Internet Cafe
8 Sackville Street
Piccadilly

London
W1X 1DD
Tel: 020 7734 0983
Email: alex@offshorecafe.co.uk
Website: www.offshorecafe.co.uk

Planet Connect Café
5/5a Cross Belgrave Street
Leeds Centre
LS2 8JP
Tel: 0113 270 5918
Email: planet@miaht.demon.co.uk

Planet Electra
36 London Road
Liverpool
L3 5NF
Tel: 0151 708 0303
Email: info@planetelectra.u-net.com
Website: www.planetelectra.com

The Playing Fields
139–143 Whitfield Street
London
W1P 5RY
Tel: 020 7383 5850
Fax: 020 7383 7470
Email: Gamesmaster@ThePlayingFields.co.uk
Website: www.theplayingfields.co.uk

Portobello Gold
95–97 Portobello Rd
Notting Hill
London
W11 2QB
Tel: 020 7460 4910
Fax: 020 7460 4911
Email: mike@portobellogold.com
Website: www.portobellogold.com

ProvaNet Internet Cafe
Shandwick Square
Easterhouse
Glasgow
Tel: 0141 783 0783
Email: info@provanet.co.uk

Website: www.provanet.co.uk/café

Rainbow Cybercafe
5 Kings Place
Chiswick High Road
London
W4 4HT
Tel: 020 8994 0053
Email: d-bell@dircon.co.uk
Website: www.d-bell.dircon.co.uk/cafe/

Reality X Interactive
54 Broughton Street
Edinburgh
Tel: 0131 478 7099
Fax: 0131 662 4800
Email: info@reality-x.co.uk
Website: www.reality-x.co.uk

Revelations Internet Cafe
Revelations
27 Shaftesbury Square
Belfast
BT2 7AB
Tel: 01232 320337
Fax: 01232 278702
Email: info@revelations.co.uk
Website: www.revelations.co.uk

SURFIN INTERNET CAFE
81 St Georges Road
Charing Cross
Glasgow
G3 6JA
Tel/Fax: 0141 332 0404
Email: nav010@hotmail.com
Website: www.surf-in.co.uk

Surf.net Cafe
13 Deptford Church Street
London
SE8 4 RX
Tel: 020 8488 1200
Email: richard@surfnet.co.uk
Website: www.surfnet.co.uk

surfpost internet cafe
39 Park Parade
Harlesden
London
NW10 1JY
Tel: 020 8961 8272
Fax: 020 8961 9287
Email: edward@freemarkuk.com
Website: www.surfpost.net

The Tinsley Lockhart Group Internet Centre
66–68 Thistle Street
Edinburgh
EH2 1EN
Tel: 0131 225 5000
Fax: 0131 225 2000
Email: info@inform.org.uk
Website: www.t2lg.net

Web 13
13 Bread Street
Edinburgh
EH3 9AL
Tel: 0131 229 8883
Fax: 0131 229 9899
Email: queries@web13.co.uk
Website: www.web13.co.uk

Webshack
15 Dean Street
London
W1V 6AS
Tel: 020 7439 8000
Fax: 020 7287 0333
Email: rupal@webshack-cafe.com
Website: www.webshack-cafe.com

Wet
28 Oldham Street (off Piccadilly)
Manchester
Tel: 0161 236 5920
Email: dry@wet1.u-net.com

whereto?
103 High Riggs
Tollcross

Edinburgh
TD6 9PQ
Tel: 0131 229 6886
Fax: 0131 229 6896
Email: whereto@why.co.uk
Website: www.why.co.uk

World Cafe
394 St John Street
London
EC1V 4NJ
Tel: 020 7713 8883
Email: theworldcafe@earthling.net
Website: www.worldcafe.smallplanet.co.uk/
main.html

zd computers
11 Bloomsbury Plaza
56A New Oxford Street
London
WC1A
Tel: 020 7580 0855
Fax: 020 7637 7344
Email: zdcomputer@yahoo.com
Website: www.angelfire.com/ky/zdcomputers

Libraries

There are thousands of libraries in the UK and tens of thousands elsewhere in the world, between them containing more desk research data than any entrepreneur could ever require. As well as the fairly conventional lending services in the area of business books, these libraries also contain all the reference and research databases listed in this section and many hundreds more besides. Libraries, in particular the reference libraries in larger towns and cities, also have Internet access to their data, in various forms, and many offer fee-paying research services for business users, at fairly modest rates.

Apart from public libraries, there are hundreds of university libraries, specialist science and technology libraries and government collections of data, which can be accessed with little difficulty.

Librarians are trained, amongst other things, to archive and retrieve information and data from their own libraries and increasingly from Internet data sources. As such they represent an invaluable resource that entrepreneurs should tap into early in the research process. If their personnel resources are limited, you may need to write or call ahead and schedule an appointment. It will help if you take the time to familiarize yourself with some standard types of business reference materials.

Libraries and library information sources

The following directory contains a small number of libraries by way of an indication of the sort of business-related services you can expect from reasonably sized public library (Birmingham Library, City Business Library and The Mitchell Library, Glasgow). It also contains details of websites that provide details of virtually every useful business library in the world, giving not only details of the libraries themselves, where they are, opening hours, membership costs and so forth, but also details of the services they offer via the Internet.

123 World.com
Website: www.123world.com/libraries/

This site claims to be the ultimate source of authentic and reliable information about the library resources of the world on the Internet. Using 123world.com you can find out about all the libraries in your vicinity or anywhere else in the world. Their list of libraries includes public libraries, research libraries, state libraries, national archives, libraries of different educational institutions, agricultural and technical libraries, business libraries, science libraries and many other specialist libraries. Their listing also provides helpful information about various libraries.

Birmingham Library
Business Insight
Information Direct
Central Library
Chamberlain Square
Birmingham

B3 3HQ

Tel: 0121 303 3333

Fax: 0121 233 0182

Email: information.direct@birmingham.gov.uk

Website: www.birmingham.gov.uk/businessinsight

As well as having an excellent conventional library, which is all well and good if you happen to live in or near the centre of Birmingham and want to travel there, Birmingham Library has a great business information service, called Business Insight. Apart from nominal charges for copies and prints, their authoritative business information, 'garnered by information professionals', is free. They can provide you with the very latest information covering all aspects of business, whether you are concerned with local suppliers or global business trends. The aim is to enable businesses to make the right decisions by providing them with authoritative business information.

They also offer a rapid response research and enquiry service exploiting Birmingham Library's business and technical information resources on your behalf.

Their principal areas of work are listed below, but do not hesitate to contact Information Direct if you have a business enquiry that does not fall into the categories listed.

- **Mailing lists:** There are many sources for mailing lists in the UK, but most will only provide their own data. Information Direct acts as a broker, selecting the most suitable and accurate database for your criteria. Criteria typically include:
  - geographical location
  - sales size
  - number of employees
  - SIC or product code.

  Results can be provided on labels, as printed lists or on disk in various formats, and can be delivered to you by fax, email or post.
- **Company profiles:** Information Direct offers a full range of company information reports

on businesses in the UK and overseas. Considerable experience with company information sources means that Information Direct are able to find a product to suit your deadline and your budget.

They have access to material from a number of different company agents, including:

- ICC
- Experian
- Dun & Bradstreet.

In addition to financial information, ratio analysis and credit details, they can provide product information and articles from trade and national press or, if preferred, collect published annual reports and product literature on your behalf.

- **Statistics:** Information Direct has access to TradStat Plus, the most comprehensive database source for tracking global trade statistics. They are able to build accurate, timely customized trade reports for any commercially traded product in the world. This database can also be used to monitor imports of products into the UK or anywhere else in the world.
- **Market information:** Information Direct can provide market overviews of areas as diverse as the designer kitchen market to the UK entertainment attractions market.

  Overviews may include:
  - **market evaluation:** market size, share, dynamics, key issues and customer profiles
  - **new product development:** product launches, trade predictions, technical developments
  - **competitor information:** accounts, products, industry ratio comparisons.

It will cost you absolutely nothing to get a quote for the work you want done. Indicative prices are as follows:

- Minimum charge: £15 + VAT
- Mailing lists: From 0.20p per company + VAT
- Company profiles: From £15 each + VAT

- Market information & desk research: £60/hour + VAT

Information Direct also has access to additional online resources.

The British Library
Business Information Service (BIS)
96 Euston Road
London
NW1 2DB
Tel: 020 7412 7454
Fax: 020 7412 7453
Email: business-information@bl.uk
Website: www.bl.uk/services/information/business.html

BIS holds one of the most comprehensive collections of business information in the UK. Business information sources published in the UK are collected as comprehensively as possible; sources published elsewhere are taken selectively. They aim to cover the manufacturing, wholesale trading, retailing and distribution aspects of major industries and the following service sectors: financial services, energy, environment, transport, food and drink.

The information is practical rather than theoretical in nature. It is particularly useful for company news and financials, competitor information, and market research, including trends and statistics.

The information is in both print and electronic form.

- **Print:** The print collections include the following types of material:
  - **directories:** provide basic company information including contact details
  - **company annual reports:** provide information on current and future developments within a company
  - **business and trade journals:** useful for company news, competitor information, industry trends
  - **market research reports and journals:** pro-

vide information on market segmentation, current issues affecting the market, profiles of key players, product developments and market forecasts
  - **trade literature:** useful for product information.
- **Electronic:** The electronic sources of information provide access to company data, business news, statistics and full text market research. Staff at the Business Enquiry Desk can:
  - help you identify material relevant to your research project
  - provide assistance in using the catalogues
  - provide initial training on how to use the electronic sources of information
  - advise on whether material can be photocopied.

There is a range of catalogues and indexes to help you identify relevant material. In addition to the Library's Online Catalogue, there are a number of specialist catalogues available in the library itself. These include:

- **market:** indexes all the market research reports and articles from key market research journals in the open access collections
- **journal:** indexes all the business, and most of the trade journals, in the open access collections
- **company:** indexes all the post-1940 company annual reports and trade literature held in science, technology and business collections.

The British Library–Lloyds TSB Business Line
Tel: 020 7412 7454; 020 7412 7977
Email: You can submit your enquiries via the enquiry form at www.bl.uk/services/information/bis_enq.html

The British Library–Lloyds TSB Business Line is an enquiry service that is partially funded through sponsorship from Lloyds TSB. The information provided may be used to gain new clients, find new suppliers, or contribute to either the business plan or marketing strategy.

The following information can be provided:

- **company information:** contact details, names of key personnel and shareholders, turnover figure
- **market information:** market size, names of major players
- **product information:** suppliers of particular products or services, name of the company that manufactures a product with a specific trade name.

If you prefer to carry out your own research, they may be able to help by providing:

- assistance to those trying to find relevant information via the web
- advice and guidance for those wishing to use the British Library's business collections
- signposting to other organizations for more specialist information.

Staff are available to answer enquiries 0900–1700, Monday to Friday. Telephone calls will be answered within 15 seconds; email enquiries will be answered within two working days. The maximum length of research time per enquiry is 15 minutes.

City Business Library

1 Brewers' Hall Garden
London
EC2V 5BX
Tel: 020 7332 1812
Fax: 020 7332 1847
Website: www.cityoflondon.gov.uk/ [Follow the link to Services, then to Libraries]

Opening hours: Monday to Friday, 0930–1700
The City Business Library is one of the leading business information sources in the country, situated in the heart of the City of London. The collection is used by the City and the wider community of London, the UK and overseas. Their experienced staff are on hand to help you find the business information you require. If they do not hold the information you need, they will try to advise you of a more appropriate source. The library has a collection of directories, market reports, books, periodicals and newspapers, plus CD-ROMs and Internet sources. They have specialist collections covering the City, companies, countries, directories, European Union, markets, periodicals and newspapers.

Business Information Focus is the research service of the City Business Library. They can save you time by providing the answers you need, using the extensive resources of the City Business Library and their specialist knowledge of online databases. Each request is researched by an experienced business information specialist and they aim to provide a tailor-made service at a competitive price.

The information they can find includes:

- company information
- market research
- mailing lists and contacts
- document delivery
- news and information
- pretty well any other business-related research.

Their minimum charge is £12 + VAT, including delivery by fax or post. They will give you a specific quote once you have outlined your research requirements.

They can invoice UK companies, associations or partnerships on a monthly basis and are happy to accept Visa, Mastercard, Switch or Delta. Sterling cheques are also accepted. No charges are incurred until you confirm that you want them to proceed with the work as quoted.

If you are contacting them by email or fax, include an outline of your request, including sources you may have already used, your contact details, your deadline for the project and an idea of your budget. Their researchers will assess how they can best help you, and then contact you with a quote.

Consortium of University Research Libraries (CURL)

Website: www.curl.ac.uk

This is a searchable database of some of the elite UK university research libraries. Many of these universities offer market data gathering services similar to that on offer at the City Business Library or Birmingham Library.

The Internet Public Library

Website: www.ipl.org

The Internet Public Library (IPL) is a public service organization run by the University of Michigan School of Information. Their goal is to provide library services to Internet users. Activities include finding, evaluating, selecting, organizing, describing and creating information resources. There are lots of useful links to directories and databases.

Libdex Library Index

Website: www.libdex.com

Libdex is a worldwide directory of library homepages. The directory software has been created by Northern Lights Internet Solutions. Mostly US libraries.

Library Spot

StartSpot Mediaworks, Inc.
Attn: LibrarySpot.com Team
1840 Oak Avenue
Evanston
IL 60201
Tel: (847) 866-1830
Fax: (847) 866-1880
Email: info@startspot.com
Website: www.libraryspot.com

LibrarySpot.com is a free virtual library resource centre for just about anyone exploring the web for valuable research information. Forbes.com selected LibrarySpot.com as the Best Reference Site on the web for 2001 and 2000, *USA Today*

described it as '… an awesome online library' and *The Chicago Tribune* calls it '… the most useful single reference site on the Web … superb and then some.'

The site is run by StartSpot Mediaworks, Inc. in the Northwestern University/Evanston Research Park in Evanston, Ill.

M25 Consortium of Higher Education Libraries

Website: www.m25lib.ac.uk

InforM25 enables simultaneous access to over 120 college and university library catalogues in the London (UK) area. It provides users with simultaneous searching of member libraries' catalogues using standardized protocols (www.M25lib. ac.uk/M25link/).

Mitchell Library

The Mitchell Library
North Street
Glasgow
G3 7DN
Tel: 0141 287 2905 (business information)
Email: business_information@cls.glasgow.gov.uk
Website: www.mitchelllibrary.org

The Mitchell Library is Glasgow's main public reference library, and was founded in 1877 from the bequest of Stephen Mitchell, a tobacco merchant. It provides an extensive service to both the business community and other library users. Many of the services are free; however, there are subscription services on offer to business and corporate users.

Hard copy reports available for immediate access include Keynote, Mintel LI, ICC Business Ratio Plus, Marketline, and a range of Euromonitor publications. Many other reports can be accessed using online resources. All in all, they have over 1000 online and CD-ROM databases, covering such fields as:

- directories of UK business and the professions
- UK trade journals

- overseas business directories
- company annual reports and reviews
- company dissolution
- British Standards
- worldwide statistics
- market research reports
- company financials
- UK legislation
- government publications
- press cuttings
- UK and foreign patent specifications and search indexes
- trade marks and industrial brand names.

The library carries out bespoke market research at a charge out rate of £30 an hour for those within the Glasgow City Council Administrative area and £50 an hour for those outside that area, provided they pay a £200 initial deposit. Casual users not paying a deposit will be charged a 50% premium.

They also run a service known as TED (Tenders Electronic Daily), a daily electronic journal listing tender opportunities within the public sector. With very few exceptions, every contract which has a financial value above a certain threshold must be advertised throughout Europe in the 'S' Supplement to the Official Journal before it can be published elsewhere. TED is the online alternative to this publication, and a simultaneous notice is published on it, enabling instant access for all European Community countries. For an annual subscription of £900 (£750 to those inside Glasgow), the library will ensure you receive daily updates on tendering opportunities for one specified product or service.

Opening hours: 0900–2000 (Monday to Thursday); 0900–1700 (Friday and Saturday).

Public Libraries of Europe
Website: http://dspace.dial.pipex.com/town/square/ac940/eurolib.html

Started in 1996, this site gives a listing of European public libraries on the World Wide Web. They cover the whole of Europe, 42 countries so far, and their intention is to provide a complete country by country listing. For some countries a full listing already exists, in which case they just provide a pointer to it.

The WWW Virtual Library (VL)
Website: www.vlib.org

The VL is the oldest catalogue of the web, started by Tim Berners-Lee, the creator of HTML and the web itself. Unlike commercial catalogues, it is run by a loose confederation of volunteers, who compile pages of key links for particular areas in which they are expert; even though it isn't the biggest index of the web, the VL pages are widely recognized as being amongst the highest-quality guides to particular sections of the web. The central affairs of the VL are now co-ordinated by a newly-elected council, which took office in Jan 2000.

Whilst they cover almost every field of human endeavour, they have a large section on business with a subheading for marketing, amongst other business headings, and marketing itself has a further dozen headings. For example, the market research section has these further subheadings:

- basics of marketing research.
- company information
- government data
- directories
- expert sources
- Internet marketing research
- market research reports
- online searching and using databases.

Following the thread down 'company information' comes up with this list:

- **14 Steps for Researching an Industry or Specific Company:** This includes some generally good suggestions for getting started on a research project.
- **Company Information on the Web:** This guide provides a useful basic framework for using the Internet to find company information.

- **Locating Company Information on the Internet:** Nicely compiled reference site with many good links and suggestions for finding company information.
- **Researching Companies Online:** A well done free tutorial for learning how to find company information on the Internet. Broken down by research need such as finding sales leads, finding financial information, locating company home pages and more.

It's pretty mind-blowing stuff, as you might expect from the creator of the Internet. There are thousands of threads, and much of the information, including tutorials and 'lessons' are absolutely free.

UK Higher Education & Research Libraries
Website: www.ex.ac.uk/library/uklibs.html

This is perhaps the most comprehensive listing of UK higher education libraries. Currently there are over 150 libraries and information services listed, including those of universities, university colleges, and institutes and colleges of higher education. Although these libraries are intended for use by students, if you attend a business course at one of the colleges (see Section 8 for college business training courses), you will have free use of their resources. Otherwise, usually for a modest fee, you can make use of their business information service.

UK Libraries Plus
Website: www.roehampton.ac.uk/uklibrariesplus/index.html

UK Libraries Plus is a co-operative venture between higher education libraries. It enables part-time, distance and placement students to borrow material from other libraries. In addition, there is provision for full-time students and for staff to use other libraries on a reference-only basis. Membership is open to any higher education institution in the UK and over half are now members. A full list for participating institutions is given, with direct links to their websites.

The UK Public Libraries Page
Website: http://dspace.dial.pipex.com/town/square/ac940/ukpublib.html

The aim of these pages, started in 1995, is to present the most complete and up-to-date picture of public library Internet activity in the United Kingdom. This provides a good way to find the best public library near to you, review what it has on its shelves, and find out if they operate an information service for business users.

Many of the pages you can reach from their list are fairly dull. Some are little more than directories of services – the kind of information you find in library leaflets. There are, however, exceptions. To make it easy for you to find them a star has been added to the listing for libraries which they think are making an effort to use the Internet effectively. About a third of the libraries have a star.

Market research agencies

If the market research information you need can't easily be found either by yourself or by the information service of a library, then you may well have to call on a professional market researcher. This will almost certainly be a more expensive way to gather market data, but on the other hand you will undoubtedly save time and may well get more relevant and timely data.

The organizations listed below should, between them, provide links to a market researcher or market research firm anywhere in the world.

BizMiner Industry Data Reports Online
The Brandow Company/BizMiner
2601 Market Street
Suite 2 Camp Hill
PA 17011
Tel: 00 1 (717) 909 6000
Fax: 00 1 (717) 763 1232
Email: jbrandow@bizminer.com
Website: www.bizminer.com

BizMiner Industry Profiles consist of seven pages full of trends and benchmarks for 19,000 business segments. New measures include total US market volume, start-up activity rates, industry consolidation trends, concentrations of high growth firms (employment and sales) and new branch development. Profiles provide industry survival rates, employment, sales, growth and sales per employee for both average and 'survivor' firms, as well as three years of balance sheet benchmarks and over a dozen financial ratios. Profiles are available in business, small business and start-up versions. Samples of the new reports are available on their website.

Reports can be generated online, with prices as low as $38 per area. Three year business sector reports cost $55–65. Online BizMiner industry profiles are $55–65; online area vitality profiles are $45-$90. Customized work can cost $300 and up. Samples are available at website.

Cobweb Information Ltd
1st Floor
Northumbria House
5 Delta Bank Road
Metro Riverside Park
Gateshead
Tyne and Wear
NE11 9DJ
United Kingdom
Tel: +44 (0191) 461 8000
Fax: +44 (0191) 461 8001
E-mail: enquiries@cobwebinfo.com

Cobweb is a specialist provider of information services for businesses, their advisers and other professional intermediaries. Their content is of particular benefit to start-ups and SMEs. Their production team continually research, create, update and publish a practical and authoritative range of business titles, subjects and products.

Published services are available in hard copy, on CD-ROM and via the Internet.

As well as off-the-shelf information packages, Cobweb can customise any individual service to a particular client's requirements, to give it their brand, add their own content, or produce customized content from scratch.

ESOMAR®
Vondelstraat 172
1054 GV Amsterdam
The Netherlands
Tel: 00 31 20 664.21.41
Fax: 00 31 20 664.29.22
Email: email@esomar.nl
Website: http://www.esomar.org/

ESOMAR's mission is to promote the use of opinion and marketing research for improving decision making in business and society, worldwide. Founded in 1948, ESOMAR currently unites 4000 members in 100 countries, both users and providers of opinion and marketing research. All ESOMAR members and the management of companies with a full entry in the Directory have entered into a written undertaking to act in full conformance with the ICC/ESOMAR International Code of Marketing and Social Research Practice in all their research dealings. Non-political in its policies, ESOMAR is open to all persons who are actively involved in, or concerned with, marketing and opinion research.

The membership listing, which includes the UK's Market Research Society, is listed on their website.

The European Information Researcher's Network
c/o Instant Library Ltd
Charnwood Wing
GRTC
Ashby Road
Loughborough
LE11 3BJ
Tel: 01509 268292
Fax: 01509 232748
Email: eirene@instant-library.com
Website: www.eirene.com

EIRENE is a professional association representing

over 65 information brokers from the EU, EFTA and Eastern European countries. Members have adopted and are adhering to the European Code of Practice, which is subject to arbitration. Their online directory lists and describes the services of all their members, including details of their specializations and their fee structure.

The Market Research Society
15 Northburgh Street
London
EC1V 0JR
Tel: 020 7490 4911
Fax: 020 7490 0608
Email: info@mrs.org.uk (general)
Website: www.mrs.org.uk

The Market Research Society is the world's largest professional body for individuals employed in market research or with an interest in it. Founded in 1946, it is the largest body of its kind, with over 8000 members working in most organizations currently undertaking market research in the UK and overseas.

The Research Buyer's Guide, produced annually, is perhaps their most useful service for entrepreneurs. This directory provides research buyers with crucial information on over 750 companies and consultants offering market research and related services throughout the UK and Republic of Ireland. It includes details of research markets, services and locations, contacts and an overview of each organization's activities.

The online version of *The Research Buyer's Guide* is available at www.rbg.org.uk/. As well as searchable up-to-date listings, this website also offers a bulletin board to display potential research projects.

Hard copy of the Guide costs £40, but use of the online guide is both free, more useful and more up to date. There you can browse listings of organizations and freelancers, or use the QuoteMail facility to email selected suppliers

Field research

If the market information you need is not already available – and the chances are it will not all be – then you will need to find the answers yourself. This activity is known as 'field research', sometimes called 'primary research' by marketing professionals. This allows you to gather information directly related to your venture. For instance, entrepreneurs interested in opening a classical music shop in Exeter, aimed at young people, were encouraged when desk research showed that of a total population of 250,000, 25% were under 30. However, it did not tell them what percentage of this 25% was interested in classical music nor how much money each potential customer might spend. Field research (questionnaire in street) provided the answer of 1% and £2 a week spent, suggesting a potential market of only £65,000 a year (250,000 x 25% x 1% x £2 x 52)! The entrepreneurs sensibly decided to investigate Birmingham and London instead. But at least the cost had been only two damp afternoons spent in Exeter, rather than the horror of having to dispose of a lease of an unsuccessful shop.

Most fieldwork carried out consists of interviews, with the interviewer putting the questions to a respondent. We are all becoming accustomed to it, whether being interviewed while travelling or resisting the attempts of enthusiastic salesmen posing as market researchers on doorsteps ('slugging', as this is known, has been illegal since 1986). The more popular forms of interviews are:

- personal (face-to-face) interview (especially for consumer markets)
- telephone (especially for surveying businesses)
- post (especially for industrial markets)
- test and discussion group
- Internet surveys.

Personal interviews and postal surveys are clearly less expensive than getting together panels of interested parties or using expensive telephone time. Telephone interviewing requires a very positive attitude, courtesy, an ability not to talk too quickly and listening while sticking to a rigid questionnaire. Low response rates on postal surveys (normally less than 10%) can be improved by carefully written accompanying letters, explaining the purpose of the survey and why respondents should reply; by offering rewards for completed questionnaires (small gift); by associating the survey with a charity donation based on the number of respondents; by sending reminder letters and, of course, by providing prepaid reply envelopes.

Internet surveys using questionnaires similar to those conducted by post or on the telephone are growing in popularity. On the plus side, the data only has to be entered once, and that costs you nothing as the respondent does it. The other survey methods involve having the data entered or transcribed at your expense. Internet survey software also comes with the means to readily analyse the data, turning it into useful tables and charts. Such software may also have a statistical package to check out the validity of the data itself and so give you some idea of how much reliance to place on it.

Although buying the software to carry out Internet surveys may be expensive, you can 'rent' it and pay per respondent for each survey you do.

The negative aspect of using the Internet is that, at present at any rate, the sample of users is heavily biased. Students, big companies and university academics would be well represented in any sample you chose, but other sectors, for example the over-70s (up to a fifth of the population) may not.

All methods of approach require considered questions. In drawing up the questionnaire, attention must be paid to:

- defining your research objectives: what exactly is it that you vitally need to know? (e.g. how often do people buy, how much?)
- identifying the customers to sample for this information (e.g. for DIY products, an Ideal Home Exhibition crowd might be best)
- how best to undertake the research (e.g. face-to-face in street?)

- how you will analyse the data. If it involves complex multi-choice questions, or a large sample size, you may need to plan in advance to use a computer and the appropriate software to help you process the data. This will involve coding the questions. An even better idea is to keep it so simple you don't need a computer!

Now you need someone to ask your questions to. If it's a street survey, then you will have to make do with whoever comes along (note also points 4 and 5 below). Otherwise, to carry out a survey, your best bet is to buy or rent a mailing list. Typically, you'll pay a fee to the list owner, such as a magazine with its list of subscribers. You'll negotiate a fee for how many times you are allowed to use the list. Note that you are not the owner of the list.

There are several individual freelancers who specialize in brokering lists and building lists (see Listbroker.com below). You may want to consider hiring an individual for a consultation or to manage the entire process. Marketing professionals claim there's a science to buying lists, but it's quite possible to master this science on your own, especially if you are trying to reach a local or regional market. Think of publications, organizations and businesses whose lists would most likely contain people who could buy your product or service. Don't overlook trade magazines, regional magazines or non-competing businesses with a similar customer base. You can then select and narrow your lists by looking at nearly any demographic variable to arrive as close to a description of your target market as possible.

When you are sure of the above, and only then, you are ready to design the questionnaire. There are six simple rules to guide this process.

1. Keep the number of questions to a minimum. A dozen or so should be enough and fifty is getting ridiculous.
2. Keep the questions simple. Answers should be either Yes/No/Don't Know or offer at most four alternatives.
3. Avoid ambiguity – make sure the respondent really understands the question (avoid vague

words such as 'generally', 'usually' and 'regularly'). Seek factual answers; avoid opinions.

4   Make sure that you have a cut-out question at the beginning, to eliminate unsuitable respondents (e.g. those who could never use your product or service).

5   At the end, make sure you have an identifying question(s) to get a suitable cross-section of respondents. For example, you may want to identify men from women, people living alone from those with children, or certain age groups.

6   Finally, make sure you have an identifying question to show the cross-section of respondents.

The introduction to a face-to-face interview is important; make sure you are prepared, either carrying an identifying card (e.g. student card, watchdog card) or with rehearsed introduction (e.g. 'Good morning, I'm from Cranfield University [show card] and we are conducting a survey and would be grateful for your help'). You may also need visuals of the product you are investigating (samples, photographs), to ensure the respondent understands. Make sure these are neat and accessible. Finally, try out the questionnaire and your technique on your friends, prior to using them in the street. You will be surprised at how questions that seem simple to you are incomprehensible at first to respondents!

Construct the research sample population

It is rarely possible or even desirable to include every possible person in a survey. Imagine trying to talk to all pet owners if you were planning to launch petfeed.com.

Instead you would select a sample of people who represent the whole population being surveyed. You need to take care and ensure you have included all the important customer segments in your research sample.

Sampling saves time and money and can be more accurate than surveying an entire population. Talking to all pet owners may take months.

By the time you have completed your survey the first people questioned may have changed their opinion, or the whole environment may have changed in some material way.

There are two methods of sampling, each having three variants.

- **Probability sampling:** This is done to statistical rules with each member of the sample population having a known chance of being selected. In *simple* random sampling, a selection is made from the whole of a population using a method that ensures randomness. This could be achieved by picking names out of a hat or by using random number tables. In the *stratified* random sampling technique, the total population is divided into subgroups, each of which is treated as a simple random sample. This would be used if certain subgroups of the population could be expected to behave differently, but were all important to the study. It is often not possible or practical to get a list of the whole of a population – for example a city – but parts of it can easily be obtained. Area postcodes within the city will be easier to obtain and use. An *area* or *cluster* sample is chosen simply by taking a random sample of the postcodes on the list. These are then the people to include in the survey.

- **Non-probability sampling:** This is used when probability sampling is not possible, when no list of the population exists or when the population is not stable over time – for example, an airport booking hall. *Convenience* sampling includes such methods as calling for volunteers, on the street interviews and using students as guinea pigs in an experiment. In *judgement* sampling, the researcher selects people or groups of people that they believe will result in a group that is representative of the population as a whole. *Quota* sampling is a refinement of judgement sampling where the people sampled represent the overall population in some important respect. For example, if we know that 60% of pet owners are women, then we

Table 5.1   Relationship between sample size and accuracy of survey.

With random sample of ...	95% of surveys are right within ... %
250	6.2
500	4.4
750	3.6
1000	3.1
2000	2.2
6000	1.2

might construct our sample with that proportion of women in it.

The accuracy of your survey will increase with the sample size, as Table 5.1 shows.

For most basic research a growing business will find the lower sample sizes accurate enough given the uncertainty surrounding the whole area of entering new markets and launching new products.

Remember, above all, however, that questioning is by no means the only or most important form of fieldwork. Sir Terence Conran, when questioned on a radio programme, said that he undertook few formal interviews and implied that he did no market research fieldwork at all. Later in the programme, however, he confessed to spending nearly half of his time visiting competitors, inspecting new and rival products, etc. Visiting exhibitions and buying and examining competitors' products (as the Japanese have so painfully done, in disassembling piece by piece competitive cars, deciding in the process where cost-effective improvements could be made) are clearly important fieldwork processes. Just as importantly, test marketing by selling off stalls on a Saturday, or taking part in an exhibition, gives an opportunity to question interested customers and can be the most valuable fieldwork of all.

One other form of field market research you should undertake is to get out and look at your competitors' premises, get their catalogues and price lists, go to exhibitions and trade fairs relevant to your chosen business sector and get competitors' accounts and financial data. One would-be business starter on a Cranfield small business programme found out from the accounts that the 'small' competitor near to where he planned to locate was in fact owned by a giant public company who were testing out the market prior to a major launch themselves.

All methods can be equally valid, depending only on the type of market data you need to gather. The results of each piece of market research should be carefully recorded for subsequent use in presentations and business plans. Once the primary market research (desk and field research) and market testing (stalls and exhibitions) are complete, pilot testing of the business should take place in one location or customer segment before launching fully into business. Only then can you make a reasonably accurate prediction of sales and the cash flow implications for your business.

Marketing organizations

These organizations can help with your marketing and market research. There are other marketing organizations who can also help and these are listed and described elsewhere in this section, close to where their services are most relevant.

The first part of this directory covers predominantly UK organizations whilst the second part covers those concerned with international trade.

UK organizations

The Advertising Association
Abford House
15 Wilton Road
London
SW1V 1NJ
Tel: 020 7828 2771
Fax: 020 7931 0376
Email: aa@adassoc.org.uk
Website: www.adassoc.org.uk

The Advertising Association is a federation of 24 trade associations and professional bodies representing the advertising and promotional marketing industry, including advertisers, agencies, the media and support services. They provide information, research and statistics about the advertising business.

Association of Exhibition Organisers
The Red & White House
113 High Street
Berkhamsted
HP4 2DJ
Tel: 01442 873331
Fax: 01442 875551
Website: www.exhibitions.co.uk

The Association of Exhibition Organisers has 92 members and oversees the exhibitions website, which is the official website for the UK exhibition industry, sponsored by Trade Partners UK, the UK government organization responsible for all trade promotion and development work.

The website offers a comprehensive listing of all the consumer, public, industrial and trade exhibitions to be held in major venues around the UK. You can search the list by exhibition type, by exhibition date, by exhibition organizer, or by exhibition venue. It is a user-friendly service for exhibitors, exhibition organizers and exhibition visitors to find out which exhibitions are being held in the UK for up to two years ahead. The data is updated regularly at the beginning of each month.

BMRB (British Market Research Bureau) International
Ealing Gateway
26-30 Uxbridge Road
Ealing
London W5 2BP
Telephone: +44 (0)20 8433 4000
Fax: +44 (0)20 8433 4001

One of the biggest and longest-established market research companies in Britain, whose full-service capability means they can tackle virtually any research project, regardless of size or nature. For small firms their Omnibus Research Surveys pro-

vide a cost-effective way to link in with a major research study that is being run regularly for others. In this way you only have to ask the handful of questions you want answers to, and BMRB does all the hard work for you.

As well as providing lots of free information on market research, they also: run a series of free seminars as part of their Centre for Excellence programme; provide copies of reports, conference papers; have free downloadable software for market research for such tasks as desktop analysis; and provide research hints.

British Promotional Merchandise Association (BPMA)
Bank Chambers
15 High Road
Byfleet
KT14 7QH
Tel: 01932 355660
Fax: 01932 355662
Email: enquiries@bpma.co.uk
Website: www.bpma.co.uk

BPMA provide information on promotional products and services to both members and non-members.

British Web Designers Marketing Association
BWDMA
PO Box 3227
London
NW9 9LX
Tel: 020 8204 2474
Fax: 0870 2020 800
Email: info@bwdma.com
Website: www.bwdma.com

The BWDMA seeks to assist all industries with the adoption and application of Internet and related technologies to encourage development in the digital economy. The BWDMA provides a gateway for businesses to purchase with confidence from reputable suppliers through the free procurement service, Web Project Guide.

Direct Mail Information Service (DMIS)
5 Carlisle Street
London
W1D 3JX
Tel: 020 7494 0483
Fax: 020 7494 0455
Email: info@dmis.co.uk
Website: www.dmis.co.uk

Founded in 1991, DMIS undertakes major research into the direct mail industry in the UK. The research varies from gauging the volume of direct mail sent to more complex projects that deal with specific issues affecting the industry. Some of the most important work undertaken is on consumers' and business people's attitudes to direct mail. DMIS acts as the central source for industry information, and as a point of reference for enquiries.

Direct Selling Association
29 Floral Street
London
WC2E 9DP
Tel: 020 7497 1234
Fax: 020 7497 3144
Email: info@dsa.org.uk
Website: www.dsa.org.uk

This is the association for firms involved in selling to people at home, including party plan selling. Provides information and statistics on the industry, organizes conferences, training and exhibitions and has a free guide on its website, 'How to start up'. There is also a directory of members on the website.

The Institute of Sales Promotion
Arena House
66–68 Pentonville Road
Islington
London
N1 9HS
Tel: 020 7837 5340
Fax: 020 7837 5326
Email: enquiries@isp.org.uk

Website: www.isp.org.uk

This is the professional association for everyone in the sales promotion industry. Their consultants register is available to non-members and they provide general information on what the industry does for their clients.

Internet Service Providers Association (ISPA)
23 Palace Street
London
SW1E 5HW
Email: secretariat@ispa.org.uk
Website: www.ispa.org.uk

ISPA was established in 1995 to represent Internet Services Providers in the UK and promote the development of the UK Internet industry. Over 100 companies involved in the provision of Internet services in the UK are members of ISPA and they currently represent around 90% of the dial-up market. A regularly updated list of members is available on their website, along with recent press releases, policy statements and useful links.

Members receive a weekly information bulletin on national, European and international political developments and industry activity. Members also discuss current issues, sales opportunities and technical problems at meetings and via email discussion lists.

Listbroker.com
www.listbroker.com
This is a site of a list broker who supplies lists of all types – consumer, business-to-business – mostly in the UK, but there are some overseas. All list details including prices are available on the site. Their database is updated daily and offers consumer and business-to-business lists with over 1.6 billion names for rental. To use the search facilities you have to register, but there is no charge. You can put in your specific requirements and see the types of list that are available. Useful for constructing market research survey populations.

List-Link Networks Limited
PO Box 6378
Derby
DE73 1XS
Tel: + 44 (0) 1332 86 56 52
Fax: + 44 (0) 1332 86 55 72
Email: info@list-link.net
Website: www.list-link.net

List-Link's aim is to deliver detailed information on commercially available mailing lists world-wide. Just go to the main search page, enter a few topic words into the boxes, choose a country if necessary and click Go to display a list of possible matches.

You can also get a quote or contact from a professional direct marketing agency on a particular product or service by completing a short form online.

Mail Order Traders' Association
PO Box 51909
London SW99 0WZ
Tel: 020 7735 3410
Fax: 020 7735 9592

The Market Research Society
15 Northburgh Street
London
EC1V 0JR
Tel: 020 7490 4911
Fax: 020 7490 0608
Email: info@mrs.org.uk (general)
Website: www.mrs.org.uk

The Market Research Society is the world's largest professional body for individuals employed in market research or with an interest in it. Founded in 1946, it is the largest body of its kind, with over 8000 members working in most organizations currently undertaking market research in the UK and overseas.

Their *Research Buyer's Guide* provides research buyers with information on over 750 companies and consultants offering market research and related services throughout the UK and Republic of Ireland. It includes details of research markets, services and locations, senior contacts and an overview of each organization's activities. Hard copy of the directory is free to members and costs £40 (+ p&p) for non-members.

A free online version of *The Research Buyer's Guide* is available on the MRS website. There is also a bulletin board to display potential research projects.

You can browse listings of organizations and freelancers, or use the QuoteMail facility to email selected suppliers asking them to price your requirements.

Public Relations Consultants Association
Willow House
Willow Place
London
SW1P 1JH
Tel: 020 7233 6026
Fax: 020 7828 4797
Email: flora@prca.org.uk
Website: http://www.prjobseek.com/contact.htm

Represents 70% of the country's public relations consultancies. Its members are 128 consultancy brands of all sizes, working for clients in all business sectors across the UK. The PRCA holds conferences and seminars on consultancy management and current industry issues, and has annual awards to showcase the best talent in the industry at all levels.

The association commissions a number of key industry research projects, including the annual Benchmarking Survey, which is carried out independently and looks at areas such as salaries, property costs by region, staff benefits and clients' costs.

It has a directory of members, which helps identify the right firm for your needs.

International organizations

The British Chambers of Commerce
65, Petty France
London SW1H 9EU
Tel: 0207 654 5800

Fax: 0207 654 5819
Email: info@britishchambers.org.uk
Website: www.britishchambers.org.uk/exportz-
one/emrs/

The British Chambers of Commerce run the Government Export Marketing Research Grants Scheme.

Their professional export marketing research staff can help you to draw up an appropriate specification for the research work to be carried out by yourself or by a professional marketing research consultant of your choice. In addition, companies with fewer than 500 employees may be eligible for a grant of up to 50% of the agreed cost of approved marketing research projects.

British Exporters
24 Old Market Street
Bristol
BS2 0SS
Tel: 0117 909 9990
Fax: 0117 949 8000
Email: info@export.co.uk
Website: www.export.co.uk

They arrange for UK company catalogues and brochures to be distributed free to business visitors at venues worldwide, which is a cost-effective way for small UK companies to promote their products and services in new global markets.

Business Language Information Service
c/o Languages National Training Organisation
20 Bedfordbury
London
WC2N 4LB
Tel: 020 7379 5101
Fax: 020 7379 5082
Email: info@cilt.org.uk
Website: www.languagesnto.org.uk

The Languages NTO supports the providers of language services through offering information, training and advice on specific aspects of their work. It also addresses the concerns of businesses wanting to access language services, and individuals wishing to develop their careers through attaining language skills.

British International Freight Association
Redfern House
Browells Lane
Feltham
TW13 7EP
Tel: 020 8844 2266
Fax: 020 8890 5546
Email: bifa@bifa.org
Website: www.bifa.org

The British International Freight Association advise on the movement of goods worldwide and have an online directory of freight firms.

DEFRA (Department for Environment, Food & Rural Affairs)
Nobel House
17 Smith Square
London
SW1P 3JR
Tel: 020 7238 6000
Fax: 020 7238 6609
Website: www.defra.gov.uk

DEFRA offers help for exporters in the agricultural, food and environmental industries.

It is an authoritative source of information on the health conditions for international trade in live animals and animal products to, from or through Great Britain. It also provides general information relevant to such trade.

It advises on plant health for both imports and exports to help guard against the spread of harmful pests and diseases. Official controls apply to the import, movement and keeping of plants, plant pests and other material.

It jointly sponsors eFishBusiness, together with the Environment Agency and the National Assembly for Wales, to facilitate the legal movement of fish.

ExpoCentral.com
3646 W. Brown St.,
Suite A,
Phoenix,
AZ 85051,
USA
Fax: (602) 942-6734Email: admin@expocentral.
com
Website: www.expocentral.com

A link to data on all the world's major trade fairs
and exhibitions plus the opportunity to participate in virtual exhibitions provided by ExpoCen-
tral.com.

Export USA
Website: www.tradepartners.gov.uk/exportusa/
overview/introduction/introduction.shtml

A package of help which has been put together by
Trade Partners UK (see below) to tackle the issues
which have been identified as the most important
facing companies exporting to the US market for
the first time. To be eligible to apply for Export
USA, you should:

- have fewer than 250 employees
- have an established record of trading in the
  UK
- have a new or innovative product, system or
  process
- be new to the US market although not necessarily new to exporting
- be nominated by your local Business Link or
  trade association as being likely to succeed.

Once you have applied and your application has
been endorsed by your Business Link or trade
association, the final choice of those to be supported through Export USA will be made by Trade
Partners UK and the British Trade Office in New
York.

Companies selected for Export USA will be
expected to pay a one-off fee of £1000 (including
VAT) before they can access the package of help.

Successful applicants will be have access to all five
elements of the package:

- ongoing contact with a named Trade Officer at
  one of the British Consulates in the US
- an initial market assessment, and advice on
  how to proceed, from the Trade Officer
- participation in a two- or three-day course at a
  university business school on marketing to the
  US, as arranged by Trade Partners UK
- a visit to a US trade fair or event relevant to the
  individual company's particular industry and
  needs
- advice on commercial publicity, including a
  New Product from Britain press release.

Once accepted onto the Export USA programme
you will receive one year's free membership with
the British American Chamber of Commerce.

Euro Info Centres
Website: www.euro-info.org.uk

Euro Info Centres (EICs) provide local access to a
range of specialist information and advisory services to help companies develop their business in
Europe.

EICs are multilingual teams accustomed to the
demands of a transnational environment, familiar
with local, regional and European circumstances
and practices, and trained to use advanced tele-
communication and information tools. They have
direct links to the European Commission in Brussels and can plug into a business support network
comprising more than 250 centres across Europe.
EICs are therefore a powerful local resource.

EICs offer a range of services which are of practical assistance to SMEs seeking to develop new
markets and products. These include:

- specialist business enquiry services dealing
  with the spectrum of questions which different companies have on the European business
  environment, ranging from EU and national
  legislation to technical standards, from research
  and development programmes to EU funding

- help with market information through their network contacts and specialist information services. They utilise the various business contact and business co-operation initiatives also provided by the European Commission, thereby opening up further business opportunities for local companies
- alerts regarding invitations to tender issued by public agencies in Europe and beyond. By tapping into an up-to-the-minute database, EICs can supply SMEs with a daily, weekly or monthly selection of opportunities relevant to their business.

With the breadth and diversity of their services, and their local knowledge, EICs can help you develop your business in Europe. The contact points in the UK are as follows.

Euro Info Centre
Ledu House
Upper Galwally
Belfast
BT8 6TB
Tel: +44 (0) 2890 239090
Fax: +44 (0) 2890 490490
Email: eic@investni.com
Website: www.investni.com

Chamber of Commerce House
75 Harborne Road
Edgbaston
Birmingham
B15 3DH
Tel: 0121 455 0268
Fax: 0121 455 8670
Email: birmingham@euro-info.org.uk
Website: www.birmingham-chamber.com

West Yorkshire EIC
The Bradford Design Exchange
34 Peckover Street
Bradford BD1 5BD
Tel: 01274 434262
Fax: 01274 432136
Email: eic@bradford.gov.uk

Website: www.bradford.gov.uk/euroinfocentre

Bristol Chamber of Commerce & Industry
Leigh Court Business Centre
Abbots Leigh
Bristol
BS8 3RA
Tel: 01275 373 373
Fax: 01275 370 706
Email: eic@businesswest.co.uk

Essex County Council
Aquila House
Waterloo Lane
Chelmsford
Essex
CM1 1BD
Tel: 01245 702460
Fax: 01245 702461
Email: eic@essexcc.gov.uk
Website: www.essexeic.org.uk

Euro Info Centre East Anglia
Norfolk & Norwich Millennium Library
Millennium Plain
Norwich
NR2 1AW
Tel: 01603 774775
Fax: 1603 774779
Email: eic.lib@norfolk.gov.uk
Website: www.euro-info.org.uk

Euro Info Centre Small Business Gateway
150 Broomielaw
Atlantic Quay
Glasgow
G2 8LU
Tel: 0141 228 2797
Fax: 0141 228 2327
Email: euroinfocentre@scotent.co.uk
http://www.scottish-enterprise.com/euroinfo-centre

European Business Services
Euro Info Centre
81A Castle Street

Inverness
IV2 3EA
Tel: 01463 702560; 01463 715400
Fax: 01463 715600
Email: eic@euro-info.co.uk
Website: www.euro-info.co.uk

Kent Euro Info Centre
26 Kings Hill Avenue
Kings Hill
West Malling
ME19 4AE
Tel: 0345 226655
Fax: 01732 841109
Email: eic@kent.businesslink.co.uk
Website: None

Mid Yorkshire Euro Info Centre
The Learning Centre
Leslie Silver Building
Leeds Metropolitan University
City Campus
Leeds
LS1 3HE
Tel: 0113 283 3126
Fax: 0113 283 6779
Email: eic@lmu.ac.uk
Website: www.lmu.ac.uk/lss/eic/

Leicester Euro Info Centre
10 York Road
Leicester
LE1 5TS
Tel: 0116 255 9944
Fax: 0116 258 7333
Email: fiona.bell@leicestershire.businesslink.co.uk
Website: www.leicestershire.businesslink.co.uk

Euro Info Centre
The International Trade Centre for Greater Merseyside
No 1 Old Hall Street
Liverpool
L3 9HS
Tel: 0151 237 5005
Fax: 0151 237 5000

Email: dawn.mcloughlin@gme.org.uk
Website: www.eicnw.co.uk

Euro Info Centre
33 Queen Street
London
EC4R 1AP
Tel: 020 7489 199
Fax: 020 7203 1812
Email: europe@londonchamber.co.uk
Website: www.londonchamber.co.uk

Euro Info Centre UK564
Churchgate House
56 Oxford Street
Manchester
M60 7HJ
Tel: 0161 237 4020
Fax: 0161 236 1341
Email: euroinfo@c-b-e.co.uk
Website: www.tvc.org.uk/services/

North of England EIC
St George's House
Team Valley
Gateshead
NE11 0NA
Tel: 0191 497 7660
Fax: 0191 487 5690
Email: eic@onenortheast.co.uk
Website: www.eic-northofengland.com

Euro Info Centre Nottingham
Nottinghamshire Chamber of Commerce
309 Haydn Road
Nottingham
NG5 1DG
Tel: 0115 962 9633
Fax: 0115 985 6612
Email: info@nottschamber.co.uk
Website: www.nottschamber.co.uk

South Yorkshire European Information Centre
Adsetts Centre
Sheffield Hallam University
Pond Street

Sheffield
S1 1WB
Tel: 0114 201 2595
Fax: 0114 201 2552
Email: eic@shu.ac.uk
Website: www.shu.ac.uk/services/lc/eic/

Thames Valley Chamber of Commerce/Thames Valley Euro Info Centre

Commerce House
2–6 Bath Road
Slough
SL1 3SB
Tel: 01753 870530
Fax: 01753 524644
Email: enquiries@thamesvalleychamber.co.uk
Website: www.thamesvalleychamber.co.uk/eic/about.htm

Southern Area Euro Info Centre

Northguild
Civic Centre
Southampton
SO14 7LW
Tel: 023 8083 2866
Fax: 023 8023 1714
Email: southarea.eic@southampton.gov.uk
Website: http://www.euro-info-centre.co.uk/

Cardiff University Guest Building

PO Box 430
Cardiff
CF10 3XT
Tel: 0290 20 229525
Fax: 0290 20 229740
Email: info@waleseic.org.uk
Website: www.waleseic.org.uk

Fair Guide

Email: info@fairguide.com
Website: www.fairguide.com

The Fair Guide is a global business-to-business and trade fair directory. You can find out where and when which fair is scheduled using their online database.

This global directory also contains fair exhibitors and a list of the fairs in which they had participated.

The Federation of International Trade Associations

11800 Sunrise Valley Drive
Suite 210
Reston
VA 20191
Tel: 00 1 703 620 1588
Fax: 00 1 703 620 4922
Email: info@fita.org
Website: www.fita.org

The Federation of International Trade Associations (FITA), founded in 1984, fosters international trade by strengthening the role of local, regional and national associations throughout the United States, Mexico and Canada.

FITA affiliates are 450 independent international associations which fall into six categories:

- world trade clubs (world trade clubs, centres, councils; international trade associations, etc.) (examples: Washington International Trade Association; World Trade Center Miami; World Trade Club of St. Louis; Women in International Trade Chapters)
- associations/chambers of commerce with regional/bi-lateral interests (examples: the German American Business Association; the British-American Chamber of Commerce; the US-Russia Business Council)
- associations focused on international logistics (examples: National Customs Brokers & Freight Forwarders Association; Women in Transportation; Containerization & Intermodal Institute)
- associations supporting international trade (such as small business development centres/organizations, etc.) (examples: Coalition for Employment through Exports; Florida Trade Data Center)
- associations supporting exporters (examples: Small Business Exporters Association; National

Association of Export Companies; Export Managers Association of California; National Association of Export Companies)

- professional associations (examples: British Academy of Film & Television Arts Los Angeles; Foundation for International Meetings; International Licensing Industry Merchandisers' Association; American Translators Association)

The 400,000 organizations linked to FITA through their membership in a FITA member association represent a broad cross-section of the international trade community: manufacturers, trading companies, contractors, freight forwarders, customs house brokers, airlines, shipping companies, port authorities, banks, insurance brokers and underwriters, associations and a wide range of service providers including telecommunications companies, law firms and consultants.

FITA does not offer membership to companies or individuals, but rather proves a direct link to one of their member organizations.

HM Customs and Excise Statistics and Analysis of Trade Unit (SATU)

Alexander House
21 Victoria Avenue
Southend on Sea
Essex, SS99 1AA.
Tel: +44 (0) 1702 367 485
Fax: +44 (0) 1702 367 331
E-mail: uktradeinfo@hmrc.gsi.gov.uk
Website: www.uktradeinfo.com

SATU has developed a free database that will allow you to build your own trade statistics tables. The raw data you can directly access includes:

- UK Trade Statistics Database (2000 to 2001 (year to date))
- UK Regional Trade Summary Tables (to Qtr 2, 2001)
- UK World Trade Summary Tables (1994 to 1999)

- lots of downloadable Excel files with data on imports and exports by product and regions.

HM Customs & Excise also run a National Advice Service (tel: 0845 010 9000; website: www.hmce.gov.uk/). Local email contact points can be found on the website or in your telephone directory.

Their website contains all you need to know about importing and exporting and the systems and procedures you need to follow, from high level introductory guidance to in-depth information on everything from Intrastat to tariff quotas. You can now access most of the necessary systems and forms online.

Institute of Translation & Interpreting

Fortuna House
South Fifth Street
Milton Keynes
MK9 2EU
United Kingdom
Tel: +44 (0)1908 325250
Fax: +44 (0)1908 325259
Email: info@iti.org.uk
Website: www.iti.org.uk

Founded in 1986, this is an independent professional association of practising translators and interpreters in the United Kingdom. It is now one of the primary sources of information on these services to government, industry, the media and the general public. They have a free guide to getting business translations right and links to translation providers.

The Institute of Export

Export House
Minerva Business Park
Lynch Wood
Peterborough
PE2 6FT
Tel: 01733 404400
Fax: 01733 404444
Email: institute@export.org.uk
Website: www.export.org.uk

The Institute of Export is the UK's only national professional awarding body offering professional qualifications in international trade and graduate membership of the Institute of Export – MIEx (Grad). Courses of study leading to the qualification are offered nationally and globally.

Over 50 institutions of further and higher education and 12 universities throughout the UK provide a network of training supported by the Institute of Export. These offer tuition for the Institute's own examinations, the Advanced Certificate in International Trade (previously the Advanced Certificate in Overseas Trade) and the Diploma in International Trade (previously the Diploma in Export Management).

The Institute of Export also runs its own distance learning home study course, and is involved in the production of interactive computer-based learning materials. Almost 2000 registered students are currently engaged in courses of study leading to the Institute's professional qualification. The home study course is available internationally through online delivery.

Specialized training is available to both members and non-members through the Institute's seminar training programme. A comprehensive range of trade-related publications, including a series of standard texts, is published by the Institute, covering the four modules of the Advanced Certificate, and is offered to members and non-members.

They keep market information on all overseas countries trading with the UK and hold an extensive collection of statistical, marketing and contact information as electronic resources.

International Trade
The Federation of International Trade Associations

11800 Sunrise Valley Drive, Suite 210
Reston, VA 20191
USA
Tel: 800-969-FITA (3482)
+1-703-620-1588
Fax: +1-703-620-4922
Email: info@fita.org

Website: www.internationaltrade.org/webindex/index.html

This is a comprehensive searchable database of international trade with more than 4000 links to international trade/import-export web sites. The links are annotated and indexed.

You can browse through the categories, search by entering a keyword or phrase in the search box or search by country or region.

The One-Stop Internet Shop for Business
Website: europa.eu.int/business/en/

If you need advice on how to do business in the European Internal Market, how to certify your product, how to find a business partner in the EU, want to know about bidding for public contracts, or simply want a source of reliable information about the European Internal Market, then this site should prove useful.

The One-Stop Internet Shop for Business can help with these issues and many more because it brings together data, information and advice from many sources. It is part of the European Commission's 'Dialogue with Business', a service to help you to make the best of the Internal Market.

There is also information about European business news and trade shows and other practical information.

The site in all key European languages.

SITPRO
Oxford House
8th Floor
76 Oxford Street
London
W1D 1BS
Tel: 020 7467 7280
Fax: 020 7467 7295
Email: info@sitpro.org.uk
Website: www.sitpro.org.uk

SITPRO (The Simpler Trade Procedures Board), set up in 1970, is the UK's national trade facilitation agency. It is dedicated to encouraging and helping business trade more effectively and to simplifying the international trading process. Its field is the procedures and documentation associated with international trade.

SITPRO offers a wide range of services, including advice, briefings, publications and checklists covering various international trading practices. It manages the UK-aligned system of export documents and licenses the printers and software suppliers who sell the forms and export document software.

Trade Partners UK

Kingsgate House
66–74 Victoria Street
London
SW1E 6SW
Tel: 020 7215 8000; 020 7215 2471
Fax: 020 7215 4231
Website: www.tradepartners.gov.uk

Trade Partners UK is the government's central site for all their services and schemes to help exporters and to a lesser extent, importers. Their services include:

- Information Centre, a free self-service reference library for exporters, designed to help you identify, select and research the export markets offering the most potential for your products or services
- providing access to all the data you are likely to need to find an export market or export partner
- help with both finance and arrangements for visiting overseas markets
- support in exhibiting at international exhibitions
- help in joining other British companies on trade missions to major markets
- English-speaking commercial experts in every major international market to help you make the most of your visit
- help for all businesses and organizations involved in exporting from the UK to promote

goods and services abroad at overseas seminars.

UK Overseas Missions Directory

Website: www.fco.gov.uk/directory/posts.asp

Directory with links to all the UK's overseas embassies, from Afghanistan to Zimbabwe.

The second of their eight objectives is to ensure 'Enhanced competitiveness of companies in the UK through overseas sales and investments'.

WebSurveyor Corporation

505 Huntmar Park Drive, Suite 225
Herndon, VA 20170
Tel: 800.787.8755
Fax: 703.783.0069
Email: sales@websurveyor.com
Website: www.websurveyor.com

WebSurveyor offers the tools you need to create, publish, announce and analyse results from online surveys easily, quickly and professionally. Using their software you can control every aspect of each survey's appearance, results and respondent list.

The process operates in four steps.

1 Create your survey using WebSurveyor Desktop software, publishing on their server with the click of a button.
2 Invite participants to take your survey, directing them to the unique URL created automatically when you published your survey.
3 Your participants answer using a standard web browser. Their encoded responses are stored on WebSurveyor's server.
4 Download survey data to the WebSurveyor Desktop software to review and analyse the automatically-graphed results.

They can also convert your existing paper surveys to WebSurveyor online surveys quickly.

They offer a free evaluation for 10 days to test their software and service.

Costs are $449 per survey or they offer a $1500 a year subscription plan for frequent web surveys.

World Business Exchange
Website: www.wbe.net

WBE.Net generates hundreds of new trade leads from around the world on a daily basis through a variety of marketing avenues. These buyers and sellers are organized in databases that members may access as often as they want. There is no limit on the number of trading partners or key word searches a member can perform on any visit. To find buyers, you search the Trade Opportunities database. To find sellers, search for trading partners.

The membership fee ($499) includes:

- first month access fee
- training video
- user guide
- 1 full year coaching & support.

Continued Monthly Access – which can be paid by automatic debit per month – $25.00.

Books on marketing

- *Advertising for the Small Business* by Nick Daws. Corpus Publishing Limited, £9.95, Jul 2000.
- *Complete Guide to Marketing Research for Small Business* by Holly Edmunds. NTC/Contemporary Publishing Company, $29.95, Aug 1996.

  11 practical, easy-to-use chapters that show the non-research specialist how to conduct useful research on a limited budget. The information is organized conveniently, with handy checklists and worksheets in every chapter. The final section of the book comprises in-depth case studies showing how small businesses have used the techniques presented in the book to tackle market research problems – quickly and inexpensively.

- *Market Research*, Paul Hague, Kogan Page, Apr 2002, £24.95.
- *The Handbook of Online Market Research*, Joshua Grossnickle and Oliver Raskin. McGraw-Hill Education, Sep 2000, £29.99.
- *Marketing Plans,* by Malcolm McDonald. Butterworth-Heinemann, Apr 2002, £26.99.
- *Marketing Ideas for the Small Business*, P.F. Sterrett and P.W. Sterrett, Management Books 2000, Mar 2001, £12.99.
- *Small Business Marketing for Dummies*, Barbara Findlay Schenck, Hungry Minds, May 2001, £15.

Do I have enough market information?

Check out if you know enough about your market yet by answering the questions in Table 5.2.

Complete the questionnaire by entering the score in the box that most describes your behaviour. For example, if you don't know how your competitors recruit key staff, put a zero in the left-hand column. If you do know which websites your customers are most likely to visit, enter the figure 2 in the right-hand column. Try to be honest and perhaps get someone else who knows your business area well to do so, too. Add up all your scores and rate whether or not you know enough about your market yet.

- **Less than 10:** It seems unlikely that you know enough to start up yet.
- **10–15:** You still have a lot more to find out, but at least you have made a start.
- **15–25:** You have got a handle on the basic information, but there are still a few more important bits of data to research.
- **Over 25:** A high score is no guarantee of success, but you seem to have the right level of sector knowledge to start this type of business. Superior information can in itself be a source of competitive advantage, so keep up the good work.

Table 5.2   Self-assessment: test your market knowledge.

	No (0)	Have some idea (1)	Yes, have a detailed information (2)
Do you know the likely age, sex or income group of your prospective (or actual) customers?			
Do you know their buying habits and preferences?			
Do know what other related products and services they buy?			
Do you know which of your competitors they also use?			
Do you know how much of their business you want or have?			
Do you know who else operates in this market place?			
Do you know how successful they are in terms of sales and profits?			
Do you know how they promote their goods and services?			
Do you know how satisfied their customers are with their service?			
Do you know how much your competitors charge?			
Do you know the overall size of your market?			
Do you know if your market is growing or contracting, and by how much?			
Do you know what papers, journals and magazines your customers read?			
Do you know which websites your customers are most likely to visit?			
Do you know how your competitors recruit their best staff?			

Section 6

RAISING THE MONEY

Setting up a business requires money – there is no getting away from that. There will be bills such as rent to pay, materials and equipment to purchase, and all before any income is received. Starting a business on the road to success involves ensuring that you have sufficient money to survive until the point where income continually exceeds expenditure.

Raising this initial money and the subsequent financial management of the business is therefore vital, and great care should be taken over it. Unfortunately, more businesses fail due to lack of sufficient day-to-day cash and financial management than for any other reason. This section will help you avoid these pitfalls and establish strong financial controls, as well as helping you find the right type of money for your business.

How much money do you need?

The first objective is to establish how much money is needed. You will need to look at every possible cost you may need and divide them into one-off, fixed or variable categories.

The fixed costs are those that you will have to pay even if you make no sales (rent, rates, possibly some staff costs, repayments on any loans, etc.) as well as some one-off costs such as buying a vehicle or computer, which will not be repeated once the business is up and running. Variable costs are those that vary dependent on the level of your sales (raw materials, production and distribution costs, etc.).

Your finance requirements will be shown very clearly on your cash flow forecast. This is a table (see Table 6.1 below) showing, usually on a monthly basis, the amount of money actually received into the business, and the amount of money paid out.

In this example the owner has put in £12,000 and the business looks like needing a further £48,233 by month 5. After that, cash flow improves as sales income starts to flow and start-up costs cease. If this pattern looked set to continue, this business would be prudent to raise at least £60,000 of additional finance, to allow a margin for errors.

When looking to raise finance, the cash flow forecast (see Table 6.1 for an example) is one of the crucial documents that any lender will examine in detail, so it pays to be prudent when preparing these figures (see also Section 11 on the business plan).

According to a Bank of England report on small business finance, the average start-up costs for a new business in the UK are just over £19,000. However, that average conceals some wide variations. Some start-ups, particularly those in technology or manufacturing, may require hundreds of thousands or even millions, whilst others, such as those run from home, may cost little or nothing.

Six out of every 10 people starting up a business use personal funds as their initial source of finance. Survey evidence suggests that in recent years SMEs generally have become markedly less dependent on external finance. For example, a decade or so ago (1990), less than four in ten business starters used their own funds exclusively to get their businesses under way. Naturally, using your own money – your savings, your unmortgaged prop-

Table 6.1   Example of a cash flow forecast.

Newbiz Pro forma cash flow statement: Year one								
Month:	**1**	**2**	**3**	**4**	**5**	**6**	**7**	**8**
Receipts								
Sales		6,000	6,500	7,500	8,500	9,500	11,000	13,000
Owner's cash invested	12,000							
Total receipts	**12,000**	**6,000**	**6,500**	**7,500**	**8,500**	**9,500**	**11,000**	**13,000**
Payments								
Rent and rates	1,500	1,500	1,500	1,500	1,500	1,500	1,500	1,500
Heat, light and power			875			875		
Telephone system leasing	166	166	166	166	166	166	166	166
Computer systems and software leasing	416	416	416	416	416	416	416	416
Marketing and promotion	1,041	1,041	1,041	1,041	1,041	1,041	1,041	1,041
Post and stationery	270	270	270	270	270	270	270	270
Telephone			893			893		
Insurance and legal	3,500							
Wages (not Karen's)	3,000	3,000	3,000	3,000	3,000	3,000	3,000	3,000
Consultancy services (database and website)	10,000	10,000			5,000			
Memberships and subscriptions	1,500							
Travel and subsistence	1,250			1,000			2,000	
Training and staff development		2,000			2,000			2,000
Fixtures, fittings, furniture	15,000		2,500					
Bank interest and charges			1,250			1,250		
Total payments	**37,643**	**18,393**	**11,911**	**7,393**	**13,393**	**9,411**	**8,393**	**8,393**
	(25,643)	(12,393)	(5,411)	107	(4,893)	89	2,607	4,607
	0	(25,643)	(38,036)	(43,447)	(43,340)	(48,233)	(48,144)	(45,537)
	(25,643)	(38,036)	(43,447)	(43,340)	(48,233)	(48,144)	(45,537)	(40,930)

erty, your life insurance and your other assets – is a logical starting point. You may not feel you can put all of your worth behind a business because of the risks involved, but whichever route you go down, you will normally be expected to invest some of your own assets. Banks seek personal guarantees, venture capitalists like to see owners taking risks with their own money – why should they risk their clients' money if you will not risk yours?

If you can fund the project from your own resources there are attractions to doing so. Only in this way do all of the rewards of success flow to you. As soon as you bring in other sources of finance they slice off some of the reward, be it interest, share of the value on the sale of the business, or dividends. They may also constrain the business through the use of covenants, borrowing limits and the placement of financial obligations on the business – potentially not only carving off part of your rewards but also capping them by restricting your operation. But if not at the outset, at some stage in their growth most firms require outside finance to realize their full potential.

Where do small firms raise money from?

There are many sources of funds available to small firms. However, not all are equally appropriate to all firms at all times. These different sources of finance carry very different obligations, responsibilities and opportunities for profitable business. The differences have to be understood to allow an informed choice.

Most small firms confine their financial strategy to bank loans, either long-term or short-term, viewing the other financing methods as either too complex or too risky. In many respects the reverse is true. Almost every finance source other than banks will to a greater or lesser extent share some of the risks of doing business with the recipient of the funds.

The great attraction of bank borrowing lies in the speed with which facilities can usually be arranged. Most small businesses operate without a business plan, so most events that require addi-

tional funds such as sudden expansion or contraction come as a surprise, either welcome or unwelcome. It is to this weakness in financial strategy that banks are ultimately appealing, so it is hardly surprising that many difficulties arise.

Lenders and investors compared

At one end of the financing spectrum lie shareholders, either individual business angels or corporates such as venture capital providers. These share all the risks and vagaries of the business alongside the founder and expect a proportionate share in the rewards if things go well. They are less concerned with a stream of dividends, which is just as well as few small companies ever pay them, and instead hope for a radical increase in the value of their investment. They expect to realize this value from other investors who want to take their places for the next stage in the firm's growth cycle, rather than from any repayment by the founder. Investors in new or small businesses don't look for the security of buildings or other assets to underpin their investment. Rather, they look to the founder's vision and the core management team's ability to deliver results.

At the other end of the financing spectrum are the banks, who try hard to take no risk, but expect some reward, irrespective of performance. They want interest payments on money lent, usually from day one. Whilst they too hope the management is competent, they are more interested in securing a charge against any assets they may own, either business or private. At the end of the day, and that day can be sooner than the borrower expects, a bank wants all its money back – no more and certainly no less. It would be more prudent to think of banks as people who will help you turn a proportion of an illiquid asset such as property into a more liquid asset such as cash at some discount.

Understanding the differences in expectation between lenders, who provide debt, and investors, who provide equity or share capital, is central to a sound grasp of financial management (see Fig. 6.1).

Lenders ... risk averse	Investors ... risk takers
Interest paid on outstanding loan	No dividends, except if profits warrant it; frequently not even then
Capital repaid either at end of term or sooner if they have concerns	Capital returned with substantial growth by new shareholders
Security given either from assets or personal guarantees	Security comes from belief in people and their business vision.

Fig. 6.1   Lenders' and investors' expectations.

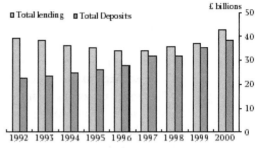

Fig. 6.2   Small firms borrowing from banks.

In between the extremes of shareholders and the banks lie a myriad of other financing vehicles, who have a mixture of lending or investing criteria. A business needs to keep its finances under constant review, choosing the most appropriate mix of funds for the risks it plans to take and the economic climate ahead. The more risky and volatile the road ahead, the more likely it is that taking a higher proportion of risk capital will be appropriate. In times of stability and low interest, higher borrowings may be more acceptable.

Bank loans

Banks are the principal and frequently the only source of finance for nine out of every ten new and small businesses. Small firms in the UK have borrowed nearly £45 billion from the banks, a substantial rise over the past few years, but not especially high taking a longer term view (see Fig. 6.2). When this figure is compared with the £38 billion that small firms have on deposit at anyone time, the net amount borrowed is around £7 billion.

Bankers, and indeed any other sources of debt capital, are looking for asset security to back their loan and the near certainty of getting their money back. They will also charge an interest rate that reflects current market conditions and their view of the risk level of the proposal.

Bankers like to speak of the five 'C's of credit analysis, factors they look at when they evaluate a loan request. When applying to a bank for a loan, be prepared to address the following points.

- **Character:** Bankers lend money to borrowers who appear honest and who have a good credit history. Before you apply for a loan, it makes sense to obtain a copy of your credit report and clean up any problems.
- **Capacity:** This is a prediction of the borrower's ability to repay the loan. For a new business, bankers look at the business plan. For an existing business, bankers consider financial statements and industry trends.
- **Collateral:** Bankers generally want a borrower to pledge an asset that can be sold to pay off the loan if the borrower lacks funds.
- **Capital:** Bankers scrutinize a borrower's net worth, the amount by which assets exceed debts.
- **Conditions:** Whether bankers give a loan can be influenced by the current economic climate as well as by the amount.

Types of bank funding

Overdraft

The principal form of short-term bank funding is an overdraft, secured by a charge over the assets of the business. A little over a quarter of all bank finance for small firms is in the form of an overdraft. The overdraft was originally designed to cover the timing differences of, say, having to acquire raw materials to manufacture finished goods which are later sold.

Starting out in a contract cleaning business, say, with a major contract, you need sufficient funds initially to buy the mop and bucket. Three months into the contract they will have been paid for and so there is no point in getting a five year bank loan to cover this, as within a year you will have cash in the bank and a loan with an early redemption penalty!

However, if your overdraft does not get out of the red at any stage during the year then you need to re-examine your financing. All too often companies utilize an overdraft to acquire long-term assets, and that overdraft never seems to disappear, eventually constraining the business.

The attraction of overdrafts is that they are very easy to arrange and take little time to set up. That is also their inherent weakness. The key words in the arrangement document are 'repayable on demand', which leaves the bank free to make and change the rules as they see fit (this term is under review and some banks may remove this term from the arrangement). With other forms of borrowing, as long as you stick to the terms and conditions, the loan is yours for the duration. Not so with overdrafts.

Term loans

If you are starting up a manufacturing business, you will be buying machinery to last probably five years, designing your logo and buying stationery, paying the deposit on leasehold premises, buying a vehicle, and investing funds in winning a long-term contract. As the profits on this are expected to flow over a number of years, then they need to be financed over a similarly long period of time, either through a bank loan or by inviting someone to invest in shares in the company – in other words, a long-term commitment. *Term loans*, as these long-term borrowings are generally known, are funds provided by a bank for a number of years. The interest can be either variable, changing with general interest rates, or fixed for a number of years ahead. Fixed rate loans have increased from a third of all term loans to around one in two. In some cases it may be possible to move between having a fixed interest rate and a variable one at certain intervals. It may even be possible to have a moratorium on interest payments for a short period, to give the business some breathing space. Provided the conditions of the loan are met in such matters as repayment, interest and security cover, the money is available for the period of the loan. Unlike having an overdraft, the bank cannot pull the rug from under you if their circumstances (or the local manager) changes.

Just over a third of all term loans are for periods greater than 10 years and a quarter are for three years or less.

Loan guarantee schemes

These are operated by banks at the instigation of governments in the UK, and in Australia, the US and elsewhere. These schemes guarantee loans from banks and other financial institutions for small businesses with viable business proposals which have tried and failed to obtain a conventional loan because of a lack of security. Loans are available for periods between 2 and 10 years on sums from £5000 to £250,000. The government guarantees 70–90% of the loan. In return for the guarantee, the borrower pays a premium of 1–2% per year on the outstanding amount of the loan. The commercial aspects of the loan are matters between the borrower and the lender.

Different countries have different conditions and these can change from year to year. But the basic concept of governments taking a hand to encourage banks to be a little bolder in their approach to new and small firm lending has been well entrenched for over two decades. In recent years between 4000 and 8000 government guaranteed loans have been granted each year in the UK, for total sums of £200–300 million.

Other types of bank lending

Banks are usually a good starting point for almost any type of debt financing. If you import raw materials, the bank provide you with Letters of Credit. If you have a number of overseas suppliers who prefer settlement in their own currency for which you will need foreign currency checking facilities or buying forward, banks can make the necessary arrangements. They are also able to provide many of the other cash flow and asset-backed financing products described below, although they are often not the only, or the most appropriate, provider.

Shopping around for a bank

Its important to remember that banks are in business too. As well as the main clearing banks, a number of the former building societies and smaller regional banks are competing hard for small firms lending.

Abbey (National), for example, set out to recruit around 600 staff across the United Kingdom as part of a push to snatch market share from its rivals in the business banking market, in a drive to challenge the 'big four' clearing banks in the business banking and finance markets. The move comes hot on the heels of an aggressive push by rivals HBOS, the merged Halifax and Bank of Scotland, into the small business banking market. Both groups have announced plans to offer a current account for small businesses paying interest of 2%.

Usage among small firms of telephone and Internet banking has significantly increased over the past few years. In 1998, 15.7% of small firms used telephone banking, rising to 33% by 2005. For Internet banking, the proportion has risen from 14.4% to 38%. Branch location seems less likely to be a significant factor to bank customers in the future, so you no longer have to confine your search for a bank to those with a branch nearby. All the major clearing banks offer telephone banking and Internet services to their small business customers or are in the process of doing so.

Credit unions

If you don't like the terms on offer from the high street banks, as the major banks are often known, you could consider forming your own bank. It's not quite as crazy an idea as it sounds. Credit unions formed by groups of small business people, both in business and aspiring to start up, have been around for decades in the US, UK and elsewhere. They have been an attractive option for people on low incomes, providing a cheap and convenient alternative to banks. Some self-employed people such as taxi drivers have also formed credit unions. They can then apply for loans to meet unexpected

capital expenditure, either for repairs, refurbishments or technical upgrading.

The popularity of credit unions varies from country to country. In the UK, for example, less than 1 in 300 people belong to one, compared with more than 1 in 3 in Canada, Ireland and Australia. Certainly, few could argue about the attractiveness of an annual interest rate 30% below that of the high street lenders, which is what credit unions aim for. Members have to save regularly to qualify for a loan, though there is no minimum deposit and, after 10 weeks, members with a good track record can borrow up to five times their savings, though they must continue to save while repaying the loan. There is no set interest rate, but dividends are distributed to members from any surplus, usually about 5% a year. This, too, compares favourably with bank interest on deposit accounts.

Local Exchange Trading Systems (LETS)

Almost 450 LETS have been set up, more than half of those since 1995. Some have only a dozen members while the largest, in Manchester, has over 380. All in all, over 40,000 people are involved in this method of trading. Anyone who joins a scheme offers skills or services, such as plumbing, gardening or the use of a photocopier, to other members. A price is agreed in whatever notional currency has been adopted, but no money changes hands. The system is more ambitious than straight barter. The provider receives a credit on his or her account kept by a local organizer and a debit is marked up against the user. The person in credit can then set this against other services. The trades that have used LETS successfully include restaurateurs, plumbers, carpenters, lawyers, retailers of all descriptions, cycle shops, freelance writers, piano teachers, translation agencies, cleaners, typists, gardeners, tree surgeons, security guards, book-keepers and child-minders. No interest is paid on LETS, but all the usual tax and Value Added Tax rules apply to businesses trading in this way. The benefits of using LETS are that you can start trading and grow with virtually no start-up capital. All you need are time and saleable skills – once you have 'sold' your wares, payment is immediate by way of a LETS credit. Also, by using LETS the wealth is kept in the local community, which means customers in your area may be able to spend more with you. For example, one shop that used to accept 25% of the value of its goods in LETS was surprised at how sharply its turnover increased when it increased the proportion to 50%. One of the keys to success in using LETS is to have an enterprising organizer who can produce, maintain and circulate a wide-ranging directory of LETS services and outlets.

Borrowing from family and friends

Those close to you can often lend you money or invest in your business. This helps you avoid the problem of pleading your case to outsiders and enduring extra paperwork and bureaucratic delays. Help from friends, relatives, and business associates can be especially valuable if you've been through bankruptcy or had other credit problems that would make borrowing from a commercial lender difficult or impossible.

Their involvement brings a range of extra potential benefits, costs and risks that are not a feature of most other types of finance. You need to decide if these are acceptable.

Some advantages of borrowing money from people you know well are that you may be charged a lower interest rate, may be able to delay paying back money until you're more established, and may be given more flexibility if you get into a jam. But once the loan terms are agreed to, you have the same legal obligations as you would with say a bank or any other source of finance.

In addition, borrowing money from relatives and friends can have a major disadvantage. If your business does poorly and those close to you end up losing money, you may well damage a good personal relationship. So in dealing with friends, relatives, and business associates, be extra careful not only to establish clearly the terms of the deal and put it in writing, but also to make an extra effort to explain the risks. In short, it's your job to make sure your helpful friend or relative won't suffer a true hardship if you're unable to meet your financial commitments.

Many types of businesses have loyal and devoted followers, people who care as much about the business as the owners do. A health food restaurant, a specialist bookstore or an art gallery, for example, may attract people who are enthusiastic about lending money to or investing in the business because it fits in with their lifestyle or philosophy.

Their decision to participate is driven to some extent by their feelings and is not strictly a business proposition. The rules for borrowing from friends and relatives apply here as well. Put repayment terms in writing, and don't accept money from people who can't afford to risk it.

Financing cash flow

Customers often take time to pay up. In the meantime you have to pay those who work for you and your less patient suppliers. So the more you grow, the more funds you need. It is often possible to 'factor' your creditworthy customer's bills to a financial institution, receiving some of the funds as your goods leave the door, hence speeding up cash flow.

Factoring is generally only available to a business that invoices other business customers, either in their home market or internationally, for its services. Factoring can be made available to new businesses, although its services are usually of most value during the early stages of growth. It is an arrangement which allows you to receive up to 80% of the cash due from your customers more quickly than they would normally pay. The factoring company in effect buys your trade debts and can provide a debtor accounting and administration service. In other words, it takes over the day-to-day work of invoicing and sending out reminders and statements. This can be a particularly helpful service to a small expanding business. It allows the management to concentrate on expanding the business, with the factoring company providing expert guidance on credit control, 100% protection against bad debts, and improved cash flow.

You will, of course, have to pay for factoring services. Having the cash before your customers pay will cost you a little more than normal overdraft rates. The factoring service will cost between 0.5 and 3.5% of the turnover, depending on volume of work, the number of debtors, average invoice amount, and other related factors. You can get up to 80% of the value of your invoice in advance, with the remainder paid when your customer settles up, less the various charges just mentioned.

If you sell direct to the public, sell complex and expensive capital equipment, or expect progress payments on long-term projects, then factoring is not for you. If you are expanding more rapidly than other sources of finance will allow, this may be a useful service that is worth exploring.

Invoice discounting is a variation on the same theme. However, the majority of small firms continue to prefer factoring to invoice discounting because it enables them to outsource their financial management controls. Factors collect in money owed by a firm's customers, whereas invoice discounters leave it to the firms themselves, although some fear that this might reduce their contact with clients. Invoice discounting is in any case typically available only to businesses with a turnover in excess of £1 million.

Cash flow financing accounts for £8 billion of business financing, up from £2 billion in 1990.

Asset-backed financing

Physical assets such as cars, vans, computers, office equipment and the like can usually be financed by leasing them, rather as a house or flat may be rented. Or they can be bought on hire purchase. This leaves other funds free to cover the less tangible elements in your cash flow.

Leasing is a way of getting the use of vehicles, plant, and equipment without paying the full cost at once. Operating leases are taken out where you will use the equipment for less than its full economic life, for example a car, photocop-

ier, vending machine or kitchen equipment. The lessor takes the risk of the equipment becoming obsolete, and assumes responsibility for repairs, maintenance and insurance. As you, the lessee, are paying for this service, it is more expensive than a finance lease, where you lease the equipment for most of its economic life and maintain and insure it yourself. Leases can normally be extended, often for fairly nominal sums, in the latter years.

The obvious attraction of leasing is that no deposit is needed, leaving your working capital free for more profitable use elsewhere. Also, the cost is known from the start, making forward planning more simple. There may even be some tax advantages over other forms of finance. However, there are some possible pitfalls, which only a close examination of the small print will reveal. So do take professional advice before taking out a lease.

Hire purchase differs from leasing in that you have the option to eventually become the owner of the asset, after a series of payments.

Trade credit

Once you have established creditworthiness, it may be possible to take advantage of trade credit extended by suppliers. This usually takes the form of allowing you anything from seven days to three months from receiving the goods before you have to pay for them. Even if you are allowed time to pay for goods and services, you will have to weigh carefully the benefit of taking this credit against the cost of losing any cash discounts offered. For example, if you are offered a 2.5% discount for cash settlement, then this is a saving of £25 for every £1000 of purchases. If the alternative is to take six weeks' credit, then the saving is the cost of borrowing that sum from, say, your bank on overdraft. So if your bank interest rate is 8% per annum, that is equivalent to 0.15% per week. Six weeks would save you 0.92%. On £1000 of purchase you would save only £9.20 of bank interest. This means that the cash discount is more attractive.

Your suppliers will probably run a credit check on you before extending payment terms. You should run a credit check on your own business from time to time, just to see how others see you (see the information on Company Plus and Dun & Bradstreet in Section 7).

You also need to be aware of the Late Payment of Commercial Debts (Interest) Act, which took effect from 1 November 1998. Since then, small businesses (up to 50 employees) have been able to charge interest on any late paid commercial debts due from larger businesses and the public sector. From 1 November 2000, small businesses have also been able to charge interest to other small businesses. The third phase of the legislation was introduced in November 2002, and gives the right to statutory interest to all firms. Recent research, however, shows that over 90% of small businesses have not noticed any improvement in late payment since the introduction of the Act.

Resources and contacts

Help or advice on lending matters

Association of British Credit Unions
Holyoak House
Hanover Street
Manchester
M60 0AS
Tel: 0161 832 3694
Fax: 0161 832 3706
Email: Infor@abcul.org
Website: www.abcul.coop

Banks

ABN AMRO
Website: www.abnamro.com/ (main business website)
Website: www.abnamro.com/com/Productsand-services/commercial/commercial.asp (financing your business website)

ABN AMRO's share of the small business banking market in both the US Midwest and the Netherlands is over 30% and they are growing in Belgium, Italy, Thailand, India, Taiwan and Hong Kong. Some presence in the UK.

Abbey National Business
Website: www.anbusinessbank.co.uk/ (main business website)
Website: www.anbusinessbank.co.uk/html/information/startup_intro.html (briefing for small business start-ups)

AIB (Allied Irish Bank)
Website: www.aib.ie/gb/ (main UK business website)
Website: www.aib.ie/gb/business/finance/financeyourbusiness.asp (small business finance website)

Alliance and Leicester
Website: www.mybusinessbank.co.uk (small business banking website)

Barclays
Website: www.barclays.com/ (main website)
Website: www.smallbusiness.barclays.co.uk/ (small business website)

Co-operative Bank
Website: www.co-operativebank.co.uk/ (main website and information on financing your business)

HBOS (Halifax Bank of Scotland)
Website: www.hbosplc.com/ (website with links to all banking services)
Website: www.bankofscotland.co.uk/ (business website, with link to services for small business)

HSBC
Website: www.hsbc.co.uk/ (main business banking website)
Website: www.ukbusiness.hsbc.com/sab/sab00001.jsp (starting a business website)

Lloyds TSB

Website: www.success4business.com/ (main business banking website)
Website: www.smallbusiness.co.uk/ (helpful hints on finance, with a strong Lloyds TSB bias)

NatWest

Website: www.natwest.co.uk/ (main website)

Royal Bank of Scotland

Website: www.royalbankscot.co.uk/ (main business website)
Website: www.royalbankscot.co.uk/small_business/ (small business website)

Yorkshire Bank

Website: www.ybonline.co.uk/business/ (main business website)

General funding advice

Business Money Ltd

Strode House
10 Leigh Road
Street
Somerset
BA16 OHA
Tel: 01458 841112
Fax: 01458 841286
Website: http://business-money.com/

The online version of *Business Money*, an independent review of finance and banking for business, offers articles from the current edition plus links to pages supplying current financial news.

ECGD

PO Box 2200
2 Exchange Tower
Harbour Exchange Square
London
E14 9GS
Tel: 020 7512 7000
Fax: 020 7512 7649
Website: www.ecgd.gov.uk

ECGD, the Export Credits Guarantee Department, is the UK's official export credit agency. They are a separate government department, reporting to the Secretary of State for Trade and Industry.

They have over 80 years' experience of working closely with exporters, project sponsors, banks and buyers to help UK exporters compete effectively in overseas markets where the private sector may be unable to help. They do this by arranging finance facilities and credit insurance for contracts, ranging from around £20,000 up to hundreds of millions of pounds. There is special help for smaller exporters. They also provide overseas investment insurance for UK-based companies investing overseas.

Factors and Discounters Association

Administration Office
2nd Floor
Boston House
The Little Green
Richmond
TW9 1QE
Tel: 020 8332 9955
Fax: 020 8332 2585
Website: www.factors.org.uk

Finance and Leasing Association

Imperial House
15–19 Kingsway
London
WC2B 6UN
Tel: 020 7836 6511
Fax: 020 7420 9600
Email: info@fla.org.uk
Website: www.fla.org.uk

Funds4Growth

Blue Chip Publishing Ltd
51 Newhall Street
Birmingham
B3 3QR
Tel: 0121 248 0437
Fax: 0121 248 0439
Email: shaunmallen@bluechippublishing.co.uk
Website: www.funds4growth.com

Complete a brief registration form, select a funding category, and Funds Finder will give you a shortlist of likely providers. Detailed information on each is available within their database. You can then email requests to any or all via a secure link. They take no fees for any transactions, either from you or from your chosen provider. You deal directly with the lender.

LETSLINK UK

(Local Exchange Trading Systems)
12 Southcote Road,
London N19 5BJ
Tel: 020-7607-7852
Fax: 020-7609-7112
Email: lets@letslinkuk.org
Website: www.letslinkuk.org

UK Banks Guide

Website: www.ukbanksguide.co.uk

UK Banks Guide is an easy way to locate high street banks and building societies. They provide a comprehensive directory of UK bank sites on the Internet covering online banking, business banking, private banking, offshore banks and international banks.

Business angels

One likely first source of equity or risk capital will be a private individual, with their own funds, and perhaps some knowledge of your type of business. In return for a share in the business, they will put in money at their own risk. They have been christened 'business angels', a term first coined to describe private wealthy individuals who backed theatrical productions, usually a play on Broadway or in London's West End. By their very nature, such 'investments' were highly speculative in nature, as shows tend to either soar or bomb. The angel would typically have a personal interest in the production, the arts in general, or perhaps in a member of the cast. They may also have wanted to play some role in the production or in negotiating an aspect of the business relationship between the players and the theatre or some other outside party. In any event they were – indeed are, for theatrical angels still exist – determined upon some involvement beyond merely signing a cheque. There is no rational way to calculate either risk or reward in such ventures. A great writer and a great cast are not guarantors of success. In the same way, total unknowns can also triumph. The chances of losing money are high.

Business angels are a similar breed. They are informal suppliers of risk capital to new and growing businesses, often taking a hand at the stage when no one else will take the chance. A sort of investor of last resort. But whilst they often lose their shirts, they sometimes make serious money. One angel who backed Sage with £10,000 in their first round of £250,000 financing, saw his stake rise to £40 million.

These angels often have their own agenda and frequently operate through managed networks. Angel networks operate throughout the world. In some cases, these networks operate on the Internet. In the UK and the US there are hundreds of networks with tens of thousands of business angels prepared to put several billion pounds each year into new or small business.

Research has unravelled the following sketchy facts about business angels as a breed. Knowing them may help you find the right one for your business.

1 Business angels are generally self-made, high net worth individuals, with entrepreneurial backgrounds. Most are in the 45–65 age group and 19% are millionaires. Only 1% of business angels are women.

2 Half of all angels conduct minimal or no sector research, meet their entrepreneur an average of 5.4 times before investing (compared with venture capitalists, who meet on average 9.5 times) and 54% of angels neglected to take up independent personal references, compared with only 6% of venture capitalists.

3 Typically, business angels are investing 5–15% of their investment portfolio in this way and their motivation is, first and foremost, finan-

cial gain through capital appreciation, with the fun and enjoyment of being involved with an entrepreneurial business an important secondary motive. A minority are motivated in part by altruistic considerations, such as helping the next generation of entrepreneurs to get started, and supporting their country or state.

4   Business angels invest in only a very small proportion of investments that they see: typically at least seven out of eight opportunities are rejected. More than 90% of investment opportunities are rejected at the initial screening stage.

5   Around 30% of investments by business angels are in technology-based businesses. Most will tell you that they vigorously avoid investing in industries they know nothing about.

6   The majority of business angels invest in businesses located in close proximity to where they live – two-thirds of investments are made in businesses located within 100 miles of their home or office. They are, however, prepared to look further afield if they have specific sector-related investment preferences or if they are technology investors.

7   Ninety-two per cent of angels had worked in a small firm, compared, for example, with only 52% of venture capitalists who had similar experience.

8   On average, business angels sell their shareholding in the most successful investments after four years (and 75% after seven years). Conversely, half of the investments in which business angels lost money had failed within two years of the investment being made.

9   Angels fundamentally back people rather than propositions.

10   Business angels are up to five times more likely to invest in start-ups and early stage investments than venture capital providers in general.

One estimate is that the UK has approximately 18,000 business angels and that they annually invest in the region of £500 million. Fig. 6.3 gives an indication of the amounts they invest.

UK Business Angels

Beer & Partners Limited

Masters Yard,
South Street,
Dorking,
Surrey,
RH4 2ES
Tel: 08701 633033
Fax: 08701 633044
Website: http://www.beerandpartners.com/

Advantage Business Angels (ABA)
Edgbaston House

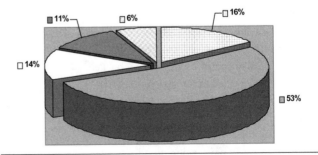

Fig. 6.3   Amount invested by UK business angels.

3 Duchess Place
Birmingham
West Midlands
B16 8NH
Tel: 0121 456 7940
Fax: 0121 455 8547
Email: info@abangels.com
Website: www.advantagebusinessangels.com

c2Ventures
Ashridge House
121 High Street
Hertfordshire
HP4 2DJ
Tel: 07050 263500
Fax: 0870 7062199
Email: info@c2ventures.com
Website: www.c2ventures.com

E-Synergy
Bride House
18-20 Bride Lane
London
National
EC4Y 8JT
Tel: 0207 5833503
Fax: 0207 5833474
Email: c.hart@e-synergy.com
Website: www.e-synergy.com

Business Link – Bedfordshire & Luton
Chamber Business
Kimpton Road
Luton
LU2 0LB
Tel: 0845 850 8822
Fax: 01582 522450
Email: info@chamber-business.com
Website: www.chamber-business.com

Business Link – Berkshire
Emlyn Square
Swindon
SN1 5BP
Tel: 0845 600 41 41
Fax: 01793 485186

Email: info@blbw.co.uk
Website: http://www.blbw.co.uk/Default.aspx/
loadindex.241

Business Link – Buckinghamshire
Unit B
The Firs
Bierton
HP22 5DX
Tel: 0845 606 4466
Fax: 0870 161 5860
Email: info@businesslinksolutions.co.uk
Website: www.businesslinksolutions.co.uk

Business Link – Cambridgeshire
Cambridge Business Services Ltd
Centenary House
St Mary's Street
Huntingdon
PE29 3PE
Tel: 0845 6097979
Fax: 01480 846478
Email: chiefexecutive@cambs.businesslink.co.uk
Website: www.cambs.businesslink.co.uk/

Business Link – Essex
Alexandra House
36a Church Street
Great Baddow
Chelmsford
CM2 7HY
Tel: 01245 241 400/01245 241510
Fax: 01245 241 500
Email: info@BL4E.co.uk
Website: http://www.bl4e.co.uk/desktopdefault.
aspx

Business Link – Hertfordshire
45 Grosvenor Road
St Albans
AL1 3AW
Tel: 01727 813813
Fax: 01727 813404
Email: info@mybusinesslink.co.uk
Website: www.hertsdirect.org

Business Link – Kent
26 Kings Hill Avenue
Kings Hill
West Malling
ME19 4AE
Tel: 0845 722 6655
Fax: 01732 841 109
Email: info@businesslinkkent.com
Website: http://www.businesslink.gov.uk/bdotg/
action

Business Link for London
Link House
292–308 Southbury Road
Enfield
EN1 1TS
Tel: 0845 6000 787
Fax: 020 8443 7270
Email: hotline@bl4london.com
Website: www.bl4london.com

Business Link for Norfolk
2nd Floor
EcoTech Centre
Turbine Way
Swaffham
PE37 7HT
Tel: 08457 218 218
Fax: 01760 726 727
Email: success@businesslinknorfolk.co.uk

Business Link for Suffolk
Felaw Maltings,
42 Felaw Street,
Ipswich IP2 8PN
Tel: 08457 254 254
Fax: 01473 417070
Website: http://www.bls.org.uk/

Business Link – Surrey
5th floor
Hollywood House
Church Street East
Woking, Surrey
GU21 1HJ
Tel: 0845 7494949

Fax: 01483 771507
Email: success@businesslinksurrey.co.uk
Website: www.businesslinksurrey.co.uk

Business Link – Sussex
Greenacre Court
Station Road
Burgess Hill
West Sussex
RH15 9DS
Tel: 0845 6788867
Fax: 01444 259255
Email: info@sussexenterprise.co.uk
Website: http://www.esib.co.uk/businesslinks.
asp?PageId=50

Business Link West
The Link Centre
Oldmixon Crescent
Weston-super-Mare
BS24 9AY
Tel: 01934 418 118/0845 768 100
Fax: 01934 629 541
Email: enquiries@businesswest.co.uk
Website: http://www.northsomersetenterprisea-
gency.co.uk/northsomersetenterpriseagency.htm

Capital Match
Dallas,
Texas
75230 USA
Email: info@capmatch.com
Website: http://www.capmatch.com/index.
cfm?fuseaction=home

Capital Network Ltd
2nd Floor
Don Valley House
Savile Street East
Sheffield
S4 7UQ
Tel: 0114 281 3831
Fax: 0114 281 2772
Email: capnet@blsheffield.co.uk
Website: www.bvca.co.uk/publications/busines-
sangels/ angelsdetails/capitalnetwork.html

Cavendish Management Resources (CMR)
31 Harley Street,
London
W1G 9QS
Tel: 020 7636 1744
Fax: 020 7636 5639
Email: cmr@cmruk.com
Website: www.cmruk.com

Entrust
Portman House
Portland Road
Newcastle upon Tyne
NE2 1AQ
Tel: 0191 244 4000
Fax: 0191 244 4001
Email: enquire@entrust.co.uk
Website: www.entrust.co.uk

Envestors
London House
100 New Kings Road
London
SW6 4LX
Tel: 020 73486171
Fax: 020 73486172
Email: funding@envestors.co.uk
Website: www.envestors.co.uk

Equity Link - owned and organized by Examplas Ltd
45 Grosvenor Road
St Albans
Hertfordshire
AL1 3AW
Tel: 01727 813533/813813
Fax: 01727 813443
Email: questions@exemplas.com
Website: www.equitylink.co.uk

Finance South East Limited (FSE)
Devonshire Place
New Road
Crowthorne
Berkshire

RG45 6NA
Email: sally.goodsell@financesoutheast.com
Tel: 01344 758540
Fax: 01344 762002
Website: www.financesoutheast.com

FirstCapital Ltd
Elsinore House
77 Fulham Palace Road
London
W6 8JA
Tel: 020 8563 1563
Fax: 020 8563 2767
Email: info@firstcap.co.uk
Website: www.firstcap.co.uk/

Gorilla Park
1-9 Memel Street,
London
EC1 OTA
Tel: +44 020 7014 8905
Email: anthony@gorillapark.com
Website: www.gorillapark.com

Great Eastern Investment Forum
Richmond House
16–20 Regent Street
Cambridge
CB2 1DB
Tel: 01223 357131
Fax: 01223 720258
Email: geif@nwbrown.co.uk
Website: www.geif.co.uk

IDJ Limited
81 Piccadilly
London
W1J 8HY
Tel: 020 7355 1200
Fax: 020 7495 1149
Email: mail@idj.co.uk
Website: www.idj.co.uk

The Great Eastern Investment Forum
Richmond House

16/20 Regent Street
Cambridge
CB2 1DB
Tel: 01223 357131
Fax: 01223 720258
Email: john.Goodger@nwbrown.co.uk
Website: www.geif.co.uk

LEntA Ventures

London Business Incentive Scheme (LBIS) Ltd
28 Park Street
London
SE1 9EQ
Tel: 020 7236 3000
Fax: 020 7403 1742
Email: lenta.ventures@gle.co.uk
Website: www.businessangels-london.co.uk

LINC Scotland

Queens House
19 St Vincent Place
Glasgow
G1 2DT
Tel: 0141 221 3321
Fax: 0141 221 2909
Email: info@lincscot.co.uk
Website: www.lincscot.co.uk

Katalyst

10 Fenchurch Avenue
London
EC3M 5BN
Tel: 0207 6655454
Fax: 0871 9906338
Email: info@katalystventures.com
Website: www.katalystventures.com

Kingston Business Angels (KBA)

3 Kingsmill Business Park
Chapel Mill Road
Kingston-Upon-Thames
London
KT1 3GZ
Tel: 0208 5452875
Fax: 0208 5438748

Email: angels@kingstoninnovation.org
Website: www.kingstoninnovation.org

London Business Angels Network

London Business Angels
5th Floor
52–54 Southwark Street
London
SE1 1UN
Tel: 0207 089 2317
Email: enquiries@lbangels.co.uk
Website: www.gle.co.uk/commercialfinanc e/lba.
htm

Oxford Early Investments (OEI)

OCFI
Mill Street
Oxford
OX2 0JX
Contact: Alastair Cavanagh
Tel: 01865 811120
Fax: 01865 209044
Email: a.cavanagh@omn.co.uk

The Oxfordshire Investment Opportunity Network (OION)

OCFI
Mill Street
Oxford
OX2 0BH
Tel: 01865 811143
Fax: 01865 209044
Email: j.cox@oxin.co.uk
Website: www.oion.co.uk

The Solent Investment Opportunity Network

Portsmouth Technopole
Kingston Cresent
Portsmouth
PO2 8FA
Contact: Arthur Monks
Tel: 02392 658268
Email: sion-bbaa@sion.org.co.uk
Website: www.sion.org.uk

South West Investment Group
Trevint House
Strangeways Villas
Truro
TR1 2PA
Tel: 01872 223883
Fax: 01872 242470
Email: info@southwestinvestmentgroup.co.uk
Website: www.southwestinvestmentgroup.co.uk

TEChINVEST
North West Development Agency
Renaissance House
PO Box 37
Centre Park
Warrington
WA1 1XB
Tel: 01925 400301/400302
Fax: 01925 400400/830456
Email: tecinvest@nwda.co.uk
Website: www.techinvest.org

Triodos Match
Brunel House
11 The Promenade
Clifton
Bristol
BS8 3NN
Tel: 0117 973 9339
Fax: 0117 973 9303
Email: mail@triodos.co.uk
Website: www.triodosmatch.co.uk

VentureNet
2 North 20th Street
Suite 510
Birmingham
Alabama 35203
USA
Tel: 205-978-9230
Email: info@venturenet.net
Website: http://www.venturenet.net/93.0.html

The Venture Site
5 The Maltings

Walkern
SG2 7NP
Tel: +44 (0) 7092 161866
Fax: +44 (0) 7092 396143
Email: info@venturesite.co.uk
Website: www.venturesite.co.uk

Winsec Corporate Exchange Ltd
1 The Centre
Church Road
Tiptree
Colchester
CO5 0HF
Tel: 0870 421 4301
Fax: 0870 421 4302
Email: corpex@winsec.co.uk
Website: www.winsec.co.uk

Xenos – The Wales Business Angel Network
3rd Floor
Oakleigh House
Park Place
Cardiff
CF10 3DQ
Tel: 029 2033 8144
Fax: 029 2033 8145
Email: kathryn.jellings@xenos.co.uk
Website: www.xenos.co.uk

Xenva Ltd
79 George Street
Ryde
PO33 2JF
Tel: 01983 817017
Fax: 01983 817001
Email: info@xenva.com
Website: www.xenva.com

Yorkshire Association of Business Angels
Unit 1 Hornbeam House
Hornbeam House
Hookstone Road
Harrogate
HG2 8QT
Tel: 01423 810149
Fax: 01423 810086

Email: admin@yaba.org.uk
Website: www.yaba.org.uk

Online directories of UK business angels can be found at www.startups.co.uk/directories.asp and for most other European countries at www.eban.org

Venture capital

Venture capital providers are investing other people's money, often from pension funds. They have a different agenda to that of business angels and are more likely to be interested in investing more money for a larger stake.

Venture capital is a means of financing the start-up, development, expansion or purchase of a company. The venture capitalist acquires an agreed proportion of the share capital (equity) of the company in return for providing the requisite funding. Venture capital firms often work in conjunction with other providers of finance in putting together a total funding package for a business. Venture capital has its origins in the late eighteenth century when entrepreneurs found wealthy individuals to back their projects.

Venture capital is a medium- to long-term investment, not of just money, but of time and effort. The venture capital firm's aim is to enable growth companies to develop into the major businesses of tomorrow.

VCs will go through a process known as 'due diligence' before investing. This process involves a thorough examination of both the business and its owners. Past financial performance, the directors' track record and the business plan are all subjected to detailed scrutiny, usually by accountants and lawyers. Directors are then required to 'warrant' that they have provided *all* relevant information, under pain of financial penalties. The cost of this process will have to be borne by the firm raising the money, but will be paid out of the money raised, if that is any consolation.

In general, VCs would expect their investment to have paid off within seven years. But they are hardened realists. Two in every ten investments they make are total write-offs, and six perform averagely well at best. So the one star in every ten investments they make has to cover a lot of duds. VC's have a target rate of return of over 30%, to cover this poor hit rate.

Raising venture capital is not a cheap option. The arrangements costs will almost always run to six figures. They are not quick to arrange either. Six months is not unusual and over a year has been known. Every VC has a deal done in six weeks in their portfolio, but that truly is the exception.

Venture capital providers will want to exit from their investment at some stage. Their preferred route is via a public offering (see 'Going Public' on page **282**), but a trade sale is more usual (see Fig. 6.4).

Although venture capital is big business, the value of funds invested in early stage UK companies has remained modest, at just a few per cent of all the funds invested. While this is mainly attributable to the risk-reward relationship, the due diligence and transaction costs involved in investing

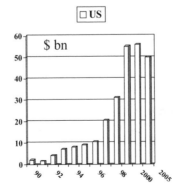
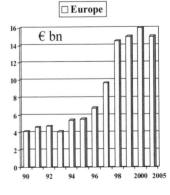

Fig. 6.4   Venture capital explodes: annual investment in the US and Europe.

in small companies are similar to those associated with investments in large companies, and so they are far higher per unit of funds invested.

But don't despair. New venture capital funds are coming on stream all the time and they too are looking for a gap in the market.

UK venture capital providers

Some of these firms are very focused, only serving a single industry or a small geographic area of the UK. Others have a wider vision and see the world as their market and will consider almost any business sector. One VC even suggests they would be prepared to consider a business in sufficient trouble to require rescuing!

	Minimum investment	Stage of investment*	Industry preferences	Geographic preferences
3K Digital Level 4, 16 Old Bond Street, London W1X 3DB Tel: 020 7355 3322 Fax: 020 7355 3407 Email: info@3kdigital.com Website: www.3kdigital.com	£0.5 million	All	IT	UK, USA, Western Europe, Scandinavia
Aberdeen Murray Johnstone Private Equity 55 Spring Gardens, Manchester M2 2BY Tel: 0161 233 3500 Fax: 0161 233 3550 Email: gary.tipper@aberdeen-asset.com Website: www.aberdeen-asset.com	£0.5 million	Expansion upwards	All	UK
Abingworth Management Ltd Princes House, 38 Jermyn Street, London SW1Y 6DN Tel: 020 7534 1500 Fax: 020 7287 0480 Email: info@abingworth.co.uk Website: www.abingworth.com	£0.5 million	Early stage	Medical/health care, biotech, service, manufacturing industries, technology-related	UK, USA, some Europe
ABN AMRO Capital Limited 199 Bishopsgate, London EC2M 3XW Tel: 020 7678 8000 Fax: 020 7678 2050 Email: ian.taylor@uk.abnamro.com Website: www.privateequities.com	£3 million	Expansion	All	UK, W Europe
Accelerator Media (UK) Limited 30 St James's Square, London SW1Y 4AL Tel: 020 7968 4288 Fax: 020 7968 4298 Email: proposals@acceleratormedia.com Website: http://www.astahost.com/info.php/accelerator-media_t3343.html	£0.5 million	Early stage upwards	Communications	UK

	Minimum investment	Stage of investment*	Industry preferences	Geographic preferences
Aberdeen Murray Johnstone Private Equity 10 Queens Terrace Aberdeen AB10 1YG Tel: 01224 631999 Fax: 01224 425916 Website: http://www.aberdeen-asset.co.uk/ecms.nsf/PrivateEquity/PrivateEquityWelcome	£1.4 million	Early stage	Communications	Worldwide
F&C Asset Management plc Exchange House Primrose Street London EC2A 2NY Telephone: +44 (0)20 7628 8000 Facsimile: +44 (0)20 7628 8188 Email: enquiries@fandc.com Website: http://www.isisam.com/index.asp?locale=UK	£0.5 million	Seed, start-up	All	UK, Ireland
Advent International plc 123 Buckingham Palace Road, London SW1W 9SL Tel: 020 7333 0800 Fax: 020 7333 0801 Email: info@uk.adventinternational.com Website: www.adventinternational.com	£5 million	Early stage	All	World
Advent Venture Partners 25 Buckingham Gate, London SW1E 6LD Tel: +44(0)20 7932 2100 Fax: 020 7828 1474 Email: info@adventventures.com Website: www.adventventures.com	£0.5 million	Seed, start-up onwards	Biotech, service, manufacturing industries, chemicals	UK, USA, W Europe
Albany Venture Managers Limited Forth House, 28 Rutland Square, Edinburgh EH1 2BW Tel: 0131 221 6510 Fax: 0131 221 6511 Email: info@albanyventures.co.uk Website: www.albanyventures.co.uk	£1 million	Early stage	Communications, IT	UK

	Minimum investment	Stage of investment*	Industry preferences	Geographic preferences
Albemarle Private Equity Limited 1 Albemarle Street, London W1S 4HA Tel: 020 7491 9555 Fax: 020 7491 7245 Email: Albemarle@btinternet.com Website: http://64.233.183.104/ search?q=cache:UpcCw5GDV4UJ:www. shafe.co.uk/companies/3248.asp+Albema rle+Private+Equity+Limited&hl=bg&lr=lang _en|lang_bg	£1.5 million	Expansion	All	UK
Alchemy Partners 20 Bedfordbury, London WC2N 4BL Tel: 020 7240 9596 Fax: 020 7240 9594 Email: jmoulton@alchemypartners.co.uk Website: www.alchemypartners.co.uk	£5 million	Re-financing	All	UK, Austria, Germany, Switzerland
Alta Berkeley Venture Partners 9–10 Savile Row, London W1S 3PF Tel: 020 7440 0200 Fax: 020 7734 6711 Tim Brown Tel: +44 20 7440 0229 tb@altaberkeley.com Barun Dutta Tel: +44 20 7440 0225 bd@altaberkeley.com Kevin Fielding Tel: +44 20 7440 0238 kf@altaberkeley.com Website: www.alta-berkeley.com	£0.1 million	Early stage	Communications, healthcare	UK, W Europe
Amadeus Capital Partners Limited Mount Pleasant House, 2 Mount Pleasant, Cambridge CB3 0RN Tel: 01223 707000 Fax: 01223 707070 Email: info@amadeuscapital.com Website: www.amadeuscapital.com	£0.1 million	Early stage	Communications, IT	UK, W Europe
Apax Partners Ltd 15 Portland Place, London W1B 1PT Tel: 020 7872 6300 Fax: + 44 (0)20 7666 6441 Email: info@apax.com Website: www.apax.com	£3 million	Early stage	IT	World

	Minimum investment	Stage of investment*	Industry preferences	Geographic preferences
Atlas Venture Ltd 55 Grosvenor Street, London W1K 3BW Tel: 020 7529 4444 Fax: 020 7529 4455 Email: london@atlasventure.co.uk Website: www.atlasventure.com	£0.3 million	Early stage	IT, biotech, service, manufacturing industries	UK, USA, W Europe
Avlar Bioventures Highfield Court, Church Lane, Madingley, Cambs, CB3 8AG Tel: +44(0) 1954 211 515 Fax: +44(0) 1954 211 516 Email: info@avlar.com Website: www.avlar.com	£0.25 million	Early stage	Biotech, service, manufacturing industries, healthcare	UK, Europe
Bamboo Investments plc 4 Crown Place , London, EC2A 4BT Tel: +44 (0)20 7422 7841 Fax: +44 (0)20 7422 7849 Email: james@bamboo-investments.com Website: www.bamboo-investments.com	£0.15 million	Early stage	IT	UK
BancBoston Capital Bank of Boston House, 39 Victoria Street, London SW1H 0ED Tel: 020 7932 9053 Fax: 020 7932 9117 Website: www.bancboscap.com	£1 million	Early stage	All	UK, USA, W Europe, C Europe, S America, Asia
Artemis International Ltd Regus House, 268 Bath Road, Slough Berks, SL1 4DX Contact: UK Sales & Marketing Tel: (44) 1753727100 Fax: (44) 1753727099 Email: info@uk.aisc.com Website: http://www.aisc.com/	£5 million	Expansion	All	World
Barclays Private Equity Limited 5 The North Colonnade, Canary Wharf, London E14 4BB Tel: 020 7512 9900 Fax: 020 7773 4805 Website: www.barcap.com	£3 million	Expansion	IT	UK, Europe

	Minimum investment	Stage of investment*	Industry preferences	Geographic preferences
Barclays Ventures Third Floor, 50 Pall Mall, London SW1Y 5AX Tel: 020 7441 4213 Fax: 020 7441 4212 Email: barclays.ventures@barclays.co.uk Website: www.barclaysventures.com	£0.25 million	Expansion	All	UK
Baring Private Equity Partners Ltd 33 Cavendish Square, London W1M 0BQ Tel: + 44 20 7290 5088 Fax: 020 7290 5020 Email: mail@bpep.com Website: www.bpep.com	£0.5 million	Expansion	All	UK, Europe, Asia
BC Partners Limited 43–45 Portman Square, London W1H 6DA Tel: 020 7009 4800 Fax: 020 7009 4899 Email: london@bcpartners.com Website: www.bcpartners.com	£50 million	MBO, MBI	All	UK, W Europe
Birmingham Technology (Venture Capital) Ltd Aston Science Park, Faraday Wharf, Holt Street, Aston Science Park, Birmingham B7 4BB Tel: +44 (0)121 260 6000 Fax: +44 (0)121 250 3567 Email: info@astonsciencepark.co.uk	£0.02 million	Early stage	IT, healthcare	UK, Europe
BNFL Enterprise (Investment Management) Ltd 65 Buckingham Gate, Off Victoria Street, London SW1E 6AP Tel: +44 (0) 20 7222 9717 Fax: +44 (0) 20 7222 1935 Website: www.bnfl.com	£0.02 million	Early stage	All	UK
Botts & Company Ltd 41-44 Great Queen Street, London WC2B 5AA Tel: +44 (0)20 7841 1550 Fax: +44 (0)20 7849 3221 Email: postmaster@bottscompany.com Website: www.bottscompany.com	£5 million	Expansion	All	UK, W Europe

	Minimum investment	Stage of investment*	Industry preferences	Geographic preferences
Bridgepoint Capital Ltd 101 Finsbury Pavement, London EC2A 1EJ Tel: 020 7374 3500 Email: info@bridcap.com Fax: 020 7374 3600 Website: www.bridgepoint-capital.com	£5 million	Expansion	All	UK, W Europe
Bulldog Partners Albemarle House, 1 Albemarle Street, London W1S 4HA Tel: 020 7529 7800 Fax: 020 7529 7801 Email: bulldog@bulldogpartners.co.uk	£0.5 million	Early stage	All	UK, W Europe
Cabot Square Capital Advisors Ltd Byron House, 7–9 St James's Street, London SW1A 1EE Tel: 020 7579 9320 Fax: 020 7579 9330 Email: contact@cabotsquare.com Website: www.cabotsquare.com	TBA	Early stage	Communications	UK, W Europe
Cairnsford Associates Ltd 32 Hampstead High Street, London NW3 1JQ Tel: 020 7435 9100 Fax: 020 7435 7377 Email: vince@cairnsford.co.uk Website: http://www.globalfinanceonline.com/featuredcompanies/cairnsford/	£0.15 million	Seed, start-up	Communications	UK, W Europe
Cambridge Research & Innovation Ltd 13 Station Road, Cambridge CB1 2JB Tel: 01223 312856 Fax: 01223 365704 Email: enquiries@cril.co.uk	£0.5 million	Seed, start-up	Biotech, service, manufacturing industries, other	UK
Candover Investments plc 20 Old Bailey, London EC4M 7LN Tel: 020 7489 9848 Fax: 020 7248 5483 E-mail: info@candover.com Website: http://www.candover.com/candover/contact/contact.jsp	£50 million	MBO, MBI	All	UK, Europe

	Minimum investment	Stage of investment*	Industry preferences	Geographic preferences
Capricorn Ventures International Ltd c/o Capricorn Associates St Mary's House, 42 Vicarage Crescent, London SW11 3LD Tel: 020 7223 9130 Fax: 020 7326 8547	£0.5 million	Other early stage, MBO, MBI	Consumer, financial	UK, Africa, USA, Australasia
Catalyst Fund Management & Research Limited 15 Whitcomb Street, London WC2H 7HA Tel: 020 7747 8600 Fax: 020 7930 2688 Email: lucy@catfund.com Website: www.catfund.com	£0.25 million	Seed, start-up	Financial	UK, C Europe, E Europe, W Europe
Cazenove Private Equity 12 Moorgate, London, EC2R 6DA Tel: +44 (0)20 7155 5700 Fax: 020 7588 9887 Email: group@cpe.cazenove.com Website: www.cazenove.com	£2 million	Expansion	Communications	EU
Charterhouse Capital Partners LLP 7th Floor, Warwick Court, Paternoster Square, London EC4M 7DX Tel: 020 7334 5300 Fax: 020 7334 5333 Website: www.charterhouse.co.uk	£20 million	Expansion, MBO, MBI	All	UK, W Europe
Cinven Warwick Court, Paternoster Square, London EC4M 7AG Tel: 020 7661 3333 Fax: 020 7661 3888 Email: info@cinven.com Website: www.cinven.com	£50 million	MBO, MBI, etc.	All	UK, W Europe
Classic Fund Management Ltd Marble Arch Tower, 55 Bryanston Street, London W1H 7AJ Tel: 020 7868 8883 Fax: (020) 7868 8719 Email: info@classicfunds.co.uk Website: www.classicfunds.co.uk	£0.25 million	All	All	UK

	Minimum investment	Stage of investment*	Industry preferences	Geographic preferences
Clayton Dubilier & Rice Limited 55 Grosvenor Street, London SW11 6HT Tel: 020 7290 5800 Fax: 020 7290 5801 Email: bvonschroder@cdr-ltd.com Website: www.cdr-inc.com	£50 million	Rescue, MBO, MBI	Chemicals and related	UK, USA, Europe
Close Brothers Private Equity 10 Throgmorton Avenue, London EC2N 2DL Tel: +44 (0) 20 7065 1100 Fax: +44 (0) 20 7588 6815 Email: enquiries@cbpel.com Website: www.cbpel.com	£1 million	Expansion, MBO, MBI	All	UK
Company Guides Limited 13 Christopher Street, London EC2A 2BS Tel: 020 7247 6300 Fax: 020 7247 6900 Email: enquiries@companyguides.com Website: www.companyguides.com	£0.5 million	Seed, start-up	Biotech, service, manufacturing industries, etc.	UK, W Europe
Compass Investment Management Ltd 33 Cork Street, London W1S 3NQ Tel: 020 7434 4484/3488 Fax: +44 (0) 20 7434 3374 Email: info@compass.uk.com Website: www.compass.uk.com	£0.5 million	Early stage, MBO	Biotech, service, manufacturing industries, etc.	UK, USA, Canada, W Europe
Crédit Agricole Indosuez Private Equity 122 Leadenhall Street, London EC3V 4QH Tel: 020 7971 4405 Fax: 020 7971 4362 Email: pat.hudson@indosuez.co.uk Website: http://www.credit-agricole.fr/legroupe/uk/highlights-2001.shtml	£1 million	Early stage, MBO, MBI	All	UK, Ireland
Credit Suisse First Boston Private Equity Credit Suisse First Boston (Europe) Limited, One Cabot Square, London E14 4QJ Tel: +44 20 7888 8888 Fax: +44 20 7888 1600 Email: julie.harper@csfb.com Website: www.csfb.com	£15 million	Expansion, MBO, MBI	All	World
Crescent Capital NI Limited 5 Crescent Gardens, Belfast BT7 1NS Tel: 028 90 233633 Fax: 028 90 329525 Email: mail@crescentcapital.co.uk Website: www.crescentcapital.co.uk	£0.25 million	All	Biotech, service, manufacturing industries, etc.	N Ireland

	Minimum investment	Stage of investment*	Industry preferences	Geographic preferences
CVC Capital Partners Limited 111 Strand, London WC2R 0AG Tel: 020 7420 4200 Fax: 020 7420 4231 Email: info@cvceurope.com Website: www.cvceurope.com	£10 million	Expansion, MBO, MBI	All	World
DB eVentures One Great Winchester Street City London, EC2N 2DB Tel: 44.20.7545.8836 Fax: 44.20.7545.4314 Email: roger.bates@db.com Website: www.dbeventures.com	£3 million	Early stage	Technology	UK, USA, Asia, W Europe
Derbyshire First Investments Limited 95 Sheffield Road, Chesterfield, Derbyshire S41 7JH Tel: 01246 207390 Fax: 01246 221080 Email: info@dfil.co.uk (general enquiries); ahay@dfil.co.uk (investment) Website: www.dfil.co.uk	£0.5 million	Early stage	Chemicals, etc.	E Midlands
Dilmun Investments Ltd 27 Berkeley Square, London W1J 6EL Tel: 020 7495 8974 Fax: 020 7499 6768 Email: smallet@dilmun.com Website: www.dilmun.com	£5 million	Expansion, MBO, MBI	Communications	UK, USA, Near East, Middle East, W Europe
Duke Street Capital Almack House, 28 King Street, London SW1Y 6XA Tel: 020 7451 6600 Fax: 020 7451 6601 Email: mail@dukestreetcapital.com Website: www.dukestreetcapital.com	£30 million	Expansion, MBO, MBI	All	UK, W Europe
Dunedin Capital Partners Limited 10 George Street, Edinburgh EH2 2DW Tel: 0131 225 6699 Fax: 0131 718 2300 Email: info@dunedin.com Website: www.dunedin.com	£3 million	MBO, MBI	Chemicals	UK

	Minimum investment	Stage of investment*	Industry preferences	Geographic preferences
ECI Ventures Ltd Brettenham House, Lancaster Place, London WC2E 7EN Tel: 020 7606 1000 Fax: 020 7240 5050 Email: janet.brooks@eciv.co.uk Website: www.eciv.co.uk	£3 million	Expansion, MBO, MBI	All	UK
Elderstreet DrKC Limited 32 Bedford Row, London WC1R 4HE Tel: 020 7831 5088 Fax: 020 7831 5077 Email: admin@elderstreet.com Website: www.elderstreet.com	£0.25 million	Early stage	Communications	UK, W Europe
Electra Partners Europe Limited Paternoster House, 65 St Paul's Churchyard, London EC4M 8AB Tel: +44 (0)20 7214 4800 Fax: +44 (0)20 7214 4801 Email: info@electraeurope.com Website: www.electraeurope.com	£20 million	MBO, MBI-related	All	UK, W Europe
Enterprise Equity (NI) Limited 78a Dublin Road, Belfast BT2 7HP Tel: 028 90 242500 Fax: 028 90 242487 Email: info@eeni.com Website: www.eeni.com	£0.25 million	Seed, start-up	All	N Ireland, Ireland
Enterprise Ventures Limited Lancaster House, Centurion Way, Leyland PR26 6TX Tel: +44(0)1772 819 000 Fax: 01772 819046 Email: ventures@enterprise.plc.uk Website: www.enterprise.plc.uk	£0.5 million	Early stage	Communications	North West & Merseyside
Episode 1 Partners 1 Hinde Street, London W1U 2AY Tel: 020 7486 4841 Fax: 020 7935 7963 Email: info@episode1.com Website: www.episode1.com	£0.5 million	Seed, start-up	Hi-tech	UK, W Europe
Equity Ventures Ltd 23 Berkeley Square, London, W1J 6HE Tel: 020 7665 6611 Email: david@equityventures.co.uk Website: www.equityventures.co.uk	£0.5 million	Expansion, MBO, MBI	Chemicals	UK, W Europe

	Minimum investment	Stage of investment*	Industry preferences	Geographic preferences
ETCapital Ltd St John's Innovation Centre, Cowley Road, Cambridge CB4 0WS Tel: 01223 422010 Fax: 01223 422011 Email (for ICT enquiries): martin@etcapital.com (for bio enquiries): david@etcapital.com Website: www.etcapital.com	£0.2 million	Seed, start-up	Biotech, service, manufacturing industries-related	Southern England
far blue ventures limited 1 Marble Quay, London E1W 1UH Tel: 020 7481 8002 Fax: 020 7481 8003 Email: enquiries@farblue.com Website: www.farblue.com	£0.5 million	Seed, start-up	Communications	UK, W Europe
Ferranti Ltd 43 Rosary Gardens, London SW7 4NQ Tel: 020 7835 1325 Fax: 020 7244 8387 Email: info@ferranti.com Website: www.ferranti.com	£0.25 million	All	Communications	UK, USA, Europe
Fresh Capital Group Limited 14–16 Hans Road, London SW3 1RS Tel: 020 7581 1477 Fax: 020 7589 3542 Email: info@freshcapital.com Website: www.freshcapital.com	£0.5 million	Early stage	All	UK, USA, W Europe
Friends Ivory & Sime Private Equity plc 100 Wood Street, London EC2V 7AN Tel: 020 7506 1601 Fax: 020 7600 4163 Email: wol.kolade@friendsis.com Website: www.friendsis.com	£2 million	Expansion, MBO, MBI	Biotech, service, manufacturing industries related	UK, W Europe
GE Equity Europe Clarges House, 6–12 Clarges Street, London W1J 8DH Tel: 020 7302 6310 Fax: 020 7302 6810 Website: www.geequity.com	£2 million	Early stage, MBO, MBI	Communications	UK, Europe

	Minimum investment	Stage of investment*	Industry preferences	Geographic preferences
GLE Development Capital 52–54 Southwark Street, London SE1 1UN Tel: 020 7089 2320 Fax: 020 7089 2321 Email: tracy.m@gledc.co.uk Website: http://www.gle.co.uk/ commercialfinance/index.htm	£0.25 million	Early stage	All	UK
GMT Communications Partners Limited Sackville House, 40 Piccadilly, London W1J 0DR Tel: 020 7292 9333 Fax: 020 7292 9390 Website: www.gmtpartners.com	£6 million	Seed, start-up, MBO, MBI	Communications	UK, Europe
Granville Baird Capital Partners 5th Floor, Walsingham House, London EC3N 4AH Tel: +44(0) 20 7667 8400 Fax: 020 7667 8481 Email: private.equity@granvillebaird.com Website: http://www.gbcp.com/en/ contactus.html	£2 million	Early stage, MBO, MBI	Communications	UK, Europe
Graphite Capital Berkeley Square House, Berkeley Square, London W1J 6BQ Tel: 020 7825 5300 Fax: 020 7825 5399 Email: info@graphitecapital.com Website: www.graphitecapital.com	£4 million	All	All	UK, W Europe
Gresham Trust plc One South Place, London EC2M 2GT Tel: 020 7309 5000 Fax: 020 7374 0707 Email: info@greshamtrust.co.uk Website: www.greshamtrust.co.uk	£2 million	Expansion, MBO, MBI	All	UK
Henderson Private Capital Ltd 4 Broadgate, London EC2M 2DA Tel: + 44 (0)20 7818 1818 Fax: + 44 (0)20 7818 1819 Email: kathryn.fisher@henderson.com Website: www.henderson.com	£5 million	Seed, start-up, MBO, MBI	Communications	UK, Europe, Far East

	Minimum investment	Stage of investment*	Industry preferences	Geographic preferences
Herald Investment Management Limited 12 Charterhouse Square, London EC1M 6AX Tel: 0171 5536314 Fax: 0171 4908026 Email: sr@heralduk.com Website: www.heralduk.com	£0.25 million	Early stage	Communications	UK
Hermes Private Equity Management Limited Lloyds Chambers, 1 Portsoken Street, London E1 8HZ Switchboard: 020 7702 0888 Andrew Raisman, Marketing Director Tel: +44 (0)20 7680 2815 Email: a.raisman@hermes.co.uk Colin Melvin, Director of Corporate Governance Tel: (020) 7702 0888 Email: governance@hermes.co.uk Website: www.hermes.co.uk	£5 million	Expansion, MBO, MBI	All	UK, Europe, Far East
HgCapital 3rd Floor, Minerva House, 3–5 Montague Close, London SE1 9BB Tel: 020 7089 7888 Fax: 020 7089 7999 Email: info@hgcapital.net Website: www.hgcapital.net	£5 million	Expansion, MBO, MBI	All	UK, W Europe
HSBC Private Equity Vintners Place, 68 Upper Thames Street, London EC4V 3BJ Tel: 020 7336 9955 Fax: 020 7336 9961 Email: chris.masterson@hsbcib.com Website: www.hsbcib.com	£1 million	All	All	UK, S America, Far East, Europe
HSBC UK Enterprise Fund for the South East The Cadmus Organisation Ltd, Suite G, Kings Business Centre, Reeds Lane, Sayers Common, Hassocks, West Sussex BN6 9LS Tel: 01273 835455 Fax: 01273 835466 Email: cadmus@globalnet.co.uk Website: www.thecadmusorganisation. ltd.uk	£0.25 million	Seed, start-up	All	S East, London

	Minimum investment	Stage of investment*	Industry preferences	Geographic preferences
HSBC Ventures (UK) Ltd 8 Canada Square, London E14 5HQ Tel: 08457 404 404 Fax: 020 7260 6767 Email: Venturesuk@hsbc.com Website: www.hsbc.co.uk	£0.25 million	MBO, MBI	All	UK
Industrial Development Board for Northern Ireland Corporate Finance and Restructuring Division, IDB House, 64 Chichester Street, Belfast BT1 4JX Tel: 028 233233 Fax: 028 545000 Email: idbni@idb.dedni.gov.uk	Open	Seed, start-up	Biotech, service, manufacturing industries	N Ireland
Industrial Technology Securities Ltd Surrey Technology Centre, Surrey Research Park, Guildford, Surrey GU2 5YG Tel: 01483 457398 Fax: 01483 568710 Email: Industrial.technology@btinternet.com Website: www.itsvc.co.uk	£0.25 million	Seed, start-up	Communications	UK, S Wales
Inflexion plc 40 George Street, London W1V 7DW Tel: 020 7487 9888 Fax: 020 7487 2774 Email: info@inflexion.com Website: www.inflexion.com	£2 million	Expansion	Communications	UK, W Europe
Innvotec Limited 1 Castle Lane, London SW1E 6DN Tel: 020 7630 6990 Fax: 020 7828 8232 Email: cvk@innvotec.co.uk Website: www.innvotec.uk.com	£1 million	Seed, start-up	Biotech, service, manufacturing industries	N Ireland, UK
Interregnum plc 22–23 Old Burlington Street, London W1S 2JJ Tel: 020 7494 3080 Fax: 020 7494 3090 Email: enquiries@interregnum.com Website: www.interregnum.com	£0.25 million	Seed, start-up	Communications	UK, W Europe

	Minimum investment	Stage of investment*	Industry preferences	Geographic preferences
JAFCO Investment (UK) Ltd Nomura House, 1 St Martin's-le-Grand, London EC1A 4NP Tel: 020 7489 8066 Fax: 020 7248 5070 Email: info@jafco.co.uk Website: www.jafco.co.uk	£0.5 million	Seed, start-up	Communications	UK, W Europe
JPMorgan Partners 125 London Wall, London EC2Y 5AJ Tel: 020 7777 3365 Fax: 020 7777 4731 Email: contactus@jpmorganpartners.com Website: www.jpmorganpartners.com	£3 million	Expansion, MBO, MBI	All	World
Katalyst Ventures Limited 10 Fenchurch Avenue London EC3M 5BN Tel: 0870 420 2565 Fax: 0871 990 6338 Email: invest@katalystventures.com Website: www.katalystventures.com	£1 million	Seed, start-up, MBO, MBI	All	UK
Kennet Capital Ltd St James's House, 23 King Street, London SW1Y 6QY Tel: 020 7839 8020 Fax: 020 7839 8485 Email: info@kennetcapital.com Website: www.kennetcapital.com	£3 million	Seed, start-up	Communications	UK, USA Europe
Kleinwort Capital Ltd 10 Bedford Street, Covent Garden London, WC2E 9HE Tel: 020 7632 8200 Fax: 020 7632 8201 Email: info@kleinwortcapital.com Website: www.kleinwortcapital.com	£2 million	Expansion, MBO, MBI	Communications	UK, Europe
Legal & General Ventures Limited 5th Floor, Bucklersbury House, 3 Queen Victoria Street, London EC4N 8NH Tel: 020 7528 6456 Fax: 020 7528 6444 Email: enquiries@ventures.landg.com Website: www.legalandgeneralventures.com	£20 million	MBO, MBI	All	UK, W Europe

	Minimum investment	Stage of investment*	Industry preferences	Geographic preferences
LF Europe Limited 85 Wimpole Street, London W1G 9RJ Tel: 020 7224 3883 Fax: 020 7224 0110 Email: contacteurope@lfvc.com Website: www.lfvc.com	£1 million	All	Consumer	UK, W Europe
LICA Development Capital Ltd 12 Stratford Place, London, W1C 1BB Tel: 020 7839 7707 Fax: 020 7839 4363 Email: enquiries@lica.co.uk Website: www.lica.co.uk	£0.25 million	Early stage, MBO, MBI	Communications	UK
Lloyds TSB Development Capital Limited 45 Old Bond Street, London W1S 4QT Tel: 020 7499 1500 Fax: 020 7647 2000 Website: www.ldc.co.uk	£2 million	Expansion, MBO, MBI	All	Scotland, Wales, England
London Ventures (Fund Managers) Ltd 4th Floor, 17 Golden Square, London W1F 9JH Tel: 020 7434 2425 Fax: 020 7434 2426 Email: lvfm@compuserve.com Website: www.londonventures.co.uk	£0.5 million	Seed, start-up, MBO, MBI	Communications	London
Loxko Venture Managers Ltd 22 Henrietta Street, London WC2E 8ND Tel: 020 7240 5024 Fax: (020) 7420 3993 Email: enquiries@loxko.com Website: www.loxko.com	£0.5 million	Expansion, MBO, MBI	All	UK, World
LTG Development Capital Ltd Chelsea House, West Gate, London W5 1DR Tel: 0208 991 8920 Fax: 0208 991 1678 Email: info@ltgdevcap.com Website: http://www.ltgdevelopmentgroup.co.uk/abt.htm	£0.25 million	Early stage	Biotech, service, manufacturing industries	UK, USA, Near East, Middle East, W Europe
The Manchester Technology Fund Ltd Incubator Building, Grafton Street, Manchester M13 9XX Tel: 0161 606 7235 Fax: 0161 606 7300 Email: mail@mantechfund.com Website: www.mantechfund.com	£0.25 million	Seed, start-up	Biotech, service, manufacturing industries	N West, Merseyside

	Minimum investment	Stage of investment*	Industry preferences	Geographic preferences
Matrix Private Equity 9–10 Savile Row, London W1S 3PF Tel: 020 7439 6050 Fax: 020 7287 2312 Email: info@matrixpe.com Website: www.matrixpe.com	£0.25 million	Seed, start-up	Communications	UK
Merlin Biosciences Limited 33 King Street, St James's, London, SW1Y 6RJ Tel: + 44 (0) 20 7811 4000 Fax: + 44 (0) 20 7811 4001 Email: enquiry@merlin-biosciences.com Website: www.merlin-biosciences.com	£0.25 million	Seed, start-up	Biotech, service, manufacturing industries	W Europe
Midven Limited 37 Bennetts Hill, Birmingham, B2 5SN Tel: 0121 710 1990 Fax: 0121 710 1999 Email: enquiries@midven.com Website: www.midven.com	£0.2 million	Seed, start-up, MBO, MBI	Biotech, service, manufacturing industries	East Midlands, West Midlands
Catalyst Investment Group Limited 10-13 Lovat Lane, London, EC3R 8DN Telephone: 020 7929 5090 Fax: 020 7929 5086 Website: http://www.catalystinvestment.co.uk/	£0.2 million	Seed, start-up	Hi-tech, finance	UK, Europe
Moorfield Investment Management Ltd Premier House, 44–48 Dover Street, London W1S 4NX Tel: 020 7399 1900 Fax: 020 7499 2114	£0.5 million	–	Property	UK
MTI MTI Partners Limited, Langley Place, 99 Langley Road, Watford, Herts WD1 4BE Tel: 01923 250244 Fax: 01923 24 7783 Email: headoffice@mtifirms.com Website: www.mtifirms.com	£0.25 million	Seed, start-up	Biotech, service, manufacturing industries	UK
NatWest Development Capital Ltd 21 Castle Gate, Nottingham NG1 7AQ Tel: 0115 959 0049 Fax: 0115 938 8400 Email: david.lambert@nwdevcap.co.uk Website: www.rbdc.co.uk	£1 million	Expansion, MBO, MBI	All	UK

	Minimum investment	Stage of investment*	Industry preferences	Geographic preferences
NBGI Private Equity Old Change House, 128 Queen Victoria Street, London EC4V 4BJ Tel: 020 7661 5678 Fax: 020 7661 5667 Email: info@nbgipe.co.uk Website: www.nbgiprivateequity.co.uk	£2 million	Expansion, MBO, MBI	All	UK
nCoTec Ventures 40 Portman Square, London W1H 6LT Tel: 020 7947 8800 Fax: 020 7947 8801 Email: info@ncotec.com Website: www.ncotec.com	£0.3 million	Seed, start-up	Communications	UK, Europe, Nordic
NewMedia SPARK plc 33 Glasshouse Street, London W1B 5DG Tel: 020 7851 7777 Fax: 020 7851 7770 Email: enquiries@newmediaspark.com Website: www.newmediaspark.com	£0.5 million	Seed, start-up	Communications	UK, Asia, W Europe
Nichimen Europe plc 3 Shortlands, London, W6 8DA Tel: 020 7886 7000 Fax: 020 7886 7090 Email: info@nichimen.co.uk Website: www.nichimen.co.uk	£1 million	Early stage	Biotech, service, manufacturing industries	UK, Japan, W Europe
Northern Enterprise Limited 3 Earl's Court, 5th Avenue, Team Valley, Gateshead NE11 0HF Tel: 0191 442 4300 Fax: 0191 442 4301 Email: enquiries@nel.co.uk Website: www.nel.co.uk	£0.25 million	Seed, start-up, MBO, MBI	Biotech, service, manufacturing industries	UK
Northern Venture Managers Limited Northumberland House, Princess Square, Newcastle upon Tyne NE1 8ER Tel: 0191 244 6000 Fax: 0191 244 6001 Email: new@nvm.co.uk Website: www.nvm.co.uk	£0.5 million	Seed, start-up, MBO, MBI	All	UK

	Minimum investment	Stage of investment*	Industry preferences	Geographic preferences
Orange Ventures 50 George Street, London W1U 7DZ Tel: 020 7984 1697 Fax: 020 7984 2061 Email: deborah.hylton@orange.co.uk Website: www.orangeventures.com	£0.5 million	Seed, start-up	Communications	UK, USA, Ireland, Scandinavia
Pacific Investments 124 Sloane Street, London SW1X 9BW Tel: 020 7225 2250 Fax: 020 7591 1650 Email: jlb@beckwithlondon.com	£1 million	All	Finance	UK, World
Parallel Ventures Managers Limited 49 St James's Street, London SW1A 1JT Tel: 020 7600 9105 Fax: 020 7491 3372	£1 million	Expansion, MBO, MBI	Biotech, service, manufacturing industries	UK, W Europe
Penta Capital Partners Ltd 150 St Vincent Street, Glasgow G2 5NE Tel: 0141 572 7300 Fax: 0141 572 7310 Email: info@pentacapital.com Website: www.pentacapital.com	£1 million	Expansion, MBO, MBI	Communications	UK, Ireland
Permira Advisers Limited (formerly Schroder Ventures Europe) 20 Southampton Street, London WC2E 7QH Tel: 020 7632 1000 Fax: 020 7240 5072/497 2174 Email: lucy.du-sautoy@permira.com Website: www.permira.com	£10 million	Early stage, MBO, MBI	Biotech, service, manufacturing industries	World
Phoenix Equity Partners 33 Glasshouse Street, London W1B 5DG Tel: 020 7434 6999 Fax: 020 7434 6998 Email: enquiries@phoenix-equity.com Website: www.phoenix-equity.com	£10 million	Expansion, MBO, MBI	Chemicals	UK, Europe
Pi Capital 7 Old Park Lane, London W1K 1QR Tel: 020 7629 9949 Fax: 020 7491 1015 Email: contact@picapital.co.uk Website: www.picapital.co.uk	£1 million	Early stage, expansion	All	UK

	Minimum investment	Stage of investment*	Industry preferences	Geographic preferences
Piper Private Equity Limited Eardley House, 182–184 Campden Hill Road, London W8 7AS Tel: 020 7727 3842 Fax: 020 7727 8969 Email: info@piperprivateequity.com Website: www.piperprivateequity.com	£0.5 million	Expansion, MBO, MBI	Consumer	UK
Pond Venture Partners Ltd Marpol House, 6 The Green, Richmond, Surrey TW9 1PL Tel: 020 8940 1001 Fax: 020 8940 6792 Email: office@pondventures.com Website: www.pondventures.com	£0.8 million	Seed, start-up	Communications	UK, W Europe
Prelude Technology Investments Limited Sycamore Studios, New Road, Over, Cambridge CB4 5PJ Tel: 01954 288090 Fax: 01954 288099 Email: Prelude@prelude-technology.co.uk Website: www.prelude-technology.co.uk	£1 million	Seed, start-up	Biotech, service, manufacturing industries	UK, Europe
Postern Fund Management Limited Adam House, 7-10 Adam Street, London WC2N 6AA Tel: +44 (0) 20 7520 9362 Fax: +44 (0) 20 7520 9363 Email: Ptaylor@postern.com Website: www.postern.com	£0.5 million	Rescue	All	UK, W Europe
PPM Ventures Ltd 1 New Fetter Lane London EC4A 1HH Tel: (020) 7822 1000 Fax: (020) 7822 1001 Email: nfo@ppmcapital.com Website: www.ppmventures.com	£15 million	Expansion	All	UK, Far East, Australasia
Primary Capital Limited Augustine House, Austin Friars, London EC2N 2HA Tel: +44 (0) 20 7920 4800 Fax: +44 (0) 20 7920 4801 Email: primary@primaryeurope.com Website: www.primaryeurope.com	£1 million	Expansion, MBO, MBI	All	UK, W Europe

	Minimum investment	Stage of investment*	Industry preferences	Geographic preferences
ProVen Private Equity Limited 42 Craven Street, London WC2N 5NG Tel: 020 7451 6500 Fax: 020 7839 8349 Email: info@proven.co.uk Website: www.provenprivateequity.com	£0.75 million	Expansion, MBO, MBI	All	UK, USA, Nordic
Quester Capital Management Limited 29 Queen Anne's Gate, London SW1H 9BU Tel: 020 7222 5472 Fax: 020 7222 5250 Email: contact@quester.co.uk Website: www.quester.co.uk	£0.75 million	Seed, start-up	Communications	UK, W Europe
YFM Private Equity Saint Martins House 210-212 Chapeltown Road Leeds LS7 4HZ Tel: 0113 294 5050 Fax: 0113 294 5002 Email: leeds@yfmprivateequity.co.uk Website: http://www.yfmprivateequity.co.uk/	£10 million	Expansion, MBO, MBI	Chemicals	UK, W Europe
Noble Fund Managers Limited 76 George Street Edinburgh EH2 3BU Tel: 0131 225 9677 Fax: 0131 225 5479 Email: NFM@noblegp.com Website: http://www.noblegpweb.com/webapps/komplete/index.php?KTURL=mod_page.html&page=227	£1 million	Early stage	Communications	UK, W Europe
Rutland Fund Management Ltd Rutland House, Rutland Gardens, London SW7 1BX Tel: 020 7556 2600 Fax: 020 7581 8766 Email: info@rutlandpartners.com Website: www.rfml.co.uk	£10 million	Refinancing	All	UK
RVC-Greenhouse Fund 11 Upper Grosvenor Street, London W1K 2NB Tel: 44 20 7355 5700 Fax: 020 7355 5701 Email: greenhouse@reuters.com Website: www.rvc.com	£1 million	Seed, start-up	Communications	UK, World

	Minimum investment	Stage of investment*	Industry preferences	Geographic preferences
Sagitta Private Equity Berkeley Square House, Berkeley Square, London W1J 6BL Tel: 020 7543 1500 Fax: 020 7495 8546 Email: srauf@sagitta.co.uk Website: www.sagitta.co.uk	£2 million	Expansion, MBO, MBI	All	UK, W Europe
Sand Aire Private Equity Ltd 101 Wigmore Street, London W1U 1QU Tel: 020 7290 5200 Fax: 020 7495 0240 Email: private.equity@sandaire.co.uk Website: www.sandaire.co.uk	£2 million	Expansion, MBO, MBI	All	UK
Schroder Ventures Life Sciences 71 Kingsway, London WC2B 6ST Tel: 020 7421 7070 Fax: 020 7421 7077 Email: lifesciences@schroders.com Website: www.svlifesciences.com	£0.6 million	Seed, start-up	Biotech, service, manufacturing industries	UK, USA, W Europe
SCI Private Equity Limited 9 Upper Belgrave Street, London SW1X 8BD Tel: +44 20 7259 4400 Fax: +44 20 7259 4409 Email: jmasri@sofaer.com Website: www.sofaer.com	£1 million	All	All	UK, W Europe
Scottish Equity Partners 17 Blythswood Square, Glasgow G2 4AD Tel: 0141 273 4000 Fax: 0141 273 4001 Email: enquiries@sepl.co.uk Website: www.sepl.co.uk	£1 million	Seed, start-up	Biotech, service, manufacturing industries	UK
Seed Capital Limited The Magdalen Centre, The Oxford Science Park, Oxford OX4 4GA Tel: 01865 784466 Fax: 01865 784430 Email: lucius@oxfordtechnology.com Website: www.oxfordtechnology.com	£0.5 million	Seed, start-up	Biotech, service, manufacturing industries	UK
Sovereign Capital Limited 25 Buckingham Gate, London SW1E 6LD Tel: 020 7828 6944 Fax: 020 7828 9958 Email: info@sovereigncapital.co.uk Website: www.sovereigncapital.co.uk	£2 million	Early stage, MBO, MBI	Communications	UK

	Minimum investment	Stage of investment*	Industry preferences	Geographic preferences
Springboard Plc 7 Duke of York Street, London SW1Y 6LA Tel: 0207 004 2600 Fax: 0845 600 8009 Email: g.downes@springboardplc.com Website: www.springboardplc.com	£0.2 million	Seed, start-up, MBI	All	UK
Standard Life Investments (Private Equity) Limited 2nd Floor, 1 George Street, Edinburgh EH2 2LL Tel: 0131 225 2345 Fax: 0131 245 6105 Email: Private_equity@standardlife.com Website: www.standardlifeinvestments.com	£5 million	Expansion, MBI, MBO	All	UK, Europe
Strathdon Investments Ltd 14–15 Jewry Street, Winchester, Hants SO23 8RZ Tel: 01962 870492 Fax: +44 (0)1962 844 064 Email: info@strathdon.com Website: www.strathdon.com	£0.5 million	Seed, start-up	Communications	UK, USA, W Europe
STAR Capital Partners 39 St James's Street, London SW1A 1JD Tel: 020 7016 8500 Fax: 020 7016 8501 Email: mail@star-capital.com Website: www.star-capital.com	£15 million	Expansion, MBO, MBI	Chemicals	UK, W Europe
The Summit Group Ltd The Pavilion, 3 Broadgate, London EC2M 2QS Tel: 020 7614 0000 Fax: 0207 614 0066 Email: kit.huntergordon@summit-group.co.uk Website: www.summit-group.co.uk	£0.25 million	Seed, start-up	Communications	UK, USA, Canada, W Europe
Thompson Clive & Partners Limited 24 Old Bond Street, London W1S 4AW Tel: 020 7491 4809 Fax: 020 7493 9172 Email: mail@tcvc.com Website: www.tcvc.com	£1 million	Early stage, MBO, MBI	Communications	UK, USA, Europe

	Minimum investment	Stage of investment*	Industry preferences	Geographic preferences
Top Technology Ventures Limited Warwick Court, 5 Paternoster Square London EC4M 7BP Tel: 020 7489 5200 Fax: 020 7489 5201 email: ttv@toptechnology.co.uk Website: www.toptechnology.co.uk	£0.5 million	Seed, start-up	Communications	UK
Transatlantic Capital Ltd 95 Wilton Road, Suite 3 London, SW1V 1BZ Email: info@transatlantic-capital.com Website: http://www.transatlantic-capital.com/	£0.25 million	Seed, start-up	Biotech, service manufacturing industries	UK, USA, W Europe
Trinity Venture Capital 1 Lombard Street, Belfast BT1 1BN Tel: 028 90 233222 Fax: 028 90 330032 Email: hal@tvc.com Website: www.tvc.com	£1 million	Seed, start-up	Hi-tech	UK, W Europe, Ireland
TTP Venture Managers Ltd Melbourn Science Park, Cambridge Road, Melbourn, Royston SG8 6EE Tel: 01763 262626 Fax: 01763 262265 Email: mailventures@ttpventures.com Website: www.ttpventures.com	Open	Seed, start-up	Biotech, service, manufacturing industries	UK, W Europe
UBS Capital 100 Liverpool Street, London EC2M 2RH Tel: 020 7568 9000 Fax: 020 7568 9022 Email: ubs.capital@ubscapital.com Website: www.ubscapital.com	£3 million	Seed, start-up	Chemicals	UK, World
UK Steel Enterprise Ltd (formerly British Steel (Industry) Ltd) The Innovation Centre, 217 Portobello, Sheffield S1 4DP Tel: 0114 270 0933 Fax: 0114 224 2222 Email: yorks@uksteelenterprise.co.uk Website: www.uksteelenterprise.co.uk	£0.2 million	Seed, start-up, MBO, MBI	Biotech, service, manufacturing industries	UK (Steel making areas)

	Minimum investment	Stage of investment*	Industry preferences	Geographic preferences
VCF Partners Swiss Life House, South Park Sevenoaks Kent TN13 1DU Tel: 01732 471800 Fax: 01732 471810 Email: info@foresightventurepartners.com Website: www.vcf.co.uk	£0.75	Early stage	Communications	UK
Wales Fund Managers Limited Cedar House, Greenwood Close, Cardiff Gate Business Park, Cardiff CF23 8RD Tel: 029 20 546250 Fax: 029 20 546251 Email: info@wfml.co.uk Website: www.wfml.co.uk	£0.25 million	All	All	UK
Warburg Pincus Almack House, 28 King Street, St James's, London SW1Y 6QW Tel: 020 7306 0306 Fax: 020 7321 0881 Email: dpathak@warburgpincus.com Website: www.warburgpincus.com	£5 million	Early stage	Biotech, service, manufacturing industries	UK, USA, Far East, W Europe
WL Ventures Limited Geddes House, Kirkton North, Livingston EH54 6GU Tel: 01506 415144 Fax: 01506 415145 Email: investment@wlventures.co.uk Website: www.wlventures.co.uk	£1 million	Seed, start-up, MBO, MBI	All	Scotland (Lothian region)
WM Enterprise Wellington House, 31–34 Waterloo Street, Birmingham B2 5TJ Tel: 0121 236 8855 Fax: 0121 233 3942 Email: mail@wm-enterprise.co.uk Website: www.wm-enterprise.co.uk	£0.5 million	Expansion, MBO, MBI	Chemicals	UK
Yorkshire Fund Managers Ltd (part of the Yorkshire Enterprise Group) Saint Martins House, 210–212 Chapeltown Road, Leeds LS7 4HZ Tel: 0113 294 5050 Fax: 0113 294 5002 Email: YFM@yorkshire-enterprise.co.uk Website: www.yorkshire-enterprise.co.uk	£0.15 million	Seed, start-up, MBO, MBI	Biotech, service, manufacturing industries	UK

	Minimum investment	Stage of investment*	Industry preferences	Geographic preferences
Young Associates Limited Harcourt House, 19 Cavendish Square, London W1M 9AB Tel: 020 7447 8800 Fax: 020 7447 8849 Email: info@youngassoc.com Website: www.youngassoc.com	£0.5 million	Seed, start-up, expansion	Communications	UK, W Europe, Israel

* MBO = management buy-out; MBI = management buy-in.

Online directories of venture capital providers

British Venture Capital Association
3 Clements Inn, London, WC2A 2AZ
Tel: 020 7025 2950
Fax: 020 7025 2951
Email: bvca@bvca.co.uk
Website: www.bvca.co.uk

Online directory of all UK members, plus lots of helpful information about raising VC money.

European Venture Capital Association
Minervastraat 4
B-1930 Zaventem (Brussels)
Belgium
Tel: 00 32 2 715 00 20
Fax: 00 32 2 725 07 04
Email: evca@evca.com
Website: www.evca.com

Over 850 members to be found on their online search engines. The directory can be searched by country, amount of money you are looking for and in a variety of other ways.

NVCA (National Venture Capital Association)
1655 North Fort Myer Drive
Suite 850
Arlington
VA 22209
Tel: 703 524 2549
Fax: 703 524 3940
Email: www.nvca.org
Website: www.nvca.org

An online directory of 250 mostly US VCs, and lots of useful information about raising money, preparing business plans and finding advisers.

Venture Capital: On the Net (1000)
Website: www.advocacy-net.com/venturemks. htm

Just what it says. Links to 1000 VC websites around the world.

Going public

Taking your business to a stock market and raising risk capital from the general public is also a possibility. Not many do it, but at its peak a few hundred firms a year were funded in this way. There are two possible types of stock markets on which to gain a public listing. A full listing on the London Stock Exchange, the New York Stock Exchange or any of the other major exchanges calls for a track record of making substantial profits with decent seven figure sums being made in the year you plan to float, as this process is known. A full listing also calls for a large proportion of the company's shares being put up for sale at the outset. (In the UK this would be at least 25% of the company's shares.)

In addition, you would be expected to have 100 shareholders now and be able to demonstrate that 100 more will come on board as a result of the listing. This is rarely an appealing idea to entrepreneurs, who expect to see their share price rise in later years, and are loath to sell off so much of the business at what they believe to be a bargain basement price. There is also the threat of a takeover with so many of the shares in so many other peoples' hands. However, if going public appeals to you, the US market may be the best place to float. The value placed on new companies on those stock markets is between three and five times that of UK and European markets.

Junior markets such as London's Alternative Investment Market (AIM) or the Nouveau Marché in Paris are a much more attractive proposition for entrepreneurs seeking equity capital. Formed in mid/late 1990s specifically to provide risk capital for new rather than established ventures, these markets have an altogether more relaxed atmosphere.

The AIM market is the largest junior market in Europe. Since 1995, more than 1900 companies have been admitted and over £17bn in new capital raised. AIM is particularly attractive to any dynamic company of any size, age or business sector which has rapid growth in mind. The smallest firm on AIM entered at under £1 million capitalization and the largest at over £330 million. The formalities are minimal, but the costs of entry are high and you must have a nominated adviser, such as a major accountancy firm, stockbroker or banker.

Where to float ... and why it matters

Going public also puts a stamp of respectability on you and your company. Table 6.2 outlines some of the options. It will enhance the status and credibility of your business, and it will enable you to borrow more against the security provided by your new shareholders, should you so wish. Your shares will also provide an attractive way to retain and motivate key staff. If they are given, or rather are allowed to earn, share options at discounted prices, they too can participate in the capital gains you are making. With a public share listing you can now join in the takeover and asset-stripping game. When your share price is high and things are going well, you can look out for weaker firms to gobble up – and all you have to do is to offer them more of your shares in return for theirs. You do not even have to find real money.

Who to talk to

London Stock Exchange
Old Broad Street
London
EC2N 1HP
Tel: 020 7797 4404
Fax: 020 7797 2001
Website: www.londonstockexchange.com

Table 6.2 Comparison of criteria for flotation on various exchanges.

Market	Number of stocks	Floatation cost	Entry requirements	Minimum market capitalization	Comparable price/earnings ratios (P/E)
Alternative Investment Market (AIM)	1200	£0.5 million	Low	None	1
London Stock Exchange	2500	£1 million +	High	£1 million +	1
techMARK	200	£0.75 million +	High	£50 million +	x3
New York Stock Exchange	2600	£7 million	Very high	£12 million +	x2
NASDAQ	5500	£6 million	Very high	£10 million +	x5

Grants, awards and competitions

Unlike debt, which has to be repaid, or equity, which has to earn a return for the investors, grants and awards are not refundable. So, although they are often hard to get, they can be particularly valuable.

Almost every country has incentives to encourage entrepreneurs to invest in particular locations or industries. The US, for example, has an allowance of Green Cards (work and residence permits) for up to several hundred immigrants each year prepared to put up sufficient funds to start up in a substantial business in the country.

In the UK, if you are involved in the development of a new technology, then you may be eligible for a Small Firms Merit Award for Research and Technology (SMART). This is open to individuals or businesses employing fewer than 50 people. The grant is in two stages and can be for amounts as high as £100,000 in total. You may also get help with the costs of training staff, gaining quality recognition, or carrying out market research to identify export opportunities (see Section 5).

Support for business comes in a very wide variety of forms. The most obvious is the direct (cash) grant, but other forms of assistance are also numerous. The main types are as follows.

- **Direct grant:** This is a cash item, which may be offered for activities such as training, employment, export development, recruitment or capital investment projects.

  It is rare to obtain 100% grant funding. Most schemes require the recipient company to put up a proportion of the cost, with a figure 50% being typical.
- **Repayable grant:** This is where cash funding is offered for a project with the intention that the sums are repaid out of future revenues. The grant is not repayable in the event the project fails.
- **Soft loan:** This is a loan where the terms and conditions of repayment are more generous (or softer) than those which would prevail if the loan were made available under normal commercial terms. The interest rate may be less than the ongoing commercial rate for a similar loan and/or the repayment term may be longer. Sometimes the loan may be interest-free.
- **Equity finance:** Here a capital sum is injected into the business where the provider does not expect interest or repayment of the loan itself. Rather, the provider of funds takes an equity share of the business, in the hope/expectation that the value of the stake will appreciate at some time in the future, enabling a sale of the stake, thus facilitating a return on the original investment.
- **Free or subsidized consultancy:** Often it is the lack of a particular skill or skills which a company feels – this is particularly so in the case of start-ups and new companies. Some schemes provide these skills at free or subsidized rates by paying, in whole or in part, the fees of accredited or approved consultants who possess the skills the organization lacks.
- **Access to resources:** A number of schemes provide access to valuable publicly owned facilities (e.g. research facilities operated by the Ministry of Defence).
- **Best practice transfer:** There are now a number of well-established quality and best practice initiatives such as Investors in People and ISO 9000 .The cost of transferring such 'best practice' procedures to small firms is often subsidized by government.
- **Shared cost contract:** The costs of research and development programmes can be prohibitive for small firms acting alone. Sharing the costs of such programmes with others, whereby all participants share in the costs and the consequent resulting know-how, can be a solution. Such arrangements are often brokered, and sometimes part financed, by public bodies or institutions.
- **Subsidies:** Some awarding bodies, whilst not always advancing direct cash grants, will subsidize the costs of approved products or services used by firms.
- **Location:** Many grants are location-specific. There are several schemes that operate across the whole of the UK, and are available to all businesses that satisfy the outline criteria, but in

addition to these there are a myriad of schemes that are administered locally. Thus the location of your business will be absolutely crucial, and funding that might be available to you will be strongly dependent on the area into which you intend to grow or develop. Additionally, there may well be additional grants available to a business investing in or into an area of social deprivation, particularly if it involves sustainable job creation.

- **Industry type:** In order to satisfy the local economic or political agenda, many funding schemes are allocated towards the development of particular industry sectors.

Improving your chances of getting a grant

The assistance provided for enterprise is limited, so you will be competing for grants against other applicants. You can enhance your chances of success by following these seven rules.

1 **Keep yourself informed about which grants are available:** Grants are constantly being introduced (and withdrawn) but there is no system that lets you know automatically. You have to keep yourself informed.

2 **Do not start the project for which you want a grant before you make the application:** The awarding body will almost certainly take the view that if you can start the project without a grant you must have had sufficient funds to complete it without assistance. Better still, show the project is dependent on the grant being made.

3 **Make sure your application is in respect of a project:** Usually, grants are given for specific projects, not for the normal organic growth of a business. If, for example, you need new equipment to launch a product, make sure your application emphasizes the project, not the equipment. State the advantages of the project's success (for example, it will safeguard or create jobs) and explain that the purchase of the equipment is a prerequisite for that success.

4 **Try to get in first:** The chances of a successful application are always highest just after a scheme is launched. That is when there is the most money 'in the pot', and it's also the time when those administering the scheme are keenest to get applications in and grants awarded. Competition is likely to be less fierce.

5 **Make your application match the awarding body's objectives:** The benefits of your project should fit in with the objectives of the awarding body and the grant scheme itself. So if the grant is intended to help the local community, or the country in the form of potential exports, for example, make sure these are included. Most grant applications require the submission of a business plan, so make sure you have an up-to-date one.

6 **Make sure you have matching funds available:** It is unusual for a grant to finance 100% of the costs of any project. Typically nowadays a grant will contribute 15–50% of the total finance required. Those making the decision about the grant are spending public money. They have a duty to ensure it is spent wisely and they will need to be absolutely convinced that you have, or can raise from other sources, the balance required.

7 **Talk to the awarding body before you apply:** Make contact with an individual responsible for administering the scheme. You will be given advice on whether it is worth your while applying, before you start spending time and effort on making the application. You may get some help and advice on completing the application form. You may also get an insight into how you should shape your application.

Help with grants

Business Link
www.businesslink.org

Department of Trade and Industry
www.dti.gov.uk

E-Commerce Awards
www.ukonlineforbusiness.gov.uk

The awards are run by UK online for business and InterForum, a not-for-profit campaign group of companies that helps British business to trade electronically. The awards have been designed to recognize and reward those small companies that have demonstrated business excellence through the use of e-commerce.

Funders online
51 rue de la Concorde
B-1050 Brussels
Belgium
Tel: 00 32 2 512 8938
Fax: 00 32 2 512 3265
Email: webmaster@fundersonline.org
Website: www.fundersonline.org

This directory is designed to help you track down in a quick and efficient way specific types of information provided on a funder's website, such as its grants list, programmes description or newsletter; to enable you to find funders according to their country of location and fields of activities.

Grants On-line
75 Hazelwood Drive
Verwood
BH31 6YG
Tel: 01202 828674
Email: services@mycommunity.org.uk
Website: www.co-financing.co.uk

This site provides access to the latest information on grants from the European Union, UK government, National Lottery, Regional Development Agencies (RDA) grants and UK grant making trusts.

The site is designed to guide you through the external funding maze, save you valuable time in identifying relevant external funding opportunities and ensure that you have the most up-to-date information available. There is a 14 day free trial offer, and standard subscription is £150 per annum.

j4b
51 Water Lane
Wilmslow
SK9 5BQ
Email: enquiries@j4b.co.uk
Website: www.j4b.co.uk

The mission of j4b is to help businesses everywhere to find out about any grants, financial assistance, subsidies and help-in-kind that may be available to them. j4b was set up in 2000 to find easier ways through the information jungle that puts most businesses off trying to find out about their possible entitlement. The site is updated continuously. It is free to use. There are no up-front fees for applicants to pay and j4b does not receive a commission on successful applications. Registered users receive targeted alerts about grants that might apply to them.

UK Fundraising
www.fundraising.co.uk/grants.html
Has free links to grants and funding resources, listed by geographical region.

Business competitions

If you enjoy publicity and like a challenge then you could look out for a business competition to enter. Like government grants, business competitions are ubiquitous and like national lotteries they are something of a hit or miss affair.

But one thing is certain: if you don't enter, you can't win. There are more than 100 annual awards in the United Kingdom alone aimed at new or small businesses. For the most part, these are sponsored by banks, the major accountancy bodies, chambers of commerce and local or national newspapers, business magazines and the trade press. Government departments may also have their own competitions as a means of promoting their initiatives for exporting, innovation, job creation and so forth. The nature and the amount of the awards change from year to year, as do the sponsors. But looking out in the national and local press, or contacting one of the organizations mentioned below, should put you in touch with a competition organizer quickly, as will an Internet search. Money awards constitute 40% of the main competition prizes. For the most part, these cash sums are less than £5000. However, a few do exceed £10,000 and one UK award is for £50,000. Other awards are for equally valuable goods and services, such as consultancy or accountancy advice, training and computer hardware and software.

Business competitions directory

Book-Look Awards

Categories: Three awards to websites that are exceptionally well constructed. Sites are judged based on ease of navigation, content, graphic quality, page layout and design by Book-Look's award team.

Book-Look
Email: support@book-look.co.uk
Website: www.book-look.co.uk/awards/awards.htm

UK Bioscience Business Plan Competition

Categories: The competition aims to increase awareness of the issues involved in developing a bioscience business and help the formation of new bioscience business ventures. The competition comprises two rounds.

* Round 1: participants have access to training in key commercialization issues.
* Round 2: 18 ideas are selected for development into full business plans.

The costs of participation in the competition are fully met by funds provided by sponsors. Those progressing to Round 2 receive up to £4000. The ultimate winners will receive a prize of £20,000 and two runners-up will receive £10,000 to assist with further development of their business.

Biotechnology & Biological Sciences Research Council (BBSRC)
Polaris House

North Star Avenue
Swindon
SN2 1UH
Tel: 01793 413200
Fax: 01793 413201
Website: www.bbsrc.ac.uk/business/skills/plan/Welcome.html

Business in the Community Awards for Excellence
Categories

The awards are run in association with the *Financial Times*, sponsored by the Department of Trade and Industry, and recommended by the British Quality Foundation.

Criteria

* Celebrate and recognize achievement.
* Identify and share best practice.
* Inspire others to consider how they make an impact on society.
* Encourage companies to continually improve the impact of their core business.
* Raise awareness of the benefits of responsible business practice.

All finalists of the Awards for Excellence will be entitled to use the Impact Endorsement Mark.

Business in the Community
137 Shepherdess Walk
London
N1 7RQ
Tel: 0870 600 2482
Email: rebecca.fowkes@bitc.org.uk
Website: www.bitc.org.uk/awards.html

Business Weekly Awards
Categories

* **Innovation One to Watch:** For companies and consultancies with innovative technology – starting-up or developed – which appear to the judges to have strong commercial potential.
* **Growth & Expansion:** For companies demonstrating strong growth in the last 12 months,

in turnover, staff numbers, physical premises, new products or markets.

- **Private Company of the Year:** For the private business which, in the opinion of the panel of judges has made the most commercial progress in the previous 12 months.
- **Quoted Company of the Year:** For public business which the judges feel has made the most commercial progress in the previous 12 months.

Business Weekly Awards

Email: awards@businessweekly.co.uk
Website: www.businessweekly.co.uk

Cambridge Evening News Business Excellence Awards

Launched in the early 1990s, these awards are now firmly established as the premier awards of their kind in the region. The winners are invited to a glittering awards presentation.

Categories

- Businesswoman of the Year
- Businessman of the Year
- Small Business of the Year
- Business of the Year
- Business Investment
- Business Innovation
- Business Training.

Cambridge Newspapers Ltd

Winship Road
Milton
Cambridge
CB4 6PP
Tel: 01223 434203
Fax: 01223 434211
Email: editorial@cambridge-news.co.uk
Website: www.cambridge-news.co.uk/businessawards/

Centrica-New Statesman Upstarts Awards

There are three winners for these awards, each receiving a cheque for £15,000; the fourth receives a cheque for £5000 towards R&D.

Criteria

- All entrants must be aged 18 or over and live in the United Kingdom.
- All entrants must be nominated by a business or organization operating within the local community.
- Entrants are required to supply contact details of two referees who will be able to vouch for them, e.g. doctor, JP, MP, solicitor, local councillor, religious denomination leader, company, charity or community organization director, etc.
- Organizer application forms must be duly completed. Individuals may present more than one proposed project.
- Entrants must provide information explaining the entry; a typed or written summary, a cash flow projection to show how the award will be spent, a description of how the project or business will be promoted, brief details of any team members, etc.

Upstarts Awards

New Statesman
7th Floor
Victoria Station House
191 Victoria Street
London
SW1E 5NE
Email: upstarts@newstatesman.co.uk
Website: www.upstarts.org.uk

Dragon Awards
Categories

- **Local Regeneration Award:** Recognizing organizations that have developed an ongoing programme that is seen to support the social and economic regeneration of their local area.
- **The Heart of the City Award:** Recognizing firms located in the City, Docklands or City limits that participate in community involvement activities.
- **The Small Business Award:** Recognizes small businesses that have worked with their local community. Businesses with fewer than 100

staff and a turnover of less than £3 million can apply.

- **Corporate Community Involvement Newcomer Award:** Recognizing organizations that have implemented corporate community involvement activities with distinction within the last 18 months.
- **The London Partnership Award:** Recognizing a single community project that has actively engaged business partners from a number of organizations.
- **The Lord Mayor's Award:** Rewarding organizations that use their purchasing power to support local businesses by buying goods from the local community.

The Corporation of London's Economic Development Unit

Tel: 020 7332 3608
Email: dragonawards@corpoflondon.gov.uk
Website: www.cityoflondon.gov.uk/urban_
regeneration/engaging_the_city/dragon_awards.
htm

EBusiness Innovation Awards
Categories

- International eGovernment Awards
- Awards for Small/Medium Businesses
- Global eBusiness Innovations.

Submit by email a 600 word text in three paragraphs explaining:

- the challenge
- the solution
- the achievement.

EBusiness Innovation Awards

Tel: 01489 872802
Email: awards@abfl.co.uk
Website: www.ecommerce-awards.com

Ecommerce Awards

The E-Commerce Awards are organized by UK online for business and InterForum. The awards are sponsored by Cisco Systems and The Royal Bank of Scotland Group. There are prizes worth over £125,000. There is no charge for entry.

Ecommerce Awards

Stuart Hillston (project director)
Tel: 01296 641856
Fax: 01296 641857
Email: stuart@ecommerce-awards.co.uk;
info@ecommerce-awards.co.uk
Website: www.ecommerce-awards.co.uk
Erica Kellaway (administrator)
Tel: 01784 473005
Fax: 01784 473006
Email: erica@interforum.org

Entrepreneur of the Year
Criteria

- A regional national and international annual award scheme identifying and recognizing the achievements of outstanding entrepreneurs within successful growing dynamic businesses. The programme celebrates their successes and the spirit that entrepreneurs bring to the economy in terms of job creation and the UK's competitiveness. The awards are endorsed by the Department of Trade and Industry, the British Chambers of Commerce, the Design Council, Community Action Network and the Institute of Directors.
- The overall UK Entrepreneur of the Year will go forward to the Ernst & Young World Entrepreneur of the Year Awards the following year.

Entrepreneur of the Year

Ernst & Young
Becket House
1 Lambeth Palace Road
London
SE1 7EU
Contact: Will White (Media Relations Manager)
Tel: 020 7951 3264
Email: wwhite@uk.ey.com
Website: www.ey.com/global/gcr.nsf/

Evening Press Business Awards

Categories

- Small Business of the Year
- Exporter of the Year
- Growth Business of the Year
- Best Environmental Company
- Progress through People
- Use of New Technology
- New Business of the Year
- Business Personality of the Year.

There is an online entry form for those wishing to submit via the web.

Evening Press Business Awards

Evening Press
76–86 Walmgate
York
YO1 9YN
Contact: Sky Ferrey (PA to the editor)
Website: www.thisisyork.co.uk/york/busines-sawards2002/

Growing Business Awards

Categories

- New Product of the Year
- International Initiative of the Year
- Most Promising Young Company
- Innovative Company of the Year
- Entrepreneur of the Year
- Best Business Advisor
- Company of the Year
- E-Business of the Year

Entries will be judged by a panel of eminent and impartial adjudicators. Entering one or more category is allowed. Award winners may state in advertising/promotional activity and on their stationery that they are a winner, but this must include the category and year in which the award was won.

The Growing Business Awards

Real Business
23rd Floor Millbank Tower
Millbank
London
SW1P 4QP
Contact: Iona Reid Scott
Tel: 020 7828 0999
Fax: 020 7630 0733
Email: awards@caspianpublishing.co.uk
Website: www.growingbusinessawards.co.uk

Human Resources Excellence Awards

Categories

- Best contribution of HR to business strategy
- Best HR contribution to merger and acquisition integration
- Excellence in attracting and developing high potential talent
- Excellence in change management
- Best transformation of the HR function using IT
- Best work/life solutions.

An entry fee of £250 + VAT is required for each category that you enter. A further fee of £100 + VAT is payable if your organization is shortlisted.

The following other awards cannot be entered directly as they are chosen from all the entrants and category winners:

- the KPMG Consulting Special Award
- the Human Resources Award.

Human Resources Excellence Awards

174 Hammersmith Road
London
W6 7JP
Contact: Samantha Graham (Events Manager)
Tel: 020 8267 4145
Fax: 020 8267 4331
Email: sam.graham@haynet.com
Website: www.haynet.com

The Internet Industry Awards

Categories

- Consumer Awards
- Business Awards
- Industry Awards
- Internet Watch Foundation Award.

Fifteen awards split into separate categories, governed by different rules and procedures for each section. A summary is published on the ISPA website.

ISPA UK
23 Palace Street
London
SW1E 5HW
Tel: 020 7233 7234
Fax: 020 7233 7294
Email: secretariat@ispa.org.uk
Website: www.ispaawards.org.uk

Mayor's Awards for Business Achievement
Introduced in 1989 by the Mayor of the time to publicly recognize the achievements of local businesses. The Awards are launched in October of every year, and visits to shortlisted companies take place in mid/late January of the following year. The process culminates at the Presentation Dinner at the Town Hall (King's Lynn) at the end of February/beginning of March.

Criteria
* Businesses with over 100 employees (2)
* Businesses with less than 100 employees (3)
* Staff Development and Training (4)
* Local Service Enterprise with 20 employees (or part-time equivalents).

Prizes range from money to advertising (in the *Lynn News* and on KL.FM), and from marketing assistance (from Business Link) to handmade engraved shields.

Borough Council of King's Lynn & West Norfolk
King's Court
Chapel Street
King's Lynn
West Norfolk
PE30 1EX
Tel: 01553 616200
Website: www.west-norfolk.gov.uk

The London Excellence Commitment to Excellence Recognition
Provides recognition of an organization's commitment to the use of the excellence model and to continuously improving their organization. Organizations may apply for an award at any time. Organizations are required to submit a portfolio showing how they apply the principles of excellence in their organization and can demonstrate their continuous improvement activities.

The award comprises a framed certificate and a logo that may be used on the winner's materials.

London Excellence
Tel: 020 7232 5380
Email: excellence@london-excellence.org.uk
Website: www.london-excellence.org.uk

East of England Excellence
Tel: 01223 713939
Website: www.eee.org.uk

Excellence North East
Tel: 0191 515 3603

Excellence North West
Tel: 01204 399097

Excellence South East
Tel: 01489 570704
Website: www.excel.se.com

Excellence South West
Tel: 0117 905 5721
Website: www.org.uk

Excellence Yorkshire
Tel: 01274 233193
Website: www.excellence-yorkshire.org.uk

Midlands Excellence
Tel: 020 7232 5380
Website: www.midlandsexcellence.org.uk

Northern Ireland Quality Centre
Tel: 028 90 468999

Website: www.niqc.com

Quality Scotland Foundation
Tel: 0131 556 2333
Website: www.qualityscotland.co.uk

Wales Quality Centre
Tel: 01978 293196

Merseyside 21 Awards
Environmental awards for the five boroughs of Merseyside.

At the first Earth Summit, countries of the world gathered to set a new agenda for the twenty-first century. Agenda 21 was the result. The Merseyside 21 Business and Community Awards are the creation of Groundwork on Merseyside, working in partnership with Government Office, North West, local authorities, local chambers, business links and industry. The Merseyside 21 Awards are a showcase to the world for the efforts of Merseyside people to create a better environment.

Merseyside 21 Community Awards
- The Lord Winstanley Changing Places Award
- Changing Lives Award
- Changing Schools Award
- Cared for Places Award.

Merseyside 21 Business Awards
- Tony Bonner Environmental Business of the Year Award
- Public Authority Environmental Best Practice Award
- Environmental Management System Award
- Community Stewardship Award
- Waste Minimiser Award
- Energy Award
- Physical Environmental Improvement Award
- Environmental Innovation & Technology Award.

Merseyside 21 Awards
Tel: 01744 739396
Website: www.businessenvironmentpark.co.uk

Oxford University Business Plan Competition
(Oxford Science Enterprise Centre)
Criteria
- Should be original, or a significant improvement on an existing business.
- Can be a product, process or service.
- Must make 'significant use of design or technology'.

Invitations are open to:

- entrepreneurs
- researchers
- students
- new companies.

Process
- Write a two-page summary of your idea.
- If accepted, you can enter a full business plan outlining how your business would work.
- Shortlisted business plans are showcased at Venturefest for judging.
- Winner receives a £10,000 prize; £1000 for best new idea.

Oxford Centre for Innovation
Mill Street
Oxford
OX2 0JX
Tel: 01865 811145
Fax: 01865 204950
Email: info@venturefest.com
Website: www.venturefest.com

Parcelforce Worldwide Small Business Awards
These awards are designed to recognize and reward the UK's leading small businesses. Entrants benefit from:

- recognition for the efforts of their employees
- public relations – winners stories are always in demand – which generates great coverage that's seen by competitors, customers and employees alike
- prizes worth up to £130,000

- new business – the opportunity to meet and network with other SMEs.

Criteria
- Company independently owned, UK based and have 30 or less employees.
- Company turnover is £50,000+ per annum.
- Company established at least two years before entry deadline.

Website: www.parcelforce.com/awards/qualify.asp

Prime Faraday Spark Awards
Prime Faraday Parnership, in conjunction with the DTI, is running this pilot scheme of PFSA awards to build relationships between SMEs and HEIs (Higher Education Institutes). These grants are intended to help resource small, confidence-building measures towards SME and HEI partnerships that are likely to lead to a longer term relationship. The grants have a fixed value of £5000 and are to be awarded to the HEI to tackle a problem relevant to the SME. The aim of the scheme is to provide quick approval with minimal bureaucracy. The grant is payable in arrears and will be paid on receipt of a report on how the grant was used. Applications will be considered by the PRIME Faraday executive committee and ranked according to the following criteria:

- relevance to the PRIME domain
- HEI track record
- creation of new long-term relationships within the PRIME community
- relevance and benefit to the HEI and SME partnership
- quality of the work proposed
- new partnerships that have not jointly received funding from any source.

Only applications made using the online form will be acceptable. This form has been tested with a variety of browsers and platforms. In the event of a problem sending your application form, please email Paul Palmer for advice.

The Prime Faraday Partnership
Wolfson School of Mechanical and Manufacturing Engineering
Loughborough University
Loughborough
LE11 3TU
Contact: Paul J. Palmer (Technical Manager)
Tel: 01509 227672
Email: p.j.palmer@lboro.ac.uk
and

The Prime Faraday Partnership
School of Mechanical Materials Manufacturing Engineering and Management
University of Nottingham
Coates Building
University Park
Nottingham
NG7 2RD
Contact: Steve Fewkes (Technology Manager)
Tel: 0115 951 4363
Email: Steve.Fewkes@nottingham.ac.uk

The Queen's Awards for Enterprise
The UK's top awards for business performance are awarded in three categories:

- international trade
- innovation
- sustainable development.

General information can be downloaded from the website.

The Queen's Awards Office
Tel: 020 7222 2277
Email: info@queensawards.org.uk
Website: www.queensawards.org.uk

SDC Innovation Awards
Introduced to nurture and encourage innovation in every sector of the colouration industry, each category carries a prize of £2500, to be spent on education and/or research in the field of colour.

Criteria

- **Colour in Design:** for innovation in the use of colour in design as applied to any material in any format
- **Colour in Process:** for the innovative application of colour in industry, with particular emphasis on productivity, styling, energy savings and environmental improvements
- **Colour in Research:** for innovation in colour research into the development of colorants and the use, application and control of colour

SDC Innovation Awards
Tel: 01274 725138 ext 203
Fax: 01274 392888
Email: secretariat@sdc.org.uk
Website: www.sdc.org.uk/general/innovawards. htm

Smart: Scotland

Entries for Smart: Scotland can be submitted at any time of the year by individuals planning to start a business in Scotland and small existing firms/groups with less than 50 employees. Applicants should have either an annual turnover not exceeding approx. £4.35 million (€7 million) or a balance sheet total not exceeding approx. £3.11 million (€5 million). Smart aims to help small businesses improve their competitiveness by developing new, highly innovative and commercially viable products and processes to be benefit of the national economy. Winners receive a grant of 75% of the costs of carrying out a feasibility study with a time-scale of between 6 and 18 months. The maximum award is £45,000.

Entries are actively encouraged from companies spun off from the science base.

Smart: Scotland
SEELLD
Meridian Court
5 Cadogan Street
Glasgow
G2 6AT
Contact: Caroline Caniffi
Tel: 0141 242 5560

Fax: 0141 242 5589
Email: caroline.caniffi@scotland.gov.uk
Website: www.scotland.gov.uk
For application pack, contact: Janice Leitch
Email: janice.leitch@scotland.gov.uk

UK Green Chemistry Awards

Three annual awards for green chemistry technology that offers significant improvements in chemical processes, products and services through research and commercial exploitation of novel chemistry to achieve a more sustainable cleaner and healthier environment.

- Annual Academic Award of £10,000 to young academic (under 40) preferably working in collaboration with industry.
- Two annual awards to UK companies for technology, products or services, one company at least being an SME.

UK Green Chemistry Awards
Contact: Mike Lancaster (Green Chemistry Network Manager)
Tel: 01904 434549
Fax: 01904 434550
Email: greennet@york.ac.uk
Website: www.chemsoc.org.uk

Women into Business Conference and Awards

The Women into Business awards are seeking to reward women whose achievements and genuine commitment through their influence have made a significant contribution to their business throughout the year.

The Small Business Bureau Ltd
Curzon House
Church Road
Windlesham
GU20 6BH
Tel: 01276 452010; 01276 452020
Fax: 01276 451602
Email: info@sbb.org.uk
Website: www.smallbusinessbureau.org.uk

The Irish Republic

This section gives details of organizations that can help with raising finance in the Irish Republic. Many of the organizations listed in Section 2 as providers of general advice also provide funding advice or directly supply funding of various sorts:

- County Enterprise Boards
- Enterprise Ireland
- Údarás na Gaeltachta
- Shannon Development
- The Crafts Council of Ireland (CCI)
- Business Incubators and Innovation Centres
- The Smurfit Job Creation Enterprise Fund
- First Step.

For more detailed information and contact details for these organizations, see pages **22–32**.

Venture capital providers in Ireland & Northern Ireland

ACT Venture Capital Ltd

Jefferson House
Eglington Road
Donnybrook
Dublin 4
Tel: 00 353 1 260 0966
Fax: 00 353 1 260 0538
Email: info@actvc.ie

ACT Venture Capital is an Irish private equity company which has been providing venture capital for over 20 years. Financed by Ireland's leading institutional investors and many well-known international funds, ACT provides capital in the range €50,000 to €15 million to globally focused technology-based SMEs, traditional companies in manufacturing and services, and buy-outs.

- Preferred industries/sectors: Development/ expansion including technology, MBO, MBI, secondary purchase/replacement capital, early stage/start-ups with exceptional promise.

- Preferred stage of investment: 1st round/2nd round/pre-IPO.
- Preferred amount (of initial investment): €2 million.
- Geographical regions: Ireland, UK and Continental Europe.

Alliance Investment Capital

CFI House
Clonskeagh Square
Dublin 14
Tel: 00 353 1 283 7656
Fax: 00 353 1 283 7256
Email: frank.traynor@allinv.com
Website: www.allianceireland.com

Alliance Investment Capital is a IR£7.5 million/ €9.5 million fund focusing on equity investments in companies which operate in Ireland in established Irish companies across a wide spectrum of manufacturing, distribution and services businesses with an emphasis on technology-based firms.

- Preferred industries/sectors: Established business in any growth sector.
- Preferred stage of investment: Prefer to invest where business has been in existence for at least two years.
- Geographical regions: Republic of Ireland.

Campus Companies Venture Capital Fund

Molesworth House
8–9 Molesworth Street
Dublin 2
Tel: 00 353 1 679 0818
Fax: 00 353 1 679 9014
Email: info@campuscapital.com
Website: www.campuscapital.com

Campus Companies Venture Capital Fund is Ireland's leading early stage development capital fund. The fund is focused on investing in businesses promoted by staff and/or graduates of Irish universities. The fund can provide capital in amounts ranging from IR£30,000 to IR£500,000/

€38,100–635,000 for minority equity stakes in qualifying businesses. Investments in any industry will be considered, but they must be market-focused and have good growth prospects. The ethos of the fund is business partnership. The Fund will seek to work with management in developing the business and increasing the value of the company through strategic, operational and development guidance as well as introductions to commercial contacts where appropriate.

- Preferred industries/sectors: All businesses that show exceptional promise for commercial development. All sectors will be considered, with particular emphasis on information technology and new economy.
- Preferred stage of investment: Seed and early stage development.
- Geographical regions: Ireland.

Crescent Capital (N.I.) Ltd.

5 Crescent Gardens
Belfast
BT7 1NS
Tel: 00 353 1 2890 233633
Fax: 00 353 1 2890 329525
Email: mail@crescentcapital.co.uk
Website: www.crescentcapital.co.uk

Crescent Capital (N.I.) Ltd. is a Belfast-based venture fund specializing in development capital investments in Northern Ireland-based companies in the manufacturing, tradeable services and information technology sectors. They typically invest up to one million pounds, with larger deals undertaken via syndication. They actively support the development of portfolio companies and one of their executives generally joins the board. Added value includes strategic management advice, corporate finance support and assistance in negotiating major transactions and further fundraising.

- Preferred industries/sectors: Manufacturing, tradeable services and information technology.
- Preferred stage of investment: Early stage and expansion.

- Preferred amount (of initial investment): £250,000–750,000.
- Geographical regions: Northern Ireland.

Cross Atlantic Capital Partners

Unit 13 Richview Office Park
Clonskeagh
Dublin 14
Ireland
Tel: 00 353-1-218-2100
Fax: 00 353-1-218-2132
Email: info@xacp.com
Website: www.xacp.com

Cross Atlantic Capital Partners is a venture capital management firm that manages several venture partnerships, the first of which is Cross Atlantic Technology Fund, L.P. This fund has raised €146 million for investment in innovative technology companies in the US, Ireland and the UK, with offices in all three countries. Cross Atlantic also works closely with The Crucible Corporation, which is focused on early stage venture capital investments in Ireland.

- Preferred industries/sectors: Information and communications technology.
- Preferred stage of investment: Early stage and expansion.
- Preferred amount (of initial investment): €1.8–11.7 million.
- Geographical regions: US, Ireland and UK.

Deal Management Ltd.

74 Pembroke Road
Dublin 4
Tel: 00 353 1 660 9313
Fax: 00 353 1 660 7904
Email: dealman@eircom.net
Website: www.ivca.ie

Set up in 1998, the AWG Investment Fund has IR£5 million/€6.35 million to invest in start-up and expanding business in Ireland. They have an appetite for investment in a wide range of sectors, not just technology and food. While maintaining a commercial approach, they place a strong emphasis on being supportive and helpful to individual investments.

- Preferred industries/sectors: General sectors.
- Preferred stage of investment: Early stage expansion, new investment, follow-on investment.
- Preferred amount (of initial investment): IR£250,000–500,000/€317,500–635,000
- Geographical regions: Ireland.

Delta Partners Ltd.
South County Business Park
Leopardstown
Dublin 18
Tel: 00 353 1 294 0870
Fax: 00 353 1 294 0877
Email: venture@delta.ie
Website: www.delta.ie

Delta Partners, founded in 1994, invests in start-up and early stage technology-based companies. Financed by a range of Irish and international institutions and funds, Delta has in excess of €100 million under management, and has made investments in more than 30 companies. It aims to be the first venture capital investor in a company and is an active investor, working with management to build the company.

- Preferred industries/sectors: E-commerce, IT, communications, life sciences.
- Preferred stage of investment: Start-up and early stage.
- Preferred amount (of initial investment): €250,000 to 4 million, with access to higher amounts through syndication.
- Geographical regions: Principal focus in Ireland and UK.

Dublin Business Innovation Centre
The Tower
TCD Enterprise Centre
Pearse Street
Dublin 2

Tel: 00 353 1 671 3111
Fax: 00 353 1 671 3330
Email: info@dbic.ie
Website: www.dbic.ie

Dublin Business Innovation Centre manages the Dublin Seed Capital Fund, Business Innovation Fund and Irish BIC's Seed Capital Fund, with a combined value of €6.8 million. These funds were established by Dublin BIC to provide seed and early stage equity capital to emerging, start-up and developing companies across a range of technology-led sectors including IT, telecoms, software and other sectors.

- Preferred industries/sectors: Technology-led IT, telecoms, software and other sectors.
- Preferred stage of investment: Seed/early stage
- Preferred amount (of initial investment): £50,000–200,000/€64,000–254,000.
- Geographical regions: Dublin region & Republic of Ireland.

Eircom Enterprise Fund Ltd.
114 St Stephen's Green West
Dublin 2
Tel: +353 1 4785492
Fax: 00 353 1 679 7253
Email: mmoore@eircom.net
Website: www.eircom-enterprise-fund.ie

The fund provides risk capital for investment in early stage communications businesses with growth potential. It aims to support sound business proposals from committed people likely to succeed. In addition, the new company must operate within a growth market segment with particular emphasis on TMT (telecoms, media, technology) companies.

- Preferred industries/sectors: Communications.
- Preferred stage of investment: Seed and early stage.
- Preferred amount (of initial investment): IR£30,000–300,000/€38,100–381,000.

- Geographical regions: Republic of Ireland.

Enterprise 2000 Fund Ltd.
43 Pearse Street
Dublin 2
Tel: 00 353 1 677 5570
Fax: 00 353 1 677 5588
Email: capital@enterprise2000fund.ie
Website: www.enterprise2000fund.ie

This fund provides early stage capital to companies with significant growth potential through competitive advantage. It is a joint initiative between Bank of Ireland and Enterprise Ireland. Capital in the range of €35,000–200,000 is provided to qualifying companies. Access to second round funding up to a maximum of €400,000 is available provided certain business objectives are achieved. The fund has a broad industry sector focus.

- Preferred industries/sectors: All sectors except property, financial services, retail.
- Preferred stage of investment: Early stage.
- Preferred amount (of initial investment): €35,000–200,000.
- Geographical regions: Republic of Ireland.

Enterprise Equity (Irl.) Ltd.
Dublin Road
Dundalk
Co Louth
Tel: 00 353 42 9333 167 (Ireland)
Fax: 00 353 42 933 4857 (Ireland)
Email: info@enterpriseequity.ie
Website: www.enterpriseequity.ie

Enterprise Equity (NI) Ltd.
78A Dublin Road
Belfast
BT2 7HP
Tel: 028 90 242500 (Northern Ireland)
Fax: 028 90 242487 (Northern Ireland)
Email: info@eeni.com
Website: www.eeni.com

Enterprise Equity (Irl.) Ltd and its sister company Enterprise Equity (NI) Ltd., established and wholly owned by the International Fund for Ireland operate as commercial venture capital companies providing venture capital to new and expanding businesses in the Southern Border counties, Connaught and throughout the whole of Northern Ireland (i.e. Counties Donegal, Sligo, Leitrim, Louth, Cavan, Monaghan, Galway, Mayo and Roscommon, as well as the whole of Northern Ireland).

- Preferred industries/sectors: All sectors except property or retail.
- Preferred stage of investment: All stages of growth from start-up onwards.
- Preferred amount (of initial investment): IR£250,000 to 1 million/€318,000 to 1.27 million.
- Geographical regions: Northern Ireland and Counties Donegal, Cavan, Monaghan, Leitrim, Sligo, Louth, Galway, Mayo and Roscommon.

Hibernia Capital Partners Ltd
Beech House
Beech Hill Office Campus
Clonskeagh
Dublin 6
Ireland
Tel: 00 353 1 2057770
Fax: 00 353 1 2057771
Email: equity@hcp.ie
Website: www.hcp.ie

One of Ireland's largest private equity funds at IR£61 million (€77.5 million). Provides equity and equity-related finance for development capital management buy-outs and buy-ins, corporate recapitalizations, acquisitions and public to private transactions. Although locally based, Hibernia has significant international presence through its worldwide network of sponsors and investors. Hibernia's geographic focus is Ireland.

Hibernia is part of The Reihill Venture Capital Group, which also includes Trinity Venture Capital.

- Preferred industries/sectors: All.
- Preferred stage of investment: MBO/recapitalization/development capital.
- Preferred amount (of initial investment): IR£3–12 milion/€3.8–15.3 million.
- Geographical regions: Ireland and Great Britain.

ICC Venture Capital

72–74 Harcourt Street
Dublin 2
Tel: 00 353 1 415 5555
Fax: 00 353 1 475 0437
Email: ventcap@icc.ie
Website: http://www.iccvc.ie/home.html

ICC Venture Capital

ICC House
46 Grand Parade
Cork
Tel: 00 353 21 277666
Fax: 00 353 21 270267
Email: ventcap@icc.ie
Website: www.icc.ie

ICC Venture Capital is a leading provider of private equity to the software, technology and general industry sectors in Ireland. It manages funds of IR£300 million/€381 million and has invested over IR£65 million/€82.55 million in software/technology companies.

- Preferred industries/sectors: All, excluding property.
- Preferred stage of investment: Expansion capital, MBO/MBI, some early stage.
- Preferred amount (of initial investment): £1 million/€1.27 million (minimum); IT/software: £500,000/€635,000 (minimum).
- Geographical regions: Ireland.

NCB Venture Ltd.

3 George's Dock
Irish Financial Services Centre
Dublin 1
Tel: 00 353 1 661 5611

Fax: 00 353 1 661 5987
Email: michael.murphy@ncb.ie; mark.mulqueen@ncb.ie
Website: www.ncbdirect.com

NCB Ventures manages the €26 million(£21 million) Guinness Ireland Ulster Bank Equity Fund, which was established in 1997 to provide private equity to early stage growth-oriented companies. The fund investors comprise financial institutions, industrial companies and government agencies, and the fund invests in technology and general industry sectors. Portfolio companies are supported through the appointment of nominee directors, and assistance with further fundraising initiatives.

- Preferred industries/sectors: All excluding property, financial services, exploration, alcoholic beverages, fisheries and cold storage services.
- Preferred stage of investment: Start-up, early stage.
- Preferred amount (of initial investment): €375,000 to 1.25 million.
- Geographical regions: Republic of Ireland.

Smurfit Venture Capital Management Services Ltd

Beech Hill
Clonskeagh
Dublin 4,
Ireland.
Tel: 00 353 (0) 1-202 7000
Fax: 00 353 (0) 1 662 8700
Email: info@smurfit-venture.iol.ie
Website: www.smurfit.ie/venture
Fund fully invested.

- Preferred industries/sectors: Fund fully invested.
- Preferred stage of investment: N/A.
- Preferred amount (of initial investment): N/A.
- Geographic regions: N/A.

Trinity Venture Capital
Beech House
Beech Hill Office Campus
Clonskeagh
Dublin 4
Ireland
Tel: 00 353 1 205 7700
Fax: 00 353 1 205 7701
Email: info@tvc.com
Website:http://www.tvc.com/

Trinity Venture Capital
Northern Ireland Office
1 Lombard Street
Belfast
BT1 1BN
Tel: 028 90 233222
Fax: 028 90 330032
Email: info@tvc.com
Website: www.tvc.com

Trinity Venture Capital provides equity for early stage and expanding private technology companies, particularly in Ireland. Established in September 1997, it currently has €120 million under management and has an investment portfolio which reflects Ireland's strong performance in the technology sector.

- Preferred industries/sectors: IT, telecoms, software, e-commerce, Internet technology, communications.
- Preferred stage of investment: Early stage and expanding technology companies.
- Preferred amount (of initial investment): €1–6 million.
- Geographical regions: Ireland and Europe.

Irish Venture Capital Association (IVCA)
Tel: 00 353 1 276 46 47
Fax: 00 353 1 274 59 15
Email: administrator@ivca.ie
Website: www.ivca.ie

The IVCA website has links to its members.

Keeping the books

To survive and prosper in business you need to know how much cash you have and what your profit or loss on sales is. These facts are needed on at least a monthly, weekly or occasionally even a daily basis to survive, let alone grow.

While bad luck plays a part in some business failures, a lack of reliable financial information plays a part in most. However, all the information needed to manage well is close at hand. The bills to be paid, invoices raised, petty cash slips and bank statements between them are enough to give a true picture of performance. All that needs to be done is for that information to be recorded and organized so that the financial picture becomes clear. The way financial information is recorded is known as 'bookkeeping'.

But it is not only the owner who needs these financial facts. Bankers, shareholders and tax inspectors will be unsympathetic audiences to anyone without well-documented facts to back them up. If, for example, a tax authority presents a business with a tax demand, the onus then lies with the businessperson, using their records, either to agree or dispute the sum claimed. If you are unable to adequately explain a bank deposit, the tax authority may treat it as taxable income. A bank manager, faced with a request for an increased overdraft facility to help a small business grow, needs financial facts to work with. Without them the bank will generally have to say no, as they are responsible for other people's money.

In any event, if you plan to trade as a limited company (see Section 7), you are required under the Company Act 1985 'to keep adequate records sufficient to show and explain the company's transactions.'

Keeping even the simplest of records, perhaps as little as writing down the source of the deposit on the slip or in your cheque book and recording the event in a book or ledger, will make your relations with tax inspectors and bankers go much more smoothly.

Starting simple

If you are doing books by hand and don't have a lot of transactions, the single entry method is the easiest acceptable way to go. Single entry means you write down each transaction in your records once, preferably on a ledger sheet. You record the flow of income and expenses through your business by making a running total of money taken in (gross receipts) and money paid out (payments or as they are sometimes called, disbursements). Receipts and payments should be kept and summarized daily, weekly or monthly, as the business needs require. At the end of the year, the 12 monthly summaries are totalled up. You are ready for tax time.

Table 6.3 shows an example of a 'cash book', as this simple record system is known, is given below.

In the left-hand four columns, the month's expenses are entered as they occur, together with some basic details and the amount. At the head of first column is the amount of cash brought forward from the preceding month.

On the right, expenses are listed in the same way. The total receipts for the month are £1408.15 and for expenses £672.01. The difference is the amount of cash now in the business. As we have brought in more cash than we have spent, the figure is higher than the amount we brought forward at the beginning of the month. This figure of £808.14 is the amount we 'carry down' to be 'brought forward', to use the technical terms, to the next month. The total of the month's payments and the amount 'carried down', is equal to the sum of all the receipts in the left-hand columns.

If there are a reasonably large number of transactions it would be sensible to extend this simple cash book to include some basic analysis of the figures.

An example of the payments side of an analysed 'cash book', as this type of bookkeeping system is known, is shown in Table 6.4 (the receipts side is similar, but with different categories). You can see at a glance the receipts and payments both in total and by main category. This breakdown lets you see, for example, how much is being spent on each major area of your business, or who your most important customers are. The payments are the same as in the example above, but now we can see how much we have spent on stock, vehicles and telephone expenses. The sums totals both down the amount columns and across the analysis section, to arrive at the same amount. £672.01. This is both useful bits of management information, as well as being essential for your tax return.

Table 6.3 A simple cash book system.

Receipts				Payments			
Date	Name	Details	Amount (£)	Date	Name	Details	Amount (£)
1 June	Balance	Brought forward	450.55				
4 June	Anderson	Sales	175.00	4 June	Gibbs	Stock purchase	310.00
6 June	Brown	Sales	45.00	8 June	Gibbs	Stock purchase	130.00
14 June	Smith & Co.	Refund on returned stock	137.34	12 June	ABC Telecoms	Telephone charges	55.23
17 June	Jenkins	Sales	190.25	18 June	Colt Rentals	Vehicle hire	87.26
20 June	Hollis	Sales	425.12	22 June	VV Mobiles	Mobile phone	53.24
23 June	Jenkins	Sales	56.89	27 June	Gibbs	Stock purchase	36.28
							672.01
				30 June	Balance	Carried down	**808.14**
			1,480.15				**1,480.15**
1 July	Balance	Brought forward	808.14				

Table 6.4   Example of an analysed cash book.

Payments				Analysis			
Date	Name	Details	Amount (£)	Stocks	Vehicles	Telephone	Other
4 June	Gibbs	Stock purchase	310	310			
8 June	Gibbs	Stock purchase	130	130			
12 June	ABC Telecoms	Telephone charges	55.23			55.23	
18 June	Colt Rentals	Vehicle hire	87.26		87.26		
22 June	VV Mobiles	Mobile phone	53.24			53.24	
27 June	Gibbs	Stock purchase	36.28	36.28			
Totals			**672.01**	**476.28**	**87.26**	**108.47**	

If you are taking or giving credit then you will need to keep some more information as well as the cash book, whether analysed or not.

You will need to keep copies of paid and unpaid sales invoices and the same for purchases, as well as your bank statements. The bank statements should then be 'reconciled' to your cash book to tie everything together. For example, the bank statement for the example given in the simple cash book system above should show £808.14 in the account at the end of June. Figure 6.5 outlines how this works.

Double entry bookkeeping

If you operate a partnership, trade as a company, or plan to get big, then you will need a double entry bookkeeping system. This will call for a series of day books and ledgers, a journal, a petty cash book

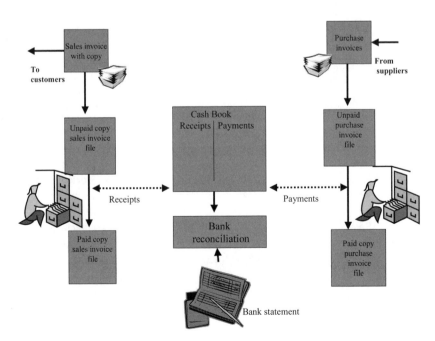

Fig. 6.5   A simple system of business records.

and a wages book, as well as a number of files for copies of invoices and receipts.

This bookkeeping system requires two entries for each transaction, which provides built-in checks and balances to ensure accuracy. Each transaction requires an entry as a debit and as a credit. This may sound a little complicated, but you only need to get the general idea.

A double entry system is more complicated and time-consuming if done by hand, since everything is recorded twice. And if done manually, this method requires a formal set of books – journals and ledgers. All transactions are first entered into a journal and then are posted (written) on a ledger sheet – the same amount is written down in two different places. Typical ledger accounts are titled income, expenses, assets, and liabilities (debts) (see Table 6.5).

To give an example, in a double entry system a payment of rent might result in two separate journal entries – a debit for an expense of, say, £250 and a corresponding credit of £250 – a double entry. The debits in a double entry must always equal the credits. If they don't, you know there is an error somewhere. So, double entry allows you to balance your books, which you can't do with the single entry method.

The records to be kept come in the following main categories.

Day books

Day books, sometimes called journals or books of original entry, are where every transaction is initially recorded in date order. Each day book is used to cater for one kind of transaction, so if there are enough transactions of a particular kind, you open a day book for it. For example, there are always enough cash transactions to warrant a cash

Table 6.5 Example of a double entry ledger.

General journal of Andrew's Bookshop			
Date	Description of entry	Debit	Credit
10 July	Rent expense	£250	
	Cash		£250

day book. If a firm sells on credit, then there will be a sales day book. Cash day books are described below.

Cash books

Many small businesses trade in both notes and coins and cheques. For bookkeeping purposes these are all called cash, although initially a separate record is kept of each.

The petty cash book is used to record transactions in notes and coins. Money in is on the left-hand page and money out on the right. The money out could include such items as stamps or office coffee. Always keep receipts, as one day you may have to verify these records. Once a week, or daily if the sums involved justify it, total the money in and out to get a cash balance. Check that it agrees with actual cash from the till or cash box.

The cash book records all receipts and payments made by cheque. Once again, money in is on the left-hand page and money out on the right. Every week, add up both pages to arrive at a cash at bank balance. This should be checked against your bank statement at least once a month to ensure that the basic information you are working with is correct.

Sales and purchase ledger

If your business gives credit to customers, or takes credit from suppliers, you will need a sales and a purchase ledger. Each ledger should ideally have a separate page for every business that you deal with.

On the right-hand side of the purchase ledger are listed the date, description, amount and cost of each item bought on credit. On the left-hand side a record is kept of all payments made to the supplier, with the items for which the payments were made. Each month, by deducting the left-hand total from the right, you can see how much each supplier is owed. Suppliers ought to send you a statement and you can use that to check your own view of the situation.

The sales ledger deals with customers in much the same way. One important difference is that credit sales are shown on the left-hand side of the ledger, while customers' payments appear on the right. This is simply an accounting convention to deal with credits and debits. It would also be very useful to keep a note of customers' (and suppliers') addresses, telephone numbers and contact names with each entry in the ledgers. This will ensure you have all the relevant information when chasing up payments or dealing with queries.

Capital or asset register

Limited companies have to keep a capital register. This records capital items they own, such as land, buildings, equipment and vehicles, showing the cost at date of purchase. It also records the disposal of any of these items and the cumulative depreciation.

The nominal ledger (or private ledger)

This is usually kept by your accountant or bookkeeper. It brings together all the information from the primary ledgers, as these other basic records are called. Expenses from the cash books and purchase ledger are 'posted' to the left-hand side of the nominal ledger. Income from sales (and any other income) is posted to the right. Normally each type of expense or income has a separate page, which makes subsequent analysis an easier task.

The trial balance

Every month each page in the nominal ledger is totalled, and used to prepare a trial balance. In other words, the sum of all the left-hand totals should end up equalling the sum of all the right-hand totals. This is the basis of double entry bookkeeping, and is what gives you confidence that the figures are correctly recorded.

Using a computer

With the cost of a basic computerized accounting system starting at barely £50, and a reasonable package costing between £200 and £500, it makes good sense to plan to use such a system from the outset. Some advantages of using a computerized system are:

- No more arithmetic errors. As long as the information is entered correctly, it will be added up correctly. With a computer, the £250 rent expenditure in the example above is input as an expense (a debit), and then the computer automatically posts it to the rent account as a credit. In effect, the computer eliminates the extra step or the need to master the difference between debit and credit.

- Routine tasks such as filling in the tax and VAT returns take minutes rather than days. The system can ensure your returns are accurate and fully reconciled. With a computerized system, invoices will always be accurate. You can see at a glance the customers who are regularly taking too long to pay. Reminder statements can be automatically prepared.

- If your business holds a stock of raw materials or goods for sale, a computerized system can help you match stock levels to demand. It could even provide profit margin information quickly by product, so you can see which products are worth promoting and which are less attractive.

Choosing a bookkeeping system

There are several main options when choosing a system to work with.

Use a manual system

You can buy off-the-shelf manual sets of books from any office stationer's outlet. These will cost anything from £10 to £20 for a full set of ledgers. Or you could buy a book describing a bookkeeping process and then just draw up the pages yourself.

Hingston Publishing Co. produce small business accounts systems for both VAT and non-VAT registered business for about £15.

Hingston Publishing Co.
Honeymoor Lodge
Eaton Bishop
Hereford

HR2 9QT
Tel: 01981 251621
Email: sales@hingston-publishing.co.uk
Website: www.hingston-publishing.co.uk

Use a bookkeeping service
Accountants and freelance bookkeepers will do all the work for you, at a price. The rate will be anything from £20 per hour upwards. The most routine but vital task may be doing the payroll. If you don't get this done on time and correctly, both staff and the Inland Revenue, for whom you have to collect PAYE (Pay As You Earn), will become restless. A weekly payroll service for up to 10 employees will cost upwards of £85 per month. If everyone is paid monthly this will drop to about a third of that figure.

It's probably best to get someone local if you go this route, so ask around to find someone who uses someone and is satisfied. Alternatively, use Yell or yellow pages.

Bookkeeping services range from a basic 'write up the entries and leave the rest to you' approach, through to providing weekly or monthly accounts, perhaps with pointers as to what might be going wrong. There are even services that act as a virtual finance director, giving you access to a senior accountant who may even sit on your board.

Most bookkeeping services will have a computerized system which you will have to plug into.

Choose your own accounting software
There are myriad software providers who serve the small business market with software for bookkeeping. Here are some of the household names and a few that are not so well known.

Money 2002
Microsoft Limited
Microsoft Campus
Thames Valley Park
Reading
RG6 1WG
Tel: 0870 50 30 400
0870 60 10 100
01 450 2113

Website: www.microsoft.co.uk

The personal and business edition of Microsoft's Money 2002 includes tools for managing your personal finances and keeping track of business accounts within the same product. It is really only suitable for sole traders and small partnerships. If you're looking for an accounting package that will meet the needs of a more complex business, Money 2002 doesn't provide a sufficiently broad set of features. It does, however, support trading in euros as a standard feature.

In general, it uses little in the way of specialist accounting terms and there's a good range of online help to support you through tasks. In addition to the standard online help, there are also some useful information sources, such as links to online guidance on VAT regulations prepared by Customs and Excise and data from the DTI on raising small business funding.

The product includes a selection of accounting reports. These cover essential analyses such as Profit and Loss and VAT summaries. However, there's little in the way of drill-down facilities to view data behind the high level figures.

It is an inexpensive product, between £25 and £35 depending on the version you buy, and there's no yearly support cost for Money 2002. It's not a suitable product for any business that expects to expand quickly or might require extra add-ons such as payroll facilities in the future, but it has some good features to offer sole traders.

MYOB 10
MYOB UK Ltd
Westec House
West Gate
London
W5 1YY
Tel: 020 8997 5500
Email: sales.uk@myob.com
Website: www.myob.co.uk

The product's set-up includes a series of five wizards that let you configure the way the system operates and create accounts tailored to a specific business type. Although getting started is straight-forward, it relies on accounting terms to describe processes, such as creating an invoice, and supplements these with confusing vocabulary of its own. Customer and supplier contact details are stored in a Card File that contains features such as an Identifiers list which can be useful, as it provides a means of creating customer groups.

MYOB 10 also divides customers' accounts into lower level jobs, which is particularly useful for service-based industries. In terms of analysis, there are some drill-down tools within the program's reporting screens and you can export data to Microsoft Excel from within the package for more in-depth analysis.

MYOB 10 is an all-round small-business tool, which includes payroll and stock control capabilities as standard. One year's support is £111.63 (including VAT) and costs £235.

TAS Books Small Business Edition

TAS Books Small Business Edition
Technical Support Department
TAS Software
North Park
Newcastle Upon Tyne
NE13 9AA
Tel: 0845 245 0220
Website: www.tassoftware.co.uk

The Small Business Edition (SBE) is the latest addition to TAS Software's accounting software range. As such, it's aimed specifically at the needs of new, smaller companies, and in general, online support within the product is comprehensive and there's a manual that helps to explain more advanced features.

Businesses that need to track IR35 payments can specify whether they want to track IR35 in general, as well as determine if each invoice posted will be subject to the tax. Taxation support is generally good within the product and there are some useful tools for creating a VAT 100 report from your accounting data. There's no euro support and you can only create entries in sterling.

There is a £117 (excluding VAT) a year support cost and a purchase price of £199 (excluding VAT).

QuickBooks 2002

QuickBooks 2002
Intuit Ltd
Statesman House
Stafferton Way
Maidenhead
Berkshire
SL6 1AD
Tel: (Sales & Support): +44 870 609 0601
Website: www.intuit.co.uk/quickbooks/

The reporting tool within QuickBooks 2002 is similar to that of its predecessor. However, there are also new features for batch printing and some additional reports.

It also handles all major currencies including the euro and it is possible to store item prices in two different currencies. This is beneficial if you need to display consistent prices in an additional currency, rather than fluctuating costs based on variable conversion rates. The product also takes account of VAT codes for EC businesses.

Invoice management has been improved, and includes tools for creating variable pricing schemes. These will be particularly useful to businesses that charge a different rate for overseas customers.

The system allows you to prepare multiple estimates for a single job, to track time, expenses and create sales orders. It can integrate with Microsoft Office and can grow with your business by adding an integrated payroll.

The basic version is £139.85 (including VAT) and the Pro version is £259.90 (including VAT).

Instant Accounting

Website: www.uk.sage.com

At £149 including VAT, Sage's entry product Instant Accounting bears reasonable comparison with some of the other products on the market.

It's one of the more basic packages available, offering none of the features, such as multiple currency support, available elsewhere.

Creating a new set of accounts is straightforward. Like most of these packages, Instant Accounting offers an Easy Startup Wizard that collects data about your business.

The program is tailored to meet the needs of businesses selling goods at set unit prices. For companies offering more consultancy-based services, the product isn't sufficiently flexible to support varying price levels or more unusual one-off charges that can be associated with service businesses. Sterling is the only currency supported by the product and there's no ability to track current tax charges, such as IR35.

Instant Accounting is the ideal single user program for a start-up business or a company with very basic accounting processes and top-line reporting requirements.

Other accounting software systems

These are some other bookkeeping and accounting systems designed for small firms and in some cases for particular industry sectors.

- Acnsof Corporation (www.acnsof.com): Developer who has made available an accounting package for the smaller business.
- Asseance Software (www.asseance.com): Integrated accounting and information management system with a small business orientation.
- A21 (www.a21.net/): A business accounting solution, e-commerce enabled, designed for SMEs.
- Banana Accounting for European Companies (www.banana.ch): Double entry accounting program for European small businesses, associations and financial companies. Czech firm.
- Business Management System for Book Publishers (www.acumenbook.com/): Business management software, including royalty accounting and job costing, designed specifically for book publishers.

- Cashier 2000 (http://members.aol.com/legalac/): Solicitors' accounting software with optional time recording, legal aid franchising and client database.
- C.A.T. (www.catsoftware.com): Software packages addressing the specific accounting tasks that are unique to the carnival business.
- CheckMark Software Inc (www.checkmark.com/): Payroll and accounting software: checkmark for Macintosh and Windows machines.
- Creative Solutions (www.creativesolutions.com/): Integrated tax, accounting and practice management software designed exclusively for practising accountants.
- DBA Software (www.dbasoftware.com/): A small business software package focused exclusively on the needs of manufacturers and job shops.
- Deltanet (www.deltanet2.com/): Integrated accounting program for all uses. Free downloads.
- Dosh (www.dosh.co.uk:): This small business specializes in accounting software for the self-employed and businesses with less than 10 employees. DOSH Cashbook assumes no bookkeeping knowledge, but provides help through onscreen steps and a comprehensive manual., The software allows users to produce a complete record of all receipts and payments, a cash flow summary, a VAT account and bank reconciliation statements for any period and prints reports on to A4 paper. Trial versions of the software can be downloaded from the web site.
- MagiCalc 2000 (www.magcalc.com): An accounting software package that enables people with little to no accounting knowledge to do bookkeeping.
- Micro Key Software Inc. (www.microkey.cc): Alarm company management and central station automation software for dealers.
- MoneyWare 2000 (http://money-ware.com): Investment management and small business accounting software.

- Paragon (www.goparagon.com): Small business management and accounting software, custom access database design and applications and employee time clock software solutions.
- Peachtree Accounting (www.peachtree.com/epeachtree/): web-enabled accounting software for small businesses.
- PageUltra. (www.pageultra.com/): Shareware integrated accounts software for UK businesses.
- QuickUSE Accounting (www.quickuse.com): Integrated accounting software – free downloads from the site.
- Red Wing (www.redwingsoftware.com): Mid-range software systems designed for growing SMEs.
- RentBook Software (www.rentbookplus.co.uk): Property management and integrated accounting system.
- R.T.I. (www.internetRTI.com): Accounting and operational software for restaurants.
- SBC Systems (www.sbcsystemsinc.com): Software solutions for service contractors and wholesale distributors.
- Simplex (www.simplex.net): The popular Simplex D accounting program for retailers and small businesses.
- Software Options (www.software-options.com): Accounting, telesales, order processing and stock control for food products distributors.
- TAAME – Travel Agents Accounting Made Easy (www.taame.com): Bookkeeping and administration software for travel agencies.
- Vertex (www.vertexsoftware.com/accounting-software.htm): Software for today's rehabilitation professional.

If you want some help in choosing a system try visiting the Exelco website.

Exelco
8233 Via Paseo Del Norte
Suite E-300
Scottsdale
AZ 85258
Fax: 00 1 480 922 6504
Tel: 00 1 480 922 6500
Website: www.exelco.com

This is a site that features unbiased information and reviews of over 150 accounting systems. They do, however, have something to sell. Their Accounting Library (TAL) is a software evaluation tool that uses data provided by the software publishers. It has been used for several years, and has helped hundreds of companies and consultants gather the information and thoroughly evaluate the capabilities of a wide field of candidate systems. It starts at $395 for the basic system.

If you know exactly what you want, visit ebay's auction site, which has 20 pages of second-hand accounting software for small business, from $10 upwards: http://listings.ebay.com/aw/plistings/list/category3769/index.html.

Choosing an accountant

Keeping your financial affairs in good order is the key to staying legal and winning any disputes. A good accountant inside or outside the firm can keep you on track. A bad accountant is in the ideal position to defraud you at worst, or derail you through negligence or incompetence. What attributes should you look for and how can you find the right accountant for your business? The key steps to choosing a good accountant are:

1   Check they are members of one of the recognized accounting bodies.
2   Have a clear idea of what services you require. You need to consider how complete your bookkeeping records are likely to be: will you need the VAT return done, budgets and cash

flow forecasts prepared and updated, as well as an audit?

3 Clarify the charges scale at the outset. It may well make more sense to spend a bit more on bookkeeping, both staff and systems, rather than leaving it all to a much higher charging qualified accountant.

4 Use personal recommendations from a respected fellow businessman. Pay rather less attention to the recommendation of bankers, government agencies, family and friends, without totally ignoring their advice. There is nothing like hearing from a fellow 'consumer' of a product or service.

5 Find out who else they act for. You don't want them to be so busy they can't service your needs properly, or to be working for potential competitors.

6 Find out what back-up they have for both systems and people. The tax authorities will not be very sympathetic, whatever the reason for lateness. It would be doubly annoying to be fined for someone else's tardiness.

7 Take references from the accountant's clients, as well as from the person who recommended them. It could just be a lucky event that they get on. They may even be related!

8 See at least three accountants before making your choice, making sure they deal with companies your size and a bit bigger. Not so much bigger as to have no relevant advice and help to offer, but big enough for you to have some room for growth without having to change accountants too quickly.

9 Make the appointment for a trial period only, and set a specific task to see how they get on.

10 Give them the latest accounts of your business and ask them for their comments based on their analysis of the figures. You will quickly see if they have grasped the basics of your financial position.

Finance and accounting organizations

Association of Accounting Technicians
154 Clerkenwell Road
London
EC1R 5AD
Tel: 020 7837 8600
Fax: 020 7410 6970
Email: aat@aat.org.uk
Website: www.aat.co.uk

The Association of Accounting Technicians has a database of self-employed people able to keep your books on its website. It's not easy to find, so this is the exact URL: www.aat.co.uk/current/currmembers/key/searchpage.cfm.

Chartered Institute of Management Accountants
26 Chapter Street
London
SW1P 4NP
Tel: +44 (0) 20 8849 2251
Fax: 020 7631 5309
Website: www.cimaglobal.com

Institute of Chartered Accountants in England and Wales
PO Box 433
Chartered Accountants Hall
Moorgate Place
London
EC2P 2BJ
Tel: 020 7920 8100
Fax: +44 (0) 20 7920 0547
Website: www.icaew.co.uk

The Institute of Charted Accountants in England and Wales (ICAEW) provides accountancy news and information, together with the full text of ICAEW reports on accounting in business, self-assessment taxation and other subjects.

Institute of Chartered Accountants of Scotland
CA House,
21 Haymarket Yards,
Edinburgh
EH12 5BH
Tel: +44 (0)131 347 0100
Fax: 0131 225 3813
Website: www.icas.org.uk

Institute of Financial Accountants
UK Headquarters
Burford House
44 London Road
Sevenoaks
TN13 1AS
Tel: 01732 458080
Fax: 01732 455848
Email: mail@ifa.org.uk
Website: www.ifa.org.uk

Section 7

BUSINESS AND THE LAW

Everyone is affected in some way or another by the law, and ignorance does not form the basis of a satisfactory defence. Businesses are also subject to specific laws, and a particular responsibility rests on those who own or manage them. The fact is that, in business, you know that one day you will need a lawyer. The complexity of commercial life means that, sooner or later, you will find yourself taking, or defending yourself against, legal action. It may be a contract dispute with a customer or supplier, or perhaps the lease on your premises turns out to give you far fewer rights than you hoped. A former employee might claim you fired them without reason. Or the Health and Safety Inspector will call and find some aspect of your machinery or working practices less than satisfactory.

The range of possibilities is extensive, and when things do go wrong, the time and money required to put them right can be an unexpected and unwelcome drain on your cash. By doing things right from the start, you can avoid at least some of the most common disputes and cope more easily with catastrophes.

In addition to ensuring that contracts are correctly drawn up, leases are free from nasty surprises, and the right health and safety procedures are followed, a solicitor can also advise on choosing the best structure for your company, on protecting your intellectual property, and on how to go about raising money.

It makes sense either to see your solicitor before your problems arise, and find out what they can do for you, or at the very least to make yourself conversant with the relevant laws. Taking timely action on legal issues may help you gain an advantage over competitors and will almost certainly save you money in the long run.

If you are going to see a lawyer, it is always best to be well prepared. Have all the facts to hand and know what you want help with.

The information set out below is not intended to represent the whole gamut of legal issues a small or new business might face. Rather, it covers an outline of the issues that most firms are likely to face either before or shortly after they set up, together with some guidance as to how to find out about the current rules that affect this particular area, as the law like every other aspect of business is constantly evolving.

Although an indication of some of the main legal implications is given here, there is no substitute for specific professional advice. A lawyer will probably know the way in which your particular business will be affected by the laws mentioned here and other laws. In the area of taxation an accountant can earn his fee several times over. Other organizations and professionals who can advise you are listed at the end of each subsection. This section also identifies and outlines some of the key services or publications that can help you get a better understanding of business and the law. You would be well advised to at least take up the offer from Lawyers For Your Business, of a free consultation.

General legal help sources

Lawyers For Your Business

The Law Society's Hall
113 Chancery Lane
London
WC2A 1PL
Tel: 020 7405 9075
Fax: 020 7831 0344
Website: www.lfyb.lawsociety.org.uk

Lawyers For Your Business (LFYB) represents some 1400 firms of solicitors in England and Wales which have come together to help ensure that all businesses, and especially the smaller owner-managed ones, get access to sound legal advice whenever they need it.

LFYB is administered by The Law Society, and backed by Business in the Community, the Federation of Small Business and the Forum of Private Business.

To remove the risk of incurring unexpectedly high legal costs, all LFYB members offer a free consultation, lasting at least half an hour, to diagnose the problem and any need for action, with full information in advance on the likely costs of proceeding.

Call The Law Society on the number above and they will send you a list of Lawyers For Your Business members in your area, and a voucher for a free consultation.

Simply choose one of the firms in the list and arrange an appointment, mentioning LFYB and the voucher. You will need to give up the voucher to the solicitor at your first meeting.

Company Law Club

Incorporation Services Limited
1 Saville Chambers
5 North Street
Newcastle upon Tyne
NE1 8DF
Tel: 0191 261 5545
Email: info@incorporationservices.co.uk
Website: www.incorporationservices.co.uk

Company Law Club provides a range of services to members, all swiftly and expertly conducted and competitively priced. Many can be ordered by completing the online order forms. Payment can be made by credit card. Account facilities may be opened in appropriate cases. If the service you require is not listed, just email them with your requirements and they will help if they can.

Membership is free – all you need to do is register – and help comes in four ways.

- **Library:** The Company Law Club library provides the most accessible source of UK company law material available online, including:
  - an extensive database of company law topics with a comprehensive index and search facility
  - links to other company law related websites
  - company forms library download facility
  - or you can go straight to a list of the main UK companies legislation.
- **Meeting rooms:** A bulletin board for company law topics, including specific boards to keep you up to date on changes. This section of the website contains:
  - newsletter
  - digest of reported cases
  - new legislation (including statutory instruments)
  - news and views on company law issues
  - book notices
  - new websites on legal matters that concern business.
- **Services:** Company formations, ready-made companies, document drafting, company secretarial services and statutory registers. Priced from about £120 for company formations down to a 'do it yourself' company formation kit for £25.
- **Start in Business (www.startinbusiness. co.uk/quotes/lawyers.htm):** Here you can obtain a free quotation for the services of a lawyer specializing in the field of your choice. You will be asked to fill in a form with your details and the service required and in a short while you will receive, with no obligations,

email offers from those lawyers who are able to assist you.

Publications

Two useful books that cover most of this field are:

*   *Law for the Small Business* by Patricia Clayton. Kogan Page, £14.99, 10th edition 2001
*   *Business Law* by Ewan Macintyre. Pearson Higher Education, £29.99, 2001.

Choosing the legal form of your business

There are different legal frameworks for the ownership of a business and not all are equally appropriate for everyone. For example, not all sources of finance are open to every type of business, so once you know how much money is needed either to start up or to grow and what that money is needed for, you will be in a better position to make an informed choice as to legal structure. In general, the more money that is required and the more risky the venture, the more likely it is that a limited company will be a more appropriate structure.

Most businesses in the UK trade as sole proprietorships, as Fig. 7.1 shows.

Each legal structure has a range of advantages and disadvantages and confers different responsibilities, liabilities and opportunities for creating personal wealth. Most successful businesses are likely to change their ownership structure as they grow.

Ways to organize your business

Co-operatives and franchising were examined in Section 3, where you will find all the basic information and pointers as to where to look for further information (see also Table 7.1).

Sole proprietor

The vast majority of new businesses are essentially one-man bands. As such, they are free to choose the simplest legal structure. They are known by terms such as sole trader or sole proprietor. This structure has the merit of being relatively free of formality and there are few rules about the records you have to keep. There is no requirement for your accounts to be audited, or for financial information on your business to be filed.

As a sole trader there is no legal distinction between you and your business. Your business is one of your assets, just as your house or car is. It follows from this that if your business should fail, your creditors have a right not only to the assets of the business, but also to your personal assets, subject only to the provisions of local bankruptcy rules (these often allow you to keep only a few absolutely basic essentials for yourself and family). It may be possible to avoid the worst of these consequences by *distancing your assets* (see 'Business Failure' on page **355**).

The capital to start and run the business must come from you, or from loans. There is no access to equity capital, which has the attraction of being risk-free. In return for these drawbacks, you can have the pleasure of being your own boss imme-

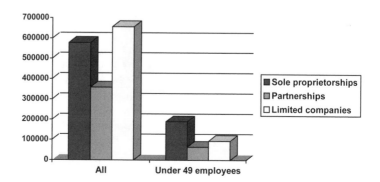

Fig. 7.1 Legal structure of VAT-registered businesses in the UK in 2001.

Table 7.1 Ways to organize your business.

Type of entity	Main advantages	Main drawbacks
Sole proprietorship	Simple and inexpensive to create and operate. Owner reports profit or loss on his or her personal tax return.	Owner personally liable for business debts. No access to external capital. Life of business restricted to life of owner. Limited potential for value creation.
General partnership	Simple and inexpensive to create and operate. Owners (partners) report their share of profit or loss on their personal tax returns.	Owners (partners) personally liable for business debts. Life of business restricted to life of first partner to die. Access to outside capital restricted to partners. Some potential for value creation.
Limited partnership	Limited partners have limited personal liability for business debts as long as they don't participate in management. General partners can raise cash without involving outside investors in management of business. Wider access to outside capital. Some potential for value creation.	General partners personally liable for business debts. More expensive to create than general partnership. Life of business restricted to life of first partners to die.
Limited company	Owners have limited personal liability for business debts. Some benefits (pensions etc.) can be deducted as a business expense. Owners can split corporate profit among owners and corporation, paying lower overall tax rate. Access to full range of external capital. Business can live on after founders' death. Potential for value creation.	More expensive to create and run than partnership or sole proprietorship. Owners must meet legal requirements for stock registration, account filing and paperwork. Separate taxable entity.
Co-operative	Owners have limited personal liability for business debts. Owners report their share of corporate profit or loss on their personal tax returns. Owners can use corporate loss to offset income from other sources.	More expensive to create than a sole proprietorship. Owners must meet legal requirements for account filing, registration and paperwork. Restricted access to outside capital. Limited potential for value creation.
Franchise chain	Has all the same advantages and drawbacks of a company, plus access to a stream of capital and income from new franchisees, to fund expansion.	

diately, subject only to declaring your profits on your tax return and if necessary applying for a trade licence. (In practice you would be wise to take professional advice before doing so.)

Partnerships

Partnerships are effectively collections of sole traders or proprietors.

It is a common structure used by people who started out on their own, but want to expand.

There are very few restrictions to setting up in business with another person (or persons) in partnership, and several definite advantages. By pooling resources you may have more capital; you will be bringing, hopefully, several sets of skills to the business; and if you are ill the business can still carry on.

The legal regulations governing partnerships in essence assume that competent businesspeople should know what they are doing. The law merely provides a framework of agreement which applies 'in the absence of agreement to the contrary'. It follows from this that many partnerships are entered into without legal formalities and sometimes without the parties themselves being aware that they have entered a partnership! Just giving the impression that you are partners may be enough to create an 'implied partnership'.

In the absence of an agreement to the contrary, the following rules apply to partnerships.

- All partners contribute capital equally.
- All partners share profits and losses equally.
- No partner shall have interest paid on their capital.
- No partner shall be paid a salary.
- All partners have an equal say in the management of the business.

It is unlikely that all these provisions will suit you, so you would be well advised to get a partnership agreement drawn up in writing before trading.

Partnerships have three serious financial drawbacks that merit particular attention.

First, if your partner makes a business mistake, perhaps by signing a disastrous contract, without your knowledge or consent, every member of the partnership must shoulder the consequences. Under these circumstances your personal assets could be taken to pay the creditors even though the mistake was no fault of your own.

Second, if your partner goes bankrupt in their personal capacity, for whatever reason, their share of the partnership can be seized by their creditors. As a private individual you are not liable for your partner's private debts, but having to buy them out of the partnership at short notice could put you and the business in financial jeopardy.

Third, if your partnership breaks up for any reason, those continuing with it want to recover control of the business, and those who remain shareholders will want to buy back shares; the leaver wants a realistic price. The agreement you have on setting up the business should specify the procedure and how to value the leaver's share, otherwise resolving the situation will be costly.

The traditional route to value the leaver's share is to ask an independent accountant. This is rarely cost-effective. The valuation costs money and worst of all it is not definite and consequently there is room for argument. Another way is to establish a formula, an agreed eight times the last audited pre-tax profits, for example. This approach is simple but difficult to get right. A fast-growing business is undervalued by a formula using historic data unless the multiple is high; a high multiple may overvalue 'hope' or goodwill, thus unreasonably profiting the leaver.

Under a third option, one partner offers to buy out the others at a price he specifies. If they do not accept his offer, the continuing partners must buy the leaver out at that price. In theory, such a price should be acceptable to all.

Even death may not release you from partnership obligations and in some circumstances your estate can remain liable. Unless you take public leave of your partnership by notifying your business contacts and legally bringing your partnership to an end, you will remain liable indefinitely.

Limited partnerships

One possibility that can reduce the more painful consequences of entering a partnership is to have your involvement registered as a limited partnership. A limited partnership is very different from a 'general' partnership. It is a legal animal that, in certain circumstances, combines the best attributes of a partnership and a corporation.

A limited partnership works like this. There must be one or more general partners with the same basic rights and responsibilities (including unlimited liability) as in any general partnership, and one or more limited partners, who are usually passive investors. The big difference between a general partner and a limited partner is that the limited partner isn't personally liable for debts of the partnership. The most a limited partner can lose is the amount that he or she:

- paid or agreed to pay into the partnership as a capital contribution; or
- received from the partnership after it became insolvent.

To keep this limited liability, a limited partner may not participate in the management of the business, with very few exceptions. A limited partner who does get actively involved in the management of the business risks losing immunity from personal liability and having the same legal exposure as a general partner.

The advantage of a limited partnership as a business structure is that it provides a way for business owners to raise money (from the limited partners) without having to either take in new partners who will be active in the business or having to form a limited company. A general partnership that's been operating for years can also create a limited partnership to finance expansion.

Forming a company

The concept of limited liability, where the shareholders are not liable in the last resort for the debts of their business, can be traced back to the Romans. However, it was rarely used, only being granted as a special favour to friends by those in power. Some two thousand years later the idea was revived when in 1811 New York State brought in a general limited liability law for manufacturing companies. Most American states followed suit and eventually Britain caught up in 1854. Most countries have a legal structure incorporating the concept of limited liability.

As the name suggests, in this form of business your liability is limited to the amount you contribute by way of share capital.

A limited company has a legal identity of its own, separate from the people who own or run it. This means that, in the event of failure, creditors' claims are restricted to the assets of the company. The shareholders of the business are not liable as individuals for the business debts beyond the paid-up value of their shares. This applies even if the shareholders are working directors, unless of course the company has been trading fraudulently. In practice, the ability to limit liability is restricted these days, as most lenders, including the banks, often insist on personal guarantees from the directors. Other advantages include the freedom to raise capital by selling shares.

Disadvantages include the legal requirement for the company's accounts to be audited and filed for public inspection.

A limited company can be formed by two shareholders, one of whom must be a director. A company secretary must also be appointed, who can be a shareholder, a director or an outside person such as an accountant or lawyer.

The company can be bought 'off the shelf' from a registration agent, then adapted to suit your own purposes. This will involve changing the name, shareholders and articles of association and takes a couple of weeks to arrange. Alternatively, you can form your own company. But before you can form a company you need to decide which of the two main structures of company to use.

A LTD company is the most common type. This is a private company limited by shares. A LTD company can be started with, say, an authorized share capital of £1000. This is then divided into 1000 ×

£1 shares. You can then issue as few or as many of the shares as you want. As long as the shares you have issued are paid for in full, if the company liquidates, the shareholders have no further liabilities. If the shares have not been paid for, then the shareholders are liable for the value, i.e. if they have 100 £1 shares, they are only liable for £100.

A PLC company is a public company and may be listed on the Stock Exchange. Before a PLC can start to trade it must have at least £50,000 of shares issued and at least 25% of the value must have been paid for. A PLC company has a better status due to its larger capital

A company must have on its notepaper the company's full name, the address of the registered office, the fact that it is registered in England or Scotland, etc., and the company number. However, the names of the directors need not be stated but, if any are (other than as signatory), all must be stated.

When a company is first registered it must send to Companies House a copy of its memorandum and articles of association and form 10, which contains the address of the company's registered office and details of its directors and company secretary. The directors' details are: current names, any former names, date of birth, usual residential address (currently under review), occupation, nationality and other directorships. For the secretary only the names and address are required.

Both accountants (see Section 6) and lawyers can help you with choosing your legal form.

The business name

A business name is a name used by any person, partnership or company for carrying on a business, unless your own name is used. You are reasonably free to use your last name for the name of your business. The main consideration in choosing a business name, however, is its commercial usefulness. You will want one that will let people know as much as possible about what you do. It is therefore important to choose a name that will convey the right image and message.

Whichever business name you choose, it will have to be legally acceptable and abide by the rules in the Business Names Act 1985. To check if your business name will be acceptable, you will need to find out the following.

- Are any other businesses already using your name? You could check this in your local phone directory, relevant trade journals or via an Internet search as outlined in Section 5.
- Does your business name conflict with a registered trade mark or is it similar to another name? To check this, visit the Trade Marks Registry of the Patent Office at www.patent.gov.uk
- Does your business name have words that imply national or international pre-eminence, representative status, specific objects or functions? If so, you will need the approval of the Secretary of State for Trade & Industry before you can use it. More detailed information and examples are available from the business names section at Companies House, Cardiff or Edinburgh – or visit www.companieshouse.gov.uk and click on 'Guidance Booklets & FAQ' and then 'Business Names'.

Logos

It is not mandatory to have a logo for your business, but it can build greater customer awareness. A logo could be a word, typeface, colour or a shape. Choose your logo carefully. It should be one that is easily recognizable, fairly simple in design and which can be reproduced on everything associated with your business. As far as the law is concerned a logo is a form of trade mark (see page **321**).

Registering a domain name

A domain name is your own web address, which you register so that your business will have the exclusive right to use. It identifies your business or organization on the Internet, and it enables people to find you by directly entering your name into their browser address box. Registering a domain name is a fairly simple, although deciding on a domain name that is not already taken can sometimes be a process of elimination. Thousands of domain names are registered every day, up to 50,000 a week according to some industry experts, and you must choose a name that has not already been registered. It is therefore important to have a selection of domain names before registering in case your first choice is unavailable. You can check whether your choice of name is available by using a free domain search service available at websites that register domain names such as www.yourname.com.

If your company name is registered as a trade mark (see below), you may (as current case law develops) be able to prevent another business from using it as a domain name. Once you have decided on a selection of domain names, you can choose several different registration options.

- Use Nominet UK (www.nic.uk/), which is the registry for .uk Internet domain names. Just as Companies House holds authoritative records for company names, or the DVLA for driving licences, so Nominet maintains the database of .uk registered Internet names. They charge £80 + VAT for two years' registration. (The me.uk second level domain was introduced on 14 January 2002.)

   Most countries have a central registry to store these unique domain names. Two sites that maintain world directories of Internet domain registries are www.internic.net/ and www.norid.no/domreg.html, between them covering pretty well every registration authority in the world.

   In order to be eligible to register direct you must provide the Internet protocol (IP) addresses of two named servers that are permanently connected to the Internet.
- Use Internet service providers (ISPs), which act as agents for their customers and will submit a domain name application for registration.

- Register online. Hundreds of websites now offer domain name registration online; it's a good idea to search the Internet for these sites, as they often sell domain names as loss leaders. Most of these providers also offer a search facility so you can see if your selected name has already been registered.
- Obtain free domain names along with free web space by registering with an Internet community. These organizations offer you web pages within their community space as well as a free domain name, but most communities only offer free domain names that have their own community domain tagged on the end – this can make your domain name rather long and hard to remember.

Once your domain name has been registered and paid for, you will receive a registration certificate, either directly or through your ISP. This is an important document as it confirms you as the legal registrant of a domain name. If any amendments need to be made at any point during the registration period, the registry and your ISP must be informed. Key points to remember are:

- a successful application remains valid for two years, after which your ISP should make contact to notify you that your domain name is due for renewal, after which you have the first option to renew for a further period of one or two years
- choose a domain name that is easy to remember – the shorter and snappier it is, the more likely it is to be remembered
- if possible, choose a domain name that actually says what you do as a business, although this will depend on the availability of your chosen names
- make sure the company with which you register your domain name sends you a registration certificate as verification
- register all the core domain-name suffixes, including '.com', '.net', '.org', '.co.uk', '.uk', at the outset to avoid falling foul of 'copycat' sites.

Protecting your ideas

Intellectual property, often known as IP, allows people to own their creativity and innovation in the same way that they can own physical property. The owner of IP can control and be rewarded for its use, and this encourages further innovation and creativity to the benefit of us all.

In some cases IP gives rise to protection for ideas but in other areas there will have to be more elaboration of an idea before protection can arise. It will often not be possible to protect IP and gain IP rights (or IPRs) unless they have been applied for and granted, but some IP protection such as copyright arises automatically, without any registration, as soon as there is a record in some form of what has been created.

Patent law, for example, can give you temporary protection for technological inventions. The registration of a design can protect the appearance or shape of a commercial product; copyright protects literary, artistic or musical creations and, more recently, computer programs; a trade mark protects symbols, logos and pictures. The period of the protection which these laws can give varies from five years, for the initial registration of the design, to 50 years after your death, for the copyright on an 'artistic' work. The level and scope of protection varies considerably, and it is a field in the process of constant change. So, for example, it is now possible with a single patent application made in the UK to secure a whole series of protections throughout Europe. The Patent Co-operation Treaty is extending that protection to the USA, Russia and Japan. In practice, however, defending 'intellectual' property is an expensive and complex process for a new or small business. If you have a unique business idea, you should investigate the four categories of protection: patenting, which protects technological and other inventions; design registration, which protects the shape or appearance of a commercial product; copyright, which protects literary, artistic and musical works; and trade mark registration, which protects symbols, logos and pictures. Some products may be covered by two or more categories, e.g.

the mechanism of a clock may be patented while its appearance may be design-registered. Each category requires a different set of procedures, offers a different level of protection and extends for a different period of time. They all have one thing in common, though; in the event of any infringement your only redress is through the courts, and going to law can be wasteful of time and money, whether you win or lose.

James Dyson's book, *Against The Odds* (Texere Publishing, £8.99, December 2000) gives a salutary warning to all would-be inventors and entrepreneurs as to how hard the task of defending intellectual property is. Dyson's website (www.dyson. com/news/) will keep you up to date on his long-running patent infringement battle with Hoover. The site also has a helpful section giving advice to would-be inventors.

Patents

The patent system in its current form was introduced over 100 years ago, although some type of protection has been around for about 350 years, as an incentive to get inventors to disclose their ideas to the general public and so promote technical advancement in general.

A patent can be regarded as a contract between an inventor and the state. The state agrees with the inventor that if he/she is prepared to publish details of his/her invention in a set form and if it appears that he/she has made a real advance, the state will then grant him/her a 'monopoly' on his/her invention for 20 years: 'protection in return for disclosure'. The inventor uses the monopoly period to manufacture and sell his/her innovation; competitors can read the published specifications and glean ideas for their research, or they can approach the inventor and offer to help to develop his/her idea under licence.

However, the granting of a patent doesn't mean the proprietor is automatically free to make, use or sell the invention himself/herself, since to do so might involve infringing an earlier patent which has not yet expired. A patent really only allows the inventor to stop another person using the particular device which forms the subject of his/her patent. The state does not guarantee validity of a patent either, so it is not uncommon for patents to be challenged through the courts.

Which inventions can you patent?

- **Be new:** The invention must never have been made public in any way, anywhere in the world, before the date on which an application for a patent is filed.
- **Involve an inventive step:** An invention involves an inventive step if, when compared with what is already known, it would not be obvious to someone with a good knowledge and experience of the subject.
- **Be capable of industrial application:** An invention must be capable of being made or used in some kind of industry. This means that the invention must take the practical form of an apparatus or device, a product such as some new material or substance or an industrial process or method of operation. 'Industry' is meant in its broadest sense as anything distinct from purely intellectual or aesthetic activity. It does not necessarily imply the use of a machine or the manufacture of an article.

An invention is not patentable if it is:

- an article or process alleged to operate in a manner clearly contrary to well-established physical laws, such as perpetual motion machines, for example:
- a discovery
- a method of treatment of the human or animal body by surgery or therapy, or a method of diagnosis
- a new animal or plant variety
- a scientific theory or mathematical method
- a rediscovered or long-forgotten idea (knowingly or unknowingly)
- an aesthetic creation such as a literary, dramatic or artistic work
- a scheme or method for performing a mental act, playing a game or doing business

- the presentation of information, or a computer program.

If the invention involves more than these abstract aspects so that it has physical features (such as a special apparatus to play a new game) then it may be patentable.

If you want to apply for a patent, it is essential not to disclose your idea in non-confidential circumstances. If you do, your invention is already 'published' in the eyes of the law, and this could well invalidate your application. Ideally, the confidentiality of the disclosure you make should be written down in a confidentiality agreement and signed by the person to whom you are making the disclosure. This is particularly important if you are talking to a commercial contact or potential business colleague. The other way is to get your patent application on file before you start talking to anyone about your idea. You can talk to a Chartered Patent Agent in complete confidence as they work under strict rules of confidentiality.

There are two distinct stages in the patenting process:

- from filing an application up to publication of the patent
- from publication to grant of the patent.

Two fees are payable for the first part of the process and a further fee for the second part. The Patent Office Search and Advisory Service will give some estimate of the costs associated with a specific investigation. They suggest, for example, that subject matter searches will cost upwards of £500, validity searches from £1000 and infringement searches from £1500. And these are just the costs for the very start of the procedure.

The whole process takes some two and a half years. Relevant forms and details of how to patent are available free of charge from the Patent Office, or can be viewed online. It is possible – and cheaper – to make your own patent application but this is not really recommended. Drafting a specification to give you as wide a monopoly as you think you can get away with is the essence of patenting and this is the skill of professional patent agents. They also know the tricks of the trade for each stage of the patenting procedure. A list of patent agents is available from the Chartered Institute of Patent Agents.

What can you do with your idea once it's patented? If you have dreamt up an inspired invention but don't have the resources, skill, time or inclination to produce it yourself, you can take one out of three courses.

- **Outright sale:** You can sell the rights and title of your patent to an individual or company. The payment you ask should be based on a sound evaluation of the market.
- **Sale and royalty:** You can enter into an agreement whereby you assign the title and rights to produce to another party for cash but under which you get a royalty on each sold unit.
- **Licensing:** You keep the rights and title but sell a licence for manufacturing and marketing the product to someone else. The contract between you and the licensee should contain a performance clause requiring the licensee to sell a minimum number of units each year or the licence will be revoked.

Whichever option you select, you need a good patent agent/lawyer on your side.

Trade mark

A trade mark is the symbol by which the goods of a particular manufacturer or trader can be identified. It can be a word, a signature, a monogram, a picture, a logo or a combination of these. To qualify for registration the trade mark must be distinctive, must not be deceptive and must not be capable of confusion with marks already registered. Excluded are misleading marks, national flags, royal crests and insignia of the armed forces. A trade mark can only apply to tangible goods, not services (although pressure is mounting for this to be changed). The Trade Mark Act 1994 offers protection of great commercial value since, unlike other forms of protection, your sole rights to use the trade mark continue indefinitely.

To register a trade mark you or your agent should first conduct preliminary searches at the Trade Marks Branch of the Patent Office to check there are no conflicting marks already in existence. You then apply for registration on the official trade mark form and pay a fee (currently £200). Your application is then advertised in the weekly *Trade Marks Journal* to allow any objections to be raised. If there are none, your trade mark will be officially registered and you pay a further fee (currently £200). Registration is initially for 10 years. After this, it can be renewed for further periods of 10 years at a time, with no upper time limit. It is mandatory to register a trade mark. If an unregistered trade mark has been used for some time and could be construed as closely associated with the product by customers, it will have acquired a 'reputation' which will give it some protection legally, but registration makes it much simpler for the owner to have recourse against any person who infringes the mark.

After you have applied for a trade mark, you are not allowed to amend it, and they will not refund your application fee should your mark turn out not to be registrable for any reason. Using their Search and Advisory Service could save you the expense of making an application that has little or no chance of being accepted for registration. That will cost you £82.25 (VAT included)) per mark.

Design registration

You can register the shape, design or decorative features of a commercial product if it is new, original, never published before or – if already known – never before applied to the product you have in mind. Protection is intended to apply to industrial articles to be produced in quantities of more than 50. Design registration only applies to features which appeal to the eye – not to the way the article functions. To register a design, you should apply to the Design Registry and send a specimen or photograph of the design plus a registration fee (currently about £100). This is examined to see whether it is new or original and complies with other requirements of the Registered Designs Act. If it does, a certificate of registration is issued which gives you, the proprietor, the sole right to manufacture, sell or use in business articles of that design. Protection lasts for five years but can be renewed for four further five-year periods.

There is no such thing as an all-embracing international registration for designs. If you want protection of your design outside the UK, you generally have to make separate applications for registration in each country in which you want protection.

You can handle the design registration yourself but, again, it might be preferable to let a specialist do it for you.

Copyright

Copyright gives protection against the unlicensed copying of original artistic and creative works – articles, books, paintings, films, plays, songs, music, engineering drawings. To claim copyright the item in question should carry the © symbol with the author's name and date.

The type of works that copyright protects are:

- original literary works, e.g. novels, instruction manuals, computer programs, lyrics for songs, articles in newspapers, some types of databases, but not names or titles which come under Trade Mark law
- original dramatic works, including works of dance or mime
- original musical works
- original artistic works, e.g. paintings, engravings, photographs, sculptures, collages, works of architecture, technical drawings, diagrams, maps, logos
- published editions of works, i.e. the typographical arrangement of a publication
- sound recordings, which may be recordings on any medium, e.g. tape or compact disc, and may be recordings of other copyright works, e.g. musical or literary

- films, including videos and
- broadcasts and cable programmes.

The above works are protected by copyright, regardless of the medium in which they exist – which includes the Internet. You should also note that copyright does not protect ideas. It protects the way the idea is expressed in a piece of work, but it does not protect the idea itself.

No action is required to take out copyright, though you can take the further step of recording the date on which the work was completed with the UKCS (United Kingdom Copyright Service) for a registration fee of £30 for 5 years or £60 for 10 years. This, though, is an unusual precaution to take and probably only necessary if you anticipate any infringement. Copyright is infringed only if more than a 'substantial' part of your work is reproduced (i.e. issued for sale to the public) without your permission, but since there is no formal registration of copyright, the question of whether or not your work is protected usually has to be decided in a court of law.

Copyright does not last forever. The duration is dependent on the type of copyright involved and can be anything from 25 to 70 years after the creator's death.

- **For literary, dramatic, musical or artistic works:** 70 years from the end of the calendar year in which the last remaining author of the work dies or the work is made available to the public (by authorized performance, broadcast, exhibition, etc.).
- **Sound recordings and broadcasts:** 50 years from the end of the calendar year in which the last remaining author of the work dies, or the work is made available to the public (by authorized release, performance, broadcast, etc.).
- **Films:** 70 years from the end of the calendar year in which the last principal director, author or composer dies, or the work is made available to the public (by authorized performance, broadcast, exhibition, etc.).

- **Typographical arrangement of published editions:** 25 years from the end of the calendar year in which the work was first published.

The computer programs regulations in 1992 extended the rules covering literary works to include computer programs.

Help and advice with intellectual property

Patent offices

These three organizations can help direct you to most sources of help and advice across all of the intellectual property field. They also have helpful literature and explanatory leaflets and guidance notes on applying for intellectual property protection. See also the organizations listed in Section 4.

UK Patent Office
www.patent.gov.uk

European Patent Office
www.european-patent-office.org

US Patent and Trade Mark Office
www.uspto.gov

Other organizations
Business Software Alliance
79 Knightsbridge
London
SW1X 7RB
Tel: 020 7245 0304
Fax: 020 7245 0310
Email: info@bsa.org
Website: www.bsa.co.uk

BSA is a worldwide organization devoted to eradicating the illegal copying of software, often referred to as 'software piracy'.

The Chartered Institute of Patent Agents
Staple Inn Buildings
High Holborn
London

WC1V 7PZ
Tel: 020 7405 9450
Fax: 020 7430 0471
Email: mail@cipa.org.uk
Website: www.cipa.org.uk

The Chartered Institute of Patent Agents hold regular clinics at a number of sites around the United Kingdom giving free basic advice to innovators who are at the early stages of developing an idea.

Below are listed the current sites for clinics and contact details for arranging an appointment. Many firms of patent agents will also offer the first consultation free of charge, so if there is not a clinic listed locally, you could contact local firms of agents – a geographically-sorted list appears on the Institute's website.

Birmingham
Patents & Technology Section
Birmingham Central Library
Chamberlain Square
Birmingham
B3 3HQ
Contact: Ted Hunt
Tel: 0121 303 4537

Every Wednesday evening. Appointment necessary.

Liverpool
Science and Technology Library
Central Library
William Brown Street
Liverpool
L3 8EW
Contact: Ruth Godner
Tel: 0151 233 5842

Every alternate Tuesday evening. Appointment necessary.

London
The Chartered Institute of Patent Agents
Staple Inn Buildings
London

WC1V 7PZ
Contact: Margaret Mitchell
Tel: 020 7405 9450
Email: clinics@cipa.org.uk

Every Tuesday evening. Appointment necessary.

Manchester
Manchester Central Library
St. Peter's Square
Manchester
M2 5PD
Tel: 0161 234 1987
Email: technic@libraries.manchester.gov.uk

Every third Tuesday of the month, 1400–1800. Appointment necessary.

Yorkshire
Contact: Kathy Pitt
Tel: 01274 754262

Monthly patent clinics covering all aspects of intellectual property are being organized by the Technical Information Service at various centres in the West Yorkshire area. Alongside these clinics the Leeds Patent Information Unit is providing demonstrations of patent searching. Due to the popularity of these clinics, they are only open to companies and individuals within the Yorkshire and Humber Region.

Copyright Licensing Agency
90 Tottenham Court Rd
London
W1T 4LP
Tel: 020 7631 5555
Fax 020 7631 5500
Email: cla@cla.co.uk
Website: www.cla.co.uk

Federation Against Copyright Theft
7 Victory Business Centre
Worton Road
Isleworth
TW7 6DB

Tel: 020 8568 6646
Fax: 020 8560 6364
Website: www.fact-uk.org.uk

FACT enforces rights in UK films and other products by seeking and collecting evidence of piracy and bringing legal (usually criminal) proceedings against infringers.

Federation Against Software Theft
1 Kingfisher Court
Farnham Road
Slough
SL2 1JF
Tel: 01753 527999
Fax: 01753 532100
Email: fast@fast.org.uk
Website: www.fast.org.uk

The Institute of Trade Mark Agents
ITMA Office
Canterbury House
2–6 Sydenham Rd
Croydon
CRO 9XE
Tel: 020 8686 2052
Fax: 020 8680 5723
Website: www.itma.org.uk

Mechanical Copyright Protection Society
Elgar House
41 Streatham High Road
London
SW16 1ER
Tel: 020 8769 4400
Fax: 020 8378 7300
Email: info@mcps.co.uk
Website: www.mcps.co.uk

MCPS authorizes on behalf of its members (composers, authors and publishers of music) use of their work in the UK and abroad by recording companies, background music operators and other recording bodies and individuals, as well as in recordings made by radio and television organizations.

Office for Harmonization in the Internal Market (Trade Marks and Designs)
Apartado de correos 77
E-03080 Alicante
Spain
Tel: (34) 965 139 100
Fax: (34) 965 139 173
Email: information@oami.eu.int
Website: http://oami.eu.int

If you want to have wider European protection for your trade mark.

Patents Information
The British Library
96 Euston Road
London
NW1 2DB
Tel: 020 7412 7919 (British patents); 020 7412 7902 (foreign patents)
Email: patents-information@bl.uk
Website: www.bl.uk/services/information/ patents/patentsnetork.html

The Trade Marks Registry
The Patent Office
Harmsworth House
13–15 Bouverie Street
London
EC4 8DP
Tel: 020 7438 4718
Fax: 020 7438 4780
Website: www.patent.gov.uk

The Trade Marks Registry
The Patent Office
Cardiff Road
Newport
NP10 8QQ
Tel: 01633 814000
Fax: 01633 813600
Website: www.patent.gov.uk

UKCS (United Kingdom Copyright Service)
4 Tavistock Avenue
Didcot

OX11 8NA
Email: information@copyrightservice.co.uk
Website: www.copyrightservice.co.uk

World Intellectual Property Organisation (WIPO)
Small and Medium-Sized Enterprises Division
World Intellectual Property Organization
34 chemin des Colombettes
1211 Geneva 20
Switzerland
Fax: 00 41 22 338 8760
Email: sme@wipo.int
Website: www.wipo.int

Premises

If you can avoid taking on premises, perhaps by working from home or going into a business incubator (see Section 4), so much the better. If that is not an option, then read on. Buying or leasing business premises entails a number of important and often complex laws affecting your decisions. To some extent these laws go beyond the scope of the physical premises, into areas such as opening hours and health and safety.

Working from home

If you plan to work from home you need to check that you are not prohibited from doing so by the house deeds or the terms of your mortgage. Clearly if your business activity is noisy, dangerous or operates over anti-social hours your neighbours will be unhappy and may take action to curb your behaviour. You will also have to notify your insurance company, as they will certainly view this change as a material fact. That said, hundreds of thousands of people work unhindered from their spare room. With the growth of telecommuting this trend is likely to grow. Many major public enterprises started out on the kitchen table.

Planning permission

An important first step is to make sure that the premises you have in mind can be used for what you want to do. There are nearly a score of different 'use classes', and each property should have a certificate showing which has been approved. The classes include retail, offices, light industrial, general industrial, warehousing and various special classes. Certain changes of class do not need planning permission – for example, from general industrial to light industrial. Also, changes of use within a class – say, from one type of shop to another – may not need planning permission. Permission will usually only be refused where the business would cause a nuisance or a safety or health hazard. This in effect means that running a business from home does not necessarily require planning permission. Once you have taken on premises, then the responsibilities for 'conforming' fall on your shoulders, so take advice.

Building regulations

Even if you have planning permission, you will still have to conform to building regulations. These apply to the materials, structure and building methods used, in either making or altering the premises. So if you plan any alterations you may need a special approval.

The lease

Before taking on a lease, look carefully at the factors below.

Restrictions

If you are taking on a leasehold property, then you must find out if there are any restrictions in the lease on the use of the property. Often shop leases have restrictions protecting neighbouring businesses. The lease will often stipulate that the landlord cannot 'unreasonably' withhold consent to a change in use. He may, however, insist on the premises being returned to its original shape before you leave.

You should also check if you can sublet part or all of the premises if your circumstances change.

Repairs

Most leases require the tenant to take on either internal repairing liability or full repairing leases. Resist the latter if at all possible, particularly if the property is old. If you have to accept a full repairing lease, then it is essential to get a Schedule of Condition. This is an accurate record of the condition of the premises when you take it over. It is carried out by your own and the landlord's surveyor. It is one expense you may be tempted to forgo – don't.

Rent reviews

However long (or short) your lease is, it is likely that a rent review clause allowing rent reviews every three to seven years will be included. Look very carefully at the formulas used to calculate future rents.

Security of tenure

The Landlord and Tenant Act protects occupiers of business premises. When your lease ends you can stay on at the same rent until the steps laid down in the Act are taken. These steps are fairly precise, and you would be well advised to read the Act and take legal advice. You will get plenty of warning, as the landlord must give you six months' notice in writing, even if you pay rent weekly. The landlord cannot just ask you to leave. There are a number of statutory grounds for repossession. The two main types of grounds are: that you are an unsatisfactory tenant, an allegation you can put to the test in court; or that the landlord wants the premises for other purposes. In that case you must be offered alternative suitable premises. These are obviously matters for negotiation, and you should take advice as soon as possible.

Health and safety

You have to provide a reasonably safe and healthy environment for your employees, any visitors and for members of the general public who may be affected by what you do. This applies to both the premises you work from and the work itself. An inspector has the right to enter your premises to examine it and enforce legal requirements if your standards fall short in any way.

Once you have employees you must take some or all of the following measures, dependent on the number of people you employ. However, a prudent employer should take all these measures, whether or not required by law. Doing so sets the standard of behaviour that is common in the very best firms.

- Inform the organization responsible for health and safety at work for your business of where you are and what you do. For most small business this will be the Environmental Health Department of your local authority and in some cases it will be the Health and Safety Executive.
- Get employer's liability insurance to cover you for any physical injury or disease your employees may get as a result of their work. The amount of cover must be at least £2 million and the insurance certificate must be displayed at all your places of work.
- If you have five or more employees you must have a written statement on your policy for health and safety at work and you must bring it to your employees' notice. You must also make any breach of that safety policy a subject of your disciplinary procedure.

- Display the Health and Safety Law poster or hand out to employees the equivalent leaflet.
- Make an assessment of the fire risk of your workplace and keep a written record if you have five or more employees.
- Ensure you have a safe place to work with safe systems, safe access, adequate materials and protection from unnecessary risks. This is a wide-ranging requirement and includes things such as fire exits, fire extinguishers, electrical fittings, storage, machinery and equipment, hygiene, clothing and first aid
- Make sure all your employees are given adequate instruction and training so that they are competent and not a hazard to themselves or others.
- If you have 10 or more employees you must keep an accident book to record accidents at work (see Fig. 7.2). If you have a 'factory', you have to keep an accident book regardless of the number of employees. Also, for all businesses, certain types of accidents must be notified to the authority which regulates your business.

You, as an employer, can in turn expect your employees:

- to take reasonable care of their own health and safety at work and of other persons who may be affected by their acts or omissions
- to co-operate with their employer in ensuring that the requirements imposed by the relevant statutory provisions are complied with.

Date and method of reporting (e.g. personal report, memo, letter, etc.): ....

Date, time and place of event: ....
....
....

Personal details of those involved: ....
....
....
....

Brief description of the nature of the event or disease: ....
....
....
....

Fig. 7.2 Accident book.

Special trades

Restaurants and all places serving food, hotels, pubs, off-licences, employment agencies, nursing agencies, pet shops and kennels, minicabs, taxis, betting shops, auction sale rooms, cinemas and hairdressers are among the special trades that have separate additional regulations concerning their premises and/or need a special license to trade. Your local authority Planning Department will be able to advise you on the regulations that apply specifically to your trade. It would be as well to confirm the position whatever you plan to do. They can also tell you if any local by-laws are in force that could affect you.

Opening hours

Sunday trading and opening hours may be the subject of local restrictions. Once again, your local authority Planning Department will be able to advise you whether or not special local rules apply.

Advertising signs

There are some restrictions on the size and form that the name or advertising hoarding on your premises can take. A look around the neighbourhood will give you an idea what is acceptable. If in doubt, or if you are going to spend a lot of money on signage, take advice.

Sources of help and advice

The Building Centre
26 Store Street
London
WC1E 7BT
Tel: 020 7692 4000
Fax: 020 7580 9641
Email: manu@buildingcentre.co.uk
Website: www.buildingcentre.co.uk

Health and Safety Executive
HSE Information Services

Caerphilly Business Park
Caerphilly
CF83 3GG
Tel: 0870 154 5500
Fax: 02920 859260
Website: www.hse.gov.uk

The HSE runs InfoLine, which is a public enquiry service that provides information about Health and Safety at Work.

HSE Books
PO Box 1999
Sudbury
CO10 2WA
Tel: 01787 881165
Fax: 01787 313995
Website: www.hsebooks.co.uk

Book service covering all aspects of health and safety.

Licensing

Business activities which may require a licence should contact these organizations:

- For: cinemas, theatres, child minding, taxi and private hire vehicles, indoor sports venues, public entertainment (in any venue), nightclubs, pet shops, pet boarding kennels, scrap metal dealing, sex shops, nurses' agencies and street trading – apply to: Local Authority Licensing Department.
- For: residential care homes – apply to: Local Authority Registration and Inspection Unit.
- For: nursing homes – apply to: Local Health Authority.
- For: waste management, abstraction of water or discharge of effluent, scrap metal processing – apply to: Environment Agency (tel: 0845 9333111 (England); 0292 0770088 (Wales); website: www.environment-agency.gov.uk/) or Scottish Environment Protection Agency (tel: 01786 457700).
- For: hotels (including guesthouses), restaurants, abattoirs, hairdressers, mobile shops

(food sales) and other premises selling food, massage, skin piercing (including tattooing, acupuncture and cosmetic piercing), work with asbestos – apply to: Local Authority Environmental Health Department.
* For: goods or public service vehicle operators – apply to: Department of Transport and the Regions (tel: 0131 529 8500 (Scotland); 0113 283 3533 (North England); 0121 608 1000 (West Midlands); 0117 975 5000 (West Country); 01323 451400 (South East and London); website: www.detr.gov.uk/).
* For: possession or sale of weapons – apply to: police.
* For: sale of alcohol in shops, public houses, clubs, nightclubs, restaurants, hotels, (betting shops, and other gaming establishments) – apply to: magistrate; in Scotland apply to Local Authority Licensing Board.
* If your business involves: lending money, offering or arranging credit, debt collecting, issuing credit cards, offering debt adjusting or debt counselling services, operating a credit reference agency, hiring, leasing or renting out goods you may need a credit licence – apply to: Office of Fair Trading, Consumer Credit Licensing Bureau, Craven House, 40 Uxbridge Road, Ealing, London W5 2BS (tel: 020 7211 8608; website: www.oft.gov.uk/).

Trading laws

There are a raft of laws that govern trading for businesses in the UK and a mix of national and local organizations responsible for enforcing them. The main laws that are likely to impact on a new business are the following.

Agriculture Act 1970
* Provides for controls of fertilizers and animal feeding stuffs.
* Statutory labelling of fertilizers and animal feeding stuffs.
* Prevents excess deleterious materials in animal feeding stuffs.

Agricultural Produce (Grading and Marking) Acts 1928 and 1931
* Provides for the grading and marking of agricultural produce.

Animal Health Act 1981
* Provides for the control of animal diseases.
* Provides for the welfare of animals on the farm, in transit and at market.
* Deals with animal diseases that can be caught by humans.

Protection Of Children (Tobacco) Act 1986 and the Children and Young Persons (Protection From Tobacco) Act 1991
* Prohibits the sale of tobacco to children.
* Controls the siting of cigarette vending machines.

Clean Air Act 1993
* Controls the lead content of petrol and the sulphur content of diesel fuel in order to reduce atmospheric pollution.

Consumer Credit Act 1974
* Provides for control of consumer credit and hire.
* Requires licensing of credit and hire traders.
* Controls credit and hire advertising.
* Controls credit and hire documentation.
* Controls format used to indicate credit charges.
* Provides powers to revoke licences of traders offering credit or hire facilities.
* Controls debt-collecting and credit reference agencies.

Consumer Protection Act 1987
* Provides for liability for damage caused by defective products.
* Prohibits the supply of goods not in accordance with the general safety requirement.
* Provides for the protection and safety of consumers by enabling Regulations/Orders to be made controlling consumer goods.

- Provides for approved safety standards to enable compliance with general safety requirements.
- Prohibits the supply of unsafe goods.
- Provides powers for seizing and forfeiture of unsafe goods.
- Provides powers to suspend the sale of suspected unsafe goods.
- Requires persons to publish notices warning consumers of unsafe goods previously supplied.
- Prohibits misleading price indications.

Control of Pollution Act 1974
- Controls the sale of anti-fouling paints and treatments.

Development of Tourism Act 1969
- Requires price of accommodation to be displayed by hotels.

Education Reform Act 1988
- Restricts the ability to award degrees to bodies authorized by Royal Charter, Act of Parliament or in other cases designated by the Secretary of State.
- Restricts the use of terms 'Bachelor', 'Master' or 'Doctor'.

Energy Act 1976
- Requires the publication of data relating to passenger car fuel consumption.

Energy Conservation Act 1981
- Permits Regulations requiring the labelling of certain domestic appliances as to their fuel consumption (none in force).

Estate Agents Act 1979
- Governs accounts in respect of clients' money.
- Controls certain activities in connection with the disposal and acquisition of interests in land by estate agents.
- Provides powers to ban 'unfit' persons from estate agency.

European Communities Act 1972
- Implements community obligations.
- Prohibits supply of goods not of prescribed standard or composition.
- Imposes safety restrictions on certain goods.

Explosives Acts 1875 and 1923 and the Explosives (Age of Purchase) Act 1976
- Control registration of explosives stores and sellers of fireworks.
- Prevents sales of fireworks to under-age children.

Fair Trading Act 1973
- Promotes fair trading.
- Provides controls on persistent offenders who contravene trading laws.

Food Safety Act 1990
- Prohibits sale of unfit food.
- Controls the quality and standards of food.
- Controls description, advertising and labelling of food, controls claims made for food.
- Prohibits adulteration of food.

Food and Environment Protection Act 1985
- Protects the public from food rendered unsafe as a result of the escape of harmful substances such as radioactive fall-out.
- Protects the public from the misuse of pesticides.

Hallmarking Act 1973
- Provides protection for purchasers of precious metals in relation to composition, assaying, marking and description.
- Provides for recognition of international markings on gold, silver and platinum.

Health and Safety At Work Act 1974
- Controls the classification, packaging, labelling, carriage and storage of dangerous substances.

Medicines Act 1968

- Provides controls for medicinal products on production, composition, labelling, advertising and controls the incorporation of medicinal products in animal feeding stuffs.

Merchant Shipping Act 1979

- Controls the loading of ships with cargo. Trading Standards has responsibilities with respect to weighbridges (including attendants) used to check loads (i.e. the weight of heavy goods vehicles).

Motor Cycle Noise Act 1987

- Regulates the sale of exhaust systems for motorcycles.

Nurses Agencies Act 1957

- Controls the licensing of agencies providing nurses in the home.

Olympic Symbol etc (Protection) Act 1995

- Prevents unauthorized use of the Olympic Games symbols and similar labels.

Petroleum (Consolidation) Act 1928 and the Petroleum (Transfer Of Licences) Act 1936

- Require businesses storing petroleum spirit to hold a licence and to comply with stringent safety rules.

Poisons Act 1972

- Controls the sale of poisons.
- Provides for registration of the sellers of poisons.

Prices Acts 1974 and 1975

- Provides power to regulate the price display of certain goods, for example in restaurants, pubs, cafes and petrol stations. The act is intended to promote fair trading. and to control the manner in which prices and sale prices of goods may be indicated.

Property Misdescriptions Act 1991

- Prescribes various illegal practices associated with buying and selling of property.

Timeshare Act 1992

- Regulates the conduct of the sale of timeshare properties.

Trade Descriptions Act 1968

- Prohibits misdescription of goods.
- Prohibits false claims for services, accommodation and facilities.

Trade Marks Act 1994

- Creates an offence for the fraudulent application or use of a trade mark.

Trading Representations (Disabled Persons) Acts 1958 and 1972

- Controls representations made by traders in respect of the employment or assistance of blind or disabled persons in the production, packing or sale of goods.

Video Recordings Acts 1984 and 1993

- Requires classification and labelling of videos.

Weights and Measures Act 1985

- Controls weighing and measuring equipment used for trade.
- Protects against deficient quantity in sale of goods.
- Allows provision of metrological technology service to trade and industry.
- Provides guidance and control on packers' quantity control systems.
- Helps to promote the free flow of goods within the EEC.

Other criminal legislation

Local authorities generally have no statutory duty to enforce the following legislation, but can authorize their Trading Standards service to do so.

Accommodation Agencies Act 1963

- Controls the taking of money for providing services in connection with the letting of property.

Administration of Justice Act 1970

- Creates offence for harassment of debtors or alleged debtors.

Business Names Act 1986

- Requires a business carried on under a name other than that of its owner must display particulars of ownership on premises and stationery.

Cancer Act 1939

- Prohibits claims that there is a cure for cancer.

Companies Act 1985

- Requires limited companies to state their trading details on business premises and in documents.

Copyright, Designs and Patents Act 1988 as amended by the Broadcasting Act 1990

- Establishes legal protection for designs.
- Creates criminal offence to combat counterfeiting.
- Controls making, importing or distributing infringing copies of copyright material.

Dogs Act 1906 as amended by the Dogs (Amendment) Act 1928

- Deals with unburied animal carcasses.

Farm and Garden Chemicals Act 1967

- Controls labelling and marking of products.
- Prohibits transactions in unlabelled products.

Forgery and Counterfeiting Act 1981

- Prohibits forgery and counterfeiting of documents.

Insurance Brokers (Registration) Act 1977

- Requires brokers to be registered.

Intoxicating Substances (Supply) Act 1985

- Prevents sale of intoxicating substances, and equipment to aid misuse of such substances, to children.

Knives Act 1997

- Prevents the marketing of dangerous knives, and prohibits their sale to minors.

Malicious Communications Act 1988

- Makes provision for the punishment of persons who send or deliver letters or other articles with the purpose of causing distress or anxiety.

Mock Auctions Act 1961

- Prohibits certain practices in relation to sales purporting to be sales by auction.

Motor Vehicles (Safety Equipment for Children) Act 1991

- Amends the Road Traffic Act 1988 to provide regulation making powers for the shape, construction or other quality of restraining devices used for children.

Protection Against Cruel Tethering Act 1988

- Prohibits animals from being tethered in certain circumstances.

Protection of Animals Act 1911 as amended by the Protection of Animals (Amendment) Act 1954 and the Agriculture (Miscellaneous Provisions) Act 1968

- Deals with the cruelty aspect of animal welfare.
- Gives courts powers to ban persons from keeping animals.

Road Traffic Acts 1988 and 1991

Road Traffic Act (Consequential Provisions) Act 1988 and the Road Traffic Offenders Act 1988 and the Road Traffic (Foreign Vehicles) Act 1972

- Prohibits the overloading of goods vehicles.

- Prohibits sale of unroadworthy vehicles.
- Imposes minimum safety requirements of certain vehicles.

Solicitors Act 1974
- Controls unlicensed conveyancing.

Telecommunications Act 1984
- Controls advertising, marketing and labelling of telephones and associated equipment.

Theft Acts 1968 and 1978
- Prohibits obtaining property or obtaining a pecuniary advantage by deception or false accounting.

Trading Stamps Act 1964
- Regulates the issue, use and redemption of trading stamps.

Unsolicited Goods and Services Acts 1971 and 1975
- Controls the supply of unsolicited goods.
- Provides penalties for demanding payment for unsolicited goods.
- Controls trade directory entries.

Civil legislation

Local authorities have no responsibility for the following Acts. However, they provide the basis for contract law, which is applicable to consumers and businesses alike, and are fundamental to the conduct of trading activities.

Consumer Arbitration Agreements Act 1988
- Prevents compulsory arbitration clauses in consumer contracts.

Misrepresentation Act 1967
- Gives consumers civil redress for misrepresentations of goods.

Unfair Contracts Terms Act 1977
- Makes void unfair contract terms.

Torts (Interference With Goods) Act 1977
- Allows holders of other people's goods to sell them if certain conditions are complied with.

Sale Of Goods Act 1979 as amended by the Sale Of Goods (Amendment) Act 1994, Sale and Supply of Goods Act 1994 and the Sale of Goods Act 1995
- Details the rights of purchasers and the duties of sellers in the sale of goods. In summary the act states that the seller has three obligations. First, the goods must be of merchantable quality – that is, they must be reasonably fit for their normal purpose. Second, those goods must be fit for any particular purpose that the seller claims for them. This makes sellers responsible for any advice given as to the suitability of a particular product. Third, the goods sold must be as described. This includes such matters as, for example, colour and size.

Limitation Act 1980
- Prevents action being taken by parties to a contract after six years.

Supply of Goods and Services Act 1982
- For contracts other than for the sale of goods, details the rights of purchasers and the duties of sellers (see Sale of Goods Act).

Cheques Act 1992
- Enables consumers to protect payment by cheque.

Contract law

All business life is affected by contracts. Almost everything done in business, whether it be for the supply of raw materials, the sale of goods and services or the hire of a fax machine, is executed under contract law. This is true whether the contract is in writing or whether it is verbal – or even merely implied. Only contracts for the sale of land, hire purchase and some insurance contracts have to be in writing to be enforceable.

To make life even more complicated, a contract can be part written and part oral. So statements made at the time of signing a written contract can legally form part of that contract. For a contract to exist three events must take place:

- there must be an offer
- there must be an acceptance
- there must be a consideration – some form of payment.

By Internet or mail order the contract starts when the supplier 'posts' an acceptance letter, a confirmation or the goods themselves – whichever comes first.

Under the Distance Selling Regulations brought into effect in October 2001, customers have seven working days after they have received the goods to change their minds and return them. They do not need a reason and can get a full refund. Consumers must also be given:

- information about the company they are dealing with
- written confirmation of the order – by fax, letter or email
- a full refund if their goods do not arrive by the date agreed in the original order; if no date was agreed, they must be delivered within 30 days
- information about cancellation rights
- protection against credit card fraud.

A study by the Office of Fair Trading in collaboration with the trading standards service around the country examining 637 UK business websites found that they fell short in providing any accessible information on both refund and exchange policies.

Standard terms and conditions

Certain standards have to be met by law for the supply of goods and services. Over and above these you will need your own terms and conditions if you are not to enter into 'contracts' you did not intend. You will need help to devise these

terms. The following four basic propositions will govern your conditions.

- The conditions must be brought to the other party's attention before he makes the contract.
- The last terms and conditions specified before acceptance of an offer apply.
- If there is any ambiguity or uncertainty in the contract terms they will be interpreted against the person who inserted them.
- The terms may be interpreted as unreasonably unenforceable being in breach of various Acts of Parliament.

Checklist for standard terms and conditions

General

- Do they exclude any variation unless this is written and signed by a director of the company or the proprietor of the business or a partner?
- Quotations: How long are these open for? 30 days, 60 days, etc? Do different prices apply to exports?

Price

- Can the seller increase the price? If so, under what conditions?
- Is the price ex works exclusive of VAT? Does it include carriage, insurance or freight?

Terms of payment

- What time is given to pay?
- Is there a prompt payment discount?.
- If it is an export contract, in what currency is payment made?.
- Interest is now due on unpaid invoices over a certain date? If so, at what rate and from when is it charged? You also need to be aware of the Late Payment of Commercial Debts (Interest) Act, which took effect from 1 November 1998. Since then, small businesses (up to 50 employees) have been able to charge interest on any late paid commercial debts due from

larger businesses and the public sector. From 1 November 2000, small businesses have also been able to charge interest to other small businesses. The third phase of the legislation is due to be introduced in November 2002, and will give the right to statutory interest to all firms.

Delivery
- Who delivers and to where?
- Are delivery dates estimates only?

Risk and property
- When does the buyer take the risk of damage to or loss of the goods (i.e. when do they need insurance cover from)?
- Does the seller reserve title in the goods until paid for?
- Is the buyer obliged to store the goods separately and mark them as being the property of the seller?

Warranties
- Does the seller seek to limit his obligations as to merchantable quality, fitness for purpose or correspondence with samples under the Sale of Goods Act or the equivalent obligations in respect of services?
- Does the seller seek to limit his liability for any losses arising under the contract so that his liability for negligence, delay, consequential loss, etc. is limited, e.g. to the value of the goods sold?
- Does the seller need a *force majeure* clause, i.e. one which prevents him being liable for any loss caused by his failure to fulfil his obligations under the contract for reasons beyond his control, e.g. fire, bad weather, strikes, destruction of premises?

Arbitration
- In the event of a dispute should this be left to the courts rather than arbitration?
- If arbitration is necessary, who will appoint the arbitrator?

Termination
- How is the contract to be ended if it is more than a one-off agreement?
- What notice should be given?
- What happens if there is a breach of contract by one party and does that automatically give the other the right to terminate?

Governing law
- Does the contract stipulate which legal system is to regulate any disputes? This is very important, as otherwise large sums can be spent just deciding which legal system applies. This is relevant even for trading within the United Kingdom as English and Scottish law differs.

Help and advice with trading laws

Centre for Effective Dispute Resolution
Exchange Tower
1 Harbour Exchange Square
London
E14 9GB
Tel: 020 7356 6000
Fax: 020 7356 6001
Email: info@cedr.co.uk
Website: www.cedr.co.uk

CEDR Solve, CEDR's dispute resolution and prevention service, is a provider of commercial mediation and other assisted dispute resolution processes.

The Chartered Institute of Arbitrators
International Arbitration Centre
12 Bloomsbury Square
London
WC1A 2LP
Tel: 020 7421 7444
Fax: 020 7404 4023
Email: info@arbitrators.org
Website: www.arbitrators.org

The Chartered Institute of Arbitrators maintain a Register of Arbitrators, a panel of Chartered Arbitrators and a Register of Expert Witnesses, as well as advising on the process of arbitration.

Office of Fair Trading

Fleetbank House
2–6 Salisbury Square
London
EC4Y 8JX
Tel: 020 7211 8000
Fax: 020 7211 8800
Email: enquiries@oft.gov.uk
Website: www.oft.gov.uk

The OFT's job is to make markets work well for consumers. Markets work well when businesses are in open, fair and vigorous competition with each other for the consumer's custom. As an independent organization, the OFT have three main operational areas which make up three divisions – Competition Enforcement, Consumer Regulation Enforcement, and Markets and Policies Initiatives.

Their Consumer Regulation Enforcement department:

* ensures that consumer legislation and regulations are properly enforced
* takes action against unfair traders
* encourages codes of practice and standards
* offers a range information to help consumers understand their rights and make good choices
* liaises closely with other regulatory bodies that also have enforcement powers.

The Trading Standards Institute

4–5 Hadleigh Business Centre
351 London Road
Hadleigh
SS7 2BT
Tel: 0870 872 9000
Fax: 0870 872 9025
Email: institute@tsi.org.uk
Website: www.tradingstandards.gov.uk/itsa/index.htm

The Trading Standards Institute keep details of all relevant regulations on their website. They have an Award, gained by completing a short course of study, through which an individual may achieve the standard laid down by the Institute of Trading Standards Administration. The Award is gained by the candidate sitting an examination at a licensed centre, after having undertaken a training course made up of at least 25 hours of tuition.

Trading Standards Service

This is operated at the county level throughout the country to ensure trading laws are met. You can usually get contact details by contacting your council by phone or via their website. Alternatively, see www.tradingstandards.gov.uk/.

Employment law

Job descriptions

Employees have to be given a written statement of a defined list of terms and conditions of their employment within two months of starting working for you.

You should also keep written records on all employment matters, which will be invaluable in the case of dispute.

The list of terms which go into a job description will include the following.

* The names of the employer and the employee.
* The date the employee's employment began.
* The date the employee's period of continuous employment began.
* The scale or rate of remuneration or the method of calculating it.
* The intervals at which remuneration is paid.
* Any terms and conditions relating to hours of work (including normal working hours).
* Any terms and conditions relating to holidays, including public holidays, and holiday pay (sufficient to enable the employee's entitlement, including entitlement to accrued holiday pay

on termination of employment, to be precisely calculated).

- The employee's job title or a brief description of his or her work.
- The employee's place of work or, where the employee is required or permitted to work at various places, an indication of that fact and of the address of the employer.
- Where the employment is not intended to be permanent, the period for which it is expected to continue.
- Where the employment is for a fixed term, the date when it is to end.
- Any collective agreements which directly affect the terms and conditions of the employment including, where the employer is not a party, the persons by whom they were made.
- The person (specified by description or otherwise) to whom the employee can apply if dissatisfied with any disciplinary decision, and the manner in which the application should be made.
- The person (specified by description or otherwise) to whom the employee can apply for the purpose of seeking redress of any grievance relating to his or her employment, and the manner in which the application should be made.
- Any terms and conditions relating to incapacity for work due to sickness or injury, including any provision for sick pay.
- Any terms and conditions relating to pensions and pension schemes.
- Any disciplinary rules applicable to the employee.
- Requirements to work away from the employee's home country, including details of pay, any additional benefits, the duration of any overseas work and the terms and conditions of their return.
- The period of notice required, which increases with length of service. A legal minimum of one week's notice per year of service is required, up to a maximum of 12 weeks. This may be overridden by express terms in the contract.

The contractual situation

The job description forms the cornerstone of the contract of employment that exists between employer and employee. However 'the contract' is rarely a single document and may not even be completely documented. A contract comes into existence as soon as someone accepts an offer of paid employment, even if both offer and acceptance are only oral. In practice, the most important contractual document may be the letter offering a person the job together with the salary and other basic employment conditions.

The contract consists of four types of conditions.

- Express terms, which are those specifically agreed between employer and employee, whether in writing or not.
- Implied terms, which are considered to be so obvious that they don't need spelling out. These include such matters as the employee complying with reasonable instructions and taking care of business property and equipment. For the employer these can include taking reasonable care of the employee and paying them for work done.
- Incorporated terms are those terms imported into individual contracts from outside sources, most commonly from trade union agreements.
- Statutory terms include any work requirements laid down by law. These, for example, would cover safety regulations.

Working Time Directive

Whilst the owner of a business may be content to work all hours, since 1999 the law has strictly governed the amount of time employees can be asked to put in. The Working Time Regulations, as these are known, are summarized in the following 10 points.

1 The regulations apply to any staff over the minimum school leaving age. This includes

temporary workers, home workers and people working for you overseas. The regulations do not cover the self-employed.

2 One of the most important parts of the rules is that staff cannot be forced to work more than 48 hours a week. However, an employee may work over those hours if he or she agrees to it by signing an opt-out agreement. A worker can also cancel an opt-out, but must give the employer at least seven days' notice or longer (up to three months) if this has been agreed.

3 You cannot force an employee to sign an opt-out agreement from any aspect of the regulations. But if a staff member is known to have a second job, the employer should agree an opt-out if the total time worked is over 48 hours.

4 Working time includes travelling when it is part of the job, working lunches and job-related training. It does not include travel between home and work, lunch breaks or off-site training such as evening classes.

5 For night workers, there is a limit of an average of eight hours' work in 24. They are also entitled to receive a free health assessment.

6 All workers are entitled to 11 hours' rest a day, a day off each week, and an in-work rest break of at least 20 minutes if the working day is longer than six hours.

7 If you miss some rest, 'compensatory rest' is another period of rest that lasts the same time as the part of the period of rest missed. Workers should be able to take this rest reasonably soon after the time missed – normally within a couple of weeks for daily rest, and within a couple of months for weekly rest.

8 Full-time staff are also entitled to four weeks' paid holiday a year after a 13-week qualification period. However, they do not have the right to choose when to take leave. It must be agreed with the employer.

9 However, workers have no statutory right to bank holidays. If they take a bank holiday, it can count as one day of annual leave under the regulations.

10 As an employer, you must keep records that show you comply with the working time limits and that you have given night workers the opportunity for a health assessment. You do not need to record every hour worked.

As a guide, government inspectors may ask to see the following records for a particular worker:

- any relevant agreements
- pay records or time-recording systems, if you have these systems and
- if your worker does standard contract hours, contract details and the results of any monitoring to check these hours are kept.

Regulations do not require records to be kept for workers who have opted out of the working time limit. Having a simple list of those who have opted out is sufficient.

You do not have to record rest breaks, rest periods or annual leave, for the purposes of this regulation at any rate, though you would need to record details of annual leave elsewhere.

Unfair dismissal

Dealing with any disciplinary matter, particularly in circumstances that may lead to dismissal, have to be carefully managed. In most circumstances you have a year to assess employees, during which time you can dismiss them without fear of legal retribution. You can't, of course, dismiss anyone at any stage for an unfair reason such as sex, race, pregnancy or trade union activity. Nor can you dismiss someone who would qualify for paid suspension on medical grounds after they have been employed for one month, without risking a case of unfair dismissal.

Taking dismissal, the most serious area of discipline, first, there are five reasons that may mean a dismissal is fair.

- If an employee is incapable of doing the job either through lack of skill or competence, through ill health or because they are mentally or physically unable to meet the requirements of the job. Lack of skills or competence is the most common reason for dismissing people in small firms as once the business becomes successfully established the standard of work it expects from employees inevitably rises and some just can't keep up. Some circumstances are set out below.

- If an employee commits a misconduct such as theft, insolence, persistent bad time-keeping, laziness or horseplay, damage to company property, incapability through drink or drugs, or serious negligence causing unacceptable damage, loss or injury.
- If you are cutting down generally on the number of employees, or if your need for a particular skill ceases or diminishes, you may be able to make an employee redundant. In these circumstances you will have to give them between one and twelve weeks' notice, depending on their length of service, and redundancy pay of between one and one-and-a-half weeks' pay, depending on their age, for each year they have been with you.
- If it would be illegal to continue employing someone, perhaps because their right to work in this country had expired, then you can fairly dismiss them.
- If you have some other substantial reason. For a small firm this is usually where the firm's financial viability is threatened.

You can, of course, discipline staff and even in the circumstances described above dismiss them, but you need a procedure to make sure you comply with the law.

Maternity and paternity rights

Maternity rights

All pregnant employees have rights in four main areas. These include the right to reasonable time off to have antenatal care; the right not to be unfairly dismissed; the right to maternity leave; and the right to return to work. There are many conditions and exceptions, so you need to examine each case carefully to see how to proceed.

- Reasonable paid time off work must be provided so a pregnant employee can have antenatal care. Clearly the guiding word here is 'reasonable' and you may well have to rely on the employee's medical advice.
- Do not dismiss an employee because she is pregnant. A woman will automatically be held to be unfairly dismissed if any part of the reason for her dismissal is that she is pregnant. You can, however, dismiss a women fairly because of pregnancy if:
  - her condition makes it impossible for her to do her job properly
  - it would be illegal for her to do that particular job while pregnant.

If either of these conditions applies then you must offer your employee suitable alternative employment. In any event your employee is entitled to Statutory Maternity Pay (SMP) and the right to return to work, provided she otherwise qualifies.

- You must give your employee SMP if they qualify – and almost all pregnant employees now qualify. The amount of SMP is 90% of average earnings for six weeks, followed by a further 12 weeks at a rate set by the government. Women who have worked for their employer for more than a year are able to take a further 22 weeks' leave. Generally only 92% of SMP is reimbursed to employers; however, most firms with very few employees will come within 'small employers' relief', and so recover the full amount. Many employers are more generous in respect of the amount of maternity pay they give and this certainly seems to pay dividends if you want them to come back to work for you.
- You must give your employee the right to return to work, unless you have five or fewer employees at the time your employee's maternity absence began and it is not reasonably practical to take her back in her old job or to offer her another suitable vacancy. The law here is under review,

so do, as with the rest of this section, check up on the current legislation.

Otherwise, your employee has the right to return to work if she has worked for you continuously for one year at the beginning of the eleventh week before the baby is due.

Your employee may lose the right to return to work if:

- her job no longer exists because of redundancy and there is no suitable alternative job – in which case the normal redundancy conditions, including redundancy pay, may apply
- it is not practicable for her to return to her old job and you have offered suitable alternative work which she refuses
- your employee fails to meet some rules about giving you written notification of her condition and plans.

Paternity rights

Parental leave is time off to care for a child. It applies to men and women who have been employed by their employer for more than one year and have responsibility for a child as a biological, foster, adoptive or step-parent.

To qualify, the employee's child must have been born, adopted or placed for adoption on or after 15 December 1999.

The minimum period of parental leave that can be taken in one go is one week (unless the child is entitled to disability living allowance) and the maximum is four weeks. Employees are protected against unfair dismissal and detrimental treatment for taking parental leave.

Entitlement

An employee is entitled to 13 weeks' unpaid leave for each child, which must be taken before the child's:

- fifth birthday
- eighteenth birthday, if the child is entitled to a disability living allowance

- eighteenth birthday or, if placed on adoption, before the fifth anniversary of the placement commencing (whichever is earlier).

Employees must apply for leave at least 21 days before the:

- day it is to begin
- beginning of the expected week of childbirth where a father wants leave to begin when a child is born
- beginning of the week of a child's placement for adoption or, if not, as soon as is reasonably practicable when the child is to be placed.

Employers may require documentary evidence to support an application and may postpone parental leave for up to six months if it would disrupt the business. If so, the employer must give the employee written notice within seven days of receiving the request, stating reasons and the revised leave dates.

An employer cannot, however, postpone parental leave without the employee's agreement where the employee is the father and wants it to begin when his child is born, or if the child is to be placed with the employee for adoption and the leave is to begin on the day of placement.

Emergency leave

Employees have the right to reasonable unpaid leave where their 'dependants' are affected by:

- illness, injury, assault or childbirth
- breakdown in childcare/other care arrangements
- the consequences of a death
- where a child is in a serious incident at school or during school hours.

Dependants are: spouses, children, parents and other people living in an employee's house (except lodgers), and others who might rely on an employee in emergencies, such as elderly neighbours.

To take this leave, your employee should give notice as soon as reasonably practicable giving the reason for, and likely duration of, absence. 'Reasonable' time off is not defined but, usually, one or two days will suffice.

Discriminating at work

By and large, business owners can employ whoever they want to employ. However, when setting the criteria for a particular job or promotion it is usually illegal to discriminate on the grounds of sex, race, marital status or union membership. If you employ more than 15 people, then disabled employees have the right not to be discriminated against either in the recruitment process or when they are employed.

Whether you can impose age limits on job applicants or on your employees is debatable. You may find that by imposing an age limit you are indirectly discriminating against women, for example, who have had time off work to have children.

New regulations designed to prevent part-time employees from being treated less favourably than comparable full-time employees – that is, someone doing broadly similar work and with a similar level of skills and qualifications – are coming into force in the UK. Business owners will have to ensure part-time employees receive equal sick pay and maternity pay (on a pro rata basis), equal hourly rates of pay and equal access to pension schemes. Employers will also be obliged to ensure that part-time employees have equal access to training opportunities and that part-time employees are not treated less favourably than full-timers in a redundancy situation.

Discrimination against any of these groups starts right from when vacancies are advertised, where you cannot include such phrases as 'no women' or 'no men', or 'no blacks' or 'no whites'. It extends to the pay, training and promotion of those who work for you, where it is unfair to discriminate against any of these groups. It is also illegal to victimize by treating unfairly someone who has complained about being discriminated against. Sexual harassment is also a form of discrimination. That is defined as 'unwanted conduct of a sexual nature or other conduct based on sex affecting the dignity of men and women at work'. This can include unwelcome physical, verbal or non-verbal conduct. Finally, it is unfair to include in your reason for dismissing an employee that they are a member of one of these groups.

To avoid discriminating in your employment you need to ensure that all your policies and procedures meet the following criteria.

- They are applied equally to all who work for you irrespective of sex, race and so forth.
- They don't limit the proportion of one such group who comply compared with the other.
- They don't disadvantage an individual.
- They can be objectively justified. For example, there is no case to argue when being a man or woman is a genuine occupational qualification – for example, for the purpose of a particular photographic modelling assignment or an acting role. The same would be true when you have a part-time vacancy and so have no need of a full-time employee.

To make sure you are not discriminating at work, follow this six-point checklist.

- Ensure your business has an equal opportunities policy.
- Train staff in equal opportunities.
- Keep records of interviews showing why candidates were rejected.
- Ensure complaints are taken seriously, fully investigated and addressed if needed.
- Conduct staff surveys to help determine where discrimination may exist within your business.
- Examine the payroll – pay should reflect an employee's job title, not their gender.

Paying wages

Generally you can decide how much and how often you pay your employees. It will be a matter of negotiation between the parties and should be incorporated in the contract of employment. You can also negotiate on the amount and structure of any bonuses, commission and on overtime rates, holiday pay and sick pay.

As an employer you are also responsible for making certain deductions from employees' pay as laid down by law, or if you have the written agreement of your employee.

The main issues to consider when it comes to pay are as follows.

- **Minimum wage:** Since April 1999 a statutory minimum wage has been introduced in the UK. Minimum wage legislation also operates throughout Europe and in other developed economies including in the United States. The amount of the minimum wage varies from country to country and in the US from state to state. The amount is also governed by the age of the employee and whether an employee is undergoing training. The hourly rate also changes over time, so you need to keep abreast of the latest rates.
- **Holiday pay:** All employees in the UK have been entitled to at least three weeks' paid holiday since October 1998. This is kept under review and you need to check to see what current holiday entitlement is. There is no statutory entitlement to bank holidays, so, depending on the contract of employment, taking a bank holiday counts as a day off an employee's holiday entitlement. To be eligible, an employee must have been employed for at least 13 weeks. Part-time workers have the same holiday entitlement on a pro-rata basis. For example, if they work a three day week, then their paid holiday week is three days long.
- **Sick pay:** You can agree sick pay as part of a contract of employment. If you don't, then your only obligation is to give Statutory Sick Pay (SSP). Employees qualify for SSP if they are aged 16 or over, under 65 and are sick for at least four days in a row, including over weekends and public holidays. For absences of four to seven days it is usual to ask employees to sign a self-certification form (your own or one

available free from the Social Security offices). For absences of more than seven days it is usual to ask for a medical certificate. In the case of illnesses that last more than eight weeks you can ask for a full medical report and a prognosis.

The weekly rate of SSP is about £60 (this changes from time to time). Employers are able to reclaim the SSP paid out in any month where it comes to more than 13% of the business's total National Insurance contributions. This is to protect employers from the heavy cost they might otherwise face if there were an epidemic.

- Other factors that effect pay include Statutory Maternity Pay (SMP) and Equal Pay, both covered earlier. Equal Pay is a by-product of the legislation against discriminating against people at work.
- **Pension contributions:** The UK government is in the throes of a major review of pension provisions in the UK. The much-heralded stakeholder scheme has been all but abandoned, and at the time of writing several competing schemes are under consideration.

From April 2006, pensions known as a SIPP (Self Invest Pension Plan) will be widely marketed, and whose contributions attract generous tax breaks as the Government pays 22p for every 78p you chip in, or 40p if you are a higher rate taxpayer. This is set to become a popular way for business owners to invest in premises for business purposes whilst getting generous tax breaks.

A higher rate taxpayer putting a property into their SIPP would only have to pay out £60,000 for every £100,000 worth of property. Once inside the SIPP, any capital gain and income from rent is free of UK tax. Your SIPP is allowed to borrow up to half the value of the fund. So if you had £300,000 in the fund, it could borrow £150,000, enough to buy a modest property or warehouse.

That all sounds too good to be true, yet in essence it is. But there are a few issues to consider in deciding if this is right for your pension.

- If you transfer a current property into a SIPP you will be liable for CGT (Capital Gains Tax) on any profits. This could be a hefty bill, as property prices have doubled over the past five years.
- You can't get at any property or cash in a pension fund until you are 50 (55 from 2010). Even then you can only draw out 25% of the fund in tax-free cash and a pension equivalent to 120% of what an annuity would buy you. The pension can only pay out if the fund has cash, say from renting out the property.
- If your business uses any property that you have put into the pension, you will have to pay the market rent to your pension fund.
- Pension contributions, however made, are subject to an annual limit of £215,000 and a lifetime cap of £1.5 million.

These are all uncharted waters; as the rules are still being made, take professional advice from a tax expert and a pension provider.

These organizations can help you find out more about SIPPs and if they are right for you: OPAS, the Pensions Advisory Service, is an independent non-profit organization (Tel: 0845 6012923; www. opas.org) and a good place to start to get some general information. Then look up The Association of Independent Financial Advisors (Tel: 020 7628 1287; www.aifa.net); and check out the UK Tax Directory of UK Tax Professionals (www.tax-ationweb.co.uk/directory). Both have directories putting you in contact with professional advisers.

Union recognition

As an employer you may find that you have employed members of a trade union.

You may even find that some of your current employees want to join a union, or get you to recognize that union as their negotiating body. This latter point is fairly unlikely unless you employ dozens of people and it has to be said that unions are more likely to be active in the public sector and in large scale manufacturing operations. As the typical small business fits neither of these descriptions, this may not be an issue to consider.

However, there are a number of points to keep in mind.

- Everyone has the right to belong or not to belong to a trade union.
- As an employer you cannot discriminate against someone for being or not being a member of a trade union.
- You can't refuse to employ someone because they are a union member.
- You must allow union members to take part in union activities, for example meetings, at the appropriate time, which is normally outside working hours.
- You may need to consider union-negotiated pay rates as a factor in arriving at pay rates in your business, even if you have no union members in the business.
- If sufficient (40%) members of a workforce want to join a union, or are members of that union, they can ask for that union to be recognized. Recognition, in the context of employee relations, gives a union a whole raft of defined legal rights to exercise on behalf of its members, including the right to engage in collective bargaining.

Employing overseas staff

The number of people detected by the Immigration Service working illegally in the UK (and in other advanced industrialized countries) has risen significantly in recent years. The Asylum & Immigration Act (1996) took effect on 27 January 1997 and is intended to ensure that only those legally entitled are offered employment and employers can be held liable. Employers can be fined a maximum penalty for this criminal offence (£5000 for each person being employed illegally).

You can protect yourself by making certain basic checks before taking on new employees and asking to see (and copying) one of the following.

- A document issued by a previous employer, the Inland Revenue, the Benefits Agency, the Contributions Agency or the Employment Service which states the NI number of the person named.
- A passport or national identity card issued by a member state of the EC and which describes the holder as a national of that state.
- A passport describing the holder as having the right of abode in the UK.
- A certificate of registration or naturalization as a British citizen.
- A birth certificate issued in the UK or Republic of Ireland.
- A passport or other travel document endorsed to show that the person named is exempt from immigration control, has indefinite leave to enter or remain in the UK, or current leave, and is not precluded from taking the employment in question, or has no time limit on their stay.
- A letter issued by the Home Office confirming the same.
- A passport or other travel document endorsed to show that the holder has a current right of residence in the UK as a family member of a named national of a member state of the EC and who is resident in the UK.
- A letter issued by the Immigration and Nationality Directorate or the Home Office indicating that the person is a British citizen or has permission to take employment.
- A work permit or other approval issued by the Department for Employment & Education.
- A passport describing the holder as a British Dependent Territories citizen.

You do not need to, and should not, make checks on employees who were working for you before 27 January 1997.

The Human Rights Act

In October 2000 the Human Rights Act came into effect in the UK. As an employer you need to pay particular attention to the following issues.

- **Surveillance:** If you conduct any form of surveillance over your employees, whether it's recording phone conversations, monitoring emails or examining computers, you will need a clear policy and that policy must be made known to your employees. You are only allowed to use surveillance for legitimate reasons. So, for example, you are allowed, even required, to record phone conversations between employees and customers in certain industries (financial services) and you may use video surveillance for security reasons, including protection from staff theft.

  You can also read emails to ensure employees are not sending abusive messages or using the Internet to access pornography.
- **Dress codes:** You will still be able to insist that staff follow your instructions on dress code. However, the onus is on you as the employer to show why that dress code is necessary. It may be that 'anything goes as long as it is clean' gradually becomes the norm in most small firms, except when safety or the attitude of customers is concerned.
- **Disciplinary procedures:** Employees with less than 12 months' continuous service can't bring an action for unfair dismissal. But under this Act they may be able to bring a claim for damages if you haven't followed correct disciplinary procedures.
- **Religion:** The new law outlaws discrimination on the grounds of religion. This means you must take extra care in such areas as giving employees time off to observe religious holidays and allowing them to wear clothes that conform with their religious requirements.

Taking out legal expense insurance

The growing burden of employment legislation facing small firms is forcing more and more businesses to take out legal expense insurance, as the risk of being prosecuted for law-breaking rises. But it is not only the risk that is rising. The consequences are spiralling upwards too. The ceiling for unfair dismissal awards has risen from £12,000 to £50,000, just one example of the burden of new employment laws.

In 2001 there was a 40% rise in payouts for discrimination claims, and employment tribunals awarded £3.53 million for sex, race and disability claims.

The advent of no-win, no-fee legal support is encouraging more individuals to feel confident enough to take on companies both big and small, often in circumstances where their chances of success are not immediately obvious.

The remedy for the small firm without its own human resources department to keep it operating clearly within legal boundaries and a legal department to fend off any legal threats, is to take out legal expense insurance.

Firms that sign up for this type of insurance can not only expect any fines and awards to be paid, but their costs associated with defending themselves against allegations will also be met. In many cases, whether the employer wins or loses, they will pay their own legal costs, which makes insurance cover especially attractive. For the small employer, who often takes on the task of handling disputes with employees themselves, this is a great benefit, not only saving time but lifting the concerns and anxieties that inevitably accompany litigation.

Sources of help and advice on employment law

Advisory, Conciliation and Arbitration Service (ACAS)

Brandon House
180 Borough High Street
London
SE1 1LW
Tel: 020 7396 5100
Website: www.acas.org.uk

Although you may mostly hear of ACAS in big public disputes between management and 'worker', a large part of their work is spent preventing disputes, dispensing information and working with small firms.

British Safety Council

Tel: 020 8741 1231
Fax: 020 8741 4555
Email: info@britsafe.org
Website: www.britishsafetycouncil.org

Membership organization costing £199 + VAT per annum for firms with between 1 and 50 employees. One of the most valuable benefits of being a member of the British Safety Council is free access to the Information Service. You can then use the service every working day of the year to ask occupational health, safety and environmental questions by letter, fax, telephone and email. A team of qualified safety professionals is available to talk to you, address your questions and respond quickly with information. Most information requests are classified as immediate (answered within two hours), urgent (answered the same day) or non-urgent (answered within two days).

Emplaw

Tel: 0870 751–8905
Email: info@emplaw.co.uk
Website: www.emplaw.co.uk

The Emplaw website has a free area covering basic British employment law information and you can find a lawyer in your area who specializes in the aspect of employment law you are concerned with.

Equity Direct

Tel: 0845 600 3444.
Website: www.equalitydirect.org.uk

This service, provided by ACAS, the Commission for Racial Equality, the Small Business Service and others is designed to give business managers easy access to authoritative and joined-up advice on a wide range of equality issues. It's available across England for the cost of a local call from 0800–2000, Monday to Saturday and 1000–1600 on Sunday.

Advisers provide practical, down-to-earth advice on specific questions to help you make decisions which are right for your company. Your conversation will be in complete confidence.

This site provides general guidance on some of the main topics. It will be developed over time in response to your questions and comments. If you cannot find the answer to your question quickly, however straightforward, then call an adviser on the helpline above.

The Work Foundation

Peter Runge House
3 Carlton House Terrace
London
SW1Y 5DG
Tel: 0870 1656800
Fax: 020 7479 1111
Website: www.theworkfoundation.com

Annual associate membership starts from £150 plus VAT and membership costs £450 plus VAT for companies with between 1 and 50 employees, which gives you:

- The Information Service: unlimited access to a library of work-related journals and publications, HR statistics and information, including examples of company policies
- Employment Law Helpline: experienced HR practitioners to help your organization with a realistic view of the law and personnel issues
- *the gist*: a monthly magazine to keep you informed of changes in the world of work
- Membership website: to help keep you up to date, with online access to Managing Best Practice research and summaries
- online factsheets: concise overview of facts, legal pointers, latest state of play and crucial best practice guidance on management issues
- discounts on vetting service for your HR policies to ensure that they are legally correct and meet current thinking on best practice
- a discount on an organizational audit for your organization on joining as a member of The Industrial Society.

Tailored Interactive Guidance on Employment Rights (TIGER)

Website: www.tiger.gov.uk

A government website, TIGER is designed to provide a user-friendly guide through UK employment law.

Insurance

Insurance forms a guarantee against loss. You must weigh up to what extent your business assets are exposed to risk and what effect such events could have on the business if they occurred. Insurance is an overhead, producing no benefit until a calamity occurs. It is therefore a commercial decision as to how much to carry, and it is a temptation to minimize cover. You must carry some cover, either by employment law, or as an obligation imposed by a mortgager. You will have to establish your needs by discussing your business plans with an insurance broker. Make sure you know exactly what insurance you are buying; and, as insurance is a competitive business, get at least three quotations before making up your mind.

Employer's liability

You must carry at least £2 million cover to meet your legal liabilities for death or bodily injury incurred by any employee during the course of business. In practice, this cover is usually unlimited, with the premiums directly related to your wage bill.

Personal accident

Employer's liability only covers those accidents in which the employer is held to be legally responsible. You may feel a moral responsibility to extend that cover to anyone carrying out an especially hazardous task. You may also have to cover your own financial security, particularly if the business depends on your being fit.

Product liability insurance

Obligations are placed on producers or importers of certain types of goods under both the Consumer Protection Act 1987 and the Sale of Goods Act 1979. In addition, the common law rules of negligence also apply. In a partnership, for example, with unlimited liability, it would be quite possible to be personally bankrupted in a law suit concerning product liability. Even if the business was carried out through a limited company, although the directors may escape personal bankruptcy, the company would not. If you believe the risks associated with your product are real, then you need to consider taking out product liability insurance

Director's and officer's liability insurance

Risks insured under this heading include: negligent performance of duties; and breach of the Companies Acts – particularly the Insolvency Act, which can hold directors personally liable to a company's creditors.

Public liability

This protects employers against legal liability for death or injury to a third party on their property. These events can occur through defects in your premises, negligent acts by your employees or from liabilities arising from the product that you market.

Professional liability

Solicitors, accountants and management and computer consultants are obvious examples. Anyone involved in giving professional advice should consider their possible liability arising from wrongful advice and negligence to their client.

Business premises, plant and equipment

These obviously need cover. There are, however, a number of ways of covering them. 'Reinstatement' provides for full replacement cost, while 'indemnity' meets only the current market value of your asset, which means taking depreciation off first. There are other things to consider too. Removal of debris, architect's fee, employees' effects and (potentially the most expensive of all) local authorities sometimes insist that replacement buildings must meet much higher standards than the ones they replace.

Stock

From raw materials through to finished goods, stock is as exposed as your buildings and plant in the event of fire or another hazard. Theft from commercial property runs to hundreds of millions of pounds per annum.

Consequential loss

Meeting the replacement costs of buildings, plant, equipment and stock will not compensate you for the loss of business and profit arising out of a fire or other disaster. Your overheads, employees' wages, etc. may have to continue during the period of interruption. You may incur expenses such as getting subcontracted work done. Insurance for consequential loss is intended to restore your business's finance to the position it was in before the interruption occurred.

Goods in transit

Until your goods reach your customer and he accepts them, they are still at your risk. You may need to protect yourself from loss or damage in transit.

Commercial vehicle policy

Although you may have adequate private-use cover for your present vehicle, this is unlikely to be satisfactory once you start to use the vehicle for business purposes. That and any other vehicles used in the business should be covered by a commercial-use policy.

Fidelity guarantee and other thefts

Once in business you can expect threats from within and without. A fidelity guarantee can be taken to protect you from fraud or dishonesty on the part of key employees. Normal theft cover can be taken to protect your business premises and its contents.

Key man insurance

You may be required by anyone putting money into your business to have key man insurance. This will provide a substantial cash cushion in the event of your death or incapacity. This is particularly important in small and new firms where one person is disproportionately vital in the early stages. Partners may also consider this a prudent protection.

Pensions

You may have to provide your employees with access to a stakeholder pension and in any event you will probably want to consider one for yourself.

Help and advice with insurance

Association of British Insurers (ABI)
51 Gresham Street
London
EC2V 7HQ
Tel: 020 7600 3333
Email: info@abi.org.uk
Website: www.abi.org.uk

Association of Pension Lawyers
4–7 Artillery Lane
London
E1 7LS
Website: www.apl.org.uk

British Insurance Association (BIBA)
14 Bevis Marks
London

EC3A 7NT
Tel: 020 7623 9043
Email: enquiries@biba.org.uk
Website: www.biba.org.uk

Life Assurance Association (LIA)
LIA House
Station Approach
Chorleywood
Rickmansworth
WD3 5PF
Tel: 01923 285333
Email: info@lia.co.uk
Website: www.lia.co.uk

The Pensions Advisory Service (OPAS)
11 Belgrave Road
London
SW1V 1RB
Tel: 020 7233 8080.
Fax: 020 7233 8016
Email: enquiries@opas.org.uk
Website: www.opas.org.uk

The Society of Pension Consultants,
St Bartholomew House
92 Fleet Street
London
EC4Y 1DG
Tel: 020 7353 1688
Fax: 020 7353 9296
Website: www.spc.uk.com

Taxation: sole traders, partnerships, companies, PAYE, VAT, National Insurance

The more successful a small business is, the greater its exposure to tax liabilities. Its exact tax position will depend on the legal nature of the business. A limited company will be subject to corporation tax at a set rate announced each year by the government. If the business is not a limited company, its proprietor is likely to be subject to income tax and subject to tax rates applying to the general public. Simply monitoring pre-tax ratios, which in themselves are satisfactory measures of trading performance only, is not enough. The owner/manager is concerned with the net profit after tax. This, after all, is the money available to help the business to grow, or to meet unforeseen problems.

Managing the tax position is one area where timely professional advice is essential. This is made even more important because tax rules can change every year. Good advice can both help to reduce the overall tax bill and so increase the value of profits to the business.

Sole traders, partnerships and limited companies are treated differently for tax purposes so we will look at each in turn.

Sole traders and partnerships

Partnerships are treated as a collection of sole traders for tax purposes, and each partner's share of that collective liability has to be worked out. Sole traders (self-employed) have all their income from every source brought together and taxed as one entity. In the UK the taxes that need to be calculated are:

1 income tax, on profits
2 Class 4 national insurance, on profits
3 capital gains tax, on the disposal of fixed assets at a profit, or when the business is sold
4 inheritance tax, paid on death or when certain gifts are made.

Neither of the last two taxes are likely to occur on a regular basis, so we will not be dealing with them. When those taxes do come into play the sums involved are likely to be significant and professional advice should be taken from the outset.

Under the self-assessment tax system in the UK the basis of a period of a year of assessment is the accounting year ending within that tax year. So if you made up your accounts to 31 December, the basis period for income tax year 2002/2003 would be 6 April 2002 to 5 April 2003. There are special rules that apply for the first year and the last year of trading that should ensure tax is charged fairly.

If your turnover is low, currently in the UK less than £15,000 per year, you can put in a three line account. Sales, expenses and profit. If it is over whatever the current low figure is, then you have to summarize your accounts to show turnover, gross profit and expenses by main heading.

You will have a personal allowance – that is, the current threshold below which you don't pay tax. That amount is deducted from the profit figure. Then a figure is added for Class 4 national insurance based on taxable profits between a certain band. In the UK that band is currently between about £8000 and £26,000 and the tax rate is 6%. This is paid in addition to the flat rate Class 2 contributions of about £7 per week.

All these rates and amounts are constantly changing, but the broad principles remain.

Company taxation

Companies have a separate legal identity from those who work in them, whether or not they are shareholding directors. Everyone working in the business is taxed as an employee. The company is responsible in the UK, through the PAYE (Pay As You Earn) system for collecting tax and passing it to the tax authorities.

Directors' pay is a business expense, just as with any other wages, and is deducted from the companies revenues in arriving at its taxable profits.

Companies in the UK pay tax in three main ways.

- Tax on the company's profits for the year, as calculated in the tax adjusted profits. This is called corporation tax. As of 2005/6, corporate income tax rates start at 0% on the first £10,000 of taxable income, then quickly move up to a 23.75% rate on taxable income in the range of £10,000 to £50,000 and drop back to a 19% rate on taxable income of more than £50,000 up to £300,000. Between £300,001 and £1.5 million the tax rate is 32.75%, after which it drops back to 30%.
- On the distribution of profit to the shareholders in the dividend payment. This gives the appearance of taxing the same profit twice,

but through a process of *tax credits* this double taxation doesn't generally occur. When a shareholder gets a dividend from a company, it comes with a tax credit attached. This means that any shareholder on the basic rate of tax won't have to pay any further tax. Higher rate tax payers, however, have a further amount of tax to pay.

- If an asset – say, a business property – is sold at a profit, then the company will have made a capital gain. This gain will be taxed along the general lines of corporation tax, with lower rates applying to smaller companies.

Which legal structure is best?

The most important rule is never to let the 'tax tail wag the business dog'. Tax is just one aspect of business life. If you want to keep your businesses finances private then the public filing of accounts required of companies will not be for you. On the other hand, if you feel that you want to protect your private assets from creditors if things go wrong, then being a sole trader or partner is probably not the best route to take.

Company profits and losses are locked into the company, so if you have several lines of business using different trading entities you cannot easily settle losses in one area against profits in another. But as sole traders are treated as one entity for all their sources of income, there is more scope for netting off gains and losses. Here are some points to bear in mind.

- If your profits are likely to be small, say below, £50,000, for some time, then from a purely tax point of view you may pay less tax as a sole trader. This is because as an individual you get a tax-free allowance. Your first few thousand pound of income are not taxable. This amount varies with personal circumstances – married or single for example – and can be changed in the Budget each year.
- If you expect to be making higher rates of profit (above £50,000) and want to reinvest a large portion of those profits back into your business, then you could be better off forming a company. That is because as a companies don't start paying higher rates of tax until their profits are £300,000. Even then, they don't pay tax at 40%. A sole trader would be taxed at the 40% rate by the time their profits had reached about £30,000, taking allowances into account. So a company making £300,000 taxable profits could have £54,000 more to reinvest in financing future growth than would a sole trader in the same line of work.
- Non-salary benefits are more favourably treated for the sole trader. You can generally get tax relief on the business element of costs that are only partly business related, such a running a vehicle. A director of a company will be taxed on the value of the vehicle's list price and will not be allowed travel to and from work as a business expense.

PAYE

Income tax is collected from employees through the PAYE system. The employee's liability to income tax is collected as it is earned instead of by tax assessment at some later date. If the business is run as a limited company then the directors of the company are employees. PAYE must be operated on all salaries and bonuses paid to them, yourself included.

The Inland Revenue now issue booklets in reasonably plain English, explaining how PAYE works. The main documents you need to operate PAYE are as follows.

1 A deduction working sheet (Form P11) for each employee.
2 The PAYE Tables. There are two books of tax tables in general use, which are updated in line with the prevailing tax rates:
   - Table A – Pay Adjustment Tables: show the amount that an employee can earn in any particular week or month before the payment of tax
   - Tables B to D and SR – Taxable Pay Tables:

show the tax due on an employee's taxable pay.

3 Form P45, which is given to an employee when transferring from one employment to another.

4 Form P46, which is used when a new employee does not have a P45 from a previous employment (e.g. a school leaver starting work for the first time).

5 Form P60, which is used so that the employer can certify an employee's pay at the end of the income tax year in April.

6 Form P35 – the year-end declaration and certificate. This is used to summarize all the tax and National Insurance deductions from employees for the tax year.

7 Form P6, the tax codes advice notice issued by the Inspector of Taxes telling you which tax code number to use for each employee.

The tax deduction for each employee is worked out as follows (for week read month, if that is the payment interval).

1 Add this week's gross pay to the previous total of gross pay to date, so as to show the total gross pay to and including this week of the tax year.

2 By checking the tax code number of the employee on Table A, arrive at the figure of tax-free pay for that particular week.

3 Deduct the amount of tax-free pay from the total pay to date, to get the amount of taxable pay.

4 Using Table B, work out the tax due on the total taxable pay for the year to date. Then make the appropriate deduction to allow for the tax due.

5 Deduct the amount of tax already accounted for in previous weeks, from the total tax due, to work out the tax due for the week.

National Insurance

As well as deducting income tax as an employer you must also deduct National Insurance (NI) contributions. There are three rates of contributions for NI purposes:

- **Table A:** the most common rate, used in all cases except those mentioned below
- **Table B:** used for certain married women who can produce to you a certificate for payment at reduced rate
- **Table C:** used for employees who are over pension age.

For Tables A and B there are two amounts to calculate; the employee's contribution and the employer's contribution. For Table C there is no employee's contribution. The amounts of contributions are recorded on the same deduction working sheets used for income tax purposes. In 2003/4, the first £4,628 of annual wages are exempt from NI charges. Up to £30,940 the employer pays 12.8% and the employee pays 11%. Above £30,940 employees pay 1% National Insurance, whilst the employer still keeps paying out at the 12.8% level.

The accounting records you will need

When you pay out wages and salaries to your staff you need to record the net pay in your cash book. This will also record the PAYE and NI paid to the Collector of Taxes.

If you only have one or two employees then the record of the payments in the cash book, together with the other PAYE documentation, will probably do. But if you have any more you should keep a wages book. The deductions working sheet gives you a record of the payments made to each employee throughout the year. You also need a summary of the payments made to all employees on one particular date.

Payslips

The law requires that employees *must* provide their staff with itemized pay statements. These must show:

- gross pay
- net pay
- any deductions (stating the amounts of each item and the reason why the deductions are made).

Value added tax (VAT)

VAT is a tax on consumer spending. It is a European tax system, although most countries have significant variations in VAT rates, starting thresholds and in the schemes themselves. Every business over a certain size has to become, in effect a tax collector. There is no reward for carrying out this task, but there are penalties for making mistakes or for making late VAT returns.

VAT is complicated tax. Essentially, you must register if your taxable turnover, i.e. sales (not profit), exceeds £60,000 in any 12 month period, or looks as though it might reasonably be expected to do so. This rate is reviewed each year in the budget and is frequently changed. (The UK is significantly out of line with many other countries in Europe, where VAT entry rates are much lower). The general rule is that all supplies of goods and services are taxable at the standard rate (17.5%) unless they are specifically stated by the law to be zero-rated or exempt. In deciding whether your turnover exceeds the limit you have to include the zero-rated sales (things like most foods, books and children's clothing), as they are technically taxable; it's just that the rate of tax is 0%. You leave out exempt items. There are three free booklets issued by the Customs & Excise: a simple introductory booklet called 'Should you be registered for VAT?' and two more detailed booklets called 'General Guide' and 'Scope and Coverage'. If in doubt (and the language is not easy to understand), ask your accountant or the local branch of the Customs & Excise; after all, they would rather help you to get it right in the first place than have to sort it out later when you have made a mess of it.

Each quarter you will have to complete a return, which shows your purchases and the VAT you paid on them, and your sales and the VAT you collected on them. The VAT paid and collected are offset against each other and the balance sent to the Customs & Excise. If you have paid more VAT in any quarter than you have collected you will get a refund. For this reason it sometimes pays to register even if you don't have to – if you are selling mostly zero-rated items for example; also, being registered for VAT may make your business look more workmanlike and less amateurish to your potential customers.

VAT records

The simple bookkeeping system discussed in Section 6 may need to be extended to accommodate VAT records. So the analysed cash book, if you are using a simple system, will need some more columns to accommodate, for example, the pre-vat sales, the amount of VAT and the total of those two figures.

Doing the sum

Calculating the VAT element of any transaction can be a confusing sum. These simple rules will help you always get it right. Take the gross amount of any sum – that is, the total including any VAT – and divide it into 117.5 parts (if the VAT rate is 17.5%) or a figure that corresponds to the VAT rate + 100. All this means is that we are saying that the bill we have received is 100% of the net bill with another 17.5% on top.

Then we can take a 117.5th part of the bill and multiply it by 100 to get the pre-VAT total and by 17.5 to arrive at the VAT element of the bill.

Doing the VAT return

This has to be where a computer-based bookkeeping system wins hands down. VAT returns (or sales tax returns in the US) are automatically generated by the accounting package. All you have to do is enter the current VAT rate. If you take web-enabled software updates you may not even have to do this. Basically, the VAT inspectors are interested in five figures. How much VAT you have collected on their behalf on the goods and services you have sold. How much VAT has been collected from you by those who have sold you goods and services. The difference between those two sums is the VAT due to be paid, if positive, and the amount to be reclaimed from the VAT, if negative. For businesses, VAT is a zero sum game – it's the end consumer who picks up the tab.

The final two numbers are a check on the reasonableness of the whole sum. Here you must show the value of your sales and purchases, net of VAT for the period in question. The VAT return has to be signed by the person registered for VAT. It's important to remember that a named person is responsible for VAT, a limited company being treated as a 'person' in this instance. Not only are you acting as an unpaid tax collector, but there are penalties for filing your return late or incorrectly. Your VAT records have to be kept for six years and periodically you can expect a visit from a VAT inspector.

Filing the audited accounts

As a sole trader or partnership, you do not have to get your accounts audited, if you do not want to. You may want to consider doing so, if the cost would not be too steep, as it can help in dealings with your tax inspector. It may also help you if you need confirmation of income from your business – for example, to get a mortgage to buy a house. If your business form is a limited company, you may have to get your accounts audited by an accountant.

If your company has sales of less than £350,000, you will not need to do so. Companies with turnover above that figure have to have audited accounts and they must be filed at Companies House.

Preparing abbreviated accounts

All companies must prepare full accounts for presentation to the company's shareholders, but SMEs can send abbreviated accounts to the Registrar of Companies. Abbreviated accounts contain very little information that could be of use to a competitor. Nothing is given away on turnover or margins, for example, a luxury denied to larger companies. Small companies' accounts (ones with less than £350,000 turnover, balance sheet totals less than £1.4 million and fewer than 50 employees on average, to be precise) delivered to the Registrar must contain:

- an abbreviated balance sheet
- selected notes to the accounts, including accounting policies, share capital, particulars of creditors payable in more than five years and the basis of any foreign currency transactions
- a special auditor's report (unless exempt).

The rules of disclosure are complex and the above only gives a brief outline of the requirements. If you are unsure about the information that you have to provide then you should take professional advice. Where a company files abbreviated accounts it must have a special auditor's report confirming that the exemptions have been satisfied and the directors must make a statement at the foot of the balance sheet saying that they have relied upon the exemptions.

The audit

Most companies will be required to appoint an auditor and have their accounts audited. It is the job of the auditor to report to the members (shareholders) of the company as to whether the accounts have been properly prepared taking notice of the appropriate accounting rules. The auditor must also report as to whether the accounts give a *true and fair* view of the state of the company's affairs. In order to arrive at their conclusion the auditor will carry out an examination of the records on a test basis to ensure that the accounts are not materially incorrect. This does not mean that the auditor will check every detail, but they will look at a representative sample of transactions to get a feel for whether or not the books are being properly kept.

If your bookkeeping records are poorly kept, inaccurate or missing, then expect a hefty bill and a lot of your time being spent in answering questions about long gone and often fairly trivial financial events.

If you have a computerized system, the year-end audit is made much simpler for you and your accountant. In fact, with some accounting software, you can do much of the work for the accountant before he sets foot on your premises. You can, for example, produce reports which all auditors will require, such as the trial balance. Some packages have utilities which enable the auditor to run random checks on the transactions and postings and some have facilities for the pre-production of debtors' confirmation letters. Auditors will normally send those out to debtors to check that the transaction did take place .In this way, the auditor's life is made much simpler and, hopefully, it will take less time to conduct the audit, your personnel will be free to carry on with their work sooner, there will be a smaller fee for you to pay and, if you require it, your accountant can get on with some work that will be of rather more benefit to the business. For example, they could advise on how you could tighten up on credit control or stocktaking or get better and more timely management accounts; all infinitely more valuable to the owner-manager than a set of audited accounts.

Filing your accounts late

If you are trading as a company then your accounts have to be filed with the appropriate government agency. In the UK that is Companies House.

Late filing penalties were introduced in 1992 to encourage directors of limited companies to file their accounts on time because they must provide this statutory information for the public record.

The amount of the penalty depends on how late the accounts reach the Registrar, as shown in Table 7.2.

Unless you are filing your company's first accounts, the time normally allowed for delivering accounts to Companies House is 10 months from the end of the relevant accounting period for private companies. If you are filing your company's first accounts and they cover a period of more than 12 months, they must be delivered to the Registrar

within 22 months of the date of incorporation for private companies.

Sources of help with tax matters

Accountancy bodies are listed in Section 6.

HM Revenue & Customs (HMRC)
Website: www.hmrc.gov.uk

Their Website will direct you either to Inland Revenue and tax matters, or to VAT and other duty matters.

- **Starting Up In Business:** This is a campaign to get people starting their own business to register immediately with HMRC. There is a guide available which aims to help you understand some of the many things you need to think about when you're running a business, especially the main tax and National Insurance issues. They also highlight some other important areas of the law which aren't the Inland Revenue's responsibility – and suggest where to go for further, more detailed information.
- **Business Support Teams:** Local Business Support Teams provide a series of half-day workshops to support new and small employers and businesses. They can also offer you detailed advice on all aspects of payroll, talk you through any problems you may be experiencing and, if you wish, check that your payroll systems process information accurately and reliably.

  Their workshops cover:
  - starting in business
  - taking on your first employee
  - workshops covering specific payroll issues

Table 7.2 Penalties for filing your accounts late.

Length of delay, measured from the date the accounts are due	Private company
3 months or less	£100
3 months and one day to 6 months	£250
6 months and one day to 12 months	£500
More than 12 months	£1,000

- end of year procedures
- businesses in the construction industry.

There is no charge for this service, and advisers will see you at a place that suits you.

Business failure

Many businesses don't enjoy the luxury of a dignified exit. They are forced into failure, usually with unpleasant repercussions. Something can usually be salvaged from the wreckage, but that requires you to know something of the likely events that lie ahead. Fortune favours the prepared mind.

The ways that small, and for that matter not so small, businesses go under can be divided into several categories.

Bankruptcy

Bankruptcy is a way of dealing with your financial affairs if you cannot pay your debts. While it is not a criminal offence to get into debt, becoming a bankrupt has serious implications. You can be made bankrupt if you owe £750 or more and fail to pay it within three weeks of receipt of a statutory demand; or if you fail to satisfy a judgment debt.

Under these circumstances a creditor can apply to the court for an order of bankruptcy, or the debtor can apply himself. If the debtor has paid the bill(s) in question, or the court feels he has made a reasonable offer to his creditors which has been unreasonably refused, then a bankruptcy order will not be made.

As soon as the bankruptcy order is made, the debtor becomes an undischarged bankrupt. With the exception of the tools of the bankrupt's trade, clothing, bedding and household equipment – all of a basic nature – all of the bankrupt's personal and business assets come under the control of the official receiver, who becomes his trustee in bankruptcy.

A bankrupt cannot: act as a director or be involved in the management of a company; be an MP, counsellor or JP; obtain credit of more than £250 without revealing he is an undischarged bankrupt; or engage directly or indirectly in any business other than in the name he was adjudged bankrupt without disclosing his bankruptcy. Any money a bankrupt earns belongs to his trustee in bankruptcy, less anything the trustee feels is necessary to maintain or motivate him. The trustee uses all the bankrupt's assets to pay off first the secured creditors (the bank), then the preferential creditors (PAYE, VAT, National Insurance and wages) and then everyone else.

On the bright side, bankruptcy frees the debtor from financial worry and allows him to make a fresh start. And unless the bankrupt makes a habit of this offence the stigma is short-lived. If the debts are less than £20,000 the bankrupt is automatically discharged after two years. In all other cases a bankrupt will be discharged after three years.

These conditions only apply to people who have not been bankrupted before in the last 15 years. These will have to wait five years or longer for their discharge.

Voluntary arrangements

These were brought into being by the Insolvency Act 1986. Until then it was not possible for a debtor to make a legally binding compromise with all his creditors. Any single creditor could scupper the plans.

Now a debtor can make a proposal to his creditors to pay all or part of the debts over a period of time. The mechanics are simple. The debtor applies to the court for an interim order stating that he intends to make a proposal naming a qualified insolvency practitioner who will be advising him. The position is then frozen, preventing bankruptcy proceedings until the insolvency practitioner reports back to the court.

A creditors' meeting will be called, notifying all creditors, and if the proposal is approved by more than 75% by value of the creditors' meeting, it will be binding on all creditors.

This course of action avoids all the less attractive features of bankruptcy – but it will only work if you have something credible to offer your creditors.

Receivership

This occurs when a borrower (a company) fails to meet its obligations to a mortgagee. The most usual scenario is where a company gives a charge over assets (such as property or equipment) to its bankers. This in turn allows the banker to advance funds to the company.

In these circumstances, if the company fails to meet its obligations to its bankers, for example by not repaying money when due, then the bank can appoint a receiver. The receiver has wide powers to step in and run the business or sell off its assets for the benefit of the person who appointed him. The existing director's authority will be suspended and existing contracts with the company only have to be carried out by the receiver if he believes it worthwhile to do so.

Money generated by the receiver first goes to paying the costs of selling assets (auctioneers' fees), then to paying the receiver's own fees. Only then will the person appointing the receiver get his debt paid. Once that too has been discharged, others further down the pecking order, such as preferential debts (see 'Bankruptcy' above), may get paid.

Winding up and liquidation

Winding up is to limited companies what bankruptcy is to sole traders and partnerships. A limited company is considered to be unable to pay its debts if a creditor leaves a demand for a debt of £750 or more in a certain prescribed form at its registered office and that debt is not paid within 21 days. Once this position is reached an application can be made for the company to be wound up. The company itself can ask to be wound up, as can any creditor, or in some circumstances various government officials can so ask.

Before a winding up order is made the court appoints a provisional liquidator – always called 'the official receiver'. Once the winding up order is made, all court proceedings against the company are stopped, all employees' contracts are terminated and its directors are dismissed.

The liquidator's job is to get in the company's assets and pay off the creditors. The order of payment is the same as under receivership.

Administration

The Insolvency Act 1986 introduced legislation to help companies in serious financial difficulties to trade their way back to financial health. The thinking here is similar to that behind that of voluntary arrangements, although administration usually involves much more substantial sums.

While in administration the company is protected from its creditors while an approved rescue plan is implemented. Administration orders will only be made where the court is satisfied that the company has cash available from either shareholders or lenders to finance the rescue plan. It follows that not many administrations are granted – and not many are successful.

Director's responsibilities

Over 1500 directors are disqualified each year in the UK alone. The reasons for their disqualification range from fraud to the more innocuous wrongful trading, which means carrying on doing business whilst the business is insolvent. This latter area is more difficult for a director to recognize before the event, but you need to be aware of the danger signs and remedies

In practice, a director's general responsibilities are much the same as those for a sole trader or partner, and indeed they can be better. This is because by forming a company you can separate your own assets from the business assets (in theory at any rate, unless personal guarantees have been extracted). But this separation is conditional upon 'responsible business behaviour'. However, a director also has to cope with some technical, more detailed requirements, for example sending in your accounts to Companies House. More onerous than just signing them, a director is expected and required in law to understand the significance of the balance sheet and profit and loss account and the key performance ratios. Some of a director's duties, responsibilities and potential liabilities are as follows.

1 To act in good faith in the interests of the company. This includes carrying out duties diligently and honestly.
2 Not to carry on the business of the company with intent to defraud creditors or for any fraudulent purpose.
3 Not knowingly to allow the company to trade while insolvent ('wrongful trading'). Directors who do so may have to pay for the debts incurred by the company while insolvent.
4 Not to deceive shareholders.
5 To have a regard for the interests of employees in general.
6 To comply with the requirements of the Companies Acts, such as providing what is needed in accounting records or filing accounts.

How not to get disqualified as a director

The most dangerous of these areas of a director's responsibilities are ones that could get you disqualified. In summary, the areas to avoid at all cost are the following.

1 Trading while insolvent, which occurs when your liabilities exceed your assets. At this point the shareholders' equity in the business has effectively ceased to exist and when shareholder equity is negative, directors are personally at risk, and owe a duty of care to creditors – not shareholders. If you find yourself even approaching this area you need the prompt advice of an insolvency practitioner. Directors who act properly will not be penalized, and will live to fight another day.
2 Wrongful trading can apply if, after a company goes into insolvent liquidation, the liquidator believes that the directors (or those acting as such) ought to have concluded earlier that the company had no realistic chance of survival. In these circumstances the courts can remove the shelter of limited liabilities and make directors personally liable for the company's debts.

3 Fraudulent trading is rather more serious than wrongful trading. Here the proposition is that the director(s) were knowingly party to fraud on their creditors. The full shelter of limited liability can be removed in these circumstances.

Former directors of insolvent companies can be banned from holding office for periods of up to 15 years. Fraud, fraudulent trading, wrongful trading or a failure to comply with company law, for example filing your annual accounts, may result in disqualification.

Breaches of a disqualification order can lead to imprisonment and/or fines. Also you can be made personally liable for the debts and liabilities of any company in which you are involved. Neither can you issue your orders through others, having them act as a director in your place. This will leave them personally liable themselves. A register of disqualified directors is available for free access on the Companies House website.

Sources of help with business failure

The Insolvency Practitioners Association
Bow Bells House
11 Bread Street
London
EC4M 9BE
Tel: 020 7329 0777
Email: secretariat@ipa.uk.com
Website: www.ipa.uk.com

The Insolvency Practitioners Association have an online directory of insolvency practitioners around the UK, with basic contact details.

The Insolvency Service (Publications Orders)
Records Management
4th Floor East
Ladywood House
Birmingham
B2 4UZ
Tel: 0121 698 4241
Website: www.insolvency.gov.uk

Government department that has a range of guidance publications covering bankruptcy, insolvency, directors' disqualification and how to wind up your own company.

Registry Trust Limited
173–175 Cleveland Street
London
W1P 5PE
Tel: 020 7380 0133

Each year there are around 700,000 County Court judgments (CCJs) made against individuals and companies. You can find out if any have been made against you, or against any other business, for a fee of £4.50 for a postal search of the register for each name and address searched.

The Small Claims Court

Many countries, including the US and the UK, have a procedure for getting legal disputes concerning payment from customers settled quickly and inexpensively.

This court aims to provide a speedy, inexpensive resolution of disputes that involve relatively small amounts of money. The advantage of the Small Claims Court is that if you cannot afford a solicitor and you are not entitled to Legal Aid you can still bring your case to the court yourself. Even if you can afford a solicitor, their fees may be more than the amount you are claiming. If you do not manage to get your opponent to pay your costs then you will not be any better off.

The jurisdictional limits (the amount for which you can sue) in these courts are rising fairly quickly. In the US you can sue for $5000 or sometimes more and in the UK if the amount of money claimed is under £5000 that is likely to come under the jurisdiction of the Small Claims Court.

However, if your claim is for personal injury it will only be heard in the Small Claims Court if the claim for the injury itself is not more than £1000.

For housing cases involving a landlord's failure to repair the property the claim will be heard in the Small Claims Court if the cost of repairs or the compensation claimed is not more than £1000. You are entitled to ask for Interest on the amount you are claiming; this is currently 8% per year. If you want to claim interest you must put that on your claim.

A businessperson can use the Small Claims Court to collect bills, to obtain a judgment for breach of contract, or to seek money for minor property damage claims – for example, suing someone who broke a fence around your property or parking area. The Small Claims Court offers you an opportunity to collect money that would otherwise be lost as it would be too expensive to sue for in regular court. True, for very small cases, it's not always cost-effective, and occasionally you'll have problems collecting your judgment. But the Small Claims Court should still be part of the collection strategies of your businesses.

Before you start the legal, investigate alternatives. If your case involves a written contract, check to see if the contract requires mediation or arbitration of disputes. If so, this may limit or cut off your right to go to any court, including the Small Claims Court. Second, consider other cost-effective options, such as free or low-cost publicly operated mediation programmes. If you're in a dispute with a customer, or perhaps another business, and you still have hopes of preserving some aspect of the relationship, mediation – even if not provided for in a contract – is often a better alternative than going to court. Any litigation tends to sour people's feelings.

Starting the process

You can make a claim by getting a Claim Form from your local County Court. On the 'Particulars of Claim' form you state what your claim is for and why you are claiming and also include the amount you are claiming and say if you want interest.

In personal injury cases you must also file a medical report giving details about your injury. You will need to send to the court the Claim Form plus a copy for the court and a copy for each opponent if there is more than one.

The court is then responsible for sending copies to your opponent together with a form for defending the claim, a form for admitting the claim and a form for acknowledging service, which your opponent must complete and send back to the court.

The court will then send you a copy together with a set of instructions on what you should do next or they may fix a hearing date when you will have to go to court.

Hearings will usually last no more than one day, but an hour or so is more likely. The court can even deal with your case without holding a hearing. They just consider your case 'on paper'. If the judge decides your case is suitable to be dealt with without a hearing they will tell you and your opponent. The court can also deal with your case by a 'telephone hearing' if you and your opponent agree and as long as you are both legally represented. This will be arranged using a BT conference 'call out' system.

If the court has video conferencing facilities it may also be possible to hold a hearing by video link.

You do not have to attend the hearing as long as you give seven days' notice before the hearing to the court and your opponent telling them you will not be attending.

You can send written evidence to the court and the court will take your evidence into account when reaching its decision. The court must tell you the reasons for its decision.

Getting paid

One of the frustrating things about any legal process is that winning the argument could in the end resolve nothing. If the person you are suing has no money, or decides to ignore the judgment against them, then the ball could be back in your court.

If your opponent looks as though they could pay, but won't, you have a number of options.

Oral examination is where your opponent is told to come to court to provide the court with details of his or her income, capital and savings. You can then decide from this information whether they are able to repay the debt.

To apply for an oral examination you should get a 'Request for Oral Examination' form from the court, sending a small fee, together with details of the amount of money which remains unpaid under the judgment.

The court will serve an order telling your opponent to come to court – some courts prefer to send an affidavit, or questionnaire to the opponent to complete first. When your opponent attends court he or she will be questioned by either a District Judge or an officer of the court. You don't have to be present, but you can give details of any questions you would like asked of your opponent.

If your opponent refuses to answer any questions or produce documents you can apply to the court for an order that he must do so. This is called a 'penal notice'. If your opponent still fails to obey the order they will be in 'contempt of court' and if the order has a penal notice attached you can apply to the court to commit your opponent to prison for breach of the order.

If your opponent does not attend court then a new date has to be fixed to give them the opportunity to attend. Your opponent could ask that you pay their travel expenses for attending court. If they do, you must pay these not less than seven days before the hearing. You must then file a certificate at court to say either that your opponent has not requested any money or that you have paid it. This certificate must be filed with the court four days before the hearing.

It will not have escaped your notice that you have not yet been paid anything and might even have had to fork out something by way of expenses for the person you are suing.

Garnishee proceedings may be a simpler option if your opponent is owed money by a third party, a not infrequent defence offered by late payers. You can get an order requiring the third party pays that money direct to you. Your debt must be at least £50 and the third party must be within England and Wales.

To apply you must send to the court an affidavit to say the money owed has not been repaid as the court ordered and that it is still outstanding. You will need to pay a court small fee for a temporary order which you must serve on the third party. A hearing date will then be fixed when the third party can attend and make objections about the order.

Warrant of delivery is a possibility if your opponent has a particular item or goods belonging to you and you want their return. If the judgment or order says the goods are to be returned you can apply for a 'Request for a Warrant of Delivery'. No hearing is necessary; the court bailiff will contact your opponent to fix an appointment to remove the goods.

Attachment of earnings could be useful route as long as the debt is not less than £50 and your opponent is working. You can apply for an order that your opponent's employer deduct a certain amount from their wages each week or month in to pay the debt. The court will fix a hearing date and serve you and your opponent with details.

Your opponent is entitled to have part of their earnings protected against deductions. The judge will decide how much this will be and also decide the amount to be deducted and how often.

Getting a *charging order* is yet another route to ensure payment, if your opponent owns property. You can apply to the court to 'register a charge' at the Land Registry against your opponent's property to show that you have an interest in the sale proceeds of the property. This forewarns any person intending to buy your opponent's property and will make it more difficult for them to sell. It may just be enough of an irritation to make them pay up and be done with it. If there are other charges, such as a mortgage or bank loan, registered before you on the Land Register, then they will be paid first.

Whilst the Small Claims Court, or indeed any court, is one way to claim money that is owed, it is, as you can see, neither easy nor certain. First, you want to be relatively sure of your legal position. You must have a valid legal basis for a lawsuit. Do you have a decent chance of proving in court that the defendant refused to pay a fair and just bill, or broke a contract, or negligently damaged your property? If not, any talk about going to court is just an idle threat that may hurt your credibility.

Online writs

Since January 2002 anyone claiming up to £100,000 may now sue through the Internet at any time, day or night. If the claim is undefended, the money can be recovered without anyone having to go to court. The service, called Money Claim Online, can be reached at www.courtservice.gov.uk/.

To start the process, click on a picture of a blindfolded figure of Justice superimposed on a claim form. The service is open to individuals and businesses claiming a fixed sum from people or companies in England and Wales. After registering online, claimants fill in the names of the parties and a summary of the claim. The fee – £27 minimum – is calculated automatically and must be paid by credit or debit card before proceedings are issued. People on legal aid cannot use the service. Claimants 'sign' a statement of truth in support of their claims by typing in their names. Dishonesty can be punished as a contempt of court. The service cannot be used by vexatious litigants – people who have been banned from issuing further legal proceedings without court permission.

Help with making a small claim

ClaimsLink (UK) Ltd
PO Box 1312
Bristol
BS99 2GP
Tel: 0117 909 0162
Fax: 0117 909 9941
Email: admin@claimslinkuk.co.uk
Website: www.small-claims.co.uk

Since 1993 ClaimsLink (UK) Ltd have been processing legal claims through the Small Claims Courts. They are an independent company with an in-house legal team dedicated to the detailed requirements of modern County Court procedures. Their head office is based in Bristol, where all claims are filed.

CompactLaw

Website: www.compactlaw.co.uk

Website with full details of small claims procedures.

Data protection

The first Data Protection Act was passed in 1984
and grew out of public concern about personal
privacy in the face of rapidly developing computer technology. However, even at the time it was
passed it was virtually inconceivable that computers would permeate every sector of business and
society to the extent to which they now have. The
Act was also passed to enable the United Kingdom to ratify the Council of Europe Convention
on Data Protection, allowing data to flow freely
between the United Kingdom and other European
countries with similar laws, preventing damage to
the economy and international trade which might
otherwise have occurred.

The latest Data Protection Act, 1998, came into
effect on 1 March 2000.

Who needs to register?

Every business and organization irrespective of
size is governed by the Data Protection Act, so
the answer is fairly straightforward: if you hold
personal information about living individuals on
computer or have such information processed on
computer by others (for example, by a computer
bureau or your accountant), then you probably
do need to register under the Data Protection Act.
This need not be particularly sensitive information and can be as little as a name and address.

The Data Protection Act 1998 also covers
some records held in paper form. These records
do not have to be notified to the Commissioner,
but should be handled in accordance with the data
protection principles. Manual records are covered
by the Act if they form part of a relevant filing
system. The Act defines a relevant filing system as
'any set of information relating to individuals and

structured, either by reference to individuals or by
reference to criteria relating to individuals, in such
a way that specific information relating to a particular individual is readily accessible.'

The maximum penalty for non-registration is
£5000 plus costs in the Magistrates' Court and an
unlimited fine in the Higher Courts. This amount
has not changed since the 1984 Act came into
force.

What does the Act cover?

The Act is concerned with 'personal data' which is
'automatically processed'. Personal data is information about living, identifiable individuals. The
Act works in two ways, giving individuals (data
subjects) certain rights, while requiring those who
record and use personal information on computer (data users) to be open about their use of that
information and to follow sound and proper practices (the Data Protection principles).

- Data users are those who control the contents
  and use of a collection of personal data. This
  can be any type of company or organization,
  large or small, within the public or private
  sector. A data user can also be a sole trader,
  partnership or an individual. A data user need
  not necessarily own a computer.
- Data subjects are the individuals to whom the
  personal data relate.

What are the data protection principles?

Even if you are exempt from notification, you
are still required to comply with the eight data
protection principles. The principles are rules of
good information handling practice and are laid
down in the Act. Essentially, the principles must be
applied to individual situations by individual data
controllers and the onus is on you, the data controller, to ensure your use of data does not breach
these principles.

The first five principles establish general standards of data quality.

They specify that data must be:

- obtained fairly and lawfully
- held only for specific and lawful purposes and not processed in any matter incompatible with those purposes
- relevant, adequate and not excessive for those purposes
- accurate and where necessary kept up to date
- not kept for longer than necessary.

The sixth principle says that the data should be processed in accordance with the rights of data subjects under the Act. This means that individuals have the right, amongst other things, to:

- be informed upon request of all the information held about them by a particular data controller
- prevent the processing of their data for the purposes of direct marketing
- compensation if they can show that they have been caused damage by any contravention of the Act
- the removal or correction of any inaccurate data about them.

The seventh principle requires you to ensure that you have adequate security precautions in place to prevent the loss, destruction or unauthorized disclosure of the data. If you use another company or individual to process your data on your behalf (data processor), you must have a written contract in place to ensure that the processor has adequate security and will only process the data according to your instruction.

The eighth principle requires you not to transfer data outside the European Economic Area unless you are satisfied that the country in question can provide an adequate level of security for that data, except where you have the data subject's consent.

Conforming to these principles requires for the most part little more than common sense and good business practice. You will need, however, to take some elementary precautions, including the following.

- Decide how long individual records need to be kept. For example, for employee's records, in practice you will only need these for as long as the threat of an action for unfair dismissal remains or until any other dispute is resolved.
- The fourth principle is one you should apply rigorously when designing your record-keeping system. You don't want it cluttered up with volumes of useless information in any event.
- You need to make sure manual records are kept under lock and key and computerized records are password protected. Access should be restricted to yourself and anyone you appoint to supervise this area. You also need to take some measures to protect the data from accidental loss. For computerized systems this can be done by having regular back-ups. With manual records, protection is more complex. At the most basic level you need a secure filing cabinet that can withstand any normal hazard. You could consider having key documents scanned and retained offsite. But doing so would be more complicated than having computerized records in the first place. Your guiding principle should be that employee and customer records are kept at least as securely as other key business records, such as your accounting information.

Sensitive data

The Act defines eight categories of sensitive personal data. These are:

- the racial or ethnic origin of data subjects
- their political opinions
- their religious beliefs or other beliefs of a similar nature
- whether they are a member of a trade union
- their physical or mental health or condition
- their sexual life
- the commission or alleged commission by them of any offence or

- any proceedings for any offence committed or alleged to have been committed by them, the disposal of such proceedings or the sentence of any court in such proceedings.

If you hold personal data falling into these categories it is likely that you will need the explicit consent of the individual concerned. You will also need to ensure that your security is adequate for the protection of sensitive data.

Exemptions from registration

There are a number of exemptions from registration under the requirements of the Act for individuals and organizations which make only very limited use of personal data. There is no procedure for officially claiming an exemption and data users are not obliged to notify the Registrar that they are relying on one. However, you should be aware that you may need to defend your decision to rely on an exemption in the criminal or civil courts. You may be surprised to see that the exemptions look much the same as some of the purposes on the registration application form. This is because exemptions can easily be lost if you use information in many of the normal ways you would want to in running a business, for instance, using pay and pensions records for other personnel purposes. Often data users find it easier to proceed as though an exemption were not available rather than to continually monitor their compliance with its terms. Bear in mind also that although an exemption may cover you now, your circumstances may change later. It is also important to realize that two exemptions cannot be claimed at the same time for the same data. In other words, it is often safer to register.

Further information

The above information gives only a general idea of the scope of the act. The Data Protection Registrar's website has a downloadable word file with the full provisions of the act, running to some 111 pages. Though wordy, as these documents tend to be, it is full of useful examples and cases.

How to register

There are currently two ways to make an application to notify.

- **On the Internet:** You can complete the notification form online, print it and send the form in with the notification fee or your direct debit instruction.
- **By telephone:** You can telephone the notification helpline. You will be asked to provide your name, address, contact details and to specify the nature of your business. When you receive your form you need to check the details on Part 1, provide some additional information on Part 2, and then return the form together with the annual notification fee, currently £35, or your direct debit instruction.

Keeping your register entry up to date

Once you have notified you must keep your register entry up to date.

When any part of your entry becomes inaccurate or incomplete you must inform the Registrar. This action must be taken as soon as practicable and in any event within a period of 28 days from the date on which your entry became inaccurate or incomplete. Failure to do so is a criminal offence.

Changes must be notified in writing quoting your security number. Change forms are available online or can be obtained by phone. One is for adding an additional purpose to your notification and the other is for making any other amendment to your notification. Changes can be made free of charge.

Changes of legal entity

A register entry is not transferable from one data controller to another. If there is a change in the legal entity of the data controller a new entry must be made in the register. Examples of changes in legal entity are when a sole trader becomes a partnership or a partnership becomes a limited company. In these cases you should telephone the notification helpline to start the process of notifying the new legal entity.

A changing environment

The Information Code, which is being introduced in stages and aims to enforce the Data Protection Act, will give, amongst other things, workers the right to see any company record which mentions them. For a £10 fee a worker can see any record concerning them and this includes confidential personnel records and file notes from appraisals or disciplinary meetings.

Sources of help and advice with data protection

British Standards Institute
389 Chiswick High Road
London
W4 4AL
Tel: 020 8996 9000

Fax: 020 8996 7400
Email: info@bsi-global.com
Website: www.bsi-global.com

BSI have information and literature on best practice in complying with the Data Protection Act.

Data Protection Commissioner
Wycliffe House
Water Lane
Wilmslow
SK9 5AF
Tel: 01625 545700
Fax: 01625 524510
Email: mail@dataprotection.gov.uk
Website: www.dataprotection.gov.uk

Full text of the Data Protection Act, explanatory guidelines for small businesses and online registration procedures can be found on the website. The Information Helpline number is 01625 545 745.

Section 8

'THE KNOWLEDGE': TRAINING FOR SMALL BUSINESS

There are now more opportunities for education and training, at every level, in the small business and management field than ever before. No formal academic qualifications are required for most of the courses, and costs are generally modest. In certain cases, participants may be eligible for grants or subsidized training. The bulk of the activities are concentrated in universities and colleges throughout the whole of the UK. However, there are a growing number of opportunities for the less mobile to take up some form of home study in the business field in general, and small business opportunities in particular. With the growth of the Internet it is now practical and worthwhile for UK-based entrepreneurs to get their learning experience from virtually any part of the world.

There is now some reliable evidence to show that people attending small business courses can significantly improve their chances of success.

The courses on offer for small businesses generally fit into the following main categories.

Start-up courses

These are for people considering starting up a business. These are usually of short duration, charging a modest fee. They concentrate on giving an introduction on how to start your own business. As well as providing lectures, the courses give an opportunity for those who have recently started up in business to talk about their experiences. The demand for these courses is high and it certainly forms the most cost-effective method of finding out very quickly a lot about what is going on in the 'new and small business world'. These courses are frequently run at weekends and sometimes on evenings during the week.

Topic courses

These are usually run over a few days or weeks, for those already in business. They cover topics such as financial management, marketing, bookkeeping, exporting, e-business, employing people and strategy/business planning. Accountants and colleges also run courses after the Budget, giving tax update courses.

Business growth

These programmes are aimed at those already running a business and who are actively seeking ways to expand profitably. The Cranfield Business Growth Programme is one of the pioneers in this sector. Some 600 entrepreneurs have been through their programme and many have achieved substantial growth. One company going through the programme has grown from £8 million turnover to £50 million in a six year period and recently sold up for £530 million. Business growth programmes usually start with a comprehensive review of company strategy, analysing strengths and weaknesses; go on to review the business opportunities and threats ahead; set goals, objectives and business strategy; and culminate in business and action plans to show how growth will be achieved. Classroom sessions focus on real issues in participants' companies, and are often led by successful entrepreneurs with exciting stories to tell. As well as classroom sessions, each participant will have a personal tutor, whose task is to help that individual prepare plans. Often, being able to meet with other-like minded entrepreneurs is the major benefit – there being so few forums where owner-managers can debate and discuss their ideas with a peer group whose views they can fully respect.

Where to find a course

There are three routes explained here to finding the right training course to help you start and run your business. You can look up a convenient course run at a UK college or university. These are listed in the directory of UK university and college small business courses. Alternatively, you can take an online or distance learning programme. There is a small selection of these programmes in the directory of online small business courses, by way of illustration. If an online course looks like the best route to knowledge for you, then you could also use the directory of online small business training programmes databases.

Directory of training for small business in UK universities and colleges

Key to initials (topic courses):
F = Finance
M = Marketing
B = Bookkeeping
EX = Exporting
IT = Information Technology
INT = Internet
MA = Management
ST = Strategy
? = Contact college

	Start-up courses	Topic courses	Business growth	Consultancy/ advice	Research activity	Business/ e-club	Special small business unit
Aberdeen College, Gallowgate Centre, Gallowgate, Aberdeen AB25 1BN Tel: 01224 612000 Fax: 01224 612001 Email: enquiry@abcol.ac.uk Website: http://abcol.ac.uk	–	F, B, M, INT, IT, MA	–	–	–	–	–
Abingdon and Witney College, Abingdon Campus, Northcourt Road, Abingdon OX14 1NN Tel: 01235 555 585 Fax: 01235 553 168 Email: inquiry@abingdon-witney.ac.uk Website: http://www.abingdon-witney.ac.uk/	–	IT, INT	–	–	–	–	–
Abingdon and Witney College, Witney Campus, Holloway Road, Witney OX28 6NE Tel: 01993 703 464 Fax: 01993 703 006 Email: inquiry@abingdon-witney.ac.uk Website: www.abingdoncollege.ac.uk	–	IT, INT	–	–	–	–	–
Accrington and Rossendale College, Sandy Lane, Accrington, Lancs BB5 2AW Tel: 01254 389933 Fax: 01254 354001 Email: kcoupe@across.ac.uk Website: http://www.accross.ac.uk	–	F, IT, MA	–	–	–	–	–

	Start-up courses	Topic courses	Business growth	Consultancy/ advice	Research activity	Business/ e-club	Special small business unit
Alton College, Old Odiham Road, Alton GU34 2LX Tel: 01420 592200 Fax: 01420 592253 Email: enquiries@altoncollege.ac.uk Website: www.altoncollege.ac.uk	–	IT	–	–	–	–	–
Amersham and Wycombe College, High Wycombe Campus, Spring Lane, Flackwell Heath, High Wycombe HP7 9HW Tel: 01494 735555 Fax: 01494 735577 Website: www.amersham.ac.uk	–	F, M, IT, MA, ST	–	–	–	–	–
Angus College, Marketing Department, Business Development Centre, Keptie Road, Arbroath DD11 3EA Tel: +44 (0)1241 432600 Fax: 01241 876169 Email: marketing@angus.ac.uk Website: www.angus.ac.uk	■	F, IT, MA, ST ■	■	–	–	–	■
Anniesland College, Balshagray Campus, 27 Broomhill Avenue, Glasgow G11 7AE Tel: 0141 357 4310 Fax: 0141 339 8895 Email: reception@anniesland.ac.uk Website: www.anniesland.ac.uk	–	B, F, IT, MA	–	–	–	–	–

Anniesland College, Hatfield Campus, 19 Hatfield Drive, Glasgow G12 0YE Tel: 0141 357 3969 Email: reception@anniesland.ac.uk Fax: 0141 357 6557 Website: www.anniesland.ac.uk	–	B, F, IT, MA	–	–	–	–
Askam Bryan College, Bedale Centre, Benkill Drive, Bedale DL8 2EA Contacts: Heather Amy; Jackie Scarth Tel: 01677 422344 Email: hla@askham-bryan.ac.uk Website: http://www.askham-bryan.ac.uk/en/webpage.asp?wpid=17	–	F, M, B, EX, IT, INT, MA, ST	–	–	–	–
Askham Bryan College, Guisborough Centre, Avenue Place, Redcar Road, Guisborough TS14 6AX Contacts: Jonathan Murray; Jo Lamb Tel: 01287 633870 Email: th@askham-bryan.ac.uk Website: http://www.askham-bryan.ac.uk/en/webpage.asp?wpid=17	–	B, INT, IT	–	–	–	–
Askham Bryan College, Harrogate Centre, Hornbeam, Hookstone Road, Harrogate HG2 8QT Contact: Elaine Stainton Tel: 01423 870600 Email: es@askham-bryan.ac.uk Website: http://www.askham-bryan.ac.uk/en/webpage.asp?wpid=17	–	B, IT, INT	–	–	–	–

	Start-up courses	Topic courses	Business growth	Consultancy/ advice	Research activity	Business/ e-club	Special small business unit
Askham Bryan College, Pickering Centre, Swainsea Lane, Pickering YO18 8NE Contacts: Rodger Kennedy; Rita Spence Tel: 01751 473431 Fax: 01751 473431 Email: res@askham-bryan.ac.uk Website: http://www.askham-bryan.ac.uk/index.asp?wpid=1	–	B, IT, INT	–	–	–	–	–
Barking College, Dagenham Road, Romford RM7 0XU Tel: 01708 770000 Fax: 01708 770007 Email: admissions@barkingcollege.ac.uk Website: www.barking-coll.ac.uk	■	F, M, B, EX, IT, INT, ST	■	■	–	–	–
Barry College, Colcot Road, Barry CF62 8YJ Tel: 01446 725063; 01446 725000 Fax: 01446 732667 Email: enquiries@barry.ac.uk Website: www.barry.ac.uk	■	All	■	■	–	–	–
Birmingham Technology Ltd, Faraday Wharf, Holt Street, Aston Science Park, Birmingham B7 4BB Tel: 0121 250 3503 Fax: 0121 250 3567 Email: shaunw@astonsciencepark.co.uk Website: www.astonsciencepark.co.uk	■	MA, ST	■	■	■	■	■

Institution			Courses			
Bolton Business School, Deane Road, Bolton BL3 5AB Tel: 01204 903111 Fax: 01204 900516 Email: enquiries@bolton.ac.uk Website: www.bolton.ac.uk/business	–	F, M, IT, INT, MA, ST ■	■	–	–	–
Borders College Commercial Road, Hawick TD9 7AW Tel: 08700 50 51 52 Fax: (01450) 377164 Email: ksmeaton@borderscollege.ac.uk Website: www.bcconsultants.co.uk	–	M, IT, INT, MA, ST ■	■	–	–	■
Bournemouth University Business School, The Business School, Talbot Campus, Poole, Dorset BH12 5BB Contact: John Gatrell Tel: +44 (0)1202 965467 Fax: +44 (0)1202 965261 Email: business@bournemouth.ac.uk Website: http://business.bournemouth.ac.uk/	■	ST ■	■	–	–	■
Bristol City Council Community Education Service, Stoke Lodge Community Education Centre, Shirehampton Road, Stoke Bishop, Bristol BS9 1BN Tel: 0117 903 8844 Fax: 0117 903 8802 Email: admissions@bristolandbath.com Website: http://www.bristol-lea.org.uk/lifelong/commed.html	■	F, M, B, EX, IT, INT, MA, ST ■	–	–	–	–
Burton College, Lichfield Street, Burton on Trent DE14 3RL Tel: 01283 494400 (main switchboard); 01283 494411 (course enquiries) Fax: 01283 494800 Website: www.burton-college.ac.uk	–	IT, INT, MA –	–	–	–	–

	Start-up courses	Topic courses	Business growth	Consultancy/ advice	Research activity	Business/ e-club	Special small business unit
Cambridge Regional College, Science Park Campus, King Hedges Road, Cambridge CB4 2QT Tel: 01223 418200 Email: enquiry@camre.ac.uk Website: www.camre.ac.uk	■	F, M, B, EX, IT, INT, ST	■	■	–	–	–
Cardonald College Glasgow, 690 Mosspark Drive, Glasgow G52 3AY Tel: 0141 272 3333 Fax: 0141 272 3444 Email: enquiries@cardonald.ac.uk Website: www.cardonald.ac.uk	■	F, B	■	–	–	–	–
Cavendish College, 35–37 Alfred Place, London WC1E 7DP Tel: 0207 580 4074 Fax: 0207 255 1591 Email: learn@cavendish.ac.uk Website: www.cavendish.ac.uk	–	M, EX, INT, MA	–	–	–	–	–
Central Ryedale Community Education Service, Course Enquiries, Community Education Office, 68 Lanton Road, Norton, Malton YO17 9AE Tel: 01653 694 122 Fax: 01653 696 753 Email: enquiries@northyorks.gov.uk Website: www.northyorks.gov.uk	■	F, B, IT, INT	■	–	–	–	–
City College Coventry, Tile Hill Centre, Tile Hill Lane, Coventry CV4 9SU Tel: 024 7679 1000 Fax: 024 7646 4903 Email: info@tilehill.ac.uk Website: http://www.covcollege.ac.uk/home/	–	All	–	–	–	–	–

Organization							
City of Wolverhampton College, Course Enquiries, Wulfrun Campus, Paget Road, Wolverhampton WV6 0DU; Tel: 01902 836000; Email: vaughand@wolvcoll.ac.uk; Website: www.wolverhamptoncollege.ac.uk	■	?	–	–	–	–	–
City University, (Courses for Adults Information), Northampton Square, Islington, London EC1V 0HB; Tel: +44 (0)20 7040 5060; Fax: +44 (0)20 7040 5070; Email: info@city.ac.uk; Website: www.city.ac.uk	■	F, B	■	–	–	–	–
Connect Internet Solutions (Training Bookings), 1st Floor Faraday House, Liverpool Digital, Edge Lane, Liverpool L7 9NJ; Tel: +44 (0) 151 282 4321; Fax: +44 (0) 151 282 4322; Email: admin@connect.org.uk; Website: www.connect.org.uk	–	IT, INT	■	–	–	–	–
Cornwall Business School, Cornwall College, Pool, Redruth, Cornwall TR15 3RD; Contact: Sue Lloyd; Tel: (0209) 616161; Fax: (0209) 616107; Email: cbs@cornwall.ac.uk; Website: www.cbs.ac.uk	■	F, M, B, IT, INT, MA, ST	■	–	–	–	■
Croydon CETS, Coombe Cliff CETS Centre (within Park Hill), Coombe Road, Croydon, CR0 5SP; Tel: 020 8253 1850 (enrollment line); Fax: 0208 667 0078; Email: admin@cets.co.uk; Website: www.cets.co.uk		?					

	Start-up courses	Topic courses	Business growth	Consultancy/ advice	Research activity	Business/ e-club	Special small business unit
Dewsbury College, Admissions, Halifax Road, Dewsbury, West Yorkshire WF13 2AS Tel: 01924 436221 Fax: 01924 457047 Email: info@dewsbury.ac.uk Website: www.dewsbury.ac.uk	–	F, M, B, EX, IT, INT, MA, ST	■	–	–	–	–
Falmouth and Penryn Adult Education Centre, Clare Terrace, Falmouth, Cornwall TR11 3ET Contact: The Admissions Tutor Tel: 01326 319275 Fax: 01326 212363 Email: aefalmouth@cornwall.uk Website: www.cornwall.gov.uk	■	F, M, B, IT, MA, ST	–	–	–	–	·
Fife College of Further & Higher Education, St Brycedale Avenue, Kirkcaldy KY11EX Tel: 01592 268591 Fax: 01592 640225 Email: enquiries@fife.ac.uk Website: www.fife.ac.uk	■	F, M, B, IT, INT, MA, ST	■	■	–	–	–
Grantham College, College Reception, Stonebridge Road, Grantham NG31 9AP Tel: 01476 400200 Fax: 01476 400291 Email: enquiry@grantham.ac.uk Website: www.grantham.edu	–	F, B	■	–	–	–	

Organization						
Harlow and Bishop's Stortford Adult Learning Centre, Harlow College, Velizy Avenue, Harlow CM20 3LH Tel: 01279 868000 (national admissions) Email: enquiries@harlow-college.ac.uk Website: www.harlow-college.ac.uk	—	—	—	■	■ F, M, B, EX, IT, INT, ST	■
Havering College of Further Education, Ardleigh Green Road, Essex RM11 2LL Tel: 01708 455011 Email: info@havering-college.ac.uk Website: www.havering-college.ac.uk	—	—	—	—	■ F, M, B, EX, IT, INT, MA, ST	—
Heriot Watt University, Scottish Institute for Enterprise, Edinburgh EH14 4AS, Tel: +44 (0) 131 449 5111 Fax: +44 (0) 131 449 5153 Email: enquiries@hw.ac.uk Website: http://www.hw.ac.uk/sitemap.htm	■	—	—	—	— MA, ST	■
Ideal Schools, 6 Dixon Street, Glasgow G1 4AX Tel: 0141 248 5200 Fax: 0141 248 5085 Email: idlschools@aol.com Website: http://www.idealschools.co.uk/	—	—	—	■	■ F, B, IT	■
Institute of Management, Management House, Cottingham Road, Corby NN17 1TT Tel: +44 (0)1536 204 222 Fax: +44 (0)1536 201 651 Email: enquiries@managers.org.uk Website: wwwbinst-mgt.org.uk	—	—	—	■	■ MA	■

	Start-up courses	Topic courses	Business growth	Consultancy/ advice	Research activity	Business/ e-club	Special small business unit
Kendal College, Milnthorpe Road, Kendal LA9 5AY Tel: 01539 814700 Email: enquiries@kendal.ac.uk Website: www.kendal.ac.uk	–	F, M, B, EX, IT, INT, ST	■	■	–		■
Kidderminster College, The Business Development Unit, Hoo Road, Kidderminster DY10 1LX Student Services: 01562 512003/4 Fax: 01562 512006 Email: studentservices@kidderminster.ac.uk Website: http://www.kidderminster.ac.uk/index.htm	■	F, M, B, IT, INT, MA, ST	■	■	–	–	–
Kite Human Resource Consultants, Kite Training, 45 Belvedere Avenue, Chesterfield S40 3HY Tel: 01246 220284 Fax: 01246 550682 Email: Training@Kite-UK.com Website: www.Kite-UK.com	–	MA, ST	■	–	–	–	–
Knowsley Community College, Rupert Road, Roby L36 9TD Tel: 0151 477 5777 Fax: 0151 477 5703 Email: info@knowsleycollege.ac.uk Website: http://www.knowsleycollege.ac.uk/kcc_frameset.html	■	F, M, B, IT, INT, MA, ST	–	■			
Malvern Hills College, Malvern Open Access Centre, Albert Road North, Malvern WR14 2YH Tel: 01684 565351 Fax: 01684 561767 Email: information@evesham.ac.uk Website: www.worcs.com	■	F, B	■	–	–	–	–

Ming-Ai (London) Institute, Denver House, 1 Cline Road, London N11 2LX
Tel: 0208 361 7161
Fax: 0208 361 4207
Email: enquiry@ming-ai.org.uk
Website: www.ming-ai.org.uk

B, EX, IT   –   –   –   –   –

Newman College of Higher Education, Genners Lane, Bartley Green, Birmingham B32 3NT
Contact: Chris Wormwell
Tel: 0121 476 1181 ext 2366
Fax: 0121 476 1196
Email: registry@newman.ac.uk
Website: www.newman.ac.uk

IT, INT, MA   –   –   –   –   –

North West Centre for Business & Management, Edge Hill, ■ St Helens Road, Ormskirk L39 4QP
Tel: 01695 584274
Fax: 01695 584675
Email: Choneker@edgehill.ac.uk; enquiries@edgehill.ac.uk
Website: www.edgehill.ac.uk

F, M, IT, MA, ■ ST   ■   ■   –   ■

Norton Radstock College, South Hill Park, Radstock, Bath BA3 3RW
Contact: Course Information
Tel: 01761 433161
Fax: 01761 436173
Email: courses@nortcoll.ac.uk
Website: www.nortcoll.ac.uk

MA, ST   –   –   –   –

	Start-up courses	Topic courses	Business growth	Consultancy/ advice	Research activity	Business/ e-club	Special small business unit
Oldham Chamber of Commerce, Business Training Managers, Oldham Business Centre, Cromwell Street, Oldham OL1 1BB Tel: 0161 620 0006 Fax: 0161 620 0030 Email: businesstraining@oldhamchamber.co.uk Website: www.oldhamchamber.co.uk	■	All	■	■	–	–	■
Otley College, (Otley & Orwell Training Ltd), Charity Farmhouse, Charity Lane, Ipswich IP6 9EY Tel: +44 (0)1473 785543 (national admissions) Fax: +44 (0)1473 785353 Email: info@otleycollege.ac.uk Website: www.otleycollege.ac.uk	–	F, M, B, EX, IT, INT, MA, ST	■	■	–	–	–
Oxford Brookes University, Business School. The Enterprise Centre, Wheatley, Oxford OX33 1HX Tel: +44 (0)1865 485908 Fax: 01865 485830 Email: query@brookes.ac.uk Website: http://www.business.brookes.ac.uk/bs/	■	All	■	■	■	–	■
Oxford Computer Training, 30 Market Place, Westminster, London W1W 8AW Tel: 0207 436 4872 Fax: 0207 323 4582 Email: info@oxfordhouse.co.uk Website: http://oxfordhouse.co.uk	■	F, B, IT	■	–	–	–	–

Organisation					Codes	
Park Lane College, Course Enquiries, Park Lane Site, Park Lane, Leeds LS3 1SS Contact: Course Enquiries Tel: 0845 045 7275 Fax: 0113 216 2020 Email: course.enquiry@parklanecoll.ac.uk Website: www.parklanecoll.ac.uk	■	–	–	–	F, M, B, EX, IT, INT, MA, ST ■	–
Pitman Training Centre, 1st Floor, Northumberland House, 303–306 High Holborn, WC1V 7JZ Tel: 020 7025 4700 Email: info@tap.co.uk Website: http://tap.co.uk	■	–	–	–	F, B, IT, ■	–
Portsmouth University Business School, University House, Winston Churchill Avenue, Portsmouth, Hampshire PO1 2UP Contact: Nick Capon Tel: +44 (0)23 9284 8484 Fax: +44 (0)23 9284 3082 Email: info.centre@port.ac.uk Website: www.port.ac.uk/departments/	–	■	–	–	F, M, IT, INT, MA, ST ■	■
Professional Training Centre, Colchester Institute, Sheepen House, Sheepen Road, Colchester CO3 3LH Tel: 01206 518181 Fax: 01206 518182 Email: info@theptc.co.uk Website: www.theptc.co.uk	–	■	–	–	F, M, IT, INT, MA, ST ■	–

	Start-up courses	Topic courses	Business growth	Consultancy/ advice	Research activity	Business/ e-club	Special small business unit
Rother Valley College, Doe Quarry Lane, Dinnington, South Yorkshire S25 2NF Contact: Julie Williams Tel: 0800 328 8008 Fax: 01909 559003 Email: studentservices@rothervalley.ac.uk; J.williams@rothervalley.ac.uk Website: www.rothervalley.ac.uk	■	F, M, B, IT, INT, MA, ST	–	■	–	–	–
Scarborough Centre for Regeneration, The University of Hull, Hull HU6 7RX Tel (General enquiries): +44 (0)1482 346311 (Order a prospectus): +44 (0)870 126 2000 Email: admissions@hull.ac.uk Website: www.hull.ac.uk	■	F, M, B, EX, IT, INT, MA, ST	■	–	–	–	–
School for Social Entrepreneurs, 18 Victoria Park Square, London E2 9PF Tel: 0208 981 0300 Fax: 0208 983 4655 Email: sandra.wynter@sse.org.uk Website: www.sse.org.uk	■	F, M, B, EX, IT, INT, ST	■	■	■	■	■
Services to Business, Coleg Llandrillo, Llandudno Road, Rhos-on-Sea, Colwyn Bay LL28 4HZ Contact: Admin assistant, Barbara Meadow Tel: 01492 546666 Ext: 239 Fax: 01492 542339 Email: admissions@llandrillo.ac.uk Website: www.llandrillo.ac.uk	■	F, M, B, IT, INT, MA, ST	■	■	–	–	–

Organization		Type					
Sheffield College, PO Box 345, Sheffield S2 2YY Tel: +44 (0) 114 260 3603 Tel: +44 (0) 114 2603655 Fax: 0114 260 2251 Email: enquiries@sheffcol.ac.uk Website: www.sheffcol.ac.uk	–	ST	■	–	–	–	–
Small Firms Enterprise Development Initiative (SFEDI Ltd), 12 Stephenson Court, Fraser Road, Priory Business Park, Bedford MK44 3WH Tel: +44 (0)1234 831222 Fax: +44 (0)1234 831222 Email: info@sfedi.co.uk Website: www.sfedi.co.uk	■	F, M, B, EX, IT, INT, ST	■	■	■	–	–
South Molton Community College, Old Alswear Road, South Molton EX36 4LA Tel: 01769 572129 Fax: 01769 573351 Email: PBerry5082@aol.com	■	F, B	■	–	–	–	–
South Thames College, Wandsworth Centre, Wandsworth High Street, Wandsworth, London SW18 2PP Contact: Student Services Tel: 020 8918 7777; 0208 9188 7150 Fax: 0208 918 7136 Email: enquiries@south-thames.ac.uk Website: www.south-thames.ac.uk	■	F, M, B, EX, IT, INT, MA, ST	–	–	–	–	–
Southend Adult Community College, Southcurch Centre, Ambleside Drive, Southend on Sea SS1 2UP Tel: 01702 445700 Fax: 01702 445739 Email: info@southend-adult.co.uk Website: www.southend.gov.uk	–	F, B	■	–	–	–	–

	Start-up courses	Topic courses	Business growth	Consultancy/ advice	Research activity	Business/ e-club	Special small business unit
Speak First Ltd, 353 Kentish Town Road, London NW5 2TJ Tel: 0870 841 4111 Fax: 0870 841 4222 Email: info@speakfirst.co.uk Website: www.speakfirst.co.uk	–	MA, ST	■	–	–	–	–
Spelthorne College, Church Road, Ashford TW15 2XD Contact: Admissions Tel: 01784 248666 Fax: 01784 254132 Email: info@spelthorne.ac.uk Website: www.spelthorne.ac.uk	■	F, M, B, EX, IT, INT, MA, ST	–	–	–	–	–
Stockport College of Further and Higher Education, Stockport College, Wellington Road South, Stockport SK1 3UQ Contact: Course Enquiries Tel: +44 (0)845 230 3106 Fax: 0161 480 6636 Email: enquiries@stockport.ac.uk Website: www.stockport.ac.uk	■	F, B	■	–	–	–	–
Study House Ltd, Sales Office, The Woodside Centre, Catchdale Moss Lane, Eccleston, St Helens WA10 5QJ Tel: 01744 6167980 Fax: 01744 731122 Email: info@study-house.co.uk Website: www.study-house.co.uk	–	F, M, B, EX, IT, INT, MA, ST	■	■	–	–	–

Organization						
Swadlincote Centre for Guidance and Learning, Rinkway, Swadlincote, Derbyshire DE11 8JL. Tel: 01283 228400. Fax: 01283 228401. Email: fionaeaglesham@swadlincotecentre.co.uk; susanlangridge@swadlincotecentre.co.uk. Website: www.swadlincotecentre.co.uk	■	M, IT, ST	■	–	–	■
The Enterprise Partnership Ltd, PO Box 38451, London SE16 5WD. Tel: 020 7232 0325. Fax: 0207 498 1803. Email: info@entpart.demon.co.uk. Website: http://entpart.demon.co.uk	–	MA, ST	■	–	–	–
University of Abertay, Centre for Business Development & Enterprise, Dundee Business School, Bell Street, Dundee DD1 1HG. Tel: + 44 (0) 1382 308401. Fax: 01382 308400. Email: r.d.kirk@tay.ac.uk. Website: www.tay.ac.uk	■	M, B, ST	–	–	–	■
University of Brighton, Business Services, Mithras House, Lewes Road, Brighton BN2 4AT. Contact: Business Services Information Desk. Tel: 01273 643222. Fax: 02773 643 227. Email: business.services@brighton.ac.uk. Website: www.brighton.ac.uk	–	INT, MA	–	–	–	■

	Start-up courses	Topic courses	Business growth	Consultancy/ advice	Research activity	Business/ e-club	Special small business unit
University of Central England, ERDC Business School. Perry Barr, Birmingham B42 2SU Tel: +44 (0)121 331 5200 Fax: +44 (0)121 331 6366 Email: business.school@uce.ac.uk Website: http://www.bs.uce.ac.uk/default.asp?pageID=3	■	IT, MA, ST	■	■	–	–	–
University of Central Lancashire, Business Development, Preston PR1 2HE Tel: +44 (0)1772 201201 Fax: 01772 892917 Email: mgibson@uclan.ac.uk Website: www.uclan.ac.uk	–	F, M, INT, MA, ST	■	■	–	–	■
University of Derby, Derbyshire Business School. Kedleston Road, Derby DE22 1GB Tel: +44 (0) 1332 590500 Fax: +44 (0) 1332 294861 Email: d.rae@derby.ac.uk Website: www.derby.ac.uk	■	MA	■	■	–	–	–
University of Glasgow, Department of Business & Management, West Quadrangle, Gilbert Scott Buildings, University Avenue, Glasgow G12 8QQ Tel: +44 (0) 141 330 3993 Fax: +44 (0) 141 330 4939 Email: r.paton@mgt.gla.ac.uk Website: www.gla.ac.uk/departments/ managementstudies	–	M, MA, ST	■	–	–	–	■

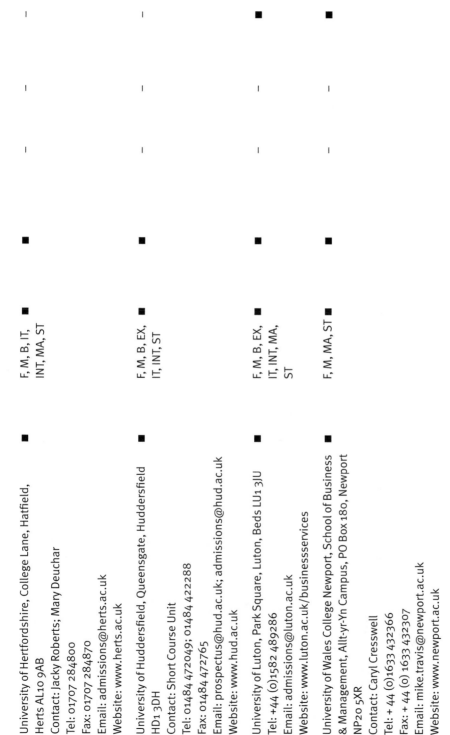

University of Hertfordshire, College Lane, Hatfield, Herts AL10 9AB
Contact: Jacky Roberts; Mary Deuchar
Tel: 01707 284800
Fax: 01707 284870
Email: admissions@herts.ac.uk
Website: www.herts.ac.uk
F, M, B, IT, INT, MA, ST

University of Huddersfield, Queensgate, Huddersfield HD1 3DH
Contact: Short Course Unit
Tel: 01484 472049; 01484 422288
Fax: 01484 472765
Email: prospectus@hud.ac.uk; admissions@hud.ac.uk
Website: www.hud.ac.uk
F, M, B, EX, IT, INT, ST

University of Luton, Park Square, Luton, Beds LU1 3JU
Tel: +44 (0)1582 489286
Email: admissions@luton.ac.uk
Website: www.luton.ac.uk/businessservices
F, M, B, EX, IT, INT, MA, ST

University of Wales College Newport, School of Business & Management, Allt-yr-Yn Campus, PO Box 180, Newport NP20 5XR
Contact: Caryl Cresswell
Tel: + 44 (0)1633 432366
Fax: + 44 (0) 1633 432307
Email: mike.travis@newport.ac.uk
Website: www.newport.ac.uk
F, M, MA, ST

	Start-up courses	Topic courses	Business growth	Consultancy/ advice	Research activity	Business/ e-club	Special small business unit
Walsall College of Arts and Technology, PO Box 4203, WS1 1WY Tel: 01922 657000 Email: info@walcat.ac.uk Fax: 01922 657083 Website: www.walcat.ac.uk	-	MA	-	-	-	-	-
Waltham Forest College, Forest Road, Waltham Forest, Greater London E17 4JB Tel: 0208 501 8000 Fax: 0208 501 8001 Email: info@waltham.ac.uk Website: www.waltham.ac.uk	■	F, M, B, IT, INT, ST	■	-	-	-	-
West Cheshire College, Eaton Road, Handbridge, Chester CH4 7ER Contact: Course Admissions Hotline: 01244 670600 or 0151 356 7800 Tel: 01244 677677 Fax: 01244 670676 Email: info@west-cheshire.ac.uk Website: www.west-cheshire.ac.uk	■	F, B	■	-	-	-	-
West Cumbria Adult Education, Cumbria County Council, The Courts, Carlisle CA3 8NA Contact: Course Enquiries Tel: 01228 606060 Fax: 01228 606327 Email: information@cumbriacc.gov.uk Website: www.cumbriaadulteducation.co.uk	■	F, M, B, EX, IT, INT, MA, ST	■	-	-	-	-

			Codes			
West Suffolk College, Bury St Edmunds, Out Risbygate, Bury St Edmunds IP33 3RL Tel: 01284 701301 Fax: 01284 750561 Email: info@westsuffolk.ac.uk Website: www.westsuffolk.ac.uk	■	■	F,	–	–	–
Westminster Adult Education Service (WAES), Maida Vale Centre, Elgin Avenue, London W9 2NR Tel: 0207 297 7297 Fax: 0207 641 8140 Email: info@waes.ac.uk Website: www.waes.ac.uk	■	■	F, M, B, EX, IT, INT, ST	■	–	–
Wigan & Leigh College, PO Box 53, Parsons Walk, Wigan WN1 1RS Tel: 01942 76 16 00; 01942 76 11 11 Fax: 01942 76 16 03 Email: do.morris@wigan-leigh.ac.uk Website: www.wigan-leigh.ac.uk	■	■	F, MA, ST	■	–	■
Wrexham Business School, North East Wales Institute of Higher Education, Plas Coch, Mold Road, Wrexham LL11 2AW Tel: 01978 293444 Fax: 01978 290008 Email: services@newi.ac.uk Website: www.newi.ac.uk	■	■	F, M, EX, IT, INT, MA, ST	–	–	■
Yeovil College, Mudford Road, Yeovil BA21 4DR Tel: 01935 423921 Fax: 01935 429962 Email: info@yeovil.ac.uk Website: www.yeovil-college.ac.uk	■	■	F, B	■	–	–

Directory of online small business programmes

This is a small cross-section of the thousands of online and distance learning courses for business starters and small businesses.

Business Teacher (now taken into the Exams Tutor business)

Website: www.businessteacher.co.uk

This site was devised by a group of business lecturers to aid delivery of advanced business courses through the use of online study material. As an individual subscriber at a cost of £19.99 a year you'll get 12 months' full access to all the content, which has been written and developed by subject specialists who are qualified business lecturers. They are an approved content provider for the National Grid for Learning, (NGfL), the government body set up to ensure the quality of learning material on the web. They are also listed on the BBC's Education Web Guide – 'Best of the Web'.

Canada/British Columbia Business Services

Website: www.smallbusinessbc.ca

A free resource by the Canada/British Columbia Business Service Centre. The mandate of the Canada/British Columbia Business Services is to serve as the primary source of timely and accurate business-related information and referrals on Federal and Provincial government programmes, services and regulations, without charge.

They provide an excellent series of small business tutorials: Starting With A Good Idea; Marketing Basics; Financing Your Business; Planning Fundamentals; and Business Regulations for Getting Started.

Economic Development Online

Website: www.edo.umn.edu

Economic Development Online is a series of high-quality economic development courses provided by leading universities and hosted by the University of Minnesota. Their E-Commerce for Small Business course, for example, costs $100.00.

Education to Go

Website: www.ed2go.com

Education to Go have a range of small business courses on line, including How to Grow Plants for Fun and Profit, and Starting Your Own Construction Management Business.

E-Learn.uk.com

Website: www.e-learn.uk.com

E-Learn.uk.com offers distance learning through the Internet, providing you with an interactive educational experience and the opportunity to study through accredited learning providers. You can choose from a wide variety of online business courses and programmes, including:

*   Basic Bookkeeping and Accounts
*   Communication Techniques Certificate
*   Customer Relations Certificate
*   Business Studies
*   Stress Management Diploma Course
*   Stress Management – Corporate & Professional
*   Telemarketing Professional.

You'll learn at your own pace and decide on your own method of learning, all with a choice of payment options. Just register as a new student and select a course from the online prospectus. You can work online or print out course materials and get started right away.

Ideal Schools

60 St Enoch Square
Glasgow
G1 4AG
Tel: 0141 248 5200
Website: www.idealschools.co.uk

Provides online bookkeeping courses aimed at small businesses

Oxford Open Learning International
4 King's Meadow
Oxford
OX2 0DP
Tel: 01865 792790
Fax: 01865 200154
Email: enquiries@ool.co.uk
Website: www.ool-international.com

Oxford Open Learning offers a wide range of 'A' level, GCSE and vocational training courses and programmes, both online and via CD-ROM, including:

* Certificate Entrepreneurial Skills
* Diploma in Accounting
* Diploma in Business Studies
* Principles of Management
* Retirement Homes Management
* Small Business Skills
* Mediation and Negotiation.

Personal Traveler
PO Box 4481
San Dimas
CA 91773
USA
Tel: 00 1 909 592 9473
Email: sales@europejam.com
Website: www.europejam.com

Personal Traveler offers its Take Charge! course for small business owners and managers, which provides a simple, step-by-step method to increasing profits. Organized into 12 weekly sections of seven lessons each, the programme provides 84 straightforward and effective problem-solving and business-growing strategies. Each lesson also has a corresponding worksheet that helps you to take immediate action on what you have learned. Costs $49.95.

Start Right
Website: www.businesspark.barclays.co.uk/seminars_events/sems_events_startright.htm

Barclays and the National Federation of Enterprise Agencies are joint organizers of this seminar programme, which has helped thousands of people throughout England and Wales start and run their own business.

The events are very informal. Content and duration may vary from event to event. However, they will cover aspects such as:

* the pros and cons of being your own boss
* the legal and financial implications involved in running a business
* preparing a business plan
* marketing
* cash flow
* funding.

The seminars are delivered by experts who know the concerns of starting a business, and have experience of the different market sectors. The majority of seminars are free of charge. However, in some circumstances it may be necessary for a charge to be levied.

Study House Ltd
Sales Office
8 Hillswood Avenue
Kendal
LA9 5BT
Tel: 01539 724622
Fax: 01539 734270
Email: info@study-house.co.uk
Website: www.study-house.co.uk

Study House Ltd is a UK provider of distance learning courses and qualifications and offers a wide variety of business and professional qualification certificate programmes, including:

* Certificate in Business Planning
* Certificate in Business Management

- Certificate in Executive Office Skills
- Certificate in Conflict Management
- Start Your Own Business Pack
- Certificate in Business Finance
- Small Business Finance Diploma.

The business certificate courses are available on CD-ROM or in hard copy format, with student support via telephone and email, enabling students to complete their studies at work or at home and over a time-scale which suits their other commitments. No formal attendance at college is required but tutor support is included.

Directory of online small business training programmes databases

These databases give you access to most of the English speaking world's providers of online and distance learning for entrepreneurs and small businesses.

Association of British Correspondence Courses

PO Box 17926
London
SW19 3WB
Tel: 020 8544 9559
Fax: 020 8540 7657
Email: info@HomeStudy.org.uk
Website: www.homestudy.org.uk

Online database of members, with direct links to hundreds of small business-related home learning programmes.

British Association for Open Learning

Suite 12
Pixmore Centre
Pixmore Avenue
Letchworth
SG6 1JG
Tel: 01462 485588
Fax: 01462 485633
Email: sarah@baol.co.uk
Website: www.baol.co.uk

Has a region-by-region directory of distance learning and online learning providers.

Providing informed objective advice and information on all aspects of learning and learning innovation.

Compendium of Entrepreneur Programs

Website: www.marshall.usc.edu/web/Lloydgreif.cfm?doc_id=1070

Lloyd Greif Center, run by Marshal School of Business is designed to help students develop an entrepreneurial attitude of being open to change, developing new ideas and thinking outside the box and beyond the limitations of existing paradigms. This blend of tools, skills and attitude equips the graduates to organize and manage new ventures. Their website's aim is to provide a convenient source of information about university programmes in entrepreneurship.

For each school there are two pages devoted to a description of its entrepreneurship programme in a format intended to make it easy to scan for similarities and differences. Schools are listed in alphabetical order by name. At the end of most descriptions is an online home page reference for seeking additional information about the school and its activities devoted to entrepreneurship. A total of 128 mostly US and European schools are included in the database that have programmes truly focused on entrepreneurship.

Hotcourses.com

Website: www.hotcourses.com

This website lists and describes 285 courses for small businesses in the UK. They range from topic programmes on bookkeeping or business start-up, through to e-commerce and employing key staff. It has many other training programmes in its extensive database.

International Centre for Distance Learning

Walton Hall
Milton Keynes
MK7 6AA

Tel: 01908 653537
Fax: 01980 654173
Email: icdl-enquiries@open.ac.uk
Website: www-icdl.open.ac.uk

Based at the Open University, this database contains details of over 1000 institutions worldwide offering distance learning courses. These institutions range from small private accredited colleges to large distance teaching universities.

Twenty-four UK providers are listed as providing How To Start Your Own Business programmes. They range from Bed and Breakfast Hotel Management through to Starting A Successful Horse Management Business.

My Own Business Inc.
PO Box 8039
Rowland Heights
CA 91748
USA
Email: support@myownbusiness.org
Website: www.myownbusiness.org

This has to be the place to start. It's good and it's free. My Own Business is an online, 11-session course providing the basic 'do's and 'don't's for entrepreneurs. The course is intended for both start-up and already operating entrepreneurs. With audio sound bites, quizzes, feedback and a tool to create your own business plan, the site is fully interactive.

In response to the 1992 Los Angeles riots, successful entrepreneur Phil Holland founded My Own Business, Inc. to share his expertise and experience in creating businesses with the people whose neighbourhoods most required rebuilding. The first classes were held in Compton, California.

Over a span of 10 years, MOBI has improved, updated and refined the course to support the development of new businesses. You can see and hear over 50 entrepreneurs talk about the problems and successes they have encountered on the way and there is also an online business plan writing package.

Eleven topics are covered: Deciding on a Business; the Business Plan; Organization and Insurance; Location and Leasing; Accounting and Cash Flow; How to Borrow Money; E-Commerce; Buying a Business or Franchise; Marketing; Expanding; and Handling Problems.

National Grid for Learning
Website: www.ngfl.gov.uk

This is the UK government's gateway to educational resources on the Internet. The NGfL provides a network of selected links to websites that offer high quality content and information.

Small Business Learning Centre
ASBDC
1205 University Avenue
Suite 300
Columbia
MO 65211
USA
Tel: 00 1 573 882 9098
Email: mengj@missouri.edu
Website: www.smallbusinesslearning.com

A partnership between the US Small Business Administration and the Association of Small Business Development Centres listing hundreds of online courses for entrepreneurs, business people, anyone interested in starting a business and marketing it.

Small Business Research Portal
Website: www.smallbusinessportal.co.uk

This site includes in a wide range of information about small business conferences and UK institutions that run training programmes for small business. Mostly an academic site, but some useful links.

Tap into Learning
Website: www.tap.org.uk

This is an online database of thousands of learning

opportunities. It is compiled from information supplied by providers in Avon, Dorset, Gloucestershire and Somerset. ('Avon' is used to describe the unitary authorities of Bath & NE Somerset, Bristol, North Somerset, South Gloucestershire.) The database allows you to search for a learning opportunity that suits your requirements by selecting from a number of options including:

- subject
- geographical area (county, district, town)
- method of study
- qualification
- attendance
- provider.

On 10 February 2002, tapping in 'small business' came up with the following offering of programmes:

- small business finance (10 courses)
- small business management (30 courses)
- small business marketing (3 courses)
- small business operations (5 courses)
- small business personnel (2 courses).

University for Industry
Website: www.ufiltd.co.uk

UFI's learning services are being delivered through learndirect (www.learndirect-business.co.uk/), which provides access to innovative and high quality courses, over 80% of them online. learndirect will enable people to fit learning into their lives, learning wherever they have access to the Internet – at home, at work, or in one of over 1000 learndirect centres. They have information and advice on over 500,000 courses nationwide online and aim to show you how learndirect can help you unlock the potential of your small business.

World Wide Learn
World Wide Learn
Suite 4
2521 17th Avenue SW
Calgary

Canada
T3E 0A2
Tel: (403) 686–6162
Website: www.worldwidelearn.com

The primary goal of this site is to help you find online education resources as quickly and easily as possible. Started in 1998, World Wide Learn is a directory of hundreds of online courses in 64 subject categories (and growing).

Other major small business training resources

New Deal
Website: www.newdeal.gov.uk/english/self_employment/

New Deal is a key part of the government's Welfare to Work strategy. A part of its service is to offer help for people who want to set up and run their own business. Help with a business plan and a period of test trading is available whilst on New Deal. Work Based Learning for adults (in England and Wales), Training for Work (in Scotland), or a Jobfinder's Grant are other avenues available for people wishing to work for themselves.

New Deal personal advisers will refer people who want to find out more about the self-employment option of New Deal to an awareness session. This will be a brief introduction to the most important aspects of self-employment. Following on from this there will be a short course – usually one day a week for four weeks – or one-to-one counselling. This course will help you:

- decide whether self-employment is the best choice for you
- get further information and training
- produce a business plan.

Once you've come up with an approved business plan or are independently trading, you will enter the 'Test Trading period' of the self-employment option. For up to six months you will get advice and support from training providers while setting up and running your own business, plus the opportunity to train towards an approved qualification.

Training providers will offer a range of help, from dealing with day-to-day queries to help with finding start-up finance. They will also meet with you regularly to check your progress. Help and advice will continue to be available for up to two years after the option has ended.

There is also help for people who want to earn a living as a performing musician (vocalist, instrumentalist or DJ) through New Deal for Musicians.

When you take up the self-employment option, you will receive an allowance plus a grant of up to £400 paid in equal weekly or fortnightly instalments. Any money the business earns during the six months on the option can either be ploughed back into the business or stored in a special bank account until the option has ended.

The Learning and Skills Council

If you are looking to train and educate new staff for your business, then your local Learning Skills Council may be able to help. They may also be able to signpost you towards training to meet your own needs as a business starter. The Learning and Skills Council replaced the Training and Enterprise Councils and the Further Education Funding Council in 2001. They are now responsible for all post-16 education and training.

The Council has brought together the skills of the Training and Enterprise Councils and the Further Education Funding Council to work with partners, employers, learning providers, community groups and individuals to develop and implement strategies that meet the Government's aims set out in the 'Learning to Succeed' White Paper.

It works alongside the Employment Service, the Small Business Service, Connexions, the National Training Organisations, further education and sixth form colleges, and representatives of community groups, to understand, define and then meet training and education needs. The Learn-

ing and Skills Council's national office is based in Coventry, with 47 local Learning and Skills Councils across England.

East of England
Learning and Skills Council (Bedfordshire and Luton)
Woburn Court
2 Railton Road
Woburn Road Industrial Estate
Kempston
MK42 7PN
Tel: 0845 019 4160
Fax: 01234 843211
Email: bedsandlutoninfo@lsc.gov.uk
Website: www.lsc.gov.uk

Learning and Skills Council (Berkshire)
Pacific House
Imperial Way
Reading
RG2 0TF
Tel: 0845 019 4147
Fax: 0118 975 3054
Email: berkshireinfo@lsc.gov.uk

Learning and Skills Council (Birmingham and Solihull)
Chaplin Court
80 Hurst Street
Birmingham
B5 4TG
Tel: 0845 019 4143
Fax: 0121 345 4503
Email: birminghamsolihullinfo@lsc.gov.uk

Learning and Skills Council (Bournemouth, Dorset and Poole)
Provincial House
25 Oxford Road
Bournemouth
BH8 8EY
Tel: 0845 019 4148
Fax: 01202 299457
Email: bdpinfo@lsc.gov.uk

Learning and Skills Council (Cambridgeshire)
Stuart House
St Johns Street
Peterborough
PE1 5DD
Tel: 0845 019 4165
Fax: 01733 895260
Email: cambridgeshireinfo@lsc.gov.uk

**Learning and Skills Council
(Cheshire and Warrington)**
Dalton House
Dalton Way
Middlewich
CW10 0HU
Tel: 0845 019 4163
Fax: 01606 320082
Email: cheshireandwarringtoninfo@lsc.gov.uk

Learning and Skills Council (County Durham)
Allergate House
Belmont Business Park
Belmont
Co. Durham
DH1 1TW
Tel: 0845 019 4174
Fax: 01325 372302
Email: countydurhaminfo@lsc.gov.uk

**Learning and Skills Council
(Coventry and Warwickshire)**
Oak Tree Court
Binley Business Park
Harry Weston Road
Coventry
CV3 2UN
Tel: 0845 019 4156
Fax: 024 7645 0242
Email: CWinfo@lsc.gov.uk
Website: www.lsc-cw.org

Learning and Skills Council (Cumbria)
Venture House
Regents Court
Guard Street

Workington
CA14 4EW
Tel: 0845 019 4159
Fax: 01900 733302
Email: cumbriainfo@lsc.gov.uk

Learning and Skills Council (Derbyshire)
St Helen's Court
St Helen's Street
Derby
DE1 3GY
Tel: 0845 019 4183
Fax: 01332 292188
Email: derbyshireinfo@lsc.gov.uk

**Learning and Skills Council
(Devon and Cornwall)**
Foliot House
Budshead Road
Crownhill
Plymouth
PL6 5XR
Tel: 0845 019 4155
Fax: 01752 754040
Email: devonandcornwallinfo@lsc.gov.uk

Learning and Skills Council (Essex)
Redwing House
Hedgerows Business Park
Colchester Road
Chelmsford
CM2 5PB
Tel: 0845 019 4179
Fax: 01245 451430
Email: essexinfo@lsc.gov.uk

Learning and Skills Council (Gloucestershire)
Conway House
33–35 Worcester Street
Gloucester
GL1 3AJ
Tel: 0845 019 4189
Fax: 01452 450002
Email: gloucestershireinfo@lsc.gov.uk

Learning and Skills Council (Greater Manchester)
9th Floor, Arndale House
Arndale Centre
Manchester
M4 3AQ
Tel: 0845 019 4142
Fax: 0161 261 0370
Email: GrManchesterinfo@lsc.gov.uk

Learning and Skills Council (Greater Merseyside)
3rd Floor
Tithebarn House
Tithebarn Street
Liverpool
L2 2NZ
Tel: 0845 019 4150
Fax: 0151 672 3533
Email: merseysideinfo@lsc.gov.uk

Learning and Skills Council (Hampshire and Isle of Wight)
Eagle Point
Little Park Farm Road,
Segensworth
Fareham
PO15 5TD
Tel: 0845 019 4182
Fax: 01329 237733
Email: hampshire-IOWinfo@lsc.gov.uk
Satellite office: Mill Court, Furlongs, Newport
PO30 2AA

Learning and Skills Council (Herefordshire and Worcestershire)
Progress House
Central Park
Midland Road
Worcester
WR5 1DU
Tel: 0845 019 4188
Fax: 01905 721403
Email: HWinfo@lsc.gov.uk

Learning and Skills Council (Hertfordshire)
45 Grosvenor Road
St Albans
AL1 3AW
Tel: 0845 019 4167
Fax: 01727 813443
Email: hertsinfo@lsc.gov.uk

Learning and Skills Council (Humberside)
The Maltings
Silvester Square
Silvester Street
Hull
HU1 3HA
Tel: 0845 019 4153
Fax: 01482 213206
Email: humberinfo@lsc.gov.uk

Learning and Skills Council (Kent and Medway)
26 Kings Hill Avenue
Kings Hill
West Malling
ME19 4AE
Tel: 0845 019 4152
Fax: 01732 841641
Email: kentandmedwayinfo@lsc.gov.uk

Learning and Skills Council (Lancashire)
Caxton Road
Fulwood
Preston
PR2 9ZB
Tel: 0845 019 4157
Fax: 01772 443002
Email: lancashireinfo@lsc.gov.uk

Learning and Skills Council (Leicestershire)
17a Meridian East
Meridian Business Park
Leicester
LE19 1UU
Tel: 0845 019 4177
Fax: 0116 228 1801
Email: leicestershireinfo@lsc.gov.uk
Website: www.enterprisenet.co.uk

**Learning and Skills Council
(Lincolnshire and Rutland)**
Lindum Business Park
Station Road
North Hykeham
Lincoln
LN6 3FE
Tel: 0845 019 4178
Fax: 01522 561563
Email: lincsrutlandinfo@lsc.gov.uk

Learning and Skills Council (London Central)
Centrepoint
103 New Oxford Street
London
WC1A 1DR
Tel: 0845 019 4144
Fax: 020 7896 8686
Email: londoncentralinfo@lsc.gov.uk

Learning and Skills Council (London South)
Canius House
1 Scarbrook Road
Croydon
CR0 1SQ
Tel: 0845 019 4172
Fax: 020 8929 4706
Email: londonsouthinfo@lsc.gov.uk

Learning and Skills Council (London East)
Boardman House
64 Broadway
London
E15 1NT
Tel: 0845 019 4151
Fax: 020 8929 3802
Email: Londoneastinfo@lss.gov.uk

Learning and Skills Council (London North)
Dumayne House
1 Fox Lane
Palmers Green
London
N13 4AB
Tel: 0845 019 4158
Fax: 020 8882 5931

Email: londonnorthinfo@lsc.gov.uk

Learning and Skills Council (London West)
Central House
Lampton Road
Hounslow
Middlesex
TW3 1HY
Tel: 0845 019 4164
Fax: 020 8929 8403
Email: londonwestinfo@lsc.gov.uk
Website: www.westlondon.com/ResearchCentre

Learning and Skills Council (Milton Keynes, Oxfordshire and Buckinghamshire)
Latimer House
Langford Business Park
Langford Locks
Kidlington
Oxford OX5 1GG
Tel: 0845 019 4154
Fax: 01235 468200
Email: MKOBinfo@lsc.gov.uk

Learning and Skills Council (Norfolk)
St Andrews House
St Andrews Street
Norwich
NR2 4TP
Tel: 0845 019 4173
Fax: 01603 218802
Email: norfolkinfo@lsc.gov.uk

Learning and Skills Council (North Yorkshire)
7 Pioneer Business Park
Amy Johnson Way
Clifton Moorgate
York
YO30 4TN
Tel: 0845 019 4146
Fax: 01904 385503
Email: northyorkshireinfo@lsc.gov.uk

**Learning and Skills Council
(Northamptonshire)**
Royal Pavilion

Summerhouse Road
Moulton Park Industrial Estate
Northampton
NN3 6BJ
Tel: 0845 019 4175
Fax: 01604 533046
Email: northantsinfo@lsc.gov.uk

Learning and Skills Council (Northumberland)
Suite 2
Craster Court
Manor Walk
Cramlington
NE23 6XX
Tel: 0845 019 4185
Fax: 01670 706212
Email: northumberlandinfo@lsc.gov.uk

Learning and Skills Council (Nottinghamshire)
Castle Marina Road
Castle Marina Park
Nottingham
NG7 1TN
Tel: 0845 019 4187
Fax: 0115 872 0002
Email: nottsinfo@lsc.gov.uk

Learning and Skills Council (Shropshire)
The Learning Point
3 Hawksworth Road
Central Park
Telford
TF2 9TU
Tel: 0845 019 4190
Fax: 01952 235556
Email: shropshireinfo@lsc.gov.uk

Learning and Skills Council (Somerset)
East Reach House
East Reach
Taunton
TA1 3EN
Tel: 0845 019 4161
Fax: 01823 226074
Email: somersetinfo@lsc.gov.uk

Learning and Skills Council (South Yorkshire)
The Straddle
Victoria Quays
Wharf Street
Sheffield
S2 5SY
Tel: 0845 019 4171
Fax: 0114 275 2634
Email: southyorkshireinfo@lsc.gov.uk

Learning and Skills Council (Staffordshire)
Festival Way
Festival Park
Stoke-on-Trent
ST1 5TQ
Tel: 0845 019 4149
Fax: 01782 463104
Email: staffordshireinfo@lscstaffordshire.org.uk

Learning and Skills Council (Suffolk)
Felaw Maltings
42 Felaw Street
Ipswich
IP2 8SJ
Tel: 0845 019 4180
Fax: 01473 883090
Email: suffolkinfo@lsc.gov.uk

Learning and Skills Council (Surrey)
Technology House
48–54 Goldsworth Road
Woking
GU21 1LE
Tel: 0845 019 4145
Fax: 01483 755259
Email: surreyinfo@lsc.gov.uk
Website: www.surreyllsc.org.uk

Learning and Skills Council (Sussex)
Prince's House
53 Queen's Road
Brighton
BN1 3XB
Tel: 01273 783555
Fax: 01273 783507
Email: sussexinfo@lsc.gov.uk

Learning and Skills Council (Tees Valley)
2 Queens Square
Middlesbrough
TS2 1AA
Tel: 0845 019 4166
Fax: 01642 232480
Email: teesvalleyinfo@lsc.gov.uk

**Learning and Skills Council
(The Black Country)**
1st Floor
Black Country House
Rounds Green Road
Oldbury
Warley
B69 2DG
Tel: 0845 019 4186
Fax: 0121 345 4777
Email: blackcountryinfo@lsc.gov.uk

Learning and Skills Council (Tyne and Wear)
Moongate House
5th Avenue Business Park
Team Valley
Gateshead
NE11 0HF
Tel: 0845 019 4181
Fax: 0191 491 6159
Email: tyneandwearinfo@lsc.gov.uk

Learning and Skills Council (West of England)
St Lawrence House
29–31 Broad Street
Bristol
BS99 7HR
Tel: 0845 019 4168
Fax: 0117 922 6664
Email: WestofEnglandinfo@lsc.gov.uk
Website: www.lsc.gov.uk

Learning and Skills Council (West Yorkshire)
Mercury House
4 Manchester Road
Bradford
BD5 0QL
Tel: 0845 019 4169

Fax: 01274 444009
Email: westyorkshireinfo@lsc.gov.uk

**Learning and Skills Council
(Wiltshire and Swindon)**
The Bora Building
Westlea Campus
Westlea Down
Swindon
SN5 7EZ
Tel: 0845 019 4176
Fax: 01793 608003
Email: Wiltswindoninfo@lsc.gov.uk

Training plan

Starting a business will call upon a whole range of new skills that you may have never needed before. Don't be tempted to claim to be too busy or to hope to pick those skills up as you go along. The link between training and business success is undisputed, but if for no other reason, make time for training as banks will sometimes be more generous if they see business skills training in a business plan.

It's important to remember also that training is not just for you. As the business starts to grow, you will need to delegate tasks to staff members, and they will need to learn new skills too. It is important for everyone connected with your business to obtain the range of skills that are necessary to run a successful business. Cover the following areas in your audit.

- **What skills do you need?** Make a short list of broad-based business skills – bookkeeping, marketing, sales techniques, customer care, market research, IT, e-commerce and so forth. Restrict the list to those areas applicable to the business.
- **When do you need them by?** Your own business plan will identify the priority in which you need to acquire the skills. Try to set specific target time-scales against the acquisition of each skill.
- **How will you acquire them?** Consider a variety of methods including formal structured

courses, more informal courses, self-paced learning programmes and books.

- **Make a Training Plan:** Review the courses and institutions listed here to find if any of these offer the type of training you need. Show and discuss your training requirements with your business adviser, accountant or any other experienced business contact. They may have access to a wide range of suitable courses, some of which are subsidized or even free.

Review this audit on a regular basis so that your skills needs and acquisitions always match your business development.

Section 9

OPPORTUNITIES FOR YOUNG ENTREPRENEURS

Young, as far as starting a business is concerned, is a fairly elastic term. For the purposes of this section it is taken as meaning anyone between around 15 and 30 years of age. The organizations listed below have between them helped over a million young people set up in business, and help a further 100,000 each year.

The Prince's Trust, one of the main forces in the field, helps 5000 British teenagers to set up their own business, most of who are successful and 10% of whom have achieved annual sales in excess of £1 million each.

The following case study is just one example of a business started at school that has grown into a stunningly successful venture.

Codemasters

www.codemasters.com

David Darling, a schoolboy entrepreneur, has created a multi-million-pound company from modest beginnings – his first venture operated from his grandparents' garden shed. As a teenager growing up in the early 1980s, he developed his first digital game and placed an advert in a specialist magazine. The exercise was a success. Darling, 34, is now head of Codemasters, a group that employs more than 380 people and in 2001 made profits of £22 million.

David and his brother, Richard, were fascinated by the new technology of computer games. They were avid readers of Popular Computing Weekly (PCW), a specialist magazine for Atari, Commodore and Sinclair users. One section of the publication was devoted to programming, featuring computer code listings for popular games as well as tuition and advice. The technology was primitive and with the help of the magazine, the two brothers were able to copy simple codes for games such as P Space Invaders. Next they started to develop games, initially for themselves.

Thus they decided to test the market and saved up the money for a half-page advertisement in PCW. The price was £70, which they raised by missing school dinners for weeks.

They created their own advert and logo – a Superman-type character – with the help of a friend whose father ran an advertising design company. Under the name Galactic Software, they offered '14 great games from America' for £10. They had hoped merely to make enough money to cover the cost of the advert, but in the event 40 readers replied, generating £400 of sales. Encouraged by their success, the brothers ran a second and third advert in consecutive issues. After the third, some 500 orders came in, which was more work than two people could manage, especially with exams approaching. In response Darling employed the services of a music duplication business in Bridgwater, Somerset. It made copies of tapes for local bands and he struck a deal paying the company to copy the 14 games at the rate of 50p per tape.

The first company vehicle was a very secondhand Honda moped bought for £60 to collect the tapes, while he used his grandparents' garden shed as a warehouse.

After the Darling brothers sat their exams, they went into business full-time.

Organizations which can help young people start up in business

Although some of these organizations are based outside the UK, the information on their websites and some of their services are available to anyone anywhere and certainly of value to any entrepreneur.

Graduates for Growth
www.graduatesforgrowth.org.uk

A website run out of Durham University to help graduates start a business or get work in a small business.

Independent Means
126 Powers Avenue
Santa Barbara
CA 93103
USA
Tel: 00 1 805 965 0475
Website: www.anincomeofherown.com

Independent Means is a provider of products and services for girls' financial independence, and for parents trying to raise financially fit kids. It's an American site that aims to be the first stop for news and know-how on starting a business; making, saving, giving and growing money.

They provide on-the-ground programmes and seminars, books, games and activities for teens, parents and mentors, and the companies that serve them.

Independent Means was founded by CEO Joline Godfrey, an entrepreneur, activist and writer who has been featured on *Oprah*, the *Today Show*, *The Wall Street Journal*, *The New York Times*, and countless other news programmes.

IMI has an experienced staff with diverse backgrounds in business, including work at major corporations. Five of the company principals also have experience as entrepreneurs with their own companies.

IMI also has a network of over 400 certified trainers qualified to run and deliver IMI pro-

grammes worldwide. Although their corporate office is in Santa Barbara, California, they run programmes all over the US as well as in Australia, New Zealand and they are expanding their reach every day.

Junior Achievement
National Headquarters and Service Center
One Education Way
Colorado Springs
CO 80906
USA
Tel: 00 1 719 540 8000
Fax: 00 1 719 540 6299
Website: www.juniorachievement.org

This is a movement that seeks to educate and inspire young people to value free enterprise, business and economics to improve the quality of their lives. Located in Colorado Springs, Junior Achievement's National Headquarters and Service Center provides support for 156 local offices and their international affiliate serves another 100 countries, with offices around the world.

Altogether, Junior Achievement reaches approximately 5.2 million students worldwide. Through age-appropriate curricula, Junior Achievement programmes begin at the elementary school level.

The JA Company Program provides basic economic education for high school students. By organizing and operating an actual business enterprise, students learn how businesses function.

They have a wide range of documents to support participants on any JA Company Program to help you track progress.

You can also visit a Product Ideas site for a list of JA Company Program vendors that offer products for resale that could be a first step to generating an independent income for a young entrepreneur.

Livewire
Shell Live Wire
Hawthorn House
Forth Banks
Newcastle upon Tyne

NE1 3SG
Tel: 0191 261 5584
Fax: 0191 261 1910
Email: shell-livewire@pne.org
Website: www.shell-livewire.org

Livewire is a national programme supported by Shell to help young entrepreneurs start their own business.

A part of the Shell UK community investment programme, Shell Livewire helps young people (aged 16–30) set up in business with information, advice and support, including how to write a business plan and how to carry out market research.

There are free downloadable booklets on how to carry out market research and how to write a business plan on the website. There is also a 1000 page business encyclopedia covering many topics essential to would-be entrepreneurs.

There are also annual Young Business Start Up Awards, where the winner of the UK final wins £10,000.

The National Youth Agency

Eastgate House
19-23 Humberstone Road
Leicester
LE5 3GJ
Tel: 0116 242 7350 (minicom available)
Fax: 0116 242 7444
Email: nya@nya.org.uk
Website: www.nya.org.uk

Youth work helps young people learn about themselves, others and society, through informal educational activities which combine enjoyment, challenge and learning. Youth workers work with young people aged between 11 and 25, particularly those aged between 13 and 19, in order to promote their personal and social development and enable them to have a voice, influence and place in their communities and society as a whole.

They maintain on their website:

- training information on youth work courses
- contact details of key agencies and local youth services.

The Prince's Trust

18 Park Square East
London
NW1 4LH
Tel: 020 7543 1234
Fax: 020 7543 1200
Freephone: 0800 842842
Email: webinfops@princes-trust.org.uk
Website: www.princes-trust.org.uk

The Prince's Trust London Regional Office

3rd Floor
Tribute House
120 Moorgate
London
EC2M 6TS
Tel: 020 7382 5100
Fax: 020 7382 5199
Email: webinfolo@princes-trust.org.uk

The Prince's Trust helps 14–30 year olds to develop confidence, learn new skills and get into work. They offer opportunities when no one else will. So if you've got an idea for a business but no one will give you the money to get it off the ground, they can offer you finance and advice.

The Prince's Trust can offer:

- a low interest loan of up to £5000
- test marketing grants of up to £250
- grants of up to £1500 in special circumstances
- advice from a volunteer 'business mentor' during your first three years of trading
- extra support including discounted exhibition space and specialist advice.

Last year The Prince's Trust helped more than 4800 young people to set up in business. Over 71% of all start-up applications to The Prince's Trust were converted into new ventures – creating almost 18,000 businesses in just five years. One in ten of those businesses had a turnover in excess of £1 million.

The top 50 Prince's Trust businesses turn over £148 million and employ over 1600 people and since the Trust was established it has helped 43,000 young people to set up in business to 2002.

Even those entrepreneurs who started up with the Trust's help but subsequently had to close their business found advantages from the experience. 51% of young people whose businesses did not succeed went straight into full-time employment, despite the fact that most were out of work before receiving assistance from the Trust. 74% reported that the experience of running their own business had been positive, feeling they had gained skills and increased their confidence.

Training and mentor support are key factors in enterprise success. Success was boosted by pre-start up training. The mentoring and support offered by the Trust also contributed significantly to business success.

The Prince's Trust has many Regional Offices that support the Trust's business start-up activities.

The Prince's Trust – Scotland

Head Office
1st Floor
The Guildhall
57 Queen Street
Glasgow
G1 3EN
Tel: 0141 204 4409
Fax: 0141 221 8221
Email: webinfosc@princes-trust.org.uk

The Prince's Trust – Northern Ireland

Block 5
Jennymount Court
North Derby Street
Belfast
BT15 3HN
Tel: 028 9074 5454
Fax: 028 9074 8416
Email: webinfoni@princes-trust.org.uk

The Prince's Trust – Cymru

Baltic House
Mount Stuart Square
Cardiff
CF10 5FH
Tel: 029 20 437000
Fax: 029 2043 7001
Email: webinfowa@princes-trust.org.uk

The Prince's Trust East of England Regional Office

3a Princes Street
Ipswich
Suffolk
IP1 1PN
Tel: 01473 228844
Fax: 01473 228845
Email: webinfoea@princes-trust.org.uk

The Prince's Trust – North East Regional Office

Tynegate Business Centre
5th Floor
Aidan House
Sunderland Road
Gateshead
Tyne & Wear
NE8 3HU
Tel: 0191 4788488
Fax: 0191 4788487
Email: webinfone@princes-trust.org.uk

The Prince's Trust North West Regional Office

Northbridge House
Elm Street Business Park
Burnley
Lancashire
BB10 1PD
Tel: 01282 714161
Fax: 01925 442074
Email: webinfonw@princes-trust.org.uk

The Prince's Trust South East Regional Office

Headway House
Crosby Way
Farnham
Surrey GU9 7XG
Tel: 01252 891330
Email: webinfose@princes-trust.org.uk

The Prince's Trust South West Regional Office
66 Ringwood Road
Bath BA2 3JL
Tel: 01225 489 930
Fax: 01225 489 931
Email webinfosw@princes-trust.org.uk

The Prince's Trust – East Midlands Regional Office
Mansion House
41 Guildhall Lane
Leicester
LE1 5FQ
Tel: 0116 253 7824
Fax: 0116 253 7866
Email: webinfoem@princes-trust.org.uk

The Prince's Trust West Midlands Regional Office
Lye Business Centre
Enterprise Drive
Hayes Lane
Lye
Stourbridge
West Midlands
DY9 8QH
Tel: 01384 892100
Fax 01384 895381
Email: webinfowm@princes-trust.org.uk

The Prince's Trust Yorkshire and The Humber Regional Office
1st Floor
King Charles II House
Headlands Road
Pontefract
WF8 1DD
Tel: 01977 698 000
Fax: 01977 698 001
Email: webinfoyh@princes-trust.org.uk

The Prince's Trust
Queen Elizabeth's Training College
Leatherhead Court
Woodlands Road
Leatherhead

KT22 0BB
Tel: 01372 844101

The Prince's Trust
Beech House
Witham Park
Waterside South
Lincoln
LN5 7BL
Tel: 01522 808518

The Prince's Trust
Bedford House
Oxford Street
Liverpool University
Liverpool
L69 3BX
Tel: 0151 794 3197

The Prince's Trust
5 The Pavement
London
SW4 0HY
Tel: 020 7498 2774

The Prince's Trust
Bedfordshire Youth Enterprise Service
The Business Centre
Kimpton Road
Luton
LU2 OLB
Tel: 01582 410011

The Prince's Trust
Kent Foundation
Session House
County Hall
Maidstone
ME14 1XQ
Tel: 01622 694280

The Prince's Trust
Queen's Court
Newport Road
Middlesborough
TS1 5EH

Tel: 01642 245400

The Prince's Trust
Northamptonshire Chamber of Commerce
Royal Pavilion
Summerhouse Road
Moulton Park
Northampton
NN3 6BJ
Tel: 01604 533036

The Prince's Trust
4th Floor
Intercity House
Plymouth Station
Plymouth
PL4 6AA
Tel: 01752 251051

The Prince's Trust
42 Grosvenor Road
Ripley
DE5 3DG
Tel: 01773 513753

The Prince's Trust
45 Grosvenor Road
St Albans
AL1 3AW
Tel: 01727 813769

Students in Free Enterprise
The Jack Shewmaker SIFE World Headquarters
Robert W. Plaster Free Enterprise Center
Jack Kahl Entrepreneurship Center
1959 East Kerr Street
Springfield
MO 65803–4775
USA
Tel: 00 1 417 831–9505
Fax: 00 1 417 831–6165
Email: sifeteams@sife.org
Website: www.sife.org

This is a grassroots student movement that is sweeping the world. Active on more than 1000 college and university campuses in more than 20 countries, its mission is to encourage students with the idea of seizing their opportunities and making a difference. Through a collaborative effort between business and education, SIFE teams teach the principles of market economics, entrepreneurship, business ethics and personal financial success.

UK Youth
Kirby House
20–24 Kirby Street
London
EC1N 8TS
Tel: 020 7242 4045
Fax: 020 7242 4125
Email: mark@youth.org.uk
Website: www.youth.org.uk

This is a community for young people using the Internet for learning. The project is managed by UK Youth and is part of The National Grid for Learning. The website, www.youth.org.uk, seeks to empower young people and youth workers to learn together. Its aims are to support youth by:

- developing a virtual community to link and empower young people using the Internet for learning
- providing resources, information and advice for young people using the Internet.

Some of their services are particularly valuable to young people starting up their own business.

- **Web tutorials:** Designed to help the beginner use the Internet and publish on the web.
- **Over 1000 links:** Indexed by the National Youth Agency Focused Access Information System (NYAFAIS).
- **World directory:** The site also has links to other youth sites around the world. One link, for example, is to Youth Industry, in the Bay Area of San Francisco. Their mission is to provide a safe and productive environment in which 15–22 year olds can learn marketable

skills through the creation and operation of small businesses.

Wandsworth Youth Enterprise

Broadway Studios
28 Tooting High Street
London
SW17 0RG
Tel: 020 8672 2832
Fax: 020 8767 7701
Email: admin@wyec.org.uk
Website: www.wyec.org.uk

WYEC is a registered charity that offers a range of business start-up services for young people aged 17–30 in the Wandsworth, Kingston & Merton boroughs. They offer:

- Free half-day awareness seminar designed for young people who are exploring the idea of starting their own business.
- Free one-to-one business counselling to help young people develop a viable business plan, raise finance, and launch a business venture. With further counselling up to two years after starting a business to help young people establish their business.
- Business planning course designed to provide young people with core business planning skills and information. Successful completion can lead to a NVQ level 3 qualification.
- Subsidized offices, studios, workshops and business support services, available for up to two years. Worth an average of up to £6790 per business in subsidies for qualifying clients.
- Subsidized mailing address, telephone message taking, and business support services available for up to two years. For start-up clients and businesses trading less than 12 months.
- A High Flyers Programme with free specialist counselling for 12 months, a £500 working capital grant, and a £400 training grant available to clients meeting the programme's acceptance criteria

YEO (Young Entrepreneurs Organization)

500 Montgomery Street
Suite 500
Alexandria
VA 22314
USA
Tel: 00 1 703 519 6700
Fax: 00 1 703 519 1864
Website: www.yeo.org

The Young Entrepreneurs' Organization is a volunteer group of business professionals, all of whom are under 40 years of age and are the owners, founders, co-founders or controlling shareholders of a company with annual sales of $1 million or more.

The YEO's objective is to support, educate and encourage young entrepreneurs to succeed in building companies and themselves. They are striving to be the premier, peer-to-peer, global network, community and resource for young entrepreneurs and have active chapters all over the world, including the UK, France and Germany in Europe.

Young Enterprise UK

Peterley House
Peterley Road
Oxford
OX4 2TZ
Tel: 01865 776845
Fax: 01865 775671
Email info@young-enterprise.org.uk
Website: www.young-enterprise.org.uk

Young Enterprise is a national education charity with a mission: to inspire and equip young people to learn and succeed through enterprise. Founded in 1963, their aim is to give young people between the ages of 15 and 19 the opportunity to set up and run a company selling products they have designed and made.

In the UK alone they have around 36,000 young people or 'achievers' running their own companies.

Their Company Programme helps people aged 15–19 set up and run their own company over the course of one academic year. They elect a board of directors from amongst their peers, raise share capital, and market and finance a product or service of their own choice. At the end of the year they liquidate the company and present a report and accounts. Formal recognition of the skills and abilities developed through the Company Programme is offered via the Young Enterprise Examination, which all Company Programme participants are invited to sit.

Their Entrepreneurship Master classes are one-day seminars designed mainly for students who have already experienced the highs and lows of running their own company in Young Enterprise's Company Programme. The Master classes are designed to encourage students to think about starting their own business as a career option and to identify the key entrepreneurial skills required in starting their own business. They also help students to understand the main issues and practicalities of starting their own business, for example: who to approach concerning financial matters, who to approach for help and advice.

YoungandSuccessful.com

Email: info@youngandsuccessful.com
Website: www.youngandsuccessful.com

YoungandSuccessful.com is an online network that supports the needs of young people from around the world as they attempt to build and thrive in both their personal and professional lives. To do this they have built this site in the form of a community, so people can not only have a place to gather and find others in similar situations, but can have their questions acknowledged and addressed by their peers.

The website's goal is to open up a whole new world of opportunities, relationships, resources and information to help young people succeed in, amongst other things, starting their own business.

YoungBiz (A KidsWay Company)

PO Box 7987
Atlanta, GA 30357

USA
Tel: 00 1 888 543 7929
Website: www.youngbiz.com

YoungBiz is all about the business of being young. 'As a teenager,' so YoungBiz proclaim, 'there are tons of decisions you have to make every day, decisions that can be as small as what cereal to have for breakfast to which college you want to attend.' YoungBiz is there to take those awesome decision-making skills and use them to make great financial and business decisions. Their entrepreneurs section is full of articles, hints, case studies and links aimed at young people starting up. They feature case examples of 17-year-old school children turning hobbies into cash, and have lots of links to helpful websites.

Youth Enterprise Centre Network

Kendal Crescent Industrial Estate
Alness
Easter Ross
Website: www.highland-opportunity.com/Young-Enterprise.html

Highland Opportunity Limited has opened the first of its network of Youth Enterprise Centres. These centres are intended to offer low rental short-term access to business space for young people starting out on the business property ladder.

There are five units available at Alness in the 12 to 16 sq.m. range, with rentals around £20 per week including business rates, heat, light and common services. There are disabled access and facilities.

Highland Opportunity Limited

Contact Moira McRonald at HOL Head Office:
81A Castle Street
Inverness
IV2 3EA
Scotland
Tel: +44(0)1463 228340
Email: info@highland-opportunity.com
Website: http://www.highland-opportunity.com

Youth Entrepreneurship Program

Website: www.entreplexity.ca/programs/youth_enterprise.htm

The Youth Entrepreneurship Program is one of the longest running programmes at the Institute for Enterprise Education, in partnership with Brock University in the US. This highly interactive and experiential learning based programme, which runs for 30 weeks, is for youths between the ages of 18 and 29.

By the time the participants have finished their 30 weeks, they will have researched and documented the results of their planning and they will have produced an extensive and defendable Business Action Plan.

Section 10

STARTING UP OVERSEAS

Hundreds of thousands of UK entrepreneurs have set up in business in almost every country in the world. Although some countries have restrictions on who can and cannot come into the country, most do not. The most usual form of restriction is the requirement that local directors and even shareholders have to 'front' the organization. But these barriers are coming down fast. Even countries such as Russia and China are more open to incoming entrepreneurs.

Some countries are more than just open. For example, the US, Canada, Australia, Israel, Ireland, Italy and South Africa are among a growing band of countries who offer a fast track to citizenship for people who will bring money and innovative ideas.

The directory below is an eclectic list of organizations that help entrepreneurs in their own country. Some, such as the SBA in America, are official government departments with assistance budgets running into billions of dollars and hundreds of regional and city offices. Others are more modest affairs, perhaps one-man bands recently established in countries coming to terms with both free enterprise and democracy for the first time. Some of these organizations are clustered under one umbrella, such as the European BICs, with 200 separate organizations in a score of countries.

The organizations listed here all provide at least basic information in English and are a useful starting point at the very least in finding out about how to set up in business in their country.

Directory of associations and help organizations

Afghanistan
Afghan Chamber of Commerce and Industry
Representing Businesses in Afghanistan
Mohammad Jan Khan Watt
Kabul
Tel: 93 02 290 090
Fax: 92 01 287 458

Africa
The Africa Business Network
Email: abn@ifc.org.
Website: www.ifc.org/abn/
Site gives business data and contact details for whole continent.

Albania
Union of Chambers of Commerce and Industry of Albania
RR Kavajes 6
Tirana
Tel/Fax: 355 4 222934
Email: uccial@abissnet.com.al

Argentina
Argentina Business
Tel/Fax: 54 11 43 427723
Website: www.invertir.com

Australia
Business Entry Point
Email: support@business.gov.au
Website: www.business.gov.au

Department of State and Regional Development Programme
Head Office
GPO Box 4509 RR
Melbourne
Victoria 3001
Tel: 61 3 9651 9387
Email: enquiries@dsrd.vic.gov.au
Website: www.dsrd.vic.gov.au; www.sbv.vic.gov.au

Small Business Development Corporation
553 Hay Street
Perth 6000
Tel: 1800 199 125
Email: info@sbdc.com.au
Website: www.sbdc.com.au

Small Business Enterprise Association of Australia and New Zealand (SEAANZ)
PO Box 36
Abbotsford 3067
Tel: 03 9415 1299
Email: creid@vcta.asn.au
Website: www.seaanz.asn.au

Austria
BIC Burgenland GmbH
Technologiezentrum
7000 Eisenstadt
Contact: Johann Binder
Tel: 43 2682 704.220
Fax: 43 2682 704.2210
Email: office@bice.at
Website: www.burgenland.at

Azerbaijan
Entrepreneurship Development Foundation (EDF)
3 Rashid Behbudov Street
4th floor
Baku
Azerbaijan 370000
Contact: Sabit Bagirov (President)

Tel: 99 412 93 14 38
Fax: 99 412 93 89 31; 99 412 98 19 27
Email: far@monitor.baku.az

Bangladesh
Foreign Investors Chamber of Commerce & Industry
35-1 Purana Paltan Line
Inner Circular Rd
GPO Box 4086
1000 Dhaka
Tel: 880 2 831 9448
Fax: 880 2 8319449
Email: ficci@fsbd.net

Barbados
Barbados Investment and Development Corporation
Pelican House
Princess Alice Highway
St Michael
Tel: 246 427 5350
Fax: 246 436 1447
Website: www.BDIC.com

Belarus
The Belarusian Chamber of Commerce and Industry
14 Masherova Avenue
220035 Minsk
Tel: 375 17 2269127
Fax: 375 17 2269860
Email: mbox@cci.by
Website: www.cci.by

Belize
Belize Enterprise for Sustainable Technology (BEST)
PO Box 35
Forest Drive
Belmopan
Tel: 501 8 23 043 23 150
Fax: 501 8 22 563
Email: BEST@btl.net

Belgium
Bekaert-Stanwick Management Consultants
AXXES Business Park
Gebouw B
Guldensporenpark 20
B-9820 Merelbeke
Tel: 32 9 210 59 50
Fax: 32 9 210 59 51
Email: guido.giebens@bekaertstanwick.com
Website: www.bekaertstanwick.com

Bolivia
Bolivia Small Business Association
Centro de Fomento a Iniciativas Económicas
(FIE)
Calle General Gonzáles No 1272
La Paz
Tel: 02 32 2933
Fax: 02 32 2840
Website: www.boliviabiz.com/business/assoc.
htm

Bosnia and Herzegovina
Chamber of Economy of Bosnia & Herzegovina
Branislava Djurdjeva 10
71000 Sarajevo
Tel: 387 33 663631
Fax: 387 33 663632
Email: madziahmetovic@komorabih.com
Website: www.komorabih.com

Brunei
Brunei Darussalam Small and Medium Enterprise
Ministry of Industry and Primary Resource
Bandar Seri Begawan BB3910
Tel: 673 2 380048, 673 2 382822
Fax: 673 2 381381
Email: resctr01@brunet.bn
Website: www.brunet.bn/org

Bulgaria
Bulgarian Chamber of Commerce and Industry (BCCI)
42 Parchevich Str
1000 Sofia
Tel: 359 2 9872631
Fax: 359 2 9873209
Email: bcci@bcci.bg
Website: www.bcci.bg

Canada
Canada/British Columbia Business Service Centre
601 W Cordova Street
Vancouver BC
V6B 1G1
Tel: 1 800 667 2272
Fax: 604 775 5520
Website: www.smallbusinessbc.ca

Centre d'Entreprises et d'Innovation de Montréal
Rue du Prince 33
H3C 2M7
Montréal
Contact: Jacques Pelland
Tel: 1 514 866.05.75
Fax: 1 514/866.35.91
Email: info@ceim.org
Website: www.ceim.org

Canadian Federation of Independent Business
Email: info@cfibmail.com
Website: www.cfib.ca

Social and Enterprise Innovations (SEDI)
1110 Finch Avenue West
Suite 406
North York
Ontario
M3J 2TZ
Tel: 416 665 2828
Fax: 416 665 1661
Email: info@sedi.org
Website: www.sedi.org/html

China
British Chamber of Commerce – Chengdu
Room 1410
610015
Chengdu

Tel: 86 28 6277802
Fax: 86 28 6250424
Email: info@bccchina.org
Website: www.bccchina.org

China Council for the Promotion of International Trade (CCPIT)

China Chamber of International Commerce (CCOIC)
No 1 Fuxingmenwai Street
Beijing (100860)
Tel: 86 10 68013344; 86 10 68034830
Fax: 86 10 68030747; 86 10 68011370
Email: ccpitweb@public.bta.net.cn
Website: www.ccpit.org/engVersion/indexEn

China Economy

Department of International Cooperation
State Information Center
CEInet Data Co Ltd
No 58 Sanlihe Road
Beijing 100045
Email: ceco@mx.cei.gov.cn
Website: www.ce.cei.gov.cn

English language site linking to small business initiatives in China.

SME Forum

Website: www.forum.tdctrade.com/cgi-bin/Ultimate.cgi

Discussion group on SME issues in the region.

State Economic and Trade Commission

Email: cpoffice@public.bta.net.cn
Website: www.setc.gov.cn/english/index_e.htm

Enterprise reform and development website, English version.

Colombia
Centro de Servicios para la Innovación Technológica Universidad Javeriana – CITE

Calle 40, 6–23
piso 8 Edificio Gabriel Giraldo

Bogotá
Tel: 338 085
Fax: 2 857 289
Email: vvaldés@javercol.javeriana.edu.co

Croatia
Croatian Chamber of Commerce

Roosveltov trg 2
10000 Zagreb
Tel: 385 1 4561712/3
Fax: 385 1 4828380
Email: hgk@hgk.hr
Website: www.hgk.hr

Cyprus
Cyprus Chamber of Commerce and Industry

38 Grivas Dighenis Avenue. & 3 Deligiorgis Street
PO Box 21455
1509 Nicosia
Tel: 357 2889840
Fax: 357 2668630
Email: chamber@ccci.org.cy
Website: www.ccci.org.cy

Czech Republic
BIC Prague

Plzenska 221/130
15000 Prague 5
Contact: Pavel Komarek
Tel: 420 2 572.12.873
Fax: 420 2 572.12.340
Email: komarek@bic.cvut.cz
Website: www.bic.cvut.cz

Economic Chamber of the Czech Republic

Seifertova 22
Prague 3
Tel: 420 2 24096111
Fax: 420 2 24096222
Email: info@komora.cz
Website: www.komora.cz

Denmark
BIC Nord

Niels Jernes Vej 10
9220 Aalborg O

Tel: 45 96 35 44 30
Fax: 45 96 35 44 25
Email: bic@bic-nord.dk
Website: www.bic-nord.dk

Danish Invention Center – Danish Technological Institute
Gregersensvej
PO Box 141
DK-2630 Taastrup
Tel: 45 72 20 20 00
Fax: 45 72 20 27 51
Email: fk@dtu-innovation.dk

Dominican Republic
Instituto Dominicano De Tecnologia Industrial (INDOTEC)
Av. Núñez de Cáceres
Santo Domingo
Contact: Olef Palmer
Tel: 809 566 8121
Fax: 809 227 8809
Email: INDOTEC@Tricom.net

Ecuador
National Association of Entrepreneurs
Avenida Amazonas 1429 y Colon
Edificia Espana, Piso 6
Oficina 67
Casilla 17–07–9103
Quito
Tel: 59 32 238 507/550 879
Fax: 59 32 550 879/509 806
Email: ande@uio.satnet.net
Contact: Patricio Rivadeneira, Executive Director

Estonia
Estonian Association of Small and Medium-Sized Enterprises (EVEA)
Liivalaia 9
EE-10118 Tallinn
Tel: 372 6 403 935
Fax: 372 6 312 451
Email: sme@evea.ee

Europe
European Association of Craft, Small and Medium-Sized Enterprises
Rue Jacques de Lalaing 4
B-1040 Brussels
Tel: 32 2 230 75 99
Fax: 32 2 230 78 61
Email: ueapme@euronet.be
Website: www.ueapme.com

European Business & Innovation Centres Network (EBN)
Network of 150 European Business and Innovation Centres
Tel: 32 2 772 89 00
Fax: 32 3 772 95 74
Email: ebn@ebn.be
Website: www.ebn.be

Female Europeans of Medium and Small Enterprises (FEM)
4 Rue Jacques de Lalaing
B-1040 Bruxelles
Tel: 32 2 285 07 14
Fax: 32 2 230 75 99

Jeunes Entrepreneurs de l'Union Europeenne – JEUNE
4 Rue Jacques de Lalaing
B-1040 Bruxelles
Tel: 32 2 230 75 99
Fax: 32 2 230 78 61
Email: jeune@kmonet.be
Website: www.jeune-entrepreneurs.org

Finland
B.I.C. Carelia
Lânsikatu 15 Carelian Science Park
80110 Joensuu
Contact: Aula Pirkka
Tel: 358 13 263 72 10
Fax: 358 13 263 71 11
Email: pirkka.aula@carelian.fi
Website: www.carelian.fi

Small Business Institute
Website: www.tukkk.fi/sbi/

The Former Yugoslav Republic of Macedonia
Ministry of Economy
Small Business Department
Tel: 389 91 113 677
Fax: 389 91 111 541

France
PME-France
Website: www.pme-france.com

Agence pour la Création d'Entreprises
14 rue Delambre
75682
Paris Cedex 14
Contact: Christian Perreau
Tel: 33 1 42 18 58 58
Fax: 33 1 42 18 58 00
Email: info@apce.com
Website: www.apce.com

Georgia
Georgian Chamber of Commerce & Industry
11 Chavchavadze Ave.
380079 Tbilisi
Tel: 995 32 29 33 75
Fax: 995 32 23 57 60
Email: ktm@ean.kheta.ge
Website: www.gcci.org.ge

Germany
Association of German Technology and Business Incubation Centres (ADT)
Rudower Chaussee 29
D-12489 Berlin
Tel: 49 30 63 92 62 21
Fax: 49 30 63 92 62 22
Email: adt@adt-online.de
Website: www.adt-online.de

INNO – Gesellschaft fur innovative Unternehmensentwicklung mbH
Karlstrasse 45b
D-76133 Karlsruhe

Tel: 49 721 91 345 0
Fax: 49 721 91 345 99
Email: m.schaettgen@inno-group.com

Berlin Chamber of Small Business and Skilled Crafts
Handwerkskammer Berlin
Blücherstrasse 68
10961 Berlin
Tel: 030 259 03 01
Fax: 030 259 03 235
Email: info@hwk-berlin.de
Website: www.hwk-berlin.de;
www.mittelstandsportal.de

British Chamber of Commerce in Germany
50678 Cologne
Tel: 49 221 31 44 58
Fax: 49 221 31 53 35
Email: generaloffice@bccg.de
Website: www.bccg.de

Gibraltar
Gibraltar Federation of Small Business
Tel: 350 47722
Fax: 350 47733
Email: dghio@gfsb.gi
Website: www.gfsb.gi

Greece
BIC of Attika
Stadiou Street 7
8th Floor
10562 Athens
Contact: Dimitris Karachalios
Tel: 30 1 331 42 30
Fax: 30 1 331 42 32
Email: bicofattika@hol.gr
Website: www.bicofattika.gr

Hellenic Technology Transfer Center
17 Mitseon Street
GR-11742 Athens
Tel: 30 1 921 09 35
Fax: 30 1 923 55 55
Email: httcat@athensnet.gr

Website: www.httc.gr

Thessaloniki Chamber of Small and Medium-Sized Industries
546 24 Thessaloniki
Tel: 30 31 241668
Fax: 30 31 232667

Grenada
National Development Foundation of Grenada
PO Box 659
Lucas Street
St George's
Tel: 473 440 1869
Fax: 473 440 6644
Email: ndf@caribsurf.com

Hong Kong
SME Office
Room 609, 6/F
Trade and Industry Department Tower
700 Nathan Road
Kowloon
Tel: 852 2398 5133
Fax: 852 2737 2377
Email: smeenq@mail.gcn.gov.hk
Website: www.sme.gcn.gov.hk

Hong Kong General Chamber of Commerce
Website: www.chamber.org.uk

Hong Kong Trade Development Council
Website: www.tdctrade.com

Hong Kong Trade Development Council
Website: www.tdctrade.com

Hungary
Hungarian Chamber of Commerce and Industry
H-1055 Budapest
Kossuth Lajos ter 6–8
Tel: 36 1 4745100
Fax: 36 1 4745105
Email: mkik@mail.mkik.hu
Website: www.mkik.hu

Innostart Hungary National Business and Innovation
Fehervari ut 130
1116 Budapest
Contact: Kinga Garab
Tel: 36 1 382 15 00
Fax: 36 1 382 1510
Email: garab@innostart.hu
Website: www.innostart.hu

Iceland
Iceland Chamber of Commerce
Kringlan 7
103 Reykjavik
Tel: 354 510 7100
Fax: 354 568 6564
Email: mottaka@chamber.is
Website: www.chamber.is

India
Entreprenurship Development Centre of India
Ahmedabad
PO Bhat 382 428
Gujarat
Tel: 91 79 3969151; 91 79 3969153; 91 79 3969163
Fax: 91 79 3969164
Email: ediindiaad1@sancharnet.in
Website: www.ediindia.org

PHD Chamber of Commerce & Industry (PHD)
PHD House
Opp. Asian Games Village
New Delhi 100016
Tel: 91 11 686 3801 04
Fax: 91 11 686 3135 05
Email: phdcci@del2.vsnl.net.in

National Small Industry Extension Training (NISIET) Institute
Yousufguda
Hyderabad 500 045
Tel: 91 40 3608544 218; 91 40 3608316 217
Fax: 91 40 3608547; 91 40 3608956; 91 40 3541260
Cable: SIETINSTITUTE, Hyderabad

Website: www.nisiet.com

Trade-India
Website: www.trade-india.com

Indonesia
Indonesian Chamber of Commerce and Industry
Jl. HR Rasuna Said Block X-5 Kav 2–3
Ariobimo Sentral
9th Floor
12950 Jakarta
Tel: 62 21 527 44 85
Fax: 62 21 527 44 86
Email: adm_dj@indonesia.kadin.net.id
Website: www.kadinnet.com

Israel
Federation of Israeli Chambers of Commerce
84 Ha'hashmonaim Street
PO Box 20027
61200 Tel Aviv
Tel: 972 3 563 1020/1
Fax: 972 3 561 9027
Email: chamber@chamber.org.il
Website: www.chamber.org.il

Israel Small and Medium Enterprise Authority
www.asakim.org.il/index.html

Italy
Aster S. cons.a.r.l. – Emilia Romagna Technological Development Agency
c/o CNR Area della Ricerca
Via Cobetti 101
I-40129 Bologna
Tel: 39 051 639 80 99
Fax: 39 051 639 81 31
Email: info@aster.it
Website: www.aster.it

BIC Lazio SpA
Viale Parioli 39b
00197 Roma
Contact: Luigi Campitelli
Tel: 39 06 807 94 35

Fax: 39 06 807 88 39
Email: bic@biclazio.it
Website: www.biclazio.it

Entrepreneurial Promotion and Development
Via Guglielmo Saliceeto
00161 Rome
Tel: 39 06 854 541
Fax: 39 06 8545 4375
Email: lsozio@spi-net.com
Website: www.spi-net.com

Italian Union of Chambers of Commerce, Industry, Agriculture and Handicraft (Unioncamere)
Piazza Sallustio
21 – Roma 00187
Tel: 39 06 47041
Fax: 39 06 4704240
Email: internazionale@unioncamere.it
Website: www.unioncamere.it

Jamaica
Jamaica Promotions Corporation (JAMPRO)
35 Trafalgar Road
Kingston 10
Tel: 809 929 9450
Fax: 809 924 9650
Email: jampro@uwimona.edu.jm

Japan
Japanese Federation of Small Business
Website: www.chuokai.or.jp/english/

Japan Small and Medium Enterprise Corporation
Email: KB-joho@jasmec.go.jp
Website: www.partner.sme.ne.jp

Korea
British Chamber of Commerce in Korea
Rm. 201
Anglican Church Bldg
3–7 Chong-dong
Chung-gu
Seoul

Tel: 02 720 9406
Fax: 02 720 9411

Korea Chamber of Commerce and Industry
Website: www.kcci.or.kr/kccinew/08/dbk1/de

Korean Federation Of Small Business
Website: www.kfsb.or.kr/english/

The Small and Medium Business Administration (SMBA)
Email: webmaster@digital.smba.go.kr
Website: www.smba.go.kr

Lithuania
Lithuanian Entrepreneurs Employers Confederation (LVDK)
Rotundo str.5
LT-2600 Vilnius
Tel: 370 2 629729/617992
Fax: 370 2 220 448/262 352
Email: lvdk@post.omnitel.net

Lithuanian Innovation Centre
T. Sevecenkos 13
2600 Vilnius
Lithuania
Tel: 370 2 23 27 80
Fax: 370 2 23 27 81
Email: kgecas@ktl.mii.lt
Website: www.lic.lt

Luxembourg
Centre de Récherche Public Henri Tudor
6, rue de Coudenhove-Kalergi
1359 Luxembourg
Contact: Claude Wehenkel
Tel: 352 42 59 911
Fax: 352 43 65 23
Email: claude.wehenkel@crpht.lu
Website: www.crpht.lu

Macao
Macao's Euro-Chinese Entrepreneurs Club
Suite 1109
Macao Landmark

Av. Da Amiza de Macao
Guangzhou
Contact: Lu Dong
Tel: 853 68 77 191
Fax: 853 93 89 46
Email: mecec@euro-china.net
Website: www.euro-china.net

Macedonia
Economic Chamber of Macedonia
St Dimistrie Cupovski 13
1000 Skopje
Email: ic@ic.mchamber.org.mk
Website: www.mchamber.org.mk

Malaysia
The Malaysian Industrial Development Authority (MIDA)
Website: www.jaring.my/mida/

Malta
Institute for the Promotion of Small Enterprise (IPSE)
Small Enterprise Centre
Marsa Industrial Estate
Marsa LQA 06
Contact: Ray Muscat
Tel: 356 23 38 38
Fax: 356 23 40 45
Email: rmuscat@ipse.org.mt
Website: www.ipse.org.mt

Moldova
Chamber of Commerce and Industry of the Republic of Moldova
MD-2012
Kishinev
Eminescu str 28
Tel: 3732 221552
Fax: 3732 241453
Email: camera@chamber.md
Website: www.chamber.md

The Netherlands
The Royal Association MKB-Nederland
Brassersplein 1 delft

The Netherlands
PO Box 5096
Tel: 31 15 2191212
Fax: 31 15 2191414
Website: www.mkb.nl/mkbnederland/english.
shtml

New Zealand
Ministry of Economic Development
PO Box 1473
Wellington
New Zealand
Tel: 64 4 472 0030
Fax: 64 4 472 4638
Website: www.med.govt.nz

Nigeria
Nigerian Association of Chambers of Commerce, Industry, Mines and Agriculture
15-A Ikorodu Road
Maryland By-Pass
Lagos
P.M.B. 12816
Tel: 234 1 496 4727
Fax: 234 1 496 4737 or 493–2481
Email: naccima@supernet300.com
Website: www.nigeriabusinessinfo.com/naccima.
htm

Norway
Forskningsparken As
Gaudstadalleen 21
0371 Oslo
Contact: Torp Svenning
Tel: 47 22 95 85 33
Fax: 47 22 60 44 27
Email: svenning.torp@sposlo.no
Website: www.fposlo.no

Norwegian Trade Council
Website: www.ntc.no

Philippines
European Chamber of Commerce of the Philippines
Representing Europe's business interests in the
Philippines
Sen. Gil J. Puyat Avenue
19th Floor
PSBank Tower CPO 1302
Metro Manila 1253
Makati City
Tel: 63 2 759 6680
Fax: 63 2 759 6690
Website: www.eccp.com

Poland
Ministry of Economy
Department of Craft, Small and Medium-Sized
Enterprises
Ul. Pl. Trzech Krzyzy ¾
00–507 Warsaw
Tel: 48 22 621 83 14; 48 22 621 27 54
Fax: 48 22 629 23 11
Email: dms@mg.gov.pl
Website: www.mg.gov.pl

Polish Chamber of Commerce
00–074 Warsaw
ul. Trebacka 4
Tel: 48 22 6309600
Fax: 48 22 8274673
Email: infodata@kig.pl
Website: www.kig.pl

Polish BICs Association
Ul. Polanka 3
61 131 Poznan
Contact: Krzysztof Zasiadly
Tel: 48 061 877 17 5
Email: biuro@sooipp.org.pl
Website: www.sooipp.org.pl

Zwiazek Rzemioska Poskiego – ZRP
Ul. Miodowa 14
PL-00–950 Warschau
Tel: 48 22 6335 79 81
Fax: 48 22 635 79 81

Email: zrp@zrp.pl
Website: www.peryt.waw.pl/bior/

Portugal
Agencia de Inovaçao
Edificio Green Park Av. Dos Combatentes, 43A
1600 042 Lisboa
Contact: Manuel Laranja
Tel: 351 21 721 09 10
Fax: 351 21 727 17 33
Email: mdl@adi.pt
Website: www.adi.pt

INOV – Inesc Inovacao
Instituto de Novas Tecnologias
Rua Alves Redol 9
P-1000 029 Lisboa
Tel: 351 21 310 04 50
Fax: 351 21 310 04 99
Email: inov@inov.pt
Website: www.inov.pt

Romania
Chamber of Commerce and Industry of Romania and of Bucharest Municipality
2 Octavian Goga Blvd
74244 Bucharest 3
Tel: 401 322 9535 38
Fax: 401 322 9542
Email: dre@ccir.ro
Website: www.ccir.ro

National Agency for Regional Development (NARD)
11 Poterasi Street
Sector 4
Bucharest
Fax: 40 1 336 1843

Private Entrepreneurs Confederation from the Timis County (PECT)
Gen. Praporgescu Str. Nr. 2
1900 Timisoara
Contact: Radu Nicosevici (President)
Tel/Fax: 40–56–221–426

Russia
The Academy of Management and the Market
Website: www.morozov.ru

Russia Small Business Support
Website: www.english.pravda.ru/economics/2001/12/19/24004.html

Russian Association of Small and Medium Enterprises
Website: www.rasme.ru

The Russian Small and Medium Business Support Agency
Website: www.delo.ru

Russian SME Resource Centre
Website: www.rcsme.ru/addr-eng/

The mission of the Russian SME Resource Centre since 1997 is to provide assistance to private entrepreneurship development in the Russian Federation. Their site also contains a database of more than 1000 regional and federal SMEs support organizations in Russia (www.rcsme.ru/eng/).

Singapore
Ministry of Finance
Ministry of Finance Headquarters
100 High Street
#06–03
The Treasury
Singapore 179434
Website: www.mof.gov.sg

Slovakia
BIC Bratislava
Zochova 5
811 03 Bratislava
Contact: Roman Linczenyi
Tel: 421 7 544 11 195
Fax: 421 7 544 17 522
Email: femirc@bicba.sk
Website: www.bicba.sk

Ministry of Economy
Enterprise Development and Regional Policy
Department
Mierova 19
827 15 Bratislava
Tel: 42 17 4854 1527
Fax: 42 17 4333 0158

Slovak Chamber of Commerce and Industry
HQ – Gorkeho 9
SK-81603 Bratislava 1
Tel: 421 2 54131228/54131136
Fax: 421 2 54430754
Email: sopkurad@scci.sk; foreign@scci.sk
Website: www.scci.sk; www.sopk.sk

Slovenia
Chamber of Commerce and Industry for Slovenia
Dimiceva 13
SI-1504 Ljubljana
Tel: 386 1 58980000
Fax: 386 1 5898100
Email: infolink@gzs.si
Website: www.gzs.si/eng/index.htm

South Africa
BRAIN (Business Referral and Information Network)
Website: www.brain.org.za

The Free Market Foundation (FMF)
2nd Floor
Export House
Corner of West & Maude Streets
PO Box 785121
Sandton 2146
Tel: 27 11 884 0270
Fax: 27 11 884 5672
Email: fmf@mweb.co.za
Website: www.freemarketfoundation.com; www.mbendi.co.za/werksmns/sabus01.htm; www.ntsika.org.za/frames.htm

Spain
Fundacion Universidad Empresa de Leon (FUELE)
Avda Facultad N25
Edif. El Albeitar
E-24071 Leon
Tel: 34 987 29 16 51
Fax: 34 987 29 1644
Email: fuele@unileon.es
Website: www.unileon.es

PIMEC SEFES
Viladomat 174
E-08015 Barcelona
Tel: 34 93 49 64 500
Fax: 34 93 49 64 501
Email: europa@sefes.es
Website: www.sefes/es

Parc BIT
Cami de Ca'n Manel s/n
E-07120 Son Espanyol
Palma de Mallorca
Tel: 34 971 43 51 51
Fax: 34 971 43 51 52
Email: pimeb@intercom.es
Website: www.pimeb.net

Sweden
BIC Mid Sweden AB
Terminalvägen, 10
861 36 Timra
Contact: Nils Karlsen
Tel: 46 60 19 09 00
Fax: 46 60 19 09 09
Email: info@bicmid.se
Website: www.bicmid.se

Federation of Swedish Industries
PO Box 5501 114 85
Stockholm
Tel: 46 8 783 80 00
Fax: 46 8 662 35 95
Website: www.industriforbundet.se/eng/news-eng.nsf

Switzerland
Swiss Research Institute of Small Business and Entrepreneurship
University of St.Gallen
Kirchlistrasse 44
CH-9010 St Gallen
Tel: 41 71 243 07 00
Fax: 41 71 243 07 01
Website: www.igw.unisg.ch/org

Taskforce PME
Website: www.pmeinfo.ch

Taiwan
Small and Medium Enterprise Administration
Website: www.moeasmea.gov.tw/english.html

Thailand
Department of Industrial Promotion
Rama IV Road
Tatchathewi
Bangkok 10400
Website: www.dip.go.th

Thai Chamber of Commerce
Website: www.thaicommerce.com/thai.htm

Trinidad and Tobago
Caribbean Association of Industry and Commerce
PO Box 442
Room 351 Trinidad Hilton
Lady Young Road
St Ann's
Tel: 868 623 4830
Fax: 868 623 6116
Email: caic@trinidad.net
Website: www.trinidad.net/caic

Turkey
SISECAM
Barbaros Bul. 125
Besiktas
TR-80706 Instanbul
Tel: 90 212 274 72 00
Fax: 90 212 266 66 83

Email: bkuban@sisecam.com.tr
Website: www.sisecam.com.tr

United States
Hispanic Chambers of Commerce
Website: www.hcoc.org/resource.htm

Small Business Administration (SBA)
409 Third Street, SW
Washington DC 20416
Tel: 800 827 5722
Website: www.sba.gov

The US Small Business Administration, established in 1953, provides financial, technical and management assistance to help Americans start, run, and grow their businesses. With a portfolio of business loans, loan guarantees and disaster loans worth more than $45 billion, in addition to a venture capital portfolio of $13 billion, SBA is the nation's largest single financial backer of small businesses. Last year, the SBA offered management and technical assistance to more than one million small business owners.

United States Federation of Small Business
Website: www.usfsb.com
Hawaii
Website: www.hawaii.com/business

Ukraine
Association of Young Entrepreneurs
16 Bulvar Shevchenko
Kiev
Tel: 380 44 225 6313

The Ukrainian Chamber of Commerce and Industry
Ukraine 252601
Kiev 33 vul.
Velyka Zhytomyrska
Tel: 380 44 21224911
Fax: 380 44 2123353
Email: ucci@ucci.org.na
Website: www.ucci.org.ua

Vietnam
Union of Associations of Industry and Commerce
51 Ben Chuong Duong
District 1
Ho Chi Minh City
Tel: 848 8293389
Fax: 848 8215448

Representing business in Ho Chi Minh City.

World
World Association for Small & Medium Enterprises (WASME)
Plot No 4
Sector 16A
Noida
Uttar Pradesh
India - 201301
Tel: 91 11 8 4515238
Fax: 91 11 8 4515243
Email: wasme@vsnl.com
Website: www.wasmeinfo.org

World Chambers Network
Email: secretariat@worldchambers.com
Website: www.worldchambers.com

World database of chambers of commerce.

Yugoslavia
Federal Market Inspectorate
Website: www.gov.yu

Books

Ernst & Young

Their 'Doing Business In …' series gives a country profiles and provides an overview of the government structure, economic climate, investment climate, tax systems, forms of business organization and accounting practices in almost every country in the world.

You can download them free of charge on: www.ey.com/GLOBAL/gcr.nsf/EYPassport/Welcome-Doing_Business_In-EYPassport.

PricewaterhouseCoopers

PricewaterhouseCoopers publish a Doing Business Guide series covering 60 countries. Details and ordering facility on their website, www.pwc-global.com.

Section 11

PREPARING THE BUSINESS PLAN

So far, this book has covered the sources of help and advice covering areas that are essential if you are to have a realistic chance of success. All businesses are risky, but with superior knowledge you have a better chance of success. The business plan is where you bring all that knowledge to bear on the task of getting your venture launched on the market, or on to its next stage of growth. Without hard data, your plan will be based on hunches and guesstimates, and not many financiers will be keen to put their money where your mouth is.

A business plan is a *selling* document that conveys the excitement and promise of your business to any potential backer or stakeholder. That audience can include outsiders such as the bank, venture capitalists or even current and prospective new employees who need to be confident that there is a future in the business for themselves. The plan needs to be prepared and written by those who are vital to its implementation. For an example of a business plan, look back at pages 14–27.

No start-up or growing business should be without a *current* business plan that has been thoroughly reviewed within the past six months.

The planning horizon ideally should be at least three years. It takes this long to implement anything of strategic merit. The first year of the business plan will form the framework for the *operating budget*. This is the line by line profit and loss style description of how you plan to execute your strategy.

The reasons for having a business plan include the following.

- **Testing your ideas:** This systematic approach to planning enables you to make your mistakes on paper, rather than in the market place. One potential entrepreneur made the discovery while gathering data for the cash flow forecast in his business plan that if he delayed purchasing some equipment, and leased others, he could halve his initial funding requirements. This had a profound effect on his financial strategy!

  Another entrepreneur found out that, at the price he proposed charging, he would never recover his overheads or break even. Indeed 'overheads' and 'break even' were themselves alien terms before he embarked on preparing a business plan.

- **Confidence:** Once completed, a business plan will make you feel more confident in your ability to set up and operate the venture. It may even compensate for lack of capital and experience, provided of course you have other factors in your favour, such as a sound idea and a sizeable market opportunity for your product or service.

- **Financing:** Your business plan will show how much money is needed, what it is needed for and when and for how long it is required.

  As under-capitalization and early cash flow problems are two important reasons why new business activities fail, it follows that those with a soundly prepared business plan can reduce these risks of failure. They can also experiment with a range of alternative viable strategies and so concentrate on options that make the most economic use of scarce financial resources.

It would be an overstatement to say that your business plan is the passport to sources of finance. It will, however, help you to display your grasp of the financial dynamics of your business to the full and to communicate your ideas to others in a way that will be easier for them to understand and to appreciate the reasoning behind your ideas. These outside parties could be bankers, potential investors, partners or advisory agencies. Once they know what you are trying to do, they will be better able to help and advise you.

- **Planning experience:** Preparing a business plan will give you an insight into the planning process. It is this process itself that is important to the long-term financial health of a business, and not simply the plan that comes out of it. Businesses are dynamic, as are the commercial and competitive environments in which they operate. No one expects every event as recorded on a business plan to occur as predicted, but the understanding and knowledge created by the process of business planning will prepare the business for any changes that it may face, and so enable it to adjust quickly.

Despite these many valuable benefits, thousands of would-be entrepreneurs still attempt to start without a business plan. The most common among these are businesses that either appear to need little or no capital at the outset, or whose founders have funds of their own; in both cases it is believed unnecessary to expose the project to harsh financial appraisal.

The former hypothesis is usually based on the easily exploded myth that customers will all pay cash on the nail and suppliers will wait for months to be paid. In the meantime, the proprietor has the use of these funds to finance the business. Such model customers and suppliers are thinner on the ground than optimistic entrepreneurs think. In any event, two important market rules still apply: either the product or service on offer fails to sell like hot cakes and mountains of unpaid stocks build up, all of which eventually have to be financed; or it does sell like hot cakes and more financially robust entrepreneurs are attracted into the market. Without the staying power that adequate financing provides, these new competitors will rapidly kill the business off.

Those would-be entrepreneurs with funds of their own or, worse still, funds borrowed from friends and relatives, tend to think that the time spent in preparing a business plan could be more usefully (and enjoyably) spent looking for premises, buying a new car, or installing a computer. In short, anything that inhibits them from immediate action is viewed as time-wasting.

As most people's initial perception of their business venture is flawed in some important respect, it follows that jumping in at the deep end is risky, and unnecessarily so. Flaws can often be discovered cheaply and in advance when preparing a business plan; they are always discovered in the market place, invariably at a much higher and usually fatal cost.

What financiers look out for

All successful businesses need finance at some stage in their development, so as well as the operational benefits of preparing a business plan, it is important to examine what financiers expect from you, if you are to succeed in raising those funds.

It is often said that there is no shortage of money for new and growing businesses, the only scarce commodities are good ideas and people with the ability to exploit them. From the potential entrepreneur's position, this is often hard to believe. Out of every thousand business plans received by venture capital providers, only 100 or so are examined in any detail, less than 10 are pursued to the negotiating stage, and only one of those is invested in.

To a great extent the decision whether to proceed beyond an initial reading of the plan will depend on the quality of the financial arguments and the revenue model used to support the investment proposal. The business plan is the ticket of admission giving the entrepreneur their first and often only chance to impress prospective sources of finance with the quality of their proposal.

It follows from this that to have any chance at all of getting financial support, your business plan must pay regard to the likely requirements of potential financiers.

Bankers, and indeed any other sources of debt capital, are looking for asset security to back their loan and the near certainty of getting their money back. Essentially banks are in the business of converting illiquid assets such as property or stock into liquid assets such as cash or overdraft facilities. They will also charge an interest rate which reflects current market conditions and their view of the level of risk of the proposal. Depending on the nature of the business in question and the purpose to which the money is being used, bankers will take a 2 to 5 year view.

Bankers will usually expect a business to start repaying both the loan and the interest on a monthly or quarterly basis immediately the loan has been granted. In some cases a capital holiday of up to two years can be negotiated, but in the early stages of any loan the interest charges make up the lion's share of payments, like mortgage repayments. You need to allow for this in your cash flow projections.

Bankers hope that a business will succeed so that they can lend more money in the future and provide more banking services, such as insurance or tax advice to a loyal customer.

It follows from this appreciation of lenders' needs that they are less interested in rapid growth and the consequent capital gain than they are in a steady stream of earnings almost from the outset.

As most new or fast-growing businesses generally do not make immediate profits, money for such enterprises must come from elsewhere. Risk or equity capital, as other types of funds are called, comes from venture capital houses, as well as being put in by founders, their families and friends.

Because the inherent risks of investing in new and young ventures are greater than for investing in established companies, venture capital fund managers have to offer their investors the chance of larger overall returns. To do that, fund managers must not only keep failures to a minimum, they have to pick some big winners too – ventures with annual compound growth rates above 35% – to offset the inevitable mediocre performers. With this in mind it is hardly surprising that the New Economy has sucked in so much equity finance. Typically, a fund manager would expect of any 10 investments: one star, seven also-rans, and two flops. However, it is important to remember that despite this outcome, venture capital fund managers are only looking for winners, so unless you are projecting high growth, the chances of getting venture capital are slim.

Not only are venture capitalists looking for winners, they are looking for a substantial shareholding in your business. There are no simple rules as to what constitutes a fair split. However, as a rough rule of thumb these proportions offer some guidance:

- for the idea: 33%
- for the management: 33%
- for the money: 33%.

So if the venture capital firm sees you have a great idea and a first class team, they may aim for a third of your business as their reward for putting up the money. If your team is weak they may want to put in a non-executive director and work with you in other ways to strengthen the team. In which case they may aim for more than a third of your business in return for their investment

It all comes down to how much you need the money, how risky the venture is, how much money could be made, and your skills as a negotiator. However, it is salutary to remember that 100% of nothing is still nothing, so all parties to the deal have to be satisfied if it is to succeed.

As fast-growing companies typically have no cash available to pay dividends, and in the case of many e-businesses may not have made any profits in any case, investors can only profit by selling their holdings. With this in mind the venture capitalists need to have an exit route, such as a stock exchange or a potential corporate buyer, in view at the outset.

Unlike many entrepreneurs (and some lending bankers), who see their ventures as life-long commitments to success and growth, venture capitalists have a relatively short-term horizon. Typically, they are looking to liquidate small company investments within two to six years, allowing them to pay out individual investors and to have funds available for tomorrow's winners. So your financial plan needs to accommodate this time-scale.

To be successful, your business must be targeted at the needs of these two sources of finance, and in particular at the balance between the two. Lending bankers ideally look for a ratio of 1:1, which means half the businesses finances are borrowed and half comes from risk capital. Banks have been known to go to 4:1, but rarely willingly or at the outset of their involvement. Venture capital providers will almost always encourage entrepreneurs to take on new debt capital to match the level of equity funding.

If you are planning to raise money from friends and relatives, either as debt or equity, then their needs must also be taken account of in your business plan.

Entrepreneurs are naturally ebullient when explaining the future prospects for their businesses. They frequently believe that 'the sky's the limit' when it comes to growth, and money (or rather the lack of it) is the only thing that stands between them and their success.

It is true that if you are looking for venture capital, then the providers are also looking for rapid growth. However, it is as well to remember that financiers are dealing with thousands of investment proposals each year, and already have money tied up in hundreds of business sectors. It follows, therefore, that they already have a perception of what the accepted financial results and marketing approaches currently are, for any sector. Any new company's business plan showing projections that are outside the ranges perceived as acceptable within an industry will raise questions in the investor's mind.

Make your growth forecasts believable; support them with hard facts where possible. If they are on the low side, then approach the more cautious lending banker, rather than venture capitalists. The former often see a modest forecast as a virtue, lending credibility to the business proposal as a whole.

General content

The following elements need to be taken account of in preparing a well constructed business plan.

1 The recipient

Clearly a business plan will be more effective if it is written with the reader in mind. This will involve some research into the particular interests, foibles and idiosyncrasies of those readers. Bankers are more interested in hearing about certainties and steady growth, whilst venture capitalists are also interested in dreams of great things to come.

It is a good idea to carry out your reader research before the final editing of your business plan, as you should incorporate something of this knowledge into the way it is presented. You may find that slightly different versions of the 'deal on offer' have to be made for different audiences. This makes the reader feel the proposal has been addressed to them rather than just being the recipient of a 'Dear Sir or Madam' type of missive. The fundamentals of the plan, however, will remain constant.

2 Packaging

Every product is enhanced by appropriate packaging and a business plan is no exception. Most experts prefer a simple spiral binding with a clear plastic cover front and back. This makes it easy for the reader to move from section to section, and it ensures the document will survive the frequent handling that every successful business plan is likely to get.

A letter quality printer, using 12 point type, double spacing and wide margins, will result in a pleasing and easy to read plan.

3 Layout and content

There is no such thing as a universal business plan format. That being said, experience has shown that certain styles have been more successful than others. Following these guidelines will result in an effective business plan which covers most requirements. Not every subheading will be relevant, but the general format is robust.

First, the cover should show the name of your business, its address, phone, fax, email address, website and the date on which this version of the plan was prepared. It should confirm that this is the business's current view on its position and financing needs.

Second, the title page, immediately behind the front cover, should repeat the above information and also give the founder's name, address and phone number. A home phone number can be helpful, particularly for investors, who often work irregular hours too.

The Executive Summary. Ideally one page, but certainly no longer than two, this should follow behind the title page.

Writing this is the most difficult task, but it is the single most important part of the business plan. Done well it can favourably dispose the reader from the outset. Done badly, or not at all, then the plan may not get beyond the mail room. These two pages must explain:

- the current position of the business, including a summary of past trading results, if you have any
- a description of the products or services, together with details on any rights or patents and details on competitive advantage
- the reasons why customers need this product or service, together with some indication of market size and growth

- a summary of forecasts of sales and profits, together with short and longer term aims and the strategies to be employed
- how much money is needed to fund the growth and how and when the provider will benefit.

The executive summary can be written only after the business plan itself has been completed.

The table of contents follows the executive summary and is the map that will guide readers through the business proposal. If that map is obscure, muddled or even missing, then you are likely to end up with lost or irritated readers who are in no mind to back your proposal.

Each main section should be listed, numbered and given a page identity. Elements within each section should also be numbered, e.g. 1, 1.1, 1.2, etc.

The contents should include:

- **The business and its management:** A brief history of the business and its performance to date and details on key staff, current mission, legal entity, capital structure and professional advisers.
- **Products and services:** A description of products and services, their applications, competitive advantage and proprietary position. Include details on state of readiness of new products and services and development cost estimates.
- **Marketing:** Provide a brief overview of the market by major segment showing size and growth. Explain the current and proposed marketing strategy for each major segment, covering price, promotion, distribution channels, selling methods, location requirements, and the need for acquisitions, mergers or joint ventures, if any.
- **Management and staffing:** Give details on current key staff and on any recruitment needs to achieve the planned goals. Include information on staff retention strategies, reward systems and training plans.

- **Operations:** Describe how your products and services are 'made', how quality standards are assured and how output to meet the varying levels of demand implied in the business plan can be met.
- **E-commerce:** This is not simply about selling goods and services online. It covers a range of activities that can be carried out online to make your business more efficient. These solutions extend across the supply chain from ordering your raw materials right through to after sales service. It can incorporate market intelligence gathering, customer relationship management and a whole range of back office procedures. Your business plan should show how you plan to tackle this area.
- **Financial forecast and controls:** At the heart of every investment or lending proposition is the need to demonstrate that the business will deliver a satisfactory financial result. The business plan needs to show, in summary form, the key results to be achieved. This should cover sales, cash flow, profits, margins and investment returns for a sufficient period to give confidence.

  Provide a summary of the key financial data, including ratios, together with a description of the key controls used to monitor and review performance.
- **Financing requirements:** Show the finances needed to achieve the planned goals, together with timings. You should also demonstrate how the business would proceed using only internal funding. The 'gap' is what the extra money will help to deliver.

Appendices could include: CVs of the key team members; technical data; patents, copyrights and designs; details on professional advisers; audited accounts; consultants' reports; abstracts of market surveys; details of orders on hand and so on.

4 Writing and editing

The first draft of the business plan may have several authors and it can be written ignoring the niceties of grammar and style. Now would be a good time to talk over the proposal with your legal adviser to keep you on the straight and narrow, and with a friendly banker or venture capitalist. This can give you an insider's view as to the strengths and weaknesses of your proposal.

When the first draft has been revised, then comes the task of editing. Here grammar, spelling and a consistent style do matter. The end result must be a crisp, correct, clear and complete plan, no more than 20 pages long. If you are not an expert writer you may need help with editing. Your local librarian or college may be able to help here.

5 The oral presentation

Anyone backing a business does so primarily because they believe in the management. They know from experience that things rarely go to plan, so they must be confident that the team involved can respond effectively to changing conditions. You can be sure that any financier you are presenting to will have read dozens of similar plans, and will be well rehearsed. They may even have taken the trouble to find out something of your business and financial history.

Keep the following points in mind when preparing.

- Rehearse your presentation beforehand, having found out how much time you have. Allow at least as much time for questions as you take in your talk.
- Use visual aids and if possible bring and demonstrate your product or service. A video or computer-generated model is better than nothing.
- Explain your strategy in a businesslike manner, demonstrating your grasp of the competitive market forces at work. Listen to comments and criticisms carefully, avoiding a defensive attitude when you respond.
- Make your replies to questions brief and to the point. If they want more information, they can ask. This approach allows time for the many

different questions that must be asked either now or later, before an investment can proceed.

Your goal is to create an empathy between yourself and your listeners. Although you may not be able to change your personality, you could take a few tips on presentation skills. Eye contact, tone of speech, enthusiasm and body language all have a part to play in making a presentation go well.

Maintaining confidentiality

Finding an investor or a bank to lend to your business may take weeks or months. During that time they will diligently gather information about the business so that they won't have surprises later about income, expenses or undisclosed liabilities. The business plan will only be the starting point for their investigations.

If you and the prospective financiers are strangers to one another, you may be reluctant to turn over sensitive business information until you are confident that they are serious. (This is not so sensitive an issue with banks as it is with business angels and venture capital providers.) To allay these fears, consider asking for a confidentiality letter or agreement.

A confidentiality letter will suffice in most circumstances. But if substantial amounts of intellectual property are involved, you may prefer a longer, more formal, confidentiality agreement drafted by a lawyer. That's OK, but you (and perhaps your lawyer as well) should make sure that the proposed document contains no binding commitment on you. The confidentiality letter should be limited to their agreement to treat the information as strictly confidential and to use the information only to investigate lending or investing in the business, and to the other terms set out in the letter.

Don't be surprised if the investor wants to learn about your own financial status, job or business history. They are interested in your financial stability, your reputation for integrity and your general business savvy because they will, in effect, be extending credit to you until you deliver them the interest or return they are expecting on their money.

Making your business plan stand out

Most business plans are dull, badly written and frequently only read by the most junior of people in the financing organization. One venture capital firm in the US went on record to say they received 25,000 business plans asking for finance last year and invested in only 40.

Getting money from is expensive, time-consuming and hard work. Having said that, it is possible to get a quick decision. One recent start-up succeeded in raising £3 million in eight days, the founder having turned down an earlier offer of £1 million made just 40 minutes after his business plan was presented. Here is a summary of how to make your business plan stand out from the crowd.

- **Hit them with the benefits:** You need to spell out exactly what is it you do, for whom and why that matters. 'Our website makes ordering office supplies for small businesses simple. It saves the average customer five hours a week browsing catalogues and £5000 a year through bank discounts not otherwise available to firms this size. We have surveyed 200 local small firms, who rate efficient purchasing as a key priority.' This statement has the ring of practical authority about it.
- **Believable projections:** Future charts always look like a hockey stick. That's fine, if you can explain exactly what drives growth, how you capture sales and what the link between activity and results is.
- **Say how big the market is:** Financiers feel safer backing people in big markets. Small percentages of massive markets may be hard to achieve – but if you get it, at least it's worth it. Going for 10% of a market measured in millions

rather than billions may come to the same number, but it won't be as interesting.

- **Who are you and who are the team?** You need to sound like winners with a track record of great accomplishments.
- **Have some non-executive directors:** But they need to have relevant experience or be able to open doors and do deals.
- **Financial forecasts:** You need projected cash flows, profit and loss accounts and balance sheets for at least three years out. No one believes them after Year One, but the thinking behind them is what's important.

The profit margins will be key numbers in your projections, alongside sales forecasts. These will be probed hard, so show the build-up in detail.

- **Demonstrate the product or service:** Financiers need to see what the customer is going to get. A mock-up will do; failing that, a picture or diagram. But words are not enough.

Help with writing the business plan

Accelerators and business incubators

Often the help with business planning starts as part of the 'application' process to get into the incubator in the first place. Most put business planning at the centre of their offer. Most provide visitors to their website with helpful pointers towards better business planning.

Business Links and enterprise agencies

These organization are described and contact points listed in Section 2. They have the great merit of being locally based and staffed with people well versed in the process of putting together a business plan.

Business planning software and online help

The following websites and organization are well worth visiting or contacting.

American Express
Website: http://home3.americanexpress.com/ smallbusiness/tool/biz_plan/index.asp

American Express run something they call the Small Business Exchange Business Plan Workshop. This workshop will help you create a business plan to guide your business through the start-up or growth phase, or with a search for capital.

They've distilled the typical business plan into seven key elements. For each element the site provides a description, instructions for creation and, for many, tips for avoiding common pitfalls. They have also provided 'Toolboxes' full of samples, worksheets and glossaries that will clarify and walk you through the process.

You can experiment on someone else's business in the Try It Yourself section by testing your skills on a fictional business plan and be rated on how prepared you are to create your own. In each step of this exercise you will be presented with three choices for how an element of the business plan should read. After reading the three choices, pick the one that sounds best to you. You will then be able to read why the answer you picked is right or wrong. When you are done learning on the fictional plan, you will be ready to create one of your own.

Bplans.com
Website: www.bplans.com

Bplans.com, created by Palo Alto Software, offers thousands of pages of free sample plans, planning tools, and expert advice to help you start and run your business. Their sample plans come under three main headings.

- **Sample businesses:** You can browse their full sample of over 60 real business plans created with Business Plan Pro.
- **Sample marketing plans:** You can browse their full sample of real business plans created with Business Plan Pro.
- **Sample website plans:** You can look at their website plans that were created with Web Strategy Pro to help your website be a success.

Their site has 60 free sample business plans on it and their software package, Business Plan Pro, has these plans plus a further 140. The sample business plans are tailored for every type of business from aircraft rental to wedding gowns.

Out Of Your Mind … And Into The Marketplace
Email: lpinson@business-plan.com
Website: www.business-plan.com/index.html

This is a 15-year-old US-based small business publisher, business plan software developer and consulting firm specializing in step-by-step 'how-to' information for aspiring and current business owners. Their goal is to enable entrepreneurs to create credible and defensible business plans.

They work with clients in three different ways:

- textbooks and software
- workshops and seminars
- business plan consulting services.

BizPlanit.Com
Email: biz@bizplanit.com
Website: www.bizplanit.com

'BizPlanIt.Com's website has free resources including free business plan information, advice, articles, links and resources, a free monthly newsletter, the "Virtual Business Plan", to pinpoint information. They also have an email service, Ask Mr. BizPlanIt, providing free answers to business plan questions within 24 hours.'

Dilbert Mission Statement Generator
Website: www.unitedmedia.com/comics/dilbert/career/bin/ms2.cgi

Click on the 'Regenerate' label and an endless stream of fully formed mission statements will appear. Their offerings include such sentences as:

> It is our business to competently build resource-leveling catalysts for change while promoting personal employee growth.

and:

> It's our responsibility to completely disseminate high-payoff sources and enthusiastically build high standards in benefits.

Intended to raise a smile as you struggle with your business plan. Could help relieve a tense moment as you go through the final draft of your business plan before presentation day.

Interactive Business Planner (IBP)
Website: www.smallbusinessbc.ca/cbcbsc/ibp.html

A free resource provided by the Canada/British Columbia Business Service Centre, a small firms advisory body in Canada. IBP provides an excellent series of small business tutorials: Starting With A Good Idea, Marketing Basics, Financing Your Business, Planning Fundamentals and Business Regulations for Getting Started.

Invest-Tech Limited
27 Ardmeen Park,
Blackrock
Co Dublin
Tel: 00 353 1 283 4083
Fax: 00 353 1 278 2391
Email: info@planware.org
Website: www.planware.org

PlanWare offers the following free planning tools:

- Free-Plan and Biz-Plan, business plan guides and templates for Word
- Exl-Plan Free, fully-integrated short-term financial planner for Excel
- free Business Plan eGuides, compilation of papers on business planning matters
- free On-Line Financial Planner covering a five-year planning horizon
- free On-Line Strategy Planner for compiling a strategic business plan
- free On-Line Advice Service for problems relating to the compilation of a business plan.

Free-Plan is a protected *read-only* document supplied as freeware by Invest-Tech Limited.

Once you register, it can be unprotected and freely modified. There is no charge for this, and details of the process can be found on the website.

Depending on the status and scale of the business, you will certainly need to edit Free-Plan to create the most appropriate structure and flow for your plan. They recommend that you do this initial editing by hand on a printed copy and then apply the changes to a renamed copy of Free-Plan. Start the process by tuning the section headings and deleting/moving entire sections or large blocks of text to get the right overall framework.

Once your plan's framework has been defined, review its content to ascertain the key gaps in your preparatory work. You must sort these out before starting to write the plan. In other words, do the main planning before starting to draft the detailed plan. The plan has some Excel spreadsheets built in, with both US/Canadian and UK versions.

Just in case you are wondering about Invest-Tech's apparent altruism, like American Express, and pretty well everyone else in the 'free' software and help business, they do have other wares to sell on the website.

Microsoft Business Plan Writer

This is a free business plan writer, but it's only free if you happen to have Microsoft Office 2000 and, even then, only if you have something other than the most basic edition. There is an example business plan, software including a series of Excel templates, and a comprehensive package of explanatory text for pretty well every aspect of setting up and running a small business. There are embedded links to about 200 websites such as the Patent Office and venture capital firms covering the UK, USA and Australia.

Royal Bank of Canada
Website: www.royalbank.com

This site has a wide range of useful help for entrepreneurs. At www.royalbank.com/sme/index.html, you can access their business plan writer package and three sample business plans.

Small Business Information
Website: http://sbinformation.about.com/cs/businessplans/

A 'magazine' website with links to about 100 business plan writers and other useful information about writing business plans.

Their free Business Plan Outline is a multipart template that walks you through the whole process of making a business plan.

My Own Business Inc.
PO Box 8039
Rowland Heights
CA 91748
USA
Email: support@myownbusiness.org
Website: www.myownbusiness.org

Eleven templates and two sample business plans are offered for free from this site.

You can see and hear over 50 entrepreneurs talk about the problems and successes they have encountered on the way and there is an online business plan writing package

See page **391** for more details.

MyBplans.com
Website: www.bplans.com

The PlanWizard is quick and easy to use. Answer a few questions, and the PlanWizard will display a list of sample plans, articles, and other resources that match your search. You can see how other businesses have started with their plan and read answers to common questions for these business types. According to MyBpans, more than 150,000 people have used the PlanWizard to help them find information on similar businesses. It's simple and it's free.

National Federation of Enterprise Agencies (NFEA)
Website: www.smallbusinessadvice.org.uk

The website of the NFEA has a step-by-step business planning guide with free downloads to take out some of the hard work of financial calculations.

Small Business Institute
Website: www.busplan.cc/sample/sample.htm

A website with six sample business plans, including ones for a dentist practice, a Mexican restaurant, an ice cream parlour and a small manufacturing business

Training courses

Section 8 lists courses at colleges that provide training in writing business plans. There are also distance learning courses, both off- and online, covering the area.

Business plan competitions

One spur to getting a great plan written is to get into a business plan competition. Some are relatively closed shops, but even those that are closed may have something of value to offer. For example, the Stanford website has some useful pointers for anyone writing a business plan.

European Business Plan of the Year Competition
Website: www.london.edu

The most prestigious contest in Europe, this event is hosted by Insead and the London Business School. The programme is open to all MBA programmes in Europe, with prizes of £10,000 or so and consultancy advice from big name firms. Finishes in June each year.

Hummer Winbald February Madness Start-up tournament
Website: www-rohan.sdsu.edu/dept/emc/

Run like the college basketball tournament. 64 Internet-related business plans are chosen for the first round and teams progress to the 'sweet sixteen shootout'. Organized by the Hummer Winbald venture capital group. Open to all universities. Runs from February to June.

MIT $50K Entrepreneurship Competition
Website: http://50k.mit.edu

This is the one contest where even the losers can win. Akamai, for example, lost the 1998 contest but now have a market capitalization of over $20 billion. This student-run tournament recently celebrated its eleventh anniversary. Open to MIT community only. Begins in February, ends in May.

Moot Corp Business Plan Competition
Website: www.mootcorp.org

Its been called 'the Superbowl of World Business Plan competitions'. Hosted in Austin, Texas on the first week in May. Open to all universities, Texans and foreigners. Just added $100,000 to the prize chest for 2002.

Oxford Venturefest
Website: www.venturefest.com

In 2001, Venturefest introduced some 1800 entrepreneurs, scientists, researchers and developers to funders, new business partners and new customers. The event has become a vital date in the UK's business calendar and continues to attract many of the world's major VC organizations, seed fund managers, business angels, and organizations and individuals seeking lucrative investment opportunities. As well as cash prizes of £10,000, one Venturefest sponsor, Oxford Brookes University Business, runs a Business Plan Clinic that encourages and rewards innovation by providing one-to-one coaching and advice for embryonic business ideas, with free access to enterprise experts including company directors, business advisors, banks and academics. If you are aged between 16 and 25 and have a great business idea, simply submit a one-page business summary in order to secure a clinic session.

The Stanford Entrepreneur's Challenge
Website: http://bases.stanford.edu/challenge00/index.html

Out of 104 teams that entered the competition this year, 30 advance to the semi-final round and get one step closer to $50,000 in prizes. The semi-finalists were announced on 16 February at the Venture Fest. Limited to the Stanford community, but some useful online help and prompts to aid in the preparation.

Venture Challenge
Website: www-rohan.sdsu.edu/dept/emc/

Hosted by the Entrepreneurial Management Center of the College of Business Administration/San Diego State University. This year marks the 12th anniversary of the event and will include schools from Europe, Asia, Australia, Canada, Mexico and the United States, making it one of the most international competitions to date. The Venture Challenge boasts an impressive list of sponsors including NASDAQ, Qualcomm Corp., Sempra Energy and Motorola. Runs from February to April. Open to all universities.

UC Berkeley Business Plan Contest
Website: http://groups.haas.berkeley.edu/bplan/index.htm

The winner of the last contest received funding of $6.6 million from a prominent venture capital firm. Registration on the 15 February. Over $50,000 in cash and prizes. Open to alumni and students of UC Berkeley.

Books

The Business Planning Workbook by C. Barrow and R. Brown. Kogan Page and the *Sunday Times*, Fifth Edition, 2005.

Section 12

GLOSSARY OF KEY BUSINESS TERMS

This glossary gives a meaning to words that have either been used in the book (and may or may not have been explained in context) or that you are likely to meet early on in your business life.

Account(s) Usually annual financial records of a business.

Accrual An accounting concept that insists that income and expenses for the accounting period be included, whether for cash or credit.

Ad Valorem Literally: according to value. Any charge that is applied as a percentage of value.

Added value The difference between sales revenue and material costs. See also *value added*.

Adoption curve A graphic representation of the classification of users or buyers of an innovation according to the time of adoption. These categories are as follows: innovators, first 2.5%; early adopters, next 13.5%; early majority, next 34%; late majority, next 34%; laggards, last 16%. Research has shown that these adopter groups have different characteristics, i.e. social class, age, education and attitudes. Those launching new products or businesses have to pay particular attention to the characteristics and behaviour of the innovator group in order to identify the most likely early customers, and so focus initial marketing on them.

Advertising The central purpose of all advertising activity is to secure as many favourable buying decisions as possible. As a concept, advertising has been around too long for its origins to be precisely traced. As an institution-alized business it has existed in the UK since the 1700s, when newspapers began to feature advertisements. The UK's oldest advertising agency, Charles Baker, was founded in 1812. The most surprising fact about advertising is not how much money is spent on doing it (although that is quite surprising) but how much money is misspent. Lord Leverhulme is reputed to have said, 'Half the money I spend on advertising is wasted, but I can't find anyone to tell me which half.' For the smaller firm, leaflets and brochures consume the greater proportion of advertising expenditure. Answering the following five questions before committing to any expenditure can usually ensure that this intangible activity has some concrete results.

1 What to you want to happen? (i.e. X people to buy Y quantity of produce Z)
2 How much is that worth?
3 What message will make it happen?
4 What media should be used?
5 How will the results be checked?

Advisory, Conciliation and Arbitration Service (ACAS) The name ACAS conjures up images of late-night sessions in smoke-filled rooms holding the ring between trade union bosses and company directors. The reality of their work is rather more prosaic, and is in the main concerned with preventing disputes before they can get to the public eye. They also offer advice on recruitment and selection, payment systems and incentive schemes, and manpower planning. It is in these areas that they can prove particularly helpful to new firms, and over a quarter of their 12,500+ advisory visits each year are to companies with fewer than 50 employees.

AIM   Alternative Investment Market. Market for small and new businesses to raise equity capital (see also *IPO*).

Angel   Someone who puts up risk capital for a theatrical performance, show or film. A West End musical, for example, costs upwards of £500,000. Starlight Express cost over £2.2 million, so external funding is essential. These 'angels' must be prepared to lose their money and many do. The rewards, however, can be spectacular. Investors who bought into Evita have recouped their cash six and a half times. Those who put up money for the smash hit musical Me and My Girl recouped their money and received their first profit within 10 months. The term has now been taken over by the venture capital industry to mean any private investor.

Animal spirits   A term coined by J. Maynard Keynes to describe the effects of entrepreneurial zeal on the healthiness or otherwise of an economy. Surveys such as those conducted by the Confederation of British Industry and the Small Business Research Trust regularly attempt to monitor some aspects of these animal spirits.

Annual report   see *audit*.

Arbitrage   Profiting from differences in the price of something that is traded on more than one market.

Asset   Something owned by the business which has a measurable cost.

Audit   A process carried out by an accountant (auditor) on all companies each year, to check the accuracy of financial records. The auditor cannot be the company's own accountant. The result is the annual report.

Authorized capital   The share capital of a company authorized by law. It does not have to be taken up. For example, a £1000 company need only 'issue' two £1 shares. It can issue a further 998 £1 shares without recourse to law. After that sum it has to ask the permission of its shareholders.

Back-up   Copies made of data and programs to be available in the event of originals being corrupted, damaged or lost.

Bad debts   The amounts of money due in from customers that either have become or are expected to become uncollectable. The accounting principle of conservation requires that all reasonably likely losses be anticipated. So debts that are almost certainly uncollectable are deducted from the total; debts which are reasonably likely to be uncollectable have a specific provision made against them; and in addition a general provision can be made against the rest of the debts, based on past experience. This was *creative accounting* born.

Balance sheet   A statement of assets owned by a business and the way in which they are financed, taken from both liabilities and owner's equity. This report does not indicate the market value of the business.

Bankruptcy   Imposed by a court when someone cannot meet his bills. The bankrupt's property is managed by a court-appointed trustee, who must use it to pay off the creditors as fairly as possible.

Barriers to entry   The way in which big businesses appear to pull up the drawbridge after them. The greater the barriers to entry the fewer the opportunities for new firms to enter a market. Such barriers include *economies of scale*, access to distribution channels, high capital requirements, high spending on research and development, short *product life cycles*, break-even pricing, high advertising expenditure and government policy.

Benchmark   The performance of a business against some standard or standards that other comparable businesses have achieved. Usually ranked in such a way that a firm can see if it is in the top, middle or bottom position.

Better mousetrap fallacy   Coined by Geoffrey Timmons, Professor of Entrepreneurship at Northeastern University, to describe the often unwarranted faith put into a new product or invention by entrepreneurs, especially if it has been granted a patent. His thesis is that technological ideas must indeed be sound, but that marketability and marketing know-how generally outweigh technical elegance in the success equation. To illustrate this claim, Professor Timmons' research shows that less than 0.5% of the best ideas contained in the US Patent Gazette in the last five years have returned a dime to the inventors.

Black economy Usually refers to businesses run by the self-employed who illegally avoid tax and National Insurance. There is therefore no official record, and they are collectively referred to as the black economy.

Blue chip In gambling, the high chips are usually blue. In business, this refers to high-status companies and their shares. They are usually large companies with a long successful trading history.

Bookkeeping The recording of all business transactions in 'journals' in order to provide data for accounting reports.

Book value Usually the figure at which an asset appears in the accounts. This is not necessarily the market value.

Bootstrapping Getting a business underway with the minimum of finance. Literally pulling the business through by sheer effort. Improbable, but it can be done.

Break-even point The volume of production at which revenues exactly match costs. After this point profit is made.

Browser World Wide Web client. An information retrieval tool.

Business transfer agents Analogous to estate agents, they help bring buyers and sellers of small and usually retail businesses together.

Byte A sequence of eight 'bits', used to represent one character of information. A letter, digit, symbol or punctuation mark.

Cadillac syndrome This occurs when entrepreneurs brush aside the vital price-volume issue and its relationship to the *break-even point*, with the explanation, 'We are the Cadillac of the field.' This leads to the setting of such an unreasonably high price that a market so small as to sink the business is brought about. Although

the theoretical profit margin on each unit sold is high in percentage terms, the volume sold is too low to even recover the investment. For many inventors, financial failure is often of secondary importance to their 'artistic' success (unless it is their money at stake). The fact that their product is on the market is, in itself, sufficient success. Synonymous with the Rolls Royce syndrome.

Capital It has several meanings, but unprefixed it usually means all the assets of the business.

Cash The 'money' assets of a business, which include both cash in hand and cash at the bank.

Cash flow The difference between total cash coming in and going out of a business over a period of time.

Cash flow break-even point The point below which the firm will need either to obtain additional financing or to liquidate some of its assets to meet its fixed costs.

Caveat emptor Buyer beware. The buyer must inspect and satisfy himself it is adequate for his needs. The seller is under no obligation to disclose defects but may not actively conceal a known defect or lie if asked.

Chairman (of the Board) The senior director of a company. In a small business this role is usually combined with that of *managing director*. He is responsible for presenting the *annual report* to the shareholders, along with his own comments on how the business is performing in the light of world affairs.

Common shares Securities that represent equity ownership in a company. Common shares let an investor vote on such matters as the election of directors. They also give the holder a share in a company's profits via dividend payments or the capital appreciation of the security.

Company director A person elected by the shareholders of a limited company to control for them the day-to-day management of the business, and to decide on policy. The Companies Act sets out directors' duties and responsibilities. In most companies, one-third of the directors are required to retire from office each year. The directors who retire in any one year are those who have been longest in office since their last election. A retiring director can stand for re-election.

Company doctor   Someone brought in to turn around an ailing venture. The term can also apply to someone who makes a habit of buying up loss-making ventures and returning them to profitability. Usually the measures taken by a company doctor in restoring a business to health include large-scale redundancies, closing down loss-making units, and the sale of any parts of the venture peripheral to its main trade. This may account for why such people are reticent to assume the title, but they are well known on the acquisition/merger circuit.

Company secretary   Every limited company in the UK must have a company secretary. In public companies they must be professionally qualified and in a private company they must be 'suitable' but need not have professional qualifications. They are appointed by the board of directors to carry out the legal duties of the company such as keeping certain records, sending information to the Registrar of Companies, and generally to manage the administration of the company.

Computer-aided design (CAD)   Software to produce two- and three-dimensional drawings on the screen and as hard copy.

Computer program   Instructions telling a computer to carry out a specific task.

Corruption   A distortion or elimination of data from the memory or disk, usually caused by electromagnetic impulses – e.g. when a disk is left near another electronic or magnetic device such as a loudspeaker.

Cost of goods sold   The costs of goods actually sold in any period. It excludes the cost of the goods left unsold, and all overheads except manufacturing.

Crash   What happens when a program refuses to continue. Usually the program has to be reloaded, with the loss of all work in progress – unless you have kept a back-up.

Creative accounting   The term used to describe the rather elastic treatment of accounting rules and concepts, usually in an effort to create a picture that is favourable to the entrepreneur. In its more extreme forms it becomes fraud.

Credit scoring   A statistical technique where several financial characteristics are combined to form a single score to represent a customer's creditworthiness.

Current assets   Assets normally realized in cash or used up in operations during the year. It includes such items as debtors and stock.

Current liability   A liability due for payment in one trading period, usually a year.

Database   An electronic filing program enabling data to be kept in an organized way for later retrieval and analysis.

Debenture   Long-term loan with specific terms of interest, capital repayment and security.

Debug   Computerese for 'troubleshoot'.

Demand, Law of   An economic theory that suggests that, all things being equal, the lower the price, the greater the demand. The concept is much misunderstood by new entrepreneurs who believe the only thing that has to be done to beat a competitor is to have a lower price. The theory was put to good effect by the late Sir Jack Cohen of Tesco in his philosophy of 'stack it high and sell it cheap'. He understood the need for good promotion, a good range and mix of products and above all good location for his stores, as well as having competitive prices. Unfortunately (or perhaps not!), the demand for all products or services is not uniformly elastic – that is, the rate of change of price and demand are not interlinked. Some products are actually price-inelastic. For example, Jaguar and Rolls-Royce would be unlikely to see any more cars if they knocked 5% off the price – indeed, by losing snob value they may sell less. So if they dropped their price they would simply lower profits. However, people would quite happily cross town to save 5p in the £1 on fresh vegetables and meat. This concept is closely allied to working out the *break-even point*.

Depreciation A way of measuring the cost of using a fixed asset. A set portion of the asset's cost is treated as an expense each period of its working life.

Direct costs Expenses, such as labour and materials, which vary 'directly' according to the number if items manufactured. Also called *variable costs.*

Downside risk Everyone who goes into a business venture does so with the expectation of making a profit. After the excitement of calculating the size of the prospective fortune to be made, the prudent entrepreneur also takes stock of the likely maximum to be lost if it all goes wrong. This is called the downside risk. The Midland Bank's association with Crocker in the USA shows that it's not just your original stake than can be at risk. Crocker's loans were in the main secured against farm land values, which was fine while prices were rising, but became a catastrophe when they started to fall as they did shortly after the Midland acquisition. Crocker's *bad debt* provision had to be topped up with extra money from the UK parent.

Earnings before interest and taxes (EBIT) A financial measure defined as revenues less cost of goods sold and selling, general, and administrative expenses. In other words, operating and non-operating profit before the deduction of interest and income taxes.

Earnings per share (EPS) A company's profit divided by its number of outstanding shares. If a company earned £1 million in one year and had 1 million shares of stock outstanding, its EPS would be £1 per share.

Economies of scale The gain experienced by firms that can spread their costs over a large volume of output. Other advantages, such as more efficient buying, can accrue to big producers. It is one of the *barriers to entry*, inhibiting new firms from entering certain markets successfully. However, achieving economies of scale carries some penalties. For example, it makes such businesses relatively inflexible and

less responsive to change than their smaller cousins.

Ego trip A rather more accurate description of what many entrepreneurs are up to than the more prosaic term 'business'. The ego is only recognized by such entrepreneurs when it is bruised by *bankruptcy.*

Electronic Fund Transfer Systems (EFTS) A variety of systems and technologies for transferring funds (money) electronically rather than by cheque. Includes Fedwire, Bankwire, automated clearinghouses (ACHs), and other automated systems.

ECGD Export Credit Guarantee Department.

E-business Any activity on the Internet that transforms business relationships or fundamentally changes the way in which business is done. It is not simply about selling things you already make or have, but a new way to drive efficiencies, speed up transactions, innovate new products and services and create more value for your business and for your customers. In this respect the Internet should be seen as an 'enabling technology', such as the telephone or electricity, which themselves both improved a whole variety of processes and allowed whole new industries to become established. Unlike *e-commerce*, which usually only involves relationships between suppliers and customers, e-business involves a more complex series of relationships, both inside a business, for example to change the way work is done, and outside, to improve relationships along the whole value chain that links a business and its suppliers to the market.

E-commerce One element of *e-business* that describes the trading relationship between companies and individuals exchanging goods and services using the Internet.

E-economy Also referred to as the 'Digital Economy' or 'Cyberspace', this is the whole virtual environment in which electronic business is conducted. It is here that goods and services are exchanged, relationships initiated and established and money changes hands. Activities in the e-economy can mirror similar activities taking place in the conventional market place. So, for example, a major food retailer may have alongside its 'bricks' activities, as its physical trading has become known, an Internet or 'clicks' business. In measuring the e-economy, only the 'clicks' portion of business would be counted.

Email   The modern alternative to telex and conventional paper-based mail, using computers and the Internet.

Entrepreneur   An entrepreneur is someone who recognizes an opportunity, raising the money and other resources needed to exploit that opportunity, and bears some or all of the risk associated with executing the ensuing plans. Entrepreneurship can be more correctly viewed as a behaviour characteristic than a personality trait, which explains why the 'typical' entrepreneur is difficult to describe – or to detect in advance using questionnaires.

Equity   The owner's claims against the business, sometimes called the shareholder's funds. This appears as a liability because it belongs to the shareholders and not to the business itself. It is represented by the share capital plus the cumulative retained profits over the business's life. The reward for equity investment is usually a dividend paid on profits made.

Escrow account   An escrow account is a special bank account into which earnings from sales (e.g. convertible currency proceeds from exports) are accumulated. These revenues are set aside for subsequent acquisition of goods and services from a foreign supplier. The escrowed money, usually interest-bearing, is disbursed by the bank to the foreign supplier under payment terms and against documents specified in the supplier's sale contract.

Experience curve   A graphical description of what happens to costs as a business acquires history of experience of producing a product. Typically, for each doubling of experience, as represented by the absolute volume of output, unit costs can be expected to fall by 20–30%. This axiom poses at least one threat and one opportunity for entrepreneurs.

Extraordinary general meeting (EGM)   Meeting held within the rules laid down by company law and the company's own rules to deal with unusual events, such as responding to a takeover bid and changing the capital structure of a business.

Financial ratio   The relationship between two money quantities, used to analyse business results.

Financial year   A year's trading between dates agreed with the Inland Revenue. Not necessarily the fiscal year, which starts on 5 April.

Firmware   Computer instruction stored in read-only memory (ROM).

Fixed assets   Assets such as land, building, equipment, cars, etc. acquired for long-term use in the business and not for stock in trade. Initially recorded in the balance sheet at cost.

Fixed cost   Expenses that do not vary directly with the number of items produced. For example, a car has certain fixed costs, such as tax and insurance, whether it is driven or not.

Floating charge   The security given by a borrower to a lender that floats over all his assets. So if the borrower fails to repay the loan, the lender can lay claim to any and all of his assets up until the time the full sum due has been recovered. This contrasts with a fixed charge.

Forecast   A statement of what is likely to happen in the future, based on careful judgement and analysis.

Force Majeure   The title of a standard clause in marine contract exempting the parties for non-fulfilment of their obligations as a result of conditions beyond their control, such as earthquakes, floods or war.

Forfaiting   Forfaiting is a form of supplier credit in which an exporter surrenders possession of export receivables, which are usually guaranteed by a bank in the importer's country, by selling them at a discount to a 'forfaiter' in exchange for cash. Forfaiters usually work with bills of exchange or promissory notes, which are unconditional and easily transferable debt instruments that can be sold on the secondary market. Differences between export factoring and forfaiting are:

- factors usually want access to a large percentage of an exporter's business, while most forfaiters will work on a one-shot basis
- forfaiters generally work with medium- and long-term receivables (180 days to seven years), while factors work with short-term receivables (up to 180 days).

See also *factoring*.

Free cash flows   Cash not required for operations or for reinvestment. Often defined as earnings before interest (often obtained from operating income line on the income statement), less capital expenditures, less the change in working capital.

Funds   Financial resources, not necessarily cash.

Gearing   The ratio of a business's borrowings to its equity. For example, a 1:1 ratio would exist where a bank offered to match your investment pound for pound.

Going concern   Simply an accounting concept, it assumes in all financial reports that the business will continue to trade indefinitely into the future unless there is specific evidence to the contrary – i.e. it has declared an intention to liquidate. It is not an indication of the current state of health of the business.

Goodwill   Value of the name, reputation or intangible assets of a business. It is recorded in the accounts only when it is purchased. Its nature makes it a contentious subject.

Graphics   Software to produce graphs, charts, presentation, graphics and even high quality pictures.

Gross   Total before deductions. For example, gross profit is the difference between sales income and costs of goods sold. The selling and administrative expenses have yet to be deducted. Then it becomes the net profit.

Growth vector matrix   When planning for growth, entrepreneurs tend to be led by opportunity, which more often than not leads them to select diversification strategies at the outset. By their nature diversification strategies are the most risky as they build neither on the company's proven product nor on market skills – they simply use surplus cash or borrowings to back a hunch. Successful diversification calls for strong management skills, a commodity in short supply in most small firms. The growth vector matrix was developed in 1965 by Igo Ansoff to help companies to cluster and analyse their strategies for growth and to assess their relative riskiness. The dimensions of the matrix are defined as product and market, each of which is defined in terms of the present position and the new position, resulting in four basic growth strategies: market penetration, market development, product development and diversification.

HyperText Markup Language (HTML)   The rules that govern the way documents are created so that they can be read by a *browser*. These documents are characterized by the .html or .htm file extension.

HTTP   HyperText Transport Protocol, the protocol used by web servers.

Hyperlink   A link in a given document to information within another document. These links are usually represented by highlighted words or images.

Irrevocable   This the most common instrument of credit in international trade, and carries an irrevocable obligation of the issuing bank to pay the beneficiary when drafts and documents are presented in accordance with the terms of the letter of credit. An irrevocable letter of credit, once issued, cannot be amended or cancelled without the agreement of all named parties. As such, it must have a fixed expiration date.

Income statement   See *profit and loss account*.

Insolvency   A situation in which a person or business cannot meet the bills. Differs from bankruptcy, as the body involved may have assets that can be realized to meet those bills.

Interface   Electronic device that links computer hardware together. For example, a printer or VDU to the computer itself.

Initial public offering (IPO)   A company's first sale of stock to the public. Securities offered in an IPO are often, but not always, those of young, small companies seeking outside equity capital and a public market for their stock. Investors purchasing stock in IPOs must generally be prepared to accept very large risks for the possibility of large gains. IPOs by investment companies (closed-end funds) usually contain underwriting fees which represent a load to buyers (see also *AIM*).

Insiders   These are directors and senior officers of a corporation – in effect, those who have access to inside information about a company. An insider is also someone who owns more than 10% of the voting shares of a company.

Internet   An international computer network of networks that connects government, academic and business institutions.

Invisible hand   The cornerstone of the theory of economist Adam Smith (1723–90) on the way the capitalist system works, as expounded in his book, *The Wealth of Nations* (1776). The book lends credibility to entrepreneurial activity by proposing that if all individuals act from self-interest, spurred on by the profit motive, then society as whole prospers, with no apparent regulator at work. It is, wrote Smith, as if an 'invisible hand' guided the actions of individuals to combine for the common wealth. Governments are 'selective' in the ways in which they demonstrate their belief in this theory and their all too visible hand is seen in the creation of more and more *red tape* that often seems only to inhibit enterprise.

JPEG   A method, developed by the Joint Photographic Expert Group, of storing an image in digital format.

Just-in-time inventory systems   Systems that schedule materials/inventory to arrive exactly as they are needed in the production process.

Junk bond   A bond with a speculative credit rating of BB or lower is a junk bond. Such bonds offer investors higher yields than bonds of financially sound companies. Two agencies, Standard & Poor's and Moody's Investor Services, provide the rating systems for companies' credit.

Know-how agreement   This is a promise to disclose information to a third party. If the disclosure is made for them to evaluate the usefulness of the know-how, the agreement is called a secrecy agreement. If the disclosure is made to allow commercial; production, it is called a know-how licence.

LANs and WANs   Local Area Networks (LANs) and Wide Area Networks (WANs) are generic terms referring to two important basic types of networks. The Internet can be thought of as a number of LANs interconnected by WANs. An average packet will run across a company's local Ethernet (LAN), up an ISDN or leased line or some other link (WAN) to an Internet Service Provider. The ISP has Ethernet (LAN), too, that transports the packet to the right router for delivery to a cross-country provider (WAN). The packet begins bouncing from one LAN site to another over WAN links.

Learning curve   The improvement in the performance of a task as it is repeated and as more is learned about it.

Leveraged buy-out (LBO)   A transaction used for taking a public corporation private, financed through the use of debt funds: bank loans and bonds. Because of the large amount of debt relative to equity in the new corporation, the bonds are typically rated below investment grade, properly referred to as high-yield bonds or junk bonds.

Liabilities   The claims against a business, such as loans and equity.

Letter of credit   A financial document issued by a bank at the request of the consignee guaranteeing payment to the shipper for cargo if certain terms and conditions are fulfilled.

- A Revocable Letter of Credit is subject to possible recall or amendment at the option of the applicant, without the approval of the beneficiary.
- A Confirmed Letter of Credit is issued by a foreign bank with its validity confirmed by a domestic bank. An exporter who requires a confirmed letter of credit from the buyer

is assured payment from the domestic bank in case the foreign buyer or bank defaults.

- A Documentary Letter of Credit is one for which the issuing bank stipulates that certain documents must accompany a draft. The documents assure the applicant (importer) that the merchandise has been shipped and that title to the goods has been transferred to the importer.

LIFO (Last-in-first-out)   The last-in-first-out inventory valuation methodology. A method of valuing inventory that uses the cost of the most recent item in inventory first.

Liquidation   The legal process of closing down a business and selling off its assets to meet outstanding debts.

Loan capital   Finance lent to a business for a specific period of time at either a fixed or varied rate of interest. This interest must be paid irrespective of the performance of the business.

Love money   Money put into a business by family, friends or successful business neighbours. It is a US term that has less to do with love than it has to do with tax. In the USA anyone investing in a new enterprise can do so out of pre-tax income and so have that investment effectively subsidized by the marginal tax rate.

Management buy-out (MBO)   A growing phenomenon whereby the managers of a company become its owners. They do this by setting up a new company which buys either all or, more usually, a part of their old company. The money to do so is raised from banks, venture capital funds and from the managers themselves. The reason for the buy-out often stems from the desire of the parent company to pull out of a certain activity. Or to demerge from a previous amalgamation.

Management consultant   'Someone who borrows your watch to tell you the time – then charges you for the privilege.' A rather disparaging description, but one that is instantly recognizable by anyone that has used a consulting firm. Management consultants sell professional advice on most aspects of business, including financial management, marketing, market research, strategy formulation and manpower planning. The have come into their own in the information technology area and in all aspects of managing change in organizations. Management consultants are much in evidence after takeovers where they are used to help the victor make sure of the spoils. In the UK there are about 5000 management consultants, with 2800 belonging to the Institute of Management Consultants, their professional body.

Managing Director   A company director holding special powers to manage the day-to-day affairs of a company. Next in importance to the chairman.

Marginal cost   The extra cost incurred in making one more unit of production.

Market segment   A group of buyers who can be identified as being especially interested in a particular variant of the product. For example, a cheap day return ticket for a train is a variant of a rail fare, especially attractive to people who do not have to get to their destination early, perhaps to work.

Market share   The ratio of a firm's sales of a product in a specific market during a particular period to the total sales of that product in the same period in the same market.

Marketing mix   The combination of methods used by a business to market its product. For example, it can vary its price or the type and quantity of advertising; the distribution channels can be altered; finally, the product itself can either be enhanced or reduced in quality.

Marketing strategy   Philip Kotler, the US marketing theorist, identified four basic competitive marketing strategies. While strategy is classically a big business concept, there is no reason why small businessmen should not profit by using the same principles. Indeed, there is much evidence to suggest they are more likely to succeed if they do.

Memorandum of association   A legal document drawn up as a part of the registration of a company in the UK. The memorandum must state the company's name, its registered office, its purposes and its authorized share capital. The purpose of the business, as set out in the memorandum, is very broad, deliberately so, in order not to preclude any type of trade the company may choose to embark on in the future. The memorandum is sent to the Registrar of Companies, who must also be informed of any changes.

Memory   Computers use their electronic memory to store and process data. There are two sorts of memory – ROM (read-only memory), which is a permanent store containing the computer's internal operating instructions; and RAM (random-access memory), which is a temporary store containing data and programs currently being used. When the power is turned off all data and programs in the RAM memory are lost.

Modem   A device that allows computers (and ancillary equipment) to communicate over telephone wires.

MPEG   A method, devised by the Moving Pictures Experts Group, of storing movie files in digital format.

Multi-tasking   The capability for more than one program (in the case of a network, possibly used by more than one user) to run at the same time.

National Insurance   A state insurance scheme in the UK administered by the Department of Health and Social Security, by which every employer, employee and self-employed person makes weekly payments to provide insurance against accidents, sickness and unemployment, and towards a pension and other benefits.

Networking   Linking together several computers. See *LANs and WANs*.

Non-disclosure agreement   An agreement which allows you to reveal secret commercial information – for example, about an invention – to a third party, and which prevents them from making use of that information without your agreement.

Non-executive director   A part-time director, who helps to plan and decide the policy of a company but who has no responsibility for carrying out such policies. Normally, companies

raising capital through merchant banks and other financial institutions will be 'encouraged' to have a nominee of theirs as a non-executive director.

'Off the shelf' company   A company without a trading history that has been formed and held specifically for resale at a later date. Agencies keep a large stock of such companies in numerous categories of business. They cost around £130 each, and can be up and running in a day or so. An 'off the shelf' company may have an unsuitable name, but that can be changed later for a modest fee. A tailor-made company will cost more than an 'off the shelf' company, and it takes four to five weeks to set up. So if speed is of the essence, the 'off the shelf' is the first choice.

One per cent syndrome   Also known as the market research cop-out clause. This describes the situation in which a prospective business owner starts a venture on the premise that 'If we only sell 1% of the potential market, we'll be a great success.' This argument is then advanced so that no time is wasted in doing basic market research – after all, the business only has to sell to this tiny percentage of possible buyers! In fact, this type of thinking leads to more business failures than any other single factor. If the market is so huge as to make 1% of it very profitable, then inevitably there are large and established competitors. For a small firm to try to compete head-on in this situation is little short of suicidal. It can be done, but only if sound research has clearly identified a market niche, or if there is a particular industry 'lag' that would allow a new business to obtain a special place. However, more usually the idea itself is badly thought through – as are all ideas that do not take the customers' viewpoint – and this causes the business to fail to gain even the magical 1%.

Opportunity cost   The value of a course of action open to you but not taken. For example, keeping cash in an ordinary share account at a building society will attract about 2% less interest than a five-year term the same society.

So the opportunity cost of choosing not to tie up your money is 2%.

Overhead   This is an expense which cannot be conveniently associated with a unit of production. Administration or selling expenses are usually overheads.

Overtrading   Expanding sales and production without enough financial resources – in particular, working capital. The first signs are usually cash flow problems.

Pareto principle   The rule which states that 80% of effort goes into producing 20% of the results. For a new business, this rule is usually observed first when it is seen that 20% of their customers produce 80% of sales by value. As this rule is close to impossible to change, it is only by widening the customer base and lowering the dependence on a few important customers that a new firm can hope to survive.

Peripheral   Collective name for any piece of equipment, e.g. printers, disk drives, monitors, modems and plotters, which can be attached to a computer.

Piggybacking   Usually associated with firms that market other firms' products as well as their own, but the term can be used to describe any 'free riding' activity.

Pixel   Dots on the screen produced by the computer to draw text or pictures. The greater the number of pixels on the screen, the better the definition will be.

Poison pill   Anti-takeover device that gives a prospective acquiree's shareholders the right to buy shares of the firm or shares of anyone who acquires the firm at a deep discount to their fair market value. Named after the cyanide pill that secret agents are instructed to swallow if capture is imminent.

Preference shares   These usually give their holders the right to a fixed dividend and priority over ordinary shareholders in liquidation, and confer voting power only in matters concerning the varying of the shareholders' rights or in cases when dividends have not been paid. There are four types of preference share in the entrepreneur's 'capital' armoury:

1 cumulative preference shares, which give the right to payment of any past dividends not paid

2 redeemable preference shares, which are those that the company has agreed to repay on a specified date, often at a premium over issuing price

3 participatory preference shares, which, in addition to the right to a fixed dividend, allow further profit participation in good times

4 convertible preference shares, which have the right to be changed for ordinary shares at specified dates and prices.

Product life cycle   A concept which states that every product (or service) passes through certain identifiable stages in its life. Understanding the implications of each of these stages for the company's *cash flow*, *profit* and *marketing strategy* is an important element in successfully launching a new venture.

1 **Pre-launch:** All the work done to bring the product or service to market. This includes product development, market research, etc.

2 **Introduction:** Usually featured by low sales and no profits. Innovators (*adoption curve*) are the main customers.

3 **Growth:** If all goes well and the product is accepted by the innovative customers, sales begin to grow, sharply at first.

4 **Maturity:** Sales growth stops, new competitors have probably arrived, and the original product is beginning to look a bit stale.

5 **Decline:** Unless the product is re-launched, by changing various elements in the *marketing mix*, sales will decline.

Profit   The excess of sales revenue over sales cost and expenses during an accounting period. It does not necessarily mean an increase in cash.

Profit and loss account   A statement of sales, costs, expenses and profit (or loss) over an accounting period monthly, quarterly or annually. Also known as the *income statement*.

Protocol   A planned method of exchanging data over the Internet.

Pyramid selling   A form of multi-level distributorship which typically involved the manufacture or sale by a company, under its own trade name, of a line of products through 'franchises' which appear to be regular franchise distributorships. The pyramid may include three to five levels of non-exclusive distributorships, and individuals may become 'franchisees' at any level by paying the company a fee, and agreeing to buy stock, based on the level of entry. Once in, the individual earns a commission by selling the company's products, but at higher levels in the pyramid it is made more attractive to introduce new members. This product is sold down the chain at progressively higher prices, until the final person has to sell to the public. Since most people make a profit by merely being a link in the chain, the emphasis is placed on recruiting more investors-distributors, rather than on selling to end customers. The schemes, like chain letters, are lucrative for those at the top of the pyramid. But inevitably, the market becomes saturated, no further participants can be recruited and the system then collapses. Contrary to public opinion, pyramid selling is not illegal in the UK. It is, however, controlled by the Fair Trading Act 1973 (section 118) and by the provisions of the Consumer Credit Act 1971.

QuickTime   A method of storing movie and audio files in a digital format. Developed by Apple.

RAM   Random-access memory is the space used for storing computer data as programs. It can be changed as new programs or data are called up.

Receiver   Someone called in by a troubled company's creditors to try to sort out the company's financial problems. The receiver's aim is to get the company back on the straight and narrow without it going into liquidation.

Red tape   The excessive use of or adherence to formalities. Despite protestations to the contrary, it would appear to describe accurately the relationship between Whitehall and enterprise. Research by the Forum of Private Business has shown that an entrepreneur wishing to set up a limited company as an electrician needed to make 18 telephone calls, travel 127 miles to collect papers, and spend 24 hours reading 269,200 words to understand government regulations.

- The average time spent by small businesses in complying with government regulations is 10.5 hours per week, at a cost of £2000 per year.
- Failure to comply with regulations can result in prison sentences of up to two and a half years and/or fines of up to £2000.
- At every pay day there are 34 clerical operations per employee to calculate tax and National Insurance contributions and to provide the pay slip.
- Customs and Excise requires a quarterly form, VAT 100, to be completed. But the VAT inspector will expect to see every VAT invoice and bill by way of confirmation.

With the seemingly endless encroachment of legislation, it seems unlikely that government-inspired deregulation measures will be effective in the short run. The only hope in the foreseeable future is a microcomputer with the appropriate software – alas, as yet unwritten.

Registered office   This need not necessarily be the same address as the business is conducted from. Quite frequently the address used for the registered office is that of the firm's solicitor or accountant. This is, however, the address where all official correspondence will go. EEC regulations now require the name of the company to be prominently displayed at the registered office address.

Reserves   The name given to the accumulated and undistributed profits of the business. They belong to the ordinary shareholders. They are not necessarily available in cash, but are usually tied up in other business assets.

Revenue   Usually from sales. Revenue is recognized in accounting terms when goods have been despatched (or services rendered) and the invoice sent. This means that revenue pounds are not necessarily cash pounds. A source of much confusion and frequent cash flow problems.

ROM   Read-only memory.

Royalty   The money paid to the owner of something valuable for the right to make use of it for a specified purpose. Examples include payment made to the owners of a copyright for permission to publish, or the owner of a patent for permission to use a patented design.

Schedule D   Cases I and II are the Inland Revenue rules that govern tax allowances for self-employed people.

Schedule E   Allowances for employed people.

Seasonality   A regular event, usually one that causes sales to increase or decrease in an annual cycle. For example, the weather caused by the seasons or events associated with the seasons: Christmas, spring sales, summer holidays, etc.

Secured creditor   Someone lending money to a business whose debt is secured by linking a default in its repayment to a fixed asset, such as a freehold building.

Server   A computer that serves information and software to the Internet community

Share capital   The capital of the business subscribed for by the owners or shareholders.

Share option   A facility that allow top managers and employees to have shares in the companies for which they work, on special terms. The most effective way to improve employees' attitudes, productivity and understanding of the company's position is by instituting a share option scheme. In this way they can participate in success (and failure) too. Half of all leading UK companies operate such schemes. Indeed, various Finance Acts from 1972 have relaxed the tax position in this area.

Six badges of trade   The list drawn up by the Royal Commission on the Taxation of Profits and Income, 1955 to distinguish whether an activity constitutes trading (and is therefore taxable), or is simply a hobby (and is not). The list includes:

- the frequency of the activity
- the value added, or amount of work done
- the motive
- the nature of the transaction
- the circumstances
- the methodology.

Sleeping partner   Someone who has put up capital but does not intend to take an active part in running the business. They can protect themselves against the risk of unlimited liability by having the partnership registered as a limited partnership. The Limited Partnership Act of 1908 sets out the arrangements and relationships that apply in the absence of any formal agreement being reached by the various partners. In a company the 'sleeping partner' would normally be a shareholder and so limit his financial exposure in that way.

Software   A computer term usually associated with programs and related documentation.

Spreadsheet   Computer document format designed to help financial planning. Spreadsheet software can be used to perform repetitive numerical calculations and spreadsheeets sometimes referred to as a modelling tool. It comprises rows and columns into which numbers, formulae and text can be entered.

Strategy   A general method of policy for achieving specific objectives. It describes the essential resources and their amounts, which are to be committed to achieving those objects (see *tactics*).

Sweat equity   The value that accrues to a business by virtue of the time, energy and intellectual effort required to get to the immediate pre-launch phase. It is a notional concept applied by venture capitalists to assess the commitment the entrepreneur has to his business idea; it is a substitute for the commitment that hard cash would demonstrate in the event that a proprietor has no money to put up.

SWOT analysis   SWOT is an acronym for Strengths, Weaknesses, Opportunities and Threats, the four factors that have to be considered when developing a successful business *strategy*.

Synergy   A co-operative or combined activity which is more effective or valuable than the sum of its independent activities.

Tactics   The method by which resources allocated to a strategic objective are used.

Tax avoidance   Action taken to avoid having to pay tax unnecessarily, using legal means.

Tax evasion   Using illegal means of avoiding payment of tax and making a false tax declaration. About 70,000 small businesses are investigated by the UK Inland Revenue department each year for irregularities in their tax affairs. Just short of £400 million in extra tax is recovered from these firms. Most proprietors who have gone through the experience of a tax investigation would be reluctant to do anything that might incur a repeat of the experience.

Tax loss   A loss that has been manufactured specifically to reduce or eliminate taxable profits. Such action usually consists of bringing forward expenditure. That unfortunately has the usual effect of increasing profits in the next year. However, for sole traders it can be attractive to have a loss in their first trading period as this forms the reference base for future tax.

Trade cycle   At times, the economy appears to behave like a rollercoaster, encouraging new ventures and expansion plans on the upswing, only to dash them on the rocks a short time later when the downturn comes. This effect is known as the trade cycle. No one is quite sure why there is this regularity – or rather, everyone is sure but for different reasons.

True and fair   Accounting terminology that indicates that the business financial reports have been prepared using generally accepted accounting principles.

Turnkey   Usually refers to a client-commissioned system, accepted only when you can 'turn on a key' and are satisfied with the results, or output.

Unique selling proposition   Coined in 1940 by Rosser Reeves, advertising copywriter of the leading advertising agency, Ted Bates. His thesis was that from the launch of a product or service onwards you should always seek to identify and promote a unique selling proposition. This can be done by asking two questions: what is different about me, the seller, and what is different about our product or service? If nothing is different, why on earth should anyone want to buy from you? This is a particularly powerful concept at the outset of a new venture when a firm is short on market credibility.

User group   Organization set up by computer users who have a common interest. This common interest may be a particular computer, a piece of software or an activity. Usually there is a free exchange of ideas, programs and tips and quite frequently a magazine is produced and circulated to members.

URL   Uniform Resource Locator, the address to a source of information. The URL contains four distinct parts, the protocol type, the machine name, the directory path and the file name. For example: www.ncsa.uiuc.edu/SDG/Software/Mosaic/NCSAMosaicHome.html.

Vapourware   A term, slightly derogatory in nature, used to describe wishful thinking in describing a business's advantages or strategies.

Value   In accounting it has several meanings. For example, the 'value' of a fixed asset is its costs less its cumulative depreciation. A current asset, such as stock, is usually valued at cost or market value, whichever is the lower.

Value added   The difference between sales revenue that a firm gets from selling its products (or services), and the cost to it of the materials used in making those products.

Variable costs   See *direct costs*.

Variance   The difference between actual performance and the forecast (or budget or standard).

VDU   Visual display unit – another term for monitor.

Word processor   The essential element in word processing is the ability to enter text into a computer and manipulate it so that the desired final output is obtained before the hard copy is printed.

Working capital   Current assets less current liabilities, which represents the capital used in the day-to-day running of the business.

Working life   The economically useful life of a fixed asset. Not necessarily its whole life. For example, technological development may render it obsolete very quickly.

Work in progress   Goods in the process of being produced, which are valued at the lower end of manufacturing costs or market value.

World Wide Web = WWW = W3 = the web   a distributed hypertext-based information system, originally conceived at CERN to provide its user community with an easy way to access global information.

Dictionaries online

http://archive.ncsa.uiuc.edu/SDG/Software/ Mosaic/Glossary/
A glossary of World Wide Web terms and acronyms.

www.1000dictionaries.com
A thousand free online dictionaries.

www.online-dictionary.net

www.yourdictionary.com/diction4.html

www.washingtonpost.com/wp-srv/business/ longterm/glossary/indexag.htm

INDEX